SOMETHING ABOUT THE AUTHOR®

Something about
the Author *was named
an "Outstanding
Reference Source,"*
the highest honor given
by the American
Library Association
Reference and Adult
Services Division.

ISSN 0276-816X

sometHInG ABOUT tHe AUtHor®

**Facts and Pictures about Authors
and Illustrators of Books for Young People**

volume 210

GALE
CENGAGE Learning

Detroit • New York • San Francisco • New Haven, Conn • Waterville, Maine • London

GALE
CENGAGE Learning™

Something about the Author, Volume 210

Project Editor: Lisa Kumar

Editorial: Laura Avery, Pamela Bow, Jim Craddock, Amy Fuller, Andrea Henderson, Margaret Mazurkiewicz, Tracie Moy, Jeff Muhr, Kathy Nemeh, Mary Ruby, Mike Tyrkus

Permissions: Margaret Abendroth, Savannah Gignac, Aja Perales

Imaging and Multimedia: Savannah Gignac, John Watkins

Composition and Electronic Capture: Amy Darga

Manufacturing: Drew Kalasky

Product Manager: Janet Witalec

For product information and technology assistance, contact us at
Gale Customer Support, 1-800-877-4253.
For permission to use material from this text or product,
submit all requests online at **www.cengage.com/permissions.**
Further permissions questions can be emailed to
permissionrequest@cengage.com

Gale
27500 Drake Rd.
Farmington Hills, MI, 48331-3535

LIBRARY OF CONGRESS CATALOG CARD NUMBER 62-52046

ISBN-13: 978-1-4144-4223-5
ISBN-10: 1-4144-4223-8

ISSN 0276-816X

This title is also available as an e-book.
ISBN-13: 978-1-4144-6442-8
ISBN-10: 1-4144-6442-8
Contact your Gale sales representative for ordering information.

Printed in the United States of America
1 2 3 4 5 6 7 14 13 12 11 10

Contents

Authors in Forthcoming Volumes

Below are some of the authors and illustrators that will be featured in upcoming volumes of *SATA*. These include new entries on the swiftly rising stars of the field, as well as completely revised and updated entries (indicated with *) on some of the most notable and best-loved creators of books for children.

Philippe Béha ❚ Born in France, award-winning illustrator Béha now makes his home in his adopted Québec, Canada. His colorful, modernistic mixed-media art is featured in over one hundred French-language books for children, as well as in several works for English-speaking readers, among them Jane Yolen and Heidi E.Y. Stemple's *Fairy Tale Feasts: A Literary Cookbook for Young Readers and Eaters* and Katarina Jovanovic's folktale adaptation *The King Has Goat Ears.*

Colleen Doran ❚ Graphic novelist and comic-book artist Doran is best known for *A Distant Soil,* a comic-book series she first created at age twelve and which has gone on to sell over 500,000 copies. In addition to her own work, Doran has also created art for projects by numerous other writers, such as Neil Gaiman, Tom Ligotti, and Warren Ellis, and has illustrated Peter David's picture book *Mascot to the Rescue!*

Judy Horacek ❚ Horacek is an Australian cartoonist and humorist whose wry images have been collected in anthologies that include *Life on the Edge, If the Fruit Fits . . . ,* and *I Am Woman, Hear Me Draw.* In addition to using her talent to comment on political and social issues, she has also produced whimsical children's books such as *The Story of Growl* and *Where Is the Green Sheep?*

Mireille Levert ❚ Levert is an award-winning artist and author whose work is well-known to young children in her home province of Québec, Canada, as well as in the country's English-speaking provinces in translation. Her artwork for Sharon Jennings' "Jeremiah and Mrs. Ming" stories earned Levert much acclaim and several major awards, and her original self-illustrated picture book *An Island in the Soup* was honored with the Canada Council for the Arts' Award for Illustrated Children's Literature in 2001.

***E.B. Lewis** ❚ A popular illustrator whose accolades include both a Caldecott Honor and the Coretta Scott King award, Lewis has created paintings that have enriched numerous picture books. His interest in promoting positive role models for young people of color has inspired his work in Nikki Grimes' *Talkin' about Bessie,* Jacqueline Woodson's *Coming on Home Soon,* Joseph Slate's *I Want to Be Free,* and Janet S. Wong's *Homegrown House.*

Eric Metaxas ❚ A humorist and commentator based in New York City, Metaxas served as head writer and editorial director for Rabbit Ears Productions, an award-winning animation and recording studio, and wrote scripts for the *Veggie Tales* series of computer-animated Christian-themed videos. Featuring upbeat stories that reflect their author's values, Metaxas's children's books include *Squanto and the Miracle of Thanksgiving, It's Time to Sleep, My Love,* and *God Made You Special.*

Michael Scott ❚ Scott, an Irish folklorist and mythologist, is the author of more than one hundred books for readers of all ages, including works of fantasy, science fiction, and horror. Considered an expert on Celtic lore, Scott published his first collection, *Irish Folk and Fairy Tales,* in 1983, and the well-respected work has remained in print ever since. In addition, Scott has written such acclaimed novels as *The Hallows, Silverhand,* and *The Alchemyst,* while also collaborating with actress and writer Adrienne Barbeau to create the novel *Vampyres of Hollywood.*

Steve Seskin ❚ A songwriter and author, Seskin has had a long, successful career writing hit songs for musicians that include country singers Tim McGraw, Kenny Chesney, and Colin Raye as well as Peter, Paul, and Mary. Seskin also has a successful career as a performer, having recorded seventeen albums in which he performs his own music. A regular performer at school assemblies and workshops, he treats listeners to a range of songs geared toward young audiences. Picture-book adaptations of Seskin's humorous songs include *Don't Laugh at Me* and *A Chance to Shine.*

***Melissa Sweet** ❚ Sweet is an award-winning artist whose illustration projects include James Howe's "Pinky and Rex" picture-book series, Joan Knight's "Charlotte" series of travel journals written by Claude Monet's fictional daughter, and the award-winning *The Sky's the Limit,* written by Catherine Thimmesh. Awarded a Caldecott Honor Book citation for her illustrations for Jen Bryant's picture-book biography *A River of Words: The Story of William Carlos Williams,* she has also created artwork for her own stories in *Carmine: A Little More Red, Tupelo Rides the Rails,* and *Fiddle-i-Fee: A Farmyard Song for the Very Young.*

***Paul Yee** ❚ Yee is an award-winning Canadian writer whose Chinese heritage and experiences growing up in the Chinatown region of Vancouver, British Columbia, have inspired many of his highly acclaimed books for younger readers. While Yee focuses his writing primarily on Canadian children of Chinese ancestry who desire to learn about themselves and their heritage, his books have also found audiences among children of many backgrounds living in both Canada and the United States. Among Yee's works are picture books, short-story collections such as *Tales from Gold Mountain: Stories of the Chinese in the New World,* and novels that include *Breakaway, The Curses of Third Uncle,* and *Learning to Fly.*

Introduction

Something about the Author (*SATA*) is an ongoing reference series that examines the lives and works of authors and illustrators of books for children. *SATA* includes not only well-known writers and artists but also less prominent individuals whose works are just coming to be recognized. This series is often the only readily available information source on emerging authors and illustrators. You'll find *SATA* informative and entertaining, whether you are a student, a librarian, an English teacher, a parent, or simply an adult who enjoys children's literature.

What's Inside *SATA*

SATA provides detailed information about authors and illustrators who span the full time range of children's literature, from early figures like John Newbery and L. Frank Baum to contemporary figures like Judy Blume and Richard Peck. Authors in the series represent primarily English-speaking countries, particularly the United States, Canada, and the United Kingdom. Also included, however, are authors from around the world whose works are available in English translation. The writings represented in *SATA* include those created intentionally for children and young adults as well as those written for a general audience and known to interest younger readers. These writings cover the entire spectrum of children's literature, including picture books, humor, folk and fairy tales, animal stories, mystery and adventure, science fiction and fantasy, historical fiction, poetry and nonsense verse, drama, biography, and nonfiction. Obituaries are also included in many volumes of *SATA* and are intended not only as death notices but also as concise overviews of people's lives and work. Additionally, each edition features newly revised and updated entries for a selection of *SATA* listees who remain of interest to today's readers and who have been active enough to require extensive revisions of their earlier biographies.

Autobiography Feature

Beginning with Volume 103, many volumes of *SATA* feature one or more specially commissioned autobiographical essays. These unique essays, averaging about ten thousand words in length and illustrated with an abundance of personal photos, present an entertaining and informative first-person perspective on the lives and careers of prominent authors and illustrators profiled in *SATA*.

Two Convenient Indexes

In response to suggestions from librarians, *SATA* indexes no longer appear in every volume but are included in alternate (odd-numbered) volumes of the series, beginning with Volume 57.

SATA continues to include two indexes that cumulate with each alternate volume: the Illustrations Index, arranged by the name of the illustrator, gives the number of the volume and page where the illustrator's work appears in the current volume as well as all preceding volumes in the series; the Author Index gives the number of the volume in which a person's biographical sketch, autobiographical essay, or obituary appears in the current volume as well as all preceding volumes in the series.

These indexes also include references to authors and illustrators who appear in *Gale's Yesterday's Authors of Books for Children, Children's Literature Review,* and *Something about the Author Autobiography Series.*

Easy-to-Use Entry Format

Whether you're already familiar with the *SATA* series or just getting acquainted, you will want to be aware of the kind of information that an entry provides. In every *SATA* entry the editors attempt to give as complete a picture of the person's life and work as possible. A typical entry in *SATA* includes the following clearly labeled information sections:

PERSONAL: date and place of birth and death, parents' names and occupations, name of spouse, date of marriage, names of children, educational institutions attended, degrees received, religious and political affiliations, hobbies and other interests.

ADDRESSES: complete home, office, electronic mail, and agent addresses, whenever available.

CAREER: name of employer, position, and dates for each career post; art exhibitions; military service; memberships and offices held in professional and civic organizations.

MEMBER: professional, civic, and other association memberships and any official posts held.

AWARDS, HONORS: literary and professional awards received.

WRITINGS: title-by-title chronological bibliography of books written and/or illustrated, listed by genre when known; lists of other notable publications, such as plays, screenplays, and periodical contributions.

ADAPTATIONS: a list of films, television programs, plays, CD-ROMs, recordings, and other media presentations that have been adapted from the author's work.

WORK IN PROGRESS: description of projects in progress.

SIDELIGHTS: a biographical portrait of the author or illustrator's development, either directly from the biographee—and often written specifically for the *SATA* entry—or gathered from diaries, letters, interviews, or other published sources.

BIOGRAPHICAL AND CRITICAL SOURCES: cites sources quoted in "Sidelights" along with references for further reading.

EXTENSIVE ILLUSTRATIONS: photographs, movie stills, book illustrations, and other interesting visual materials supplement the text.

How a *SATA* Entry Is Compiled

SATA editors examine a wide variety of published sources to gather information for an entry. Biographical and bibliographic sources are consulted, as are book reviews, feature articles, published interviews, and material sometimes obtained from the biographee's family, publishers, agent, or other associates. Whenever possible, the author or illustrator is sent a copy of the entry to check for accuracy and completeness.

Entries that have not been verified by the biographees or their representatives are marked with an asterisk (*).

Contact the Editor

We encourage our readers to examine the entire *SATA* series. Please write and tell us if we can make *SATA* even more helpful to you. Give your comments and suggestions to the editor:

Editor
Something about the Author
Gale, Cengage Learning
27500 Drake Rd.
Farmington Hills MI 48331-3535

Toll-free: 800-877-GALE
Fax: 248-699-8070

Something about the Author Product Advisory Board

The editors of *Something about the Author* are dedicated to maintaining a high standard of excellence by publishing comprehensive, accurate, and highly readable entries on a wide array of writers for children and young adults. In addition to the quality of the content, the editors take pride in the graphic design of the series, which is intended to be orderly yet inviting, allowing readers to utilize the pages of *SATA* easily and with efficiency. Despite the longevity of the *SATA* print series, and the success of its format, we are mindful that the vitality of a literary reference product is dependent on its ability to serve its users over time. As literature, and attitudes about literature, constantly evolve, so do the reference needs of students, teachers, scholars, journalists, researchers, and book club members. To be certain that we continue to keep pace with the expectations of our customers, the editors of *SATA* listen carefully to their comments regarding the value, utility, and quality of the series. Librarians, who have firsthand knowledge of the needs of library users, are a valuable resource for us. The *Something about the Author* Product Advisory Board, made up of school, public, and academic librarians, is a forum to promote focused feedback about *SATA* on a regular basis. The nine-member advisory board includes the following individuals, whom the editors wish to thank for sharing their expertise:

Eva M. Davis
Director,
Canton Public Library,
Canton, Michigan

Joan B. Eisenberg
Lower School Librarian,
Milton Academy,
Milton, Massachusetts

Francisca Goldsmith
Teen Services Librarian,
Berkeley Public Library,
Berkeley, California

Susan Dove Lempke
Children's Services Supervisor,
Niles Public Library District,
Niles, Illinois

Robyn Lupa
Head of Children's Services,
Jefferson County Public Library,
Lakewood, Colorado

Victor L. Schill
Assistant Branch Librarian/Children's Librarian,
Harris County Public Library/Fairbanks Branch,
Houston, Texas

Caryn Sipos
Community Librarian,
Three Creeks Community Library,
Vancouver, Washington

Steven Weiner
Director,
Maynard Public Library,
Maynard, Massachusetts

something ABOUT the AUThOR

ADKINS, Jan 1944-
   (Diego Vega)

Personal

Born November 7, 1944, in Gallipolis, OH; son of Alban Blakemore (a sheet-metal contractor) and Dixie Lee Adkins; married Deborah Kiernan, September 14, 1968 (died, June, 1976); married Dorcas Sheldon Peirce, December, 1977 (marriage ended); married Deborah Fenning (marriage ended); children: (first marriage) Sally, Samuel Ulysses, Robbie (stepchild). *Ethnicity:* "Caucasian; Welsh, German, Scots." *Education:* Ohio State University, B.A., 1969. *Politics:* "Skeptic." *Hobbies and other interests:* Tennis, hiking, sailing, singing, bicycling, cooking for friends.

Addresses

Home— Home and office—Jan Adkins Studio, 25 Wildwood Ln., Novato, CA 94947. *Office— Agent*—Writer's House, 21 W. 26th St., New York, NY 10010. *E-mail*—j.adkins@verizon.net.

Career

Author and illustrator. Ireland & Associates Architects, Columbus, OH, architectural designer, 1963-66; writer, graphic designer, and illustrator, 1969—; math and science teacher in Mattapoisett, MA, 1969-70; Buzzard Inc. (advertising agency), Marion, MA, vice president

Jan Adkins (Meg Smith Photography. Courtesy of Jan Adkins.)

and art director, 1974-76; *National Geographic* magazine, Washington, DC, associate art director, 1980-88; Design Lab, Providence, RI, art director, 1995-96. Teacher of illustration at Rhode Island School of Design and Maryland Institute College of Art, 1990-96; guest lecturer, Norman Rockwell Museum, "Master of Illustration" series. Consultant to art museums, zoos, and natural history and science museums.

Member

Society of Children's Book Writers and Illustrators.

Awards, Honors

Brooklyn Museum Art citations, 1972, 1973, 1974; Lewis Carroll Shelf Award, University of Wisconsin, and National Book Award nomination, both 1972, both for *The Art and Industry of Sandcastles*; Children's Book Showcase awards, Children's Book Council, 1974, for *Toolchest,* and 1976, for *Inside*; Children's Science Book Award, New York Academy of Sciences, 1981, for *Moving Heavy Things*; Best Science Book designation, American Society of Science Teachers, 1985, for *Workboats*; Silver Addy Award for Design, Orlando Art Directors; Gold Medal for Best Essay of 1999, International Regional Magazine Association; Elementary and Early Childhood Award, Bridgewater State College, 2001, for contributions to literacy in young readers; Gold Medal for Best Editorial Illustration, San Francisco Society of Illustrators, 2001; Author of the Year designation, Naval Institute, 2002, for contributions to young people's naval history; Nonfiction Honor List selection, *Voice of Youth Advocates,* 2003, for *Bridges: From My Side to Yours*; Best Illustration Series of the Year, *Naval History* magazine; numerous design and illustration awards from Society of Illustrators, Art Directors Clubs of Metropolitan Washington and New York, *Communication Arts,* and others.

Writings

SELF-ILLUSTRATED, EXCEPT WHERE NOTED

The Art and Industry of Sandcastles: Being an Illustrated Guide to Basic Constructions along with Divers Information, Walker (New York, NY), 1971, reprinted, 1994.
The Craft of Making Wine, Walker (New York, NY), 1971.
How a House Happens, Walker (New York, NY), 1972.
The Craft of Sail, Walker (New York, NY), 1972.
Toolchest, Walker (New York, NY), 1973.
Small Garden, Big Surprise, Ginn (Lexington, MA), 1974.
The Bakers: A Simple Book about the Pleasures of Making Bread, Scribner (New York, NY), 1975.
Inside: Seeing beneath the Surface, Walker (New York, NY), 1975.
Luther Tarbox (children's fiction), Scribner (New York, NY), 1977.

Moving On: Stories of Four Travelers, Scribner (New York, NY), 1978.
Symbols: A Silent Language, Walker (New York, NY), 1978.
Wooden Ship, Houghton Mifflin (Boston, MA), 1978, reprinted, WoodenBoat (Brooklyn, ME), 2004.
The Art and Ingenuity of the Woodstove, Everest House (New York, NY), 1978.
Moving Heavy Things, Houghton Mifflin (Boston, MA), 1980, reprinted, Wooden Boat (Brooklyn, ME), 2004.
The Wood Book: An Entertaining, Interesting, and Even Useful Compendium of Facts, Notions, Opinions, and Sentiments about Wood and Its Growing, Cutting, Working, and Burning, Little, Brown (Boston, MA), 1980.
Heavy Equipment, Scribner (New York, NY), 1980.
Letterbox: The Art and History of Letters, Walker (New York, NY), 1981.
A Storm without Rain (young-adult novel), Little, Brown (Boston, MA), 1983, reprinted, WoodenBoat (Brooklyn, ME), 2004
Workboats, Macmillan (New York, NY), 1985, reprinted, WoodenBoat (Brooklyn, ME), 2004.
String: Tying It Up, Tying It Down, Scribner (New York, NY), 1992, published as *Line: Tying It Up, Tying It Down,* WoodenBoat (Brooklyn, ME), 2004.
Machines in Our Garden ("Collections for Young Scholars" series), Open Court Publishers (Chicago, IL), 1995.
The Wonder of Light, Newbridge Communications (New York, NY), 1997.
Bridges: From My Side to Yours, Roaring Book Press (Brookfield, CT), 2002.
John Adams, Young Revolutionary, illustrated by Merle Henderson, Aladdin (New York, NY), 2002.
What If You Met a Pirate?: An Historical Voyage of Seafaring Speculation, Roaring Brook Press (Brookfield, CT), 2004.
What If You Met a Knight?, Roaring Brook Press (Brookfield, CT), 2006.

OTHER

(Illustrator) Laurence Pringle, *Chains, Webs, and Pyramids: The Flow of Energy in Nature,* Crowell (New York, NY), 1975.
Cookie (mystery novel), Harper (New York, NY), 1988.
Deadline for Final Art (adult mystery novel), Walker (New York, NY), 1990.
Solstice: A Mystery of the Season (young-adult novel), Walker (New York, NY), 1990, reprinted, WoodenBoat (Brooklyn, ME), 2004.
(Editor and illustrator) *The Ragged Mountain Portable Wilderness Anthology,* Ragged Mountain Press (Camden, ME), 1993.
(Illustrator) Bill Pinkney, *Captain Bill Pinkney's Journey* ("Collections for Young Scholars" series), Open Court Publishers (Chicago, IL), 1995.
(Illustrator) Dean Torges, *Hunting the Osage Bow: A Chronicle of Craft* (originally published in *Traditional Bowhunter* magazine), Gilliland Press (Arkansas City, KS), 1998.
(Author of text) *Dream Spinner: The Art of Roy Andersen,* Settlers West (Tucson, AZ), 2000.

(As Diego Vega) *Young Zorro: The Iron Brand* (novel), Rayo/HarperCollins (New York, NY), 2006.
Frank Lloyd Wright: A Twentieth-Century Life, Viking (New York, NY), 2007.

Contributor to periodicals, including *Air and Space, Island Journal, Chesapeake Bay, Harper's, Mother Earth News, Sail, Smithsonian,* and *WoodenBoat.* Contributing editor to magazines, including *Cricket, Smithsonian, Muse,* and *Click.* Contributor of short fiction to anthologies, including *Unusual Suspects.* Author of scripts for television documentaries produced on Public Broadcasting System and the Discovery Channel.

Adkins's books have been published in Braille editions and translated into Swedish and Danish.

Sidelights

An award-winning author and illustrator whose detailed drawings involve and inspire young readers, Jan Adkins has created books on subjects as diverse as sand castles, baking bread, and sailing, all inspired by his curiosity, desire to gain experience in certain subjects, and his enthusiasm for sharing that knowledge with others. In addition to nonfiction titles such as *How a House Happens, The Wonder of Light,* and *Moving Heavy Things,* Atkins has also penned fiction for both teens and adults.

Born in Ohio and raised across the Ohio river in Wheeling, West Virginia, Adkins inherited both his creativity and his ability to figure things out from his parents, whom he describes on his *Jan Adkins Studio* Web site as "a sheet-metal contractor who invented clever devices and could fix anything" and "a loopy, beautiful woman with wit and a lyric Welsh soprano." After graduating from high school in Ohio, he studied architecture at Ohio State University, but ultimately changed his major to English literature and creative writing. Meanwhile, Adkins apprenticed as an architectural designer, developing his illustration skills and his ability to present technical objects in clear, easy-to-understand diagrams. In 1980, he was invited to join the staff of *National Geographic,* where he worked as an associate art director, teaming up with authors, illustrators, and researchers to create the illustrated texts for which the magazine is noted. The recipient of numerous design awards from professional organizations and others for his books, magazine work, and exhibitions, Adkins cites his favorite job as writing nonfiction for young people.

Adkins' first book, 1971's *The Art and Industry of Sandcastles: Being an Illustrated Guide to Basic Constructions along with Divers Information,* is a whimsical illustrated guide to building with wet sand. More than that, it also provides readers with an introduction to the history and structure of actual castles as well as to life in medieval times. Illustrated with detailed drawings of historical castles and their sand counterparts, the book was complimented by critics who remarked on the author's unusual presentation. *Scientific American* con-

tributors Philip Morrison and Phylis Morrison dubbed the work "a small tour de force" and a "loving study of medieval life and times," while in *School Library Journal,* Ruth M. McConnell called *The Art and Industry of Sandcastles* "an instructive, fun ramble on sandcastle building that is doubtless the definitive work on the subject."

Adkins continues to bring the same combination of skillful drawing, lucid explanation, and novelty to bear on subject he tackles and includes a discussion of the tools, materials, and terminology involved in related projects. While some reviewers have expressed concern that such technical information might be unappreciated by younger readers, Adkins once commented in an interview with Norma Bagnall for *Language Arts:* "I don't want children to understand everything; I want them to read the book. . . . If children understand everything the first time around, they'll throw the book away, and they ought to."

In *String: Tying It Up, Tying It Down* (republished in 2004 as *Line: Tying It Up, Tying It Down*) Adkins creates a knot primer that includes tying techniques from the half-hitch to the square knot as well as practical uses ranging from boat docking to necktie-tying. "Using fun illustrations and text," the book "shows how to securely tie everything from shoes to ships," explained W.E. Butterworth IV in his review for *Boy's Life,* while in *Booklist* Deborah Abbott praised Adkins for creating "a text that reads like a novel—smooth flowing, carefully woven, precise, lively." While noting that the text might be too advanced for younger readers, *Voice of Youth Advocates* contributor Sherry Hoy nonetheless praised *String* as "an esoteric, eclectic blend of lore." Commending the author/illustrator for his "detailed black-and-white pencil drawings," *School Library Journal* contributor Carole B. Kirkpatrick found the book to be "more practical and far-reaching in scope" than its title would imply; "that it's enjoyable just to read through is a pleasant bonus," the critic added.

Other nonfiction titles by Adkins include *The Art and Ingenuity of the Woodstove, Moving Heavy Things, The Craft of Sail, Letterbox: The Art and History of Letters,* and *Bridges: From My Side to Yours.* Reviewing *Letterbox,* Barbara Elleman commented in *Booklist* that the work contains Adkins' "well-known precision, wit, and attentive style," while in *Kirkus Reviews* a contributor cited the book as one of the author's "earnestly high-toned, craft-looking anomalies" that contains "lots of fine calligraphy" intermixed with such a wealth of extraneous details that the book becomes a kind of "cultural collage." The more-focused *Bridges* presents a 10,000-year history of bridge construction from the days of the Roman Empire to the present. Mixing stories about engineering advances and the people who made them, Adkins reveals a "fascination with his subject," according to *Horn Book* reviewer Mary M. Burns, and "his knowledge of history is as dazzling as his understanding of engineering principles." In addition, "fascinating human interest tidbits add historical context," Mary Ann Carcich wrote in her *School Library Journal* review, praising *Bridges* as well-illustrated and a useful volume for "a wide audience."

In *What If You Met a Pirate?: An Historical Voyage of Seafaring Speculation* and its partner book *What If You Met a Knight?,* Adkins takes idealized views of life on the high seas and jousting in shining armor and places them in their real historical perspectives. *What If You Met a Pirate?* shows that the life of a sailor on a pirate vessel did not actually include much swashbuckling, and that some of the commonly believed pirate punishments were actually invented by illustrators of a later era. According to Carolyn Phelan, writing for *Booklist,* "this realistic portrayal of pirates and their activities is even more intriguing than the romanticized version [Adkins] . . . debunks." *School Library Journal* critic Laurie Edwards wrote of the book that "Adkins's detailed renderings will be as familiar to fans of his other nonfiction books as his tongue-in-cheek humor." In *What If You Met a Knight?* Adkins reveals that knighthood was more about responsibilities for an area of land, and the people who lived there than about undertaking dramatic quests. Using the example of Sir Guy of Wareham, he shows that a knight's job dealt with trade, enforcing laws, and taking care of the people who live on his lands. Lucinda Snyder Whitehurst, writing in *School Library Journal,* called *What If You Met a Knight?* "an excellent extended-reading resource and a good choice for children interested in the period." Complimenting Adkins' "colorful, detailed illustrations," *Booklist* Phelan wrote that "particularly good for visual learners, this slender book offers a fine introduction to knighthood."

Having worked as an architect in his early career, Adkins was a natural fit to pen the biography of a famous architect in *Frank Lloyd Wright: A Twentieth Century Life,* part of Viking's "Up Close" series. Calling the biography "lively," Delia Carruthers wrote in *School Library Journal* that "Adkins captures Wright's strong personality, fierce character, and emotional ups and downs." According to Gillian Engberg in *Booklist,* the author "skillfully illuminates the man's complex, brilliant character."

In addition to writing nonfiction, Adkins has found success as a fiction writer. His first self-illustrated picture book, *Luther Tarbox,* follows a lobsterman as he pulls in his traps during a dense New England fog, his work hastened by the novice boaters nearby who hope he will lead them back to shore. In her *Horn Book* review, Charlotte W. Draper praised the humorous tale for its "rich and rhythmic" language, while in the *Bulletin of the Center for Children's Books,* Zena Sutherland dubbed *Luther Tarbox* "a brisk and salty tale" that "conveys the appeal of the sea" to young listeners.

The sea also figures in *Solstice: A Mystery of the Season,* as Charlie and his father travel by motorboat to an island off the Maine coast for Christmas. When their boat engine fails, the two are taken in by a lobsterman and his family who teach father and son some simple lessons about family. A reviewer for *Publishers Weekly* called the book "slender but hypnotic," and noted that Adkins' "almost mystical novel captures the intensity of the holiday season in both its promise and its pain."

For adult readers, Adkins' *Deadline for Final Art* is a "taut mystery/thriller," according to a *Publishers Weekly* contributor. In the novel, an associate art director for *National Geographic* magazine finds himself in the center of cold war espionage involving a highly sensitive missile defense system, resulting in what the *Publishers Weekly* reviewer described as "a brisk, savvy thriller, spiced with Washington and magazine-publishing details."

Adkins ventures into sci-fi territory in his young-adult novel *A Storm without Rain.* Set in eastern Massachusetts and drawing on its author's knowledge of shipbuilding and sailing, the story follows the adventures of fifteen-year-old Jack Carter, who begins a short sailing trip in 1981 and ends up in 1904. In his family's shipyard, Jack meets his own grandfather, then a teen himself, and together the two boys try to find a way to help Jack return to his own time. Writing in the *New York Times Book Review,* Jane Langton commended Adkins for including details about turn-of-the-twentieth-century Massachusetts that bring Jack's plight to life for young readers. She also hailed Adkins' "memorable" illustrations, which with the text create "an authentic background." The critic concluded, "The reader puts down the book with admiration for craftsmanship—for that of the boatbuilders . . . and for that of the writer, who honed his fanciful tale so authentically."

In 2006, Adkins tried his hand at presenting the legendary Robin Hood of Los Angeles, Zorro, as a teen in *Young Zorro: The Iron Brand.* As in his nonfiction books, *Young Zorro* features a wealth of true-to-life historical detail about what life was like in Spanish colonial Los Angeles. Diego de la Vega, the teen who will eventually become the famous freedom fighter, and his best friend, Bernardo, investigate the disappearances of both cattle and local craftsmen. Noting that though the young vigilante is not quite as dashing as the adult he will become, Todd Morning nonetheless wrote in *Booklist* that *Young Zorro* "has enough action and rich detail of old California to engage readers."

Biographical and Critical Sources

BOOKS

Children's Literature Review, Volume 7, Gale (Detroit, MI), 1984, pp. 17-28.

PERIODICALS

American Biology Teacher, July, 1998, Teri Clark, review of *The Wonder of Light,* p. 550.

Appraisal, fall, 1981, review of *Moving Heavy Things* and *Heavy Equipment,* pp. 8-9.

Backpacker, April, 1994, Nancy Humes, review of *The Ragged Mountain Portable Wilderness Anthology,* p. 102.

Booklist, July 15, 1971, review of *The Art and Industry of Sandcastles: Being an Illustrated Guide to Basic Constructions along with Divers Information,* p. 913; October 1, 1973, review of *The Craft of Sail,* p. 168; February 1, 1976, Barbara Elleman, review of *Inside: Seeing beneath the Surface,* p. 763; February 1, 1979, Barbara Elleman, review of *Symbols: A Silent Language,* p. 862; September 1, 1981, Barbara Elleman, review of *Letterbox: The Art and History of Letters,* p. 40; April 15, 1983, Barbara Elleman, review of *A Storm without Rain,* p. 1089; April 15, 1992, Deborah Abbott, review of *String: Tying It Up, Tying It Down,* p. 1524; July, 2002, Gillian Engberg, review of *Bridges: From My Side to Yours,* p. 1838; October 15, 2004, Carolyn Phelan, review of *What If You Met a Pirate?,* p. 404; March 1, 2006, Todd Morning, review of *Young Zorro: The Iron Brand,* p. 87; August 1, 2006, review of *What If You Met a Knight?,* p. 69; November 1, 2007, Gillian Engberg, review of *Frank Lloyd Wright,* p. 57.

Boy's Life, December, 1992, W.E. Butterworth IV, review of *String,* p. 19.

Bulletin of the Center for Children's Books, June, 1971, Zena Sutherland, review of *The Art and Industry of Sandcastles,* p. 149; September, 1972, Zena Sutherland, review of *How a House Happens,* p. 1; January, 1974, Zena Sutherland, review of *The Craft of Sail,* p. 73; April, 1974, Zena Sutherland, review of *Toolchest,* p. 121; April, 1976, Zena Sutherland, review of *Inside,* p. 121; May, 1976, Zena Sutherland, review of *The Bakers: A Simple Book about the Pleasures of Making Bread,* p. 137; February, 1978, Zena Sutherland, review of *Luther Tarbox,* p. 89.

Christian Science Monitor, October 23, 1978, William Jaspersohn, review of *Wooden Ship,* p. B2.

Horn Book, February, 1978, Charlotte W. Draper, review of *Luther Tarbox,* p. 42; October, 1978, Karen M. Klockner, review of *Wooden Ship,* pp. 512-513; April, 1979, Kate M. Flanagan, review of *Symbols,* pp. 203-204; February, 1981, Karen Jameyson, review of *Heavy Equipment,* p. 65; August, 1983, Mary M. Burns, review of *A Storm without Rain,* pp. 448-449; July-August, 2002, Mary M. Burns, review of *Bridges,* p. 481.

Kirkus Reviews, May 15, 1973, review of *The Craft of Sail,* p. 569; November 15, 1975, review of *Inside,* p. 1289; February 1, 1976, review of *The Bakers,* pp. 135-136; August 1, 1980, review of *Moving Heavy Things,* p. 980; January 1, 1981, review of *Heavy Equipment,* p. 9; September 1, 1981, review of *Letterbox,* pp. 1084-1085.

Kliatt, September, 1993, Jody K. Hanson, review of *A Storm without Rain,* p. 15.

Language Arts, May, 1980, Norma Bagnall, interview with Adkins, pp. 560-566.

New York Times Book Review, November 4, 1973, Lavinia Russ, "How to Make Almost Everything," p. 62; November 16, 1975, Louise Armstrong, review of *Inside,* p. 46; May 2, 1976, Craig Claiborne, review of *The Bakers,* p. 41; October 30, 1977, Joyce Milton, review of *Luther Tarbox,* p. 34; December 10, 1978, Rex Benedict, review of *Wooden Ship,* pp. 77, 91; September 18, 1983, Jane Langton, review of *A Storm without Rain,* p. 39.

Publishers Weekly, July 5, 1971, review of *The Art and Industry of Sandcastles,* p. 50; June 24, 1983, review of *A Storm without Rain,* p. 58; June 22, 1990, review of *Deadline for Final Art,* pp. 46-47; November 30, 1990, review of *Solstice: A Mystery of the Season,* p. 70.

Reading Teacher, May, 1979, review of *Toolchest,* p. 945.

School Library Journal, September, 1971, Ruth M. McConnell, review of *The Art and Industry of Sandcastles,* p. 147; October, 1972, Barbara Gibson, review of *How a House Happens,* pp. 108-109; October, 1973, Don Reaber, review of *The Craft of Sail,* p. 111; March, 1976, review of *The Bakers,* p. 98; October, 1978, Phyllis Ingram, review of *Wooden Ship,* p. 152; January, 1979, Daisy Kouzel, review of *Symbols,* p. 50; August, 1981, Lorraine Douglas, review of *Letterbox,* p. 61; June, 1992, Carole B. Kirkpatrick, review of *String,* p. 127; July, 2002, Mary Ann Carcich, review of *Bridges,* p. 128; December, 2004, Laurie Edwards, review of *What If You Met a Pirate?,* p. 125; September, 2006, Lucinda Snyder Whitehurst, review of *What If You Met a Knight?,* p. 224; November, 2007, review of *Frank Lloyd Wright,* p. 141.

Scientific American, December, 1971, Philip Morrison and Phylis Morrison, review of *The Art and Industry of Sandcastles,* p. 112; December, 1980, review of *Moving Heavy Things,* pp. 47-48.

Voice of Youth Advocates, August, 1992, Sherry Hoy, review of *String,* p. 180.

Washington Post Book World, February 12, 1984, Michael Dirda, review of *Toolchest,* pp. 10-11.

ONLINE

Jan Adkins Studio Web site, http://www.janadkins.com/ (November 19, 2009).

Autobiography Feature

Jan Adkins

AUTOBIOGRAPHY OF TWELVE PERSONALITIES FLYING IN LOOSE FORMATION

I returned yesterday from an assignment in England where the driving was, for me at least, perilous. Last night, sleeping in my own big bed for the first time in two weeks, I had a dream with edges so sharp and colors so bright that it seemed important.

I was fixing food for friends. The unfamiliar kitchen was narrow, in an old city I have never seen. We left the house for a movie. I drove—in a red van and on the left side of the road (my driving mind still in England). The place was steep and mountainous; I compared the narrow roads, precipitous, drop-offs, and unguarded edges to what Sicily must be like. We were descending with a deep valley on our left, my friends—perhaps ten in a big van, almost a bus—were laughing, talking loudly and happily. Someone in the passenger's seat told me to be careful of the edge. Just then I saw the wheel stray right over the crumbling edge. I had misjudged the tight turn, the van lurched forward and out into the awful space, and I knew that the error was fatal. We fell. We fell clear of the van, as if it had no roof, falling into the deep valley, toward its grassy fields. I called out to my friends in anguish, "I'm sorry, forgive me, I've done this, I've ended your fine lives." They were too terrified to answer. I was terribly frightened of death, frantically thinking for a solution, an alternative, watching the turf rush toward me. The prime emotion I felt, though, was shame that I'd brought this on my friends. I looked across the falling bodies, quiet limbs in the rushing air, their eyes transfixed by the ground rising toward them, to my son, Sam, falling, and I felt his despair at having his life end at nineteen. I called to him but the ground was almost . . . we struck.

There was no pain, no sensation at all. We all rose, dazed, and tried a few steps, a few words. We were wondering if we were spared, somehow, in some way we didn't understand. A flicker of hope and even of curiosity. Could we be dead? Was this another way to be? Things were quiet, different. We were wearing soft, red sweaters, which seemed odd, and odder still that Sam was wearing bright yellow, foul-weather gear.

A small group of people wandered up to a steel gate at the edge of our field. I called to them but they didn't answer. I walked up to a woman and grabbed her rudely

but she didn't respond. They didn't know we were there. So, we were dead. I looked back to Sam: he had just fallen in love and the injustice of cutting his life short crushed me. He would never play the intricate, sweet, painful games of intimacy. He would never see his love again. I fell deeper than the valley floor into despair.

I turned toward the group of people at the gate. Surely they must hear me! "Madam," I said, "Sir," uncharacteristically formal, cautious about the politics of the dead. They did not respond. But I saw recognition: a boy, of ten or eleven, whose eyes followed me, with interest.

"Can you see me?"

He nodded, yes, of course he could.

"Can you hear me? Can you hear my voice?"

"Yes," he answered, without fear or agitation, "I can hear you."

His father looked at the boy and had a dim sense of something. With unfocused eyes he called out to the blank field in front of him, "He can hear you."

I was impatient with the father. "You can't see anything. You don't know anything. This boy can hear me, he can see me and his friend, and you, too."

I addressed the children in the group as they came forward to the gate. "Well, that's something at least," I said, seizing what comfort I could. "I'm dead, gone from the world, and only you kids can hear me or see me." I laughed; the situation seemed silly and somehow familiar, like my life writing and illustrating books. The adults I called to so urgently were deaf, but the children listened—not eagerly, but with the interest one might give a pond on the way to school, a diversion, a spark of fun in a day full of boredom designed by adults.

I shook my head, amused even in despair by my minor rôle in this life or the next, and found myself in my bed, in my tiny house by the water, and my son was still nineteen and in love, and the world was still open to the most astonishing possibilities.

It was like a gift from God: the house and the happiness and the fine summer day just dawning.

So, to celebrate it, I have risen early to write down my dream for you. I am glad to be alive, and healthy, and blessed by a son and a daughter (she was busy in an-

Jan Adkins, 1990 (Courtesy of Jan Adkins.)

other dream, no doubt), and friends, and a profession I love. What have I learned from this dream? I won't store up seven years of grain for seven famine years, and I won't find a man with magic beans, and I won't open an Arabian cave with secret words, but I will hug this summer day to me a little tighter, and the ones that follow. And I'll talk more gratefully across the gate to the people—most of them young and in in need of a little diversion—who hear me.

I suppose I will continue to shout to adults, but I am more aware of my real audience, and more satisfied to serve it. My best work speaks to young people, the smartest readers available, the freshest minds. More than other readers they need truth, and truth is a hard editor.

*

When I'm working out, sweating and breathing hard, I view the halfway mark of my exercise with interest: a street sign or a stopwatch tells me I have as far to go as I've already gone. How am I doing? Are my legs and ankles holding out? Is it easier or harder than I thought it would be? Am I making progress?

I am about to reach my halfway mark of fifty years, and I view it with interest. How am I doing? Has it been harder or easier than I thought it would be? How will the second half go? It is a good time for reflection, for subtotaling my education, and for setting out feelings about my past, my work, my future—and it seems a good time to share them.

If you mean to share my feelings, you should know more about me and my twelve or more personalities. Here is a stocky body of medium height with powerful legs, working shoulders, and what is left of a once-prosperous paunch. I am in exceptional health for a fifty year old, which mean that my joints only creak in the morning. I work out every day—powerwalking, playing tennis, fantasizing on my NordicTrak that I am cross-country skiing across frozen ice fields, delivering serum to plague-stricken Nome. Even when I'm not exercising, you would normally see me in motion, restless, pacing or fiddling with something.

The face is pleasant enough, welcoming a story or some news. From a wide battery of expressions ranging from silly to incensed, there are two more frequently used than others: an oblivious, benign frown of intense brow-furrowed concentration, and an expectant, brash smile. Here is a nose of character, and under it a grey walrus mustache. Dimples that may have been cute when I was eight have worked themselves into the face from much smiling and make parentheses that connect the nose with an aspirin chin set in a big neck. There is a tonsure of thick white hair around a bald pate that sets off a high forehead like a sperm whale's melon. A pair of muddy bluey-brown eyes, wary and myopic, behind big glasses. A keen observer would note from a characteristic craning of the neck, up and down as I examine anything, that they are bifocals. If you speak to me for any length of time, I might well ask you to repeat a phrase now and then; my hearing is, literally, shot (I did a great deal of target and trap shooting when I was in my teens, and very few shooters used ear protection then). My voice, as nearly as I can tell from inside my head, is staccato and varies widely in pitch, like the bark of an interested dog.

I am a white male and this suggests a *caveat.* I haven't noticed any enormous benefits from my standing in the power elite, but I suppose I should be thankful not to have been held back by being black or female or some other flagged minority we white males seek to suppress. I have been held back by my own failings. I could stand

Infant Adkins (Courtesy of Jan Adkins.)

up for my own victimhood and place myself in several minorities—alcoholics, manic-depressives, dyslexics—but I prefer to think that I, like you, have simply missed the boat a lot. I've said Yes when I should have said No, and I've stayed when I should have gone, and I've opened my month when I should have kept it shut. My only victimhood is the great brotherhood (and sisterhood, see below) of persistent stupidity. I like being a man, though, and admire men a great deal. I stand up for my gender: we were out there tap-dancing along the intellectual ramparts for five millennia before some miracle in the sixties convinced women to become full partners. We came up with a few interesting tidbits, and we screwed lip a lot. Yes, yes, I'm antediluvian in my beliefs, insisting that women were co-conspirators in our long minuet of I-do-this-and-you-do-that. Personally, I'm glad the old dance is through, though the music was graceful and comforting. We need full partners in this world. I'm a man with a great many close women friends. I have also had the advantage of being a mother as well as a father, and I have raised two children, alone for many years. I value women and the feminine side of my own nature. But here is my literary caveat: when I speak, it is from my standpoint, a man's, and I take it that you may want to see the world from my male eyes.

I will not say "he or she" often, though the omission is for flow rather than chauvinism. I do not think that God is a man, though I will sometimes refer to "Him" because I am a man. Chipmunks undoubtedly think God has great fur. I invite you to travel in my mind for a few pages and add gender-embracing phrases (or phrases for color, nationality, creed, or sexual orientation) for your own comfort, for I have no wish to exclude anyone.

You are reading about me because I do something that interests you. What do I do? I am an explainer. My particular talent is unraveling complicated ideas and making them understandable. My central article of faith is that virtually anything is explainable to anyone: a ten year old could understand orbital mechanics or the immune system if it were well explained. I also believe that explaining to young readers requires more skill, more knowledge, and more grace than laying out facts for adults. It is the hardest task I've ever had, and the most exciting.

There are two reasons I'm a good explainer. First, I'm a good learner. I pursue facts with appetite and store them in accessible groups. When I learn more about the atmosphere, for instance (I am designing and illustrating a poster for *Air & Space* magazine on the atmosphere), I store new facts about the volume and concentration of air at altitudes above and below 10,000 feet with what I know about migrating birds—that some geese migrate as high as 20,000 feet. This correlation interests me, makes facts more lively, and binds facts into reality. When I worked at *National Geographic* (I was an art director there for nine years) interviewing hundreds of the brightest men and women in the world, I discovered that experts are almost always poor explainers: they are too involved in digesting minute facts at the cutting edge of discovery and they lose an overall perspective; they have forgotten the paths they took to understanding. An explainer reconstructs a direct, step-by-step path to understanding, keeping facts in proportion, deleting unimportant or misleading side issues. An explainer's path is probably simpler than the wandering path an expert chooses: Lewis and Clark took a circuitous route when they explored the American West but if you need driving directions between New York City and San Francisco, you may want the less involved, less detailed, more direct AAA explanation—a road map.

A good explainer sees patterns. When I collect facts and stories and ideas, I see how they relate to each other and see the shapes of repetition behind them, and even deeper patterns behind them. Studying the Roman Empire, I see patterns in invention and fashion and communication that are similar to the patterns I see in our contemporary society, or in ancient China. Patterns help me relate an historical event to a contemporary event. They also help me create metaphors, which are patterns that help understanding. I can say, for instance, that the Space Race of the 'sixties and 'seventies was very like the medieval search for the Holy Grail, a quest for spiritual goals with worldly benefits, *spin-offs:* travel to distant lands brought technological benefits to the world of the Middle Ages; many contemporary technological benefits came from NASA's philosophical and even spiritual pursuit of space—bigger rocket engines and more reliable computer networks.

I see explanation as a craft in itself, a demanding art. It requires courage in the face of complication. Just as you must never run from a snarling dog, you must never allow a complex problem to intimidate you. Look for the patterns, the big shapes that define the problem, and work inward from them. Ask the right questions. This is a good guide to looking at a new problem: Your sharpest, most useful tool is your own ignorance. Use your ignorance carefully and do not try to cover it up by assuming that you know more than you know. How does this thing work? Why did they build it in the first place? Why wasn't the old way of doing this just as good? What happens if this thing runs out of gas . . . or road . . . or gravity . . . or funding? Your questions should go from the general to the specific: first you ask *what* a locomotive does and *why* does it do that. Later you can ask *how* it works, starting with how steam is made, how it pushes a piston, and eventually you will get to the driving wheels on the track.

I learned an important lesson in explanation from an old friend and a great editor, Jake Page: step out and sit with the audience. A difficulty of expression is often a struggle to maintain some voice you've established rather than your lack of facts or words to convey them. Step out: "You may wonder why I haven't told you what the most important part of the steam locomotive

is," you might say, "But I can't tell you. The truth is more complicated: many parts are important to the engine's power."

This stepping out is also important to style. If you can listen to your own words, the paragraph you've just written, as if you were a friend hearing it for the first time, then you might say, "Tell me the facts and don't bother with the 'wherefore's' and 'thus's.' Don't get fancy on me, just tell me." Jake Page had a motto for writing, taken from an old Jack Teagarden jazz song: "Say It Simple." If you haven't said it simple, you haven't explained it.

*

Why am I an explainer? Good question. Like all of the best questions it has many answers, all of them true. The Shop is a good place to begin.

The Shop sits on Wheeling Island, which sits in the middle of the Ohio River in the city of Wheeling, West Virginia. The Shop is really three buildings connected by stairs and catwalks; together they were the home base of Adkins Roofing Company. My grandfather started Adkins Roofing with $3.67 and a pushcart, walking through the streets of that tough little city around the turn of the twentieth century, calling out his trade, fixing roofs, drainpipes, stove flues, and gutters. He was successful—a cocky, fast-talking, sharp-eyed young man—and built the business. He bought one building of The Shop, then another, then another, all in a row.

In those days, before dams and locks controlled the river, the Ohio flooded every spring. People who lived on the Island then remember floods with annoyed pleasure (in the same way you may remember the last really big, really inconvenient, really neat blizzard). Homes and buildings on Wheeling Island were built with tall ground floors. The spring floods filled them up and the Islanders continued their lives above the water. As powerful and even dangerous as the floods were, they were like a yearly ritual, not a disaster but a rite of spring when neighbors helped one another, work slowed, stranded folk called from back porch to back porch. It was a time of generosity and occasional fun.

The Shop is the first building I can remember. I knew it thirty years after Grampa had bought it. It had a cavernous first floor filled with imperishable roofing supplies like cylinders of tar and pitch as big as fireplugs, barrels of galvanized roofing nails, hundreds of yards of downspout and gutter, rough wood crates around smooth, green glass, carboy flasks full of soldering acid, tubs of red and green roofing paint, rolled sheets of lead, and bed-size flats of sheet metal—galvanized steel, tin, stainless steel, precious copper. Above the high-water level was the working floor. In a hall with a fifteen-foot ceiling stood the machines for cutting, bending, joining, and shaping sheet metal. Shears ten feet long sliced easily through rigid, grey, galvanized steel with a booming, twanging step on the long foot pedal, making a small, timid boy cringe for his fingers and keep them in his pockets. Brakes—bending machines—stood at parade rest in varying sizes. The larger brakes were counterweighted with cantaloupe-sized spheres of iron on thick vertical rods, like cartoon weights for a circus strong man. The clamp handles were cast iron, too, shaped to a pattern made for working men's hands. High in the shadows hung patterns for metal pieces like hoods or ducts or tanks that might be made again (I still like to hang things from the ceiling in my house). Along the west wall, under the tall windows, a long wooden workbench ran almost the length of the hall. It had shelves under it, a dusty cave for seldom-used but occasionally necessary tools that crimped or rolled or seamed or scalloped or notched sheet metal. The workbench had a metal edge with square holes for setting up mandrils and forms over which sheet metal was hammered and bent. Squat, little, black iron furnaces as big as a rural mailbox were spaced along the back of the bench. They looked like big slippers with prong feet, two or three soldering irons resting on the sole, their square, stock business ends pushed into the toe, and on a busy day they were all hissing, glowing inside the toe with gas flame and the red hot irons. The irons had roughly turned wooden handles, unfinished, holding a rod and the heads, glowing dull orange-red, but the tips were ground to pyramids gleaming with silvery solder. Beside each furnace was a white block, a round tin, and a little pot of acid with a metal-handled black brush. The acid was brushed onto a seam to etch the surface and prepare it for soldering. The irons were pulled and rubbed over the white blocks, which yielded a white smoke, then dipped in the tins, which held a clear amber paste and gave forth a brief angry hiss. Now the iron would hold solder and let it into a seam. The solder, itself, was stacked beside the furnaces as heavy foot-long silver sticks with "50/50" cast into the face beside the trade name. The iron was held or rubbed along the seam, vaporizing the acid, transferring its heat, and in a few moments the solder was held along the iron, melting in curves, flowing, filling up the seam and spreading under joints, solidifying in a few seconds. Soldering was exciting to watch, but scary, too.

Welding was more frightening. It was less graceful than soldering but more dramatic. And there were differences in the kinds of welding.

Gas welding, for cutting or brazing (joining with brass) metal, was plain and logical. It made me appreciate the immediacy of chemistry. Cylinders of gas—red for acetylene, green for oxygen—hissed urgently through thick rubber hoses and a bronze handpiece as my father adjusted its heavily knurled knobs, meant to be turned by gloved hand. A grating, sparking metal striker was passed over the tip of the handpiece, popping the acetylene into a sinuous yellow flame with a black ribbon of soot curling away from its tip. The welder (and his son) pulled their black goggles down, filtering out everything in the world but that flame, and then the oxygen joined the acetylene. Instant chemical rage, the oxygen angering the acetylene to awful brightness, terrible heat that could cut metal, a flame like some biblical truth too bright to behold, a flame that—without the goggles—could actually blind.

Electric arc welding was incomprehensible. It just happened. The metal pieces to be fastened were seized by a copper-jawed clamp with red rubber handles. The welder and his boy donned armor, a grey headpiece that swung down over the whole face like a helmet's visor, a dark rectangular window in front of their eyes. The father held a handpiece, another clamp that held a thin, coated rod like a Fourth of July sparkler. The rod approached the grounded metal slowly. Unearthly light, bluish and dazzling, exploded between the rod and the metal but, unlike any other explosion, it was continuous, crackling and buzzing at a brutish sixty-cycle, unvarying, inhuman level until the rod drew back from the burned surface.

Welding was dangerous, deadly. First lessons from my father and uncle: never look at the flame, look at everything else, watch your step, think about your fingers, hands in, think about it, ask. Being around welding, even innocently, was dangerous.

*

My father was particularly good at welding. When I was born, during the war and downriver in Point Pleasant, he was a welding foreman in the Marietta Shipyards, and he was nicknamed "Flash Gordon." I believe he was proud of the name. He welded for forty-five years, even after he had dozens of men working for him, and the danger followed him. I remember another flash, the name for welder's eye-burn. The damaging light attacked your eyes when you weren't looking directly at it, burned your retina. Your peripheral vision was enough to harm you. His eyes were often burnt by the welding around him, working steel deck or steel construction, and I remember the sound of Dad walking the house at night, back and forth, carrying too much pain to sleep.

Fifty years after he was Flash Gordon, the danger has run him down. After years of working in fumes and solvents, acids, the vaporized haze of burning galvanized steel, the reek of pitch and tar, washing paint and grime from his hands in gasoline before he started home, his bone marrow has been affected, refusing to produce blood cells that will carry enough oxygen. It is called siderablastic anemia, and it causes acute shortness of breath with minor exertion. I keep a snapshot of my young father in my mind: I see him running up extension ladders, no hands, with a fifty-pound roll of roofing felt over each shoulder. Still powerful at seventy-five, barrel-chested and strong, he can walk no more than twenty feet before a rest for puffing and muttering. His mind and will are like the cutting torch, fierce and

From **Moving Heavy Things,** *written and illustrated by* **Jan Adkins** (Courtesy of Jan Adkins.)

indignant at this obstacle or any other, and he rages at his confinement. Flash Gordon is still defiant, but his old enemy Ming the Merciless lives up to his name.

My uncle Charlie is part of The Shop—a small, quick man with a handsome face, the broad Adkins forehead, sharp eyes, and a more aquiline nose than his brothers'. He moved with an acrobat's haste in a delicate bouncing stride and had a high-wire artist's balance. Even more frenetic than my father, speaking incredibly rapidly in tumbling rushes of words, humming or whistling as he rushed on, he worked roofs most of his life. With my father and Uncle Charlie I learned to appreciate the geometry of roofs, still my favorite architectural shapes. I would climb up ahead of them and walk the easier pitches, learning to step with my toes out as I walked up, sideways as I walked down. I learned ladders and angles and the dangers of trusting old masonry that seemed solid. I learned to appreciate details—in tools and techniques and in finishing the job right. I would walk through a house with Uncle Charlie and see a ruined ceiling, hanging plaster, and on the roof I would see the minor lapse in detail (a missing nail or a misplaced corner of flashing) that caused it.

I was really learning two deeper lessons: tools and risk. I was learning that the physical world is changeable, fixable. There was no mystery about it; you got the tools and the materials and you fixed it. The Adkins

Boys weren't afraid of any problem. They could fix anything, given time. The labors of Hercules? What do you think, Charles? I don't know, Al, we're going to need one big bulldozer for that stable-cleaning job and two extra trucks, but I give it ten days with four guys and the dozer driver. No, no, no, Charles, we can divert a river right through that place with some conduit, see? The Twelve Labors would have given the Adkins Boys at least two months of delight.

And the risk? This amazes me most. My father loved me and my uncle doted on me, but they encouraged me to wander around some of the most dangerous places I can imagine. I could conjure up nightmares about my own children simply walking through The Shop—massive cutting machines, acid, explosive gasses, piles of sharp metal—much less playing in it day by day. They were not neglecting me. In a way, I think, they were inoculating me, exposing me to small dangers so that larger dangers were understandable without being overwhelming. The two lessons went together: the world can be hazardous but it can be shaped; you need the tools and the willingness. It was a good lesson.

My father told me stories. Not about elves and trolls but how glass was made, or steel, or aluminum. He told me how sand was dredged out of the Ohio River and washed and graded, and where cement came from, and how it arrived in Wheeling on barges, and what mix they used in the cement trucks, and why they didn't mix it on site, and how long it took to harden, how long to cure, and the dressing that went on the surface so it didn't cure too quickly. No kings or wizards, his stories were amazing without them.

In great part The Shop and the work in it—and my father and my uncle and the dusty blue Adkins Roofing Company trucks and the stacks of metal and materials—shaped my writing. I realize now that I lived in a world of specificity and mechanical certainty, very reassuring for a child. How specifically I remember the place, the tools. Perhaps all that utilitarian clutter helped train my memory, but it also set me close to the basic simplicity of the world. I knew that my father and uncle could make or fix anything, given the tools and the plans.

A satellite looks at land beneath it with filters. One filter gives it a picture of vegetation cover, the extent of the forest. Another filter yields a heat picture, showing infrared flares in cities or industrial areas and ignores the forest. Looking back at my childhood with an emotional filter, I see a pattern of opposites, dark and light.

I see a loud and rollicking brightness of happy emotions, laughing with my father and my uncles. I see a dark somber world of anxieties surrounding my mother. With another filter I see a dark city life of grime and soot in a polluted industrial valley, and I see a bright green, airy country summer in the hills of West Virginia where the family went for weeks in the summer. But a satellite controller would ask for correlation, *ground truth.* Are these perceptions real? Or are they some attempt to oversimplify the complex terrain of my past? Surely my memory is simplifying, trying to make some order out of contradictory facts. It is trying to extrapolate some sensible line through a clutter of data points that, individually, mean nothing but have some trend as a group. Where does the trend lead? My childhood was not arranged in black and white but was, like yours, a random spattering of incidents that mixes to some value of happiness or dissatisfaction at a distance of years. The overall trend is important in its own way, but what was the ground truth?

*

The key to the ground truth may be with my mother. The memories surrounding her are so contradictory and confusing that unravelling them could unravel everything. Rosebud? Hardly. There was more substance to Dixie Lee.

Do you remember your mother as she was when you were small? I do not and my younger sister, Judy, doesn't. We remember five or six of her, very different. Some of them were wonderful, the essence of warmth and care. Some of them were tedious, and some were dangerous. Coming through the door of our home was an anxious moment: which mother would be there?

At her best she was flip and funny. Her sarcastic observation of the people around us made my sister and me laugh. Her primary target of opportunity was our father and his bluff-bowed wake through life. She was girlish and smiling, relaxed, and, judging from the photographs my sister keeps, a lovely woman. But her casual remarks could, in a few moments, become more pointed, more caustic, angrier. The distant, humorous view she had of townspeople lengthened and sharpened into paranoia and an obsessive hatred of pretentious, posturing upper crust. In this sudden, bitter transformation she saw their small-town attempts at gentility as flimsy blinds for corruption and sin. "Hypocrite" was probably the word my sister and I remember Dixie speaking most often. The banter about our father, sometimes teasing, sometimes admiring of his concentration and stamina and energy, acquired an uglier edge over the years.

My sister and I were loved and indulged. We were the beneficiaries and the victims of an escalating war of nerves and tones and sarcasm. Our parents found it difficult to care for each other, so we received their affection and attention. But it was impossible to ignore the fact that we lived in a war zone.

At this distance it is sad and plain. Our parents were two bright people with very different personalities who loved and even respected one another for alternate strengths in their personalities. Our mother's grace and filigree, in the best of all worlds, should have complemented Dad's practicality and solidity. But they had frightened one another with rejection, anger, and had made a distance each was willing to bridge only a little way. It is plain, too, that our mother was a troubled woman, suffering what is now called a "bi-polar mood disorder," cycling between deeper and deeper depression (lying in her bed, the curtains drawn shut) and more frightening bursts of silly, feckless release. A nuts-and-bolts guy, our father was confounded by her behavior: it was abnormal, it was embarrassing, it was—worst of all—impervious to any of the fixes that made up his view of the world. If she had had a broken leg or malaria, he could have dealt effectively and directly with it, but this was something unseeable, insubstantial. He couldn't weld her or put a sheet metal screw through her feelings or shore her confidence up with timber or change her spark plugs. He resented and mistrusted her malady and saw it more and more as a flaw in her character. On her part, she saw his stubborn practicality as stupidity, and his desire to get on in the world and to be accepted as hypocrisy.

He came from a loud, happy family of four brothers. They were indulged by a butterball, doting mother, kept in line by a strict, peppery, spry father, and argued constantly, happily, about everything. They lived over The Shop. They built things, they read *Popular Science,* they explored, they hunted and fished and spent time in the woods away from the city. The brothers became contractors and engineers and loved new things all their lives.

She came from a poor and dysfunctional family of twelve, packed into a dark, strange house near the Baltimore and Ohio Railroad yards where her alcoholic father worked as a steam mechanic. Her mother was more profoundly troubled than she. Her brothers and sisters were a mixed, wrangling lot. A few walked out of McMechan, West Virginia, with style and wit and a generous heart—my aunt Frieda and my uncle Garland were sweet, caring people. Most stayed, mired in depression and booze and sadness. Judy and I dreaded our obligatory trips to McMechan (just downriver from Wheeling) with Dixie. The house had a smell of creosote and sleeping people, a place of dark corners and whispered conversations and odd looks. We wondered that our father never came with us. He stopped going, I found out recently, after an incident when I was an infant: after an argument my grandmother seized me roughly from Dixie and ordered them to stay; he advised her quietly to give the child back to his wife or he would beat her senseless; he left with his family and did not return.

When I was tiny, four or six, there was a poem that terrified me, "Little Orphant Annie," with its awful refrain,

> . . . And the goblins will get you
> Ef you don't watch out!

. . . In retrospect, we were right to dread the place.

*

There was a place I loved, though, and it remains in my memory like a cup of sweet cider: Viola. Back in the mountains behind Wheeling, over many ridges and toward the Pennsylvania border, Viola was a clutch of a few houses and two taverns on the banks of Big Wheeling Creek, at the base of Sand Hill. It is no longer on maps and it no longer exists, really, as a destination for anyone. But when I was little the taverns were still open and the dirt road still smoked with the dust of cars coming and going, where or from I do not know. After a long drive on dirt roads, climbing, seeing cows and pigs and more trees than Wheeling offered, the road ran along a ridge and fell suddenly into switchbacks, down and down for ten minutes. At one switchback the driver—my father, my grandfather, my uncle—blew the horn a special way; that turn was a few miles above our own destination and we were telling them "We're Coming!" We turned north at the bottom, passed one of the taverns, and went on to Turkey Run, where the car slowly and carefully forded a stream. This was magic. It was all they could do to keep me in the car, I had to watch the wheels fighting the fast current. Then up and off toward the place, almost there, excited, and then there it was, Camp. That's all we ever called it, Camp. It was a rude cottage set into the steep hill and separated from Big Wheeling Creek by a dirt road and a patch of brush, cut early in the season with a Gravely tractor known as Old Dobbin. It had a tin, standing seam roof painted red (the Boys must have agreed that, for this application, tin was right) and a long front porch. It had a narrow garden plot, tilled by Old Dobbin, and a grape arbor that arched over the path paralleling the road and leading to the outhouse.

Patterns in light and dark. I look back to life in the city, within sight of The Shop, on a street shared with busses that made the dishes rattle in their cupboards, in an industrial valley where the air was visible and tasted coppery, where the sun broke through the manufacturing smog—from Wheeling Steel, Wheeling Pipe and Coupling, and the Blaw-Knox Foundry—only after hours of work dismantling the yellow-grey stuff above us. That was the bulk of my life but, amazingly, I see it paired equally with the few weeks a year I spent in Viola, because that green place was such a wonder, such a powerful influence.

Life in Viola was relaxed. There was a red checkered oilcloth on the big table where everyone ate, and spoons in a glass mug on the table. There was a pump and a coal cookstove. There was a rain barrel. There was the creek itself, full of life: crawdads and turtles and fish and snakes and water skeeters and birds. There was the smell of scallions peeled for lunch, of green leaves around us, of citronella skeeter chaser daubed ineffectually on me, of kerosene lamp oil and gasoline for Old Dobbin, of gunpowder when the brothers plinked at cans floating in the creek with .22's, and the not unpleasant smell of the outhouse. There was the sound of rain on the tin roof, of laughter (a lot of that), of the little generator at night, keeping two bulbs going for cards and talk, of Old Dobbin starting with a hiss-bump, hiss-bump, and then a continuous bray. There was the distant sound of a car approaching on the stone and dirt road, mounting, louder, then breaking out of the green turn beyond the outhouse and the garden and clattering, roaring past, waving to the passengers whoever they were, past, the diminishing sound, and the taste of light dust.

I loved that place. My father loved it, and most importantly I loved the way my father was in Viola, easy and fun and attentive. I knew my mother hated it and I didn't know why, but it was hard to forgive. Examining it now, I can see how easy it was for her to dislike. Coming out of a family of twelve in a cramped house, my mother wanted lace curtains and clean floors. Living rough had no charm for her. It was also the absolute domain of the Adkins Boys and their loving mother, my grandma. They were close, and Dixie was not confident enough to be one of them. Who was? None of the aunts felt at home there, I fear. They were outsiders but welcome. They had a strained look often, but in the early '50s camp life was not part of a woman's job description. Viola was such a sweet place, though, with the potential for so much joy, I still believe that the men my mother and my aunts married lived there, in their hearts. In some unrecoverable way, the best part of my father, his boyhood, stayed in Viola. He abandoned the boy in him because he thought his family needed a grown-up. Even good men make this tragic mistake. In truth we stopped going to Camp because our mother hated it, and I can understand why, but after forty years it is still hard to forgive.

It is easier to forgive the depressions and the rages. I understand those now; I've struggled with them myself. It's easy to wonder if current medication could have helped my mother. Perhaps. Drugs help some people through difficult times, but I question their long-term effects, especially with addictive people like my mother. All her life she was addicted to things that promised a confidence she perennially lacked: alcohol, tranquilizers, religion, scorn. She leaned on the frailest crutches: imagined illnesses, sympathetic doctors, vitamin shots, and even longed for old age as some kind of escape from the responsibilities of an adult. She carried a wound that was never healed, and when she died, alone (my parents divorced after my sister and I left), it was fresh and painful. How could we have helped her heal? How might we have lent her courage? I'm a good explainer, but I have never made a good job of this heavy question.

In a troubled house a child finds other realities. David Moyes and I had dozens. Picture two best friends, small bookish kids who talk about space travel and inventions and bad smells, excitable boys of ten living on Wheeling Island. David's father worked for *The Wheeling Intelligencer* and received two movie passes every week.

He was a stuffy man who had no use for mindless pastimes, thank goodness, and the wonderful tickets fell to us. There was a price, though, payable to fate. Each week the two boys, hardly the bold characters we wished to be, walked half the length of the Island and confronted the Great Void: the suspension bridge. That bridge is part of the Historical American Engineering Record now, a marvel in its time, spanning the big river across its deep commercial channel with massive cables and steel decking you can see through. We were terrified but resolute. Fortifying ourselves with a hit of chocolate, we would start talking tough blocks before the bridge ramp, and then we were on it, daring one another to look down. "See? I'm looking. I'll bet you won't, a thousand dollars." The drop, beneath our Buster Browns, seemed like a thousand feet. Unless the water table has risen, it was about fifty. But we endured, we prevailed, like Shackleton and Perry, until the blessed abutments on the east side, and then we were close to our sanctuary.

Wheeling was a gritty city. When my socks came off at bathtime, black lines of soot and grime were tattooed around my ankles. Touching a fireplug or a wall left a black smudge on the finger. The sky was more often yellow-grey than blue. I will not slight that Wheeling, though: the two boys lived in the miasma of powerful industry and its energy must have sparked across their

Daughter, Sally, in the Cascades, on the way to the top of Mt. Cameron (Courtesy of Jan Adkins.)

minds. Today Wheeling is clean and weak, all of its grime—and all of its heart-filling commerce—is gone. As David Moyes and I made our brave trek on Saturday afternoons, the whistles were still braying over the steel mills and galvanizing plants and pipe coupling factories, spewing out smoke and production and dollar reality, a practical world that seemed to have no time for fantasy. But fifty yards from the bridge abutments lay a cavern of fantasy: the Capitol Theater.

It was one of the movie palaces of the thirties, enormous, elegant. To us it was the only elegant thing in Wheeling, and we needed some touch of grace to flux our heated, ten-year-old imaginations. Art deco columns graced by art deco sculptural women without nipples threw the ceiling up into unreachable darkness. The carpet was blood red, the walls were ornate, the carpeted staircases were grand. The purple curtain that finally parted for the blaze of light and magic was velvet an inch thick that hesitated and resisted before gliding aside, swaying like a gypsy skirt. David and I huddled in the popcorn-scented darkness before this fire of imagination and threw ourselves like supplicants into it, becoming each week a part of another world far from Wheeling. We were brave explorers, projecting our hearts to enormous distances. No one knew how dedicated we were to imagination, how rigorously we trained for our chosen discipline, and no one noticed that our return across the awful bridge was bolder than our going.

The movies made me write. They gave me respect for the magic of imagination. I knew its power. I suspect that the little trial David and I faced crossing the river (no parent today would let their ten year olds wander a city as freely as we did) made the experience more vivid and more lasting. I still love the movies. I huddle with new worlds and popcorn in the dark and throw my heart to new places.

I am trying to tell you how my mind was shaped. The events and situations that influenced me most are small. They would never appear on a résumé and would fall beneath the notice of the FBI (if they should suspect me of something dangerous). The big, terrible things that shaped your perceptions are events your best friends and relatives might not have noticed as more than events or annoying habits. The mountains of your mind are wrinkles in time, mere ripples in the social fabric.

I am also trying to be honest with you, and I am an honest man—within the limits of myopia and of professional fantasy. (Never ask a writer what the tennis score is: he will most often blurt out what he thinks the score *should* be.) Being honest is not easy on me or even on you, as the reader. My mind and work have been shaped by light and dark forces, deeds and misdeeds. Some of it is not pretty scenery.

*

In the summer after third grade we moved from the city to the country. My father built a house at the edge of St. Clairsville, Ohio, about fifteen miles west of Wheeling. The house is white brick and stainless steel with aluminum windows and a flat industrial roof, a clean structure that may lack grace but will be standing firmly for the tricentennial Fourth of July. I doubt that the roof will be leaking, even then. When our house was built at the end of the road, we were surrounded by fields. The nearest structure was a hatchery with a kennel. A high, bald knob rose up beside us: the north side was planted in corn, the south side left for grazing Herefords. A woods faced us across the dirt road. It had trails that led me down, through years of exploring, to other woods, and other woods that led on to Canada and the Pacific Northwest, it seemed, or at least farther than I ever went. The best woods embraced a narrow valley and stream, going down and down, lovely and full of secrets. The bones of sheep lay scattered near a spring in a field corner. An old farmhouse bulged with stored grain. A big house, almost a mansion, sat abandoned and overgrown, open-doored and broken-windowed, with musty books still on the walnut library shelves. Far down the valley (I mean far for an eleven year old) was Three Falls, a terminal destination like Katmandu or Tierra del Fuego: a short water tumble over a ledge of rocks, a broad and shallow pool, then a sizeable waterfall with a deeper, swimmable pool that flowed on and over an impressive drop, fifteen or twenty feet, to a deeper, darker pool. Just short of Three Falls was an evil port to the underworld, a ventilation shaft for an abandoned coal mine. Skin prickling, throat aching, an eleven year old could look over the four-foot concrete collar into the black pit. A rickety wooden stair, untrodden by any sane person (except perhaps by David Valentine, a fearless black boy in my class), reached down twenty feet and ended disastrously in hanging, rotted wood. It was necessary to throw a stone, the largest you could manage, into the shaft and wait many mysterious seconds for a clatter and a doomed splash or, sometimes, a clang of metal from the blackness.

Just beyond Three Falls was the end of the world, or the end of any world you wanted to explore, since the sweet green valley broke onto a reddish, noxious coalmine tailing dump that fanned out to ragged bluffs smoking from deep inextinguishable fires.

My experience of St. Clairsville was alienating. It was an old, established town. Its families were old and settled and lived by the bones of their ancestors, it seemed. I stayed in that pleasant little town of rolling hills—so much more beautiful than stained, sooty Wheeling—for eight years before I went off to college, and I never felt comfortable or part of its inner life. I was always an outsider, certain that any real citizen could reveal my impersonation as a member of the tribe. My family, uncomfortable with its own bond—that primary bond between my mother and father—was not comfortable with other families. I remember being alone a lot at the end of the road, and of wandering the woods alone for days on end. I know I had friends but I always felt like an awkward new boy, and it is the alone part I remember.

Writing this, I'm struck by how classically neurotic it seems. What happened to make me feel so alienated? What minor ripple became my Matterhorn of separation, looming between me and the world? I could say it was something about the dysfunctional wrangling in my family. I could isolate the first awareness of some discomfort, some problem, to the move from Wheeling to St. Clairsville, which uprooted me without much preparation or involvement or explanation. I could cite fears about my mother's sudden emotional crashes, manic episodes, compulsive behavior, depressions, and the strange cloying affection she gave to my sister and me at unpredictable intervals, syrupy attention that was so self-serving it seemed impersonal.

The whole truth is more subtle and systemic, probably. The fact is that I was a strange boy. I had a secret inner life and loved aloneness as much as I hated and feared it. I loved to disappear and creep about and project my small self onto the larger images of heroes. I was alternately desperate for attention and jealous of my solitary world. Perhaps this, as much as anything else, made me a writer: I gather attention like a carnival barker with the odd products of my solitary fantasies.

As a father I can look back to the alternately timid and precocious boy I was (am) and see a more complete picture. As I watched my children grow, it became obvious that they were hard-wired with a given nature from birth. A good parent can amplify and celebrate that innate personality, a controlling parent can try to change it (succeeding only in submerging it), and parents driven by their own distractions can ignore it. Parenting is a critical skill but not as formative as we would like to believe.

I believe my parents loved me. I believe they were baffled by me and too driven by their own inner struggles to see the actual shape of their boy. I believe they gave me everything they felt a child needed and made allowances for my deviation from their model of a normal boy, but they did make me aware of my shortfall. It is easy to love them but it is also easy to believe that they resented my stubborn reluctance to fit the rôle in their minds. For Al and Dixie I was a beloved changeling, and for my father I still am an odd but fond stranger he lived with and nurtured for many years.

*

I'm going to skip over school now, because I don't think it's very important. The normal run of primary and secondary education in America was a dispiriting passage from one room to another, from one disconnected subject to another, enlivened only by a very few teachers who nurtured some secret spark not yet extinguished by the system. I had a few, but they were not enough to make school interesting or even useful. In thirteen years of being ground through the proud literacy machine like a sausage, no one told me what I was obliged to be doing, what tests were for, what study was, what or how much (or how little) I was expected to accomplish. Who was the practitioner and who was the client? We—the students in sixth grade English or biology—assumed that we were the work force, manufacturing a product for someone else, for the school board or for The State, as if our book reports had some intrinsic value to our teacher and her masters. Come to that, no one ever told me what a book report was meant to accomplish, and so I missed (along with millions of other students) the enormous importance of book reports. None of us had a notion of being clients on a deferred payment plan. We believed we were worker bees who did what we did because we did it, and we went mindlessly back and forth from book to paper without a clue.

But we were the clients of a system (mis-) designed to help us toward a primary task: learning how to learn. The central, laudable purpose was to provide a literate work force to the state. Though we were never informed of their existence, and though their shapes were hidden behind a smoke screen of tests and requirements, we had four or five plain, primary goals: learning to communicate with the common language of the state (English, literature, composition), learning simple computation (math, geometry), learning the physical basics of our life and the life around us (science, biology), and learning that we were only one society at one point in time in an old world of many differing societies (geography, history, civics). The fifth goal was meant to be taught using the first four goals as a tool: learning to gather information on specific, detailed subjects (study skills that should have prepared us to learn machining or car repair or philosophy or medicine).

We didn't know we were learning to learn—and doing so poorly that most of us would play catch-up the rest of our lives. I was not a good student. I was bright, I suppose, but erratic. I had a short, blunt attention span, and I'm not sure I knew how to excel.

But everyone knows how to do well! No.

I teach, now—editorial illustration at the Rhode Island School of Design and at the Maryland Institute College of Art. Many of my students are remarkably like I was: bright, curious, vain, awkward. I've discovered a basic learning block, the one-dog category: in any creative exercise (writing, speaking, and especially the graphic arts) students will make every effort to avoid being judged with the class. They will try to create a category to themselves: "You must judge me for my own unique qualities, not by common stuff the whole class shares." I've seen my students do this so many times. Ask for a small black-and-white drawing and the display wall blossoms with full-color paintings, sculpture, photos. Each variation from the assignment insisting, There's only one dog in this category. I've *done* this so many times: I spent most of my student energy in separating myself from my classmates, and much less in learning.

Later, in college, I wasted my time and effort in proving that I was special, the only dog in my category. I tried to believe in a flair that superceded dull competence. I held simple plodders in scorn—and of course in anguished envy. I danced as fast as I could, hoping no one would notice the fairly dull boy and his lackluster work behind the blur of footwork. Flash over substance, style over content, pretension hiding fear.

The one-dog category is an important realization for a teacher. I can see it at work in adults, too, and in the fractionalizing of our country into smaller groups, to be regarded only by their own narrow values. It's a fear of judgment and failure, of being less than anyone else, of losing. And if we live with those fears, we need our own tiny categories.

So I wandered through eight years of confusing and largely inept education in a small town in Ohio. The strain between my parents grew. I had friends but remained inside my constructed shell, alone and afraid.

One of my friends, David Henderson, was extremely bright. It was a time of great interest, little knowledge, and no sensitivity about intelligence. It was the time of the television quiz show and universal IQ testing. Teams would come to test David and would, occasionally, test me. I was bright, but I was never Henderson. This almost feeling was a fixture through my entire youth. David and I were good friends but that insecurity stayed with me.

The cold war had given the United States a paranoid suspicion of its own inferiority, and the sudden presence of *Sputnik* orbiting overhead did not help it. The society of the 'fifties and 'sixties was swollen with prosperity but deeply suspicious. The politically confounding Korean War whispered in the national ear that might and wealth *didn't always work.* We were convinced that Communism *did* work. We didn't like what it would do to us and our prosperous, open-ended lives, but we were certain that Communists played hardball smarter and with fewer scruples than we were willing to play it. We saw the pictures of Russian children sitting stiffly and attentively at their desks, speaking eight languages and figuring advanced math problems. We knew if those kids didn't get A's, the Politburo would liquidate them—harsh, but those kids could do math. We knew that intellectuals were setting up Communist cells all over the country in little towns just like ours, probably right down the block from the school. And we knew that the days of comfortable assumptions were over—the Supreme Court was desegregating the South. There was a sickness in the body of our society, our own internal crimes of oppression unpropitiated by Lincoln and the U.S. Civil War. At some simple, naive level of our unexamined consciousness, we believed that King Cotton and wicked slavers of the Deep South had tainted our seed.

We went to school with black kids and were aware that their culture was separate from ours. They lived in the black section of St. Clairsville. But so did the others.

From **Deadline for Final Art,** *written and illustrated by Jan Adkins* (Courtesy of Jan Adkins.)

This was coal mining country and we had an entire roster of minorities: hunkies and wops and bohunks and pollocks and squareheads. We had Czechs and Greeks and Slavs but we were short on Jews and Orientals. St. Clairsville was farmland and mines near steel mills. We were international but our small society still aligned itself around the prosperous, successful core of white, Protestant, goal-oriented, order-loving Americans that, presumably, attracted immigrants from all over the world to come and be part of it. It was a good notion: we'd established a central set of values and we'd shown that they worked, imperfectly but consistently. We asked everyone to jump in the melting pot, add their flavor, but stay with the basics. Work hard, obey the law, take care of your kids, contribute to the community, become one of us. It was harder for some than for others. We weren't a homogenous society like Japan, indeed we were proud of our polyglot, polychrome heritage, but the melting pot was not patient. It demanded assimilation within a reasonable time. When a group clung too long to its character, refusing to supplant it with the common slock, the Melting Pot felt its generosity had been insulted, and its pique could be ugly. In our rural area the Catholic Church was still suspect and we were casually certain that its priests received orders from the

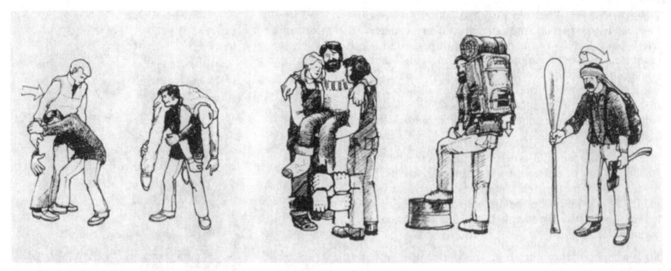

From Moving Heavy Things, *written and illustrated by Jan Adkins* (Courtesy of Jan Adkins.)

pope, a foreign potentate. The remarkable faith of Jews in keeping their society separate was both admired and suspected but theology, never sensible in our society, was too primary to remind us that Jesus had not been killed by the Jews but by an old political crisis in the Middle East. We really believed that Jesus was a white Protestant, perhaps Episcopal.

I believe that our society was impatient with black Americans for being so obvious, as if they chose to remain dark-skinned. We weren't set up to understand the systemic differences. David Valentine's picture in the yearbooks looked awful, because the camera was set for an 18 percent grey white-skin reflection. David was about 65 percent grey to the film and in order to get facial detail his picture—and every other black student's picture—was underexposed on the print. It was a ghastly effect next to all the standard printings, as if we went to school with black ghosts. There were other students at the economic level of African Americans in our town, farm families and laborers, but black members of the community were visually, obviously different, and our world was approaching the cusp of change. In my mind the great tragedy of American life, the polarization of black and white interests, may rest solely with the blank fact that one minority was graphically discernable, though the American heritage of our black fellow-students was almost certainly hundreds of years older than most of our European and east European immigrant pedigrees. In their turn the Irish and the Italians were the undesirable minorities of America but they assimilated, blended, and when the great civil rights changes came in the 'sixties, black Americans might have followed the same unpleasant but ultimately rewarding path. But they were 65 percent gray.

Over the years I spent in St. Clairsville, a painful pressure began to build at school. I was made aware that I had a terrible liability: a great potential. Teacher after teacher became impatient with my middling performance and pumped the pressure higher: "You're smart,

you can do the work, but you don't! Why not? You have such great potential!" I try to remember that intelligence and the idea of gifted students were poorly understood, but it's difficult to look back and not see a dangerous situation building. Those teachers were trapped by the education system into the test paradigm, and here was a high-IQ child who refused to test well. Not one of them asked smart questions. None of them looked at me as if I were anything but a standard issue student with an extra helping of brains. Not one of them wondered if I had any special difficulty with school or with perception. Smart was smart, test results didn't lie, and I was stubbornly refusing to fulfill my potential. This refusal was communicated to my parents repeatedly, and it broadened the gap between us. There was no way, in the late 'fifties, that another kind of attention could have reached me. It's taken me forty years to understand intelligence, and I've had the advantage of special perspective. The pressure built relentlessly through school and continued into college.

My time at college was a disaster. I was inadvertently and unavoidably set for self-destruction, as you might power up an expensive, delicate robot and set it walking, without thinking much about it, toward the rim of the Grand Canyon. But let me pause here and speak about love.

*

I am writing about my profession, which is communication. I'm an explainer in words and pictures. Though you may have decided otherwise by now, what I do best is write prose. To write, anyone needs four cardinal qualities: curiosity, introspection, courage, and love.

Why write anything if you're not curious enough to find out about everything? Writing is really the process of discovery more than reportage. A.J. Liebling, one of the writers I most admire, maintained that a great reporter had two attributes: insatiable curiosity and an almost painful shyness. He believed that curiosity drove the reporter past his reticence, and the shyness made people talk to him. Shyness, or really an air of vulnerability, helps an interviewer. When I was interviewing scientists and explorers and scholars for *National Geographic,* I discovered that interviewing is the art of making yourself the canvas, encouraging the interviewee to paint his or her story on the canvas and keeping the painting on track. My sharpest and most useful tool in interviewing was ignorance: I did my homework and established a working knowledge of the subject but was plain about what I didn't know. My vulnerability was in my ignorance, my curiosity was immense, and my interviewee was eager to work on such a receptive, unthreatening canvas. I wanted to know everything, and I wanted to connect it all. I knew there was a reason for everything and every reason related to what we were in our tribal hearts. The writer must be curious.

You can't dictate good prose. Perhaps some Cato, trained in oratory, might pass off acceptable words, but never great writing. The spoken word and the written word are two languages. The written word is meant to be polished, smoothed, reworked. Introspection is the quality that insists on change, reviews the content, demands more graceful phrasing, insists on deliberate pacing. Introspection is unblinking honesty, a difficult goal. I suspect that all writers are both troubled and blessed by self-doubt. Perhaps only people with the ability to question their own work can be writers. The inner dialogue that is constantly making critical changes is the very process of writing, and it is also the source for long nights of depression. It comes with the territory, and it's a chronic injury that you'll learn to live with, like shin splints or tennis elbow.

Courage is deciding you have something to say. Many good writers and illustrators lose their courage for a time. Their own vanity ambushes them. They want to say large and amazing things about life, to change reality with their images. It's a daunting goal and when they realize they won't write *The Origin of Species* or *The Interpretation of Dreams,* they lose the courage to say the small, homely, important things they could say. The writer and illustrator don't often provide revelations, merely their personal view of the world, but if that view has clarity, and if it carries the courage of confidence, it can be truly valuable. If a writer is brave and honest, the body of his work can be significant and can change reality for a few readers. More importantly, in seeing and speaking with courage, the writer will have perceived reality as well as he could.

A writer needs love. Without it he is dull, and so is his work. A good writer communicates his passion for the subject, for the people around it, and his passion for life. The ability to tap passion is the basis of art, and the ability to do it on cue is the hallmark of a professional. To have a fiery affair with the nuts and bolts of life, so that writing about perfectly fried perch or the masonry of the Renaissance cathedrals is as exciting as writing erotica, is a great writer's gift. Romantic love always resides behind that love of life, like the constant pilot light that ignites a furnace's larger flame. Most writers are constantly in love, one way or another. I know one well-known writer who identifies each of her novels with the affair that fueled her through the process. Look at any dedication and reflect on this: no one writes for money; no one can pay you enough for the difficulty, and damn few pay you at all; you only write for the glory of the thing, which is love.

In St. Clairsville I fell in love, sometime late in the fourth grade, and I continued steadfastly to love the same girl through high school and most of college. I suppose I love her today, though love has become such a complicated concept in fifty years that it is difficult to say the word without obscuring the object of love with overlays of caution and fear. Loving the girl in St. Clairsville was wonderful. It was also disastrous.

I have had the fortune—good and bad—to be in love half a dozen times, and a few spates of infatuation between. I know that I am predisposed to an unhealthy obsession with women who are not quite available.

From **Moving Heavy Things,** *written and illustrated by* **Jan Adkins** (Courtesy of Jan Adkins.)

They may have other fish to fry, they may be healing from old wounds, they may have other preferences. Compounding my choices are choices women make: I am an odd creature to be sure. I am voluble and seem close, but a part of me is stubbornly alone. I intimidate most likely women, and the hardy souls that persist are often as troubled as I am. I believe I ask the women I love to pursue that solitary part or me, and I bark at them when they do, wanting to keep my aloneness and wanting them to storm and subdue it. Once again, the experience or maturity is that two opposing feelings are not only possible, but likely.

If one of my twelve personalities is a lover, and if you could look at his face, it would be scarred and beaten like a bad prizefighter who stayed too long in the ring. But I still believe in love. It's the only game in town, and for a writer it is air or water, basic.

At the end of my time in St. Clairsville I launched myself toward college, totally unprepared in any way, unsupported in anything but funds, unaware of what this new life could require. I was fecklessly, obliviously doomed. I had left the airplane without a parachute, and I was actually enjoying the view on the way down, expecting something wonderful to happen near the ground.

I don't want to spend too much time on this disaster because it was so inevitable that the real importance is only in the healing afterward. I will note that no one helped me in any way to make an intelligent, sensitive choice of colleges, that no one suggested some alternative to walking out of high school and into college, that I seriously considered only one college, that my family was expectedly incapable of viewing this as a problem with more than the most obvious solution, and that I enrolled in the fall term at what must have been the worst choice I could have made, Ohio State University. Looking back, I can see that I should have waited and worked a year before entering college. I needed the seasoning. I should have enrolled in a small college far away, a place that might have given me some support and a sense of belonging, along with a sense of place. Ohio State University was a vast, impersonal, mechanical nightmare where I promptly became lost in the smallest currents of brutish dorm life, confused by assignments and the need for study, and reduced to insignificance in huge classes of a thousand or more. The largest classes, like differential calculus, were often taught by television, presided over by an unspeaking graduate assistant. I can barely remember one held in a tiny basement room of the Botany and Zoology building, where the temperature and the humidity were conveniently high for the plant specimens but acted like a Mickey Finn to a confused student walking in from the searingly cold winds of the huge, flat Oval, parking himself in an oak chair to watch, for the three minutes before sleep smothered him, a full professor named Fisher talk about higher mathematics. I failed that class several times. In fact, I failed almost every class, and flunked out of the university three times in a period of two years.

Did this tell anyone there was a problem? No. It brought up the spectre of my great potential, and why wasn't I doing well when I could if I really wanted to? Conclusion: I really didn't want to.

I started at Ohio State in the architecture program, an art and a science I have always loved, but a difficult course of study, especially for someone as ill-prepared as I. Architecture students took 21 hours of class each semester; education majors took 14 or 16. The study demands confounded me, and I did poorly even in design classes. I was obviously skillful at the concepts, but I could not or would not meet the requirements. I avoided the subjects entirely, separating myself in the same way I now see my illustration students avoiding judgment. I insisted on being a one-dog category. I was a colorful character, amusing, ineffective. I failed classes over and over.

Four important things happened at Ohio State. During one of the periods between failure and readmittance I was hired by a great architect, W. Byron Ireland, and worked as a designer with Byron's firm, off and on, for five years. Byron had been one of Eero Saarinen's senior designers. He was my introduction to elegance of design, the art of gracious living, and the power of style. The story of Byron's kindness to me, of the people he worked with, who became my closest friends, of his decline and of his pauper's death a dozen years later is a subject I have kept fermenting for many years, the subject of a novel one day.

In architecture I took classes with a gifted architectural historian, Professor Perry Borchers, who is my friend and one of my important mentors today. For his classes I had to make graphic reports, in words and pictures, and I credit him with the beginning of my career.

One of the best things that happened to me seems like a catastrophe. After struggling to achieve without the tools or understanding of achievement for three years, after flunking out of an academically mediocre school three times, after failing to excel even at architecture, my chosen art and profession, I was laboring under an intolerable pressure. Depression dogged every step I made. I had no support. My parents could not understand or dilute the pressure; they were a part of it themselves. My irrational and even offensive behavior, really a plea for comfort and care, drove away the girl I had loved for so long. She was dealing with her own family demons. This so often happens with people who choose one another instinctively: they have recognized similar anxieties in each other that actually exacerbate their problems. A whiff of my difficulty was all she needed to disappear. I was only barely rational during that time but always amusing enough that the people around me discounted my difficulties. I was too smart to be in such a mess. Why didn't I do something about it? I had such great potential. Of course, it was my convoluted intelligence, twisted by fantasy and pretension and desperation, that drove my prospects ever downward.

If you learn nothing else from my curious life-tale, these two lessons may be useful. First, intelligence comes in all flavors and in all band-widths. A very few people are smart across the board. Some are brilliant in one narrow area. I have known photographers and picture editors who were image-gifted but couldn't read a map or figure out why airplanes flew. I have known Nobel laureates who were hopelessly stupid at simple human interaction. I have never known a truly intelligent person who did not have complete lapses of understanding in random areas. And I have known hundreds of dull-witted people who exhibited sudden brilliance inside their area of expertise. Intelligence is one part of nobility but, in itself, it is nothing to boast of. The other part of nobility is the spiritual confidence that can only be built brick by brick, with great effort and much pain. If you find a man or woman with both, try to learn everything you can from them. I am as smart as a whip, and as stupid as a steer.

The second lesson is that intelligence is not a defense against depression or self-deceit. Rather, it indicates a vulnerability. Depression, I have concluded over the thirty years I've grappled with the Black Dog, using therapy and drugs with and without support, is a spiritual wound. I believe in therapy; it has helped me. I believe that some people can be helped by drugs; they did me less good than was expected and even retarded my progress after a time. I believe passionately that the only real help lies in facing the spiritual problems inside your deepest system of beliefs—how you feel about goals and death and love and children and the shortness of life and the paradox of God. I do not believe that Eastern philosophies or mystic visions or religious revelations or deep massage or transcendental meditation touch the spirit of an American depressive because they are outside the Western, hamburger, Chevrolet vocabulary of images and ideas that make up that inner core of belief. You might as well expect herbs and dancing to clear your clogged drain. I do not believe that arranging the practical clutter of your life addresses emotional or spiritual wounds, though it offers some breathing space (some divorces are good examples of practical solutions that send the baby flying with the bathwater). I don't believe that there are easy fixes, free lunches, or miracle diets. Recognition of a wound and working toward healing with understanding of the seriousness of the problem every day sometimes actually works. Some of the real helps are simple. Alcohol is a depressive agent; think about how you use it. Love is basic to life, if it's sensible and supportive. Being good to yourself, with the admission that you are someone who needs and deserves good care, is essential. Reward yourself and be firm with your lapses. Changing the venue, if you can, helps; making a trip is not escaping if you know you're coming back, but it can give you perspective on the questions you left behind. One of the most important parts of dealing with a spiritual wound is recognizing its pain as real: do not let any fool tell you that you shouldn't feel bad, that so many things are going well in your life that you have no right to weep, that you should count your blessings and feel ashamed that you are whining. If you hurt, you hurt. The pain is a symptom of something wrong. Admit it, embrace it, and fix it as well and as gently as you can. These Adkins Rules for depression have been hard won.

The benevolent catastrophe was a fairly complete nervous breakdown, whatever that meant or means. I flunked school yet again, at a time when the Army was hungry for warm bodies to replace the cold bodies being flown back from Vietnam. My panic overwhelmed me. It was largely despair over my failure. The draft was secondary but it offered a more immediate terror. Curiously, the terror was not death, nor was it any philosophical antipathy toward the Vietnam War. Of course I made lip service to peace and brotherhood, but in my heart I was merely confused by the spectacle. I believed in the necessity of a strong military and in my country acting out or principle, throwing its men and arms into the balance on the side of good. But which side was good? It was never clear to me or to U.S. president Lyndon Johnson, come to that. No one of my generation will ever be comfortable with their own disposition of the Vietnam War, whether they stayed at home with a good deferment, fought in Asia, or exiled themselves to Canada.

No, the terror was not the war, itself, but the Army. I can remember clearly that my greatest fear was of being imprisoned in open barracks for years with forty regular guys. This was the nightmare of the one-dog category: I could no longer be the only dog in my own customized category; I would be sent to the pound. It was desperate elitism but I had never played a team sport or felt accepted by any group, especially a cut through the very middle of America. I was an outsider, always. The fast footwork, light banter, and verbal games that kept me afloat at the edge of my collegiate society would mean nothing. I knew I would be a helpless target. I was purely terrified.

Failure, terror, panic. Some kind soul suggested that I see a doctor at the University Health Center, a sympathetic fellow who wasn't available. You don't always get what you want, but if you try real hard you get what you need. I saw Dr. Richard W. Worst, who listened with watery, benign eyes, saying very little, and concluded mildly that I should stay in the hospital for a while. If my memory bank serves, this was not a miracle diagnosis; I believe I was approaching the state of Lon Chaney Jr., just before the full moon.

So I spent some time in the hospital. I have had two breakdowns in my life: one in 1964 and one in 1987. (In 2010 I will be ready for my next inward journey.) For me and for my situation in life at those times—the pressures, the players, the coincidences, the real and imagined disasters—I *needed* a time-out. An actuary might suggest that you or someone in your life will need the same kind of institutional attention. I can reassure you or your friend this far: some of the best, brightest, worthiest, most caring, and strongest people I have ever known took their time-outs with me. It was not wasted time; it was so valuable that I cannot bring myself to be ashamed of it. Both seasons of respite left me wiser, more sensitive, and stronger.

Another benefit of my first time in the hospital was my aversion to recreational drugs. I had such vile reactions to the crude psychoactive drugs psychiatrists gave me in the mid-sixties that, out of the hospital, when I was offered mind-altering substances in the psychedelic heyday, I just said "No," adding, "This is kid stuff next to what I've taken, and it all scares the bejesus out of me."

Problems can be solved. The resolutions are never quite what you expected, but they make sense. I came out of the hospital calmer and more centered. I returned to school in a couple of semesters, this time in English. Over the next four years I became a good student. Indeed, if my early grades weren't factored into my point average, I would have graduated with honors. I loved school then, and I miss it now. Teaching is one way for me to revisit that interesting, intellectually active time.

I said that four important things happened to me at Ohio State University. Bob Canzoneri was the fourth. I took creative writing with Bob and learned a great deal from his own struggle with writing. I'm not sure that Bob ever taught me how a verb snuggles up to a noun, or if he ever warned me about using modifiers in strings (I'm beginning to warn myself about those things now), but his approach to writing was confident and unmystical. Bob was and is a storyteller. This constituted the technique of his writing (and years of hard-won technique, so personal and abstruse as to be invisible). Tell the story, do a good job. Make it interesting. It wasn't any stranger than that, and if you were *trying* to write, then you were either a tolerable storyteller or, rarely, a great storyteller, and that was just wonderful and he wanted to hear your stories.

Later I learned other creative techniques as simple, as effective, and as excruciatingly difficult to learn. Bill Decker, a great editor and writer, told me that writing a great novel was really bone-simple. You picked a verity, one of life's dozen or so truths, and you wrote a story about people working toward the verity. You went back over what you'd written, and every word that pointed toward the verity you left, and every word that didn't point toward it you took out. Simple. Bill Garrett, the brilliant, megalomaniacal, infinitely painstaking, brusque, intense, and charismatic editor-in-chief of *National Geographic* magazine, for the nine years I was an art director there, was a vastly talented photographer as well as a mystically gifted editor (I apologize for the length of this sentence but no description of Garrett was ever simple). His technical advice on photojournalism could have gone to volumes but, uncharacteristically, he confined it to five syllables:"*f*8 and be there." The explanation, for nonphotographers, is almost as simple: *f*8

is the most common setting of aperture on any camera, medium, so the Great Garrett is telling you not to sweat the tricks, just be in the right place at the right time. I cannot resist the temptation to place myself in this company, so I will pass on the "First Adkins Dictum" of illustration from the "Twenty Guides to Illustration" I issue to my students at the beginning of every semester: the most important rule of illustration is simple and foolproof: *Tell the story.* This is a guide and a diagnostic. If you tell the story, you win. If you don't tell the story, go back and try again.

After eight years of college I left Ohio State with a B.A. in the School of Adult Education (they were the only folks who would take me after I'd flunked out three times), and enough credit hours for a doctorate. I launched myself into the real world with these credentials, along with my training in practical architectural design, an untrained ability at illustration, a desire to write fiction, and an interest in science and design and history. I was bright, eager, curious, fresh, and totally unprepared.

But I had leaped into college totally unprepared! I had learned so much, had struggled so earnestly to overcome my handicaps, and I had succeeded in many ways. Was this a replay? Was this fair? As they say on the coast of Massachusetts, Ayuh. You betcha.

For I had become an apprentice Yankee on the coast of Massachusetts. In my last year of school I married a

Adkins with his son, Sam, on the Chesapeake (Courtesy of Jan Adkins.)

Massachusetts girl, Deborah Ann Kiernan. She was deep and quiet and funny and strange. We lived in Columbus, Ohio, for my last year of school and hurried to Wareham, Massachusetts, because I had been stunned and obsessed. Debbie and her family were from Wareham. The wedding was held there. I had never really seen the ocean. When I arrived, I walked innocently down to the shore of Buzzards Bay, a storage shed of the Atlantic inside Cape Cod where storms, winds, and a particularly nasty wave-chop are kept. I looked at the water, it regarded me, and I have never been the same since that day.

*

Marriage was a strange state for me. I hardly knew how to dress myself and wave bye-bye, as my mother often said, much less deal with someone else. I was a compulsively chatty, disorganized adolescent with no social abilities. I wandered through life obliviously, offending everyone as pleasantly as possible. All of us take our history into any relationship, trailing it behind us like a long plume, getting it caught in other people's doors, knocking over their best lamps with it, and dragging it through the jelly. Invariably and usually unconsciously we reconstruct our childhood family, the only model we have of adult life. To a marriage of dissimilar and often distant people I brought my father's brash, insulting humor and his false, jokey bravado in confronting the dangerous mysteries that surrounded every woman he ever knew. I brought my mother's suspicions, her indulgence in secluded dark moods, and her inadvertently socialist wariness of the broadly defined upper class (hypocrites). I was stubborn and compelled by fears inherent in my childhood model of a family, both to be controlling and to feel victimized.

I have had an enormous advantage in my work of seeing life from a simple, childish perspective. A kind of arrested development has helped me write simpler and communicate my enthusiasm with more credibility. The same arrested development has poisoned most of my important relationships. No, I don't think it's necessary for a writer to be childish; it's merely a seductive option, a crutch often taken.

I loved Debbie. She had a large, warm, honest soul, and I believed she was strong enough to supply the stability I lacked in our marriage. But we can't count on the next step. The one thing we fear most is the unexpected, the kind of sudden volcanism of fate that wounded Debbie and me and, later, brought us to an end.

We were living in her parent's guest house while I searched for a job. The bare, uninsulated cottage was a hundred yards from her parents' home on Little Harbor marsh at the head of Buzzards Bay. Debbie's father, Robert D. Kiernan, was a Yankee lawyer, a peripheral politico, clerk of courts, bailiff, and town counsel. He had a sweet boyish face and a soft voice that hid a streak of prickly will that was very apparent to his two

daughters and the people closest to him. He loved baseball and the Red Sox and gardening and good food and the marsh. Debbie's mother, Doris, was the most powerful and certainly one of the most brutal women I have ever met. She believed that the world was peopled with fools who needed direction, and keenly felt her burden to direct. She was ruthless and scornful and, in the course of her calling as the agent of order in her small New England world, she had neither the time nor the leisure for sensitivity. Her special scorn was reserved for professionals, charlatans like architects, doctors, and even lawyers. They were only fools with sheepskins. It caught up with her. It must be said that Doris was effective and appreciated. She accomplished practical wonders in her small-town arena. Who can say that the cost in embarrassment and humiliation was not worth her work? Small towns need small dictators; the New England town meeting has its administrative limits. Even today, when a new clerk at the Wareham Town Hall is driven to tears by an insulting applicant or fee-payer, an older woman will sometimes step across to her counter, put a generous arm around her shaking shoulders, and murmur after the retreating miscreant, "He wouldn't 'a said that if Doris Kiernan were here. And he wouldn't 'a." One afternoon Doris was gardening with Robert D. in their sandy patch near the guest house and she had a heart attack. She sat down on a bench and announced it to Robert D. He offered to take her to the hospital, but she brushed the suggestion aside. "What did those people know, anyway?" She died that evening.

The sudden death of Doris disconcerted everyone, in their reserved New England way. Robert D. had always been maintained by Doris and now he must be maintained by someone else. The community decided that we would live with him. We didn't have the strength to refuse.

Patterns of light and dark, always. For a struggling new citizen overqualified for most jobs and seemingly unsuited to any profession, the sudden umbrella of a home was a Godsend. Living on that exquisite marsh with a breathing space to write and try new things and explore my adopted Bay was the start of my professional career as a writer and illustrator. The dark side was powerful. Robert D. was the patriarch. Debbie became the mother of the house. I became the boarder, always an outsider in the tight, Yankee society, never really understanding the intricate play of forces under the surface. Debbie and I grew further apart. Another dark result was that Debbie grew more and more despondent. Perhaps today I could see her listless silences and flat affect as the symptoms of real clinical depression. At the time I was too caught up with my own rôle as outsider and victim. She was caught between me and Robert D., both of us self-obsessed, neither of us offering hospitable hearts.

It's difficult for me to think about those years in anything but books, and they are the least of what happened. I wrote and illustrated many books then. It would satisfy a mystic that, at Doris's funeral reception in the house, a friend from New York noticed some of my drawings on the wall and asked if I were interested in writing books. You betcha. She connected me with publishing friends in New York and a month later I was writing my first book, *The Art and Industry of Sandcastles,* a product of an expensive education and hours of fooling around on the beach in front of the marsh. My first book was completely outside publishing standards, because I really didn't know anything about them. I hand-lettered it, I illustrated it, and I designed the pages as best I could. Miraculously it was a success and was nominated for the National Book Award that year. I travelled to book fairs and guest appearances. I began other books. I got an agent. I was a writer.

Deciding that I was a writer was the hardest decision I've ever made. I really didn't know I had made it until one morning on a lobsterboat, doing research for an article later published in *Harper's* magazine on lobstering in Massachusetts. Carl Taylor, my friend and subject, introduced me to Louie, another lobsterman, as they shared coffee in the middle of the Bay, "This here's Jan Adkins, Louie. He's a writer-fellah."

To be a professional writer is to accept an enormous weight of purpose. It is not a profession of appointments and regular paychecks. For almost thirty years I have lived by my wits, month to month. I take pride that I have raised a family and bought three houses and gotten crowns and root canals and kept cars repaired on the earning strength of my cleverness, nothing more. It is an awful profession. It has gotten only a little more predictable and no easier. It is more fun, I will admit, because I am excited by the maturity of my abilities (here, again, you may disagree, and you *are* the reader).

The books followed one another but so many other things happened. The intensity of the emotion packed into that distant time is surely the reason I assign books to cover it.

My daughter, Sally, was born. She was and is a miracle. The world was endlessly fascinating to her, nothing eluded her curiosity. Her wonderful eyes and her delicate hands sought everything, every phenomenon of nature, every object, every taste. A credible amalgam of her mother and me, she was yet unmistakably herself, a unique personality. She is twenty-three now, and a scientist studying botany at the Smithsonian and in the South American rainforests. She is giving and proud and intelligent and graceful and thoughtful. Sally has more of Debbie than most daughters carry from their mothers. They were naturally, fascinatingly close, like a dual being. She carries my somewhat boggy and sad temperament at times—and resents it. I am consistently in awe of her will and her pains at making life go well around her.

My second daughter, Kate, was born, and died a few hours later. For years I dreamed painfully of Kate's confusion, ushered toward the classic River Styx and the six-headed dog's baying and the dark ferry. That I had no belief in these things did not soften the edges of my dream. I had failed little Kate, somehow, and let her go into the darkness without me.

My mother died, quite suddenly, of a cerebral aneurism. She lived alone then. She had been dead for a few days when she was found by a friend. Though I spoke to her week by week on the telephone, I did not know her well. There are so many times, sitting by the water or finishing a project, when I would like to talk with her now. There are so many things I've learned that might help. When she died, she was years younger than I am now.

My son, Samuel Ulysses Adkins, was born in 1975. Sam appeared like a sudden burst of sun on a day you thought would be cloudy. He laughed at everything and loved being with people. He had fine, white hair, as I did when very young, but his turned corn-shock yellow and thick. He blossomed in freckles and his smile became a habitual, mischievous grin, always welcome. Sam is nineteen now, and my best friend. We talk about everything and laugh about a lot. I am lucky to have Sam as close to me as Sally was to Debbie. He is studying to be a chef and is externing at a great restaurant, La Folie, in San Francisco.

I look forward to subverting Sally's and Sam's children and teaching them all the Irish and sea songs that drive my children crazy. My own fatherhood began uncertainly and vainly. But over twenty-three years I have become a better father and mean to help my children, and their children, in ways my own father could not. The songs are only a smoke screen.

I am talking about patterns of light and dark that make up a time for me that is important, joyful, and ultimately painful. I'm going to excuse myself now and step out of the room in a way my steeliest personality can march brusquely through a difficult passage that, even after twenty years, is still electric with grief and guilt and missed opportunities and tragedy.

*

In 1974 Robert D. Kiernan remarried and we were free to go. We had held back life, even refused it in ways. That time on the marsh was professionally productive but emotionally draining. Debbie and I found a house in Marion, Massachusetts, the next town along the shore. We bought it and moved to it. In looking back I see that this was my first adult home, and that I was faced with adult responsibilities for the first time. Robert D.'s patriarchy had stunted my maturity, perhaps even regressed it. Faced with a family and a home and the prospect of a real relationship, I panicked. I seized on an insubstantial romantic pretext and left my family. What was I reaching for? What snake-oil salesman had pitched my mind on such an aberrant flight? I was not searching for Freedom, which is barely definable and never a livable concept. Perhaps it was Romance, in the broader, *Lord Jim* sense. I see, though, with a sinking heart, that I was only begging my adolescence to stay a little longer. I was protecting my fantasies at the cost of my values, trading gold for glitter.

Debbie, furious and hurt and amazed, stayed in the little house in Marion as I moved around the country, staying in Washington, DC, then in Cambridge, Massachusetts, and even on a horse ranch in Cle Elum, Washington, writing and herding cattle, learning to cowboy with a patient quarter horse named Panama Red. It was a year and a few months of ignorant mis-adventures, self-pitying confusion, and deliberate refusal to think straight. Perhaps I should add another breakdown to the two I've mentioned, but giving this long lapse of sense a clinical label is too close to an excuse.

One day at the end of that buzzing, deafening, impenetrable time, I was sitting in Cambridge at the house of a kind friend, Peter Kemble. A few hours later, without knowing what had happened or what volition had moved me, I discovered myself in the driveway of the Marion house. My car's engine was ticking as it cooled, and it was a sweet early evening. I knocked and walked into the house. Debbie was watching a TV movie from the couch. I asked if she had an extra beer. "Adkins," she replied, "I've always got a beer for you." I stayed. We made plans for the rest of our lives. We were very happy. I was astounded at how well the house fit around me. Debbie had to leave the next day with friends for a play in Falmouth. "Stay here," I said, "I'll get some beers, we'll watch a movie."

"We've got the rest of our lives to watch movies together," she said happily, and she left. On the way to Falmouth she was killed when a drunken driver shot into the traffic rotary off Otis Air Force Base. Her friends were not seriously hurt. Neither was the driver who killed her.

This was not a judgment, not truly a tragedy in the Greek sense. Debbie's death was random bad luck, and the coincidence of timing was especially harsh. One part of me believes that, but only after twenty years of struggle and therapy. There is a more fatalistic personality that whispers to me when the day is long and the light is going. If you do not have such whispers in the dim light, you are lucky, but most of us hear them.

Out of the airplane once more, and once again I had neglected to take the parachute. At a time of emotional upheaval and barely budding responsibility, I was thrust into the role of father and mother. When I use this phrase my daughter rises to dispute me: Dad, you weren't a mother at all, just a father trying to do everything. She's technically correct. The real meaning in my habitual phrase is that I experienced a side of parenting most men never live, the seemingly endless march of days on duty, the watch that never ends, the combined joy and frustration of being totally respon-

Adkins, at Chowder and Marching Society (Courtesy of Jan Adkins.)

sible, night and day, for the safety, sustenance, comfort, amusement, and advancement of wonderful children. If children were disposable, the chore would be easier, but children never are, especially if you have leaned into their cribs and sniffed their tummies at night and known unmistakably, chemically, miraculously, that you are bonded forever to them. Let us say I tried to nurture and sing and comfort and provide and do everything a mother and father should do. It was a Herculean chore. I remember distinctly loving the sound of the dishwasher clumping and hissing as it started up, because it signalled a respite—Sally and Sam were in bed, the kitchen was clean (or as clean as I could manage that evening), and I had an hour or two of quiet reflection. I was still on watch but off the bridge.

*

It is a glitch in our society that men don't experience the full range of parenting. Robert Graves ascribes it to the Industrial Revolution that centralized work outside the home place and took the men away from the family, leaving both girls and boys to be raised, dominated, and modeled on a woman often resentful of her diminution in society. Feminists write it off to men's compulsive domination of society, on their lack of responsibility, their lack of nurturing ability and, hell, they wouldn't be any good at it anyway. Having some small authority in the matter, I may as well offer my opinion along anthropological and psychological lines. Until very recently we still retained remnants of our old hunter/gatherer ancestors. I believe men are dreamers and planners, theorists and stalkers, who are constantly pushing the envelope of life and territory. Hunting is planning and risk and ranging out to bring game in. Their job description involves projection and risk and effort at the limits. I love them for that. I believe that women are burdened for a significant time with the gestation and early feeding of progeny, that it was natural for women to develop better nurturing skills and to assume, in the course of a growing family, the rôle of center, the keeper of the warmth. Their job description involves stability and comfort and endurance. I love them for that. Early child care has fallen, understandably, to women. Further, I believe that parenting is such a difficult, endless, frustrating job that any excuse to leave someone else holding the bag is welcome, and men have taken that opportunity for a long time. Men are missing a worthwhile challenge in full-range parenting, a robust task more difficult and less expensive than Outward Bound. I can also attest that it is often fun and provides more hugs and rewards than anyone is likely to get on the factory floor.

I was helped in my parenting. My plight was pitiful and my limitations were well known, so a group of friends, who called themselves The Mothers (some of them were men, too, Sally), put together a fund that hired a housekeeper for me. The housekeeper was a soft and gentle older woman of Portuguese heritage named Helen Madeiros, who will always be dear to me. Debbie's sister, Judy, was constantly active for us, forgiving and understanding and cheerful and a spring of support. My closest and strongest helper was Sally, who put aside her confounding loss to seize the infant Sam, only five years younger, as her own. In great measure Sally raised Sam. In eighteen years she has not relinquished her captaincy and Sam has put up only token resistance. She was and is his stoutest defender. She was and is his fiercest critic. Sam adores and admires her, and has a respect for all women, remarkable in a very young man, because of her. They are so close that I envy them.

During the most difficult part of this single parenting I flew to New York with Sally, taking the manuscript and all the illustrations for a new book, *Luther Tarbox*. In keeping with a long literary history that includes Hemingway, T.E. Lawrence, and many others, I lost everything on the returning flight. I was so emotionally devastated by what had already happened that starting over again from sketches and manuscript notes was just one more inconvenience. I reproduced the drawings and reconstructed the manuscript, and the book was published. I learned a lesson from the loss that I now pass to my students: as long as a book or illustration is incomplete, it carries infinite possibilities and is a noble vessel for the author's hopes. As soon as the book is finished and

sent off, it gathers the leaden pall of reality, rising or falling on its own tawdry merits, a target for any hack with a blue pencil or a book review column. I never sent a new book off without a sigh. Books are lost because authors are dreamers: better to lose the book than the unflawed, undiminished dream. A professional writer or illustrator whose work arrives at the publisher's must have a hard nose.

I published a lot of books on a lot of subjects. I'm quite proud of some books and wistful about the lost opportunities in others. Reviewing my career as a whole, to this point, I see some major errors.

I neglected to build a sustained partnership with one publisher. Hopping from one publishing house to another harmed me. I didn't accumulate the momentum of support other authors with fewer and less successful books have. That support translates directly into enthusiasm at the publishing house, advertising budgets, marketing ingenuity, personal appearances, talk shows, sales . . . and royalties. I can fault my agent for shopping me out to this house for one kind of book, and to another for a different kind of book, but the fault was mine. It was my responsibility to direct my career.

I didn't keep up with my field. I sequestered myself in Marion and worked in a vacuum. I had no idea what the directions of children's literature were. I had very little contact with other authors or librarians or booksellers. My excuse for professional agoraphobia was my pace, my constant work, my struggle to make ends meet.

I didn't choose my subjects carefully or with an understanding of my audience. Some of my cleverest work is buried in books that have minimal value. I seized on the idea that interested me at the time I finished the last book.

I didn't seek better, harsher, keener criticism. It has been rare for me to ask anyone to critique my work after publication. I have relied foolishly on reviews, which are worthless to an artist. Specific, knowledgeable criticism would have driven me further, identified flaws of my own editing, suggested illustrative areas that needed work, and encouraged me to open new artistic ground.

I regarded my work as Inspired Art, and not as work in progress. My illustration students share this flaw. They have a mystic reverence for whatever their hand puts on the page, believing it to be driven by some deep mechanism of soul and experience they couldn't possibly understand. This superstitious nonsense holds any artist back. I encourage them in the way someone should have encouraged me—to lose my awe for my own image and change it boldly, fool with it, wrestle it around, put it to rights until I understand it truly. I didn't make enough mistakes before I went to finals. In short, I hadn't learned a sensible work model.

I didn't seek out a mentor. I needed a trusted guide to share the hope of my work. That guide could have been—and in the best of all possible worlds would have been—an editor. It shocks me that no editor in all the publishing houses I've dealt with has made even minor efforts to put together a critical partnership with me. A real working editorial partnership would have been valuable and profitable and rewarding for both of us. I'm at a loss for a conclusion to this conundrum. Could it be that I was such a *prima donna* that I discouraged any attempt? (I was, but was I *that*bad? Worse than all other authors? I think not.) Could it be that editors and art directors simply aren't paid enough to fiddle with the books beyond spell-checking? Could it be that they share my flaw (and my students') of Awe for Art? Could it be that publishing houses are by nature lazy and fatalistic and depend on sales figures, rather than editorial acumen, to raise one book above another?

I wasn't financially successful or psychologically confident enough to stop and consider. I rushed from one book to another with no pause for reflection. This was an error but among the most understandable mistakes I've made. The finances of a freelance writer and illustrator are at best chancy and for the most part perilous. Since I began writing and illustrating books on Little Harbor Marsh in 1970 (excepting the nine years I worked at *National Geographic*), I have been living on the thin dollar edge, from one month to another. It is a common belief that publishing a book, and indeed more than one, is a profession. The truth is that one author in several thousand makes his living by his primary work. Illustrating for magazines and books has allowed me to make up enough difference to resist grand larceny. More recently I've taught (something I should have done for years). Other authors lecture, teach, and sell real estate. I am trying to find a way to give up the fear of financial failure, by teaching more often or publishing more intelligently. Fear is antithetical to art. What I've accomplished has been eked out in spite of fear, and this in itself is a small victory.

Over the past two years I've used a more sensible work model. I learned it working with Design Lab, an excellent industrial design firm in Providence, Rhode Island, where Ralph Beckman and Henry Sharp taught me the process of iteration and reiteration. You must first establish all the needs that surround the product—the needs of the consumer, certainly, but also the manufacturer, the marketer, the retailer. The goal is to arrive at a finished product with every need met and every possible opportunity included and intact. The process is to make many mistakes, early and often, going through dozens of reiterations that progressively improve on the primary iteration, an original sketch, an "unsacrosanct" ablative model meant to fall away and reveal new things about the next sketch. For Design Lab, this meant hard thinking about the *program,* the list, of needs. The invention or device that followed was put together loosely and quickly. This first sketch was changed, rebuilt, fooled with, reconsidered entirely, rethought, scrapped, recreated, and continuously reiterated in forms closer and closer to a useful product that answered the original needs. For me, the process is closely similar in publishing. Before I make a line on paper or write a word, I must consider the program. Who is my audience? What is the market and how will this book be marketed (publisher to sales agent to bookstore to buyer, or publisher to bookstore, or mail order, or even direct mail)? What is this book's statement? What is the *verity* it aims for, in deference to Bill Decker? What is the best medium for the book's topic (watercolor, pencil, pen and ink, acrylic, ink and wash)? How much will the book cost? How much time can I afford to spend on it? How much research will it need? It is only at this point that I can sensibly begin, and then I begin with rough layouts, thumbnails that give me a loose idea of how to advance the story or idea I'm following in the book. This thumbnail stage is repeated more than once, and at every stage, now and later, I send out copies of the iteration and ask for input from the editor, the art director, and from eyes and ears I trust. Do I take their suggestions? Often. Often I will make an argument for the text or layout in my current iteration, or for a completely separate solution suggested by the argument. In all this change, I am seeking out solutions to problems of storytelling. The solutions are there. They are inherent in the story itself, which invariably directs the final form. My personality and my drawing fist and my text are subordinate to the story; they serve it. If I am lucky, I will go through a dozen or more iterations. The computer is particularly helpful in this process, producing dummies (sketch iterations of a book's pages) with current changes without great effort.

What about the finished product? I will quote my friend Luis Marden, a legendary writer at *National Geographic,* now in his active eighties. "You never finish a story, you abandon it." At some point you decide that the stage of iteration you've reached is as good as you can make it at that time, and you let it go with hope.

My last four books have been completed in this way, and they are more balanced and of more satisfaction to me than any of my previous books. They are not the best books I've done, because the subjects of these four works have been chosen for me. Earlier books like *A Storm without Rain* or *Wooden Ship* have glaring flaws but address wonderful subjects that make them superior books. I wish I could have done them properly in the iterative process I learned so late. They would have been enormously better.

*

A few years after Debbie died, I remarried. My new wife was an old friend, Dorcas, who brought her own boy, Robbie, to our family. Robbie was between Sally and Sam in age, a bright and intense boy who never quite found comfort in the recombined family. Though we became close friends over nine years, Dorcas and I never quite found our comfort either.

Adkins, at **National Geographic,** *1983* (Courtesy of Jan Adkins.)

We did good things together, often. I cooked a lot of meals, which is a joy to me. We sailed together in Massachusetts and Maine. Our children loved the water and became good sailors. We bicycled and hiked and skied and worked outside together. We were an active bunch. The best view of our family was one of red and sweaty faces, grinning in sly competition after a goal achieved—some ridge crossed or snowy field skied or road bicycled or point weathered.

I learned to become a father slowly. It is not a skill you learn once. At every age a child needs a new father, and each child needs a separate father for his or her particular age. I was not as patient with Robbie's particular needs as I was with Sally's or Sam's. It wasn't that he simply wasn't *my* boy but more that his special interests and style of attention and many fears were foreign to me. To that dissimilarity add one of Robbie's virtues, his loyalty to his father and even to his original, unsplit family. In all the years we lived together, Robbie vocally preferred his original berth as single child with Dorcas and his father, John. The new family, as interesting and full of activity as it was, never won him. I've come to respect that unswerving devotion, though I certainly whaled the daylights out of Robbie for it, one way and another, over the years. Robbie is twenty-two and a fine, handsome boy. I believe we are friends now, and that he can depend on me for support that he de-

clined years ago. It would please me if we could be closer to each other as we grow older.

When people ask me what I'm proudest of, I almost always rank my fatherhood at the head of the list. I've been a good father, over time. This is an iterative process, too; I've made grievous errors early and often, and I'm still working it out, but I'm improving. I'm proud of the trust my children and I have made, together. I am inordinately proud of navigating a boat—twiceto a tiny island in the middle of the Atlantic, using only a sextant, a chronometer, and tables of nautical data. Raising Bermuda with a margin of error of less than a mile after almost five hundred miles of open sea is a proud moment. Fog navigation in Maine is actually more difficult, sometimes more critical, and with some instruction I'm sure anyone could make a good celestial landfall, but it was one of those high-profile accomplishments that speaks to some important personality in me. I'm proud of learning to play tennis, and I look forward to learning the game for another twenty years or more. My books, the reason you are reading this self-appraisement, are important but might still rest below my satisfaction at being a part of *National Geographic* magazine, for so long.

I was invited to join the magazine in 1980 by Howard Paine, the associate editor for art. Howard is the most original and complete graphic mind I've ever known, and I've learned more about design and illustration and editing from him than from any other person. I was asked to come aboard because of my background in explaining things in words and pictures. Everyone who joined the magazine came aboard. *National Geographic* had a nautical flavor. It may have been a legacy from the real founder, Alexander Graham Bell, who lobbied hard for people answering his invention, the telephone, to shout "Ahoy!" instead of "Hello." Bell and the Grosvenor dynasty that has controlled *National Geographic* for a hundred years—starting with Bell's son-in-law, the magazine's first editor-in-chief, Gilbert Hovey Grosvenor—were all ardent sailors. This may have been another reason I came aboard, who knows?

In a life of near seclusion and alienation, *Geographic* was the only place I ever truly belonged. Before *National Geographic* I was perennially haunted by one of my darker personalities declaring that I was an outsider, a stranger to regular folks, an artsy, fussy, abstruse and abnormal being clinging at the fringe of society. In the Society I was right at home with 1,100 other oddball overachievers. Not only did I fit, I excelled in fast company.

My job was to explain things. What couldn't be photographed or simply stated fell to me. I found ways to explain science, history, anthropology, medicine, and other technical problems through pictures and diagrams. I would confer with the picture editor (the nominal job-captain of a story), the writer, and the photographer when the article was in its infancy. I would assign the subject to one of my researchers and do my own research. I went over the images sent from the field by the photographer and over the early manuscript. I correlated my research with their research, and suggested solutions to problems of understanding. With a quarter-page illustration I could clearly show the mechanism of a microchip transistor or a remotely piloted deep-sea vehicle and free the writer to address the human side of the story. I could show things a photograph could never attempt: a cross section through the Gulf Stream or the layering of spy satellite orbits or the comparative energy levels of atoms. Often I would turn up new information not handled in the text but necessary to understanding the story, and I found ways to explain these concepts in sidebars.

I did not do the illustrations but assigned illustrators to work from my research notes and layout sketches. Working with the best illustrators in the world humbled my own scratchy style. Before I came to the magazine, most of the conceptual work had been done by Howard Paine or by the illustrators themselves. Howard's work took him away from the magazine and illustrators often sought simplistic solutions, even *National Geographic* solutions (copying their dated, distorted idea of the magazine's look) that didn't advance the style of the magazine. I added another level of concept, a bolder design signature, a more aggressive research effort spe-

cifically for illustrations, a three-dimensional and iconic approach to explanation, and a new respect for the reader's ability to understand complex ideas. I changed the way art supported stories, and I changed the job description of art director at *National Geographic.* The magazine needed me. I knew I was better at my job than anyone had ever been and that I was learning to be better. I read through reams of technical data and, more exciting, I consulted original sources. If I needed to know something about sub-atomic particles, I did not consult a local assistant professor but went directly to Murray Gell-Mann, discoverer of quarks. I travelled all over the country and occasionally abroad, interviewing scientists, technicians, archaeologists, historians, surgeons, aircraft designers, explorers, microscopists, engineers, futurists, soldiers, and astronauts. I witnessed wonders and explored the world of the mind and the globe.

The political and editorial currents in the Society were swift and treacherous. Nothing was done without repercussions, nothing went unnoticed—subtle movements, bold strokes. At first I hated the internecine rivalries and department battles for ascendancy. Later I swam happily in them, playing the Society's interior Machiavellian game in earnest. I was vital to the magazine's workings but in the end I was not essential. I learned shark politics from great white sharks, swam with them, but in the end I was eaten. I am sometimes sad that I will never have the opportunity to use what I learned about management and to implement what I discovered about the positive uses of politics in an organization. It is too late for me to run a department, even though I would have done it gently, humanely, and efficiently. I like to reflect that, though I lost the game, I learned it from masters.

It is difficult to relate my feelings for the *National Geographic* magazine without sounding foolish. I finally had a home. At last someone valued my broad band curiosity and cluttered, multi-disciplinary background. My intensity and enthusiasm was not wasted there. My abundance of ideas was never discounted. I entered the building every day for nine years with a glow of pride. When I turned the corner at L Street and walked up 17th, I checked the flags: on sunny days the big ten-foot flags flew—Old Glory and the brown/green/blue Society flag; on rainy days, smaller four-foot versions flew; if a *National Geographic* employee had died, the Society flag flew at half mast. I expected it would fly at half mast for me one day, and I was content to work the rest of my life and die in harness. I never liked doing anything as much, I was never so challenged, and I was never so well-suited to any other task.

*

Patterns. Sometime in 1985 I went on assignment to Haiti, on the first of our Columbus articles. I returned with a case of giardiasis, a fairly common intestinal parasite. Parasites were so expectable at *National Geographic* that we sometimes referred to them as The *National Geographic* Diet. Misdiagnosed at first, it ruined my health for months. This was during one of the difficult times in my marriage. Dorcas had become a watch officer at Outward Bound in Maine and spent large parts of the summer there and at her parents' home in Rhode Island. Washington summers are tedious, to be sure, but Dorcas's departure left me alone and feeling abandoned. During my bout with giardiasis I became dehydrated, weak, and sometimes delirious. I could not leave my second-floor bedroom for days. It seems obvious now, that the dehydration altered my psychochemical balance and set me up for a long depression that was to have devastating results.

How simple it looks in hindsight. But how accurate is our hindsight? More than one truth lives in the events that punctuate our lives. With a simple, comfortingly logical filter, I can see one phenomenon leading to another, one domino toppling the next, one falling rock dislodging a larger boulder. Another truth is that events are strung together with fine wire that may tug but never pulls: one event may make another marginally more likely. We like looking back to firm cause and effect, though, as if our lives were shaped for a useful end.

At this remove why shouldn't I comfort myself with simplicity? But even at this remove, part of me steps out of the room again and lets my coldest personality quick-step through events.

I grew more and more depressed. My depression and the stepped-up pressure at *National Geographic,* wore at the frail bonds of my marriage to Dorcas, strained almost to breaking by foolishness and compulsion by both partners. The marriage ended in a "civilized" but nasty coda of separation in the same house. My children were upset and distant, they avoided siding with Dorcas or me. The pressure at work was coincidentally greater at that time. My emotional temperature rose. I searched for a new partner to salve my grief at feeling abandoned. A year later I met a woman going through her own separation and fell wholly, obsessively in love. A few months later the same depression and insecurity that had driven my damaged marriage under contributed to the end of the new relationship. My work began to suffer. I sank deeper and deeper into despair. I was barely functional. I wept quickly, often. I acknowledged my second breakdown grudgingly but with grateful surrender. It was more profound than my first and occasioned more destruction, required more resources, demanded more rebuilding. I was hospitalized for almost five months.

My children held me up and held me back from the brink. Blinded and deafened by storms of emotion, I could still feel their love, and it called me back to the light. Sally was brave and tough. Sam was giving and resilient. As Debbie's death allowed me to see both sides of parenting as few men have; my own sickness allowed me to see the enormous strength in my own children. Nothing happens that doesn't reveal some glimpse of God.

My sister also stood with me through my sickness and recovery and will always be a glad part of my life. She is a dentist in West Virginia, a caring woman with a raucous sense of humor. Our experience of family life together was hectic but we laugh a good deal about it now. When I want to write about strong, competent women, I have my sister and my daughter as models.

Stronger, calmer, I returned to life. I resumed my work at *National Geographic* and Sally went away to boarding school. Robert D. had died in 1984 and left a trust fund for Sam's and Sally's education. Sally chose for herself a compact, active, athletic, and intellectually vigorous school in Steamboat Springs, Colorado—the Whiteman School. She has always made shrewd judgments.

Sam remained with me and became my best friend. In the mornings we overcame our shared genetic inertia together, struggling to make the first steps of the day and gaining pace with the morning, getting Sam to his bus on time most mornings. We cooked together, shopped, entertained, watched hundreds of movies, discussed every topic, sang, . . . and grew. I hope to be near Sam for many years.

A year after I returned to *National Geographic* I was fired. My work was exemplary, my emotions were controlled, but I had lost Howard's trust. He became abusive of my work rather than critical, grew suspicious, questioned my motives and my methods, and probed every sensitive area he could find. Looking back I see that he was more politically astute than I had guessed; he had divined the great rift that would tear into the magazine and eventually diminish the Society. Difficulty between the Society's president, Gil Grosvenor, and Garrett, the magazine's editor-in-chief, was reaching critical levels, and Howard knew that the active art director at the moment of the coming crisis would safely retain his seat. I had gained too much trust with the senior editors. He rationalized my dismissal as efficient for the good of the magazine, even though I was handling most of the active stories at the time. He was also phobic about mental illness. He created a credible paper trail of difficulty between us, going so far as to accuse me of using illegal drugs. He worked the Old Boy network masterfully and had the sudden, seemingly fortuitous aid of my close friend, colleague, and confidant. (Months later this "interested friend" was instrumental in having Howard dismissed and in taking his position. Poetry is where you find it.) There was also a dark current involved: unfounded and unsubstantiated rumors of sexual harassment carried great weight but were never mentioned to me. They were never questioned, simply assumed to be true. I could not defend myself against them because I discovered their fatal influence long after the fact. They came from the woman I had loved so completely before my breakdown.

I left the National Geographic Society in its centenary year, 1988. Garrett, Howard, and most of the people for whom I had worked left the following year. Nothing in a long, disaster-prone life has hurt me more. We accept death for ourselves and even for our loved ones as God's due. The soiled machinations of frightened men scurrying behind walls to hoard up favor and position seem less divine and are harder to understand.

*

My life, as I remember it, began in Wheeling, West Virginia; that industrial cockrel city on the Ohio River is me. My life began in St. Clairsville, Ohio, where I wandered the woods and lived an outsider's life like a spy among plain people. My life began when I leaped from a small lawn to a large university; the disorientation, sudden demands, and cold impersonality of Ohio State tempered part of me. My life began again when my pretension could no longer support me in an arena that demanded achievement, when I broke completely and paused to reassemble the pieces; I continued to learn as a different person. My life began in Wareham, Massachusetts, confronting marriage and a formidable profession and the bewitching sound of the ocean; I will always be an apprentice yankee, a writer, and doubt

that I can ever live inland or go long without a boat under me. My life began after the death of a wife I loved poorly but truly; I will always be a father who tries to be more, and I can never ignore the pain I've given people who love me. My life began when I came aboard *National Geographic* magazine; the Society flag will not dip for me but the lessons I learned there will always be a part of my work. My life began when I left *National Geographic* magazine; it has taken me six years to rebuild my career, rechart my course, recharge my resources, and set out for an island I have heard of in the middle of a large ocean.

My life will begin over and over, and yours will, too. In the past six years I have continued to change. There are so many of me.

Several years ago I discovered that I am an alcoholic. I stopped drinking. I should mention that I believe in drinking—it's a fine, mild dose of comfort for those that can take it safely. But for me, alcohol is a psychoactive poison, heightening my natural tendency toward depression and melodrama. Depression and victimhood would have killed me before my liver gave out. There are legions of alcoholics who never seem drunk, look around. I was one of them. I miss good beer and, occasionally, Mount Gay rum and Irish whiskey, but I can live longer and better without them.

The author with his daughter, Sally, and his son, Sam, at Sam's graduation, Whiteman School, 1993 (Courtesy of Jan Adkins.)

Should I say that I discovered God or that God showed himself to me? I was not struck blind on the way to Tarsus, I did not start to speak in tongues, I did not have any sudden revelation. I was an agnostic, driven away from religion by my mother and by a life in the logical sciences. I came to my belief through science, studying cosmology and medicine and archaeology and oceanography. I began to perceive a pattern, an order that reached beyond my life or my city or the confines of the time I was enjoying. I began to see that every scientist I met searched fervently for simplicity. Why simplicity? There is no indication that the universe is essentially simple. That scientific hope of finding basic answers is, as Isaac Asimov observes, faith. I came to believe that God is an essential part of the fabric of our lives and of reality. I do not understand everything about my fledgling faith, and I know it has no name or support group. I know a few things about it. I know that there are no easy answers in any organized religion or in anyone book or in anyone figure. There is no organized religion that has not distorted and distanced the bond between God and Man. I call myself a Christian but this is another personal misstatement, and as Sally would rise to complain that I am not technically a *mother,* my friend Deb Fenning would certainly leap up to question my technical right to being a *Christian.* Do I embrace the Trinity and the miracles and Jesus's payment for our sins, and do I accept the central issue of Jesus as God? Well, you have me there, Deb. That's too much for me to process now. It is enough of a leap to love God as the father (and mother, Sal) of us all, and to love Jesus through his patient, revolutionary teaching. I love poetry so much that the Bible appeals to me on that level. It is an anthology of disparate teaching focusing on a semi-nomadic people in a harsh, eastern Mediterranean climate. The contributions were submitted between four to five millennia ago. The editing is spotty and the editions differ. The tone of book two differs so radically from book one that it seems a shame they are bound together. There seem to be hundreds of satisfied mullahs and loud pundits eager to interpret the original meaning of the books for me, and this makes me nervous. Relying on any one reference violates my scientific ethic. We live in a complex, connected world far away in time and technology and understanding from Judea. I am certain that I must listen for God's voice speaking now. There are no reproducible results in this field, but I have the deep, comfortable belief that you will find the face of God if you search hard and well in any direction. You can come to him through poetry or history or steam mechanics or science. If I am wrong about all this and arrive at the pearly gates to meet white-bearded Charlton Heston beyond the clouds, I will be speechlessly abashed, but I know I will also be forgiven.

*

Over the past six years I've scurried in many interesting directions. I've written scripts for The Discovery Channel and documentary films. I've designed courses in explanation and illustration for the Rhode Island School of Design, and I've taught at the Maryland Institute College of Art. I've been on design teams for toys and video controllers and medical diagnostics, and I have my name on some patents. I have researched, designed, and illustrated a project for Saudi Arabia explaining the Islamic pilgrimage, the Hajj, to Moslems all over the world. I have studied Stonehenge and neolithic Britain on site. I have helped to design museum exhibitions and interactive casino shows and historical expositions and wildlife experiences. I've written mission statements for medical centers and I've produced posters about the atmosphere. I've illustrated for twenty magazines, explaining science and history and how to add a screened-in back porch. I've designed and illustrated a journal and date book, an anthology of wilderness writing, and two textbooks for young readers. I admire the short Nobel Prize acceptance speech in Vonnegut's *Cats Cradle,* in which the scientist says, "I stand before you now because I never stopped dawdling like an eight-year-old on a spring morning on his way to school. Anything can make me stop and look and wonder, and sometimes learn. I am a very happy man. Thank you."

After all this pounding around, where am I? I live in a tiny house overlooking a backwater of Chesapeake Bay, two miles upriver of the Naval Academy at Annapolis. My boat, *Groucho,* sits jauntily at my dock, impatient with me for staying so long at the computer explaining myself to you. It is a twenty-eight-foot Rozinanate ketch designed by the great marine architect L. Francis Herreshoff, whom I knew as an old man in Marblehead, Massachusetts. I sail a classic, exquisite sailboat and drive an old Chevrolet Cavalier station wagon.

Sally is cataloguing plants at the Smithsonian Institute and is thinking about her next collecting trip to a South American rainforest. She is small, pretty, serious and funny at the same time, and after a long period of viewing me as a hopelessly confused case has reconsidered. We have good dinners and talk too long on the phone.

Sam is cooking in San Francisco and thinking about his own bistro/restaurant/market, for which I will do the graphics. He spent four years at Whiteman School (Sally insisted, another shrewd decision) and went on to the Culinary Institute of America at Hyde Park. He is tall, lean, handsome, witty, sweet, and wry. I miss him.

I am blessed with friends and am still looking for a smart, funny, warm woman, who has the good sense to drive me occasionally crazy (this prevents major madness) and pry me out of my solitude. I do not get to ski as much as I'd like but this is Maryland and not Colorado. I do not and will not own any cats. I play tennis several times a week and have fantasies about entering seniors' tournaments if I can ever control my tendency to risk low-percentage shots. I am still a superb shot and defend Saltpan Cove with a quiet, accurate air-rifle against pirates who try to invade it by hiding under tiny leaves. I still love to sing in the respectable Welsh tenor inherited from my mother. My father is still alive and grousing happily about this job or that project or my uncle Charlie (who lives near him) in Venice, Florida. My sister, Judy, is very dear to me and is starting a new dentistry office in Charleston, West Virginia.

Where is my island? What is my course? After exploring so many directions I must concentrate my efforts and mark the chart. Fifty is very young for me. Secretary of State John Hay suggested to a foreign diplomat about his president and my hero, Theodore Roosevelt, "You've got to remember this about the president: he's about twelve years old.;" I can expect to learn more about writing well for at least twenty years, and then glide with clever memoirs. It's past time to make intelligent decisions about the books I write and the way I produce them and the way they arrive in your hands. I confess that it is a struggle to make such sensible plans after fifty years of extemporizing. I have a dozen book ideas that strike me as important to young people. I have another dozen that seem merely entertaining. I would like to do two biographies of personal heroes, Hell Roaring Mike Healy and Ralph Bagnold. I need an enduring, profitable, interactive relationship with an aggressive publisher who shares my publishing goals, but publishing has changed significantly in the last ten years. I am still learning the new trade but I have hopes. Making money at doing good things is an appealing notion.

I want to own a big, capable boat and sail down the coast of the Americas to Rio or farther. I want to sing more and be afraid less. I want to redesign this tiny house to have a bigger studio and better space for the Chowder and Marching Society, the ragtag band of friends who come to dine at my table. I want to continue to learn about being a father and friend and lover and son and brother and explorer.

I have willed my stocky, bearlike skeleton to the Rhode Island School of Design illustration department, the rest to whomever might need a spare part, and I've asked that a restful stone bench be set up wherever I'm teaching when I check out. It can have my name, date of birth and death (let us hope that is ages hence), and my interlocking professions—writer, illustrator, explainer. I would also like my motto, just to give the bench a tone, the one Pliny the Elder adjured himself with: *Nulla dies sine linea* (Never a day without lines).

Jan Adkins contributed the following update to his autobiographical essay in 2009:

I just filed for Social Security and Medicare, in time for my sixty-fifth birthday. I'm shocked.

How did I get so old? Understandably, I lost track of time. A writer's life is perpetually disorienting because we play with time, flashing back and leaping forward.

We straddle space and time as we compare simultaneous events in different places or treat events separated by centuries and continents as single concepts. We even dwell outside time in that quantum, maybe-concept of "once upon a time."

We write our characters old and young, good and evil, dull and bright, yet they're all parts of us in some way. We speak for the cast of characters we know within ourselves. This odd multitude of alter-egos dwells with us, all of them resonant to the rhythm of the same thumping heart. Who am I? Shall I introduce you to all of me? Forget it: you don't have time to meet them all.

Writers deal with abstracts and imponderables, mysteries and what-ifs. This is our job description, the circus act that's required day by day. All this loosey-goosey swiveling about with time and persona and theory is no good for our hold on reality. And it plays Old Harry with our grasp of dates and years and age.

So this morning I confronted an old duffer in the mirror. I'm sure it wasn't me. I had lots of hair, dark brown— just last Tuesday, wasn't it? Crikey, it's an old bald guy with a tonsure of white buzz-cut fur. Who is that guy?

For a charitable moment I reach for the hope that this is the person I most wanted to be, a character lifted from the *Atlantic Coast Pilot* and NOAA's "Notices to Mariners." Perhaps, I thought as I gazed into the mirror, I've become that admirable and judicious fellow, The Prudent Mariner, who notices things, adopts safe practices, avoids problems, shuns shoal water, and reaches port safely. What a happy fate to be The Prudent Mariner, solid and wise. Ah, fantasy!

No, this dripping elder shivering on the rocks is the Ancient Mariner, cast temporarily onto the grim shore of reality, forced to review his tatterdemalion life and make some reckoning to the unfortunate wedding guests before he slips, seal-like, back into the nepenthean waters and resumes his professional daydreaming.

Then what have I learned? I've shot half a dozen albatrosses, watched the crew I knew fade away in the withering heat, and I've paid a heavy price for my exuberant marksmanship. Do I have any lessons to impart? Any sage observations? Where am I on the edge of geezerhood?

*

I expected to be less foolish.

I hoped that as age piled around me I might assume the assurance and dignity of a senior literary statesman. I thought I might become the *eminence gris* of nonfiction for young people.

Nope.

It's possible that dignity isn't learned; it could be genetic. Some folks are bred to caution and careful judgment. Isn't good breeding the primary purpose of the New England Social Register? My shot at dignity wasn't even a near-miss. But, honestly, I'm not entirely sure I want to be dignified.

If I'm not risking folly every day, I'm shrinking from the edge where creativity happens. Out there on the edge is an electric zone where newness and inappropriateness, balance and serendipity, divine drama and flamboyance, aren't distinctly identifiable. I find it easy to step over the line. Frequently. So I embrace being a frequent flyer fool. The risks of a pratfall out there in the breeze of ingenuity are overwhelming, daunting. But the edge is where it happens. It's where the writer and illustrator and creator live. The edge is windy and exposed and never comfortable. But the view can be lovely.

*

I expected to be wealthier. Not robber-baron, private jet, gold Rolex wealthy, but I expected to enjoy some security. I really did believe that maturity would be an easier glide. I'd have time to perfect my art at leisure and examine some of the mysteries in detail.

As a "comfortably well-off" senior figure, I'd have time to dabble. I love to paint, but I can't really afford to create art without being paid for it. There are only so many work hours. I love crafts, but they're not economically feasible. I seem to remember someone in the 1960s saying quite confidently that out in California, you can make a living on macramé. Did I really hear that?

Life has never been easy for artists—writers, illustrators, painters, actors, musicians, macramé-ists. And post-Reagan-trickle-down-economy life in the arts has become even more difficult, less viable. We live in a poor climate for fringe-dwellers.

Artists are the worst kind of dreamers: instead of selecting from a list of approved and proven dreams, they choose their own personal fantasies. Disastrously, artists expect their dreams to follow a Walt Disney plot arc— they struggle and persist as they're faithful to their dreams; they listen to their hearts, and, at last!, they succeed as the orchestra builds to a peaceful climax. Stop the projector!

I've lived long enough to know good men crushed by a life of following their shining dreams. Many of them are bitter, defeated idealists driven to extremes of rationalization to explain why they weren't rewarded for their faith. (Everyone in the movies is rewarded at the end; why weren't they?) Dear, kind men have been driven by soured dreams to political conservatism, blaming liberal conspiracies for their shortfalls. Fine, solid women have been robbed of their softness and grace by strident accusations against male-domination, sexual-bias, and glass ceilings to explain their dreams' demise.

We may be doing our children a disservice by encouraging them to follow their dreams. Dreams are dangerous. As pretty as they may be, dreams kill and maim the spirit if they're not compatible with reality. We might be better elders by counseling our children to choose their dreams more carefully, more skeptically. The simple truth is that every personal pie in the sky may not be worth our faith.

*

I expected Benny Goodman to be king forever.

I loved my father's music, and I loved his ebullient, expectant outlook. I inherited my father's outlook along with his fixation on progress. To him the world was evolving into a better and more rational place. Science, industry, technology, and social awareness would dispel hunger, want, prejudice, corns, bunions, and hemorrhoids.

Presently, I'm working on a difficult book about oil. I'm trying to put down what young people should know about oil as they enter adulthood. Much to my dismay, I'm discovering that the plot arc of the world doesn't point toward the stars. My father would object to this conclusion loudly, stubbornly, because he was an inventor, a tinkerer, a planner. Progress was his religion.

I've stumbled over a few inescapable facts that I find impossible to refute. We may search frantically for a few minor pockets of crude oil here and there, but the geologists have done their work over the past hundred years with increasingly sensitive and earth-embracing tools: we're about to run out of oil.

There is a lot of oil left, my yes. But there are more of us, and more of this inflated population is now advanced and economically viable, so whole continents now compete for the oil we've been using for ourselves. Today, North America is home to only a small fraction of the world's inhabitants, yet we use most of the oil. The United States can no longer see ourselves as the only fully mobile and industrially advanced nation. We passed the Hubbert Peak of oil production just after the turn of the new century. In 2030, we'll have only as much available oil as we produced in 1980. But that dwindling amount must be shared with more of a world population that will have grown from about 4.4 billion in 1980 to around 9 billion in 2030. Our piece of the crude oil pie will be small, indeed. In 2030—more realistically far before then—we will lose our oil-use monopoly as China and India and Indonesia claim larger shares of the world supply. And they'll get their shares.

Oil prices will rise in these United States, and oil supply will grow tight within my lifetime. The pervasive, complex, subtly interlocking American system of living is dependent on cheap oil. We're headed willy-nilly toward some undefined tipping point where the big gears of our largely unseen services—electric production, truck deliveries, clean water treatment, food transport, international price-negotiating advantages, trash pickup, and medical services on demand—will falter. Society will fray and tear. Expect change on an unpredictable and even apocalyptic scale. Teach your grandchildren to fish and farm.

Progress has already reversed itself without fanfare. Old guys like me remember their mothers as housewives, listening to Benny Goodman with an unhurried cup of coffee, taking time to bake elaborate pastries and pies or to play canasta. The present reality is that housewives are a luxury of the rich. Middle-class men and women can't be housewives and househusbands! It doesn't pay.

Why should a writer of children's book address oil-shortages in a précis of his life? Because children are my audience, my special concern. And because I'm a teacher of other writers and illustrators. I have some obligation to say, firmly, that a life in the arts may be a dream of the past. Today, being a writer or graphic artist is often the indulgence of a spouse with a damn good income.

Why didn't I find a wealthy spouse long ago?

*

Recently I learned something from Philadelphia. Our odd family gathered for my niece's wedding, a sweet little affair in a Unitarian chapel designed by the great Victorian architect, Frank Furness. We were enchanted by Philadelphia in several ways. It's a mature city with a delightful mix of scales: the comforting human scale of narrow one-way streets lined with brick and stone town houses and narrow shops, alongside the expansive monumental scale of the Ben Franklin Parkway, the Philadelphia Art Museum (*Rocky*), and the Franklin Institute.

Part of our fascination with Philadelphia was architecture. My daughter frequently cried out as we passed wonderful old building of articulated charm. I was trained as an architect and taught to appreciate the Bauhaus International style, the planes and machined curves of le Corbusier, the discipline of Mies van der Rohe. Then why was I, too, thrilled by the Victorian architecture of Philadelphia?

After a day or so I began to see that we were appreciating the Art of the Unnecessary. The Furness chapel in which I felt so happy and bemused was extravagantly decorated by wonderful wood and stone carving, by fumed-oak raised panels with intricately detailed moldings, by exquisite joinery in simple bench backs, their vertical staves locked together with holly butterfly wedges. The coffered ceiling in dark oak was relieved by beaded board squares painted deep Prussian blue, and this blue was set off by a delicate banding of light green scalloping along the coffer edges. All charming, beguiling, and amusing in the sense of musical wit. And all unnecessary.

I began to savor the decorative excesses of the Philadelphia City Hall. The floral and symbolic carvings were grace notes, noodling bits of artistic flourish to lighten the big masses of the principle parts.

We passed another church which may have been designed by that stalwart of late-nineteenth-century architecture, H.H. Richardson. What impressed me in this church was the arrangement of geometric shapes making up a playful, three-dimensional composition. One main shape was round, like the base of a tower, and carried red stonework bands that emphasized its barrel shape. A rhythmic line of gothic windows above it supported a conical slate roof with a ridiculous and amusing finial at the peak. The square bell tower beside it was balanced by the low, heavy stone walls of a fortress-like entrance. The interior shape and flow patterns of the building were expressed in the outer shapes, balanced and harmonious as a Calder mobile. It was stone and slate and heavy woodwork and shingle . . . but it was a light-hearted church praising a benevolent God.

What crept into my thoughts was the difference between contemporary architecture and these playful, enthusiastic elder-brother buildings. Philadelphia taught me that our stripped-down modern architecture is more like Soviet and Third Reich fascist architecture than an expression of freedom. It's the architecture of corporate fascism, the simplest glass and aluminum shell that will keep out the elements.

Granted, much of what delighted me was simple dollar freedom. The details of the Furness chapel sprang from weeks of drawings and revisions. Money was available. Architects could indulge in unnecessary but delightful decorations. And money was available for the artisan, so he could craft the wood joinery and sculpt the stone flowers and carve letters in the oak.

This frothy architecture was an expression of belief in the power of art to beguile and endure. Furness and Richardson built with the certainty that their designs would surely outlast any child born on the day ground was broken for construction. A great part of the architecture we see today is built to last twenty years or less.

In architecture school we were taught that architecture should express the flow and function of an inner purpose. A church shouldn't be confused with a bank. Architecture should reflect society's priorities. It was a matter of faith that this principle was reversible: workers in Wright's Johnson Wax Building were happier and more productive. Architecture could shape the lives of the people who inhabited it.

Let's say that architecture *does* mean something. What are we conveying to children in school architecture? As I've visited classrooms around the country, I've seen thousands of double-wide pre-fab classrooms parked on cheap land around hideous concrete block utility buildings. This is the common architecture of contemporary schools. What does it convey to its inhabitants? It's clearly disposable, cheap, ugly, and convenient. What message are we sending to our children through economically fascist architecture? Are we really telling them that their lives are cheap and replaceable? Are we saying that their education is a minor priority in our national life? Are we letting them know how unimportant they are?

The fact is that our society is nearly bankrupt, financially and creatively. It would be impossible to build that Frank Furness church today. First, no bank would lend the construction money or approve the plans: "too wasteful, too detailed." Second, we don't have the artisans who can still accomplish that work. Third, we're too cynical to support joyful, detailed, unnecessary design.

What did Philadelphia suggest about the state of creativity in America?

First, let's separate "shock value" of anything radically, startlingly different from "creativity," which is a conscious expression of idea or emotion. What about our traditionally "creative" avenues?

In American cinema, perhaps our most powerful medium, creativity is a drug on the market. So many new movies are remakes of former successes because studios want a sure thing more than a fresh thing.

Serious music for the concert hall stands outside normal life, since it's funded by philanthropy bound to the salon preferences of a small coterie of experts. Classical music is no longer an expression of human emotion but mathematical tone exercises constructed to impress other composers. Does new concert music stir the hearts of people who don't own white tie and tails? I can't imagine a contemporary concert piece producing the impact made in 1924 by Gershwin's "Rhapsody in Blue."

I see this in publishing, as well. Publishers demand that a book fill a niche ready-made. As much as cinema studios, publishers want a sure thing. It's doubtful that *Winnie the Pooh* would be a viable choice today because it just doesn't fit an age niche or a purpose description, doesn't have "mandated diversity" and has no female characters beyond Mrs. Kanga.

*

In my work, I expected more help from the tide.

I expected that the current of popular culture into which I was born would have momentum and that its continued flow would help my artistic journey. I expected the themes and motives of the past to persevere. But there

The author on a school visit (Courtesy of Jan Adkins.)

has been some disruptive event that tore us away from our folklore and literary roots. I didn't expect such a disruptive eddy to distance my readers from the tales and heroes on which our cultural identity was built.

The young people with whom I talk in schools, and the audience for which I write, are culturally illiterate. They don't know their own heritage tales and legends, and schools simply don't have time to bother with them.

We're a Greco-Roman, Judeo-Christian culture. Think for just a moment: what a multitude of stirring stories, vaulting heroes, wicked villains, and inspired life parables reside in those four descriptive titles!

The books that inspired me to write grew out of soil rich with history, legend, large figures, causes. Conrad, Melville, Twain, Hemingway, Steinbeck, Forester—they were storytellers explaining human mysteries and necessities in parables. Those parables sprang from our cultural library of great deeds. A man risking everything for a friend was Gilgamesh storming the underworld to find his wild friend Enkidu. A small but determined figure battling overwhelming force was young David slaying the fearsome giant Goliath. A journey torn with peril and storms was Odysseus' homeward voyage waylaid by the tempting sorceress Calypso. Leadership and dogged determination against great odds and bluster was King Henry V's band of 2,500 brothers standing fast in the rain against 20,000 French gentleman-glory-seekers at Agincourt. The failure of bureaucracy at the cost of brave lives was the Light Brigade charging in the point-blank teeth of the Russian guns. The blood runs quicker even mentioning the bright heroes of our shared past.

The rich cultural soil that grew our literature for so long has been swept aside as undesirable dirt, pejoratively dismissed as ancient history, and replaced by symmetrical and instructive new tales without violence and anger. These new tales are a cold, barely nutrient synthetic solution, concocted from the thin, insubstantial "culture of entertainment."

Where was the disconnect that cast literature adrift from our shared culture? In some important way we stopped being members of a grand society and became individuals struggling against society. We turned inward to examine our own navels in deeper and more mundane detail.

Today we have no heroes recognizable in the antique sense of sterling characters with boundless strength and exemplary morals. Most of our literature seems bent on proving that our protagonists are as depraved and mundane as our villains. Dirty Harry is the low-bar model for our heroes. But he isn't a hero; he's merely the lesser of two evils, a shade less wicked and violent than his antagonists. Both Harry and the thugs he exterminates break the law, and both believe devoutly in violence and overwhelming force as the ultimate solution to conflict.

We've become a culture of narcissists. We're comforted when historical revisionists portray shining characters of the past as scurrilous creeps in disguise. Diminishing our heroes assures us that we're not so bad, that they're no better than we are, just as self-obsessed and venal. Fallen heroes give us license to slip even further.

It's likely that we even elected a particularly inept president because folks wanted their chief executive to be a regular guy, no brighter than the rest of us, not an intellectual or a college professor but a Good Old Boy.

How did we become so self-obsessed? Perhaps Sigmund Freud opened the dikes. More likely it was the clamoring, ever-present press of American advertising insisting that our own comfort was more important than the values our tribe—our society—had worked to establish.

The door to our subconscious flew open in the 'fifties. Popular media—novels, cinema, television drama—began to recognize that the logical surface of our actions and thoughts were only a fraction of our feelings, and that those feelings were more powerful than we knew. It was important to recognize the existence of illogical anxiety and anger in our deeper, less accessible subconscious. But we may have mistaken the validity of those feelings with their rightness. I may harbor deep, neurotic anger at my Uncle Bill and it may be possible to trace those feeling to some slight or trauma. But my feelings' origins don't justify taking a hammer to Uncle Billy.

The old axiom, "There ain't no such a thing as a bad cowpoke, only a sick one," may be true. But it was still wrong for Tex to rob the Danville Train.

The fact is that there *were* heroes. There almost certainly *are* heroes now. But they make us uncomfortable. Maybe they shame us a little. Adams, Jefferson, Franklin, and their colleagues were heroes driven by principle. Theodore Roosevelt was driven by energetic morals. Sergeant York was driven by duty. What drives us?

We've made heroes of Don Corleone and Tony Soprano. In our new folklore, Mafiosi are powerful and wealthy but ruthless and vengeful. What is their allure? A large factor is, almost certainly, the simplicity of their conflict. If we dismantle the moral restraints and legal niceties, they are simply family men surrounded by enemies who must defend themselves and their families expediently, quickly, simply. "Bang."

This is the moral drama we prefer. No cloud of gray-area social and legal rules, but a direct, black and white melodrama—us and them, me and the encroaching world. Again, our narcissism blurs an ability to discern the multitude of grays that make up reality.

One advance of our age is that we've been taught to be more sensitive to feelings, diversity, and tolerance than our grandparents. It's unfortunately true that my grandparents supported a genteel but disturbing backlog of prejudice against African Americans, Jews, Hispanics, Asians, Slavs, women, homosexuals, and even Catholics. Embracing the health of American diversity is a positive shift in our consciousness.

But how did a broader tolerance lead us to deeper narcissism? How did we develop even more callous self-regard?

Perhaps it takes a geezer like me to recognize the lack of social glue, the failure of a common bond. We seem to care more about abstract groups of diversity and less about people. The level of contact and courtesy on the street is sketchy. We've become suspicious of our fellow citizens regardless of race, creed, color, or place of national origin.

Yes, we're more politically correct, but how did the edge of our morals become so dull? Weren't we the generation that confronted Jim Crow laws and segregated schooling? And won? But we've watched lackadaisically as Watergate, Iran-Contra, Enron, sub-prime junk bonds, Abu Ghraib, and gargantuan financial scams flicker past us in a blur of tawdry, casual corruption. We *expect* our government and our leaders to be corrupt. We don't protest the most outrageous transgressions.

Only a nation of self-obsessed and morally disoriented drones would entertain institutionalized torture like water-boarding as American public policy or as a political party preference. Only a government that reflects our own confusion would appear so blasé about lack of basic decency. It's like Dirty Harry in the White house.

*

I expected a new Age of Reason to sweep away superstition.

The unfolding of science in the last half of the twentieth century and our pursuit of the most basic principles of life have been thrilling—DNA, the human genome, subatomic particles, planetary probes, deep space views from the Hubble, medical advances. But each revelation is another layer of complexity, requiring a new depth of understanding.

I fear that in our time we've come to resent and even reject complication. Our national attention span has been worn away by television (especially by *Sesame Street*), and what isn't plain black-and-white within a few moments is boring.

Our boredom with "fancy knowledge" has led us back to magic and superstition. Magic is always easier to understand than quantum physics or the mathematics of evolution.

What I've encountered, especially here in California, is a new folklore of superstition in medicine. Millions of people seriously subscribe to alternative medicine. The logical progress of medical science has been an endless series of hypotheses and refutations, of theory and experiment. As our technology grew more exacting, we devised elegant proofs to disprove old theories once widely accepted. But our course always took us in the direction of logical rigor, of strong proofs and double-blind studies. This skeptical sense is now considered "insulting" to citizens who hold their own scientific views, biblically or medically. "I don't know much about science, but I know what I like."

I'm a great reader of Patrick O'Brien's"Aubrey-Maturin" series set around the Napoleonic Wars. Stephen Maturin is a physician and surgeon of great skill and delightful character. Yet his medical theory is completely wrong. He subscribes to the ancient school of humors, in which good health is the result of balancing four bodily fluids. One tenet of this disproved theory is bloodletting. In the novels Maturin discusses hundreds of drugs, yet only half a dozen have any real medicinal value. Two of those are opium and the placebo. The rest of his pharmacopoeia is not only non-therapeutic but often harmful. Some readers find this amusing.

For me, the parallels between Maturin's outdated pill-rolling and Chinese herbal, homeopathic, massage-therapy, extended chiropractic, therapeutic acupuncture, reflexology, and burning herbs is too close for amusement. Millions of people swear that homeopathic remedies available at Whole Foods will cure their ills. Exhaustive double-blind studies that find no trace of benefit in homeopathy don't dissuade them. Millions of "well-educated" people claim that Chinese herbals are sound medicine because it's been practiced for ten thousand years! They maintain their faith though in ten thousand years the herbalists never found cures for malaria, tuberculosis, cholera, typhus, or simple infection.

The basis for stubborn illogical resistance to the scientific method is emotional. When young people say, "I don't believe in Western medicine," they're really insisting that their assumptions about reality are just as valid as the assumptions of the scientific community. The American Medical Association is considered an "old boys' club" bent on making more money and not on providing scientifically underwritten health care.

Logically, scientific theory isn't assumptive. Its validity is supported by exhaustive double-blind studies, its results are transparently published and peer-reviewed, and results are duplicated hundreds of times by separate tests. But the emotional weight of a statement dismissing Western medicine is that "all ideas are equal," and "my idea is just as valid as yours."

This can be comforting in a narcissistic world-view. And the anecdotal outcomes of quack medicine are encouraging because most human maladies are self-arresting within five days to two weeks no matter what kind of medicine is applied. Good luck with that appendicitis, though.

Self-centered regard for our personal bubble of chosen belief is a return to medieval superstition that takes the form of astonishingly widespread belief in ghosts, Bigfoot, UFOs, horoscopes, and a *National Enquirer* backlog of urban legends.

No medium has ever expressed the American psyche more colorfully than Hollywood movies. The lure of new folklore is writ large in our obsessive movie themes. There are only a few serial killers currently active in the entire country, but their presence as movie villains (and even heroes, as in *Dexter*) suggests that they're as numerous as dry cleaners. Zombies: can anyone explain our fond obsession with the living dead?

Our love affair with vampires is more understandable: vampires transcend death, have way cool powers, and have active dating lives. Oddly, they always have plenty of money. But they reach into our folklore, and I include vampires and werewolves as a minor part of our literary roots. But why so many vampire themes? Why the Goth longing to believe?

An even more basic question is: What dark purposes does our popular culture of horror movies serve?

I don't write magic. Admittedly, one of my favorite books—*Solstice*—is a spooky little ghost tale with a proper shiver up the spine toward the end. But that's a literary device, a convention, and simply fun. It's also a metaphor for the persistence of family values and the tragedy of family dissolution. I'm happy that it's been reprinted by WoodenBoat Books and enjoys a brisk sale. But it isn't Harry Potter.

I hear someone say, "But Harry Potter leads children to books!" There are better guides without the magic.

When magic and illogic come into a story, reality and sensible human character evaporate. Magic is the enemy of intellect. Teaching children that magic is real, or even suggesting it, can't be moral. Our work as creators is not merely to entertain but to reflect life.

I had a basic difference with my friend Isabel Allende. When she wrote the novel *Zorro,* I was her technical advisor. As part of the Zorro package, Harper asked me to write a young-adult series, *Young Zorro,* about Diego de la Vega and his silent brother Bernardo before Diego, much later, became Zorro, the adult crusader for justice. In the first novel, *Young Zorro: The Iron Brand,* I wrote about the fifteen-year-old boys in the Los Angeles Basin in 1805. I did a great deal of historical research on the customs, dress, food, and life-patterns of the mission pueblos. I fell back on Cato the Censor's dictum of oratory: "Seize the subject; the words will come." I wrote tales out of the California pueblo life, using the locations and possibilities of real history as themes.

Isabel, a wonderful story-teller, wrote her book differently. She is famous for her "magic realism" that weaves prophecy, native shamans, ghosts, signs and magic into the lives of her characters to direct them. And she was bored to death with the dusty, rural Pueblo de los Angeles. Her characters hot-footed it to romantic Spain as soon as she was able to arrange schooner passage down the coast to the Panamanian Isthmus.

For me, the raw pueblo life was fascinating, real, and full of possibilities! My characters didn't need magic because they had grizzly bears, pirates, slavers, whalers, Gabrieleño Indian villages, wildfires, storms—an embarrassment of riches for a writer. The historic village was a settlement of a few hundred Hispanics, a couple thousand Gabrieleño converts, several thousand unconverted Gabrieleños in the mountain Indian villages, and 25,000 cattle. My protagonists, Diego and Bernardo, and their fiery girl friend Trinity, rode everywhere on horses and mules. A paradise for boys!

The first novel was not marketed well and it may have been my fault. In an effort to suggest that the stories were realistic the author was listed as "Diego Vega (as told to Jan Adkins)." The name on the spine was, mistakenly, "Vega," an unknown, so the book was reviewed only once in the United States, and by a reviewer who mistook the book as a promotion piece for the Antonio Banderas *Zorro* movies. Sales were poor. But it's a book of which I'm enormously proud. It's a great yarn

about youth. I hope the California school system will pick up the ball and spark the publication of the next two novels, *Young Zorro: The Golden Skull,* and *Young Zorro: The Feathered Cape.*

We can reflect character and real values without magic even when our protagonists are bunnies. One of the most comforting series of books I've ever discovered is Rosemary Wells' *The Bunny Planet* cycle. She should receive a prize from the National Institute for Mental Health for demonstrating how to knit up a disappointing day with a fantasy and a bit of humor. No child should be without this little nutshell library of three tiny books. I've seen these books do wonders for grownups, as well, used as an antidote for disappointing days.

We can't legislate sense or logic. But in an era of "nanomachinery" and GPS, we should agree, generally, to be more skeptical of superstition and magic. Even at the risk of being politically incorrect and intolerant of equal ideas, we could also express a more creative and poetically respectful "theological skepticism" about foolishly literal interpretations of holy writings recorded by tribal sages with large axes to grind, and meant for semi-nomadic people 4,000, 2,000, and 1,700 years ago.

*

I had hoped to become my grampa.

Johnny Adkins was a sarcastic and annoying man. An elderly gentleman once tried to hit me with his cane when he discovered that Johnny was my grandfather. He held a grudge. But I would have been sympathetic to his complaints about my grampa, who regarded me as a ninnyhammer.

Johnny had lived a long and varied life, with some adventurous turns and considerable native intellect. Like my father, he was shrewd and inventive and loved a laugh. As crusty and annoying as he was, his four boys and the citizens of the big river-island on which we lived (Wheeling Island in the Ohio River), regarded Johnny with respect and consulted him with problems. "Ask Dad," one of his boys would say, "he's probably figured this one out before." Often, he had. Even when he hadn't, he could suggest ways that might work and (more importantly) ways he'd found that simply *didn't* work. He was an elder of a tribe of tinkers, and his ability to provide solutions was acute. When he couldn't solve a problem, he could listen and encourage. This is also the function of an elder.

So I hoped to become an elder of my tribe of inkfish.

But this hasn't happened. That great tectonic shift that tore us away from our continent of fables and tales also sheared away our tie to elders. In our culture we don't consult old people. Perhaps we assume that technology has changed so much that their input can't be relevant.

I'm not sure this is the mechanism, however. It's more likely a function of our contemporary narcissism: we don't consult our elders because we can't bear criticism. We prize our ideas as pure expressions of our being, and our ideas are just as good as any other ideas, aren't they? Why should we allow some out-of-context, beyond-his-depth old guy tell us we're wrong?

Of course, it's possible that the old guy might tell you you're right, but just a hair off-direction. He might have figured this one out before. Or he might have some long-perspective input you haven't really considered. But the sting of criticism is too dangerous, and input compromises your purity of authorship.

We're not a culture of collaborators; we pat ourselves on the backs for being "rugged individualists." Collaboration may work well for sheep or for dull minds, but we insist that the brightness of our ideas can only be diminished by a committee.

As a young man I was as guilty of this sad selfishness as anyone else. Only after I had been associate art director at *National Geographic* magazine for many years did I realize that the most creative work I'd ever done was collaboration in the layout room. There, in the heady foam of cross currents and asymmetrical contributions, the photographer, writer, legend writer, photo editor, and art director created context, designs, expressions, and stories that were better and more complete than any one of us could have made. I learned a lot of humility and pride in that room. Perhaps too late.

The excitement of collaboration with brilliant creators and excited explorers is the current I miss every day. Even thinking about *National Geographic* is sometimes painful, because I loved it so much.

Out on my own, writing and illustrating, designing and researching, I have wanted to share my skills, but I'm in the wrong culture. I can't be a tribal elder.

Indeed, there may now be an imposed shelf-life for creatives. As I grow older my work becomes deeper and more understanding and less egocentric (don't take this autobiographical musing as a proper example!). My understanding is broader and softer. My images more casual but surer. My sentences less complex. My verbs are more active and my modifiers more specific. But the older I become without having written a blockbuster best-seller, the less credence I carry in my profession.

I've never written a best seller. True, I've written books that have sold consistently for almost forty years. But I've never hit the charts, and this is the only thing that counts for publishers. Publishers trust me less each year. Without major national sales figures, I'm not a sure thing. Even though I'm at the height of my powers, writing nonfiction for young people has been a poor career choice, and I'm guilty of that disastrous faith in dreams against which I've warned you.

If I thought that hitting the charts was an index of books' qualities, I'd take up bagging groceries at Trader Joe's and leave this difficult profession. But as professionals we know that marketing makes sales, and that best sellers are created in the board room and by the author. I believe I'll soldier on for a time. I knew Isaac Bashevis Singer when he was ninety-three. Ike was at the top of his game, excited about his work, looking forward to the next book. I can do that, even without the big sales.

I miss teaching. Teaching at Rhode Island School of Design was one of the most satisfying things I've ever done. Teaching at the Maryland Institute College of Art was also a hoot; the illustration studio course were exciting, the graphic design courses were fun, and I especially relished the slide-and-discussion courses I gave in the history of illustration. But RISD wanted art academics, not professionals, as staff members. ("We don't want to turn this into a trade school!") The associate professorship that would have been a reward, comfort, challenge and sustaining purpose for me was given over to someone with the proper M.F.A and Ph.D. Maryland Institute also loved wallpaper—M.F.As and Ph.D.s. Alas, illustration classes here in the San Francisco area are taught not by tribal elders but by young warriors with a fashionable edge.

So I work and exist in an eddy of the publishing world. My chance at a Harry Potter series—*Young Zorro*—

"A Convocation of Wizards": grandson Maxwell Ulysses Burger, 2.5 years; Adkins, 65 years; and grandson Lucas Kiernan Burger, 10 *months* (Photograph by Sally Adkins. Courtesy of Jan Adkins.)

flopped. My nonfiction for young people sells modestly. I write articles about boats and humor articles for coastal magazines; I consult on museum design and look for creative ways to continue comfortably.

*

Perhaps we should acknowledge our financial recession and its devastation of the arts. I hope some analytical minds recognize the failure of our education system to extend our cultural heritage.

Franklin Delano Roosevelt's Great Depression solution for artists was the Works Progress Administration, which funded murals, books, photographic exhibits, and plays. Many young people were energized in the Conservation Corps, building trails and national park facilities.

Using this precedent, maybe we need a Corps of Storytellers. Thousands of naturally loquacious raconteurs might set out from Washington, DC. They might stop in the town squares under walnut trees and elms, under skylights at the malls, or park themselves in library corners in every city and village. They might pause on benches, beside fountains, in bus-stop shelters, and tell all the old stories. Odysseus, The Light Brigade, Horatius at the Bridge, Pecos Bill, Blackbeard, Jean Lafite and Andrew Jackson meeting at the Old Absinthe House, Theodore Roosevelt descending the South American River of Doubt, Lindbergh teaching U.S. Army Air Force P-38 fighter pilots to shoot down Zeros, Thomas Jefferson planting radishes. It would be a great gig for old, talkative duffers like me, a blessing to kids, entertainment when oil gets expensive, and a way to rediscover ourselves. We need those tales. Our hearts are empty without them.

*   *   *

ARGUELLES, Francisco Xavier
See STORK, Francisco X.

*   *   *

ARNOLD, Emily
See McCULLY, Emily Arnold

*   *   *

AUGARDE, Steve 1950-
(Steven Andre Augarde)

Personal

Born October 3, 1950, in Birmingham, England; son of Eric Claude (a builder and interior decorator) and Grace Olive Augarde; married; children: two daughters. *Education:* Attended Yeovil School of Art, Somerset College of Art, and Rolle Teacher Training College.

Addresses

Home—England. *E-mail*—augarde@onetel.net; augarde@talktalk.net.

Career

Author, illustrator, paper engineer, and animator. Illustrator for advertising agencies; animator for television series *Bump,* British Broadcasting Corporation (BBC). Semi-professional musician; performed in jazz group and for two BBC series; qualified teacher. Gardener for National Trust at Montacute House, England; has also worked as a telemarketer and motorcycle dispatch rider.

Awards, Honors

Bronze medal, Nestlé Smarties Book Prize, 2003, for *The Various;* Carnegie Medal long-list inclusion, 2005, for *Celandine,* and 2008, for *Winter Wood.*

Writings

SELF-ILLUSTRATED; FOR CHILDREN

A Lazy Day, Fabbri & Partners (London, England), 1974.

The River That Disappeared, Fabbri & Partners (London, England), 1974.

The Willow Tree, Fabbri & Partners (London, England), 1974.

Pig, Deutsch (London, England), 1975, Bradbury Press (Scarsdale, NY), 1977.

Barnaby Shrew Goes to Sea, Deutsch (London, England), 1978.

Barnaby Shrew, Black Dan, and the Mighty Wedgwood, Deutsch (London, England), 1979.

Mr. Mick, Deutsch (London, England), 1980.

January Jo and Friends, Deutsch (London, England), 1981.

SELF-ILLUSTRATED; AND PAPER ENGINEER

Humpty Dumpty, illustrated by Moira Kemp, designed by Herman Lelie, Lodestar Books (New York, NY), 1996.

Tractor Trouble: A Pop-up Book, Lodestar Books (New York, NY), 1996.

Five Speckled Frogs, and Other Counting Rhymes, Cartwheel Books (New York, NY), 1997.

The Hokey Pokey, and Other Party Rhymes, Cartwheel Books (New York, NY), 1997.

The Itsy Bitsy Spider, and Other Hand Rhymes, Cartwheel Books (New York, NY), 1997.

Row, Row, Row Your Boat, and Other Play Rhymes, Cartwheel Books (New York, NY), 1997.

Fire Engine to the Rescue: A Pop-up Book, Tupelo Books (New York, NY), 1998.

Here Comes the Lifeboat!, Orion Children's (London, England), 1999.

When I Grow Up, Madcap (London, England), 1999, Grosset & Dunlap (New York, NY), 2000.

Vroom! Vroom! A Pop-up Race to the Finish!, David & Charles Children's (London, England), 2000, Little, Brown (Boston, MA), 2001.

Big Nose, Small Nose: A Book of Opposites, Mathew Price (Sherborne, England), 2001.

Garage, Charlesbridge Publishing (Watertown, MA), 2002.

Kissing Fish, Ragged Bears (Sherborne, England), 2002.

Counting Sheep, Ragged Bears (Sherborne, England, 2002.

Flying Pigs, Ragged Bears (Sherborne, England), 2002.

Dancing Bears, Ragged Bears (Sherborne, England), 2002.

The Big Yellow Digger, Ragged Bears (Sherborne, England), 2002.

We're Going on an Airplane!, Handprint/Ragged Bears (England), 2003.

The New York Yellow Bulldozer, Handprint/Ragged Bears (England), 2003.

Purple Eyes, Gingham Dog (Grand Rapids, MI), 2004.

One Paper Hat, Gingham Dog (Grand Rapids, MI), 2004.

Cover of Steve Augarde's middle-grade fantasy The Various, ***in which a girl finds a link to the world of faerie.*** (Copyright © 2004 by Steve Augarde. Used by permission of David Fickling Books, an imprint of Random House Children's Books, a division of Random House, Inc.)

Hello, Moon, Gingham Dog (Grand Rapids, MI), 2004.

ILLUSTRATOR

Bill Gillham, *Septimus Fry F.R.S.; or, How Mrs. Fry Had the Baby in the World,* Deutsch (London, England), 1980.

Eric Charles, *Bertha and the Windmills* (based on the television designs by Ivor Wood), Deutsch (London, England), 1985.

Eric Charles, *Bertha and the Great Painting Job* (based on the television designs by Ivor Wood), Deutsch (London, England), 1985.

Eric Charles, *Bertha and a Mouse in the Works* (based on the television designs by Ivor Wood), Deutsch (London, England), 1986.

Eric Charles, *Bertha and the Best Machine Competition* (based on the television designs by Ivor Wood), Deutsch (London, England), 1986.

Eric Charles, *Bertha and the Lost Tom* (based on the television designs by Ivor Wood), Deutsch (London, England), 1986.

Eric Charles, *Bertha and the Flying Bear* (based on the television designs by Ivor Wood), Deutsch (London, England), 1986.

Bertha Annual, Polystyle Publications (London, England), 1986.

This Is Bump, Kingsborn (London, England), 1987.

Bump Goes to the Seaside, Kingsborn (London, England), 1987.

ILLUSTRATOR AND PAPER ENGINEER

Elinor Bagenal, *Tractor Factory: A Pop-up Book,* Golden Books (New York, NY), 1994.

Mathew Price, *Little Red Car Gets into Trouble,* Abbeville Press (New York, NY), 2000.

Mathew Price, *Little Red Car Has an Accident,* Abbeville Press (New York, NY), 2000.

Mathew Price, *Little Red Car in the Snow,* Abbeville Press (New York, NY), 2000.

Mathew Price, *Little Red Car Plays Taxi,* Abbeville Press (New York, NY), 2000.

Matthew Price, *Patch and the Rabbits,* Orchard Books (New York, NY), 2000.

Mathew Price, *Patch Finds a Friend,* illustrated by Emma Chichester Clark, Orchard Books (New York, NY), 2000.

PAPER ENGINEER

Matthew Price, *Who Loves You Baby Bear?,* 1991.

Juan Wijngaard, *Buzz! Buzz!,* Lodestar Books (New York, NY), 1995.

Mathew Price, *Don't Worry, Alfie,* illustrated by Emma Chichester Clark, Orchard Books (New York, NY), 1999.

Mathew Price, *Where's Alfie?,* illustrated by Emma Chichester Clark, Orchard Books (New York, NY), 1999.

Cover of Augarde's young-adult novel **Winter Wood,** *featuring artwork by Melanie DeLeon.* (Jacket art copyright © 2009 by Melanie DeLeon. Used by permission of David Fickling Books, an imprint of Random House Children's Books, a division of Random House, Inc.)

Rosie Goes to Playschool (juvenile fiction), illustrated by Atsuko Morozummi, Mathew Price (Sherborne, England), 2003.

Jan Pieńkowski, *Ninja Cat,* Walker Books (London, England), 2007.

"TOUCHSTONE TRILOGY"; JUVENILE FICTION

The Various, David Fickling Books (New York, NY), 2004.
Celandine (prequel to *The Various*), David Fickling Books (New York, NY), 2006.
Winter Wood, David Fickling Books (New York, NY), 2009.

OTHER

Camion de Bomberos al Rescate, Mathew Price (Denton, TX), 2009.
Leonardo Da Vinci, Kingfisher (New York, NY), 2009.

Illustrator of "Bertha" (weekly comic strip), Kingsborn, Ltd., and "Jack in a Box" (biweekly comic strip), I.P.C., Ltd.

Sidelights

While primarily an illustrator, Steve Augarde has worked as a paper engineer for a number of children's pop-up books, and in 2003 he was awarded a bronze medal in the 2003 Nestlé Smarties' Book Prizes for his debut young-adult novel, *The Various.* Part one of Augarde's "Touchstone Trilogy," *The Various* was praised by *School Library Journal* critic Sue Giffard as an "inventive and unusual fantasy."

The Various focuses on twelve-year-old Midge. The daughter of a classical musician, Midge has been left with her uncle Brian while her mother is performing on tour. Brian owns a farm near a forest, and Midge soon discovers that magical fairies are living in Mill Farm's empty barn. Midge's uncle is planning to sell the forest land to a developer, greatly upsetting the five tribes of fairies, who live there and call themselves "the Various." Midge is drawn into the world of the Various, which features a complex, human-like society and caste system, and she attempts to prevent the forest's sale to help her new friends. "The author ably balances moments of drama with large doses of humor," a critic for *Publishers Weekly* commented in a review of Augarde's fiction debut.

Discussing the trilogy in an *Eclectica* Web site interview with Dolores D'Annolfo, Augarde noted that "the idea for *The Various* grew around a single image—that of a girl finding a winged horse. I just had this snapshot in my head: a girl kneeling in a disused barn, chinks of light coming down through the rusty tin roof, and this thing that she'd discovered, a creature, magical yet injured in some way. It was an interesting picture, strong enough to explore."

Augarde's work for toddler bookworms include creating the illustrations for Mathew Price's board book **Little Red Car.** (Copyright © 2000 by Mathew Price. Reproduced by permission.)

The second book in the trilogy, *Celandine,* is actually a prequel to *The Various.* The story's protagonist is Celantine, Midge's great aunt. Celandine is portrayed as a young girl in boarding school, and her brother is missing in action in World War I. Back on Celandine's family farm, the young protagonist learns how to contact the Gorji, ogres, and the Various. The book ends in suspense, as readers must wait for the trilogy's final installment to learn of Celandine's fate. Critics praised *Celandine* as an entertaining and well-conceived novel. According to *Booklist* contributor GraceAnne A. DeCandido, Augarde's fictional "worlds are finely imagined," and *Celandine* serves as "a fast and compelling read." Dylan Thomarie, writing in *School Library Journal,* predicted that young readers "who stick with it will be rewarded," while in *Kirkus Reviews* a critic noted that in *Celandine* "Augarde creates a familiar yet entirely original world, a very sympathetic heroine and an absolutely riveting adventure."

The "Touchstone Trilogy" concludes with *Winter Wood,* which finds twelve-year-old Midge once again helping the Various, this time in their efforts to locate the Orbis, an artifact that was separated from the Touchstone many years ago. The Various believe that if reunion occurs, their society will once again be safe, and Midge believes that her Great-Great-Aunt Celandine, who is now in a nursing home, may be the only one who can help her in her quest. Although *Winter Wood* ties together the two preceding volumes in Augarde's trilogy, Thomarie noted that readers new to the series will be able to follow the plot with little trouble. As with *The Various* and *Celandine,* added the critic, "readers will be captivated by Augarde's wonderful descriptions of the English countryside." In *Booklist* GraceAnne A. DeCandido wrote that Augarde crafts a "stirring conclusion" to his fantasy trilogy, and a *Kirkus Reviews* contributor dubbed *Winter Wood* "a perfectly paced, beautifully crafted and moving end to a memorable fantasy."

Augarde once noted: "Behind the list of book titles, of course, there are real lives going on. At least there ought

Cover of the pop-up book **Garage,** *which was written, designed, and illustrated by Augarde.* (Charlesbridge Publishing, 2002. Illustration copyright © 2001 by Steve Augarde. All rights reserved. Reproduced by permission.)

to be. I would be suspicious of anyone who spent the major part of their time in front of a typewriter or behind a drawing board. Not much going on there.

"Between 1981 and 1986 I had nothing published. This was because I was too busy—too busy having a hard time, in fact. In 1980 I had a brilliant idea and invented the electric pop-up book. To come up with a good invention in England, is, of course, to make a big mistake. In terms of progress, you may as well go rock-carving with your teeth. Still, I enlisted the help of an engineer friend, Richard Bendall, and together we made several working dummies of the book, first of all with batteries in the spine and later progressing to self-contained electronic modules mounted between the pages. We not only had pop-ups but lights and sound to accompany the pictures. We showed the dummy books to publishers who fell about with delight, shook our hands, called us geniuses, and gave us dinner. Well, at least we got the dinner.

"To give the publishers their due, they did try. But always the same reply. Too expensive. Can't be done. I still think that had we been in America, things would have been different. It is notoriously difficult in England to get a new idea funded and off the ground. Time and again we seemed to be about to break through. The tension, build up, and frustration cycle went round and round for five years. Gradually it became clear that the project would just not happen. The idea was being diluted—musical greeting cards began to appear in Japan. The impact was lost and the impetus gone.

"Disenchanted with publishing, I worked instead as a musician, playing in pubs and clubs and for a while with a theatre group. Got a job as a motorcycle dispatch rider, worked in telesales. Nearly went into selling double glazing, couldn't face it, drifted down.

"Five years on, very broke, very pissed off, I was offered the 'Bertha' books to illustrate. From January 1985 I stopped being a sunken businessman, climbed back on to the drawing board and became a floating illustrator once more. That's where the list of titles begins again."

Biographical and Critical Sources

PERIODICALS

Booklist, August 1, 2006, GraceAnne A. DeCandido, review of _Celandine,_ p. 63; April 1, 2009, GraceAnne A. DeCandido, review of _Winter Wood,_ p. 32.

Bulletin of the Center for Children's Books, October 1, 2006, April Spisak, review of _Celandine,_ p. 54.

Kirkus Reviews, July 15, 2006, review of _Celandine,_ p. 720; April 1, 2009, review of _Winter Wood;_ September 15, 2009, review of _Leonard Da Vinci._

Library Media Connection, April 1, 2004, Steve Augarde, review of _The Various._

New York Times Book Review, July 11, 2004, review of _The Various,_ p. 19.

School Librarian, March 22, 2006, Teresa Scragg, review of _Celandine,_ p. 42; June, 2009, Dylan Thomaire, review of _Winter Wood,_ p. 114.

School Library Journal, March, 2004, Sue Gifford, review of _The Various,_ p. 203; November 1, 2006, Dylan Thomarie, review of _Celandine,_ p. 129.

Voice of Youth Advocates, October 1, 2004, Mary Arnold, review of _The Various,_ p. 312; December 1, 2006, Mary Arnold, review of _Celandine,_ p. 437.

ONLINE

Eclectica Web site, http://www.eclectica.org/ (March 4, 2009), Dolores D'Annolfo, interview with Augarde.

Looking Glass Review Online, http://www.lookingglassreview.com/ (November 19, 2005), "Steve Augarde."

Steve Augarde Home Page, http://www.steveaugarde.com (October 15, 2009).*

*   *   *

AUGARDE, Steven Andre
See AUGARDE, Steve

B

BADDIEL, Ivor 1963-

Personal

Born January 31, 1963; married Sophie Jubb (a teacher and author); children: one daughter, one son.

Addresses

Home—London, England.

Career

Author and scriptwriter for television and radio. Formerly worked as a teacher.

Writings

(Compiler, with Ian Stone) *The Best Pub Joke Book Ever!*, Carlton (London, England), 1997, expanded edition, with Tim Dedopulos, 1999.

Ultimate Soccer, DK Publishers (New York, NY), 1998, published as *Ultimate Football*, Dorling Kindersley (London, England), 1998, 3rd edition, 2002.

(With Tracey Blezard) *The Supernatural: Investigations into the Unexplained*, Macdonald Young (Hove, England), 1998, Barron's Educational (Hauppauge, NY), 1999.

(With Tracey Blezard) *Extraterrestrials*, illustrated by Colin Sullivan, Macdonald Young (Hove, England), 1998.

(With Tracey Blezard) *Fantastic Creatures: Investigations into the Unexplained*, illustrated by Douglas Gray, Barron's Educational (Hauppauge, NY), 1999.

(With Tracey Belzard) *The Future: Investigations into the Unknown*, Barron's Educational (Hauppauge, NY), 1999.

(With Jonny Zucker) *Mystical Magic*, illustrated by Mike Phillips, Hippo (London, England), 2003.

(With Jonny Zucker) *David Feckham: My Backside*, Orion (London, England), 2004.

(Coauthor) Steve Fist, *Bottle: The Completely True Story of an Ex-Football Hooligan*, Mainstream (Edinburgh, Scotland), 2005.

(With Sophie Jubb) *Cock-a-Doodle Quack! Quack!*, illustrated by Ailie Busby, Picture Corgi (London, England), 2006, David Fickling (New York, NY), 2007.

(With Jonny Zucker) *Not the Highway Code: The Unofficial Rules of the Road*, Weidenfeld & Nicholson (London, England), 2006.

Author of scripts for television series, including *Star-Street*, 2001; *We Know Where You Live* 2001; *Bus Life*, 2004; *Johnny & Denise: Passport to Paradise*, 2004; and *School's Out*, 2006-07. Contributor of sports commentary to periodicals.

Biographical and Critical Sources

PERIODICALS

Booklist, September 1, 1998, Karen Hutt, review of *Ultimate Soccer*, p. 75.

Bulletin of the Center for Children's Books, July-August, 2007, Hope Morrision, review of *Cock-a-Doodle Quack! Quack!*, p. 452.

Kirkus Reviews, April 1, 2007, review of *Cock-a-Doodle Quack! Quack!*

Publishers Weekly, April 2, 2007, review of *Cock-a-Doodle Quack! Quack!*, p. 56.

School Library Journal, August, 1998, Blair Christolon, review of *Ultimate Soccer*, p. 148; March, 2007, Rachel G. Payne, review of *Cock-a-Doodle Quack! Quack!*, p. 150.*

*   *   *

BEAUDOIN, Sean

Personal

Married; wife's name Cathy; children: Stella. *Education:* B.A. (photography).

Sean Beaudoin (Reproduced by permission.)

Addresses

Home—San Francisco, CA. *Agent*—Steven Malk, smalk@writershouse.com; Jennifer de la Fuente, jennifer@ventureliterary.com. *E-mail*—SeanBeaudoin@comcast.net.

Career

Writer. Worked variously as a construction laborer, circus roustabout, busboy, used-book buyer, hotel desk clerk, camp counselor, statue repairman, and seller of jazz vinyl.

Awards, Honors

Best Book for Young Adults selection, American Library Association, 2007, for *Going Nowhere Faster.*

Writings

Going Nowhere Faster (novel), Little, Brown (New York, NY), 2007.
Fade to Blue (novel), Little, Brown (New York, NY), 2009.

Contributor to *Danger City* (anthology). Contributor of short stories to periodicals, including *Glimmer Train, New Orleans Review, Barrelhouse, Instant City, Bayou, Another Chicago Magazine, Bat City Review, Redivider,* and *Ballyhoo.*

Sidelights

Sean Beaudoin published *Going Nowhere Faster,* his debut work for teen readers, in 2007. Beaudoin, whose short fiction has appeared in such publications as *New Orleans Review, Barrelhouse,* and *Glimmer Train,* was encouraged to write the young-adult novel at the suggestion of a friend. "I never really believed writing was something I could actually do," the author told Kelly Parra in an interview on the *YA Fresh* Web site. "Not only in terms of making a living, but just finishing a book. As it turns out, more than anything else, you have to make yourself sit down and do it."

Going Nowhere Faster focuses on seventeen-year-old Stan Smith, a former child prodigy who works a dead-end job at the local video store. Although Beaudoin has worked at a number of colorful jobs, including circus roustabout, used-book buyer, and statue repairman, the author insists that the novel is not autobiographical. "Stan is a character I made up," he stated on his home page. "Like every character in every book, some of the details come from real-life experience. For instance, I

Cover of **Going Nowhere Faster,** *a novel by Beaudoin that chronicles the lackluster early adulthood of a talented young writer.* (Little, Brown, 2007. Copyright © 2007 by Sean Beaudoin. Reproduced by permission.)

did work in a video store while in high school, and I did develop an uncanny ability to recall the name and location of just about every movie on every shelf." Discussing his protagonist for the *Little Brown School Newsletter* online, Beaudoin explained that Stan's "desire to leave the small town of his youth is offset by fears of insignificance and the albatross of expectation that comes with an intelligence he has only a passing control over. Also, someone is trying to kill him." The author went on to describe *Going Nowhere Faster* as "the story of being too sensitive, too insulated, too ignored, too alone, too egotistical, too judgmental, too seventeen."

In the novel, Stan is a high-school graduate who possesses an IQ of 165. He decides against college and instead dreams of writing a hit screenplay, although his halfhearted efforts have so far made it, only to land in the trash. Stan's love life is equally depressing. He pines for the lovely Ellen Rigby even though Ellen's boyfriend, Chad Chilton, once threatened Stan and now appears to be stalking him. Stan's eccentric parents only add to his insecurities: his mother, a six-foot-tall vegan who owns an organic food store, allows a smelly, self-professed guru to live on their property, and his father, an inventor who drives a car that runs on waste oil from fast-food restaurants, has an uncanny knack for building lopsided structures. After the video store is vandalized, Stan becomes the chief suspect, and he must finally take control of his life.

Going Nowhere Faster received a number of positive reviews. "Beaudoin's breezy, conversational style quickly invites the reader to see the world through Stan's jaded, hypercritical eyes," noted *Voice of Youth Advocates* critic Steven Kral. Although a contributor in *Kirkus Reviews* praised Beaudoin's humorous prose and well-developed characters, the critic also noted that "an uneventful storyline prevents this first novel from gaining any real traction." Myrna Marler offered a more positive assessment of the book in *Kliatt*. "Written in a comically manic style, this narrative goes from one unlikely scenario to another," Marler noted, adding that Beaudoin's wacky plot "is both compelling and hilarious." *Horn Book* reviewer Lauren Adams complimented the more realistic aspects *Going Nowhere Faster*, remarking that "a romantic opportunity won and lost plays out believably, as does the satisfying ending."

In *Fade to Blue* Beaudoin treats readers to what *Horn Book* contributor Sarah Ellis dubbed a "funhouse mélange of action-adventure, romance, and dystopian science fiction," all salted with a comics interlude and social and political commentary. On her seventeenth birthday Sophie Blue had her world change when her father disappeared and she was injected with a mysterious substance. Transforming her outward self by adopting a Goth look, Sophie is now haunted by bizarre dreams and a strange incantation while trying to deal with her flaky family and a budding romance. Full of praise for Beaudoin's unique, high-energy novel, Joyce

Cover of Beaudoin's teen novel **Fade to Blue,** *featuring artwork by Wilfred Santiago.* (Little, Brown, 2009. Illustration copyright © 2009 by Wilfred Santiago. Reproduced by permission of illustrator.)

Adams Burner cited the "manic rampage of plot twists" that fuel the author's "cleverly written, inventive romp in which every detail counts." Although a *Kirkus Reviews* writer found parts of the novel to be "almost completely nonlinear," *Fade to Blue* is redeemed by Beaudoin's "stellar wit" and other sections that are "wickedly funny and creepily dreamlike." Summing up the book's many complexities, Ian Chipman noted in *Booklist* that readers will either love or hate *Fade to Blue,* "a stylishly outfitted, bafflingly structured head trip" that mixes humor, drama, and an "indescribable" plot.

Biographical and Critical Sources

PERIODICALS

Booklist, June 1, 2009, Ian Chipman, review of *Fade to Blue,* p. 50.

Horn Book, May-June, 2007, Lauren Adams, review of *Going Nowhere Faster,* p. 277; September-October, 2009, Sarah Ellis, review of *Fade to Blue,* p. 551.

Kirkus Reviews, April 1, 2007, review of *Going Nowhere Faster;* July 15, 2009, review of *Fade to Blue.*

Kliatt, March, 2007, Myrna Marler, review of *Going Nowhere Faster,* p. 8.

School Library Journal, April, 2007, Hillias J. Martin, review of *Going Nowhere Faster,* p. 128; October, 2009, Joyce Adams Burner, review of *Fade to Blue,* p. 119.

Voice of Youth Advocates, April, 2007, Steven Kral, review of *Going Nowhere Faster.*

ONLINE

Little Brown School Newsletter Online, http://www.news letterarchive.org/ (May 9, 2007), "Sean Beaudoin."

Sean Beaudoin Home Page, http://www.seanbeaudoin.com (March 1, 2008).

YA Fresh Web site, http://yafresh.blogspot.com/ (April 24, 2007), Kelly Parra, "What's Fresh with Sean Beaudoin's *Going Nowhere Faster.*"*

* * *

BERRY, Holly 1957-

Personal

Born 1957, in Kennebunk, ME; married; children: two daughters. *Education:* Rhode Island School of Design, B.F.A. (illustration), 1979; graduate study at Boston University (studio teaching).

Addresses

Home and office—Waldoboro, ME. *E-mail*—flossie. cat@verizon.net.

Career

Printmaker and children's book illustrator. *Exhibitions:* Work exhibited at Boston Printmaker's North American Juried Show, Boston, MA, 2005; Maine Art Gallery, Wiscasset; Roundtop Center for the Arts, Damariscotta, ME; Bates Mill Complex, Lewiston, ME; and Arlington Center for the Arts, Arlington, MA. Solo exhibitions include Mastcove Galleries, Kennebunkport, ME.

Awards, Honors

Golden Kite Award for illustration, 1996, for *Market Day* by Eve Bunting; silver medal, Society of Illustrators Original Art Show, 2004, for *The Impudent Rooster* by Samina I. Rascol; individual artists fellowship, Maine Arts Commission.

Writings

SELF-ILLUSTRATED

Old MacDonald Had a Farm, North-South Books (New York, NY), 1994.

Busy Lizzie, North-South Books (New York, NY), 1994.

ILLUSTRATOR

Philemon Sturges, *The Gift of Christmas,* North-South Books (New York, NY), 1995.

Elinor Pinczes, *Arctic Fives Arrive,* Houghton Mifflin (Boston, MA), 1996.

Eve Bunting, *Market Day,* HarperCollins (New York, NY), 1996.

Claire Masurel, *Where's Santa?,* Puffin (New York, NY), 1998.

Diane Stanley, *Roughing It on the Oregon Trail,* HarperCollins (New York, NY), 1999.

Laura Geringer, *The Stubborn Pumpkin,* Scholastic (New York, NY), 1999.

Joyce Carol Thomas, *The Bowlegged Rooster, and Other Tales That Signify,* HarperCollins (New York, NY), 2000.

Diane Stanley, *Joining the Boston Tea Party,* HarperCollins (New York, NY), 2001.

Sabina I. Rascol, *The Impudent Rooster,* Dutton (New York, NY), 2004.

Diane Stanley, *Thanksgiving on Plymouth Plantation,* Joanna Cotler Books (New York, NY), 2004.

Sarah Weeks, *I'm a Pig,* Laura Geringer Books (New York, NY), 2005.

Janet Squires, *The Gingerbread Cowboy,* Laura Geringer Books (New York, NY), 2006.

Lissa Rovetch, *Frog Went a-Dancing,* Kindermusik International (Greensboro, NC), 2006.

Holly Berry creates colorful artwork to capture the story in Fran Manushkin's **How Mama Brought the Spring.** (Dutton Children's Books, 2007. Illustration copyright © 2008 by Holly Berry. Reproduced by permission.)

Fran Manushkin, *How Mama Brought the Spring,* Dutton Children's Books (New York, NY), 2008.

Sarah Weeks, *Woof: A Love Story,* HarperChildrens (New York, NY), 2008.

Sidelights

Holly Berry, an artist whose linoleum-block prints are inspired by the wilderness areas surrounding her home in rural Maine, is also an award-winning illustrator of children's books. In addition to her self-illustrated titles, *Old MacDonald Had a Farm* and *Busy Lizzie,* Berry has illustrated works for such noted authors as Eve Bunting, Sarah Weeks, and Diane Stanley.

Berry made her literary debut in 1994 with *Old Mac-Donald Had a Farm,* a retelling of the familiar children's song. In Berry's version, the farmer hauls a large chest into the barn and surprises the animals by inviting them to grab an instrument. By the story's end, a fiddle-playing cat and a banjo-strumming pig have joined the fun. Writing in *Booklist,* Ellen Mandel praised "Berry's exuberant and highly promising first book." Later that year Berry published *Busy Lizzie,* an introduction to basic anatomy for young readers. The artist's "spunky colored-pencil-and-watercolor artwork makes even" the simplest daily activities "look like lots of fun," a critic observed in a review of *Busy Lizzie* for *Publishers Weekly.*

Another illustration project from Berry, *Arctic Fives Arrive* is a counting book by Elinor Pinczes. Arriving on an ice floe in groups of five, polar bears, walrus, ermine, and other cold-weather creatures spend an evening together viewing the dazzling northern lights. Berry's "simple, clean shapes give the artwork the distinctive flavor of woodcuts," noted *Booklist* critic Stephanie Zvirin, and a *Publishers Weekly* reviewer cited Berry's "clean-edged linocuts—their icy white, blue and violet areas separated with angular black outlines" as a highlight of the work. Set in an Irish village, Berry and Bunting's *Market Day* follows young Tess and her companion, Wee Boy, as they enjoy the sights, sounds, and smells of a town's busy streets. Here the artist's use of "bright natural colors convey the gaiety of the market against a backdrop of fieldstone houses and cobbled streets," a *Publishers Weekly* contributor remarked.

Berry has collaborated with Stanley on a number of works of historical fiction. In *Roughing It on the Oregon Trail* twins Lenny and Liz travel back in time to 1843 with the help of their grandmother's magical hat and join their ancestors in crossing the Great Plains. Berry's "illustrations, though very busy and rather sweet for the subject, are pleasant and colorful," Zvirin stated. The illustrator "adheres to authentic details in her sprightly cartoon-like illustrations," according to a *Publishers Weekly* critic, the reviewer adding that Berry's "balanced mix of straightforward text and speech bubbles" accommodates Stanley's narrative.

Other illustration projects by Berry include Sabina I. Rascol's folk-tale adaptation **The Impudent Rooster.** (Illustration copyright © 2004 by Holly Berry. Reproduced by permission.)

In a follow-up, *Joining the Boston Tea Party,* Lenny, Liz, and Grandma venture back to the colonial era and participate in the revolt against British taxation. "Using a lighthearted cartoon style and an upbeat palette, Berry energizes the visual narrative with kinetic compositions and eye-catching perspectives," remarked Carey Ayres in *School Library Journal,* and a *Kirkus Reviews* contributor declared that "Berry's illustrations are wonderfully detailed, from the clothing and the cooking fire, to the busy street and harbor scenes." The time-traveling trio returns in *Thanksgiving on Plymouth Plantation,* a look at the famous three-day feast that took place in 1621. "Bustling with activity, warmed with color, and full of period details, Berry's attractive illustrations light up" Stanley's tale, Carolyn Phelan observed in *Booklist.*

In *The Bowlegged Rooster, and Other Tales That Signify,* a collection of five original short stories, author Joyce Carol Thomas uses a host of barnyard birds to present lessons about human strengths and weaknesses. According to *School Library Journal* reviewer Shelley Townsend-Hudson, Berry's "whimsical artwork makes the signifying all the more fun." In *The Impudent Rooster,* an adaptation of a Romanian folktale by Sabina I. Rascol, a brave rooster turns the tables on a greedy nobleman, helping the bird's impoverished owner in the process. "Berry's oversize, comic pencil-and-watercolor pictures accent the setting with folk motifs," noted Margaret A. Bush in a *Horn Book* review of *The Impudent Rooster,* and a contributor in *Kirkus Reviews* similarly noted that the illustrator's "richly colored Romanian folk-art designs . . . reflect the humor, magic, and power of the tale."

A joyful porker extols the virtues of wallowing in the mud and hunting truffles in *I'm a Pig,* a rhyming work by Sarah Weeks. In the words of *School Library Journal* critic Robin L. Gibson, "Berry's humorous, clever illustrations enhance the deceptively simple narrative." Janet Squires offers a Wild West version of a traditional tale in *The Gingerbread Cowboy.* Here "Berry's warm palette perfectly suits the desert scenery," remarked a contributor in *Kirkus Reviews,* and Kirsten Cutler, writing in *School Library Journal,* noted that "the colorful crowd of animals and cowboys stands out dramatically against the parched landscape."

Berry's illustrations pair up with Weeks' storytelling again to create *Woof: A Love Story.* In this tale, a dog falls in love with a cat and looks for a way to express his feelings. The dog decides that he should serenade the cat with his brass bone—a trombone. In the end, the odd pairing proves that music is a universal language. Praising the whimsical work, *Booklist* contributor Daniel Kraus concluded that "everything about Berry's wildly colored and wholly unpredictable collage work has a passionate pop-art zeal."

In 2008 Berry illustrated Fran Manushkin's story *How Mama Brought the Spring.* Young Rosy is less than enthusiastic to leave her warm bed one cold winter morning in Chicago. Her mother persuades her to come into the kitchen by telling her a story about her own childhood in Belarus, where the winters were very frigid. Then the two follow a family tradition: they make special blintzes to encourage springtime to come more quickly. Julie Cummins, writing in *Booklist,* found Manushkin's account to be "more mood piece than" actual story, but added that "the happiness that radiates from it is matched by the delightful watercolor illustrations." Judith Constantinides, writing in *School Library Journal,* also cited Berry's "busy" and "colorful" images for the book, adding that younger readers "will appreciate this winning look at a different culture." A contributor to *Kirkus Reviews* concluded of *How Mama Brought the Spring* that "Berry's illustrations provide exactly the right touch, from the blue-fringed tablecloth endpapers to the folk-like art."

Biographical and Critical Sources

PERIODICALS

Booklist, June 1, 1994, Ellen Mandel, review of *Old MacDonald Had a Farm,* p. 1828; February 15, 1996, Ilene Cooper, review of *Market Day,* p. 1016; September 15, 1996, Stephanie Zvirin, review of *Arctic Fives Arrive,* p. 249; April 1, 2000, Stephanie Zvirin, review of *Roughing It on the Oregon Trail,* p. 1479; October 1, 2000, Shelley Townsend-Hudson, review of *The Bowlegged Rooster, and Other Tales That Signify,* p. 342; September 15, 2001, Helen Rosenberg, review of *Joining the Boston Tea Party,* p. 224; February 15, 2004, Hazel Rochman, review of *The Impudent Rooster,* p. 1061; September 1, 2004, Carolyn Phelan, review of *Thanksgiving on Plymouth Plantation,* p. 137; April 15, 2006, Hazel Rochman, review of *The Gingerbread Cowboy,* p. 50; January 1, 2008, Julie Cummins, review of *How Mama Brought the Spring,* p. 94; October 1, 2009, Daniel Kraus, review of *Woof: A Love Story,* p. 52.

Horn Book, November-December, 2001, Roger Sutton, review of *Joining the Boston Tea Party,* p.769; May-June, 2004, Margaret A. Bush, review of *The Impudent Rooster,* p. 339.

Kirkus Reviews, August 1, 2001, review of *Joining the Boston Tea Party,* p. 1132; April 1, 2004, review of *The Impudent Rooster,* p. 336; August 1, 2004, review of *Thanksgiving on Plymouth Plantation,* p. 749; May 1, 2005, review of *I'm a Pig,* p. 549; July 1, 2006, review of *The Gingerbread Cowboy,* p. 682; January 1, 2008, review of *How Mama Brought the Spring;* November 1, 2009, review of *Woof.*

Publishers Weekly, October 31, 1994, review of *Busy Lizzie,* p. 60; September 18, 1995, review of *The Gift of Christmas,* p. 98; February 5, 1996, review of *Market Day,* p. 89; October 14, 1996, review of *Arctic Fives Arrive,* p. 83; May 22, 2000, review of *Roughing It on the Oregon Trail,* p. 93; April 12, 2004, review of *The Impudent Rooster,* p. 64; September 27, 2004, review of *Thanksgiving on Plymouth Plantation,* p. 59; May 30, 2005, review of *I'm a Pig,* p. 59; December 10, 2007, review of *How Mama Brought the Spring,* p. 55.

School Library Journal, June, 2000, John Sigwald, review of *Roughing It on the Oregon Trail,* p. 126; November, 2000, Steven Engelfried, review of *The Bowlegged Rooster, and Other Tales That Signify,* p. 135; August, 2001, Carey Ayres, review of *Joining the Boston Tea Party,* p. 162; April, 2004, Janet M. Bair, review of *The Impudent Rooster,* p. 142; September, 2004, Julie Roach, review of *Thanksgiving on Plymouth Plantation,* p. 181; May, 2005, Robin L. Gibson, review of *I'm a Pig,* p. 103; August, 2006, Kirsten Cutler, review of *The Gingerbread Cowboy,* p. 112; January 1, 2008, Judith Constantinides, review of *How Mama Brought the Spring,* p. 92.

ONLINE

Children's Literature, http://www.childrenslit.com/ (May 22, 2009), Sylvia Firth, "Grandma Beatrice Brings Spring to Minsk."

Holly Berry Home Page, http://www.hollyberrydesign.com (November 15, 2009).*

BLACK, Holly 1971-
(Holly Riggenbach)

Personal

Born November 10, 1971, in NJ; daughter of Donald (an insurance agent) and Judy (a painter and dollmaker) Riggenbach; married Theodor Black (a painter), 1999. *Education:* Attended Temple University, 1990-92; College of New Jersey, B.A., 1995; graduate study at Rutgers University, 2001-03. *Hobbies and other interests:* Reading, fairy tales, urban fantasy, gothic decorating, collecting ball-jointed dolls (dollfies), reading teen/young-adult fiction.

Addresses

Home—Amherst, MA. *Agent*—c/o The Gotham Group, Inc., 8721 Sunset Blvd., No. 205, W. Hollywood, CA 90069. *E-mail*—holly@theblackarts.com.

Career

Writer. Worked as a production editor on medical journals and for *d8* (magazine), New York, NY.

Awards, Honors

Mythopoeic Fantasy Award finalist, Popular Paperbacks for Young Adults selection, America Library Association (ALA), Best Books for Young Adults selection, ALA, and Books for the Teen Age selection, New York Public Library, all for *Tithe;* International Reading Association/Children's Book Council Children's Choice selection, for *The Field Guide;* Quick Picks for Reluctant Readers selection, ALA, Best Books for Young Adults selection, ALA, Books for the Teen Age selection, New York Public Library, and Andre Norton Award, Science Fiction and Fantasy Writers of America, 2006, all for *Valiant.*

Writings

Tithe: A Modern Faerie Tale, Simon & Schuster (New York, NY), 2002.
Valiant: A Modern Tale of Faerie, Simon & Schuster (New York, NY), 2005.
Ironside: A Modern Faerie's Tale, Simon & Schuster (New York, NY), 2007.
(Editor with Cecil Castellucci) *Geektastic: Stories from the Nerd Herd,* Little, Brown (New York, NY), 2009.

Contributor to anthologies, including *The Faery Reel,* edited by Ellen Datlow and Terri Windling, Penguin (New York, NY), 2004; *21 Proms,* edited by David Levithan and Daniel Ehrenhaft, Scholastic (New York, NY), 2007; and *Magic in the Mirrorstone,* edited by Steve Berman, Wizards of the Coast (Renton, WA), 2008. Contributor of articles and poems, under name Holly Riggenbach, to *d8* magazine.

"SPIDERWICK CHRONICLES" SERIES

The Field Guide, illustrated by Tony DiTerlizzi, Simon & Schuster Books for Young Readers (New York, NY), 2003.
The Seeing Stone, illustrated by Tony DiTerlizzi, Simon & Schuster Books for Young Readers (New York, NY), 2003.
Lucinda's Secret, illustrated by Tony DiTerlizzi, Simon & Schuster Books for Young Readers (New York, NY), 2003.
The Ironwood Tree, illustrated by Tony DiTerlizzi, Simon & Schuster Books for Young Readers (New York, NY), 2004.
The Wrath of Mulgarath, illustrated by Tony DiTerlizzi, Simon & Schuster Books for Young Readers (New York, NY), 2004.
The Spiderwick Chronicles (boxed set; contains *The Field Guide, The Seeing Stone, Lucinda's Secret, The Ironwood Tree,* and *The Wrath of Mulgarath*), illustrated by Tony DiTerlizzi, Simon & Schuster Books for Young Readers (New York, NY), 2004.
Arthur Spiderwick's Field Guide to the Fantastical World around You, illustrated by Tony DiTerlizzi, Simon & Schuster Books for Young Readers (New York, NY), 2005.
Notebooks for Fantastical Observations, illustrated by Tony DiTerlizzi, Simon & Schuster Books for Young Readers (New York, NY), 2005.
Care and Feeding of Sprites, illustrated by Tony DiTerlizzi, Simon & Schuster Books for Young Readers (New York, NY), 2006.

"BEYOND THE SPIDERWICK CHRONICLES" SERIES

The Nixie's Song, illustrated by Tony DiTerlizzi, Simon & Schuster Books for Young Readers (New York, NY), 2007.
A Giant Problem, illustrated by Tony DiTerlizzi, Simon & Schuster Books for Young Readers (New York, NY), 2008.
The Wyrm King, illustrated by Tony DiTerlizzi, Simon & Schuster Books for Young Readers (New York, NY), 2009.

"GOOD NEIGHBORS" SERIES

Kin, illustrated by Ted Naifeh, Graphix (New York, NY), 2009.

Adaptations

The "Spiderwick Chronicles" series was adapted for film as *The Spiderwick Chronicles,* Paramount Pictures, 2008. The original screenplay was also adapted for novelizations. Some of Black's titles have been adapted as audiobooks.

Sidelights

Fantasy writer Holly Black is the author of the bestselling "Spiderwick Chronicles" novel series, about three youngsters who discover a magical world of faerie-folk, including goblins, boggarts, and sprites. Black has also written a number of titles for older readers, including *Tithe: A Modern Faerie Tale,* and has coedited the humorous anthology *Geektastic: Stories from the Nerd Herd.* "I think that I have an interest in faeries because more than any other supernatural creature, they seem to have escaped the confines of morality," Black stated on her home page. "They embody contradiction; their very nature is conflicted." She added, "Faerie ballads are terrifying."

Black recalled on her home page that she developed an early interest in the supernatural. Her mother, a painter and dollmaker, read her books about ghosts and faeries, which led Black and her sister to concoct their own witches' brews while they cared for their pet rats. Black was interested in Dungeons and Dragons role-playing as an adolescent, as well as listening to punk rock, reading, and writing poetry. She attended college in Philadelphia, where she married Theodor Black, a painter. They later moved to New Jersey, where she worked for the gaming magazine *d8.* During this time, she met illustrator Tony DiTerlizzi, who provides the artwork for her "Spiderwick Chronicles" series for young adults.

The protagonist in Black's first novel, *Tithe,* is sixteen-year-old Kaye Fierch, a high-school dropout who spends much of her time shoplifting and caring for her mother, a rock star wannabe who performs in third-rate clubs. When her mother's boyfriend becomes violent, Kaye and her mother retreat to Kaye's grandmother's house on the Jersey shore, where Kaye reunites with childhood friend Janet and Janet's gay brother, Corny.

After an encounter in an abandoned building with Janet's boyfriend, Kaye stumbles upon Roiben at the forest's edge, rescuing this beautiful, wounded knight with silver hair. Always seen as a bit different by the other girls, Kaye soon comes to understand why faeries have been a part of her life since childhood. In fact, she is a changeling pixie, and her childhood faerie playmates return and entreat her to pretend she is human, so that they can use her as an offering to release them from the power of the dark Unseelie queen. Complicating matters, however, is Kaye's attraction to Roiben, a member of the dark faeries and part of the Unseelie world Kaye's otherworldly friends wish to be free of.

Reviewing *Tithe* for *School Library Journal,* Beth Wright felt that "the greatest strength of the story lies in the settings, particularly the descriptions of the debased Unseelie Court." Writing in *Booklist,* Gillian Engberg called the book "dark, edgy [and] . . . compulsively readable." *Locus* reviewer Carolyn Cushman described *Tithe* as "an unusually powerful YA contemporary fantasy," while a *Kirkus Reviews* contributor called it a "stunning debut. . . . A labyrinthine plot with Goth sensibility makes this a luscious treat for fans of urban fantasy and romantic horror."

Cover of Geektastic, *an anthology coedited by Holly Black and Cecil Castellucci and featuring artwory by Eboy.* (Little, Brown, 2009. Reproduced by permission.)

Black returns to her faerie world in *Valiant: A Modern Tale of Faerie,* "a story weaving adolescent subculture, the dark side of the city, and those glimpses of the shadow side that most of us miss," observed *Kliatt* reviewer Michele Winship. The novel concerns seventeen-year-old Valerie Russell, who runs away to New York City after finding her boyfriend in the arms of her mother. Valerie falls in with a group of teenagers that inhabits the tunnels of the subway system, a place where the faerie world and reality coexist. She also finds herself bound to Ravus, a troll who may be involved in a plot to kill faeries. In *Valiant* "Black puts enough twists and turns into [her plot] to keep even a jaded reader from figuring out where it's going next," noted *Magazine of Fantasy and Science Fiction* reviewer Charles de Lint. "And the freshness of her work lies more in the harsh realities that fill the lives of her characters."

Discussing her inspiration for *Valiant,* Black told an interviewer on Simon & Schuster Web site, "In my life, I've had several friends and acquaintances who have, at one point or another, lived on the street. I've found the experience of homelessness to be either romanticized or demonized in much fantasy fiction. I wanted to write something that was more true to my own experiences. I attempted to portray the range of circumstances that might bring a person to live on the street—other than abuse at home—and write about some of the people I've known."

In *Ironside: A Modern Faerie's Tale,* a sequel to *Tithe,* warring factions led by Roiben, Kaye's boyfriend, and Silarial threaten both the ethereal realm of the faeries as well as New York City, known as "Ironside" to the faeries. The author "has a vigorous writing style, great dialogue, and a cast of genuinely likable characters that you can't abandon once you've started reading a book of hers," de Lint stated. According to Eva Mitnick, reviewing the work in *School Library Journal, Ironside* "will appeal to readers who like their magic served with a layer of urban grit."

Black's "Spiderwick Chronicles" series begins with *The Field Guide* and *The Seeing Stone.* In the first title, readers follow the adventures of Grace siblings Mallory, Jared, and Simon as they move with their mother to the eerie, ramshackle Victorian house owned by their great-aunt Lucinda. After hearing strange noises in the walls, Jared begins to poke around the house, eventually finding *Arthur Spiderwick's Field Guide to the Fantastical World around You,* a guide for navigating the sometimes dangerous fairy world. The second volume in the series, *The Seeing Stone,* finds Simon kidnapped and Mallory and Jared compelled to rescue their brother.

Calling the initial volume "snappy," a *Publishers Weekly* critic found *The Field Guide* to be "an inviting package," containing "appealing characters" and "well-measured suspense." Though considering the characters a bit weakly drawn in *The Field Guide* and *The Seeing Stone, School Library Journal* critic Beth L. Meister concluded that "the fast, movie-like pace will grab young readers."

In *Time* magazine Heather Won Tesoriero predicted that the "Spiderwick Chronicles" series, with its "dusty Olde Worlde charm," might attract readers too young for J.K. Rowling's "Harry Potter" books or Lemony Snicket's "A Series of Unfortunate Events" adventures. *New York Times Book Review* contributor Scott Veale offered praise for the series, citing Black's narrative as well as DiTerlizzi's artwork. "With their evocative gothic-style pencil drawings and color illustrations, rhyming riddles, supernatural lore and well-drawn characters," Veale wrote, "these books read like old-fashioned ripping yarns."

The third title in the "Spiderwick Chronicles," *Lucinda's Secret,* follows the children as they discover an old map leading them to a secret forest, despite an ominous warning from their great-aunt Lucinda. DiTerlizzi's "black-and-white Arthur Rackhamesque illustrations add a satisfyingly eerie note to this mock-gothic tale," observed *School Library Journal* contributor Elaine E. Knight of the novel. Black continues the story of the

Grace children in *The Ironwood Tree,* Here, after Mallory disappears, Jared and Simon learn that she has been taken by evil dwarves who want to construct a world made of metal and install their sister as its ruler. In the opinion of de Lint, "Black does her usual first-rate job of keeping things moving at a good pace, leavening the proceedings with equal parts whimsy and darkness."

The series continues in *The Wrath of Mulgarath,* as Mallory, Jared, and Simon must save their mother from the clutches of an evil goblin king named Mulgarath. Readers "looking for spirited YA adventure that moves along at a happy clip and plays with all the fairy elements brought up in the previous books" will be satisfied, de Lint stated. Asked to describe the success of the "Spiderwick Chronicles" series, Black noted in an interview on the Simon & Schuster Web site that "Jared, Simon, and Mallory are just regular kids in a magical world—their only powers are cleverness, compassion, and bravery. I think that kids respond to the idea of there being magic in their own backyards. I think we all like to believe that the world around us is a fantastical place, even if the magic is hidden from us most of the time."

Black and DiTerlizzi have also produced a number of companion volumes to the "Spiderwick Chronicles" books, including *Arthur Spiderwick's Field Guide to the Fantastical World around You.* The work, purported to be a reproduction of the guide discovered by the Grace children, contains descriptions and drawings of household brownies, fire salamanders, and griffins, among other creatures. "Fantasy readers will love immersing themselves in the lore of the hidden," noted Walter Minkel in *School Library Journal.* Black launched a spin-off series, "Beyond the Spiderwick Chronicles," with the publication of *The Nixie's Song.* In the story, three children help a water nixie find her missing sisters and battle a terrifying dirt giant. According to *Booklist* critic Suzanne Harold, the new work contains "the same sly humor and old-fashioned design that marked the original series." Black's Florida-based "Beyond the Spiderwick Chronicles" series continues with *A Giant Problem,* and concludes with the *The Wyrm King.*

Working with illustrator Ted Naifeh, Black initiated a new series, "The Good Neighbors," with the graphic novel *Kin.* Speaking on the Scholastic Web site, Black expounded on some of the reasons she turned to the graphic novel format: "I've always loved comics and in college I actually hung around with a bunch of comic artists. I was still trying to learn how to create a coherent plot, so although I tried to write some comic pages back then, they were very bad. Then, when I started writing novels, I felt like I'd headed off in another direction." However, after coming up with the basic idea for "The Good Neighbors," it was suggested to her that the tale might do well an extended comic or a graphic novel. As she further remarked on the Scholastic Web site: "It was a challenge to try and write for a different medium, but it was a good challenge. I think it really let me stretch and was also a lot of fun."

Kin introduces Rue Silver, a sixteen year old who begins seeing strange things around her sleepy town, including people with the wings and faces of animals. When her mother disappears, Rue's world is sundered, and now her visions take on a surreal tinge. She fears she is going insane. Then when her professor father is arrested for allegedly killing one of his students, Rue finds herself in serious trouble. Her father is also the prime suspect in her mother's disappearance, but now Rue learns the truth about her background: her mother was actually of faerie blood. This explains Rue's visions and her newfound abilities, such as becoming invisible or conversing with ivy plants. All of this is related to Rue by her grandfather, Aubrey, also of the faerie realm. When Rue finds herself torn between her human life and life in the faerie realm, she also turns investigator to find her missing mother and prove her father innocent of murder.

Kliatt reviewer George Galuschak had praise for *Kin*, noting that "Rue is a likable protagonist, a strong yet vulnerable woman who is in the process of self-discovery." *School Library Journal* contributor Lisa Goldstein was also impressed with the graphic novel, remarking that it would appeal to "fans of intelligent, otherworldly stories." Similarly, a *Kirkus Reviews* contributor predicted that, "with a healthy smattering of angst, romance and faerie lore, fans of the genre should enjoy this volume." *Horn Book* reviewer Deirdre F. Baker also had a high assessment of *Kin,* commenting that "Black demonstrates yet again that fairy-tale imagery can be a potent metaphor for the struggles of the adolescent psyche," while *Booklist* contributor Tina Coleman commended the author for doing "a wonderful job of weaving an alien faerie world through Rue's urban landscape." *ComicMix.com* contributor Andrew Wheeler called Black "a major writer for young people," and went on to note that *Kin* is "similar in plot and setting to Black's teen novels, but. . .less dark-themed and dangerous." Wheeler went on to conclude that the "Good Neighbors" books will be enjoyed by "the hordes of young readers who love stories of dangerous, seductive figures sneaking into lives very much like their own."

In an interview on the *Seven Impossible Things before Breakfast* Web site, Black noted: "I have loved faerie folklore since I was a kid and my mom brought home Brian Froud and Alan Lee's *Faeries.* That was the book that made me realize that faeries were dangerous." She added that her work has also been influenced by folklorists Dermot MacManus, Katharine Brigg, and Robert Kirk, as well as by contemporary urban fantasy authors such as de Lint, Terri Windling, and Ellen Kushner. "What I want most of all, in my own writing," Black stated, "is to evoke the sense of the numinous that both their writing and the folklore inspire."

Biographical and Critical Sources

PERIODICALS

Booklist, February 15, 2003, Gillian Engberg, review of *Tithe: A Modern Faerie Tale,* p. 1064; July, 2005, Jennifer Mattson, review of *Valiant: A Modern Tale of Faerie,* p. 1915; February 1, 2006, Carolyn Phelan, review of *Arthur Spiderwick's Field Guide to the Fantastical World around You,* p. 47; October 15, 2007, Suzanne Harold, review of *The Nixie's Song,* p. 49; September 15, 2008, Tina Coleman, review of *Kin,* p. 47.

Children's Bookwatch, December, 2008, review of *Kin.*

Horn Book, January-February, 2009, Deirdre F. Baker, review of *Kin.*

Kirkus Reviews, September 1, 2002, review of *Tithe,* p. 1303; June 1, 2005, review of *Valiant,* p. 633; November 15, 2006, review of *Care and Feeding of Sprites,* p. 1171; September 1, 2008, review of *Kin.*

Kliatt, July, 2004, Annette Wells, review of *Tithe,* p. 26; July, 2005, Michele Winship, review of *Valiant,* p. 7; November, 2008, George Galuschak, review of *Kin,* p. 32.

Locus, September, 2002, Carolyn Cushman, review of *Tithe,* p. 35.

Magazine of Fantasy and Science Fiction, March, 2004, Charles de Lint, review of *Lucinda's Secret,* p. 33; August, 2004, Charles de Lint, review of *The Ironwood Tree,* p. 32; March, 2005, Charles de Lint, review of *The Wrath of Mulgarath,* p. 27; January, 2006, Charles de Lint, review of *Valiant,* p. 35; October-November, 2007, Charles de Lint, review of *Ironside: A Modern Faerie's Tale,* p. 30.

New York Times Book Review, June 22, 2003, Scott Veale, review of *The Field Guide,* p. 23.

Publishers Weekly, October 28, 2002, review of *Tithe,* p. 74; April 14, 2003, review of *The Field Guide,* p. 70; July 16, 2007, review of *The Nixie's Song,* p. 165.

School Library Journal, October, 2002, Beth Wright, review of *Tithe,* p. 158; July, 2003, Beth L. Meister, reviews of *The Field Guide* and *The Seeing Stone,* p. 95; November, 2003, Elaine E. Knight, review of *Lucinda's Secret,* p. 88; June, 2004, Krista Tokarz, review of *The Ironwood Tree,* p. 96; June, 2005, Tasha Saecker, review of *Valiant,* p. 148; March, 2006, Walter Minkel, review of *Arthur Spiderwick's Field Guide to the Fantastical World around You,* p. 186; July, 2007, Eva Mitnick, review of *Ironside,* p. 96; November, 2008, Lisa Goldstein, review of *Kin,* p. 150.

Time, June 9, 2003, Heather Won Tesoriero, "Horror, in Pint Sizes: The 'Spiderwick Chronicles' May Have Just Enough Spookiness to Catch on with the Pre-Harry P. Set," p. 78.

USA Today, November 9, 2004, Jacqueline Blais, "'Spiderwick' Wraps the Scary in a 'Cozy' Package," p. D8.

ONLINE

ComicMix.com, http://www.comicmix.com/ (June 19, 2009), Andrew Wheeler, review of *Kin.*

Cynsations Web site, http://cynthialeitichsmith.blogspot. com/ (June 19, 2009), Cynthia Leitich Smith, interview with Black.

Holly Black Home Page, http://www.blackholly.com (June 19, 2009).

Scholastic Web site, http://www2.scholastic.com/ (June 19, 2009), "Holly Black."

Seven Impossible Things before Breakfast Web site, http:// blaine.org/ (June 19, 2009), "Holly Black: Faeries, Proms, and D&D."

Simon & Schuster Web site, http://www.simonsays.com/ (June 19, 2009), "A Conversation with Holly Black and Tony DeTerlizzi, Creators of *The Spiderwick Chronicles.*"

Spiderwick Chronicles Web site, http://www.spiderwick. com/ (June 19, 2009).

Teenreads.com, http://www.teenreads.com/ (June 19, 2009), John Hogan, review of *Kin.**

* * *

BUCKINGHAM, Royce 1966-
(Royce Scott Buckingham)

Personal

Born 1966, in Richland, WA; married; children: two sons. *Education:* Whitman College, B.A., 1989; University of Oregon, J.D., 1992.

Addresses

Home—Bellingham, WA. *Agent*—Ken Atchity, Atchity Entertainment International; kja@aeionline.com. *E-mail*—royce@demonkeeper.com; roycencara@aol. com.

Career

Writer. Whatcom County Prosecutor's Office, Bellingham, WA, attorney, 1993-2006; writer, 1993—.

Awards, Honors

QFC Video Commercial Contest winner, 1998, for *They're Worth It!;* short feature winner, Washington State Film Office Screenplay Competition, 2000, for *Milk;* feature-length winner, Pacific Northwest Writers Association Screenplay Competition, 2001, for *Oldfinger;* feature-length winner, Washington State Film Office Screenplay Competition, 2001, for *Demonkeeper* (screenplay); Seattle International Film Festival Pitchfest winner, 2003, for *Fish Tale;* Nicholl fellowship semifinalist, 2003 and 2004, for *Demonkeeper* (novel).

Writings

Demonkeeper (novel), Putnam (New York, NY), 2007.

Royce Buckingham (Photograph by Jeanne McGee. Reproduced by permission.)

Goblins! An UnderEarth Adventure (novel), Putnam (New York, NY), 2008.

Also author of screenplays, including *Demonkeeper, Goblins,* and *Oldfinger.* Author of short films, including *They're Worth It!,* produced by Buckingham and David Bialik, 1998; *Milk,* produced by See-Through Films, 2000; *Black Noise,* produced by Black Noise Productions, 2000, and *Classified,* produced by Bluescooter Productions, 2005. Contributor of stories to periodicals, including *Reed Magazine, Starblade,* and *Moonletters.* Has published articles and short stories under name Royce Scott Buckingham.

Adaptations

The *Demonkeeper* screenplay and novel were optioned for film by Fox 2000; an untitled fantasy story was adapted as a videogame storyline for Microsoft's Xbox division.

Sidelights

Attorney-turned-screenwriter and novelist Royce Buckingham is the author of *Demonkeeper,* "an enjoyable novel that is both scary and laugh-out-loud funny," according to Sharon Senser McKellar in *School Library Journal.* Buckingham was born in 1966 in Richland,

Washington, a town along the Columbia River. As a child, Buckingham loved both sports and literature, and he was especially fond of books that incorporated elements of fantasy, including Jules Verne's *20,000 Leagues under the Sea,* Norton Juster's *The Phantom Tollbooth,* and Beverly Cleary's *The Mouse and the Motorcycle.* He later gravitated to the works of J.R.R. Tolkien, Stephen King, and Robert E. Howard. "Around twelve, I discovered the fantasy role-playing game *Dungeons & Dragons* and began to create my own fantasy worlds," Buckingham stated on his home page. "I was a Little League baseball player filled with wonder and dreams and a fascination for stories."

After graduating from high school, Buckingham attended Whitman College, a small liberal arts school in Walla Walla, Washington, and majored in English literature. He later decided to pursue a career in criminal law and studied at the University of Oregon. During this time he also tried his hand at creative writing, and he published a short horror tale in *Reed* magazine. Buckingham landed a job in the Whatcom County prosecutor's office in Bellingham, Washington. He also completed a number of fantasy, science-fiction, and horror stories. "In 1993, I collected over one hundred rejection letters," Buckingham recalled. "One especially mean-spirited letter said, 'Your story is moronic, don't you have anything better to do with your time?' It was discouraging, but I made up a file titled 'Reasons to Keep Writing,' and kept all of those letters as motivation."

While still working as a prosecutor, Buckingham turned to writing novels and screenplays in addition to his short fiction. He earned several honors for his short and feature-length films, he wrote on his home page, including the "quadruple-crown" of Northwest screenwriting competitions: "the Washington State short script competition, the Pacific Northwest Writers Association feature length script competition, the Washington State feature length competition . . ., and the Seattle International Film Festival's Pitch Competition." One work in particular, however—a short story that would become *Demonkeeper*—became the author's pet project. The work was inspired by a homeless youth whom Buckingham had prosecuted in juvenile court. "He was thirteen, had a green Mohawk, and I'd see him downtown begging change," Buckingham recalled on his home page. "One day he disappeared, and nobody seemed to notice. Even his parents didn't know where he'd gone, or care. I imagined the chaos of street life as a monster that rose and ate him up while people weren't paying attention, as it does with so many lost children." Buckingham developed his tale into a screenplay and then translated it into a novel. "The script evolved into a much more lighthearted and fun tale than that short tale I wrote years earlier, but the message remained—kids need stability, family and a home."

Published in 2007, *Demonkeeper* centers on Nat, a lonely teenage orphan whose job is to manage the demonic creatures that live with him in a rambling estate filled with animate objects. When the Beast, the vilest creature in captivity, escapes from the basement and begins wreaking havoc on the streets of Seattle, Nat joins forces with Sandy Nertz, an assistant librarian, and Richie, a tough skateboarder, to recapture the monster before a rival demonkeeper can gain control of it. "*Demonkeeper* is a page turner, deftly combining humor and suspense with just a taste of horror," noted Howard Shirley in *Bookpage.com,* and a *Kirkus Reviews* contributor deemed the work "an engaging debut with some intriguing ideas and twists." Janice Corker, writing online for the *ipulp Fiction Library,* noted that Buckingham's background as a juvenile prosecutor "lends a poignant aspect to a tale that writhes with violence and gore. But not too much violence and gore—Buckingham leaves the grisliest details" to the reader's imagination. Shirley offered special praise for the novel's conclusion, calling it "a delightfully clever bit of logic that readers won't see coming but won't feel cheated by either."

In Buckingham's novel *Goblins! An UnderEarth Adventure* twelve-year-old Sam lives in the border town of Sumas, Washington, where he often gets into trouble

Cover of Buckingham's novel **Demon Keeper** *which finds a teen trying to keep a house full of demons at bay.* (Puffin, 2007. Reproduced by permission.)

while looking for ways to entertain himself. When Sam meets PJ, the town police officer's seventeen-year-old son, the pair takes the police cruiser to the border where they find goblins. Sam is captured by the goblin general, and PJ, with the help of some guardians, must rescue him.

Ginny Collier, reviewing *Goblins!* in *School Library Journal,* said that the novel would be appropriate "for those who want lots of action with some mild gross-out scenes." A contributor writing in *Kirkus Reviews* warned that "mild rough language makes an occasional appearance throughout this sometimes violent and often slimy tale," but nevertheless concluded that the adventure is "riotously good." While voicing concern over Buckingham's inclusion of "age-appropriate words," an online contributor remarked in *Kidliterate* that "there's a lot of humor in this book and PJ and Sam are both likable characters. A lot of the Goblin stuff is hilarious. . . . and the end, while drawing to a satisfying conclusion, clearly paves the path for a sequel."

Biographical and Critical Sources

PERIODICALS

Kirkus Reviews, April 1, 2007, review of *Demonkeeper;* August 1, 2008, review of *Goblins! An UnderEarth Adventure.*

News Tribune (Tacoma, WA), October 23, 2007, Rebecca Young, review of *Demonkeeper.*

School Library Journal, September, 2007, Sharon Senser McKellar, review of *Demonkeeper,* p. 192; November 1, 2008, Ginny Collier, review of *Goblins!,* p. 116.

Skagit Valley Herald (Mount Vernon, WA), October 31, 2007, Stephanie Kosonen, "Buckingham Shares the Joys and Pains of Being a Writer with B-E Students."

Tampa Tribune, July 8, 2007, Wendy Withers, "Demon Story Will Keep Readers Turning Pages," p. 6.

ONLINE

BookPage.com, http://www.bookpage.com/ (May, 2007), Howard Shirley, "Putting a Very Strange House in Order," review of *Demonkeeper.*

ipulp Fiction Library, http://www.incwell.com/ (March 1, 2008), Janice Corker, review of *Demonkeeper.*

Kidliterate Web site, http://www.kidliterate.com/ (October 13, 2008), review of *Goblins!*

Royce Buckingham Home Page, http://www.demonkeeper. com (May 25, 2009).*

* * *

BUCKINGHAM, Royce Scott
See BUCKINGHAM, Royce

BURNETT, Lindy

Personal

Daughter of an army chaplain; married (divorced); children: two. *Education:* Wesleyan College, B.F.A., 1976; further study at Portfolio Center.

Addresses

Home—Madison, GA. *Agent*—Kiki Pollard, contact@ alexanderpollard.com.

Career

Artist and children's book illustrator. Portfolio Center, Atlanta, GA, illustration instructor; Steffen Thomas Museum, Buckhead, GA, lead artist.

Illustrator

Laurel Lee, *My Jesus Pocketbook of God's Greatest Day,* Stirrup Associates (Decatur, GA), 1985.

Kana Kiley, *The Tongue Twister Prize,* Sadlier-Oxford (New York, NY), 1997.

Cindy Chang, compiler, *Thank You,* Andrews McMeel (Kansas City, MO), 1997.

Kirsten Hall, *Going Batty,* Scholastic, Inc. (New York, NY), 2001.

Janice Eaton Kilby, Deborah Morgenthal, and Terry Taylor, *The Book of Wizard Craft: In Which the Apprentice Finds Spells, Potions, Fantastic Tales, and Fifty Enchanting Things to Make,* Lark Books (New York, NY), 2001.

Kirsten Hall, *Green Thumbs,* Scholastic, Inc. (New York, NY), 2002.

Kirsten Hall, *The Big Sled Race,* Scholastic, Inc. (New York, NY), 2002.

Kirsten Hall, *Mystery at the Museum,* Scholastic, Inc. (New York, NY), 2003.

Janice Eaton Kilby, Deborah Morgenthal, and Terry Taylor, *The Book of Wizard Magic: In Which the Apprentice Finds Marvelous Magic Tricks, Mystifying Illusions, and Astonishing Tales,* Lark Books (New York, NY), 2003.

Kathleen V. Kudlinski, *The Sunset Switch,* NorthWord Press (Minnetonka, MN), 2005.

Kathleen V. Kudlinski, *The Seaside Switch,* NorthWord Press (Minnetonka, MN), 2007.

Sidelights

Lindy Burnett is an accomplished artist and commercial illustrator who has also provided the artwork for a number of children's books, including the anthology *The Book of Wizard Craft: In Which the Apprentice Finds Spells, Potions, Fantastic Tales, and Fifty Enchanting Things to Make* and Kathleen V. Kudlinski's *The Sunset Switch.* Burnett works primarily in watercolor, gouache, and colored pencil and her clients have included Quaker Oats, McDonald's, Hardee's, Coca-Cola, and Nestles. Asked what she enjoys most about her career, Burnett told *School Arts* interviewer Ande Cook: "Freedom.

Freedom to choose my jobs, to schedule my day, in how problems will be solved, and, of course, it's great to make art for a living."

In *The Book of Wizard Craft,* a work by Janice Eaton Kilby, Deborah Morgenthal, and Terry Taylor, young readers learn how to create their own secret potions, cobwebs, and magic wands. "Burnett does a fantastic job of bringing these projects to life with colorful illustrations," observed Elaine Baran Black in *School Library Journal.* A follow-up work, *The Book of Wizard Magic: In Which the Apprentice Finds Marvelous Magic Tricks, Mystifying Illusions, and Astonishing Tales,* contains instructions for dozens of fantastic deceptions. According to Cynde Suite, writing in *School Library Journal,* "Burnett's fanciful animals" and "concise diagrams against pastel backgrounds have an air of magic about them."

Burnett has teamed with Kudlinski to create *The Sunset Switch,* a "murmurous essay in natural history," as a critic in *Kirkus Reviews* noted. As night falls, diurnal animals like the swallow return to their homes at the same time as nocturnal creatures, including bats and screech owls, begin searching for food. Kathy Piehl, reviewing the work in *School Library Journal,* remarked that Burnett's "attention to detail rewards repeated viewing" and her "gouache illustrations provide plenty of visual appeal." In a companion volume, *The Seaside Switch,* Kudlinski shows how the cycle of the tides affects the life of seashore plants and animals. "Burnett's double-page fluid, gouache paintings provide the perfect setting for Kudlinski's rhythmic text," Patricia Manning remarked in *School Library Journal,* and *Booklist* contributor Gillian Engberg stated that the "the atmospheric details in the handsome paintings . . . will, like the words, spark curiosity."

Biographical and Critical Sources

PERIODICALS

Booklist, March 15, 2007, Gillian Enberg, review of *The Seaside Switch,* p. 50.

Cover of Kathleen V. Kudlinski's **The Sunset Switch,** *featuring artwork by Lindy Burnett.* (NorthWord Press, 2005. Illustration © 2005 by Lindy Burnett. Reproduced by permission.)

Kirkus Reviews, May 1, 2005, review of *The Sunset Switch,* p. 541.

Morgan County Citizen (Madison, GA), November 14, 2003, "The Artistic World of Burnett."

Publishers Weekly, April 16, 2001, "While Away the Hours," review of *The Book of Wizard Craft: In Which the Apprentice Finds Spells, Potions, Fantastic Tales, and Fifty Enchanting Things to Make,* p. 67.

School Arts, December 1, 1996, Ande Cook, interview with Burnett.

School Library Journal, June, 2001, Elaine Baran Black, June, 2001, review of *The Book of Wizard Craft,* p. 175; November, 2003, Cynde Suite, review of *The Book of Wizard Magic: In Which the Apprentice Finds Marvelous Magic Tricks, Mystifying Illusions, and Astonishing Tales,* p. 161; July, 2005, Kathy Piehl, review of *The Sunset Switch,* p. 76; May, 2007, Patricia Manning, review of *The Seaside Switch,* p. 120.

ONLINE

Portfolio Center Web site, http://www.portfoliocenter.com/ (March 1, 2008), "Illustrator Lindy Burnett."*

C

CHARLIP, Rémy 1929-

Personal
Surname is pronounced "Shar-lip"; born January 10, 1929, in Brooklyn, NY; son of Max (a house painter) and Sarah (a poet) Charlip. *Education:* Cooper Union, B.F.A., 1949; further study at Black Mountain College, Reed College, Juilliard School of Music, Merce Cunningham Studio, Connecticut College, and Art Students' League of New York.

Addresses
Home—San Francisco, CA. *E-mail*—remy@remycharlip.com.

Career
Actor, dancer, choreographer, producer, stage director and designer, and filmmaker; author and illustrator of children's books; songwriter, conductor of drama workshops. Choreographer and actor with original Living Theatre Company; choreographer with London Contemporary Dance Theatre, 1972—, Scottish Theatre Ballet, 1973, Welsh Dance Theatre, 1974, and Rémy Charlip Dance Company; costume designer and member of Merce Cunningham Dance Company for eleven years. Director, designer, actor, and dancer at Joyce Theater, Theatre Artand, Café La Mama, and Brooklyn Academy of Music Opera House; founding member of The Paper Bag Players (children's theatre group); toured with International All-Star Dance Company; director of opening piece presented by National Theatre of the Deaf on tour, 1971-72. Director, with Shirley Kaplan, of children's theatre at Sarah Lawrence College, 1967-71, and co-conductor of classes; lecturer, workshop director, or consultant at Harvard Summer School, Radcliffe College, University of California Santa Barbara, 1989, Hofstra University, 1991, and other schools. Co-designer and developer of a Black and Puerto Rican heritage museum in the Bronx, New York; artist-in-residence at Museum of Contemporary Art, Los Angeles, CA, 1988. Member of advisory panels of Connecticut Commission on the Arts, Brooklyn Children's Museum, Bay Area Dance Series, and Judson Poets' Theatre and Dance Theatre.

Awards, Honors
Ingram Merrill Award, 1961, 1963; Off-Broadway (Obie) Awards for direction, *Village Voice,* 1965, as producer and director of Paper Bag Players, and 1966, for *A Beautiful Day;* Boys' Clubs of America Gold Medal (with Burton Supree), 1967, for *Mother, Mother, I Feel Sick, Send for the Doctor, Quick, Quick, Quick;* Joseph E. Levine grant, Yale University, 1968-69; *New York Times* Best Illustrated Books citation, 1969, and first prize, Bologna Book Fair, 1971, both for *Arm in Arm;* two Gulbenkian Awards, 1972, for Scottish Theatre Ballet and London Contemporary Dance Theatre; Irma Simonton Black Award, Bank Street College of Education, 1973, for *Harlequin and the Gift of Many Colors;* Children's Science Book Award Young Honor designation, New York Academy of Sciences, 1975, for *Handtalk;* New York Times Best Illustrated Books citation, 1975, and *Boston Globe/Horn Book* Award, 1976, both for *Thirteen; New York Times* Best Illustrated Books citation, 1987, for *Handtalk Birthday;* award for professional achievement, Cooper Union School of Fine Arts, 1988; residency grant, Japan/U.S. Commission on the Arts; Guggenheim fellowship, John Simon Guggenheim Memorial Foundation, 2005. A library was named in Charlip's honor in Greenville, DE, and he was made a laureate by the San Francisco Public Library.

Writings

(With George Ancona and Mary Beth Miller) *Handtalk: An ABC of Finger Spelling and Sign Language,* photographs by Ancona, Parents' Magazine Press (New York, NY), 1974.

(With Lilian Moore) *Hooray for Me!,* illustrated by Vera B. Williams, Parents' Magazine Press (New York, NY), 1975.

What Good Luck! What Bad Luck!, Scholastic Book Services (New York, NY), 1977.

First Rémy Charlip Reader, edited by Nancy S. Smith and Lisa Nelson, Contact Editions (New York, NY), 1986.

(With Mary Beth Miller) *Handtalk Birthday: A Number and Story Book in Sign Language,* photographs by George Ancona, Four Winds Press (New York, NY), 1987.

Amaterasu (performance piece), produced in Los Angeles, CA, 1988.

Young Omelet (play), produced at Hofstra University, Hampstead, NY, 1991.

(With San Francisco Arts Education Project) *Ideas for Teaching Arts to Children,* San Francisco Arts Education Project (San Francisco, CA), 1995.

Why I Will Never Ever Ever Ever Have Enough Time to Read This Book, illustrated by Jon J. Muth, Tricycle Press (Berkeley, CA), 2000.

SELF-ILLUSTRATED

Dress Up and Let's Have a Party, W.R. Scott (New York, NY), 1956.

Where Is Everybody?, W.R. Scott (New York, NY), 1957.

(With Judith Martin) *The Tree Angel* (story and play), Knopf (New York, NY), 1961.

It Looks like Snow, W.R. Scott (New York, NY), 1962.

(With Judith Martin) *Jumping Beans,* Knopf (New York, NY), 1963.

Fortunately, Parents' Magazine Press (New York, NY), 1964.

(With Burton Supree) *Mother, Mother, I Feel Sick, Send for the Doctor, Quick, Quick, Quick,* Parents' Magazine Press (New York, NY), 1966, reprinted, Tricycle Press (Berkeley, CA), 2001.

I Love You, Scholastic, Inc. (New York, NY), 1967.

Arm in Arm, Parents' Magazine Press (New York, NY), 1969.

(With Burton Supree) *Harlequin and the Gift of Many Colors,* Parents' Magazine Press (New York, NY), 1973.

(With Jerry Joyner) *Thirteen,* Parents' Magazine Press (New York, NY), 1975.

Sleepytime Rhyme, HarperCollins (New York, NY), 1999.

Peanut Butter Party: Including the History, Uses, and Future of Peanut Butter, Tricycle Press (Berkeley, CA), 1999.

(With illustrator Tamara Rettenmund) *Little Old Big Beard and Big Young Little Beard: A Short and Tall Tale,* Winslow Press (Delray Beach, FL), 2002.

Baby Hearts and Baby Flowers, Greenwillow Books (New York, NY), 2002.

A Perfect Day, Greenwillow Books (New York, NY), 2007.

ILLUSTRATOR

Margaret Wise Brown, *David's Little Indian,* W.R. Scott (New York, NY), 1956.

Bernadine Cook, *The Curious Little Kitten,* W.R. Scott (New York, NY), 1956.

Margaret Wise Brown, *The Dead Bird,* W.R. Scott (New York, NY), 1958.

Betty Miles, *What Is the World?,* Knopf (New York, NY), 1958.

Ruth Krauss, *A Moon or a Button,* Harper (New York, NY), 1959.

Betty Miles, *A Day of Summer,* Knopf (New York, NY), 1960.

Betty Miles, *A Day of Winter,* Knopf (New York, NY), 1961.

Margaret Wise Brown, *Four Fur Feet,* W.R. Scott (New York, NY), 1961.

Sandol Stoddard Warburg, *My Very Own Special Particular Private and Personal Cat,* Houghton (Boston, MA), 1963.

Ruth Krauss, *What a Fine Day for . . .,* Parents' Magazine Press (New York, NY), 1967.

(With Demetra Maraslil) Jane Yolen, *The Seeing Stick,* Crowell (New York, NY), 1977.

Adaptations

Sidelights

Rémy Charlip is the author and illustrator of a variety of acclaimed children's books, including *Where Is Everybody?* and *A Perfect Day,* that range from simple reading exercises to elaborate word games to visually innovative narratives. Charlip's diverse artistic background has contributed to his success as a children's writer; a choreographer, dancer, and stage director, he creates books that are noted for their animated pictures as well as stories that encourage children to imagine and improvise for themselves. "He elicits humor, fun, and gaiety from readers through magnificent manipulation of [his] art," Shelly G. McNamara wrote in *Social Education.* An author who "tries to be both child and artist when he creates a story book," McNamara added, Charlip "reaches all viewers with his common life experiences."

Charlip demonstrated a talent for art from a young age; when he was in kindergarten, he filled the classroom blackboard with a brightly colored drawing of an ocean liner, complete with hundreds of portholes. When he later attended Cooper Union, a fine arts college, Charlip decided against becoming a painter, and he turned to dance to learn how to express himself more fully. He spent eleven years with the Merce Cunningham Dance Theatre and helped found a theatre company for children. Augmenting this, he also used his artistic skills to help support himself by drawing and designing for books as well as the stage. "I started as a painter, but soon began to be fascinated with art forms in which sequence, transition and continuity were possible: movies, comic strips, flip books, picture books, dances and theater pieces," Charlip told *New York Times* contributor Jennifer Dunning. "The elements common to these art forms can be interchangeable, such as how an idea or story can proceed from beginning to middle to end, close-ups or long shots, general lighting or spotlighting, and rhythm and phrasing."

Charlip began illustrating his own stories with the 1956 work *Dress Up and Let's Have a Party,* which he wrote one day while waiting for an appointment with editor May Garelick. His next book, *Where Is Everybody?,* brought him critical attention for its simple, imaginative approach to introducing reading. As a new picture is added on each page a new word appears to match the picture, and the book becomes a game of appearance and disappearance until it asks the question of the title. "Not quite like any other easy-to-read book, this one is an original invitation to learning and to look," Ellen Lewis Buell remarked in the *New York Times Book Review.* A *New York Herald Tribune* writer also praised the book, for it "will please the children, give them amusing easy-reading, and perhaps inspire them to make similar booklets for themselves."

Charlip's *Fortunately* also contains a type of game within its story. The book follows a boy on his way to a birthday party; he is rescued from one mishap after another only to meet more trouble soon after. With this story, Charlip "achieves a sense of wonder and sponta-

neity as the reader, teetering the whole time between fortunate and unfortunate adventures, is compelled to turn the pages," McNamara reported. The result is "an engagingly zany nonsense story, attractively illustrated," Zena Sutherland commented in *Bulletin of the Center for Children's Books,* and "the humor is the sort enjoyed by almost all small children."

Mother, Mother, I Feel Sick, Send for the Doctor, Quick, Quick, Quick has the same kind of contagious humor encapsulated in its catchy rhymes, and its silhouette illustrations can be the inspiration for a shadow play. In the book, a doctor cures a little boy's illness by removing first one strange object, then another, from the boy's stomach. The result is "really good slapstick," Alice Dalgliesh observed in the *Saturday Review.* Rachael R. Finne, writing in the *New York Times Book Review,* contended that the "wildly absurd plot . . . is the result of the author's appreciation of nonsense."

Charlip again indulges his sense of word play in *Arm in Arm,* which avoids telling a specific story in favor of

Rémy Charlip shares the history of a popular lunchtime treat in his self-illustrated picture book Peanut Butter Party. (Copyright © 1999, 2004 by Tricycle Press. Used by permission of Tricycle Press, an imprint of Crown Publishing Group, a division of Random House, Inc.)

Cover of Charlip's romance-themed picture book Arm in Arm. (Jacket art © 1997, 2004 by Tricycle Press. Used by permission of Tricycle Press, an imprint of Crown Publishing Group, a division of Random House, Inc.)

"creating a concentrated, imaginative awareness of language," according to Ingeborg Boudreau in the *New York Times Book Review.* The book contains illustrated puns, poems, dialogues, and riddles; the words move all over the page, and are even shaped to look like their subjects. Boudreau dubbed the book "a delight," adding that *Arm in Arm* is "one of the most kinetic picture books to appear in a long time." A *Publishers Weekly* critic likewise called *Arm in Arm* "unadulterated fun," and concluded: "Fun is *great* when it's the bright, rollicking, walking-in-space fun of Rémy Charlip." The 1969 book was brought back into print in 1997, with brightly colored pages in place of the black-and-white illustrations of the original. *Booklist* reviewer Carolyn Phelan welcomed the return of this celebration of wordplay, concluding that Charlip's "creative book will challenge and charm a new generation of children."

To research his next book, *Harlequin and the Gift of Many Colors,* Charlip and coauthor Burton Supree traveled to Bergamo, Italy, where the Commedia Dell'Arte story of the acrobat originated. According to the legend, Harlequin's bright patchwork outfit was created because he had no costume of his own for the town carnival. The book took Charlip and his partner over two years to do, for both the writing and illustrating proved more difficult than they had expected. Charlip's elaborate ef-

fort with the illustrations pays off, according to many critics. While the tale of how Harlequin's friends donate parts of their costumes to make him an outfit is appealing, "one must return to the illustrations . . . to taste the full flavor of the story," Barbara Wersba commented in the *New York Times Book Review.* "An enormous amount of thought and feeling has gone into these paintings," the critic continued, making for "a stunning book." Although *Junior Bookshelf* reviewer Marcus Crouch described the drawings as "elegant," he observed that the book seems "to turn in upon [itself] rather than to look out upon the world." But McNamara of *Social Education* found *Harlequin* a moving story; it "shows, so effectively, the importance of love, sharing, and sacrificing for another," the critic commented. In addition, Charlip's "drawings capture the authenticity of detail, yet they appear simple, direct and fanciful."

Thirteen is a more complex, unpredictable book. Created with fellow author-illustrator Jerry Joyner, the book follows thirteen separate stories on each two-page spread, sometimes with little or no text. "The unusual format will inspire all ages," Barbara Elleman commented in *Booklist,* and the book's "graphic variety allows unlimited possibilities for the simple stories to be expanded." Anita Silvey similarly wrote in *Horn Book* that "*Thirteen* is not only original in its use of imagery, but it also suggests an entirely different approach to picture books. . . . The pictures do not illustrate a story, nor are they simply drawn as works of art; the images respond to each other—not to any verbal concept." While *Thirteen* is a complex work, *New York Times Book Review* contributor Milton Glaser observed that its "absolute visual magic" is "executed with such decorative grace that it can be understood and experienced without discomfort." As a *Publishers Weekly* critic concluded, this "happy collaboration" contains "a wealth of surprises in a welcome contribution to children's books."

Charlip tapped the talents of photographer George Ancona and actress Mary Beth Miller of the National Theatre of the Deaf to explore nonverbal concepts of communication in *Handtalk: An ABC of Finger Spelling and Sign Language.* Miller and other characters act out and sign various concepts, including finger spelling of the alphabet. But *Handtalk* "is far from just another photo-illustrated handbook of finger spelling, nor is its appeal limited to those with a need to communicate with the deaf," a *Kirkus Reviews* contributor claimed. The authors' "energizing performance," the critic explained, is enough to make *Handtalk* a "mixed media hit." "Charlip has designed *Handtalk* with the same clarity, humor and refreshing good sense found in his other books," contended *New York Times Book Review* critic Cynthia Feldman. As a result, *Handtalk* "comes as close as any inanimate medium can to capturing the liveliness and sparkle of a beautiful, expressive and often humorous method of communication," a *Science Books* reviewer concluded.

Charlip rejoins collaborators Ancona and Miller for *Handtalk Birthday*. The book tells of a surprise party for Mary Beth, and "the reader-viewer is challenged to use all sorts of visual cues to read the story in clips of hands, faces, and fingers in blurred motion," a *Kirkus Reviews* critic remarked. Like the original *Handtalk*, this book "is most successful in conveying the sense of sign as a vital, expressive and often personal language." A reviewer for *Booklist* found *Handtalk Birthday* even more successful than the original: "Here the authors have presented words for all the signs; moreover, sentences are prompted by the birthday party atmosphere. . . . Mary Beth and company seem almost larger than life, and their enthusiasm is catching." "Exuberance, energy, and drama create high interest," Susan Nemeth McCarthy concluded in *School Library Journal,* and "this creative original story is an exciting way to share the joy of signing with children."

In the 1990s, several of Charlip's early books were brought back into print, their artwork often augmented by the new technologies that have revolutionized the world of children's books since Charlip began publishing in the 1950s. Among the works used to introduce a new generation of children to Charlip's brand of humor

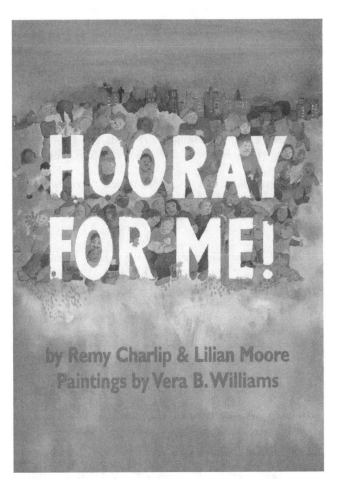

Cover of **Hooray for Me!**, *a picture book coauthored by Charlip and Lilian Moore and illustrated by Vera B. Williams.* (Illustration copyright © 1996 by Vera B. Williams. Used by permission of Tricycle Press, an imprint of the Crown Publishing Group, a division of Random House, Inc.)

are *Arm in Arm* and *Hooray for Me!* The latter title first appeared in 1975, and offers a brightly colored, self-esteem boosting narrative. The 1996 edition "gives an old favorite a new look," Carolyn Phelan remarked in *Booklist.* In a revised edition of *Mother, Mother, I Feel Sick, Send for the Doctor, Quick, Quick, Quick,* Charlip created new backgrounds for both his indoor and outdoor scenes. Charlip's "wonderfully absurd story and comical punch line" garnered praise from Phelan.

In 1999 Charlip published *Sleepytime Rhyme,* which recalls the attractive simplicity and universality of Margaret Wise Brown's best work, according to *Booklist* reviewer Marta Segal. A rhythmic text, celebrating all the parts and ways of the child the mother loves, accompanies illustrations that are "crisp, simple, and bright," Segal commented. The result is a "sweet, gentle, bedtime book," this critic concluded. A later work, *Baby Hearts and Baby Flowers,* was inspired by feedback Charlip received from children about *Sleepytime Rhyme.* A *Kirkus Reviews* critic stated that "the music of the spare verse is lulling, comforting, and full of solace and reassurance," and a contributor in *Publishers Weekly* noted that Charlip's "complex watercolor paintings reassuringly combine babies with their caregivers."

In *Peanut Butter Party: Including the History, Uses, and Future of Peanut Butter,* Charlip presents a fanciful celebration of the world's best-loved food for kids. For lovers of peanut butter, Charlip offers suggestions about making art out of it, a recipe for edible play dough, the text for a peanut butter play in which smooth and chunky face off, as well as songs, rhymes, and jokes. The book concludes with a suggestion for a solo peanut butter party that requires meditating on a jar of the stuff. "There's a touch of *A Hole Is to Dig* spontaneity here, . . . that sandwiches pleasingly with the creative approach to playing with your food," remarked Deborah Stevenson in the *Bulletin for the Center of Children's Books.* "Charlip's watercolor illustrations glorify the sticky stuff on every page," noted Lisa Gangemi Kropp in *School Library Journal,* concluding: "Like its subject, this unique book should have universal appeal."

In *Why I Will Never Ever Ever Ever Have Enough Time to Read This Book* a busy girl describes her exhausting daily schedule, which includes everything *except* having time to finish her latest literary selection. "There's more to this clever book than initially meets the eye," a *Publisher Weekly* critic remarked, and Roxanne Burg, writing in *School Library Journal,* described the work as "a light, original diversion." "This utterly charming (and more than a little surreal) picture book is winsome," concluded *Booklist* contributor GraceAnne DeCandido. In Charlip's *Little Old Big Beard and Big Young Little Beard: A Short and Tall Tale,* a work co-illustrated with Tamara Rettenmund, a pair of mismatched cowboys searches for a missing cow named Grace. "The textured watercolors feature unusual perspectives and design elements with childlike, cheery drawings of the title characters," a *Publishers Weekly* reviewer noted, and *Booklist* critic Hazel Rochman described the work as "a view of a wild West that is cozy and exciting, gentle and strong."

In 2005, Charlip suffered a debilitating stroke that affected his ability to speak and move. During his recovery, he assisted with the publication of his 2007 work, *A Perfect Day,* which he had completed before the stroke occurred. Told in verse, *A Perfect Day* depicts a father and his young son enjoying a host of comforting activities, including picnicking with friends, watching clouds, and reading a book. "Using watercolor on thick Arches paper, Charlip produces color that glistens and glows with depth," observed a critic in *Kirkus Reviews,* and a *Publishers Weekly* reviewer noted that "Charlip's festively hued art reinforces the book's upbeat tempo." Writing in *School Library Journal,* Martha Simpson described the work as "a perfect example of parent and child bonding."

As he continues to recover from his stroke, Charlip still feels the urge to create art; he evens plans to create a new dance piece. "A multitasker before that word became part of the lexicon, Charlip is an artist, choreographer, filmmaker, dancer, costume designer, poet and teacher with an impressive resume," noted Syliva Rubin in the *San Francisco Chronicle.* Whatever his activity, Charlip commented to Douglas Sadownick of the *Los Angeles Times,* the purpose is self-development: "I don't see the difference between (art) and healing. At some point, you have a dance and it has a life of its own. Or a play. Or a body. It's all the same thing. It's art. It's healing. It's education. It's therapy. The idea is to abandon the judgment of others and be more yourself."

About Charlip's books for young readers, Edith Cohen stated in the *Library of Congress Information Bulletin,* "Here is someone who transforms, embroiders and enchants ordinary experiences into magical excursions, encouraging children to imagine and improvise for themselves. His works abound in innovative narratives, wonderful word games, simple reading exercises with an appeal directly to children." In the same publication, Charlip stated, "I love sequence—how one thing follows another. That's why I love picture books. When you're reading to a child, he can't wait to get to the next page. 'Turn the page, turn the page!' That's because each new page is a door to another different world." He concluded, "It's important that we understand the way children think and feel."

Biographical and Critical Sources

BOOKS

Benbow-Pfalzgraf, Taryn, editor, *International Dictionary of Modern Dance,* St. James Press (Detroit, MI), 1998.

Children's Literature Review, Volume 8, Gale (Detroit, MI), 1985.

Shaw, John Mackay, *Childhood in Poetry,* first supplement, Gale (Detroit, MI), 1972.

Silvey, Anita, editor, *Children's Books and Their Creators,* Houghton Mifflin (Boston, MA), 1995.

Sutherland, Zena, Dianne L. Monson, and May Hill Arbuthnot, *Children and Books,* sixth edition, Scott, Foresman, 1981.

PERIODICALS

Advocate, October 12, 1999, Benoit Denizet-Lewis, "The Gay Dr. Seuss," p. 75.

Booklist, October 1, 1975, Barbara Elleman, review of *Thirteen,* p. 231; March 15, 1987, Review of *Handtalk Birthday,* p. 1125; September 1, 1997, Carolyn Phelan, review of *Arm in Arm,* p. 128; November 15, 1999, Marta Segal, review of *Sleepytime Rhyme,* p. 633; January 1, 2001, GraceAnne DeCandido, review of *Why I Will Never Ever Ever Ever Have Enough Time to Read This Book,* p. 966; March 1, 2001, Carolyn Phelan, review of *Mother, Mother, I Feel Sick, Send for the Doctor, Quick, Quick, Quick,* p. 1286; December 1, 2003, Hazel Rochman, review of *Little Old Big Beard and Big Young Little Beard: A Short and Tall Tale,* p. 683; May 1, 2007, Ilene Cooper, review of *A Perfect Day,* p. 84.

Bulletin of the Center for Children's Books, February, 1965, Zena Sutherland, review of *Fortunately,* pp. 83-84; July-August, 1999, Deborah Stevenson, review of *Peanut Butter Party: Including the History, Uses, and Future of Peanut Butter,* p. 383.

Horn Book, April, 1976, Anita Silvey, review of *Thirteen,* p. 148.

Junior Bookshelf, December, 1974, Marcus Crouch, review of *Harlequin and the Gift of Many Colors,* p. 334.

Kirkus Reviews, March 15, 1974, review of *Handtalk,* p. 304; February 15, 1987, review of *Handtalk Birthday,* pp. 306; November 15, 2001, review of *Baby Hearts and Baby Flowers,* p. 1611; April 1, 2007, review of *A Perfect Day.*

Los Angeles Times, February 18, 1988, Douglas Sadownick, "Charlip Trying to Cast Light on Sun Goddess."

New York Herald Tribune, May 12, 1957, review of *Where Is Everybody?,* p. 24.

New York Times, August 12, 1999, Jennifer Dunning, "Dancing in a New Way, from Page to Page in Children's Books."

New York Times Book Review, June 23, 1957, Ellen Lewis Buell, review of *Where Is Everybody?,* p. 22; August 21, 1966, Rachael R. Finne, review of *Mother, Mother, I Feel Sick, Send for the Doctor, Quick, Quick, Quick,* p. 20; July 20, 1969, Ingeborg Boudreau, review of *Arm in Arm,* p. 22; March 11, 1973, Barbara Wersba, "He Rose to Find His Costume Had Become the Sky," p. 8; May 5, 1974, Cynthia Feldman, "Speaking of Other Ways," p. 41; October 5, 1975, Milton Glaser, review of *Thirteen,* p. 8.

Publishers Weekly, April 14, 1969, review of *Arm in Arm,* p. 97; April 23, 1973, Paul Doebler, "Story behind the

Book: *Harlequin,*" p. 62; August 11, 1975, review of *Thirteen,* p. 117; September 11, 2000, review of *Why I Will Never Ever Ever Ever Have Enough Time to Read This Book,* p. 90; December 3, 2001, review of *Baby Hearts and Baby Flowers,* p. 58; August 11, 2003, review of *Little Old Big Beard and Big Young Little Beard,* p. 278; May 7, 2007, review of *A Perfect Day,* p. 58.

San Francisco Chronicle, October 3, 1999, Sylvia Rubin, "The Peter Pan behind *Peanut Butter Party,*" p. 37; June 15, 2006, Rachel Howard, "For Rémy Charlip, the Urge to Create Art Is So Strong, Not Even a Stroke Can Stop Him."

Saturday Review, April 16, 1966, Alice Dalgliesh, review of *Mother, Mother, I Feel Sick, Send for the Doctor, Quick, Quick, Quick,* p. 49.

School Library Journal, May, 1987, Susan Nemeth McCarthy, review of *Handtalk Birthday,* p. 83; June, 1999, Lisa Gangemi Kropp, review of *Peanut Butter Party,* p. 112; September, 2000, Roxanne Burg, review of *Why I Will Never Ever Ever Ever Have Enough Time to Read This Book,* p. 186; January, 2002, Roxanne Burg, review of *Baby Hearts and Baby Flowers,* p. 95; October, 2003, Marge Loch-Wouters, review of *Little Old Big Beard and Big Young Little Beard,* p. 115; May, 2007, Martha Simpson, review of *A Perfect Day,* p. 86.

Science Books, September, 1974, review of *Handtalk,* p. 160.

Social Education, October, 1979, Shelley G. McNamara, "Naive Mural Art as a Vehicle for Teaching Elementary Social Studies," pp. 473-476.

ONLINE

Library of Congress Information Bulletin Online, http://www.loc.gov/loc/lcib/ (June 23, 1997), John Sayers, "Young at Heart: A Celebration of Rémy Charlip."*

*   *   *

CONWAY, Celeste

Personal

Female.

Addresses

Home—New York, NY. *E-mail*—celeste@celeste conway.com.

Career

Writer and artist.

Awards, Honors

Books for the Teen Age selection, New York Public Library, 2007, for *The Melting Season.*

Writings

Where Is Papa Now? (for children), Caroline House (Honesdale, PA), 1994.

The Melting Season (young-adult novel), Delacorte Press (New York, NY), 2006.

The Goodbye Time (for children), Delacorte Press (New York, NY), 2008.

Sidelights

Celeste Conway is an American writer and artist. She published her first book, *Where Is Papa Now?,* in 1994. The book tells the story of Eliza, whose father is away on extended business on the *Lucky Goose* ship. She regularly asks her mother where in the world her father is. Eliza's mother answers as best as she can, naming a range of exotic places and describing them for her daughter. Their house is filled with the treasures of trips to foreign ports of call, including Japanese prints and English farmhouse furniture. A contributor writing in *Publishers Weekly* commented that the book's "text is emotionally flat, little more than a vehicle for Conway's sumptuous cut-paper designs."

Cover of Celeste Conway's young-adult novel The Melting Season, *featuring artwork by Sandra Speidel.* (Laurel Leaf, 2006. Used by permission of Delacorte Press, an imprint of Random House Children's Books, a division of Random House, Inc.)

Conway's young-adult novel *The Melting Season* concerns sixteen-year-old Giselle, a talented ballet student who still grieves for her father, a famous dance choreographer who died ten years earlier. Giselle's relationship with her mother, a renowned ballerina, is strained, and the teen leads a compulsively ordered life, both at her lavish New York City apartment and at her school for gifted artists. Giselle begins to emerge from her shell, however, after meeting Will, a sensitive boy from the suburbs. When she spends a night at Will's home, the teen begins to recover some painful memories from her childhood. As she learns to deal with her emotions, Giselle blossoms as a dancer.

Claire Rosser, writing in *Kliatt*, deemed *The Melting Season* "an interesting love story, concentrating on psychological factors affecting creativity," and *Booklist* reviewer Carolyn Phelan stated that the work "will capture readers with vivid imagery, emotional subtlety, and fine dialogue." Other reviewers praised Conway's ability to evoke setting. "The world of culturally elite Manhattanites is aptly drawn," Michelle Roberts noted in *School Library Journal*, and a *Kirkus Reviews* contributor remarked that the "backdrop is original and the characters who play against it are interesting and intelligent."

In *The Goodbye Time* fifth-grader Anna wonders why people celebrating a birthday view it as a new beginning in their life when, to her, a new beginning also means an end. Her brother will move out of their house for university soon, her friend Michael will be moving away after the death of his father, and she will be going to a new school at the end of the semester. With life lessons from her friends, Anna begins her own new beginning as she grows up and learns to better understand the many changes that occur in life.

Donna Volkenannt, reviewing *The Goodbye Time* on *Kidsreads.com,* commented that "the main characters, Anna and Katie, are likable. Katie is realistic, but I found Anna a bit too perfect to be believable. Nonetheless, I think middle-grade girls will enjoy reading this title." Wendy Smith-D'Arezzo observed in *School Library Journal* that the author writes through the "clear voice of a fifth grader." Smith-D'Arezzo noticed that Conway is able to present the story of less fortunate people to kids "in a way that is enlightening without being preachy." A contributor writing in *Kirkus Reviews* remarked that even though *The Goodbye Time* is marketed to a pre-teen audience, Conway gears it more toward a young-adult audience by "mixing age-appropriate feelings and observations too experienced for someone Anna's age." The same contributor added that "even the cover is ambiguous." A *Publishers Weekly* reviewer was not surprised "that Anna's emotional responses seem a little blunted" considering the large number of developments in the story. Nevertheless, the contributor claimed that "the writing is simple and clear."

Biographical and Critical Sources

PERIODICALS

Booklist, November 15, 2006, Carolyn Phelan, review of *The Melting Season,* p. 57.
Kirkus Reviews, November 15, 2006, review of *The Melting Season,* p. 1172; November 15, 2008, review of *The Goodbye Time.*
Kliatt, November, 2006, Claire Rosser, review of *The Melting Season,* p. 8.
Publishers Weekly, December 6, 1993, review of *Where Is Papa Now?,* p. 72; December 15, 2008, review of *The Goodbye Time,* p. 54.
School Library Journal, January, 2007, Michelle Roberts, review of *The Melting Season,* p. 126; February 1, 2009, Wendy Smith-D'Arezzo, review of *The Goodbye Time,* p. 97.

ONLINE

Celeste Conway Home Page, http://www.celesteconway.com (May 25, 2009).
Kidsreads.com, http://www.kidsreads.com/ (May 25, 2009), Donna Volkenannt, review of *The Goodbye Time.**

*   *   *

COOLEY, Beth
(Elizabeth Cooley)

Personal

Married; children: two daughters. *Education:* University of North Carolina at Chapel Hill, B.A., 1980, M.A., 1983, Ph.D., 1988.

Addresses

Home—Spokane, WA. *Office*—Gonzaga University, English Department, E. 502 Boone, Spokane, WA 99258. *E-mail*—cooley@gu.gonzaga.edu.

Career

Gonzaga University, Spokane, WA, associate professor of English and chair of the department.

Awards, Honors

Delacorte Press Prize, and Best Children's Books of the Year selection, Bank Street College of Education, both 2004, both for *Ostrich Eye*; Best Children's Books of the Year selection, Bank Street College of Education, 2006, for *Shelter.*

Writings

JUVENILE FICTION

Ostrich Eye, Delacorte (New York, NY), 2004.
Shelter, Delacorte (New York, NY), 2006.

Beth Cooley (Reproduced by permission.)

Sidelights

In her first novel for young adults, Beth Cooley delivers a tale that explores the feelings of a young girl who longs for a deeper connection to her family. *Ostrich Eye* centers on high-school freshman Ginger, who has not seen her father since she was very young. Ginger comes to believe that a man she encounters everywhere around town must be her real father, and she ignores other warning signs. Tragically, the man has been stalking her younger sister and ends up abducting her.

A *Publishers Weekly* reviewer praised *Ostrich Eye,* emphasizing the careful delivery of the subject matter. "Cooley sets up some delicate situations but handles them confidently; scenes involving pedophilia are shocking without being explicit," the critic noted. Claire Rosser, writing in *Kliatt,* applauded Cooley's narrative, remarking that "the style of this novel, plus Ginger's honesty, will appeal to younger YAs who like mysteries and crime stories." In *Booklist* Frances Bradburn deemed *Ostrich Eye* "a winning, if uneasy first novel," and a critic in *Kirkus Reviews* praised the novel, claiming that, "unlike ostriches, this story soars."

In *Shelter,* Cooley introduces readers to Lucy, a high-school sophomore whose world is turned upside down when she and her family are forced to move into a homeless shelter after her father dies. The transition from comfortable middle-class suburbia to a single room in a crowded facility is more than Lucy can stand. However, as she opens her eyes to the plight of those around her, including her mother who has a shocking secret, she also learns about herself.

Reviewing *Shelter* in *School Library Journal,* Janet Hilbun wrote that, "while this is not great literature, its appealing characters and smoothly flowing plot make it a satisfying read." *Booklist* contributor Debbie Carton maintained that Cooley's "strength lies in creating likable characters of all ages and finding the positive," and a *Kirkus Reviews* contributor predicted that in *Shelter* "readers will find a moving glimpse into a different kind of life."

Biographical and Critical Sources

PERIODICALS

Booklist, November 15, 2003, Frances Bradburn, review of *Ostrich Eye,* p. 606; January 1, 2007, Debbie Carton, review of *Shelter,* p. 80.

Kirkus Reviews, December 15, 2003, review of *Ostrich Eye,* p. 1448; November 1, 2006, review of *Shelter,* p. 1122.

Kliatt, January, 2004, Claire Rosser, review of *Ostrich Eye,* p. 6; November, 2006, Myrna Marler, review of *Shelter,* p. 8.

Publishers Weekly, January 26, 2004, review of *Ostrich Eye,* p. 254.

School Library Journal, January, 2004, Susan W. Hunter, review of *Ostrich Eye,* p. 128; December, 2006, Janet Hilbun, review of *Shelter,* p. 136.

Voice of Youth Advocates, February, 2007, Barbara Johnston, review of *Shelter,* p. 523.

ONLINE

Gonzaga University Web site, http://www. gonzaga.edu/ (February, 2008), "Elizabeth Cooley."

Scholastic Web site, http://www2.scholastic.com/ (October 15, 2009), biography of Beth Cooley.*

*   *   *

COOLEY, Elizabeth
See COOLEY, Beth

*   *   *

CRILLEY, Mark 1966-

Personal

Born May 21, 1966, in Hartford City, IN; son of Robert H. (a minister) and Virginia A. Crilley; married Miki Hirabayashi, May 2, 1998; children: Matthew, Mio. *Education:* Kalamazoo College, B.A., 1988. *Religion:* Presbyterian. *Hobbies and other interests:* Oil painting.

Addresses

Home—Walled Lake, MI. *Agent*—Merrilee Heifetz, Writers House, 21 W. 26th St., New York, NY 10010. *E-mail*—mark@markcrilley.com.

Career

Artist, illustrator, cartoonist, and fiction writer. Young Men's Christian Association, Changhua, Taiwan, English teacher, 1988-90, 1993-94; Morioka English Academy, Iwate, Japan, English teacher, 1991-93.

Mark Crilley (Photograph by Mary Moylan. Reproduced by permission.)

Awards, Honors

Thirteen Eisner Award nominations, for "Akiko" comic books; Great Graphic Novels for Teens selection, American Library Association, 2008, for *Spring, Summer,* and *Autumn.*

Writings

"AKIKO" SERIES; SELF-ILLUSTRATED

Akiko on the Planet Smoo, Delacorte (New York, NY), 2000.
Akiko in the Sprubly Islands, Delacorte (New York, NY), 2000.
Akiko and the Great Wall of Trudd, Delacorte (New York, NY), 2001.
Akiko in the Castle of Alia Rellapor, Delacorte (New York, NY), 2001.
Akiko and the Intergalactic Zoo, Delacorte (New York, NY), 2002.
Akiko and the Alpha Centauri 5000, Delacorte (New York, NY), 2003.
Akiko and the Journey to Toog, Delacorte (New York, NY), 2003.

Akiko: The Training Master, Delacorte (New York, NY), 2005.
Akiko: Pieces of Gax, Delacorte (New York, NY), 2006.
Akiko and the Missing Misp, Delacorte (New York, NY), 2008.

Also author and illustrator of "Akiko" comic books, beginning 1995.

"BILLY CLIKK" SERIES; SELF-ILLUSTRATED

Creach Battler, Delacorte (New York, NY), 2004.
Rogmasher Rampage, Delacorte (New York, NY), 2005.

"MIKI FALLS" SERIES; SELF-ILLUSTRATED

Spring, HarperTeen (New York, NY), 2007.
Summer, HarperTeen (New York, NY), 2007.
Autumn, HarperTeen (New York, NY), 2007.
Winter, HarperTeen (New York, NY), 2008.

Sidelights

Mark Crilley is the creator of the popular "Akiko" series of comic books featuring a spunky young Japanese-American protagonist named Akiko, and her out-of-this-world adventures. He has also penned a number of books about the plucky heroine, including *Akiko and the Great Wall of Trudd* and *Akiko and the Journey to Toog,* that have won fans among older elementary-grade readers. In addition Crilley has published two novels featuring an intrepid monster combatant named Billy Clikk as well as the critically acclaimed "Miki Falls" series of graphic novels. "Ever since I discovered that there were people out there willing to pay me to make up stories and draw strange creatures all day," he wrote on the Random House Web site, "I knew there was no turning back. 'This,' I thought, 'is the job for me.' And I still think that, every day."

Born in Indiana in 1966, Crilley moved to Detroit, Michigan, as a child and passed the time by drawing constantly. Although Crilley was a good student in school, he was also known for being shy and rather reserved . . . that is, until the fourth grade when he discovered a yet-unplumbed talent for making up humorous one-liners during a school talent show. Soon acting was vying for first-place as one of Crilley's career possibilities, although art was always a possibility. A friendship with Caldecott Medal-winning author and illustrator David Small, who then taught at Kalamazoo College, pulled the young man back into the arts arena. As Crilley recalled of Small in an interview for *Authors and Artists for Young Adults:* "He took me under his wing and got me to work harder, to learn from the masters, to always strive for excellence as an artist."

After Crilley graduated from Kalamazoo College in 1988, his career veered off both its preordained courses; moving to Asia, he taught English in Japan and Taiwan for five years. It was this time in Japan that inspired his first foray into comic books, as he penned the first incarnation of *Akiko on the Planet Smoo.* After he returned to the United States, he found a publisher in Dover, New Jersey's Sirius Entertainment, and his "Akiko" comic-book series was off and running, quickly becoming an underground phenomenon.

Inspired by both Japanese anime comics as well as by early twentieth-century cartoonist Winsor McCay's popular fantasy comic strip "Little Nemo," Crilley's "Akiko" comic features a ten-year-old protagonist. With round eyes reminiscent of the anime style, Akiko also has unwieldy braids à la Astrid Lingren's heroine Pippi Longstocking. As feisty as Pippi, Akiko finds herself drawn into otherplanetary adventures, accompanied by her unearthly sidekicks Spuckler and Mr. Beeba. Other friends include a brainy robot called Gax, and Poog, a disembodied head.

The first series of Crilley's "Akiko" comics were eventually adapted into book form. As Crilley once told *SATA,* "One of my comics found its way into the hands of Lawrence David, an editor at Random House Children's Books. Though I had no experience in writing (apart from my own comic books), Lawrence felt confi-

Cover of Crilley's middle-grade novel **Akiko and the Missing Misp,** *featuring cover art by Crilley.* (Illustration copyright © 2008 by Mark Crilley. Used by permission of Delacorte Press, an imprint of Random House Children's Books, a division of Random House, Inc.)

dent that I would be able to create a series of four novels based on the first eighteen issues of my 'Akiko' comics."

Crilley's first four novels for Random House—*Akiko on the Planet Smoo, Akiko in the Sprubly Islands, Akiko and the Great Wall of Trudd,* and *Akiko in the Castle of Alia Rellapor*—proved as popular with young readers as his comic books had. In the first work, the Japanese-American fourth grader travels to Smoo, where she is assigned by King Froptoppit to see to the rescue of the kidnaped Prince Froptoppit. The saga continues through the next three novels as Akiko and her unusual friends travel through a number of amazing lands, encounter serpents and other evil creatures, and ultimately find themselves confronted with the reason behind the prince's kidnapping.

In a *School Library Journal* review of *Akiko and the Great Wall of Trudd,* Elaine E. Knight praised Crilley's young protagonist as "a strong female character whose leadership holds her strange band together." While some critics were less than impressed with the written text of the series, others looked favorably on Crilley's efforts, *Booklist* reviewer Francisca Goldsmith praising *Akiko in the Castle of Alia Rellapor* as "a fun introduction to [the] genre" for "youngsters unfamiliar with" science fiction. Knight continued her praise of the heroine in a review of the fourth "Akiko" installment, noting that in *Akiko in the Castle of Alia Rellapor* "the bickering dialogue among the adventurers is amusing and Akiko herself shows strong leadership in helping them work as a cohesive team."

Crilley continued his "Akiko" book series with stand-alone chapter books. In *Akiko and the Intergalactic Zoo* the well-traveled preteen is rewarded by King Froptoppit with a visit to a zoo on Planet Quilk, but when the greedy zookeeper realizes that his latest guest is actually a potential specimen of an Earthian, Akiko finds herself in trouble. Escaping from this pickle, Akiko is thrust into another in *Akiko and the Alpha Centauri 5000,* when Spuckler enters his jury-rigged spacecraft in a trans-galaxy race and needs his Earth friend to sign on as pilot. In *School Library Journal* Knight remarked that the book "clearly shows its comic-book roots," while in *Booklist* Goldsmith praised Crilley for including "generous doses of wit as well as moralizing," creating "an adventure story that packs gender equity" while casting aside racial—and planetary—bias.

When Poog mysteriously disappears while en route to his home planet, Akiko (now in fifth grade) agrees to help Spuckler, Mr. Beeba, and Gax search for their ally in *Akiko and the Journey to Toog.* Knight praised the "breakneck episodic plot action, cartoon illustrations, bantering dialogue, and scores of onomatopoeic words." In *The Training Master,* the youngster heads to Zarga Baffa, where she enrolls in a demanding program for Intergalactic Space Patrollers. The series' comic-book origins "show in the anime-influenced art, derring-do adventures, and Akiko's indomitable spirit," Carolyn Lehman remarked in *School Library Journal.* Discussing his popular series on the Random House Web site, Crilley observed that the theme of the "Akiko" novels is "the important role a child plays in the world, and how, in many instances, a little kid has more sense than the adults surrounding her."

In *Akiko and the Missing Misp* the series heroine is in sixth grade. It is the first annual Middleton Mega MangaFest, and Akiko meets Akiko Robot. She then travels to planet Smoo, but Mr. Beeba mistakenly sends her back in time. Stuck twenty-five years in the past, Akiko must make sure not to alter history. She also must rescue the Misp, a powerful crown that gives the bearer absolute power over planet Smoo. Akiko meets her friends in the past, but they have not met her yet, and thus she must work alone. Critics praised *Akiko and the Missing Misp* as a delightful addition to the series. Applauding the book in *Kirkus Reviews,* a contributor noted that "this fun, light sci-fi romp fits in nicely with its predecessors and is a pleasant addition to this longstanding series."

Crilley introduces a new action-adventure hero in *Creatch Battler,* which focuses on an inquisitive twelve year old who learns that his parents—supposed owners of an extermination company—are actually employees of the Allied Forces for the Management of Extraterrestrial Creatches. The AFMEC is a secret organization that keeps the world safe from a variety of monstrous beings. When a saber-toothed orf invades the Taj Mahal, Billy accompanies his parents to India, where they encounter an even greater danger. "As with the Akiko books, the pace is breathless," observed Francisca Goldsmith in *Booklist,* and Knight commented that Crilley's "story incorporates comic-book-style action . . . and lively, wisecracking dialogue with a subtle message about courage and responsibility." In a sequel, *Rogmasher Rampage,* the youngster, now an AFMEC trainee, joins forces with Ana Garcia to defend a secluded Chinese village from hideous beasts. "The writing is slick and clean," noted *School Library Journal* contributor Tasha Saecker, and Goldsmith also complimented the tale, applauding Crilley for including "broad humor, a dash of suspense, and lots of delicious made-up words."

Spring is the first title in Crilley's "Miki Falls" series, a quartet of graphic novels about a young woman's usual relationship with a spiritual being. Influenced by manga-style comics, the works center on a curious and independent high-school senior named Miki Yoshida. While pursuing Hiro Sakurai, a handsome and brooding new student, Miki learns that he harbors a secret: Hiro is a Deliverer, a supernatural being who is entrusted to preserve love in the world. "The soft, gentle romance between Miki and Hiro is brilliantly juxtaposed with the darker elements of the story," observed a critic in *Kirkus Reviews,* and a contributor in *Children's Bookwatch* praised *Spring* as a "gentle, at times hopeful, and at

times heartbreaking story about young love." Writing in *Booklist,* Stephanie Zvirin cited Crilley's colored-pencil art as a highlight of the work, noting that his "pictures cleverly instill the story with abundant emotion, humor, and drama." According to *Publishers Weekly* reviewer Brigid Alverson, "the style of the book is Crilley's own. . . . His storytelling style is cinematic, with closeups, reaction shots and frequent cuts back and forth between scenes."

Continuing the "Miki Falls" series with installments for each season, Crilley followed *Spring* with *Summer* and then with *Autumn,* in which Miko and Hiro continue their forbidden romance. Another Deliverer, Reika, tells Hiro and Miki that they should run away or face the consequences. The couple travels to the home of Toshiko Yamada, an older man who used to be a Deliverer. Critics applauded the book's romantic story and soft pencil drawings. According to *School Library Journal* contributor Sarah Krygier, the characters "are recognizable as Japanese," but "Crilley clearly has an American influence, and his fashions look to be straight out of a neighborhood Target store." Jennifer Sweeney, writing in *Kliatt,* was also impressed with the story. She remarked that "readers will cheer for Miki and Hiro and will be captivated to see this plucky young couple overcome the odds stacked against them."

In the final book in the series, *Winter,* the reasons behind Miki's fall through a window in *Spring* are finally revealed. Indeed, the Deliverers, it seems, are behind the incident. Hiro and Miki are almost able to escape and build a life together, but just as they appear to have succeeded, the Deliverers catch up to them. Yet, Miki refuses to leave Hiro, and the couple must make a sacrifice if they wish to be together. The illustrations in this installment reflect the turmoil the couple must go through, with images bleeding from frame to frame and taking up overlapping pages. Sweeney, again writing in *Kliatt,* noted that "Miki is a strong, dynamic female character, who is both headstrong and naive, creating a pleasing blend of easily relatable traits."

"I've been blessed," Crilley once told *SATA.* "Very few people are lucky enough to do something creative and get paid for it. On one level simply getting by in this way is all the achievement I'll ever need."

Biographical and Critical Sources

BOOKS

Authors and Artists for Young Adults, Volume 50, Gale (Detroit, MI), 2003.

PERIODICALS

Booklist, March 1, 2000, Chris Sherman, review of *Akiko on the Planet Smoo,* p. 1243; January 1, 2001, Shelle Rosenfeld, review of *Akiko in the Sprubly Islands,* p.

958; January 1, 2002, Francisca Goldsmith, review of *Akiko in the Castle of Alia Rellapor,* p. 856; May 15, 2003, Francisca Goldsmith, review of *Akiko and the Alpha Centauri 5000,* p. 1660; April 15, 2004, Francisca Goldsmith, review of *Creach Battler,* p. 1453; September 1, 2005, Francisca Goldsmith, review of *Rogmasher Rampage,* p. 132; March 15, 2007, Stephanie Zvirin, review of *Spring,* p. 58.

Children's Bookwatch, August, 2007, review of *Summer.*

Entertainment Weekly, June 26, 1998, "Mark Crilley: Cult Cartoonist," p. 90.

Family Life, March 1, 2001, review of *Akiko in the Sprubly Islands,* p. 87.

Kirkus Reviews, April 1, 2007, review of *Spring;* October 1, 2008, review of *Akiko and the Missing Misp.*

Kliatt, July, 2007, George Galuschak, review of *Spring,* p. 34; September, 2007, George Galuschak, review of *Summer,* p. 28; March 1, 2008, Jennifer Sweeney, review of *Autumn,* p. 31; March 1, 2008, Jennifer Sweeney, review of *Winter,* p. 31.

Library Talk, September-October, 2000, David Linger, review of *Akiko on the Planet Smoo,* p. 41.

Publishers Weekly, January 17, 2000, review of *Akiko on the Planet Smoo,* p. 57; June 18, 2001, review of *Akiko on the Planet Smoo* and *Akiko and the Sprubly Islands,* p. 83; August 27, 2001, review of *Akiko in the Castle of Alia Rellapor,* p. 86; September 29, 2003, review of *Akiko and the Journey to Toog,* p. 67; May 24, 2004, review of *Creach Battler,* p. 63; August 21, 2007, Brigid Alverson, "Harper Hopes Teens Fall for Miki Falls."

School Library Journal, February, 2000, Lisa Prolman, review of *Akiko on the Planet Smoo,* p. 92; November, 2000, Lisa Prolman, review of *Akiko in the Sprubly Islands,* p. 113; April, 2001, Elaine E. Knight, review of *Akiko and the Great Wall of Trudd,* p. 105; November, 2001, Elaine E. Knight, review of *Akiko in the Castle of Alia Rellapor,* p. 113; October, 2002, Susan Weitz, review of *Akiko and the Intergalactic Zoo,* p. 100; September, 2003, Elaine E. Knight, review of *Akiko and the Alpha Centauri 5000,* p. 176; December, 2003, Elaine E. Knight, review of *Akiko and the Journey to Toog,* p. 112; July, 2004, Elaine E. Knight, review of *Creach Battler,* p. 104; July, 2005, Carolyn Lehman, review of *Akiko: The Training Master,* p. 72; October, 2005, Tasha Saecker, review of *Rogmasher Rampage,* p. 156; July, 2007, Alana Abbott, reviews of *Spring* and *Summer,* both p. 123; May 1, 2008, Sarah Krygier, review of *Autumn,* p. 153; July 1, 2008, Alana Abbott, review of *Winter,* p. 119.

USA Today, July 15, 2003, Penny Schwartz "'Akiko' Series Soars on Fun, Fanciful Flights," p. D4.

ONLINE

Mark Crilley Home Page, http://www.markcrilley.com (June 2, 2009).

Random House Web site, http://www.randomhouse.com/ (April 1, 2008), "Mark Crilley."

TeenReadsToo.com, http://teensreadtoo.com/ (April 1, 2008), interview with Crilley.

Worlds of Westfield Web site, http://westfieldcomics.com/ (August 30, 2002), Roger Ash, "Mark Crilley Interview."*

*   *   *

CUSHMAN, Doug 1953-

Personal

Born May 4, 1953, in Springfield, OH. *Education:* Attended Paier School of Art, 1971-75. *Hobbies and other interests:* Cooking, kayaking, reading.

Addresses

Home—Redding, CA; and Paris, France.

Career

Illustrator. Apprentice to book illustrator Mercer Mayer, 1975-77; writer and illustrator, 1977—. Instructor at Paier College of Art, 1980, and Southern Connecticut State University, 1981.

Member

Society of Children's Book Writers and Illustrators, National Cartoonists Society, Mystery Writers of America.

Awards, Honors

Reuben Award for Book Illustration, National Cartoonists Society, 1996, and Notable Trade Books for Young People selection, National Council of Teachers of English, both for *The Mystery of King Karfu;* Christopher Award, 2004, for *Never, Ever Shout in a Zoo.*

Writings

FOR CHILDREN; SELF-ILLUSTRATED

(Compiler) *Giants* (stories and poems), Platt & Munk (New York, NY), 1980.

(Compiler) *Trolls* (stories), Platt & Munk (New York, NY), 1981.

(Compiler) *Once upon a Pig,* Platt & Munk (New York, NY), 1982.

Nasty Kyle the Crocodile, Grosset & Dunlap (New York, NY), 1983.

Aunt Eater Loves a Mystery, Harper & Row (New York, NY), 1987.

The Missing Mystery, Checkerboard (New York, NY), 1987.

Uncle Foster's Hat Tree, Dutton (New York, NY), 1988.

Mouse and Mole, Grosset & Dunlap (New York, NY), 1989.

Possum Stew, Dutton (New York, NY), 1990.

Camp Big Paw, Harper & Row (New York, NY), 1990.

Doug Cushman (Photograph by John Massimino. Reproduced by permission.)

Aunt Eater's Mystery Vacation, HarperCollins (New York, NY), 1992.

The ABC Mystery, HarperCollins (New York, NY), 1993.

Mouse and Mole and the Year-Round Garden, Scientific American Books for Young Readers (New York, NY), 1994.

Mouse and Mole and the Christmas Walk, Scientific American Books for Young Readers (New York, NY), 1994.

Mouse and Mole and the All-Weather Train Ride, Scientific American Books for Young Readers (New York, NY), 1995.

Aunt Eater's Mystery Christmas, HarperCollins (New York, NY), 1995.

The Mystery of King Karfu, HarperCollins (New York, NY), 1996.

Aunt Eater's Mystery Halloween, HarperCollins (New York, NY), 1998.

The Mystery of the Monkey's Maze, HarperCollins (New York, NY), 1999.

Inspector Hopper, HarperCollins (New York, NY), 2000.

Inspector Hopper's Mystery Year, HarperCollins (New York, NY), 2003.

Space Cat, HarperCollins (New York, NY), 2004.

Mystery at the Club Sandwich, Clarion (New York, NY), 2004.

Dirk Bones and the Mystery of the Haunted House, HarperCollins (New York, NY), 2006.

ILLUSTRATOR

H.L. Ross, *Not Counting Monsters,* Platt & Munk (New York, NY), 1978.

Lillie Patterson, *Haunted Houses on Halloween,* Garrard (Champaign, IL), 1979.

Elizabeth Norine Upham, *Little Brown Bear,* Platt & Munk (New York, NY), 1979.

F. Kaff, *Monster for a Day; or, The Monster in Gregory's Pajamas,* Gingerbread House (Westhampton Beach, NY), 1979.

Leonard Kessler, *The Silly Mother Hubbard,* Garrard (Champaign, IL), 1980.

Leonard Kessler, *Hickory Dickory Dock,* Garrard (Champaign, IL), 1980.

Michaela Muntean, *Bicycle Bear,* Parents Magazine Press (New York, NY), 1983.

The Pudgy Fingers Counting Book, Grosset & Dunlap (New York, NY), 1983.

Ida Luttrell, *Tillie and Mert,* Harper (New York, NY), 1985.

Suzanne Gruber, *Chatty Chipmunk's Nutty Day,* Troll (Mahwah, NJ), 1985.

Mickey Takes a Bow, Little, Brown (Boston, MA), 1986.

Michael J. Pellowski, *Benny's Bad Day,* Troll (Mahwah, NJ), 1986.

Jack Long, *The Secret of the Nile,* Checkerboard (New York, NY), 1987.

Jack Long, *The Sunken Treasure,* Checkerboard (New York, NY), 1987.

Jack Long, *The Vanishing Professor,* Checkerboard (New York, NY), 1987.

Rose Greydanus, *Bedtime Story,* Troll (Mahwah, NJ), 1988.

C.S. White, *The Monsters' Counting Book,* Platt & Munk (New York, NY), 1988.

Sharon Gordon, *The Jolly Monsters,* Troll (Mahwah, NJ), 1988.

Terry Webb Harshman, *Porcupine's Pajama Party,* Harper & Row (New York, NY), 1988.

Melanie Martin, *Itsy-Bitsy Giant,* Troll (Mahwah, NJ), 1989.

Michael J. Pellowski, *Mixed-up Magic,* Troll (Mahwah, NJ), 1989.

Dorothy Corey, *A Shot for Baby Bear,* Albert Whitman (Morton Grove, IL), 1989.

Thomas P. Lewis, *Frida's Office Day,* Harper & Row (New York, NY), 1989.

Michaela Munteen, *Bicycle Bear Rides Again,* Parents Magazine (New York, NY), 1989.

Marcia Leonard, *The Three Little Pigs,* Silver Press (Parsippany, NJ), 1990.

Marcia Leonard, *The Elves and the Shoemaker,* Silver Press (Parsippany, NJ), 1990.

Teresa Noel Celsi, *The Fourth Little Pig,* Raintree (Milwaukee, WI), 1990.

Michael Berenstain, *1 + 1 Take Away Two!,* Western (Racine, WI), 1991.

Lois G. Grambling, *An Alligator Named Alligator,* Barron's (Hauppauge, NY), 1991.

Joan Davenport Carris, *Aunt Morbelia and the Screaming Skulls,* Little, Brown (Boston, MA), 1992.

William H. Hooks, *How Do You Make a Bubble?,* Bantam (New York, NY), 1992.

William H. Hooks, *Feed Me! An Aesop Fable,* Bantam (New York, NY), 1992.

Gary Richmond, *The Early Bird,* Word Publishing (Dallas, TX), 1992.

Naomi Baltuck, *Crazy Gibberish: And Other Story-Hour Stretches from a Storyteller's Bag of Tricks,* Linnets Books (Hamden, CT), 1993.

Mary Packard, *The Witch Who Couldn't Fly,* Troll (Mahwah, NJ), 1994.

Patricia Lakin, *Get Ready to Read,* Raintree Steck-Vaughn (Austin, TX), 1995.

Patricia Lakin, *A Good Sport,* Raintree Steck-Vaughn (Austin, TX), 1995.

Patricia Lakin, *A True Partnership,* Raintree Steck-Vaughn (Austin, TX), 1995.

Bethany Roberts, *Halloween Mice!,* Clarion (New York, NY), 1995.

Gail Herman, *Teddy Bear for Sale,* Scholastic (New York, NY), 1995.

Patricia Lakin, *The Mystery Illness,* Raintree Steck-Vaughn (Austin, TX), 1995.

Patricia Lakin, *Trash and Treasure,* Raintree Steck-Vaughn (Austin, TX), 1995.

Patricia Lakin, *Up a Tree,* Raintree Steck-Vaughn (Austin, TX), 1995.

Patricia Lakin, *Where There's Smoke,* Raintree Steck-Vaughn (Austin, TX), 1995.

Patricia Lakin, *Signs of Protest,* Raintree Steck-Vaughn (Austin, TX), 1995.

Patricia Lakin, *Aware and Alert,* Raintree Steck-Vaughn (Austin, TX), 1995.

Patricia Lakin, *A Summer Job,* Raintree Stack-Vaughn (Austin, TX), 1995.

Patricia Lakin, *Information, Please,* Raintree Steck-Vaughn (Austin, TX), 1995.

Patricia Lakin, *Red Letter Day,* Raintree Steck-Vaughn (Austin, TX), 1995.

Alice Cary, *Nat the Crab,* Open Court (Chicago, IL), 1995.

Robin Dexter, *Frogs,* Troll (Mahwah, NJ), 1996.

William H. Hooks, reteller, *Feed Me! An Aesop Fable,* Gareth Stevens (Milwaukee, WI), 1996.

Bethany Roberts, *Valentine Mice!,* Clarion (New York, NY), 1997.

Susan Goldman Rubin, *The Whiz Kids Plugged In,* Scholastic (New York, NY), 1997.

Rita Balducci, *Halloween Pigs,* WhistleStop/Troll (Mahwah, NJ), 1997.

Shelagh Canning, *The Turkey Saves the Day,* Troll (Mahwah, NJ), 1997.

Susan Goldman Rubin *The Whiz Kids Take Off!,* Scholastic (New York, NY), 1997.

Douglas Wood, *What Dads Can't Do,* Simon & Schuster (New York, NY), 2000.

Bethany Roberts, *Christmas Mice!,* Clarion (New York, NY), 2000.

Douglas Wood, *What Moms Can't Do,* Simon & Schuster (New York, NY), 2001.

Lilian Moore, *Little Raccoon,* Henry Holt (New York, NY), 2001.

Bethany Roberts, *Thanksgiving Mice!,* Clarion (New York, NY), 2001.

Joan M. Lexau, *Crocodile and Hen: A Bakongo Folktale,* HarperCollins (New York, NY), 2001.

Jane Yolen, *Animal Train,* Little Simon (New York, NY), 2002.

Douglas Wood, *What Teachers Can't Do,* Simon & Schuster (New York, NY), 2002.

Kay Winters, *But Mom, Everybody Else Does,* Dutton Children's Books (New York, NY), 2002.

Bethany Roberts, *Birthday Mice!,* Clarion Books (New York, NY), 2002.

Barbara Williams, *Albert's Impossible Toothache,* Candlewick Press (Cambridge, MA), 2003.

Bethany Roberts, *Easter Mice!,* Clarion Books (New York, NY), 2003.

John Schindel, *What Did They See?,* Henry Holt (New York, NY), 2003.

Bethany Roberts, *Halloween Mice!,* Clarion (New York, NY), 2003.

Katherine Brown Tegen, *Dracula and Frankenstein Are Friends,* HarperCollins (New York, NY), 2003.

Douglas Wood, *What Santa Can't Do,* Simon & Schuster (New York, NY), 2003.

Judy Sierra, *What Time Is It, Mr. Crocodile?,* Gulliver Books (Orlando, FL), 2004.

Bethany Roberts, *Fourth of July Mice!,* Clarion (New York, NY), 2004.

Karma Wilson, *Never Ever Shout in a Zoo,* Little, Brown (New York, NY), 2004.

Matt Mitter, *ABC: Alphabet Rhymes,* Gareth Stevens (Milwaukee, WI), 2004.

Matt Mitter, *1, 2, 3, Counting Rhymes,* Gareth Stevens (Milwaukee, WI), 2004.

Douglas Wood, *What Grandmas Can't Do,* Simon & Schuster (New York, NY), 2005.

Susan Schafer, *Where's My Tail?,* Marshall Cavendish (New York, NY), 2005.

Shirley Mozelle, *The Bear Upstairs,* Henry Holt (New York, NY), 2005.

Jacklyn Williams, *Happy Easter, Gus!,* Picture Window Books (Minneapolis, MN), 2005.

Jacklyn Williams, *Happy Halloween, Gus!,* Picture Window Books (Minneapolis, MN), 2005.

Jacklyn Williams, *Happy Valentine's Day, Gus!,* Picture Window Books (Minneapolis, MN), 2005.

Jacklyn Williams, *Merry Christmas, Gus!,* Picture Window Books (Minneapolis, MN), 2005.

Jacklyn Williams, *Happy Thanksgiving, Gus!,* Picture Window Books (Minneapolis, MN), 2006.

Jacklyn Williams, *Happy Birthday, Gus!,* Picture Window Books (Minneapolis, MN), 2006.

Jacklyn Williams, *Welcome to Third Grade, Gus!,* Picture Window Books (Minneapolis, MN), 2006.

Pat Mora, *¡Marimba!: Animales from A to Z,* Clarion (New York, NY), 2006.

Jack Prelutsky, *What a Day It Was at School!,* Greenwillow (New York, NY), 2006.

Barbara Williams, *Albert's Gift for Grandmother,* Candlewick Press (Cambridge, MA), 2006.

Stephanie Calmenson, *Birthday at the Panda Palace,* HarperCollins (New York, NY), 2007.

Carol Roth, *Here Comes the Choo-choo!,* Harcourt (Orlando, FL), 2007.

Sarah Weeks, *Ella, Of Course!,* Harcourt (Orlando, FL), 2007.

Jacklyn Williams, *The Haunted Schoolhouse: A Spooky Lift-the-flap Book,* Simon & Schuster (New York, NY), 2007.

Jacklyn Williams, *Let's Go Fishing, Gus!,* Picture Window Books (Minneapolis, MN), 2007.

Jacklyn Williams, *Make a New Friend, Gus!,* Picture Window Books (Minneapolis, MN), 2007.

Jacklyn Williams, *Pick a Pet, Gus!,* Picture Window Books (Minneapolis, MN), 2007.

ILLUSTRATOR; "HANDS-ON EARLY-LEARNING SCIENCE ACTIVITIES" SERIES

Seymour Simon and Nicole Fauteux, *Let's Try It out in the Water,* Simon & Schuster (New York, NY), 2001.

Seymour Simon and Nicole Fauteux, *Let's Try It out in the Air,* Simon & Schuster (New York, NY), 2001.

Seymour Simon and Nicole Fauteux, *Let's Try It out on the Playground,* Simon & Schuster (New York, NY), 2002.

Sidelights

Doug Cushman is an author and illustrator of well-received books for children, many of them mystery stories featuring the detective characters Aunt Eater, Seymour Sleuth, and Inspector Hopper. A popular collaborator, he has provided artwork for picture books penned by authors that include Jane Yolen, Douglas Wood, Marcia Leonard, Jack Prelutsky, and Michael Berenstain. "To use the old cliché, I draw for the child I was," Cushman told *Cynsations* online interviewer Lawrence Schimel. "I've always believed that there is no drawing, no art, especially geared for children. It's all either good art or bad art. I think it was [Maurice] Sendak who said 'You cannot write for children . . . you can only write books that will interest them.'"

In the works that Cushman has written and illustrated, including *The Mystery of King Karfu, Space Cat,* and *What a Day It Was at School!,* his emphasis on character is evident in both text and artwork. As he once commented: "A good character will almost write a book by himself with a little nudge or two from the author." Indeed, vivid characters abound in books such as *Possum Stew,* wherein mischievous Possum ties together Bear and Gator's fishing lines, tricking the friends into believing they have hooked the "Big Catfish." When the two fall into the water trying to pull in their enormous catch, Possum sneaks off with their full baskets of fish. Wanting to even the score, Bear and Gator plan a surprise of their own for Possum. Beth Herbert, writing in *Booklist,* called *Possum Stew* a "knee-slapping tale,"

while a reviewer for *Kirkus Reviews* noted that the story's humor is enhanced by the "expressive faces" in Cushman's "uncluttered illustrations." *School Library Journal* contributor Sally R. Dow also commented favorably on the author/illustrator's fictional creations, maintaining that Cushman's "light-hearted" illustrations "capture the mischievous spirit of the animals."

The ABC Mystery, another of Cushman's self-illustrated stories, is an alphabet primer charged with a mystery. The letter "A" states the crime—stolen Art—and the mystery, told in rhyming couplets, continues to unfold as Detective McGroom, a badger, pursues clues attached to successive letters of the alphabet. Calling the book a "fresh approach to the ABC's," *School Library Journal* contributor Jody McCoy claimed that *The ABC Mystery* would attract children with its "bright cartoon creatures skillfully rendered." *Booklist* reviewer Deborah Abbott suggested the book be used as a "kickoff for mystery units in the primary grades," and praised Cushman's illustrations for their "touches of melodrama and humor." A *Publishers Weekly* commentator stated that repeated readings would give "budding detectives" more chances to "spot new clues," describing the picture book as a "cunning twist on the traditional ABC" primer.

Cushman has followed the success of his *ABC Mystery* with more tales of intrigue, among them *Aunt Eater's*

Cushman's art adds to the party atmosphere in Pat Mora's picture book **Marimba! Animales from A to Z.** (Illustration copyright © 2006 by Doug Cushman. Reprinted by permission of Houghton Mifflin Company. All rights reserved.)

Mystery Christmas, The Mystery of King Karfu, and *Aunt Eater's Mystery Halloween. Booklist* reviewer Linda Perkins offered high praise for *The Mystery of King Karfu,* declaring that it will "delight mystery aficionados." In this story, wombat detective Seymour Sleuth investigates a stone chicken stolen in Egypt. Seymour and Abbott Muggs, his sidekick, catch the thief after uncovering a critical clue. Cushman designed the book as an actual detective's casebook, with investigative notes, photographs, coffee stains, and business receipts (including a camel rental) all related to the investigation. Perkins noted that the illustrated details add "silliness, suspense, and intrigue." Steven Engelfried, a *School Library Journal* contributor, described the notebook as a "clear and insightful look at how a detective puts evidence together." Engelfried also noted a "clue-filled plot, plenty of humor, and an innovative presentation" that he predicted will create a demand for more "Seymour Sleuth" mysteries.

In *Inspector Hopper* Cushman introduces two new sleuths, the dapperly dressed grasshopper Inspector Hopper and his sidekick, the bowler hat-wearing beetle McBugg. The book, intended for early elementary students who are just beginning to read independently, features three separate mystery tales. Mr. Ladybug's wife disappears in the first story, and does not return when he calls her. However, with the help of Inspector Hopper and McBugg she is soon found, safe and sound. In the second tale, "A Boat Disappears," a mosquito named Skeet loses its leaf boat. Inspector Hopper interrogates several other insects, including the Eensy Weensy Spider and a snail that jogs, before finding the culprit: Conrad the caterpillar, who ate the small vessel. In the final installment, Inspector Hopper and McBugg track down a rat—literally—with the help of the moon. Reviewers *Inspector Hopper,* Maura Bresnahan writing in *School Library Journal* that "the short sentences, catchy dialogue, and repetitive vocabulary are just right for beginning readers." Other critics praised Cushman's "handsome watercolors," as Gillian Engberg described them in *Booklist,* adding that they "will draw children in with their bug's-eye view of the world."

Inspector Hopper and McBugg return to solve four more conundrums in *Inspector Hopper's Mystery Year.* Here Cushman presents one mystery per season. In the fall, Emma Worm asks the detectives to help her figure out who is apparently haunting a pumpkin. In the winter a doctor disappears, rather inconveniently for Inspector Hopper as he has a cold that he would like to have treated. A young beetle-child goes missing in the spring, and in the summer a cricket named Holly loses her sheet music; as it turns out, it was stolen by a wasp who needed materials to help him paper over a hole in his nest. Each of these four stories "is just the right length for sharing aloud or independent reading," wrote *School Library Journal* contributor Wanda Meyers-Hines, who also called *Inspector Hopper's Mystery Year* "a fun selection for units on insects." As a *Kirkus*

Cushman's illustration projects include his work for Lynn E. Hazen's picture book **The Amazing Trail of Seymour Snail.** (Illustration copyright © 2009 by Doug Cushman. Reprinted by arrangement with Henry Holt & Company, LLC.)

Reviews contributor noted, "Cushman drops visual clues to let readers participate in the solutions to the mysteries [and] sight gags to keep the stories lively."

An elephant named Nick Trunk is the detective in *Mystery at the Club Sandwich.* The book openly spoofs classic film noir detective stories such as *The Maltese Falcon;* it is even dedicated to "Sam, Phil and Dashiell"—as in the famous noir detective Sam Spade, his creator Dashiell Hammett, and Philip Marlowe, the detective created by author Raymond Chandler. As with all good noir tales, *Mystery at the Club Sandwich* opens with "trouble" walking through the door: Maggie Trouble, a cat who works at the Club Sandwich as an assistant to star cabaret singer Lola Gale. Gale's lucky marbles have been stolen, and she wants Nick Trunk's help in recovering them. "Readers will guess the villain early on," commented *School Library Journal* reviewer Marie Orlando, "but that won't interfere with their enjoyment of the droll story."

In *Dirk Bones and the Mystery of the Haunted House* Cushman introduces another unconventional sleuth. When Dirk Bones, a skeletal reporter for the *Ghostly Tombs,* learns that residents of Ghoul Street are complaining about the spooky sounds coming from their cellars, he launches an investigation that leads him to a nearby graveyard filled with a host of surprisingly amiable creatures. "Cushman's illustrations are delightfully silly and spirited," observed *School Library Journal* contributor Gloria Koster, and a critic in *Kirkus Reviews* praised "the shivery delights that await emergent readers in this not-too-creepy caper."

Cushman has also received favorable notice for the pictures he has provided for scores of works by many different authors. Among these efforts is *Valentine Mice!*, one of a series of books by Bethany Roberts that also includes *Thanksgiving Mice!, Halloween Mice!,* and *Christmas Mice!* In this tale, four mice celebrate a wintry Valentine's Day by passing out holiday cards to all the woodland animals. Amid all the excitement, hardly anyone notices that the youngest mouse has disappeared. "Motion-filled, festive watercolors humorously document the rescue of the missing mouse," asserted a *Publishers Weekly* reviewer. Praising the successful union of words and pictures, a *Kirkus Reviews* critic claimed that the "rhythmic text and action-packed line and watercolor illustrations will draw young readers in." A shy writer who needs peace and quiet gets a noisy new neighbor in *The Bear Upstairs,* a work by Shirley Mozelle. When the two finally meet, however, they find they have more in common than they imagined. In the words of a *Publishers Weekly* critic, "Cushman's expressive, huggable creatures exude an instantly recognizable humanity."

Cushman joins forces with friend and award-winning poet Prelutsky for *What a Day It Was at School!* The volume of humorous verse depicts one exciting day at a school for critters and chronicles such adventures as an author visit and a food fight. "Cushman has created an appealing school environment with a variety of colorful cartoon animal characters," remarked *School Library Journal* contributor Carol L. MacKay, and Engberg stated that the illustrator's "active scenes extend the jokes and images in the words." In another rhyming work, Stephanie Calmenson's *Birthday at the Panda Palace,* Mouse invites her friends, including jumping monkeys and laughing hyenas, to a special dinner, and they provide an assortment of clues to help her identify her presents. According to Marge Loch-Wouters in *School Library Journal,* "Cushman's bright and cheery illustrations echo the lively rhymes."

In Judy Sierra's *What Time Is It, Mr. Crocodile?,* a hungry creature has trouble rounding up his dinner, a batch of pesky monkeys. Noting that Cushman illustrates the work in acrylics instead of his customary watercolors, *School Library Journal* reviewer Sean George remarked that "this bolder, brighter medium and method depict the action and hilarity even more effectively than his past work." A tiny pig with a knack for solving problems is the focus of *Ella, of Course!,* a tale by Sarah Weeks. When Ella gets a new umbrella as a gift, however, she creates havoc wherever she goes. To make amends, Ella must come up with a creative fix. Cushman's illustrations "make this very human theme of a

child's need to carry a much loved item come alive," noted a critic in *Kirkus Reviews.*

Although he has more than one hundred books to his credit, Cushman shows no signs of slowing down. As he stated in an essay in the *Children's Book Council Magazine,* "There are always surprises in the business of picture book writing and illustrating; the possibility of something unexpected popping up; an odd character, a new twist on an old theme, the opportunity to experiment with a different painting technique. And for me, these surprises are the greatest joy of writing for children."

Biographical and Critical Sources

PERIODICALS

Booklist, March 1, 1990, Beth Herbert, review of *Possum Stew,* p. 1338; November 15, 1993, Deborah Abbott, review of *The ABC Mystery,* p. 629; April 1, 1994, Denia Hester, review of *Mouse and Mole and the Year-Round Garden,* p. 1458; January 1 & 15, 1997, Linda Perkins, review of *The Mystery of King Karfu,* p. 869; April 15, 2000, Gillian Engberg, review of *Inspector Hopper,* p. 1555; July, 2004, Carolyn Phelan, review of *Space Cat,* p. 1850; September 15, 2004, Lauren Peterson, review of *What Time Is It, Mr. Crocodile?,* p. 254; April 15, 2005, Shelle Rosenfeld, review of *Where's My Tail?,* p. 1462; August 1, 2006, Gillian Engberg, review of *What a Day It Was at School!,* p. 96; August 1, 2006, Jennifer Mattson, review of *Dirk Bones and the Mystery of the Haunted House,* p. 84; November 1, 2006, Shelle Rosenfeld, review of *Albert's Gift for Grandmother,* p. 62; February 15, 2007, Gillian Engberg, review of *Ella, of Course!,* p. 86.
California Kids!, February, 1999, Patricia Newman, "Who Wrote That? Featuring Doug Cushman."
Horn Book, July, 2000, review of *Inspector Hopper,* p. 454; September-October, 2006, Susan Dove Lempke, review of *What a Day It Was at School!,* p. 602.
Instructor, November-December, 2001, Judy Freeman, review of *Inspector Hopper,* pp. 12-14.
Kirkus Reviews, January 15, 1990, review of *Possum Stew,* p. 103; December 1, 1997, review of *Valentine Mice!,* p. 1778; March 1, 2003, review of *Inspector Hopper's Mystery Year,* p. 381; May 15, 2004, review of *Space Cat,* p. 489; July 1, 2004, review of *What Time Is It, Mr. Crocodile?,* p. 636; September 1, 2004, review of *Mystery at the Club Sandwich,* p. 863; August 1, 2005, review of *The Bear Upstairs,* p. 855; June 1, 2006, review of *What a Day It Was at School!,* p. 578; July 1, 2006, review of *Dirk Bones and the Mystery of the Haunted House,* p. 675; October 15, 2006, review of *¡Marimba!: Animales from A to Z,* p. 1075; March 1, 2007, review of *Ella, of Course!,* p. 233; June 1, 2007, review of *Birthday at the Panda Palace.*
Publishers Weekly, December 1, 1997, review of *Valentine Mice!,* p. 52; August 2, 1998, review of *The ABC Mystery,* p. 78; December 13, 2004, review of *Mys-*

tery at the Club Sandwich, p. 68; October 24, 2005, review of *The Bear Upstairs,* p. 56; June 12, 2006, review of *What a Day It Was at School!,* p. 52.

School Library Journal, February, 1990, Sally R. Dow, review of *Possum Stew,* p. 72; February, 1994, Jody McCoy, review of *The ABC Mystery,* p. 83; February, 1997, Steven Engelfried, review of *The Mystery of King Karfu,* pp. 74-75; July, 2000, Maura Bresnahan, review of *Inspector Hopper,* p. 70; May, 2003, Wanda Meyers-Hines, review of *Inspector Hopper's Mystery Year,* pp. 110-111; September, 2004, Sean George, review of *What Time Is It, Mr. Crocodile?,* p. 180; January, 2005, Marie Orlando, review of *Mystery at the Club Sandwich,* p. 89; May, 2005, Catherine Callegari, review of *Where's My Tail?,* p. 96; July, 2005, Kathleen Whalin, review of *What Grandmas Can't Do,* p. 85; November, 2005, Wendy Woodfill, review of *The Bear Upstairs,* p. 102; July, 2006, Gloria Koster, review of *Dirk Bones and the Mystery of the Haunted House,* p. 71, and Carol L. MacKay, review of *What a Day It Was at School!,* p. 92; November, 2006, Kirsten Cutler, review of *¡Marimba!,* p. 106; December, 2006, Sherry Quinones, review of *Albert's Gift for Grandmother,* p. 118; March, 2007, Kathleen Whalin, review of *Ella, of Course!,* p. 189; September, 2007, Marge Loch-Wouters, review of *Birthday at the Panda Palace,* p. 160.

ONLINE

Children's Book Council Web site, http://www.cbcbooks. org/cbcmagazine/ (March 1, 2008), "Meet the Author/ Illustrator: Doug Cushman."

Cynsations Web site, http://cynthialeitichsmith.blogspot. com/ (March 7, 2006), Lawrence Schimel, interview with Cushman.

Doug Cushman Home Page, http://www.doug-cushman. com (March 1, 2008).*

D

DAVIS, Jack E.

Personal
Born in NE.

Addresses
Home—Port Townsend, WA. *Agent*—MB Artists, 10 E. 29th St., Ste. 40G, New York, NY 10016.

Career
Illustrator. Worked as the manager of a printing company and as a designer and senior art director at an advertising agency.

Illustrator

Martha Sacks, *Menopaws: The Silent Meow,* Ten Speed Press (Berkeley, CA), 1995.

Mark Karlins, *Music over Manhattan,* Bantam Doubleday (New York, NY), 1998.

Diane Cuneo, *Mary Louise Loses Her Manners,* Doubleday (New York, NY), 1999.

Margie Palatini, *Bedhead,* Simon & Schuster (New York, NY), 2000.

Marsha Diane Arnold, *Metro Cat,* Golden Books (New York, NY), 2001.

John Lithgow, *Marsupial Sue* (includes CD), Simon & Schuster (New York, NY), 2001.

Judy Sierra, *Monster Goose,* Harcourt (San Diego, CA), 2001.

Cathy Stefanec-Ogren, *The Adventures of Archie Featherspoon,* Aladdin (New York, NY), 2002.

Amy Axelrod, *My Last Chance Brother,* Dutton (New York, NY), 2002.

Amy Axelrod, *They'll Believe Me When I'm Gone,* Dutton (New York, NY), 2003.

Bonnie Becker, *Just a Minute,* Simon & Schuster (New York, NY), 2003.

Daniel Pinkwater, *The Picture of Morty and Ray,* Harper-Collins (New York, NY), 2003.

Lynn Downey, *Most Loved Monster,* Dial Books (New York, NY), 2004.

Margie Palatini, *Sweet Tooth,* Simon & Schuster (New York, NY), 2004.

Allan Sherman and Lou Busch, *Hello Muddah, Hello Faddah! A Letter from Camp,* Dutton (New York, NY), 2004.

Joe Fallon and Ken Scarborough, *Halfway Hank,* HarperCollins (New York, NY), 2005.

Lois G. Grambling, *T. Rex Trick-or-Treats,* Katherine Tegen Books (New York, NY), 2005.

John Lithgow, *Marsupial Sue Presents "The Runaway Pancake"* (includes CD), Simon & Schuster (New York, NY), 2005.

Karma Wilson, *Moose Tracks!,* Margaret K. McElderry Books (New York, NY), 2006.

Caralyn Buehner, *Would I Ever Lie to You?,* Dial Books (New York, NY), 2007.

Lois G. Grambling, *Here Comes T. Rex Cottontail,* Katherine Tegen Books (New York, NY), 2007.

Daniel Pinkwater, *Yo-Yo Man,* HarperCollins (New York, NY), 2007.

Lois G. Grambling, *T. Rex and the Mother's Day Hug,* Katherine Tegen Books (New York, NY), 2008.

Bill Harley, *Dirty Joe, the Pirate: A True Story,* Harper-Collins (New York, NY), 2008.

Zachary Shapiro, *We're All in the Same Boat,* Putnam (New York, NY), 2008.

Jill Esbaum, *Stanza,* Harcourt (Orlando, FL), 2009.

Marsha Hayles, *Bunion Burt,* Atheneum Books for Young Readers (New York, NY), 2009.

"ZACK FILES" CHAPTER BOOK SERIES BY DAN GREENBURG

Great-Grandpa's in the Litter Box, Grosset & Dunlap (New York, NY), 1996.

Through the Medicine Cabinet, Grosset & Dunlap (New York, NY), 1996.

A Ghost Named Wanda, Grosset & Dunlap (New York, NY), 1996.

Zap! I'm a Mind Reader, Grosset & Dunlap (New York, NY), 1996.

Dr. Jekyll, Orthodontist, Grosset & Dunlap (New York, NY), 1997.

I'm Out of My Body. . . . Please Leave a Message, Grosset & Dunlap (New York, NY), 1997.

Never Trust a Cat Who Wears Earrings, Grosset & Dunlap (New York, NY), 1997.

My Son, the Time Traveler, Grosset & Dunlap (New York, NY), 1997.

The Volcano Goddess Will See You Now, Grosset & Dunlap (New York, NY), 1997.

Bozo the Clone, Grosset & Dunlap (New York, NY), 1997.

How to Speak Dolphin in Three Easy Lessons, Grosset & Dunlap (New York, NY), 1997.

Now You See Me—Now You Don't, Grosset & Dunlap (New York, NY), 1998.

The Misfortune Cookie, Grosset & Dunlap (New York, NY), 1998.

Elvis the Turnip—and Me, Grosset & Dunlap (New York, NY), 1998.

Yipes! Grandma's a Teenager, Grosset & Dunlap (New York, NY), 1999.

How I Fixed the Year 1000 Problem, Grosset & Dunlap (New York, NY), 1999.

Hang a Left at Venus, Grosset & Dunlap (New York, NY), 1999.

Evil Queen Tut and the Great Ant Pyramids, Grosset & Dunlap (New York, NY), 1999.

This Body's Not Big Enough for Both of Us, Grosset & Dunlap (New York, NY), 2000.

How I Went from Bad to Verse, Grosset & Dunlap (New York, NY), 2000.

Don't Count on Dracula, Grosset & Dunlap (New York, NY), 2000.

The Boy Who Cried Bigfoot, Grosset & Dunlap (New York, NY), 2000.

My Grandma, Major-League Slugger, Grosset & Dunlap (New York, NY), 2001.

Greenish Eggs and Dinosaurs, Grosset & Dunlap (New York, NY), 2001.

Me and My Mummy, Grosset & Dunlap (New York, NY), 2001.

Trapped in the Museum of Unnatural History, Grosset & Dunlap (New York, NY), 2002.

Tell a Lie and Your Butt Will Grow, Grosset & Dunlap (New York, NY), 2002.

My Teacher Ate My Homework, Grosset & Dunlap (New York, NY), 2002.

Just Add Water and—Scream!, Grosset & Dunlap (New York, NY), 2002.

It's Itchcraft!, Grosset & Dunlap (New York, NY), 2003.

Sidelights

Jack E. Davis is a highly regarded illustrator of children's books, including such bestselling works as Daniel Pinkwater's *The Picture of Morty and Ray* and John Lithgow's *Marsupial Sue.* Davis, a self-trained artist who works primarily in acrylics and pencil, began his career as a designer and art director for an advertising agency before turning to freelance work. He counts among his influences the painters Charles Bragg and Fernando Botero.

Davis made his publishing debut in 1995, serving as the illustrator for *Menopaws: The Silent Meow,* a work by Martha Sacks. His first title for young readers, *Music over Manhattan* by Mark Karlins, appeared three years later. The story concerns Bernie, a youngster who finds himself overshadowed by his talented cousin until Uncle Louie teaches him to play the trumpet. "Droll caricatures cavort against a glorious Big Band-era backdrop," a *Publisher Weekly* critic observed of the book. In Diane Cuneo's *Mary Louise Loses Her Manners,* a rude little girl scours the neighborhood for her runaway sense of virtue. "Davis' full-color, exaggerated illustrations perfectly capture the humor of Cuneo's text, adding absurd details" to the story, wrote Kay Weisman in a *Booklist* review of the book's art.

Davis has collaborated with Margie Palatini on a pair of popular works for children. In *Bedhead,* young Oliver struggles with his unruly mop of hair on the very day his class will have its picture taken. Marianne Saccardi, writing in *School Library Journal,* complimented

Jack E. Davis's quirky cartoon art adds to the humor of Dan Greenberg's "Zack Files" novel **Great-Grandpa's in the Litter Box.** (Illustration copyright © 1996 by Jack E. Davis. Reproduced by permission of Grosset & Dunlap (Juvenile), a division of Penguin Putnam, Inc.)

Davis's "zany cartoon-style illustrations" and called the book "a delightful combination of text and pictures that will have readers coming back for more." A boy named Stewart is constantly nagged by his talking molar, which demands a steady diet of candy and cake in *Sweet Tooth*, "a deliciously sly story that will likely satisfy a craving for lively fun," according to a *Publishers Weekly* critic. *School Library Journal* contributor James K. Irwin maintained that Davis's "mixed-media cartoon artwork" for *Sweet Tooth* "extends the comedy of Palatini's text and enriches her characterization of Stewart."

Davis teams up with award-winning actor Lithgow on *Marsupial Sue* and *Marsupial Sue Presents "The Runaway Pancake."* In the former, a kangaroo who detests hopping tries to fit in with the koalas and platypuses. "Davis's charming illustrations, rendered in colored pencil, acrylics and ink, are full of personifying characteristics," a *Publishers Weekly* reviewer noted. In Lithgow's sequel, Sue enlists Bartholomew Koala, Sydney Wombat, and other friends to help her put on a show. "Colored-pencil, acrylic and ink illustrations packed with wacky details are entertaining in their own right," stated a *Kirkus Reviews* contributor in reviewing the second Davis-Lithgow collaboration.

Davis joins forces with celebrated author Pinkwater for *The Picture of Morty and Ray*, a work inspired by *The Picture of Dorian Gray*. After viewing the film version of Oscar Wilde's classic tale, two mischievous youngsters watch their self-portraits grow uglier with each prank they pull. According to *Booklist* critic Terry Glover, "Davis' wry, delightful illustrations bathe the rather dark, gloomy tale in a kid-friendly light." In *Yo-Yo Man*, another Pinkwater tale, a timid third-grader gains the admiration of his classmates by displaying his amazing skills with a yo-yo. Here Davis's illustrations "are colorful and jam-packed with detail, energy, and expression," remarked Marge Loch-Wouters in her *School Library Journal* review of the book.

In *T. Rex Trick-or-Treats,* a work by Lois G. Grambling, the huge dinosaur has trouble finding an appropriately scary Halloween costume. "Davis has created a non-threatening dino world with his cartoon-like line-and-watercolor illustrations," Angela J. Reynolds wrote in a *School Library Journal* reveiw of Grambling's picture book. In a follow-up, *Here Comes T. Rex Cottontail,* the tyrannosaurus agrees to help the sickly Easter Bunny deliver baskets of eggs. In the words of a *Kirkus Reviews* contributor, "T. Rex cuts a deliciously silly figure in Davis's frenzied cartoons." Davis and Grambling have also collaborated on *T. Rex and the Mother's Day Hug.*

Davis has enjoyed a long partnership with Dan Greenburg, author of the "Zack Files" series of chapter books. Inspired by Greenburg's son, the works follow ten-year-old Zack as he gets tangled up in a string of remarkable situations, many of them playing upon children's fascination with the supernatural and paranormal. In *Tell a*

Lie and Your Butt Will Grow, Zack's best friend, Andrew, watches his rear end enlarge with each yarn he spins. Davis's "amusing cartoon drawings" for this book "illustrate Andrew's posterior problem without slipping over into gross details," wrote *School Library Journal* reviewer Elaine E. Knight.

With Davis's assistance, Judy Sierra takes a macabre look at classic Mother Goose rhymes in *Monster Goose,* and here "Davis's acrylic and colored-pencil illustrations are appropriately amusing and disgusting," remarked a *Kirkus Reviews* contributor. In *Hello Muddah, Hello Faddah! A Letter from Camp,* Allan Sherman and Lou Busch's adaptation of a popular 1960s novelty song, a distressed youngster notes—with some exaggeration—the many things that have gone awry at his summer camp, including ptomaine poisoning and an outbreak of malaria. Davis presents a host of "pop-eyed young campers with oversized heads and sunburned noses," noted a *Kirkus Reviews* critic, and a reviewer in *Publishers Weekly* stated that the illustrator "brings a comic sense of heightened drama to the proceedings" in the quirky story.

Four little creatures vie for their mother's attention in Lynn Downey's *Most Loved Monster,* another book illustrated by Davis. "The pages are bursting with color and energy, as well as humorous details," observed Wanda Meyers-Hines in a *School Library Journal* review of the book. *Moose Tracks!,* featuring a story by Karma Wilson, finds a homeowner puzzled by the many

Davis contributes to the humor of Zachary Shapiro's middle-grade novel **We're All in the Same Boat.** (Illustration copyright © 2009 by Jack E. Davis. Reproduced by permission.)

hoofprints that appear throughout his house. "Viewers will like the witty, colorful art, with its expressive cartoonlike animal character," observed Shelle Rosenfeld in reviewing the story for *Booklist.* A gullible young boy has trouble distinguishing his cousin's fibs from the truth in Caralyn Buehner's *Would I Ever Lie to You?*, and here, wrote Lynda Ritterman in *School Library Journal,* Davis's "large, detailed cartoon illustrations in watercolor, acrylics, colored pencil, and ink add a great deal of interest and humor to the tale."

Zachary Shapiro's *We're All in the Same Boat* recreates the animals' journey on Noah's Ark. Initially all of the animals are excited about their cruise, but they quickly grow tired of the torrential rain. Initially they are angry with Noah, but their mood changes as they realize that they are all enduring the same misery. Kathy Piehl, reviewing the book in *School Library Journal,* described *We're All in the Same Boat* as "a humorous alphabet story with an underlying message of cooperation" and illustrations that are "hilarious." A *Kirkus Reviews* critic also enjoyed the book's art, writing that "Davis's illustrations provide clever details . . . and expressive faces convey the animals' emotions."

Jill Esbaum's *Stanza* also features illustrations by Davis. Stanza is a stray dog that writes poetry in secret for fear that his two streetwise brothers will ridicule him. When he enters a poetry contest, his secret is discovered. Calling the watercolor illustrations "hilariously busy," he is scared, a contributor to *Kirkus Reviews* enjoyed the story's humor, noting that "young writers and poets may well enjoy watching Stanza's creative process."

Biographical and Critical Sources

PERIODICALS

Booklist, August, 1998, GraceAnne A. DeCandido, review of *Music over Manhattan,* p. 2015; November 1, 1999, Kay Weisman, review of *Mary Louise Loses Her Manners,* p. 537; June 1, 2001, Amy Brandt, review of *Metro Cat,* p. 1888; September 15, 2001, Gillian Engberg, review of *Monster Goose,* p. 237; July, 2002, Julie Cummins, review of *My Last Chance Brother,* p. 1853; September 15, 2003, Terry Glover, review of *The Picture of Morty and Ray,* p. 248; October 1, 2004, Todd Morning, review of *Sweet Tooth,* p. 335; September 1, 2005, Jennifer Mattson, review of *T. Rex Trick-or-Treats,* p. 144; November 1, 2005, Julie Cummins, review of *Marsupial Sue Presents "The Runaway Pancake,"* p. 53; February 15, 2006, Shelle Rosenfeld, review of *Moose Tracks!,* p. 106; January 1, 2009, Hazel Rochman, review of *We're All in the Same Boat,* p. 96.

Kirkus Reviews, August 1, 2001, review of *Monster Goose,* p. 1131; August 15, 2001, review of *Marsupial Sue,* p. 1215; July 1, 2002, review of *My Last Chance Brother,* p. 948; June 1, 2003, review of *They'll Believe Me When I'm Gone,* p. 800; July 1, 2003, review of *The Picture of Morty and Ray,* p. 913; April 15, 2004, review of *Hello Muddah, Hello Faddah! A Letter from Camp,* p. 401; July 15, 2004, review of *Most Loved Monster,* p. 683; April 15, 2005, review of *Halfway Hank,* p. 473; August 15, 2005, review of *T. Rex Trick-or-Treats,* p. 914; September 1, 2005, review of *Marsupial Sue Presents "The Runaway Pancake,"* p. 977; January 1, 2006, review of *Moose Tracks!,* p. 47; December 15, 2006, review of *Here Comes T. Rex Cottontail,* p. 1268; June 1, 2007, review of *Yo-Yo Man;* December 15, 2008, review of *We're All in the Same Boat;* April 1, 2009, review of *Stanza.*

Publishers Weekly, July 20, 1998, review of *Music over Manhattan,* p. 219; May 31, 1999, review of *Mary Louise Loses Her Manners,* p. 92; April, 16 2001, review of *Metro Cat,* p. 64; July 23, 2001, review of *Marsupial Sue,* p. 75; August 13, 2001, review of *Monster Goose,* p. 312; July 1, 2002, review of *My Last Chance Brother,* p. 79; September 15, 2003, review of *Just a Minute,* p. 64; May 24, 2004, review of *Hello Muddah, Hello Faddah!,* p. 62; August 9, 2004, review of *Most Loved Monster,* p. 250; November 1, 2004, review of *Sweet Tooth,* p. 60; August 1, 2005, review of *T. Rex Trick-or-Treats,* p. 63; March 27, 2006, review of *Moose Tracks!,* p. 78; May 28, 2007, review of *Would I Ever Lie to You?,* p. 61; July 23, 2007, review of *Yo-Yo Man,* p. 67.

School Library Journal, July, 2000, Marianne Saccardi, review of *Bedhead,* p. 84; September, 2001, Gay Lynn Van Vleck, review of *Monster Goose,* p. 254; November, 2001, Patti Gonzales, review of *Marsupial Sue,* p. 128; September, 2002, Rosalyn Pierini, review of *My Last Chance Brother,* p. 180; April, 2003, Elaine E. Knight, review of *Tell a Lie and Your Butt Will Grow,* p. 121; September, 2003, Linda Ludke, review of *They'll Believe Me When I'm Gone,* p. 168, and Steven Engelfried, review of *The Picture of Morty and Ray,* p. 187; June, 2004, Kathleen Simonetta, review of *Hello Muddah, Hello Faddah!,* p. 132; August, 2004, Wanda Meyers-Hines, review of *Most Loved Monster,* p. 85; November, 2004, James K. Irwin, review of *Sweet Tooth,* p. 114; May, 2005, Melinda Piehler, review of *Halfway Hank,* p. 82; August, 2005, Angela J. Reynolds, review of *T. Rex Trick-or-Treats,* p. 95; April, 2006, Susan E. Murray, review of *Moose Tracks!,* p. 122; May, 2007, Lynda Ritterman, review of *Would I Ever Lie to You?,* p. 86, and Piper L. Nyman, review of *Here Comes T. Rex Cottontail,* p. 97; September, 2007, Marge Loch-Wouters, review of *Yo-Yo Man,* p. 174; March 1, 2008, Joan Kindig, review of *T. Rex and the Mother's Day Hug,* p. 164; May 1, 2008, Marge Loch-Wouters, review of *Dirty Joe, the Pirate: A True Story,* p. 100; January 1, 2009, Kathy Piehl, review of *We're All in the Same Boat,* p. 86.

ONLINE

MB Artists Web site, http://www.mbartists.com/ (March 1, 2008), "Jack E. Davis."*

DEMI 1942-
(Demi Hitz, Charlotte Dumaresq Hunt)

Personal

Born Charlotte Dumaresq Hunt, September 2, 1942, in Cambridge, MA; daughter of William Morris (an architect, actor, and entrepreneur) and Rosamond (an artist) Hunt; married John Rawlins Hitz (a teacher and writer), December 18, 1965 (marriage ended); married Tze Si (Jesse) Huang; children: (first marriage) John. *Education:* Attended Instituto Allende and Rhode Island School of Design; Immaculate Heart College, B.A., 1962; University of Baroda (Gujarat, India), M.A., 1963; additional graduate study at China Institute. *Hobbies and other interests:* Travel (has been to Mexico, Guatemala, Brazil, Chile, England, and Japan).

Addresses

Home—Carnation, WA. *Agent*—Julian Bach, Inc., 747 3rd Ave., New York, NY 10017.

Career

Artist, writer, and book illustrator. Has painted murals in Mexico, and painted the dome of St. Peter and Paul Church in Wilmington, CA. Speaker at colleges, universities, libraries, and children's events; Fulbright fellow, 1962. *Exhibitions:* Works included in exhibitions staged by Society of Illustrators.

Member

China Institute.

Awards, Honors

Awards from *Boston Globe* scholastic competitions, California State Fair, California Arts and Science Fair, Los Angeles County Museum, and Los Angeles Outdoor Art Festival, all 1961-62; Notable Book selection, American Library Association (ALA), 1980, for *Liang and the Magic Paintbrush; New York Times* Best Illustrated Children's Book selection, 1985, for *The Nightingale;* International Reading Association (IRA) Notable Book for a Global Society selection, for *Grass Sandals: The Travels of Basho;* Aesop Accolades, Children's Folklore Section of American Folklore Society, 1999, for *The Donkey and the Rock; New York Times* Best Illustrated Children's Book selection, 2001, and Oppenheim Toy Portfolio Platinum Award, both for *Gandhi;* Middle East Book Award, Middle East Outreach Council, and *New York Times* Best Illustrated Children's Book selection, both for *Muhammad;* Christopher Award, 2005, Notable Books for a Global Society selection, IRA, and 100 Titles for Reading and Sharing selection, New York Public Library, all for *The Hungry Coat;* Notable Children's Book selection, ALA, for *Mother Teresa; Storytelling World* Award, for *The Greatest Power;* Notable Books for Children selection, ALA, 2007, for *Su Dongpo.*

Writings

SELF-ILLUSTRATED

(Adapter) *Lu Pan, the Carpenter's Apprentice,* Prentice-Hall, 1978.

The Book of Moving Pictures, Knopf (New York, NY), 1979.

Under the Shade of the Mulberry Tree, Prentice-Hall (Englewood Cliffs, NJ), 1979.

Where Is It?, Doubleday (New York, NY), 1980.

Liang and the Magic Paintbrush, Holt (New York, NY), 1980.

The Leaky Umbrella, Prentice-Hall (Englewood Cliffs, NJ), 1980.

The Adventures of Marco Polo, Holt (New York, NY), 1981.

Three Little Elephants, Random House (New York, NY), 1981.

Follow the Line (wordless story), Holt (New York, NY), 1981.

Where Is Willie Worm?, Random House (New York, NY), 1981.

Cinderella on Wheels, Holt (New York, NY), 1982.

Peek-a-Boo, Random House (New York, NY), 1982.

Watch Harry Growl, Random House (New York, NY), 1984.

Demi's Find the Animal A B C: An Alphabet-game Book, Putnam (New York, NY), 1985.

Demi's Count the Animals 1, 2, 3, Putnam (New York, NY), 1986.

Dragon Kites and Dragonflies: A Collection of Chinese Nursery Rhymes, Harcourt (New York, NY), 1986.

So Soft Kitty, Putnam (New York, NY), 1986.

Fuzzy Wuzzy Puppy, Putnam (New York, NY), 1986.

Chen Ping and His Magic Axe, Dodd (New York, NY), 1987.

Cuddly Chick, Putnam (New York, NY), 1987.

Fluffy Bunny, Grosset (New York, NY), 1987.

Demi's Opposites, Grosset (New York, NY), 1987.

Downy Duckling, Putnam (New York, NY), 1987.

Fleecy Lamb, Putnam (New York, NY), 1987.

The Hallowed Horse: A Folktale from India, Putnam (New York, NY), 1987.

A Chinese Zoo: Fables and Proverbs, Harcourt (New York, NY), 1988.

Demi's Reflective Fables, Putnam (New York, NY), 1988.

Find Demi's Dinosaurs: An Animal Game Book, Putnam (New York, NY), 1989.

Jolly Koala Bear, Putnam (New York, NY), 1989.

Roly Poly Panda, Putnam (New York, NY), 1989.

Demi's Basket of Books, Grosset (New York, NY), 1989.

Demi's Christmas Surprise, Putnam (New York, NY), 1990.

The Empty Pot, Holt (New York, NY), 1990.

Find Demi's Baby Animals: An Animal Game Book, Putnam (New York, NY), 1990.

The Magic Boat, Holt (New York, NY), 1990.

Find Demi's Sea Creatures: An Animal Game Book, Putnam (New York, NY), 1991.

The Artist and the Architect, Holt (New York, NY), 1991.

Chingis Khan, Holt (New York, NY), 1991.

Little Bitty Bunny, Putnam (New York, NY), 1992.

Little Chick Chick, Putnam (New York, NY), 1992.

In the Eyes of the Cat: Japanese Poetry for All Seasons, translated by Tze Si Huang, Holt (New York, NY), 1992.

Little Baby Lamb, Putnam (New York, NY), 1992.

Demi's Dozen Farm Friends, Holt (New York, NY), 1992.

Little Lucky Ducky, Putnam (New York, NY), 1993.

Demi's Secret Garden, Holt (New York, NY), 1993.

Demi's Dragons and Fantastic Creatures, Holt (New York, NY), 1993.

Demi's Dozen Good Eggs, Holt (New York, NY), 1993.

Demi's Dozen Dinosaurs, Holt (New York, NY), 1994.

Santa's Furry Friends, Holt (New York, NY), 1994.

The Magic Tapestry: A Chinese Folktale, Holt (New York, NY), 1994.

The Firebird: A Russian Folktale, Holt (New York, NY), 1994.

The Stonecutter, Crown (New York, NY), 1995.

Buddha, Holt (New York, NY), 1995.

The Dragon's Tale and Other Animal Fables of the Chinese Zodiac, Holt (New York, NY), 1996.

Su Tong Po, St. Martin's Press (New York, NY), 1996.

Buddha Stories, Holt (New York, NY), 1997.

One Grain of Rice: A Mathematical Folktale, Scholastic (New York, NY), 1997.

The Greatest Treasure, Scholastic (New York, NY), 1998.

The Dalai Lama: A Biography of the Tibetan Spiritual and Political Leader, Holt (New York, NY), 1998.

Happy New Year! Kung-hsi Fa-Ts'ai!, Crown (New York, NY), 1998.

The Donkey and the Rock, Holt (New York, NY), 1999.

Kites: Magic Wishes That Fly up to the Sky, Crown (New York, NY), 1999.

The Emperor's New Clothes: A Tale Set in China, Margaret K. McElderry Books (New York, NY), 2000.

King Midas: The Golden Touch, Margaret K. McElderry Books (New York, NY), 2001.

Gandhi, Margaret K. McElderry Books (New York, NY), 2001.

Muhammad, Margaret K. McElderry Books (New York, NY), 2003.

The Legend of Saint Nicholas, Margaret K. McElderry Books (New York, NY), 2003.

Happy, Happy Chinese New Year!, Crown (New York, NY), 2003.

The Hungry Coat: A Tale from Turkey, Margaret K. McElderry Books (New York, NY), 2004.

The Greatest Power, Margaret K. McElderry Books (New York, NY), 2004.

Mother Teresa, Margaret K. McElderry Books (New York, NY), 2005.

Jesus: Based on the King James Version of the Holy Bible, Margaret K. McElderry Books (New York, NY), 2005.

Mary, Margaret K. McElderry Books (New York, NY), 2005.

Su Dongpo: Chinese Genius, Lee & Low Books (New York, NY), 2006.

The Boy Who Painted Dragons, Margaret K. McElderry Books (New York, NY), 2007.

The Legend of Lao Tzu and the Tao Te Ching, Margaret K. McElderry Books (New York, NY), 2007.

The Girl Who Drew a Phoenix, Margaret K. McElderry Books (New York, NY), 2008.

The Magic Pillow, Margaret K. McElderry Books (New York, NY), 2008.

Marco Polo, Marshall Cavendish (New York, NY), 2008.

Tutankhamun, Marshall Cavendish (Tarrytown, NY), 2008.

Genghis Khan, Marshall Cavendish (New York, NY), 2009.

Rumi: Whirling Dervish, Marshall Cavendish (New York, NY), 2009.

ILLUSTRATOR

Partap Sharma, *The Surangini Tales,* Harcourt (New York, NY), 1973.

Lu Yu, *The Classic of Tea,* translation by Francis Ross Carpenter, Little, Brown (Boston, MA), 1974.

Smith and Wardhough, *Feelings,* Macmillan (New York, NY), 1975.

Tom Glazer, *The Tom Glazer Guitar Book,* Warner Brothers, 1976.

Francis Ross Carpenter, *The Old China Trade: Americans in Canton, 1784-1843,* Coward, 1976.

Augusta Goldin, *The Shape of Water,* Doubleday (New York, NY), 1979.

Yushin Yoo, *Bong Nam and the Pheasants,* Prentice-Hall (Englewood Cliffs, NJ), 1979.

Jane Yolen, *Dragon Night and Other Lullabies,* Methuen (London, England), 1980.

Ann S. McGrath, *Tone's Tunnel,* Prentice-Hall (Englewood Cliffs, NJ), 1981.

Miriam Chaikin, *Light Another Candle: The Story and Meaning of Hanukkah,* Clarion Books (New York, NY), 1981.

Chaikin, *Make Noise, Make Merry: The Story and Meaning of Purim,* Ticknor & Fields (New York, NY), 1986.

Hans Christian Andersen, *The Nightingale,* Harcourt (New York, NY), 1988.

Hans Christian Andersen, *Thumbelina,* Putnam (New York, NY), 1989.

Ann Tompert, *Bamboo Hats and a Rice Cake,* Crown (New York, NY), 1993.

Aleksandr Pushkin, *The Magic Gold Fish: A Russian Folktale,* Holt (New York, NY), 1995.

J. Alison James, *Eucalyptus Wings,* Atheneum (New York, NY), 1995.

Dawnine Spivak, *Grass Sandals: The Travels of Basho,* Atheneum (New York, NY), 1997.

Illustrator of Time-Life Television's *The Wild, Wild World of Animals: The Cats,* Vineyard Books, 1976. Also illustrator of selected titles in "All about Your Name" series by Tom Glazer, Doubleday, 1978. Contributor of illustrations and stories to periodicals, including *New Yorker, Young Children, New York Times, Christian Science Monitor, Art News, China Trade Journal,* and *House and Garden.*

Sidelights

Known for crafting richly detailed and often brightly colored illustrations that are heavily influenced by Eastern themes, illustrator Demi has created more than one hundred books for children. Among these are adaptations of Chinese folktales, fables, and nursery rhymes; picture-book biographies; concept and puzzle books portraying animals from insects to dragons; and a series of novelty board books with tactile furry animals. Demi has received a number of honors during her career, including a Christopher Award for *The Hungry Coat: A Tale from Turkey* and a *Storytelling World* Award for *The Greatest Power.*

Throughout Demi's books runs the recurrent motif of things Asian, the influence not only of her travels in India and China, but also of her personal interest in

Buddhism. Reviewers have praised Demi's imaginative designs, her use of color, and her ability to blend text and illustration in her books for children. According to a contributor in the *St. James Guide to Children's Writers,* "the tales she creates and retells celebrate her ability to capture the magic of life on paper."

Born Charlotte Dumaresq Hunt on September 2, 1942, in Cambridge, Massachusetts, the illustrator would adopt her childhood nickname for her professional name. Demi was seemingly destined by biology for a career in the arts, as she grew up in one of the first families of American art. The great-granddaughter of

Demi's many self-illustrated picture books, which include **The Greatest Treasure,** *range across time and cultures.*

American painter William Morris Hunt and the great-grandniece of revered architect Richard Morris Hunt—known for his work on the Metropolitan Museum of Art—she grew up in a household where self-expression was encouraged. Her mother was a painter of note, and her father was deeply involved in the theater. She was introduced to actor Sir John Gielgud and mime Marcel Marceau as part of her family's social life.

Demi's mother encouraged and guided her daughter's education of studio art, silk-screening, jewelry-making, mural painting, and ceramics. As Demi noted in an interview with Patricia Austin in *Teaching and Learning Literature,* she always had a preference for Eastern over Western art: "Even as a little girl when my mother would take me to the Museum of Fine Arts to see something like Cezanne, I always felt something was missing and was much happier to be home looking at the Ming vases." She was also strongly influenced by the classic Chinese book *The Mustard Seed Garden Manual of Painting* and by the concept of Ch'i, "the breath and vital force and essence of all life, pervading the universe," as Demi explained in her interview with Austin. "Ch'i pervades both the paintbrush and yourself which is what I try to speak of when I speak of painting."

Attendance at the Rhode Island School of Design and a bachelor's degree from the innovative art program at Immaculate Heart College in Los Angeles helped expand Demi's sense of art. At Immaculate Heart College, she studied under Sister Maria Corita, a woman known for her silk-screen printing as well as for her rebellious stance toward the pope. These studies were followed by a master's degree in 1963 from the University of Baroda, Gujarat, India. Demi also traveled widely, visiting Brazil, then India where she was a Fulbright scholar from 1962 to 1963, and later China. She did not begin illustrating children's books until the late 1970s, but already she was an artist with a growing reputation as a painter. She painted murals in Mexico, walls for modern homes, and the dome of St. Peter and Paul Church in Wilmington, California. There have been exhibitions of her work throughout the United States and in India.

Demi's first picture book, *Lu Pan, the Carpenter's Apprentice,* appeared in 1978 and set the tone for much of her later work. Part biography and part adapted folktale, the book tells the story of a young apprentice growing up in China in the fifth century B.C. and how he ultimately becomes a master carpenter and one of China's greatest architects and inventors. The adapted text is accompanied by Demi's signature illustrations, "precise ink drawings" that are "clean and shining, their delicacy strongly evocative of the genius about whom she writes," according to Denise M. Wilms in a *Booklist* review. A critic in *Bulletin of the Center for Children's Books* pointed out how the black and white drawings are "spare and precise in the Oriental tradition."

Numerous other adaptations of folktales have followed and form what may be the core of Demi's work. Among the best known of these are *Liang and the Magic Paint-brush, Chen Ping and His Magic Axe, The Empty Pot,* and *The Stonecutter.* The story of a poor boy who wants to paint and is given a magic paintbrush that brings his pictures to life is the subject of *Liang and the Magic Paintbrush. Booklist* contributor Barbara Elleman noted of this work that Demi's "telling . . . moves gracefully in keeping with fragile lines and gentle touches of color found in the illustrations," while a *Publishers Weekly* reviewer commented that the author/illustrator's text "matches her art in fantastic effects," with delicate "shades of gold and blue" contrasting "with fiery scarlets in surpassingly beautiful [pictures]." Magic also figures into *Chen Ping and His Magic Axe,* in which a poor but honest woodcutter is rewarded with an axe that has magic properties. A *Publishers Weekly* critic observed that in this "plainly told tale of opposing moral concepts," the clear text together with the illustrations communicate "intention" well. Ilene Cooper, writing in *Booklist,* commented that Demi depicts the magical happenings of the story with paints "mixed from malachite, azurite, and cinnabar to produce a palette of both pastels and hot, bright colors."

More magic is served up in two more Chinese tales, *The Magic Boat* and *The Magic Tapestry,* and in a Rus-

In evocative water colors Demi captures the Asian origins of her story in Liang and the Magic Paintbrush. (Copyright © 1980 by Demi Hitz. Reprinted by arrangement with Henry Holt & Company, LLC.)

sian folktale by Aleksandr Pushkin, *The Magic Gold Fish.* In *The Magic Tapestry,* a loyal son is rewarded when the beautiful princess woven into his mother's tapestry comes to life to be his bride. *Booklist* reviewer Julie Corsaro noted that the "grandeur of the story is enhanced by the liberal use of shimmering gold," and concluded that Demi's "delicate paintings" are reminiscent of ancient Chinese hanging scrolls. Gold indeed is a favorite color of Demi's, and this fondness goes back to her youth when she once bought a plastic golden Buddha. She still keeps that plastic Buddha with her.

Demi's books of folktales are inspired by the legends of China, both written and passed down orally. *The Empty Pot* was one of several tales told to Demi by her husband, who she has described to Austin as "my built-in research center." In the tale, Ping is a boy who loves growing flowers. When the emperor passes out seeds to the children and proclaims that the one to grow the best flower will be the next ruler, Ping does his best to grow a magnificent flower. However, nothing comes of his work. While all the other children have glorious blossoms, Ping's flower pot is empty, and this he presents to the emperor. In the end, honesty is rewarded, for the emperor has cooked all the seeds—none should have sprouted. "Only honest Ping has the right stuff to be Emperor," commented Cooper, who noted that Demi's "precise pen-and-watercolor art works especially well here." *Horn Book* contributor Ellen Fader also praised the illustrations, which are "set in an oval in the shape of a flat Chinese fan and positioned on a pale brocade-like background, giving the pages the look of hand-painted silk."

In *The Greatest Power,* a companion volume to *The Empty Pot,* Emperor Ping wishes to bring the harmony of the heavens to his kingdom. Ping sends the children of the kingdom on a quest to find the greatest power in the world, with the advice: "A wise person must be able to see the unseen and know the unknown." Some children believe the greatest power involves money, beauty, or technology. Young Sing pays heed to the emperor's words, however, and returns with a lotus seed, which represents the life force. As her reward, Sing is named prime minister. "Demi ably combines striking artwork and a meaningful story, with quiet dignity and wisdom," observed *Booklist* critic Julie Cummins. Linda M. Kenton, reviewing *The Greatest Power* in *School Library Journal,* complimented the work's "rich palette, attention to detail, and delightful depictions of youngsters."

Artisans figure in two more Chinese folktales: *The Artist and the Architect* and *The Stonecutter. The Artist and the Architect* tells the story of a jealous artist who plots to get rid of the emperor's favorite architect, a book in which Demi's "signature style is as attractive as ever," according to Stephanie Zvirin in *Booklist.* Bright reds contrast with the "palest of peaceful pastels," noted Zvirin, and a surprise ending "is like a bolt from the blue." *The Stonecutter* is a Chinese equivalent of the

"Fisherman and His Wife," wherein a dissatisfied stonecutter wishes to be changed into something more powerful, but in the end learns his calling is the best of all. "Combine this offering with any of Demi's many other fine picture books on China to enrich a social studies unit," recommended Lauren Peterson in a *Booklist* review of *The Stonecutter.*

Demi has adapted several other folktales from India, including *The Hallowed Horse* and *One Grain of Rice: A Mathematical Folktale,* as well as *The Firebird* from Russia. Kate McMullan, reviewing the last named title in the *New York Times Book Review,* commented that "Demi's *Firebird* is a big, lavishly produced book with enough gold ink to satisfy the cravings of the greediest czar." She described Demi's elaborate illustrations, which provide "a feast for the eye," as "a cross between a Hokusai print and a Fabergé egg." In *The Hungry Coat,* Demi relates a story about thirteenth-century Turkish philosopher Nasrettin Hoca. "Inspired by Turkish art, Demi places miniature figures in frames filled with geometric patterns," noted *Booklist* contributor Linda Perkins.

Fables and nursery rhymes from China have also received the Demi treatment. Books such as *A Chinese Zoo, Demi's Reflective Fables,* and *The Dragon's Tale and Other Animal Fables of the Chinese Zodiac* provide moral lessons along with elegant artwork for young readers. Her interest in Buddhism is apparent in a collection of jatakas, Buddhist tales with a lesson, gathered in *Buddha Stories.* Based on an original book printed from woodblocks in 600 A.D., *Buddha Stories* is illustrated in gold ink against navy blue pages, resulting in "a striking visual impact," according to Janice M. Del Negro in the *Bulletin of the Center for Children's Books.*

Chinese nursery rhymes are retold in *Dragon Kites and Dragonflies,* "a book to be enjoyed and treasured," according to Hanna B. Zeiger in *Horn Book.* Additionally, Demi's poetry anthologies, such as *Demi's Secret Garden,* which includes poems from around the world, and *In the Eyes of the Cat,* which features Japanese poetry, have earned high praise. Reviewing the latter title, a collection of both haiku and tanka, Annette Curtis Klause concluded in *School Library Journal* that "the simple language and clear imagery . . . will attract young readers and perhaps instill in them a desire to explore poetry further."

Demi is also noted for her novelty books, her illustrations of the works of Hans Christian Andersen, and her biographies for young readers. Among novelty books, she has created both number and alphabet books that employ game techniques for learning. *Demi's Find the Animal A B C: An Alphabet-game Book* uses animals from A to Z to introduce the alphabet and also provides readers with the task of spotting more animals hidden in the illustrations. In *Booklist* Cheryl Penny dubbed this an "engaging puzzle book" that "will sharpen the basic prereading skill of discrimination." The artist did

Cover of* Kites, *Demi's illustrated history of the cornerstone of flight science. (Illustration copyright © 1999 by Demi. Used by permission of Crown Publishers, an imprint of Random House Children's Books, a division of Random House, Inc.)

much the same for numbers skills with *Demi's Count the Animals 1, 2, 3,* and created a fold-out introduction to the ever-popular topic of dinosaurs with *Find Demi's Dinosaurs.* More animal games and lessons in basic skills are supplied in *Demi's Opposites,* while in her adaptation of Andersen's *Thumbelina* she creates a "vividly told tale" with colors that "will undoubtedly attract children," according to *Booklist* reviewer Cooper.

Demi's biographies include *The Adventures of Marco Polo, Chingis Khan, Buddha,* and *Gandhi.* In the first, Demi details the Italian adventurer's journey from Venice to China in 1271 through both text and illustrations. Demi revisits the life of the famous explorer in *Marco Polo,* which describes Polo's twenty-four-year journey across Asia and raises questions as to whether it even happened. Charlotte Richardson, writing in *Papertigers. org,* observed that the author's "delicate stylized depictions of the Polos' experiences . . . accompany text that describes Marco's decades of adventure with clear chronology and dates." Richardson asserted that the

book "offers an inspiring antidote to the fractious attitudes of our own time," while Barbara Auerbach remarked in *School Library Journal* that "this elegant, scholarly picture-book biography brings the explorer's fantastic journey to life." Auerbach called Demi "a gifted storyteller" who is capable of weaving Marco Polo's "accounts into a seamless tale of wonder," and in *Booklist* Hazel Rochman called the "clear, double-page map showing Marco Polo's amazing route . . . a beautiful climax" to the illustrated biography.

In *Chingis Khan* Demi draws from both folklore and history to give "a terse but colorful sketch" of the notorious Mongolian leader, according to *Horn Book* critic Margaret A. Bush. "The epic adventures of this legendary figure [are] beautifully served," Bush concluded. Reviewing *Chingis Khan* in the *Bulletin of the Center for Children's Books,* Betsy Hearne noted in particular the conclusion of Demi's tale, "which is illustrated simply by layers of fused watercolor washes" that imply "time's erosion of physical conquest." In *Booklist,* Denia Hester concluded of the same book that this "handsome biography is a feast for the eyes from cover to cover, including the beautiful endpapers" and "a must for school and public libraries."

In *Buddha,* Demi brings her own affection for Buddhism to the recounting of Siddhartha's life, from his birth and the prophecies surrounding it to his ultimate path to enlightenment. *Horn Book* reviewer Stephen Dawson praised both Demi's prose and her refined illustrations, writing that "This notable achievement is not only a highly readable account of the Buddha's life but is also a thoughtful introduction to Buddhism." Demi recounts the life of the great Indian spiritual and political leader in *Gandhi.* A contributor in *Horn Book* wrote that Demi's "stylistic richness in this tale . . ., far from violating Gandhi's commitment to a spare life, honors and celebrates it." Patricia Lothrop-Green remarked in *School Library Journal* that "Demi's iconic illustrations and clear prose accord her subject's idealism the beauty and power it deserves."

After the September 11, 2001, terrorist attacks on the United States, Demi was approached by Emma Dryden of Margaret K. McElderry Books to write a book about Muhammad, the prophet who founded Islam. "I realized after this event that Americans had a lot of misconceptions about Islam and that most don't know much about the roots of the Islamic religion," Dryden told Sally Lodge in *Publishers Weekly.* "I knew that if anyone could create a balanced, sensitive book for children about Muhammad and the beginnings of Islam, it would be Demi." The artist readily accepted the assignment, telling Lodge: "I am drawn to Muslim painting and architecture. I have for years collected Eastern art and I have a huge library of books on Islam, so I didn't have to look far to find resources to write the text and create the art" for the work. *Muhammad* is an "excellent retelling of the Prophet's life that combines beauty and scholarship," according to John Green in *Booklist.* Susan Scheps, writing in *School Library Journal,* noted that "Demi's carefully designed paint-and-ink illustrations . . . are done in the style of the Persian miniature." Several critics noted that the artist takes care to portray her subject only in silhouette; Islamic tradition states that Muhammad must not be depicted directly. In the words of *Horn Book* contributor Lolly Robinson, Demi "presents the origins of Islam with great respect."

King Midas: The Golden Touch "breathes new life into one of the oldest of cautionary tales," wrote Joanna Rudge Long in *Horn Book.* Demi portrays the king as a weak, foolish man given to making poor decisions. Serving as the judge for a music contest between the god Apollo and Pan, Midas chooses the discordant Pan, so angering Apollo that he gives the king a pair of donkey's ears. Later, as a reward for helping Dionysus, Midas asks for and is granted the golden touch. In *School Library Journal* Susan Scheps took issue with Demi's decision to take liberties with the legend, stating that her "terse, choppy retelling will not appeal to those

who like classic tales left intact." A contributor to *Kirkus Reviews* was more positive, noting that "this version captures the tale's humor along with its point, and the illustrations really light up the room."

In *The Legend of Saint Nicholas* Demi offers a biography of the actual person who is closely associated with the modern-day Santa Claus. The work contains stories about the saint's life, including accounts of his good works and miracles, and it also explains the feast of Saint Nicholas, which began in the Middle Ages. "Once again Demi has created an exquisitely illustrated introduction to the life of a famous historical figure," wrote a *Kirkus Reviews* contributor, while in *School Library Journal* Eva Mitnick noted that the "greatest strength of the book is its straightforward, affectionate depiction" of Saint Nicholas. In *Booklist,* Cooper praised Demi's art, stating that "careful design work is evident right through to the endpapers."

Demi continues her study of religious figures with *Mother Teresa,* a portrait of the world-renowned nun and Nobel Peace Prize winner who devoted her life to serving the "poorest of the poor" around the globe. "Every element of this lovely book reflects Mother Teresa's simple message of service," observed *School Library Journal* contributor Linda L. Walkins, and a *Publishers Weekly* critic remarked that "Demi crafts a solid portrait of a selfless and devoutly faithful woman and her trust in Divine Providence."

In *Jesus: Based on the King James Version of the Holy Bible* Demi looks at the life of Christ through the four gospels of the New Testament. Writing in *Booklist,* Cooper called the work "a touching narrative of life, death, and resurrection," and *School Library Journal* critic Lucinda Snyder Whitehurst remarked that Demi's illustrations "are full of bright, intricate patterns, and bold touches of gold produce a feeling of awe and splendor." Using information from the King James Version of the Holy Bible as well as noncanonical sources, Demi chronicles the life of Mary, the mother of Jesus, in *Mary.* A critic for *Kirkus Reviews* described this biography as "reverential," and Cooper noted that the artwork "seems even more ornate and gilded than in Demi's previous books."

Demi profiles an eleventh-century Chinese statesman, artist, and scholar in *Su Dongpo: Chinese Genius.* Dongpo's "life embodied the enlightenment of Buddhism, the simplicity of Taoism, and the wise teachings of Confucius," Demi stated in an interview on the Lee & Low Books Web site. "He was also China's knight-errant, traveling the country and helping others with true generosity of spirit." Demi's biography "leaves readers with the sense of an extraordinary man," remarked Janet S. Thompson in *School Library Journal.* Demi looks at another legendary Chinese figure in *The Legend of Lao Tzu and the Tao Te Ching.* As she presents Lao Tzu's story, she incorporates elements of biography and myth, as well as verses from the Tao Te

Ching. In *Horn Book,* Joanna Rudge Long deemed the biography "a worthy book that's likely to require an adult's introduction to find its audience." "Clear, concise writing, thoughtfully considered design, and striking illustrations come together to make this one of the best of Demi's" profiles of spiritual figures, remarked *Booklist* critic Carolyn Phelan.

In *The Girl Who Drew a Phoenix* a young Chinese girl, Feng Huang, learns how to draw the mythical phoenix and studies its great powers in order to fill her drawing with a spirit. "Brilliant splashes of color and imaginative details bring Demi's vision of this mythical creature to life," lauded Barbara Scotto in a *School Library Journal* review of the book. A contributor writing in *Kirkus Reviews* noticed that the phoenixes are "exquisitely rendered in paint, ink, and Chinese silk brocade" in this "splendid" book. Susan Dove Lempke, reviewing *The Girl Who Drew a Phoenix* in *Horn Book,* observed that the illustrations are "meticulous as always" but felt that "the restrained format is at odds with the exclamation point-laden text." *Booklist* contributor Randall Enos predicted that "the exquisite, decorative images of the phoenixes sweeping across the pages" would be the favorite of young readers, while a contributor to *Publishers Weekly* found dubbed Demi's "artwork . . . as exquisite as ever."

The Magic Pillow, a Chinese story, follows Ping, a young boy who is excited by the tricks performed by a magician. When he sees the magician creating diamonds, Ping begins to crave wealth. The magician warns Ping about being greedy and, with the help of a magic pillow, shows the boy his future if he were to live a greedy life. Margaret Chang, reviewing the book in *School Library Journal,* mentioned that "a detailed note identifies the source for her story" and suggested that "adults may appreciate the book's message more than children." A contributor writing in *Kirkus Reviews* suggested that some readers may have wanted "to see a little more ambition in the boy, but many will appreciate the conclusion." Linda Perkins, writing in *Booklist,* claimed that "Demi's dainty, jewel-like art is the perfect vehicle for this story."

Rumi: Whirling Dervish highlights the life of Rumi, a thirteenth-century mystical poet whose writings are associated with the motion of so-called whirling dervishes, mystics of the Sufi Islam religion. A contributor writing in *Kirkus Reviews* commented that "Demi's signature luminous artwork elegantly evokes the life of one of the most revered mystical poets," even if children are not familiar with the topic. *Booklist* contributor Gillian Engberg described the book as "a handsome tribute to a figure, and a subject, rarely covered in children's books."

In her art, Demi has created a universe of marvels, including dragons and dinosaurs and elegant golden versions of reality that attract children's eyes and bring the reader into her simple straightforward text. On the surface fanciful and seemingly effortless, her illustrations are in fact the result of painstaking efforts. She recounted to Austin: "I'd draw a tiger a thousand times just to warm up and then I'd throw all those away and draw the real thing." Additionally, her delicate line drawings are often the result of a complicated layering process.

While Demi's miniaturizations and the plenitude of images in her artwork are the result of much thoughtful planning, much also comes from following her inspiration, which she calls her Ch'i. Working with children in schools, Demi attempts to develop the "magic paintbrush" technique in her work teaching young artists. Describing how she once had class after class paint all sorts of dinosaurs on long rolls of paper on the floor, she told Austin that "They found Ch'i, the essence of life, the breath, spirit and vital force of Heaven, always expansive and always growing." It is this expansive quality for which Demi's art itself is regarded.

Biographical and Critical Sources

BOOKS

St. James Guide to Children's Writers, 5th edition, St. James Press (Detroit, MI), 1999.

PERIODICALS

Booklist, July 15, 1978, Denise M. Wilms, review of *Lu Pan, the Carpenter's Apprentice,* p. 1734; September 15, 1980, Barbara Elleman, review of *Liang and the Magic Paintbrush,* p. 113; February 1, 1986, Cheryl Penny, review of *Demi's Find the Animal A B C: An Alphabet-game Book,* p. 808; May 15, 1987, Ilene Cooper, review of *Chen Ping and His Magic Axe,* p. 1444; March 1, 1989, Ilene Cooper, review of *Thumbelina,* p. 1189; April 1, 1990, Ilene Cooper, review of *The Empty Pot,* p. 1545; May 15, 1991, Stephanie Zvirin, review of *The Artist and the Architect,* p. 1802; October 1, 1991, Denia Hester, review of *Chingis Khan,* p. 329; August, 1994, Julie Corsaro, review of *The Magic Tapestry: A Chinese Folktale,* p. 2045; July, 1995, Lauren Peterson, review of *The Stonecutter,* p. 1881; April 1, 1996, Ilene Cooper, review of *Buddha,* p. 1358; September 15, 1996, Karen Morgan, review of *The Dragon's Tale and Other Animal Fables of the Chinese Zodiac,* p. 235; February 15, 1997, Ilene Cooper, review of *Buddha Stories,* p. 1017; March 1, 1997, Karen Morgan, review of *One Grain of Rice: A Mathematical Folktale,* p. 1166; May 1, 1997, Carolyn Phelan, review of *Grass Sandals: The Travels of Basho,* p. 1497; March 15, 1998, Ilene Cooper, review of *The Dalai Lama: A Biography of the Tibetan Spiritual and Political Leader,* p. 1240; August, 1998, Helen Rosenberg, review of *The Greatest Treasure,* p. 1998; March 1, 1999, Ilene Cooper, review of *Kites: Magic Wishes That Fly up to the Sky,* p. 1216; June 1,

1999, Linda Perkins, review of *The Donkey and the Rock,* p. 1832; June 1, 2000, Linda Perkins, review of *The Emperor's New Clothes: A Tale Set in China,* p. 1907; June 1, 2001, John Green, review of *Gandhi,* p. 1866; June 1, 2003, John Green, review of *Muhammad,* p. 1795; October 1, 2003, Ilene Cooper, review of *The Legend of Saint Nicholas,* p. 332; January 1, 2004, review of *Muhammad,* p. 780; February 1, 2004, Julie Cummins, review of *The Greatest Power,* p. 980; August, 2004, Linda Perkins, review of *The Hungry Coat: A Tale from Turkey,* p. 1938; January 1, 2005, Ilene Cooper, review of *Mother Teresa,* p. 848; October 1, 2005, Ilene Cooper, review of *Jesus: Based on the King James Version of the Holy Bible,* p. 68; October 1, 2006, Ilene Cooper, review of *Mary,* p. 64; November 1, 2006, Carolyn Phelan, review of *Su Dongpo: Chinese Genius,* p. 56; May 15, 2007, Carolyn Phelan, review of *The Legend of Lao Tzu and the Tao Te Ching,* p. 46; September 15, 2007, Linda Perkins, review of *The Boy Who Painted Dragons,* p. 72; July 1, 2008, Linda Perkins, review of *The Magic Pillow,* p. 72; August 1, 2008, Randall Enos, review of *The Girl Who Drew a Phoenix,* p. 76; October 1, 2008, Hazel Rochman, review of *Marco Polo,* p. 40; April 15, 2009, Gillian Engberg, review of *Rumi: Whirling Dervish,* p. 40.

Bulletin of the Center for Children's Books, September, 1978, review of *Lu Pan, the Carpenter's Apprentice,* p. 10; January, 1992, Betsy Hearne, review of *Chingis Khan,* p. 123; April, 1997, Janice M. Del Negro, review of *Buddha Stories,* p. 200; May, 2002, Janice M. Del Negro, review of *King Midas: The Golden Touch.*

Emergency Librarian, September-October, 1997, review of *Buddha Stories,* p. 51; November-December, 1997, review of *One Grain of Rice,* p. 55.

Horn Book, May-June, 1987, Hanna B. Zeiger, review of *Dragon Kites and Dragonflies: A Collection of Chinese Nursery Rhymes,* p. 349; May-June, 1990, Ellen Fader, review of *The Empty Pot,* p. 342; November-December, 1991, Margaret A. Bush, review of *Chingis Khan,* pp. 752-753; September-October, 1996, Stephen Dawson, review of *Buddha,* p. 611; March-April, 1998, Marilyn Bousquin, review of *The Dalai Lama,* p. 233; May, 2000, Joanna Rudge Long, review of *The Emperor's New Clothes,* p. 291; September, 2001, review of *Gandhi,* p. 609; May-June, 2002, Joanna Rudge Long, review of *King Midas,* p. 338; July-August, 2003, Lolly Robinson, review of *Muhammad,* pp. 477-478; March-April, 2005, Roger Sutton, review of *Mother Teresa,* p. 213; July-August, 2007, Joanna Rudge Long, review of *The Legend of Lao Tzu and the Tao Te Ching,* p. 408; July 1, 2008, Susan Dove Lempke, review of *The Magic Pillow.*

Kirkus Reviews, April 15, 2002, review of *King Midas,* p. 566; June 15, 2003, review of *Muhammad,* p. 858; November 1, 2003, review of *The Legend of Saint Nicholas,* p. 1316; February 1, 2004, review of *The Greatest Power,* p. 131; September 15, 2005, review of *Jesus,* p. 1024; August 15, 2006, review of *Su Dongpo,* p. 839; September 15, 2006, review of *Mary,* p. 950; April 15, 2007, review of *The Legend of Lao Tzu and the Tao Te Ching;* August 1, 2007, review of *The Boy Who Painted Dragons;* May 15, 2008, re-

view of *The Magic Pillow;* August 15, 2008, review of *Marco Polo;* August 15, 2008, review of *Demi: The Girl Who Drew a Phoenix;* April 1, 2009, review of *Rumi.*

Language Arts, September, 2002, review of *Gandhi,* pp. 72-73.

New York Times Book Review, April 20, 1980, Don Lessem, review of *Where Is It?,* p. 20; April 25, 1982, Elaine Edelman, review of *The Adventures of Marco Polo,* p. 33; December 3, 1990, Christopher Lehmann-Haupt, review of *The Empty Pot,* p. B2; November 14, 1993, Cynthia Zarin, review of *Demi's Dragons and Fantastic Creatures,* p. 48; January 15, 1995, Kate McMullan, review of *The Firebird: A Russian Folktale,* p. 25; September 16, 2001, review of *Gandhi,* p. 26.

Publishers Weekly, January 18, 1980, review of *Bong Nam and the Pheasants,* p. 141; March 7, 1980, review of *Where Is It?,* p. 90; June 27, 1980, review of *Liang and the Magic Paintbrush,* p. 88; November 28, 1980, Jean F. Mercier, review of *The Leaky Umbrella,* p. 50; January 2, 1981, Jean F. Mercier, review of *Dragon Night,* p. 51; January 29, 1982, review of *The Adventures of Marco Polo,* p. 66; August 30, 1985, review of *The Nightingale,* p. 422; November 8, 1985, Jean F. Mercier, review of *Demi's Find the Animal A B C,* p. 60; May 30, 1986, review of *Demi's Count the Animals 1, 2, 3,* p. 62; November 28, 1986, review of *Dragon Kites and Dragon Flies,* p. 73; April 24, 1987, review of *Chen Ping and His Magic Axe,* p. 68; September 11, 1987, review of *Demi's Opposites,* pp. 90-91; December 11, 1987, review of *The Hallowed Horse,* p. 64; October 14, 1998, review of *Demi's Reflective Fables,* p. 69; February 9, 1990, review of *The Empty Pot,* p. 59; March 1, 1991, review of *The Artist and the Architect,* p. 73; April 27, 1992, review of *In the Eyes of the Cat: Japanese Poetry for All Seasons,* p. 271; July 19, 1993, review of *Demi's Secret Garden,* p. 53; November 1, 1993, review of *Demi's Dragons and Fantastic Creatures,* p. 78; May 2, 1994, review of *The Magic Tapestry,* p. 308; October 10, 1994, review of *The Firebird,* p. 70; May 15, 1995, review of *The Stonecutter,* p. 72; October 28, 1996, review of *The Dragon's Tale and Other Animal Fables of the Chinese Zodiac,* p. 81; January 27, 1997, review of *One Grain of Rice,* p. 106; April 26, 1999, review of *The Donkey and the Rock,* p. 81; June 23, 2003, Sally Lodge, "Portrait of a Prophet: A Look at Demi's Process of Creating a Picture-book Biography," pp. 23-24; September 22, 2003, review of *The Legend of Saint Nicholas,* p. 71; February 14, 2005, review of *Mother Teresa,* p. 78; May 14, 2007, review of *The Legend of Lao Tzu and the Tao Te Ching,* p. 58; September 3, 2007, review of *The Boy Who Painted Dragons,* p. 58; August 18, 2008, review of *The Girl Who Drew a Phoenix,* p. 61.

School Library Journal, April, 1982, review of *The Adventures of Marco Polo,* p. 28; August, 1984, Beverly A. Maffei, review of *Fat Gopal,* p. 65; December, 1985, review of *Demi's Find the Animal A B C,* p. 70; December, 1986, Dana Whitney Pinizzotto, review of *Dragon Kites and Dragonflies,* p. 84; June-July, 1987, Susan Scheps, review of *Chen Ping and His Magic*

Axe, p. 81; May, 1992, Annette Curtis Klause, review of *In the Eyes of the Cat,* p. 98; January, 1996, Denise Anton Wright, review of *The Magic Gold Fish: A Russian Folktale,* p. 104; March, 1996, Susan Powers, review of *Eucalyptus Wings,* p. 176; June, 1996, Susan Middleton, review of *Buddha,* p. 136; October, 1996, Diane S. Marton, *The Dragon's Tale and Other Animal Fables of the Chinese Zodiac,* p. 112; June, 1997, Patricia Lothrop-Green, review of *Buddha Stories,* p. 107; March, 1998, Patricia Lothrop-Green, review of *The Dalai Lama,* p. 194, and Anne Connor, review of *Happy New Year! Kung-hsi Fa-Ts'ai!,* p. 194; September, 1998, Margaret A. Chang, review of *The Greatest Treasure,* p. 190; March, 1999, Margaret A. Chang, review of *The Donkey and the Rock,* p. 192; June, 1999, DeAnn Tabuchi, review of *Kites,* p. 112; August, 2001, Patricia Lothrop-Green, review of *Gandhi,* p. 167; May, 2002, Susan Scheps, review of *King Midas,* p. 136; August, 2003, Susan Scheps, review of *Muhammad,* pp. 172-173; October, 2003, Eva Mitnick, review of *The Legend of Saint Nicholas,* pp. 61-62; March, 2004, Linda M. Kenton, review of *The Greatest Power,* p. 156; July, 2004, Grace Oliff, review of *The Hungry Coat,* p. 92; February, 2005, Linda L. Walkins, review of *Mother Teresa,* p. 116; October, 2005, Lucinda Snyder Whitehurst, review of *Jesus,* p. 186; November, 2006, Lucinda Snyder Whitehurst, review of *Mary,* p. 158, and Janet S. Thompson, review of *Su Dongpo,* p. 158; May, 2007, Margaret Bush, review of *The Legend of Lao Tzu and the Tao Te Ching,* p. 152; September, 2007, Donna Atmur, review of *The Boy Who Painted Dragons,* p. 162; July 1, 2008, Margaret A. Chang, review of *The Magic Pillow,* p. 70; September 1, 2008, Barbara Auerbach, review of *Marco Polo,* p. 201; September 1, 2008, Barbara Scotto, review of *The Girl Who Drew a Phoenix,* p. 144.

Teaching and Learning Literature, May-June, 1997, Patricia Austin, "Demi's Magic," pp. 43-55.

ONLINE

Lee & Low Books Web site, http://www.leeandlow.com/ (March 1, 2008), interview with Demi.

National Public Radio Web site, http://www.npr.org/ (September 18, 2003), "Demi's *Muhammad:* Author, Artist Brings Tale of Islam to Children."

Papertigers.org, http://www.papertigers.org/ (December 31, 2003), Naomi Beth Wakan, interview with Demi; (November 30, 2008) Charlotte Richardson, review of *Marco Polo.*

Simon & Schuster Web site, http://www.simonsays.com/ (March 1, 2009), "Demi."*

*   *   *

DENISE, Anika

Personal

Married Christopher Denise (an illustrator); children: two daughters.

Addresses

Home—Barrington, RI.

Career

Children's author. Formerly worked in advertising and public relations.

Writings

Pigs Love Potatoes, illustrated by husband, Christopher Denise, Philomel (New York, NY), 2007.

Biographical and Critical Sources

PERIODICALS

Booklist, June 1, 2007, Carolyn Phelan, review of *Pigs Love Potatoes,* p. 84.

Bulletin of the Center for Children's Books, September, 2007, Deborah Stevenson, review of *Pigs Love Potatoes,* p. 15.

Kirkus Reviews, June 1, 2007, review of *Pigs Love Potatoes.*

Publishers Weekly, June 11, 2007, review of *Pigs Love Potatoes,* p. 58.

School Library Journal, July, 2007, Maryann H. Owen, review of *Pigs Love Potatoes,* p. 74.

ONLINE

Rhode Island State Council on the Arts Web site, http://www.arts.ri.gov/ (February 6, 2008).*

*   *   *

DERISO, Christine Hurley 1961-

Personal

Born 1961; married; children: Greg, Julianne. *Education:* University of Georgia, degree, 1983.

Addresses

Home—North Augusta, SC. *E-mail*—Christine@christinehurleyderiso.com; talia@christinehurleyderiso.com.

Career

Medical College of Georgia, Augusta, publications editor, 1988—; *Augusta Chronicle,* restaurant critic, 1998-2005; freelance writer.

Writings

JUVENILE FICTION

Dreams to Grow On, illustrated by Matthew Archambault, Illumination Arts Publications (Bellevue, WA), 2002.

Do-Over, Delacorte Press (New York, NY), 2006.

The Right-Under Club, Delacorte Press (New York, NY), 2007.
Talia Talk, Delacorte Press (New York, NY), 2009.

OTHER

Also author of feature articles, humor columns and essays for magazines including *Ladies' Home Journal, Parents, Family Circle,* and *Child.*

Sidelights

Christine Hurley Deriso found that the simple act of reading to her son's fourth-grade class inspired her to become an author of children's books. Although Deriso had been writing and editing professionally for many years, she had not been able to sell her fictional works. Deriso's son urged her to make up stories to tell to his fellow students. Together, they worked on a narrative that took into account things that happened in everyday life—like cleaning up rooms and doing homework. The class loved her presentations and kept asking her back. By the end of the school year, Deriso had presented dozens of stories and received much helpful criticism from her young audience. Parting was difficult, but as

Cover of Christine Hurley Deriso's young-adult novel The Right-Under Club, *featuring artwork by Monika Roe.* (Illustration copyright © 2007 by Monika Roe. Used by permission of Delacorte Press, an imprint of Random House Children's Books, a division of Random House, Inc.)

she commented in the *Dreams to Grow On* Web site, "Several wrote that because of me, they want to be writers when they grow up. I've never been so touched. Without them, I might never have discovered the joy of writing children's stories. Their inspiration was priceless. I told them that if I ever published one of my stories, I was dedicating it to them." Deriso wrote *Dreams to Grow On* an inspirational story for children, after her experience with these students.

Deriso's second book, *Do-Over,* follows Elsa, a twelve year old whose mother has passed away. After she moves away from home to live with her grandmother, she finds it less than comfortable at her new school. Elsa had always wanted to be in the popular crowd, and that dream seems farther away than ever in the new setting. Then her mother comes to her in a dream, offering an enticing wish: for one month, Elsa will be able to turn back time for ten seconds with the help of a magic locket. It's a temptation that is too difficult to resist. Elsa uses her powers to get into the popular crowd, but finds that her actions have some unexpected consequences. Carly B. Wiskoff, writing in *School Library Journal,* praised *Do-Over* for its "fast pace and lots of dialogue," while a *Kirkus Reviews* contributor maintained that "middle-schoolers who long to be popular may find this somewhat predictable story enjoyable." Renee Kirchner, a reviewer for the *Kids Reads* Web site, praised the effort, calling *Do-Over* "a tender, heartwarming novel with believable dialogue and realistic characters." As Deriso commented in *The Right Under Club* Web site, "We all have those adolescent moments that make us cringe, and I loved creating a fictional character to take the sting out of the experiences."

The Right-Under Club follows a group of five girls who feel misunderstood by their parents. They form a club to support each other through divorce, custody battles, and losing a parent through illness. A critic in *Kirkus Reviews* applauded the story, citing especially the "large cast of characters, which Deriso handles adeptly."

Talia, the middle-school protagonist of *Talia Talk* learns to negotiate various kinds of emotional relationships during the school year. She misses her deceased father and is not sure how she feels about her mother's new boyfriend, a sportscaster. She certainly resents being a major topic on her mother's morning television talk show, which broadcasts Talia's every awkward encounter and humiliating experience. The situation with her peers has also become complicated. Once part of a tight-knit group of four friends, Talia is torn when two of the girls break away and leave goofy Bridget behind. Should Talia stick with the others and be cool, or remain loyal to Bridget? Deriso adds an interesting twist to the story by having Talia win the chance to host her school's daily podcast. This turn of events, thinks Talia, will allow her to give her mother a taste of her own medicine.

Cover of Deriso's teen novel **Do-Over,** *featuring artwork by Michelle Grant.* (Illustration copyright © 2006 by Michelle Grant. Used by permission of Delacorte Press, an imprint of Random House Children's Books, a division of Random House, Inc.)

Noting that *Talia Talk* "touches on some important topics," *School Library Journal* reviewer Sari Fesko added the novel's most laudable element is its depiction of a sometimes "tense but always loving" mother/daughter bond. Focusing on the drama and humor in Deriso's story, as well as the "simple honesty" that makes its protagonist such a sympathetic character, a *Kirkus Reviews* contributor called *Talia Talk* "spunky and fun."

"Nothing is as much fun as writing about tweens," stated Deriso on her home page. These years "can be pretty excruciating . . . but they can be pretty awesome, too." Children on the cusp of adolescence are at a fascinating juncture in their lives, experimenting with different roles and trying to find out just who they really are as individuals. Inevitably they make mistakes, which are only exacerbated by the intense self-consciousness of the age—but, as Deriso's books show, there can be as much humor in these experiences as there is embarrassment. Addressing her young readers on her home page, Deriso expressed the hope that her books will provide them "a sneak previous of your inner fabulousness—the gifts vond talents you'll share with the world just as soon as you've nailed your biology final."

Biographical and Critical Sources

PERIODICALS

Children's Bookwatch, January, 2008, reviews of *Dreams to Grow On* and *The Right-Under Club.*
Kirkus Reviews, June 1, 2006, review of *Do-Over;* June 1, 2007, review of *The Right-Under Club;* October 15, 2008, review of *Talia Talk.*
School Library Journal, August, 2006, Carly B. Wiskoff, review of *Do-Over,* p. 118; December 1, 2008, Shari Fesko, review of *Talia Talk,* p. 122.

ONLINE

Christine Hurley Deriso Home Page, http://www.christine hurleyderiso.com (June 5, 2009).
Dreams to Grow On Web site, http://www.dreamstogrowon. com (June 5, 2009).
Kids Reads Web site, http://www.kidsread.com/ (March 1, 2008), Renee Kirchner, review of *Do-Over.*
Right Under Club Web site, http://www.therightunderclub. com (March 1, 2008).*

*   *   *

DURRANT, Sabine

Personal

Born in England; married; husband's name Giles; children: Mabel, Barney, Joe.

Addresses

Home—London, England.

Career

Author and journalist. *Sunday Times,* London, England, deputy literary editor; *Guardian,* London, deputy features editor and author of "The Sabine Durrant Interview." Also worked for *Observer, Independent,* and *Daily Telegraph,* all London, England.

Writings

NOVELS

Having It and Eating It, Riverhead Books (New York, NY), 2002.
The Great Indoors, Time Warner (London, England), 2003, Riverhead Books (New York, NY), 2005.
Cross Your Heart, Connie Pickles, Puffin (London, England), 2005, HarperTempest (New York, NY), 2007.
Ooh La La! Connie Pickles, Puffin (London, England), 2007, published as *Bon Voyage, Connie Pickles,* HarperTeen (New York, NY), 2008.

Sidelights

Sabine Durrant, a British journalist who is best known for her interview features in the London *Guardian,* is the author of *Having It and Eating It* and *The Great Indoors,* two highly regarded novels for adults. Durrant has also published popular romantic comedies for teen readers, including *Cross Your Heart, Connie Pickles.*

Durrant's debut work, *Having It and Eating It,* is "a satisfyingly recognisable and funny slice of middle-class parenthood," according to *Spectator* critic Nicolette Jones. The novel concerns Maggie Owen, a thirty-something London suburbanite who gave up her career as a journalist to raise her two sons. Maggie lives with her longtime boyfriend, Jake, a workaholic advertising executive and the father of her children, although he refuses to marry her. Disenchanted with the course her life has taken, Maggie experiences even more regrets after meeting an old friend, Claire Masterson, who has become a successful career woman. When Maggie suspects Claire and Jake of infidelity, she embarks on an affair of her own with an Australian gardener. *Guardian* contributor Carrie O'Grady praised Durrant's keen observations of social mores, noting that she "pulls off the Austen-like trick of bringing us nose to nose with a micro-class of society." Rachel Simhon, writing in the London *Daily Telegraph,* maintained that the author "accurately describes 'the mess and the noise and the chaos and the clobber and the palaver' of small children, along with the sheer self-centredness of a certain type of middle-class mother and her hellish toddlers." *New Statesman* contributor Rachel Cooke complimented Durrant's "lovely, wry way with words," and a *Kirkus Reviews* contributor described *Having It and Eating It* as "a standout for its rich detail and deceptively weightless prose."

Martha Bone, a London antiques shop owner, is the focus of *The Great Indoors,* a novel deemed "fresh, thoughtful and beautifully observed" by Elizabeth Buchan in the London *Sunday Times.* When her stepfather dies, Martha is charged with finding a home for the man's cat, and she quickly falls for the animal's new owner, a quirky magician with two children. At the same time, Martha's wealthy old flame, David, reappears and she must decide between the two men. "Durrant moves gently through the muddle of her characters' lives," noted a critic in *Kirkus Reviews,* and *New York Times* contributor Joanne Kaufman observed that the novel "is, in the most literal sense, a domestic drama . . . concerned with the accumulation and arrangement of furnishings—both inanimate and otherwise—and the casting off of those that don't seem to work with the others." "This well-written, intelligent book will satisfy readers hungry for romance with more substance," stated *Booklist* reviewer Aleksandra Kostovski in an appraisal of *The Great Indoors.*

In Durrant's first young-adult novel, *Cross Your Heart, Connie Pickles,* an intelligent fourteen-year-old Londoner with an interest in French culture decides the time is right for her widowed mother to remarry. Enlisting the assistance of her best friend, Connie secretly begins to plays matchmaker, with comically muddled results. The teen also grapples with her own romantic entanglements and tries to help a neighbor restore her damaged reputation. "Although light and fluffy in the telling," noted a reviewer in *Publishers Weekly,* "Connie's quest is deep-rooted, and her eventual epiphanies feel tried and true." In the words of *Kliatt* reviewer Claire Rosser, "it's all over-the-top fun, amusing for the right readers," and Jessica Lamarre, writing in *School Library Journal,* called *Cross Your Heart, Connie Pickles* "an enjoyable, lighthearted read."

Connie returns in *Ooh La La! Connie Pickles,* which was published as *Bon Voyage, Connie Pickles* in the United States. Here fifteen-year-old Connie goes on an exchange program to France but accidentally end up in Belgium after boarding the wrong train. When she manages to get to France, she finds her host family to be very strange and full of problems. She manages to help them and her own family while going through some rites of passage herself. Tina Zubak, reviewing the novel in *School Library Journal,* suggested that American "reluctant readers may be deterred by its British tone, but middle school girls looking for a light read will find much to like in Connie." Calling the book "funny and heartwarming," a contributor to *Kirkus Reviews* revealed that in *Bon Voyage, Connie Pickles* "Connie manages to stay true to herself through it all."

Biographical and Critical Sources

PERIODICALS

Booklist, April 15, 2002, Beth Warrell, review of *Having It and Eating It,* p. 1382; December 1, 2004, Aleksandra Kostovski, review of *The Great Indoors,* p. 634.

Daily Telegraph (London, England), January 26, 2002, Rachel Simhon, "Sleeping with the Gardener," review of *Having It and Eating It,* p. 1382; March 31, 2003, Philippa Stockley, "Chintz-lit—A New Sister for Chick-lit," review of *The Great Indoors,* p. 42.

Guardian (London, England), February 2, 2002, Carrie O'Grady, "Not So Common," review of *Having It and Eating It,* p. 11.

Kirkus Reviews, May 1, 2002, review of *Having It and Eating It,* p. 594; November 1, 2004, review of *The Great Indoors,* p. 1023; March 15, 2007, review of *Cross Your Heart, Connie Pickles;* April 1, 2008, review of *Bon Voyage, Connie Pickles.*

Kliatt, March, 2007, Claire Rosser, review of *Cross Your Heart, Connie Pickles,* p. 12.

Library Journal, April 15, 2002, Beth Gibbs, review of *Having It and Eating It,* p. 125; December 1, 2004, Beth Gibbs, review of *The Great Indoors,* p. 99.

New Statesman, February 11, 2002, Rachel Cooke, "Now for . . . Hen Lit," review of *Having It and Eating It,* p. 52.

New York Times, January 20, 2005, Joanne Kaufman, "A Shaggy Cat Story," review of *The Great Indoors.*

Publishers Weekly, April 29, 2002, review of *Having It and Eating It,* p. 41; December 13, 2004, review of *The Great Indoors,* p. 45; April 9, 2007, review of *Cross Your Heart, Connie Pickles,* p. 55.

School Library Journal, June, 2007, Jessica Lamarre, review of *Cross Your Heart, Connie Pickles,* p. 142; July 1, 2008, Tina Zubak, review of *Bon Voyage, Connie Pickles,* p. 96.

Spectator, April 6, 2002, Nicolette Jones, review of *Having It and Eating It,* p. 35.

Sun (London, England), June 3, 2005, Sam Wostear, review of *Cross Your Heart, Connie Pickles,* p. 62.

Sunday Mirror (London, England), February 17, 2002, Sally Morris, review of *Having It and Eating It,* p. 49.

Sunday Times (London, England), February 10, 2002, Elizabeth Buchan, review of *Having It and Eating It,* p. 45; May 4, 2003, Elizabeth Buchan, review of *The Great Indoors,* p. 45.

Times (London, England), February 9, 2002, Alex O'Connell, "The Worst of Both Worlds," review of *Having It and Eating It,* p. 12.

ONLINE

Bookbag Web site, http://www.thebookbag.co.uk/ (May 26, 2009), review of *Ooh La La! Connie Pickles.*

Teens Read Too, http://www.teensreadtoo.com/ (March 25, 2008), review of *Bon Voyage, Connie Pickles.**

E-F

ELLIOTT, Mark 1949-

Personal

Born 1949. *Education:* School of Visual Arts, B.F.A., 1990.

Addresses

Home—NY. *Agent*—Shannon Associates, 630 9th Ave., Ste. 707, New York, NY 10036. *E-mail*—art4marc@yahoo.com.

Career

Artist and illustrator. *Exhibitions:* Work exhibited at Society of Illustrators and Art Directors Guild shows.

Awards, Honors

Children's Choices selection, International Reading Association/Children's Book Council, 2000, for *Jade Green;* Society of School Librarians International Book Award Honor Book, 2006, for *Room One: A Mystery or Two;* 100 Titles for Reading and Sharing selection, New York Public Library, 2007, for *No Talking.*

Illustrator

Phyllis Reynolds Naylor, *Jade Green: A Ghost Story,* Simon & Schuster (New York, NY), 2000.

Elizabeth Levy, *Big Trouble in Little Twinsville,* HarperCollins (New York, NY), 2001.

Phyllis Reynolds Naylor, *The Grooming of Alice,* Simon & Schuster (New York, NY), 2001.

Annie Dalton, *Isabel: Taking Wing,* Pleasant Company Publications (Middleton, WI), 2002.

Grace Johnson, *The Candle in the Window: A Christmas Legend,* Revell Books (Grand Rapids, MI), 2003.

Elizabeth Levy, *Take Two, They're Small* (sequel to *Big Trouble in Little Twinsville*), HarperCollins (New York, NY), 2003.

Warren Hanson, *Grandpa Has a Great Big Face,* Laura Geringer Books (New York, NY), 2006.

Andrew Clements, *Room One: A Mystery or Two,* Simon & Schuster (New York, NY), 2006.

Jerry Camery-Hoggatt, *When Mother Was Eleven-foot-four: A Christmas Memory,* Revell Books (Grand Rapids, MI), 2007.

Andrew Clements, *No Talking,* Simon & Schuster (New York, NY), 2007.

Margaret Peterson Haddix, *Dexter the Tough,* Simon & Schuster (New York, NY), 2007.

Andrew Clements, *Lost and Found,* Simon & Schuster (New York, NY), 2008.

"PRINCESS TALES" SERIES

Gail Carson Levine, *The Fairy's Mistake,* HarperCollins (New York, NY), 1999.

Gail Carson Levine, *The Princess Test,* HarperCollins (New York, NY), 1999.

Gail Carson Levine, *Princess Sonora and the Long Sleep,* HarperCollins (New York, NY), 1999.

Gail Carson Levine, *Cinderellis and the Glass Hill,* HarperCollins (New York, NY), 2000.

Gail Carson Levine, *The Fairy's Return,* HarperCollins (New York, NY), 2002.

Gail Carson Levine, *For Biddle's Sake,* HarperCollins (New York, NY), 2002.

Gail Carson Levine, *The Princess Tales, Volume 1* (contains *The Fairy's Mistake, The Princess Test,* and *Princess Sonora and the Long Sleep*), HarperCollins (New York, NY), 2002.

Gail Carson Levine, *The Princess Tales, Volume 2* (contains *Cinderellis and the Glass Hill, The Fairy's Return,* and *For Biddle's Sake*), HarperCollins (New York, NY), 2004.

Gail Carson Levine, *The Fairy's Return and Other Princess Tales* (contains *The Fairy's Mistake, The Princess Test, Princess Sonora and the Long Sleep, Cinderellis and the Glass Hill, The Fairy's Return,* and *For Biddle's Sake*), HarperCollins (New York, NY), 2006.

Sidelights

Mark Elliott is a highly regarded artist who has also illustrated a number of children's books. Beginning in 1999, Elliott provided the artwork for Gail Carson Le-

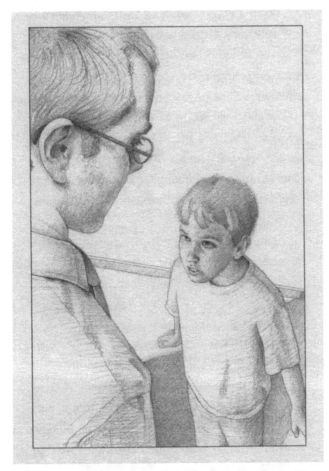

Margaret Peterson Haddix's elementary-grade novel **Dexter the Tough** *features detailed pencil artwork by Mark Elliott.* (Aladdin, 2007. Illustration copyright © 2007 by Mark Elliott. Reproduced by permission.)

vine's popular "Princess Tales" series of middle-grade novels. He garnered praise for two works in particular: *The Fairy's Mistake,* an adaptation of "Toads and Diamonds" by the Brothers Grimm, and *The Princess Test,* a retelling of Hans Christian Andersen's "The Princess and the Pea." Reviewing both titles in the *New York Times Book Review,* Meg Wolitzer noted that the works "are illustrated by spartan black-and-white line drawings . . . that give the feel of plates from some classic book of fairy tales." Reviewing the same titles, a critic in *Publishers Weekly* stated that "elegant design and Elliott's framed, black-and-white drawings create a timeless effect that plays off nicely against Levine's updated plot twists."

Another book illustrated by Elliott, Grace Johnson's *The Candle in the Window: A Christmas Legend,* is based on a story by Leo Tolstoy. In the work Gunther, a widowed cobbler, is visited on Christmas Eve by a mysterious stranger who instructs him to await a visit by the Christ Child. During the evening, Gunther aids several needy individuals who enter his shop. "Elliott's hyperrealistic, romanticized illustrations resemble posed photographs of contemporary people in a reenactment," remarked Susan Patron in *School Library Journal,* and a *Publishers Weekly* contributor stated that the artist's

pictures "match the text in their magnification of each emotion experienced and each lesson learned." In Warren Hanson's *Grandpa Has a Great Big Face,* a young boy lets his imagination run wild as he compares the size of his face, hands, and feet to those of his grandfather. "Elliott keeps a tight focus on each static image and has fun with the concept of relative size," wrote Martha Topol in *School Library Journal.*

A noisy group of fifth graders takes a surprising vow of silence in *No Talking,* a work by Andrew Clements. In this book Elliott's "black-and-white pencil drawings add immediacy to the story," Elaine Lesh Morgan remarked in *School Library Journal.* In *Dexter the Tough,* a story by Margaret Peterson Haddix, an angry and confused fourth grader makes a difficult adjustment to a new home and school with the help of an understanding teacher. "Elliott's illustrations capture the poignant emotions of these characters," Kay Weisman remarked in a *Booklist* review of *Dexter the Tough,* and Catherine Callegari, writing in *School Library Journal,* similarly noted that Elliott's "drawings nicely portray the actions and feelings of the characters in this easy chapter book."

Biographical and Critical Sources

PERIODICALS

Booklist, April 15, 1999, Susan Dove Lempke, review of *The Princess Test,* p. 1531; August, 2002, Carolyn Phelan, reviews of *The Fairy's Return* and *For Biddle's Sake,* p. 1964; January 1, 2007, Kay Weisman, review of *Dexter the Tough,* p. 102.

New York Times Book Review, August 15, 1999, Meg Wolitzer, reviews of *The Fairy's Mistake* and *The Princess Test.*

Publishers Weekly, February 15, 1999, reviews of *The Fairy's Mistake* and *The Princess Test,* p. 108; September 22, 2003, review of *The Candle in the Window: A Christmas Legend,* p. 68.

School Library Journal, October, 2003, Susan Patron, review of *The Candle in the Window,* p. 64; May, 2006, Martha Topol, review of *Grandpa Has a Great Big Face,* p. 89; January, 2007, Catherine Callegari, review of *Dexter the Tough,* p. 97; September, 2007, Elaine Lesh Morgan, review of *No Talking,* p. 193.

ONLINE

Mark Elliott Home Page, http://markelliott.artroof.com (April 1, 2009).

Shannon Associates Web site, http://www.kidshannon.com/ (April 1, 2008), "Mark Elliott."*

*   *   *

ELLIS, Ann Dee

Personal

Married; husband's name Cameron; children: two sons. *Education:* Brigham Young University, M.F.A. *Hobbies and other interests:* Books, eating, Halloween, making soup, movies, reading, snowboarding, sweating, teaching, traveling, writing, yoga.

Addresses

Home—American Fork, UT. *Office*—Brigham Young University, College of Humanities, 4110B JFSB, Provo, UT 84602. *Agent*—Edward Necarsulmer IV, McIntosh & Otis, 353 Lexington Ave., New York, NY 10016. *E-mail*—anndee@anndeeellis.com.

Career

Author and educator. Brigham Young University, Provo, UT, instructor in creative writing.

Awards, Honors

Best Books for Young Adults selection, and Quick Picks for Reluctant Readers selection, both American Library Association, both 2007, both for *This Is What I Did*.

Writings

This Is What I Did (novel), Little, Brown (New York, NY), 2007.
Everything Is Fine (novel), Little, Brown (New York, NY), 2009.

Author of blog.

Sidelights

Ann Dee Ellis is the author of *This Is What I Did*, a young-adult novel that focuses on Logan, a troubled adolescent dealing with painful and shameful memories. Ellis, who teaches creative writing at Brigham Young University, developed a love for literature at a young age. Remembering how her mother would read to her every night at bedtime, the author stated in an interview on the *Class of 2K7* Web site that "my mom made me cherish books, cherish my imagination, cherish words." Ellis decided to pursue a literary career in college, after being selected to present one of her essays at a student reading. She eventually turned to fiction as a graduate student.

The idea for *This Is What I Did* came to Ellis shortly after her wedding, as she sat in an empty, rented house. "I wasn't going to work that summer; instead we had decided I would write a novel," the author remarked in her *Class of 2K7* interview. "I remember feeling so alone that May morning. I was supposed to sit all day every day in this hollow house and write? It was a weird sense of emptiness I hadn't anticipated. I wrote five sentences and Logan, my main character was born. He was lonely. He was confused. He was awkward. He was supposed to be a normal kid happy with normal things. But he wasn't."

This Is What I Did centers on Logan, an eighth grader who is traumatized by an incident he witnessed one year earlier between his friend Zyler and Zyler's drunken father. Hoping to escape the past and help their son rebuild his life, Logan's parents move the family to a new town where Logan begins attending a different school. Logan's mother unwittingly reveals the family's background to her neighbors, however, and a twisted version of the event begins circulating among Logan's classmates. Believing Logan to be a rapist, a group of students led by his neighbor, Bruce, starts harassing and bullying him.

To boost his son's confidence, Logan's father suggests that he join the local Scout troop, which only adds to Logan's discomfort. Logan's mother offers an equally ineffective solution, as Logan refuses to talk to the therapist she locates. Finally, Logan makes a connection with Laurel, a quirky schoolmate who has a penchant for palindromes, and he lands a role in the school play. Logan also places his trust in a sympathetic counselor, and he eventually discloses the truth about that fateful night.

Cover of Ann Dee Ellis's novel Everything Is Fine, *which finds a young girl coping alone with her mother's depression.* (Little, Brown, 2009. Reproduced with permission.)

This Is What I Did garnered strong reviews. Writing in *Kliatt*, Paula Rohrlick described the work as "a valuable if disturbing story," and *Booklist* contributor Cindy Dobrez remarked that Ellis's "psychological drama effectively explores our failure to protect youth from abuse inflicted by peers or adults." Reviewing the work for *Teenreads.com*, Chris Shanley-Dillman called *This Is What I Did* "an amazing book" in which the "story's memorable characters, unique style and stirring tenderness will warm hearts and fill eyes with tears."

A number of critics applauded Ellis's unusual, fragmented prose style. In *Kirkus Reviews* a contributor cited "Logan's mumbling, realistic, terse and to-the-point narration" as a highlight of the novel, and Deborah Stevenson, writing in *Bulletin of the Center for Children's Books,* called the blend of dialogue, e-mails, and palindromic messages "a highly accessible format that also adds effectively to the tension, enhancing the tautness of Logan's account and lending a certain verisimilitude in its unpolished and choppy relation." "Part staccato prose, part transcript," a contributor in *Publishers Weekly* stated, "this haunting first novel will grip readers right from the start."

A similarly eccentric prose style, which a *Kirkus Reviews* contributor described as "impressionistic, elliptical and full of feeling," distinguishes *Everything Is Fine*. Here Ellis's teenaged protagonist and narrator, Mazzy, is forced to deal with family issues on her own after her father leaves home one summer to further his career as a sportscaster. He leaves Mazzy in charge of her mother, an art teacher who has become so clinically depressed that she cannot leave her bed or even speak to her daughter. Friends and neighbors try to help, but Mazzy keeps insisting that everything is fine. Not understanding what has caused the family's dysfunction and desperate to hold things together, Mazzy puts on a brave and even defiant face. She makes her own meals, takes care of her laundry, and tries to manage all the housework by herself, adamantly refusing to admit that she is having trouble coping—especially to a well-intentioned social worker.

Mazzy also faces issues typical for her age: the physical changes of puberty; the complexities of peer relationships; and the confusions of sexual awakening. She finds herself drawn to Colby, the boy next door, but is not sure if the feeling is mutual. Ellis has Mazzy tell her story in fits and starts, capturing the girl's conflicted feelings and frazzled nerves and echoing the frequent interruptions in her thoughts as she tries to face the unpleasant truths that are hidden from others. Calling *Everything Is Fine* "refreshingly devoid of melodrama," *School Library Journal* reviewer Riva Pollard observed that Ellis "impressively captures the voice of a sardonic, damaged, but surviving adolescent girl."

Cover of Ellis's novel This Is What I Did, *which focuses on a middle-schooler trying to escape a difficult past.* (Copyright © 2007. Reproduced by permission of Little, Brown & Company.)

Biographical and Critical Sources

PERIODICALS

Booklist, May 15, 2007, Cindy Dobrez, review of *This Is What I Did*, p. 43.
Bulletin of the Center for Children's Books, September, 2007, Deborah Stevenson, review of *This Is What I Did*, p. 19.
Kirkus Reviews, June 15, 2007, review of *This Is What I Did;* February 15, 2009, review of *Everything Is Fine*.
Kliatt, July, 2007, Paula Rohrlick, review of *This Is What I Did*, p. 12.
Publishers Weekly, July 30, 2007, review of *This Is What I Did*, p. 84.
School Library Journal, March 1, 2009, Riva Pollard, review of *Everything Is Fine*, p. 143.

ONLINE

Ann Dee Ellis Home Page, http://www.anndeeellis.com (March 1, 2008).

Class of 2K7 Web site, http://classof2k7.com/ (March 1, 2008), "Ann Dee Ellis."

Teenreads.com, http://www.teenreads.com/ (June 5, 2009), Chris Shanley-Dillman, review of *This Is What I Did;* Sarah Rachel Egelman, review of *Everything Is Fine.**

* * *

FARMER, Jacqueline

Personal

Born in Northampton, MA; married; children: two. *Education:* Wheaton College, B.A. (American history); University of Pennsylvania, M.A. (school counseling). *Hobbies and other interests:* Painting, gardening, horseback riding.

Addresses

Home—Greensboro, NC.

Career

Children's book author.

Writings

Bananas!, illustrated by Page Eastburn, Charlesbridge (Watertown, MA), 1999.

Pumpkins!, illustrated by Phyllis Limbacher Tildes, Charlesbridge (Watertown, MA), 2004.

Apples!, illustrated by Phyllis Limbacher Tildes, Charlesbridge (Watertown, MA), 2007.

Author's work has been translated into Spanish.

Biographical and Critical Sources

PERIODICALS

Booklist, August, 2004, Carolyn Phelan, review of *Pumpkins!,* p. 1938; June 1, 2007, Gillian Engberg, review of *Apples!,* p. 64.

Kirkus Reviews, June 15, 2007, review of *Apples!*

School Library Journal, March, 2000, Marian Drabkin, review of *Bananas!,* p. 224; July, 2004, Marge Loch-Wouters, review of *Pumpkins!,* p. 93; September, 2007, Grace Oliff, review of *Apples!,* p. 182.

ONLINE

Charlesbridge Web site, http://www.charlesbridge.com/ (April 10, 2009), "Jacqueline Farmer."*

G

GELBER, Lisa

Personal
Female.

Addresses
Home—Pacific Palisades, CA.

Career
Educator, artist, and author. Art teacher in Los Angeles, CA.

Writings

(With Jody Roberts) *P Is for Peanut: A Photographic ABC,* J. Paul Getty Museum (Los Angeles, CA), 2007.

Biographical and Critical Sources

PERIODICALS

Kirkus Reviews, April 1, 2007, review of *P Is for Peanut: A Photographic ABC.*
School Library Journal, May, 2007, Heide Piehler, review of *P Is for Peanut,* p. 154.*

*   *   *

GEORGE, Jessica Day 1976-

Personal
Born October 11, 1976, in ID: married; children: one son. *Education:* Brigham Young University, B.A.

Addresses
Home—UT.

Career
Writer. Worked variously at libraries, bookstores, a wedding invitation factory, a video store, and a school office.

Writings

NOVELS

Dragon Slippers, Bloomsbury (New York, NY), 2007.
Dragon Flight, Bloomsbury (New York, NY), 2008.
Sun and Moon, Ice and Snow, Bloomsbury (New York, NY), 2008.
Princess of the Midnight Ball, Bloomsbury Children's Books (New York, NY), 2009.
Dragon Spear, Bloomsbury (New York, NY), 2009.

Sidelights

Jessica Day George is the author of a number of critically acclaimed fantasy novels, including *Dragon Slippers* and *Sun and Moon, Ice and Snow.* "All I have ever wanted in this world is to read and write books," George commented on her home page. A graduate of Brigham Young University, she worked at a wedding invitation factory, a video store, and a school office while pursuing a career as an author. "I knew that I would be published eventually, because . . . well, I just had to be," she remarked on her home pages.

George's literary debut, *Dragon Slippers,* centers on Creel, an orphaned girl whose aunt decides to offer her as a sacrifice to the local dragon in the hope that the knight who comes to Creel's aid will fall in love with the girl, marry her, and share his wealth with the entire family. The feisty and intelligent Creel, however, befriends the dragon and earns his trust. After the dragon gives her a mysterious pair of blue slippers, Creel heads to the city to work as a dressmaker, but she soon finds herself embroiled in a plot to overthrow the kingdom. The novel's "exciting, fairy-tale action and vivid scenes, from glittering dragon cave to posh dress shop, are captivating," observed *Booklist* critic Gillian Engberg, and a contributor to *Kirkus Reviews* stated that George "weaves a picaresque tale with a cast of quirky characters into a medieval fantasy."

In *Dragon Flight* Prince Luka calls upon Creel and her dragon friends to help him fend off an invading army. *Dragon Spear* continues where *Dragon Flight* leaves off and maintains the growing alliance between humans and dragons. Luka's father has banished all dragons from his kingdom. The creatures now settle in the Far Isles and live happily until a foreign band of dragons kidnaps Velika, their pregnant queen. Creel, who is preparing for her marriage with Luka, is somewhat sidelined as her brother Hagen steps up to help the dragons and sort out the mess that has been created. To complicate matters, both humans and dragons are in danger from external evil forces. A contributor writing in *Kirkus Reviews* described *Dragon Spear* as "a tasty snack for dragon lovers."

Sun and Moon, Ice and Snow is a novel based on "East o' the Sun, West o' the Moon." As a child, George developed a strong interest in the country of Norway. "I

Cover of Geroge's novel **Dragon Flight,** *a fantasy featuring artwork by* **Brandon Dorman.** (Bloomsbury U.S.A., 2008. Reproduced by permission of Walker Books. All rights reserved.)

Cover of Jessica Day George's fantasy novel **Sun and Moon, Ice and Snow,** *which is based on a traditional nordic folk tale.* (Bloomsbury U.S.A. Children's Books, 2008. Reproduced by permission.)

read any book that even mentioned Norway, or was written by someone Norwegian, no matter what the topic," she recalled on her home page. George was especially intrigued by a volume of "East o' the Sun, West o' the Moon" that was illustrated by P.J. Lynch. "I knew that one day I would write my own version of the story," the author noted. *Sun and Moon, Ice and Snow* concerns a lonely, impoverished girl, known only as the lass, who agrees to live at the palace of a great white bear in exchange for great wealth. Writing in *Booklist*, Frances Bradburn called *Sun and Moon, Ice and Snow* "a vivid, well-crafted, poetic fantasy," and a *Kirkus Reviews* critic described the work as "rich in Norwegian lore and perfectly delicious to read."

George's novel *Princess of the Midnight Ball* is based on the fairy tale of the twelve dancing princesses. The story finds each of them cast under a nightly spell where they dance for King under Stone every night in a bargain for peace and stability in the kingdom. Orphaned soldier Galen discovers this strange event using an invisibility cloak. "Near the end the story spirals up in intensity . . . before a satisfyingly exciting conclusion," noted a *Kirkus Reviews* writer, and Heather Booth wrote in *Booklist* that *Princess of the Midnight Ball* "is a well-realized and fast-paced fantasy-romance that will find favor among fans of fairy tales."

Biographical and Critical Sources

PERIODICALS

Booklist, May 15, 2007, Gillian Engberg, review of *Dragon Slippers*, p. 54; February 1, 2008, Frances Bradburn, review of *Sun and Moon, Ice and Snow*, p. 42; January 1, 2009, Heather Booth, review of *Princess of the Midnight Ball*, p. 71.

Kirkus Reviews, April 15, 2007, review of *Dragon Slippers*; December 1, 2007, review of *Sun and Moon, Ice and Snow*; January 1, 2009, review of *Princess of the Midnight Ball*; April 1, 2009, review of *Dragon Spear.*

ONLINE

Jessica Day George Home Page, http://www.jessicaday george.com (May 26, 2009).*

*   *   *

GOLDBERG, Myla 1972-

Personal

Born 1972 in MD; married Jason Little (a cartoonist); children: one daughter. *Education:* Oberlin College, B.A., 1993. *Religion:* Jewish. *Hobbies and other interests:* Playing pinball; playing the accordion, banjo, flute, and other instruments; foreign and independent films.

Addresses

Home—Brooklyn, NY. *Agent*—Keppler Speakers, 4350 N. Fairfax Dr., Ste. 700, Arlington, VA 22203.

Career

Writer. Brooklyn College of the City University of New York, member of English department faculty. Worked as an English teacher in Prague, Czech Republic, and as a freelance reader for a film production company. Banjo player for Walking Hellos (all-female band).

Awards, Honors

New York Times Notable Book selection, 2000, Outstanding Book for the College Bound selection, American Library Association, Young Lions Award, New York Public Library, Hemingway Foundation/PEN Award finalist, Harold U. Ribalow Prize, Borders New Voices Prize, and Barnes & Noble Discover Award, all for *Bee Season.*

Writings

Bee Season (novel), Doubleday (New York, NY), 2000.
Time's Magpie: A Walk in Prague (essays), illustrated by Ken Nash, Crown Journeys (New York, NY), 2004.
Wickett's Remedy (novel), Doubleday (New York, NY), 2005.
Catching the Moon (picture book), illustrated by Chris Sheban, Arthur A. Levine Books (New York, NY), 2007.

Contributor of short stories to literary journals, including *McSweeneys* and *Harpers*, and to anthologies, including *Post Road 3*, Aboutface, 2001. Contributor of book reviews to *New York Times* and *Bookforum.*

Adaptations

Bee Season was adapted as a film by Naomi Foner Gyllenhaal and directed by Scott McGehee and David Siegel, Fox Searchlight Pictures, 2005.

Sidelights

Myla Goldberg is the author of the highly regarded novels *Bee Season* and *Wickett's Remedy*, and she has also published an essay collection titled *Time's Magpie: A Walk in Prague.* Goldberg's short fiction has appeared in a number of anthologies as well as in publications such as *McSweeneys* and *Harper's*, and she has also contributed book reviews to the *New York Times* and *Bookforum.* Her debut work for young readers, the picture book *Catching the Moon*, appeared in 2007.

The idea for *Bee Season* came to Goldberg after she read an essay about how spelling bees prolong the act of losing. She then, coincidentally, had dinner with a friend who regaled her with stories of her own experiences in a family dedicated to spelling bees. Before starting her novel, Goldberg had little familiarity with spelling bees: indeed, spelling the word "tomorrow" incorrectly in a fourth-grade spelling contest was the extent of her experience. To research her work, she attended the National Spelling Bee in Washington, DC.

One of the highlights of *Bee Season* that is consistently praised is the realistic voice of nine-year-old Eliza. In an interview with Linda M. Castellitto for *Booksense. com*, Goldberg mused: "The good voice has in part to do with the fact I haven't quite figured out I'm a grownup yet. I remember very clearly what it was like to be a child."

Bee Season tells the story of the Naumann family, which consists of siblings Eliza and Aaron and their parents. Their father is a cantor devoted to the study of Jewish mysticism; their mother is a practicing lawyer without whose income the family would probably starve. Aaron is a gifted sixteen year old whose father hopes will follow in his own footsteps and become a scholar, while nine-year-old Eliza is an average student from whom

Cover of Myla Goldberg's award-winning fiction debut, the coming-of-age novel Bee Season. (Anchor Books, 2000. Used by permission of Doubleday, a division of Random House, Inc.)

no one expects much. Eliza suddenly finds herself the focus of her father's attention and love when she takes first place in district and then state spelling competitions. Aaron becomes jealous and rebels by becoming involved with the Hare Krishnas. Meanwhile, hard-working Miriam goes on a crime spree for which she is arrested and committed to a mental institution. As the family falls apart, Aaron finds the courage to declare his intentions to follow his own path, and Eliza risks losing the affection of her demanding father when she finds her own voice and uses it. What looks on the surface to be tragedy for the Naumann family actually turns out to be exhilarating and emancipating for its members.

Bee Season earned numerous honors, including the Harold U. Ribalow Prize and the Barnes & Noble Discover Award, as well as garnering praise from many critics. Dwight Garner wrote in the *New York Times Book Review* that Goldberg's debut "is a dispassionate, fervidly intelligent book . . . that comes by its emotion honestly. By the time she's finished building up, and then pulling apart, the Jewish family at the center of

this story, you're likely to feel as devastated as its members all do." Reviewing *Bee Season* in *Newsweek,* Jeff Giles remarked that "it is amazing how quickly a true talent can announce itself. In the case of Myla Goldberg, it is not even a matter of pages, but of sentences." As Bill Ott observed in *Booklist,* "there is something of Holden Caulfield in Eliza, the same crazed determination to save her loved ones from themselves." Ott concluded by calling *Bee Season* "an impressive debut from a remarkably talented writer."

Set in Boston, Massachusetts, in 1918, *Wickett's Remedy* took Goldberg several years to complete. "I felt a lot of internal pressure to take risks and write something new," she explained to *Village Voice* contributor Rachel Aviv. "Writing is the reason I'm alive, basically. There's no reason to tell the same story over and over." In the novel, Goldberg introduces Lydia Kilkenny Wickett, an impoverished Irish-American shop girl who attracts the attention of aspiring medical student Henry Wickett. After they marry, Henry drops his studies to market a healing elixir that comes with a letter of encouragement, penned by Henry himself. When her husband dies during the 1918 Spanish Flu pandemic, Lydia takes a job as a research assistant to doctors who infect human volunteers with the virus. Meanwhile, Henry's partner, the unscrupulous Quentin Driscoll, transforms their humble mail-order business into a booming soft drink company.

"Like Eliza Naumann in *Bee Season,* the likable and courageous Lydia blossoms before our eyes," wrote Malcolm Jones in his *Newsweek* review of *Wickett's Remedy,* while in *Lancet* A.C. Grayling called Lydia "one of those literary creations who live in the mind, a graceful being around whom the disaster of the epidemic swirls like a hurricane." In the opinion of *Salon.com* contributor Ira Boudway, "the real reason to read *Wickett's Remedy* is for the chance to spend a few hours in the presence of the charming Lydia as she develops into a woman who, while still childlike, is no longer childish and, while still simple, is no longer a simpleton." According to Andrea Barrett, writing in the *New York Times Book Review,* the historical backdrop of Goldberg's story "serves to convey the epidemic's wider context even as it provides glimpses of various characters' fates. In addition, hundreds of comments—parallel perspectives voiced by an unnamed 'Us'—run down the margins alongside the main text until the novel's pages begin to resemble a kind of New England Talmud, replete with layers of marginalia."

Turning to younger readers, Goldberg joins forces with illustrator Chris Sheban to create *Catching the Moon,* a contemporary fable about an unlikely friendship. When the Man in the Moon notices a fisherwoman casting her line into the water each moonlit night with no success, he decides to pay her a visit. Disguised as a hiker, complete with a traveling hat, sunglasses, and a pair of boots, he stops by her shack on a moonless evening, bringing along a sea cucumber sandwich. As they share a cup of tea, the Man in the Moon notices that the high

Goldberg's picture book Catching the Moon, *features nostalgic-themes artwork by Chris Sheban.* (Illustration copyright © 2007 by Chris Sheban. Reproduced by permission of Scholastic, Inc.)

tide washes through the door of the shack and floods the floor. When he returns the next moonless night, still in disguise, the fisherwoman confesses that she is hoping to reel in the Man in the Moon and force him to stop the tide from eroding the land. Impressed with the Fisherwoman's devotion to saving her home, the Man in the Moon offers a unique solution to the problem.

Reviewers complimented Goldberg's narrative as well as Sheban's artwork in *Catching the Moon*. According to a *Kirkus Reviews* writer, the book's "lunar language and Sheban's stunningly luminous illustrations turn this contemporary tall tale into a shining winner," and a *Publishers Weekly* stated that "the gentle humor in both text and images softens the environmental theme." Elaine Lesh Morgan, writing in *School Library Journal,* also applauded Goldberg's prose, noting that her "text flows almost like the tides and includes words that will gently stretch a young child's vocabulary." *New York Times Book Review* critic Julie Just observed that the author "tells a layered story that invites rereading," while the *Publishers Weekly* reviewer called *Catching the Moon* "as captivating as moonlight shimmering on a quiet sea."

Goldberg turns to nonfiction in *Time's Magpie,* a travel-ogue that explores the Czech capital of Prague, where the author lived for a year in the early 1990s, while teaching English to government officials. Writing from the perspective of a decade, Goldberg offers readers a glimpse of Prague's most famous sites, including the Astronomical Tower, Old Town Square, and the historic Charles Bridge. She also reflects on the city's many changes, discussing its new fast-food restaurants, a neighborhood destroyed by a flood, and a variety of youthful skateboarders. *Library Journal* contributor Rita Simmons praised Goldberg's narrative, stating that she permits "her fiction writer's voice to infuse each essay with exquisite detail." Chris Springer, reviewing *Time's Magpie* for the *International Travel News,* observed that the author "strives for an all-inclusive portrait of the city, one that records much of what we tourists willfully overlook."

In addition to her writing, Goldberg teaches at Brooklyn College and plays the accordion and banjo for the Walking Hellos, an all-female rock band. Her literary success has come as a surprise, she admits, telling *USA Today* contributor Bob Minzesheimer: "I'm still amazed that's happened and hope it's something I never get used to."

Biographical and Critical Sources

PERIODICALS

Booklist, May 15, 2000, Bill Ott, review of *Bee Season,* p. 1729; September 15, 2004, Brad Hooper, review of *Time's Magpie: A Walk in Prague,* p. 201; August, 2005, Joanne Wilkinson, review of *Wickett's Remedy,* p. 1991.

Entertainment Weekly, September 30, 2005, Karen Valby, review of *Wickett's Remedy,* p. 98.

Harper's Bazaar, June, 2001, Laurel Narersen, "Write Guard: Bazaar Asks Five Fiction Masters about the Agony and Ecstasy of Modern Literary Life," pp. 116-117.

International Travel News, April, 2005, Chris Springer, review of *Time's Magpie,* p. 98.

Kirkus Reviews, July 15, 2005, review of *Wickett's Remedy,* p. 755; December 15, 2005, Bruce Allen, review of *Wickett's Remedy;* April 1, 2007, review of *Catching the Moon,* p. 321.

Lancet, December 17, 2005, A.C. Grayling, review of *Wickett's Remedy,* p. 2077.

Library Journal, April 15, 2000, Kimberly G. Allen, review of *Bee Season,* p. 122; November 1, 2004, Rita Simmons, review of *Time's Magpie,* p. 110; July 1, 2005, Jyna Scheeren, review of *Wickett's Remedy,* p. 68.

MacLean's, June 11, 2001, "The Sting of a Spelling Bee," p. 56.

Newsweek, May 29, 2000, Jeff Giles, "E Is for Eliza, a Speller at Heart," p. 70; September 19, 2005, Malcolm Jones, review of *Wickett's Remedy,* p. 62.

New York Times, June 12, 2000, Christopher Lehmann-Haupt, "Seeking Transcendence through Proper Spelling," p. B7.

New York Times Book Review, June 18, 2000, Dwight Garner, "Spellbound," p. 5; September 18, 2005, Andrea Barrett, review of *Wickett's Remedy,* p. 19; July 15, 2007, Julie Just, review of *Catching the Moon,* p. 17.

Publishers Weekly, April 17, 2000, review of *Bee Season,* p. 50; July 10, 2000, Daisy Maryles, "To Bee or Not to Bee," p. 13; July 25, 2005, review of *Wickett's Remedy,* p. 40; April 9, 2007, review of *Catching the Moon,* p. 52.

School Library Journal, November, 2000, Molly Connally, review of *Bee Season,* p. 182; December, 2005, Kim Dare, review of *Wickett's Remedy,* p. 178; June, 2007, Elaine Lesh Morgan, review of *Catching the Moon,* p. 97.

Time, July 3, 2000, Paul Gray, review of *Bee Season,* p. 62; September 26, 2005, Michele Orecklin, review of *Wickett's Remedy,* p. 76.

USA Today, September 22, 2005, Bob Minzesheimer, "Myla Goldberg Is Back, and Completely Different," p. D5.

Village Voice, September 22, 2005, Rachel Aviv, "Flu Season: A Talk with Disease-Nerd Novelist, Banjo Player, and Indie-rock Muse Myla Goldberg."

Wall Street Journal, June 16, 2000, Erica Schacter, "A Letter Perfect Debut," p. W9.

Washington Post, August 13, 2000, Louis Bayard, "Buzz Words," p. X5.

ONLINE

Booksense Web site, http://www.booksense.com/ (October 1, 2002), Linda M. Castellitto, interview with Goldberg.

Grendel Web site, http://www.grendel.org/ (March 1, 2009), interview with Goldberg.

Myla Goldberg Home Page, http://www.mylagoldberg.com (March 1, 2009).

Random House Web site, http://www.randomhouse.com/ (March 1, 2009), Laura Buchwald, interview with Goldberg.

Salon.com, http://www.salon.com/ (April 10, 2002), Gavin McNett, review of *Bee Season;* (October 1, 2005) Ira Boudway, review of *Wickett's Remedy.**

*   *   *

GRIFALCONI, Ann 1929-

Personal

Surname is pronounced "*Gree*-fal-koh-nee"; born September 22, 1929, in New York, NY; daughter of Joseph Grifalconi and Mary Hays Weik (a writer). *Education:* Cooper Union Art School, certificate in advertising art, 1950; attended University of Cincinnati, 1951; New York University, B.S., 1954; postgraduate studies at Hunter College and New School for Social Research

Ann Grifalconi (Photograph by Leslie Derusso. Reproduced by permission.)

(now New School University). *Hobbies and other interests:* Writing music, photography, archaeology, travel to Africa, Europe, and Central America.

Addresses

Home—New York, NY. *E-mail*—anngrifalconi@verizon. net.

Career

Freelance artist and illustrator, 1965—. Artist and designer in advertising and display, 1950-54; High School of Fashion Industry, New York, NY, teacher of art and display, 1954-65; Media Plus, New York, NY, president, beginning 1968; Greyfalcon House, New York, NY, producer. *Exhibitions:* Work exhibited at Vassar Library, 1989, Muscarelli Museum, 1990, and Kimberly Gallery, New York, NY, 1991. Contributor of artwork to collections, including Kerlan Collection, and to traveling exhibits.

Member

Authors Guild, Authors League of America.

Awards, Honors

New York Times Best Illustrated Book designation, and Newbery Honor Book designation, both 1968, both for *The Jazz Man; New York Times* citation, and Ad Club

Best Designed Book Award, both for *The Ballad of the Burglar of Babylon;* Coretta Scott King Illustration Award, 1985, for *Everett Anderson's Goodbye;* Caldecott Honor Award, American Library Association, 1987, for *The Village of Round and Square Houses;* Jane Addams Children's Book Award for picture book, 2003, for *Patrol: An American Soldier in Vietnam;* Jane Addams Children's Book Award honor book selection, 2003, for *The Village That Vanished.*

Writings

City Rhythms, Bobbs-Merrill (Indianapolis, IN), 1965.
The Toy Trumpet, Bobbs-Merrill (Indianapolis, IN), 1968.
The Matter with Lucy: An Album, Bobbs-Merrill (Indianapolis, IN), 1973.
The Village of Round and Square Houses, Little, Brown (Boston, MA), 1986.
Darkness and the Butterfly, Little, Brown (Boston, MA), 1987.
Osa's Pride, Little, Brown (Boston, MA), 1990.
The Flyaway Girl, Little, Brown (Boston, MA), 1991.
Kinda Blue, Little, Brown (Boston, MA), 1991.
The Bravest Flute: A Story of Courage in the Mayan Tradition, Little, Brown (Boston, MA), 1994.
Not Home (novel), Little, Brown (Boston, MA), 1995.
Electric Yancy, Lothrop (New York, NY), 1997.
Tiny's Hat, HarperCollins (New York, NY), 1999.
The Village That Vanished, illustrated by Kadir Nelson, Dial/Viking (New York, NY), 2002.
Ain't Nobody a Stranger to Me, illustrated by Jerry Pinkney, Jump at the Sun (New York, NY), 2007.

FOR CHILDREN; ILLUSTRATOR

Rhoda Bacmeister, *Voices in the Night,* Bobbs-Merrill (Indianapolis, IN), 1965.
Ina B. Forbus, *Tawny's Trick,* Viking (New York, NY), 1965.
Gladys Tabor, *Still Meadow Cookbook,* Lippincott (New York, NY), 1965.
O. Arnold, *Hidden Treasures of the Wild West,* Abelard, 1966.
Margaret Embry, *Peg-Leg-Willy,* Holiday House (New York, NY), 1966.
Edwin Palmer Hoyt, *American Steamboat Stories,* Abelard, 1966.
De Luca, editor, *Italian Poetry Selections,* Harvey House (New York, NY), 1966.
Mary Hays Weik, *The Jazz Man,* Atheneum (New York, NY), 1966.
Nancy Zimmelman, *Pepito,* Reilly & Lee, 1967.
Tillie S. Pine and Joseph Levine, *The Africans Knew,* McGraw-Hill (New York, NY), 1967.
Johanna Johnston, *A Special Bravery,* Dodd (New York, NY), 1967.
E.S. Lampman, *Half-Breed,* Doubleday (New York, NY), 1967.

Louise A. Steintorf, *The Treasure of Tolmec,* John Day, 1967.

Barbara Reid, *Carlo's Cricket,* McGraw-Hill (New York, NY), 1967.

Tillie S. Pine and Joseph Levine, *The Incas Knew,* McGraw-Hill (New York, NY), 1968.

Tillie S. Pine and Joseph Levine, *The Maya Knew,* McGraw-Hill (New York, NY), 1968.

Betsy Byars, *Midnight Fox,* Viking (New York, NY), 1968.

John and Sara Westbrook Brewton, compilers, *America Forever New,* Crowell (New York, NY), 1968.

Bronson Potter, *Antonio,* Atheneum (New York, NY), 1968.

Anton Chekov, *Shadows and Light,* translated by M. Morton, Doubleday (New York, NY), 1968.

Elizabeth Bishop, *The Ballad of the Burglar of Babylon,* Farrar, Straus (New York, NY), 1968.

Anne Norris Baldwin, *Sunflowers for Tina,* Doubleday (New York, NY), 1969.

Ruby Zagoren, *Venture for Freedom,* World Publishing (Chicago, IL), 1969.

Lois Kalb Bouchard, *The Boy Who Wouldn't Talk,* Doubleday (New York, NY), 1969.

Langston Hughes, *Don't You Turn Back: Poems,* edited by Lee Bennett Hopkins, Knopf (New York, NY), 1969.

Lee Bennett Hopkins, *This Street's for Me!,* Crown (New York, NY), 1970.

Lorenz B. Graham, *David He No Fear,* Crowell (New York, NY), 1971.

Walter Dean Myers, *The Dragon Takes a Wife,* Bobbs-Merrill (Indianapolis, IN), 1972.

Toby Talbot, *The Night of the Radishes,* Putnam (New York, NY), 1972.

Mary Hays Weik, *A House on Liberty Street,* Atheneum (New York, NY), 1972.

John Lonzo Anderson, *The Day the Hurricane Happened,* Scribner (New York, NY), 1974.

Lucille Clifton, *Everett Anderson's Year,* Holt (New York, NY), 1974.

Ann McGovern, *The Secret Soldier,* Four Winds Press (New York, NY), 1975.

Letta Schatz, *Banji's Magic Wheel,* Follett, 1975.

Lucille Clifton, *Everett Anderson's Friend,* Holt (New York, NY), 1976.

Lucille Clifton, *Everett Anderson's 1 2 3,* Holt (New York, NY), 1977.

Giovanni Boccaccio, *Stories from the Decameron,* limited edition, Franklin Library, 1977.

Lucille Clifton, *Everett Anderson's Nine Month Long,* Holt (New York, NY), 1978.

Genevieve S. Gray, *How Far, Felipe?,* Harper (New York, NY), 1978.

William Styron, *The Confessions of Nat Turner,* limited edition, Franklin Library, 1979.

Lucille Clifton, *Everett Anderson's Goodbye,* Holt (New York, NY), 1983.

Lynn Joseph, *Jasmine's Parlour Day,* Lothrop, Lee & Shepard (New York, NY), 1994.

Nancy Raines Day, *The Lion's Whiskers: An Ethiopian Folktale,* Scholastic (New York, NY), 1995.

James Berry, *Don't Leave an Elephant to Go and Chase a Bird,* Simon & Schuster (New York, NY), 1996.

Florence Parry Heide and Roxanne Heide Pierce, *Tio Armando,* Lothrop, Lee & Shepard (New York, NY), 1998.

Isaac O. Olaleye, *In the Rainfield: Who Is the Greatest?,* Scholastic (New York, NY), 2000.

Lucille Clifton, *One of the Problems of Everett Anderson,* Holt (New York, NY), 2001.

Walter Dean Myers, *Patrol: An American Soldier in Vietnam,* HarperCollins (New York, NY), 2002.

Arthur Dorros, *Julio's Magic,* HarperCollins (New York, NY), 2005.

OTHER

(With Ruth Jacobsen) *Camping through Europe by Car, with Maximum Fun at Minimum Cost* (travelogue), Crown (New York, NY), 1963.

The Right Way (play), produced in New York, NY, 1999.

Adaptations

The Village of Round and Square Houses was recorded on cassette, video, and filmstrip; *The Toy Trumpet* and *City Rhythms* were adapted as bilingual filmstrip/cassette sets.

Sidelights

Ann Grifalconi is an award-winning author and illustrator who has published more than a dozen titles for young readers and provided the artwork for books by such celebrated writers as Lee Bennett Hopkins and Walter Dean Myers. Since the mid-1960s, Grifalconi has expanded children's literature by presenting realistic characters from other cultures. Her Caldecott Honor Book *The Village of Round and Square Houses* is just one of her books that tell of African village life and traditions. Grifalconi has also written about the Mexican and Mayan peoples and has been a pioneer in the portrayal of African-American children, both with her own books and with her illustrations for others. One of Grifalconi's goals is to create works that expand her readers' horizons and "illuminate either the heart or the spirit or the mind of a child," as she once commented, adding that she hoped "to bring them something new" in the process.

Grifalconi grew up during the Great Depression of the 1930s. Her parents were divorced, and she and her brother were raised by her mother, writer Mary Hays Weik. Although it was difficult for a single parent to raise two children during trying times, Grifalconi's mother worked hard to secure a good education for them. "Basically as a survivor my mother had to move with her two children wherever the jobs were and wherever the schools were," Grifalconi once noted. Because Grifalconi rarely stayed long in any one neighborhood, books became her companions. "The reading I did expanded my worldview," she commented. "I was reading historical romances, adventures around the world." Grifalconi also began reading the *National Geographic* and other magazines that contributed even further to her appreciation of the wider world.

Ann Grifalconi's sophisticated graphic images bring to life Lucille Clifton's picture book Everett Anderson's Year. (Henry Holt, 1974. Illustration copyright © 1974 by Ann Grifalconi. Reproduced by permission.)

Grifalconi was interested in the wonderful pictures that accompanied her favorite books, such as the "Red," "White," and "Violet" story books, with illustrations by Howard Pyle and others. "When I was a little girl," she once stated, "my mother gave me Arthur Rackham's beautiful book of illustrations for *A Midsummer Night's Dream*—that thrilled me!" A comic-book reader at an early age, Grifalconi especially liked the stories that were "very realistic, such as *Tarzan* and *Flash Gordon*, all of which were done by very good illustrators of their period." Another source of excellent artwork was the *Saturday Evening Post*, which her brother sold.

When she was young, Grifalconi did not consider herself to be a good artist; she only drew doodles once in a while. However, when she was about ten years old, her mother moved the family back to her hometown in Indiana. An art teacher in her school there noticed that Grifalconi had talent. The family returned to New York City at the end of the school year, and during that summer vacation Grifalconi practiced drawing and painting.

Grifalconi's mother moved one more time before her children started high school so that they could attend the New York City public schools that specialized in art and architecture. Grifalconi's art school "was a perfect school for me because it had a creative writing class straight through, which was nongraded." In particular, Grifalconi remembered "a very gifted teacher, Miss Estelle Stiles, who taught us in a pleasant classroom where we all contributed to the school magazine. I also had another very gifted art teacher, Mrs. Julia Winston, who encouraged us all to write and illustrate our own short stories and poems. So we had a continuous art and writing experience straight through high school."

Competing against one thousand other high school graduates, Grifalconi won one of ninety competitive scholarships to attend Cooper Union, a specialized free college in New York City. "Cooper Union was one of the better opportunities for a person without money who wanted to expand their horizons and study art, architecture, or engineering," she commented. "That was a wonderful experience: we had very small classes, we were right in New York, so all sorts of famous people—artists, writer, thinkers—would visit our school, such as Dylan Thomas, the poet who was in America then, or Buckminster Fuller. We really had contact with them: we listened to their voices and were inspired by their ideas and even became students for short individual class sessions, as I did with 'Bucky' Fuller. So I think I had a great education." Also interested in printmaking and painting, Grifalconi graduated after three years with a certificate in advertising.

Grifalconi began a career in advertising but quickly became disillusioned with the work and decided to go to school again. She won a scholarship to attend New York University, where she completed a degree in art history and also pursued a minor in history, one of her longtime interests. It was a desire to teach again that brought Grifalconi back to New York to gain a college degree. "I had a 'calling' at the time, to make people ask questions, engender questions in people's minds," she commented. After earning her degree, Grifalconi joined the staff at the High School of Fashion Industry in New York City, where she taught "display, merchandising, interior design, fashion art, and a number of other things which included a sense of the world as it really was."

At the same time, the artist recalled, "I was also moving into writing and illustrating my own books. It began by example. I had been doing some woodcuts, and my mother, who was a writer, liked a woodcut I had done of a jazz musician. When Mother had said, 'Oh, I like that,' she made me realize that what I was doing might turn into something. That's how I started my first children's book called *City Rhythms*, about the sound of music and the pulse of the city." Two years later Grifalconi's mother sent her a manuscript she had written about a jazz player; this turned out to be *The Jazz Man*, the Newbery Medal honor book which Grifalconi would illustrate. Even though she had almost finished her own book, "when Mother's *Jazz Man* manuscript came back, I thought her story was such a beauty that I put my own project aside," the author continued. "Of course, Mother had always been a very fine writer—she started as a poet."

After she finished the woodcut illustrations for *The Jazz Man*, Grifalconi concluded work on *City Rhythms*. It was difficult finding the time to take her work around to publishers, especially since she was still teaching. "But I started realizing around a certain age that if I was going to carry out my art thing I'd better do it now, so even though I was teaching full-time, I would make appointments and take my portfolio around," she remembered. A knowledgeable friend suggested that Grifalconi make a "dummy" book, complete with illustrations, and show it around. The author did, and *City Rhythms* was accepted by Bobbs-Merrill and published in 1965.

Meanwhile, Grifalconi's mother was having trouble finding a publisher for her book. "*The Jazz Man* was sent to a number of people and often it was regretfully rejected and turned back. Sometimes editors literally had tears in their eyes because they liked it so much, but it was a bit controversial—it was not entirely upbeat," Grifalconi once explained. "Finally Mother said, 'Would you please take it with you while you're taking your portfolio around?'" Grifalconi took the book to Atheneum, who accepted it. "So Mother and I got to work on this project together, which was one of the great satisfactions in both of our lives." While she was working on *The Jazz Man*, Grifalconi realized that "it was a work of love, and I think it was then that I began to realize that I liked doing this more than teaching." She decided to leave her teaching job. "I felt I was shortchanging the kids."

In addition, Grifalconi perceived a need in children's books that she could fill. "I was aware that there were no really attractive black children or black families. It seemed they would make little white faces and smear them black," she remarked. Unhappy with this situation, Grifalconi decided to start making her own contributions. "I had a very good background in life drawing and figure drawing, so I felt that I could do it," she commented. "I also thought that black people were truly beautiful. Many of my friends were black, and I saw them as real people, and I hated these sort of imitation white people drawings. So when I left, I had finally decided, 'Now!' I just did it."

Grifalconi still had a desire to educate people, even though she no longer worked at a New York school. She cofounded Media Plus, a company that created interracial multimedia materials. These included films and sound filmstrips on ethnic history, women's rights, living poets, and bilingual programs in Spanish and English. There was even a filmstrip version in both languages of Grifalconi's book *The Toy Trumpet,* a book about a Mexican boy who wants an instrument of his own to play. Grifalconi and her partner later sold the company to Doubleday/Random House, but she continued to work on educational multimedia projects.

Grifalconi also began illustrating the books of other writers, taking special care to match the style of her artwork to the style of the story. "I try to sympathetically feel what the poet or writer is trying to say," she explained. "I try to follow the *word*. I think the word is very important." She gained notice for her illustrations in several of Lucille Clifton's books about Everett Anderson, a young African American. The publisher of Clifton's book allowed only one or two colors for the illustrations, so Grifalconi decided that pencil would

best relate the mood of the stories. "Because it had to be delicate and yet warm while it was also black," the artwork for *Everett Anderson's Nine Month Long* "was a delicate pencil tone because it's about waiting for a baby," Grifalconi remarked. "When I was working with *Everett Anderson's Goodbye,* where the boy is remembering the death of his father and trying to adjust to it, it seemed to me that a deeper black and white was called for. I used a much darker, bigger pencil and worked very large with *Everett Anderson's Goodbye.* I felt there was deep grief there, and I wanted to express that, so I had to go large and dark." Reviewing the graphic art in *Everett Anderson's Year,* a *Horn Book* contributor noted that the book remains "as relevant and captivating" as when it was first published. In another children's book, *One of the Problems of Everett Anderson,* "Grifalconi's soft charcoal illustrations give depth to the text, adding to the somber tone," as Shelley Townsend-Hudson remarked in *Booklist.*

Grifalconi studies and explores her subject thoroughly when she prepares to write and illustrate a book. "It's the old idea of gathering, gathering, gathering, and overgathering," she said. "I love history, and I love research. I either go to the place or I get it together here, and I do immense amounts of research—immense!" Grifalconi conducts research in the large library she keeps in her New York home, at local libraries, and in her travels around the world. "I went to Africa," she continued. "I've been going back and forth to Central America, I love it, it's one of my special places! I've been to Haiti many times, because it seems almost identical to Africa—even the earth, the plants, everything. I can see why Africans who found themselves in Haiti felt at home, it's just exactly like Equatorial West Africa." While Grifalconi was visiting a village in Cameroon, Africa, a young woman explained that in her own village the women lived in round huts while the men lived in square ones. Her trip to that village gave Grifalconi the idea for *The Village of Round and Square Houses,* which received a Caldecott honor designation.

Grifalconi used paints and chalks in her award-winning illustrations for *The Village of Round and Square Houses,* writing: "I picked the medium to suit the message." "I felt there was a lot of warmth, I remembered the sunlight, the intensity of the color, the laughter of the children, the richness of the sunlight on the trees, and I wanted to depict as much as I could that magical richness. It ended up a mixed technique. I started with watercolor, and I realized that I wanted to enhance the textures, so it became a mixed-media thing." Grifalconi's "bold, dramatic illustrations echo the rhythm of African life," Lisa Lane remarked in a *Christian Science Monitor* review of *The Village of Round and Square Houses.* "What Grifalconi has brought to these pages is master storytelling, a melding of words and pictures to communicate an imaginative piece of folklore," Bonita Brodt concluded in her review of the same work for Chicago's *Tribune Books.*

Africa has also been the backdrop for illustrations of stories by several other authors. Grifalconi's artwork for Nancy Raines Day's Ethiopian folktale *The Lion's Whiskers: An Ethiopian Folktale* is made up of "warm collage illustrations in desert shades of brown and red," according to *Booklist* contributor Hazel Rochman. A reviewer for *Publishers Weekly* felt that these collages "ably evoke the timeless quality of the parable. . . . From the vast beige expanse of the desert to the almost palpably blazing sun to the cool indigos of the sky as night falls, [Grifalconi] strikingly renders the landscape." Rochman noted that Grifalconi "draws on West African wood carvings and sculptures" for *Don't Leave an Elephant to Go and Chase a Bird,* and ranked as the best illustrations in that book were "the sly comic pictures of the conspiring elephants." Reviewing the same title, a contributor for *Publishers Weekly* felt that Grifalconi "paints in a unique, highly stylized manner patterned after African carvings."

In Isaac O. Olaleye's *In the Rainfield: Who Is the Greatest?* Wind, Fire, and Rain battle with one another in a "compelling Nigerian tale," according to Teri Markson in *School Library Journal.* Markson noted that the story is "rich with sound and imagery, yet it soars when complemented by [Grifalconi's] visually arresting mixed-media collages," a mixture of photographs with marbleized and textured papers. "Grifalconi's surreal collages explode across the pages of this eye-popping book," declared a reviewer for *Publishers Weekly.*

Grifalconi often uses Africa as a setting for her books because she believes its cultures have had a great influence on American culture. Africa is "an originating culture," she once said. "Many of us have come from that culture, and for many others, even if we're not black ourselves, nevertheless our music, our clothing, the idea of being cool, the jazz music—a lot of our originating art has come from Africa. Why did they come, where did they come from, what was the atmosphere like, you want to know the answers to those questions. How do people live in different places in the world? Why do they live differently? You want to know how, and why. So you start creating stories that present the life there, and yet you also give them human characteristics that are true of all human beings." Grifalconi employs a method of African storytelling in *The Village That Vanished,* which describes the efforts of three Yao woman to save the inhabitants of their village from invaders by invoking the spirits of their ancestors. "Both trickster tale and historical fiction, this is a valuable and unusual addition to the literature about slavery," commented Joanna Rudge Long in *Horn Book.*

Grifalconi has always been drawn to traditional cultures, in part "because I am an urban child, and I have often been an outsider. I began to wonder how this all started: what are the basics that are true of all human beings; can I present them before all these cultures have disappeared? Are there some truths that these cultures have to offer us, before we get hopelessly complicated in our urban, second-hand culture? I am trying to find and present originating cultures to our more complex civilization so that we could choose that which is good, that which is valuable, and warm and living."

In *Julio's Magic,* a book by Arthur Dorros that is set in southern Mexico, a young woodcarver forsakes his own glory and helps his aging, impoverished mentor enter an important contest. "Grifalconi's photorealistic collages capture the texture, color, and feel of village life," Linda M. Kenton stated in her *School Library Journal* review of the book, and a *Kirkus Reviews* contributor noted that Grifalconi's pictures for *Julio's Magic* "have magic of their own, establishing a strong sense of place with a touch of the surreal."

Grifalconi noted that ideas for her books come to her gradually. "It's like the way a musician might walk around listening to this and that, and finally a theme presents itself to him, becomes a persistent theme. Then you want to pin it down, so you try to find a story—or a character. When a character walks through that maze of new information with a story, it begins to come to life." *Ain't Nobody a Stranger to Me* was inspired by true events and here Grifalconi examines the relationship between a young girl and her grandfather, a former slave who fled to safety through the Underground Railroad. "Caught by the action, children will hear Finger's shining words across time, race, and generations," wrote Hazel Rochman in *Booklist,* and a critic in *Kirkus Reviews* stated that the work "makes a powerful statement across racial lines, nationalities and generations."

Grifalconi once remarked that the goal of each literary effort "is to reflect the spirit of that particular story in the most appropriate way." "In the background as well as in the story," she added, "I try to choose words carefully so that there will be just a few new words, or I try to use words the readers can easily understand. I try to present ideas on each page, so they have time to look them over. Children ought to have the satisfaction of being presented with an idea and then being presented with an accompanying image, which is also rich enough for them to go over further anytime they want to." Grifalconi uses whatever medium best suits her story, from the simple text and soft colors of *Kinda Blue* to what *Booklist* reviewer Carolyn Phelan called the "impressionistic artwork" of *The Bravest Flute.*

In *Patrol: An American Soldier in Vietnam,* a picture book for older readers that features a text by Walter Dean Myers, Grifalconi uses mixed-media collage to illustrate the story of a frightened young combat soldier. As she wrote in the *Children's Book Council Magazine,* it was necessary "to get into the head of the first-person narrator—the soldier who had just been dropped into unfamiliar country by helicopter along with this nine-man patrol and ordered to advance stealthily through forested, enemy territory. Step by step, I tried to see with his eyes, hear with his ears, and feel with his heartbeat as he moved through this unknown world, through its strange foliage, colorful plants, and wildly plumaged birds. Alone, distanced from his patrol, trying to find the sources of all the sounds: twitters, rustles, cracking shots . . . all this had to be depicted." A contributor in *Kirkus Reviews* described the artist's illustrations as "remarkable, and suitably disturbing. A jungle effect is created by overlapping photographs of trees with close-up details of leaves, marbled paper, and negative space—all of which virtually overwhelm the human figures." According to Long, "The haunting illustrations of a lovely, violated land and the taut, poetic text unite in a powerful rendering" of war's destructive capacities. Grifalconi earned the Jane Addams Children's Book Award for her work in *Patrol*.

"The audience, the person I feel I address in my mind's eye, is the child who's beginning to *feel*—like the boy who's concerned about the death of his father and is beginning to have to deal with it on his own," Grifalconi once commented. "The child who's beginning to wonder, the child who's beginning to deal with the world—just his or her first tiny, little mental and emotional steps into the world, I think that's the moment that I find quite wonderful. Possibly that relates to the fact that I was often a child who was going from one school to another. I was always in a new school, finding out a new situation, trying to figure it all out. I think I'm very interested in that process. I think that's perhaps my deepest underlying theme, exploring that with a child and with young persons."

Her goal, Grifalconi stated, is "to bring the mind and the soul in contact with new information or consideration. I think it is also to try to remain very human in that process, and to have the child come to love and understand others and himself." In the end her hope is to "give a loving, living interpretation of life as I've seen, or imagined it."

Biographical and Critical Sources

BOOKS

Hopkins, Lee Bennett, *Books Are by People,* Citation Press, 1969.

PERIODICALS

Black Issues Book Review, September-October, 2002, Lynda Jones, review of *Patrol: An American Soldier in Vietnam,* p. 61.

Booklist, February 15, 1994, Hazel Rochman, review of *Jasmine's Parlour Day,* p. 1092; September 15, 1994, Carolyn Phelan, review of *The Bravest Flute: A Story of Courage in the Mayan Tradition,* p. 143; February 15, 1995, Hazel Rochman, review of *The Lion's Whiskers: An Ethiopian Folktale,* p. 1085; February 15, 1996, Hazel Rochman, review of *Don't Leave an Elephant to Go and Chase a Bird,* p. 1023; February 15, 2000, Susan Dove Lempke, review of *In the Rainfield: Who Is the Greatest?,* p. 1118; September 15, 2001, Shelley Townsend-Hudson, review of *One of the Problems of Everett Anderson,* p. 230; March 15, 2002, Hazel Rochman, review of *Patrol,* p. 1258; September 15, 2002, Hazel Rochman, review of *The Village That Vanished,* p. 231; January 1, 2005, Gillian Engberg, review of *Julio's Magic,* p. 868; May 1, 2007, Hazel Rochman, review of *Ain't Nobody a Stranger to Me,* p. 98.

Christian Science Monitor, May 2, 1986, Lisa Lane, "Choices for Children," p. B7.

Horn Book, March-April, 1993, review of *Everett Anderson's Year,* p. 229; May-June, 1994, review of *Jasmine's Parlour Day,* p. 316; July-August, 2002, Joanna Rudge Long, review of *Patrol,* p. 449; September-October, 2002, Joanna Rudge Long, review of *The Village That Vanished,* p. 551.

Kirkus Reviews, May 1, 2002, review of *Patrol,* p. 663; September 15, 2002, review of *The Village That Vanished,* p. 1390; December 15, 2004, review of *Julio's Magic,* p. 1200; March 15, 2007, review of *Ain't Nobody a Stranger to Me.*

Publishers Weekly, April 5, 1993, review of *Kinda Blue,* p. 77; May 16, 1994, review of *Jasmine's Parlour Day,* p. 64; March 27, 1995, review of *The Lion's Whiskers,* p. 85; March 27, 1995, review of *Not Home,* p. 86; December 11, 1995, review of *Don't Leave an Elephant to Go and Chase a Bird,* p. 70; January 10, 2000, review of *In the Rainfield,* p. 67; April 22, 2002, review of *Patrol,* p. 70; August 26, 2002, review of *The Village That Vanished,* p. 68; January 31, 2005, review of *Julio's Magic,* p. 68; April 9, 2007, review of *Ain't Nobody a Stranger to Me,* p. 53.

School Library Journal, April, 2000, Teri Markson, review of *In the Rainfield,* p. 124; October, 2001, Sally R. Dow, review of *One of the Problems of Everett Anderson,* p. 113; May, 2002, Kathy Piehl, review of *Patrol,* p. 158; December, 2002, Miriam Lang Budin, review of *The Village That Vanished,* p. 97; January, 2005, Linda M. Kenton, review of *Julio's Magic,* p. 90; May, 2007, Wendy Lukehart, review of *Ain't Nobody a Stranger to Me,* p. 97.

Tribune Books (Chicago, IL), January 25, 1987, Bonita Brodt, "Just for Children," p. 4.

ONLINE

Children's Book Council Magazine Online, http://www.cbcbooks.org/cbcmagazine/ (December, 2005), Ann Grifalconi, "In the Artist's Studio."*

H

HALE, Nathan 1976-

Personal
Born 1976; married; children: two.

Addresses
Home—UT. *Agent*—Kid Shannon, 630 9th Ave., Ste. 707, New York, NY 10036. *E-mail*—nathan@spacestationnathan.com.

Career
Author and illustrator. Chase Studios (natural-history exhibit company), Cedarcreek, MO, artist.

Writings

SELF-ILLUSTRATED

The Devil You Know, Walker & Company (New York, NY), 2005.
Yellowbelly and Plum Go to School, Putnam (New York, NY), 2007.

ILLUSTRATOR

Rudyard Kipling, *Mowgli's Big Birthday* ("Jungle Book" series), adapted by Diane Namm, Sterling Publishing (New York, NY), 2006.
Rudyard Kipling, *Mowgli Knows Best* ("Jungle Book" series), adapted by Diane Namm, Sterling Publishing (New York, NY), 2007.
Shannon Hale and Dean Hale, *Rapunzel's Revenge,* Bloomsbury (New York, NY), 2008.
Dan McCann, *Balloon on the Moon,* Walker & Company (New York, NY), 2008.

Contributor of artwork to *Cricket* magazine.

Adaptations
The Devil You Know was produced as a film by 21 Laps.

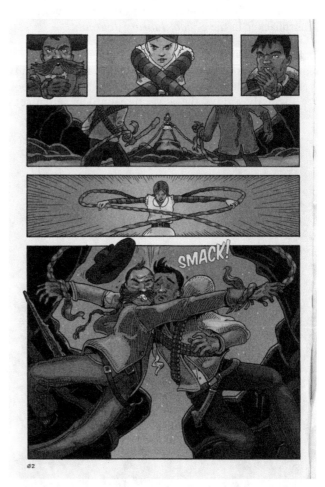

Nathan Hale's illustration projects include creating cartoon art for Shannon and Dean Hale's graphic novel **Rapunzel's Revenge.** (Illustration copyright © 2008 by Nathan Hale. Reprinted by permission of Bloomsbury Publishing Inc. All rights reserved.)

Sidelights

For several years, Utah artist Nathan Hale has worked for Chase Studios, a company that creates natural-history exhibits for museums across the United States. His illustration projects include the original picture books *The Devil You Know* and *Yellowbelly and Plum Go to School,* as well as texts written by others.

Featuring Hale's original story, *The Devil You Know* introduces the Fell family, who finds that the house they have bought is haunted. The troublesome demon who lives with them skis down the stairs and otherwise drives the family crazy its his noisy antics. Along comes Ms. Phisto, who claims she does "minor-demon removal" and "light housekeeping." The family signs her up to remove the demon, but they soon regret the decision, finding that Ms. Phisto is a more serious problem than the demon has been. "Think *Amityville Horror* with a happy ending," stated a critic for *Publishers Weekly,* who praised "Hale's considerable visual talents." "This spirited romp will appeal to readers who are not afraid of a little magic and mayhem," wrote Joy Fleishhacker in the *School Library Journal.*

Yellowbelly and Plum Go to School finds Yellowbelly, a cat-like monster, and his best friend, a purple teddy bear named Plum, preparing for their first day at school. Yellowbelly enjoys the adventure until he misplaces

Anne Meucke's quirky version of a favorite holiday tale gains a dose of humor in The Dinosaurs' Night before Christmas. (Illustration copyright © 2008 by Nathan Hale. Used by permission of Chronicle Books LLC., San Francisco. Visit ChronicleBooks.com.)

Plum in the schoolyard. A frantic search finds the missing bear, but only after other students have used poor Plum as a Frisbee and a basketball. Fleishhacker noted that young readers "will relate to Yellowbelly's childlike characteristics and be amused by his humorously exaggerated behavior and not-too-frightening appearance," and a *Kirkus Reviews* critic found that "Hale makes a common premise uncommonly appealing with illustrations that feature a gloriously multi-species cast." A reviewer for *Publishers Weekly* called *Yellowbelly and Plum Go to School* "heartwarming and clever," and concluded that Hale's "tale of friendship and loyalty will have readers awaiting more from this likable twosome."

Biographical and Critical Sources

PERIODICALS

Kirkus Reviews, June 15, 2007, review of *Yellowbelly and Plum Go to School.*
Publishers Weekly, August 1, 2005, review of *The Devil You Know,* p. 65; June 18, 2007, review of *Yellowbelly and Plum Go to School,* p. 52.
School Library Journal, August, 2005, Joy Fleishhacker, review of *The Devil You Know,* p. 96; August, 2007, Joy Fleishhacker, review of *Yellowbelly and Plum Go to School,* p. 81.

ONLINE

Kid Shannon Web site, http://www.kidshannon.com/ (April 5, 2008).
Nathan Hale Home Page, http://www.spacestationnathan.com (April 5, 2009).*

*   *   *

HARAZIN, S.A.

Personal

Born in AL; married; husband's name Tom (a business owner); children: three. *Education:* Attended Sanford University, 1970-73. *Hobbies and other interests:* Video games.

Addresses

Home—GA. *Agent*—Chudney Agency, 72 N. State Rd., Ste. 501, Briarcliff Manor, NY 10510. *E-mail*—saharazin@aol.com.

Career

Author. Worker in various hospital nursing positions; also worked in home health care. Moderator of Children's Writer's and Illustrator's Chat Board.

S.A. Harazin (Photograph by Terry Wawro. Reproduced by permission.)

Awards, Honors

Edgar Allen Poe Award nomination, Mystery Writers of America, and Quick Pick for Reluctant Readers, American Library Association, both 2007, both for *Blood Brothers.*

Writings

Blood Brothers (novel), Delacorte Press (New York, NY), 2007.

Sidelights

Nurse turned writer S.A. Harazin is the author of the young-adult novel *Blood Brothers,* which concerns the relationship between a hospital orderly and his troubled friend. Harazin's nursing career began when, at age fourteen, she started volunteering at the hospital where her mother worked. She later attended nursing school and spent years working as a hospital nurse. "I am glad I pursued that career first," Harazin remarked on the *Class of 2k7* Web site. "If I had not done that I would not have the first hand experience to write what I write."

Harazin's love of writing also began at a young age. "When I was twelve years old I bought a typewriter from Western Auto on credit," she remarked on her home page. "I began writing bad poetry and stories. . . . I hated school, but I loved journalism class." She continued writing while working as a nurse for many years, but she did not share her efforts with the world until much later. "It took me over ten years to get a book contract, and it was on the third novel I had written," Harazin told an interviewer for *TeensReadToo. com.*

Blood Brothers follows the story of Clay, a teenager from the poor part of town, and Clay's best friend Joey, who is popular and wealthy. Harazin described her protagonists to *YA Authors Café* online interviewer Catherine Atkins: "When they were seven, they spit into a bottle to become blood brothers. They dreamed of taking a cross-county bike trip, and they spent the next ten years preparing. But one evening Clay went to Joey's house and found him hallucinating and violent." Apparently on drugs, Joey attacks Clay, and in the ensuing struggle, Joey hits his head. After being taken to the hospital, he is fine at first but slips into a coma the following day. As Clay searches to find the answer to Joey's odd behavior, others begin to suspect that Clay may have been the cause.

Cover of Harizan's young-adult novel **Blood Brother,** *featuring artwork by Steve McCaffe.* (Illustration copyright © 2007 by Steve McAfee. Used by permission of Delacorte Press, an imprint of Random House Children's Books, a division of Random House, Inc.)

Blood Brothers received strong reviews. In *Kliatt,* Paula Rohrlick remarked that the book "draws a convincing portrait" of Clay, and provides a good view "of what it's like to work at a hospital, too." Shelley Huntington, writing in *School Library Journal,* noted that "it is Joey's tenuous grip on life, and Clay's deep bond with him, that will keep readers' hearts racing." As a contributor in *Kirkus Reviews* observed, Harazin's "anti-drug message is never didactic, and the story will grab readers from the first sentence."

As Harazin noted to Atkins, *Blood Brothers* "is loosely based on life experiences. It was a story that had been with me for many years. But the first grain of the story came to me at work when a patient was going through the process of brain death diagnosis. He was just a kid, and what happened next really affected me." The author credits her three children and their friends with helping her craft the realistic voices of the teens. In addition, she had other issues in mind when writing the story. "I've always hoped that readers would experience a good story and maybe have an 'aha' feeling when it's over," Harazin told Julie Bowie on the *Class of 2k7* Web log. "I never planned on having an anti-drug message or teaching anybody anything. I do hope there will be teens who decide on health care as a career."

Biographical and Critical Sources

PERIODICALS

Kirkus Reviews, June 1, 2007, review of review of *Blood Brothers.*

Kliatt, July, 2007, Paula Rohrlick, review of *Blood Brothers,* p. 14.

School Library Journal, November, 2007, Shelley Huntington, review of *Blood Brothers,* p. 124.

ONLINE

Class of 2k7 Web site, http://community.livejournal.com/classof2k7/ (September 9, 2007), Julie Bowe, interview with Harazin; (March 1, 2008), "S.A. Harazin."

S.A. Harazin Home Page, http://www.saharazin.com (March 1, 2009).

S.A. Harazin Web log, http://www.medwriter.livejournal.com (March 1, 2009).

TeensReadToo.com, http://teensreadtoo.com/ (November 21, 2007), interview with Harazin.

YA Authors Café Web log, http://www.yaauthorscafe.blogspot.com/ (July 25, 2007), Catherine Atkins, interview with Harazin.

*   *   *

HARDINGE, Frances 1973-

Personal

Born 1973, in Brighton, England. *Education:* Oxford University, M.St., 1996.

Addresses

Home—England.

Career

Author. Has worked as a technical writer for Tao Group Ltd., Reading, England, and as a graphic designer.

Awards, Honors

Sutton Writers' Circle Short-Story Competition winner, 2001, for "Borrowed Time"; Scribble Short-Story Competition winner, 2003, for "Bengal Rose"; Best Books for Young Adults selection, American Library Association, One Hundred Titles for Reading and Sharing selection, New York Public Library, William Crawford Award shortlist, London *Guardian* Children's Fiction Prize shortlist, and Branford Boase Award (with Ruth Alltimes), all 2006, all for *Fly by Night;* Carnegie Award nomination, 2007, for *Verdigris Deep.*

Writings

NOVELS

Fly by Night, Macmillan (London, England), 2005, HarperCollins (New York, NY), 2006.

Verdigris Deep, Macmillan (London, England), 2007, published as *Well Witched,* HarperCollins (New York, NY), 2008.

Gullstruck Island, Macmillan Children's Books (London, England), 2009.

The Lost Conspiracy, Bowen Press (New York, NY), 2009.

Contributor of short stories to periodicals, including *Wordplay, Alchemy,* and *All Hallows.*

Sidelights

Frances Hardinge is the author of several tales for young readers, including *Fly by Night,* winner of the Branford Boase Award for first-time children's writers, and *Verdigris Deep,* a contemporary fantasy adventure. Hardinge admits that she has been startled by her success as an author; in fact, she was in the midst of a year-long trip around the globe when she received word that Harper-Collins wanted to publish her work.

Born in 1973, in Brighton, England, Hardinge began writing at a young age, inspired in part by the rambling estate where she lived. "I can't remember a time when I didn't want to become an author," she told *Collected Miscellany* Web site interviewer Kevin Holtsberry. "I still occasionally stumble across my first literary efforts, many of which tend decidedly towards the grotesque." A voracious reader, Hardinge was drawn to the works of Susan Cooper, Alan Garner, Leon Garfield, T.H. White, and Robert Louis Stevenson, among others, and at school she enjoyed the writings of William Shakespeare and Charles Dickens. "English was a subject where I could read stories in company and discuss them," Hardinge remarked to London *Guardian* contributor Alice Wignall. "It became a lasting obsession, an enthusiasm that hasn't worn off."

In 1996 Hardinge earned a master's degree in English literature from Oxford University, where she cofounded a writer's workshop, and she took a job as a technical writer for the Tao Group, Ltd. She also began finding success with her short fiction, winning several awards and publishing stories in publications such as *Alchemy* and *All Hallows.*

Hardinge started working on her first book, *Fly by Night,* at the suggestion of Lassiter, a friend and fellow author. They began meeting weekly for brainstorm sessions, and although they generated a slew of ideas, they could not find one that satisfied both of them. Lassiter soon convinced Hardinge to attempt a work for young readers, and after she completed the first five chapters of *Fly by Night,* Lassiter took the manuscript to her editor at Macmillan. The work was quickly accepted for publication. In 2004, upon losing her job as a graphic designer, Hardinge decided to undertake her round-the-world venture. After receiving news of her book deal, she finished the trip and then returned home to begin a career as a full-time author.

Set in the Fractured Kingdom, a world that resembles eighteenth-century Britain, *Fly by Night* centers on twelve-year-old Mosca Mye, the orphaned daughter of an exiled scholar. After running away from home with her ferociously protective pet goose, Saracen, Mosca becomes the traveling companion of Eponymous Clent, a roguish wordsmith, and the trio makes its way to the city of Mandelion, where rival guilds of locksmiths and printers vie for power. Mosca and Clent soon find themselves in the employ of Mabwick Toke, the leader of the Stationers, a group that controls the distribution of literature and vows to shut down an unauthorized printing press. The intelligent and literate Mosca, however, finds herself torn between her loyalty to Clent and her personal beliefs.

In *Fly by Night* Hardinge "has created a distinctly imaginative world full of engaging characters, robust humor, and true suspense," noted *School Library Journal* contributor Steven Engelfried. A *Publishers Weekly* critic cited the novel's humor, remarking that the author's "stylish way with prose gives her sprawling debut fantasy a literate yet often silly tone that calls to mind [the work of British comedy troupe] Monty Python." "At best Hardinge's writing puts her up there with [Joan] Aiken and Leon Garfield in the recreation of an England that never was," remarked *Guardian* contributor Jan Mark, the critic also calling Hardinge "a hugely talented writer of tireless invention and vivid prose."

"From the start *Fly by Night* was designed to be a yarn that would be fun to write and to read," Hardinge remarked in her *Collected Miscellany* Web site interview.

"The ideological themes developed quite naturally from the story. The setting for *Fly by Night* developed because of my fascination with the power, danger and importance of unfettered words, but it's also a topic upon which I have certain views." In a *Bookseller* interview with Caroline Horn, the author similarly noted of her novel: "I write about challenging your belief system and testing it and seeing whether it holds up—which is what Mosca has to do. Never believe something just because it's told to you." Despite some objections, Royston applauded Hardinge's effort in *Fly by Night,* stating that the book "challenges the reader to figure out the true motives and natures of its characters, giving nothing away until near the end, and it unfolds its complications with great glee."

Hardinge's follow-up, *Verdigris Deep,* was published in the United States as *Well Witched.* The book concerns three children who gain disturbing powers in a most unusual manner. Finding themselves stranded without bus fare one evening, Josh, Ryan, and Chelle take a handful of coins from a wishing well. Soon, bizarre and unexplainable events occur: light bulbs explode in Josh's presence, Chelle begins speaking words that are not her own, and Ryan notices strange growths on his fingers. The children are then visited by the spirit of the well, a female presence whose eyes flood like a fountain, and she demands that they fulfill the wishes attached to each of the stolen coins. As time passes, they learn to harness their powers: Josh discovers that he can control electricity, Chelle becomes a conduit for the wishers' thoughts and feelings, and Ryan's warts are transformed into eyes that allow him to see the secret wishes people make. Their task initially brings great joy: the children help a man gain possession of a new motorcycle and a woman find her true love. Later, however, the spirit's directive becomes more difficult to accomplish: one individual no longer wants or needs assistance, while others have made wishes that prove to be motivated by hatred, requiring the children to perform loathsome acts.

Like *Fly by Night,* *Verdigris Deep* also earned praise from reviewers. In the words of London *Sunday Times* contributor Nicolette Jones, the novel "is often creepy and tense, although it also has humour, and the characterisation is subtle." Farah Mendlesohn, writing in *Strange Horizons* online, also complimented Hardinge's handling of her characters, calling the conclusion "deeply satisfying: it is incomplete, problematic, and flows off the edge of the page."

Reviewers in the United States also lauded the North American edition of *Verdigris Deep* as an outstanding work of fantasy, a writer for *Publishers Weekly* hailing it as an "inescapably chilling" tale with a tightly woven plot, multidimensional characters, and strikingly original use of imagery. In *Booklist* Carolyn Phelan also noted the novel's "beautiful, precise imagery," commenting further that Hardinge's exploration of "subtle ideas and reflections" indicates an admirable respect for children's ability to grapple with complex themes. A writer for *Kirkus Reviews,* describing the novel's premise as "fascinating," recommended *Well Witched* as a "vivid and imaginative" novel for young readers.

Gullstruck Island, which *Bookbag* online contributor Jill Murphy described as a "gorgeously dense fantasy," is set on a tropical island where conflict has defined the relationships between the dark-skinned and marginalized Lace tribe and the land-hungry Cavalcaste, who had arrived on Gullstruck Island years earlier as invaders. Lady Arilou and her younger sister, Hathin, are Lace, and Arilou is believed to be a "Lost"—a revered person who can detach her senses from her body and secretly send them anywhere. The first Lost to be born among the Lace, Arilou provides her tribe with the means of protecting itself against Cavalcaste, and Hathin protects and serves her sister. Arilou faces a daunting challenge when Lost Inspector Raglan Skein arrives to meet Arilou and test her Lost powers. When Skein dies under mysterious circumstances during the test, the Lace suspect that Hathin may have been responsible.

As Mendlesohn pointed out, *Gullstruck Island* "contains the classic YA motif of the protagonist learning to know herself, but the book can also be understood as entire peoples coming once again to know themselves and to know their lands. What begins as one of the simpler of Hardinge's books grows in subtlety and complexity." London *Guardian* contributor Patrick Ness expressed similar admiration for Hardinge's novel, calling it "delightfully inventive . . . and "endlessly creative." Likewise praising the book's marvelous plot and intriguing themes, Murphy also commented on the author's special talent for crafting sentences and images, noting the "sheer joy of the words as they come together." *Gullstruck Island,* concluded Murphy, "will transport its many readers."

Biographical and Critical Sources

PERIODICALS

Booklist, August 1, 2006, Jennifer Mattson, review of *Fly by Night,* p. 65; May 15, 2008, Carolyn Phelan, review of *Well Witched,* p. 60.

Bookseller, August 19, 2005, Caroline Horn, "Globetrotter Conquers the Book World," p. 17.

Guardian (London, England), January 14, 2006, Jan Mark, review of *Fly by Night;* September 5, 2006, Alice Wignall, "My Favourite Lesson: Frances Hardinge Acquired a Lasting Love of Literature at School," p. 6; February 28, 2009, Patric Ness, review of *Gullstruck Island.*

Horn Book, July 1, 2008, Deirdre F. Baker, review of *Well Witched.*

Kirkus Reviews, May 15, 2008, review of *Well Witched.*

Magpies, March, 2007, Maureen Mann, review of *Fly by Night,* p. 37.

Publishers Weekly, May 8, 2006, review of *Fly by Night,* p. 66; June 16, 2008, review of *Well Witched,* p. 48.

School Library Journal, July, 2006, Steven Engelfried, review of *Fly by Night,* p. 104; August 1, 2008, Eva Mitnick, review of *Well Witched,* p. 120.

Sunday Times (London, England), July, 2006, Steven Engelfried, review of *Verdigris Deep,* p. 104; January 4, 2009, Nicolette Jones, review of *Gullstruck Island.*

Times Educational Supplement, December 23, 2005, Elaine Williams, review of *Fly by Night,* p. 25; July 27, 2007, Nicholas Tucker, review of *Verdigris Deep,* p. 28.

ONLINE

Armadillo Online, http://www.siliconhenge.com/armadillo/ (June 25, 2009), Rhiannon Lassiter, interview with Hardinge.

Bookbag Web site, http://www.thebookbag.co.uk/ (June 8, 2009), Jill Murphy, review of *Gullstruck Island.*

Branford Boase Award Web site, http://www.branford boaseaward.org.uk/ (March 1, 2008), "Branford Boase Award 2006."

Collected Miscellany Web site, http://collectedmiscellany. com/ (July 25, 2006), Kevin Holtsberry, "Ten Questions with Frances Hardinge."

Frances Hardinge Home Page, http://www.franceshardinge. com (June 8, 2009).

Strange Horizons Web site, http://www.strangehorizons. com/ (April 26, 2006), Donna Royston, review of *Fly by Night;* (July 11, 2007) Farah Mendlesohn, review of *Verdigris Deep;* (June 8, 2009) Farah Mendlesohn, review of *Gullstruck Island.**

*　　*　　*

HILLENBRAND, Will 1960-

Personal

Born May 31, 1960, in Cincinnati, OH; son of Earl (a barber) and Alice Hillenbrand; married Jane Barnick (a teacher), June 28, 1986; children: Ian. *Education:* Art Academy of Cincinnati, 1982, B.F.A.; attended Ohio State University. *Politics:* Democrat. *Religion:* Lutheran. *Hobbies and other interests:* Painting, photography, model airplanes, spending time with family.

Addresses

Home—Terrace Park, OH. *Agent*—Tish Gayle, Literary Events Agent, 808 Lexington Ave., Terrace Park, OH 45174. *E-mail*—will@willhillenbrand.com.

Career

Illustrator and art director. Creator of e-Thology Project (educational program designed to stimulate creativity and expression).

Member

Society of Illustrators, Society of Children's Book Writers and Illustrators.

Awards, Honors

Gold Medal, Society of Illustrators, 1990; Notable Book citation, American Library Association, for *Traveling to Tondo;* Children's Choice citation, International Reading Association, for *Sam Sunday and the Mystery at the Ocean Beach Hotel* and *The House That Drac Built;* Irma S. and James H. Black Award for Excellence in Children's Literature, Bank Street College of Education, 1995, and North Carolina Children's Book Award, 1997, both for *Wicked Jack;* Ohioana Citation for Art, 2000; Please Touch Book Award, 2002, for *Kiss the Cow;* Best Books of the Year designation, *Parenting* magazine, 2002, for *Fiddle-I-Fee;* advertising awards from *Communication Arts Advertising Age, Print,* Society of Publication Designers, and Society of Illustrators.

Writings

SELF-ILLUSTRATED

Down by the Station, Harcourt (San Diego, CA), 1999.
Fiddle-I-Fee, Harcourt (San Diego, CA), 2002.
Here We Go Round the Mulberry Bush, Harcourt (San Diego, CA), 2003.
Asleep in the Stable, Holiday House (New York, NY), 2004.
My Book Box, Harcourt (Orlando, FL), 2006.
Cock-a-doodle Christmas!, Marshall Cavendish (New York, NY), 2007.
Louie!, Philomel Books (New York, NY), 2009.

ILLUSTRATOR

Elvira Woodruff, *Awfully Short for the Fourth Grade,* Holiday House (New York, NY), 1990.
Verna Aardema, reteller, *Traveling to Tondo: A Tale of the Nkundo of Zaire,* Knopf (New York, NY), 1991.
Marjorie Weinman Sharmat, *I'm the Best!,* Holiday House (New York, NY), 1991.
Elvira Woodruff, *Back in Action,* Holiday House (New York, NY), 1991.
Steven Kroll, *The Magic Rocket,* Holiday House (New York, NY), 1992.
Patricia Wittmann, *Go Ask Giorgio!,* Macmillan (New York, NY), 1992.
Natalia M. Belting, *Moon Was Tired of Walking on Air: Origin Myths of South American Indians,* Houghton (Boston, MA), 1992.
Eric A. Kimmel, *Asher and the Capmakers: A Hanukkah Story,* Holiday House (New York, NY), 1993.
Mirra Ginsburg, *The King Who Tried to Fry an Egg on His Head: A Russian Tale,* Macmillan (New York, NY), 1994.
Roxanne Dyer Powell, *Cat, Mouse, and Moon,* Houghton (Boston, MA), 1994.
Rosalind C. Wang, *The Treasure Chest: A Chinese Tale,* Holiday House (New York, NY), 1995.

Judy Sierra, *The House That Drac Built,* Harcourt (San Diego, CA), 1995.
Connie Nordhielm Wooldridge, adaptor, *Wicked Jack,* Holiday House (New York, NY), 1995.
Robyn Supraner, *Sam Sunday and the Mystery at the Ocean Beach Hotel,* Viking (New York, NY), 1996.
Barbara Diamond Goldin, reteller, *Coyote and the Fire Stick: A Pacific Northwest Indian Tale,* Harcourt (San Diego, CA), 1996.
Eric A. Kimmel, reteller, *The Tale of Ali Baba and the Forty Thieves: A Story from the Arabian Nights,* Holiday House (New York, NY), 1996.
Judy Sierra, *Counting Crocodiles,* Harcourt (San Diego, CA), 1997.
Margery Cuyler, *The Biggest, Best Snowman,* Scholastic (New York, NY), 1998.
David A. Adler, *The Many Troubles of Andy Russell,* Harcourt (San Diego, CA), 1998.
Rebecca Hickox, *The Golden Sandal: A Middle Eastern Cinderella,* Holiday House (New York, NY), 1998.
Sheila MacGill-Callahan, *The Last Snake in Ireland: A Story about St. Patrick,* Holiday House (New York, NY), 1999.
David A. Adler, *Andy and Tamika,* Harcourt (San Diego, CA), 1999.
David A. Adler, *School Trouble for Andy Russell,* Harcourt (San Diego, CA), 1999.
David A. Adler, *Parachuting Hamsters and Andy Russell,* Harcourt (San Diego, CA), 2000.
Phyllis Root, *Kiss the Cow,* Candlewick Press (Cambridge, MA), 2000.
Judy Sierra, *Preschool to the Rescue,* Harcourt (San Diego, CA), 2001.
Tom Birdseye, *Look Out, Jack! The Giant Is Back!,* Holiday House (New York, NY), 2001.
Judy Sierra, *'Twas the Fright before Christmas,* Harcourt (San Diego, CA), 2002.
Malachy Doyle, *One, Two, Three O'Leary,* Margaret K. McElderry Books (New York, NY), 2004.
Merrily Kutner, *Down on the Farm,* Holiday House (New York, NY), 2004.
Margery Cuyler, *Please Say Please! Penguin's Guide to Manners,* Scholastic (New York, NY), 2004.
Judith St. George, *The Journey of the One and Only Declaration of Independence,* Philomel (New York, NY), 2005.
Margery Cuyler, *The Bumpy Little Pumpkin,* Scholastic (New York, NY), 2005.
Margery Cuyler, *Please Play Safe! Penguin's Guide to Playground Safety,* Scholastic (New York, NY), 2006.
Jane Yolen, editor, *This Little Piggy and Other Rhymes to Sing and Play,* with musical arrangements by Adam Stemple, Candlewick Press (Cambridge, MA), 2006.
Barbara Odanaka, *Smash! Mash! Crash! There Goes the Trash!,* Margaret K. McElderry Books (New York, NY), 2006.
Jane Hillenbrand, *What a Treasure!,* Holiday House (New York, NY), 2006.
Karma Wilson, *Whopper Cake,* Margaret K. McElderry Books (New York, NY), 2007.
Myra Cohn Livingston, *Calendar,* Holiday House (New York, NY), 2007.

Lisa Shulman, *The Moon Might Be Milk,* Dutton (New York, NY), 2007.

Bobbi Miller, reteller, *One Fine Trade,* Holiday House (New York, NY), 2008.

Amy Ehrlich, *Baby Dragon,* Candlewick Press (Cambridge, MA), 2008.

Maureen Wright, *Sleep, Big Bear, Sleep!,* Marshall Cavendish (New York, NY), 2009.

Sidelights

Will Hillenbrand is an award-winning author and illustrator whose works include more than forty picture books for young readers. In addition to his self-illustrated titles such as *Down by the Station, Fiddle-I-Fee,* and *My Book Box,* he has also illustrated the works of prominent children's writers and retellers, including Eric A. Kimmel, Phyllis Root, Judy Sierra, Judith St. George, and David A. Adler, among a host of others.

Hillenbrand has lived almost all of his life in Cincinnati, Ohio, where he grew up in a family whose everyday routines centered on the neighborhood. Much of his childhood revolved around his parents' barbershop and the local baseball diamond. The youngest of four boys with diverse personalities and talents, Hillenbrand became interested in drawing. His curiosity was piqued by the cartoon sketches of an older brother, and he discovered in drawing a satisfying pastime. He exercised

Will Hillenbrand's illustration projects include creating artwork for Robyn Supraner's picture book Sam Sunday and the Mystery at the Ocean Beach Hotel. *(Illustration © 1996 by Will Hillenbrand. Reproduced by permission of Viking, a division of Penguin Putnam, Inc.)*

his art wherever he could; his crayon pictures were as likely to appear on the stairwell wall to the basement as on paper at the kitchen table, not always to his mother's delight.

Among Hillenbrand's favorite authors then and now are Maurice Sendak, Arnold Lobel, E.H. Shepard, Ashley Bryan, and Trina Schart Hyman. He finds himself caught up in the spirit of Sendak, whose characters are costumed, animated, and orchestrated across richly drawn stages. In the work of Shepard and Lobel, Hillenbrand admires the ability to create animal characters that are fully individual, yet which remain true to their unique animal nature and environment.

Although Hillenbrand was drawing from early childhood, the limited resources of his local parochial school offered little opportunity to develop his talent or interest in art. When his older brother switched to the public high school, Hillenbrand followed and, as a second-semester sophomore, enrolled in his first art class. He soon realized that he had a good eye for composition and was comfortable with graphic design. Hillenbrand decided that art was the vocational direction he wanted to take. During the summers, he produced commercial artwork at a local television station and later accepted a job at an advertising agency.

During a class in picture book art at Ohio State University taught by Ken Marantz, Hillenbrand the graphic designer and Hillenbrand the storyteller merged. His projects from this class comprised his first picture book portfolio and later he traveled to New York to submit his work to potential publishers. If he needed any further encouragement, he found it in Jane Barnick, a teacher whom he had first known as a young girl sitting on the steps of the house next to his family home. Now she kindled his interest in the illustrated book through her use of children's literature in her classroom. Their shared enthusiasm for children's picture books began a relationship that brought marriage in 1986.

After working several years as an artist and designer, Hillenbrand decided to move away from advertising art and give children's picture-book illustration a try. He later explained this decision to Ken and Sylvia Marantz in *School Arts:* "'At the time it was a risk. I'd lose my status at my job and I'd never advance in this area. But it gave me an open door. I had a goal to do picture books. It was a renewed fiery interest that had been buried for a long time. Illustrations were precious to me. I wanted to protect them somehow; they were still growing inside of me, still forming.'" Hillenbrand's artwork debuted in the 1990 picture book *Awfully Short for the Fourth Grade,* by Elvira Woodruff. Woodruff's story is about a young boy who learns the hard way the truth of the adage, "Watch out what you wish for," when his desire for his toy soldiers and alien action figures to come to life is granted—with chaotic results. Hillenbrand's second project, a collaboration with writer Verna Aardema, was *Traveling to Tondo: A Tale of the*

Hillenbrand teams up with author Tom Birdseye to give a well-known tale an amusing twist in **Look out, Jack! The Giant Is Back!** (Illustration copyright © 2001 by Will Hillenbrand. Reproduced by permission of Holiday House, Inc.)

Nkundo of Zaire, the tale of an African civet that sets out for Tondo to claim its bride and finds its journey taking longer than intended because it stops to help various friends. *Traveling to Tondo* earned an American Library Association Notable Book citation and in 1990, Hillenbrand was honored with a gold medal from the Society of Illustrators.

Another early award winner from Hillenbrand, *Sam Sunday and the Mystery at the Ocean Beach Hotel,* features a story by Robyn Supraner. This private-eye spoof takes on the trappings of "an old-time whodunit," according to Joy Fleishhacker in *School Library Journal,* and Hillenbrand's pastel illustrations "complete the illusion." Carolyn Phelan, writing in *Booklist,* called the

picture book "quirky but likable," while a contributor for *Publishers Weekly* praised Hillenbrand's "almost chameleon-like arsenal of styles," further nothing that the artwork contributes "even more verve to this funny and suspenseful tale."

Working with Barbara Diamond Goldin, Hillenbrand next illustrated a porquoi tale from native traditions in *Coyote and the Fire Stick: A Pacific Northwest Indian Tale. Booklist* contributor Karen Morgan commended the "trio of ugly-to-the-bone antagonists" that the illustrator creates for this award-winning title, and *School Library Journal* reviewer Patricia Lothrop similarly praised the realism of the artwork. "Hillenbrand's proto-Oregonians actually look like themselves," Lothrop wrote, "and not like Hollywood Indians." A contributor for *Publishers Weekly* also noted Hillenbrand's "warm and textured" illustrations which create "a thoughtfully researched portrait of Pacific Northwest Indians." Working with Eric A. Kimmel on *The Tale of Ali Baba and the Forty Thieves: A Story from the Arabian Nights,* Hillenbrand adds illustrations that "maximize the drama," according to a reviewer for *Publishers Weekly.* Reviewing that same title in *Horn Book,* Mary M. Burns commended the artist for being "particularly adept at capturing characters with a minimum of detail."

Hillenbrand has had a long and successful collaborative relationship with writer Judy Sierra, beginning with the 1995 title, *The House That Drac Built.* A cumulative Halloween tale, the book deals with the strange assortment of creatures that inhabits Drac's house. On each page, Hillenbrand introduces some new monster. Mary Harris Veeder, reviewing the work in *Booklist,* found each new monster "quite detailed, but even at their rowdiest, they aren't truly terrifying." The two have teamed up together many more times. *Counting Crocodiles* is a Pan-Asian folktale about a hungry monkey told with rhyming text by Sierra and "cleverly detailed illustrations" by Hillenbrand, remarked *School Library Journal* critic Lisa Falk. Kathleen Squires, writing in *Booklist,* praised Hillenbrand's pictures as "full of wonderful detail," and a reviewer for *Publishers Weekly* noted that "re-readers will find witty subtleties in the already uproarious mixed-media paintings" in *Counting Crocodiles.*

Further collaborative efforts with Sierra include *Preschool to the Rescue* about a maniacal mud puddle outside a school. A reviewer for *Publishers Weekly* remarked on the "soft prettiness" of the artwork which "provides a soothing counterpoint to the menacing mud puddle." *'Twas the Fright before Christmas* turns the familiar Christmas verse upside down with monsters galore. A critic for *Kirkus Reviews* praised "Hillenbrand's clever illustrations of all the nonscary monsters" for this title.

Further collaborative efforts include *The Golden Sandal: A Middle Eastern Cinderella* by Rebecca Hickox, *Kiss the Cow* by Phyllis Root, and the "Andy Russell" books by David A. Adler. In *The Golden Sandal* Hickox retells a Cinderella-type story that is taken from Iraqi folklore. In this title, "Hillenbrand uses both interior and external architectural details to re-create the limpid Middle Eastern landscape," according to *Horn Book* reviewer Susan P. Bloom. A reviewer for *Publishers Weekly* found this title a "visual treat from start to finish." *Kiss the Cow* spins more magic, but in this book the magic is bovine: when a stubborn young girl refuses to kiss the family cow for giving its milk, said cow in turn refuses to give more milk until the girl plants a kiss on the animal's nose. A reviewer for *Horn Book* felt that "Hillenbrand's sunny colors reflect the light spirit of the tale," and a contributor for *Publishers Weekly* had similar praise for the illustrations. Accord-

Hillenbrand's self-illustrated picture books include **Louie!**, *about a piglet who spreads art throughout his world.* (Philomel Books, 2009. Jacket art copyright © 2009 by Will Hillenbrand. Reproduced by permission.)

ing to this critic, the illustrator "obviously delights in depicting the extensive family's full-to-bursting life in his sunny mixed-media paintings." And writing in *Booklist,* Carolyn Phelan found that Hillenbrand's "well-conceived illustrations . . . depict a variety of scenes with style and panache." Working with Adler, Hillenbrand has also contributed illustrations for the novels featuring young Andy Russell, who always seems to get into trouble of some sort or another. Writing about *The Many Troubles of Andy Russell* in *School Library Journal,* Todd Morning found that Hillenbrand's pictures "capture the humor of the story." Christy Norris Blanchette, reviewing *School Trouble for Andy Russell* in *School Library Journal,* indicated that Hillenbrand's "black-and-white illustrations show a likable Andy."

Hillenbrand has also provided the illustrations for a number of works by Margaret Cuyler. In *The Biggest, Best Snowman,* Cuyler introduces Little Nell, a spunky, independent youngster who struggles to escape the shadows of her older siblings. Nell makes a return appearance in *The Bumpy Little Pumpkin,* which describes her efforts to create a special jack-o'-lantern from a unsightly pumpkin. "Hillenbrand's cheery, whimsical mixed-media illustrations show Little Nell's perspective," observed Gillian Engberg in *Booklist.* Penguin and his friends Hippo, Bear, and Elephant address mealtime and playtime etiquette in Cuyler's *Please Say Please! Penguin's Guide to Manners* and *Please Play Safe! Penguin's Guide to Playground Safety.* "Hillenbrand's simple, comical illustrations harness the messy chaos . . . of childhood," remarked Karin Snelson in a *Booklist* review of *Please Say Please!*

Hillenbrand joins forces with St. George in *The Journey of the One and Only Declaration of Independence,* a nonfiction picture book that offers a variety of little-known facts about the celebrated document. Here "Hillenbrand's bright mixed-media line-and-color illustrations borrow from the conventions of old political cartoons, mixing children and historical figures with familiar icons," noted *Horn Book* reviewer Vicky Smith, and *School Library Journal* contributor Lee Bock stated that the artist's "lively mixed-media illustrations . . . fill . . . the pages with visual energy and humor." The artist has also teamed with editor Jane Yolen on *This Little Piggy and Other Rhymes to Sing and Play,* a collection of songs, finger plays, and clapping games for parents and toddlers. "Hillenbrand's illustrations are a delight, featuring a largely porcine cast, soft colors and playful borders," observed a *Kirkus Reviews* writer of this picture book.

In *What a Treasure!,* a work by Hillenbrand's wife, Jane Hillenbrand, Mole uses his new shovel to find wonderful gifts for his friends Bird, Snail, and Squirrel. According to a contributor in *Publishers Weekly,* the "mixed-media artwork exudes a lighthearted tone via boldly outlined shapes and sweetly anthropomorphized characters," and Kitty Flynn, writing in *Booklist,* similarly noted that "the bold compositions lend vibrancy to the pictures' subtle coloring and shading." *Smash! Mash! Crash! There Goes the Trash!,* a tale by Barbara Odanaka, centers on a pair of piglets that wake early one morning to watch a fleet of garbage trucks roar through their neighborhood. Hillenbrand portrays "the machines as giant, mechanical toads on wheels," Julie Cummins wrote in *Booklist,* and *School Library Journal* Joy Fleishhacker remarked that the vehicles, "personified with mouthlike hoppers and red brakelight eyes, gleefully munch their way through an array of vividly colored refuse."

Hillenbrand also provides the artwork for *Whopper Cake,* a humorous story by Karma Wilson. As Grandma's birthday approaches, Grandpa determines to create a monstrous chocolate cake for her, using the bed of his pick-up truck to blend the ingredients. Wilson's "tall-tale premise provides lots of grist for Hillenbrand's oversize paintings," Jennifer Mattson observed in *Booklist,* and a *Kirkus Reviews* contributor noted that the artist "combines candy-colored egg tempura paintings with sepia-toned line drawings in jaunty double-page spreads." *Calendar,* a book version of a poem first published in 1959 by Myra Cohn Livingston, celebrates the twelve months of the year. Hillenbrand's collage pictures for this book, done in acrylic, gouache, and ink, "enhances and extends the text," as Kathleen Whalin wrote in *School Library Journal.*

For Bobbi Miller's *One Fine Trade,* a retelling of a classic Southern folk tale, Hillenbrand created pictures that, according to Wendy Lukehart in *School Library Journal,* create "convincing depth." The story recounts the adventures of a backwoods peddler whose daughter begs him to trade her skinny horse for a new silver dollar so that she can buy herself a wedding dress. It takes several outlandish exchanges—including a few episodes of magic—before the peddler gets the money and the dress is purchased. According to a *Kirkus Reviews* contributor, Hillenbrand's bright illustrations "add plenty of color and spirit" to this lively tale.

Reviewers cited Hillenbrand's illustrations for Amy Ehrlich's *Baby Dragon* as another example of artwork and text working successfully together. The book's title character is instructed by his mother to stay in one spot while she runs out on an errand. Although Baby Dragon tries hard to obey, he grows scared when the sun goes down and agrees to let a crocodile ferry him up the river to search for her. Though dangers lurk, Baby Dragon manages to avoid them easily enough—he either does not recognize them, or determinedly jumps out of harm's way to focus on getting back to his place of safety. Hillenbrand's artwork, which employs ink, colored pencil, gouache, finger paint, collage, and digitization, brings Baby Dragon's tropical forest home to life, said *School Library Journal* reviewer Mary Jean Smith. A reviewer for *Publishers Weekly* also admired Hillenbrand's contributions to *Baby Dragon,* observing that his "expressive artwork shines" and praising his compositions as "light and harmonious."

Beginning with his self-illustrated *Down by the Station,* Hillenbrand has added "author" to his list of creative talents. In his debut authorial title, he offers a "whimsical interpretation of a familiar song," according to a critic for *Publishers Weekly.* Baby animals hop aboard a multi-colored train as the engineer makes numerous stops along the line, all headed for the children's zoo. Once the train arrives at the zoo, it is followed close upon by a bus full of children come to visit. Appropriate animal noises accompany the descriptions of the odd assortment of passengers, from elephant calf to seal pup. Simple, repetitive text mixes with illustrations full of "droll detail," as the *Publishers Weekly* reviewer further commented. GraceAnne A. DeCandido, writing in *Booklist,* praised the "rainbow candy colors and . . . impish sense of humor" employed in the book, while *Horn Book* critic Nancy Vasilakis called *Down by the Station* "an enjoyable, participatory adventure for the nursery school set."

With *Fiddle-I-Fee,* Hillenbrand adapts another song into a picture book. This time he uses the old barnyard folk tune about the cat that plays fiddle-i-fee under a tree. In Hillenbrand's adaptation, the cat is supplanted by other farm animals in subsequent verses: a duck, hen, goose, cow, and others make their appearances adding to the melody with their own musical sounds. According to a *Publishers Weekly* reviewer, Hillenbrand produces a "pleasing guessing game for young readers" with his second self-illustrated title. Helen Foster James, writing in *School Library Journal,* dubbed the work "amusing," while a *Kirkus Reviews* critic commented that Hillenbrand "offers a fresh perspective on the familiar nursery rhyme." The same reviewer concluded that the book is "toe-tapping fun." Writing in *Horn Book,* Kitty Flynn remarked that, "with its pleasing repetition, animal and musical sounds, farmyard setting, and playful surprise, this picture book will have listeners clamoring for an encore."

Hillenbrand adapts another familiar song in *Here We Go Round the Mulberry Bush,* but in this case he transforms the song into a tale about "a shy pig's coming to terms with the first day of porcine kindergarten at Mulberry School," as a contributor for *Publishers Weekly* described the picture book. Ilene Cooper, writing in *Booklist,* commended the "child-friendly artwork" in this title, and *School Library Journal* critic Grace Oliff called Hillenbrand's illustrations "are engaging and include details that add both humor and interest."

Hillenbrand offers a unique take on the Nativity story in *Asleep in the Stable,* another self-illustrated title. From his spot in the rafters, a curious baby owl witnesses the birth of the Christ Child, which signting leads to a tender discussion with Mama Owl. According to Martha V. Parravano, writing in *Horn Book,* "the questioning, open-hearted, big-eyed Baby Owl is an appealing stand-in for human preschoolers." "Hillenbrand's mixed-media collage illustrations for this work are just as successful as his text," remarked a contributor in *Kirkus Reviews,* and a *Publishers Weekly* critic described *Asleep in the Stable* as "perfect for Christmas Eve sharing with little ones."

In *My Book Box,* a young elephant transforms an ordinary cardboard box into a storage vessel for his reading materials. Julie Roach, writing in *School Library Journal,* applauded Hillenbrand's mixed-media pictures, stating that his "soft illustrations . . . lend occasional humor to the simple, quiet text." A contributor in *Publishers Weekly* observed that *My Book Box* "conveys a subtle yet infectious reading-is-terrific vibe that offers universal appeal any time of year," and a *Kirkus Reviews* critic deemed it "a charming salute to books as an option for adventure and recreation."

In *Louie!* a young pig named Louie loves to draw and paint at home but is teased for this pursuit at school and gets into trouble for neglecting his lessons. His mother sends Louie to live with an aunt and uncle who run a hotel. There Louie meets Vincent, a new friend who helps the young pig develop his artistic talents. When Louie crashes his bicycle and goes to the hospital, he meets a little girl in the next room who is recovering from an appendectomy. Inspired by her experience, he writes and illustrates a book about her story. Not until the end of the book does it become evident that Louie's story is based on that of Ludwig Bemelmans, author of the childhood classic *Madeline.*

While noting that the biographical aspect of *Louie!* might not be appreciated by young children, *Booklist* contributor Gillian Engberg hailed Hillenbrand's artwork as a "textured, well-executed delight." Making a similar point, a writer for *Kirkus Reviews* dubbed the book's art as "lovely," and *School Library Journal* reviewer Susan Weitz applauded *Louie!* for both its sensitive portrayal of a creative youngster in a philistine world and its "gloriously colored, superbly executed illustrations."

In an essay on his home page, Hillenbrand stated, "I really work in three worlds at once: the world of the imagination, the world of myth, and the physical world; children seem to live comfortably in all three. Successful illustrations link these worlds together and give a visual voice to the story." When he first receives a story, he does not try to analyze it. Believing that wonder and mystery are part of a child's natural world, Hillenbrand reads and rereads the text to enter into that world. He begins with the sketches from his current journal, decides which sketches he will develop, and scans these into his computer. He then plays with scale and composition for each drawing. He also composes his book layout on the computer screen, deciding, for example, where each page will break and which type font best suits the story. Even while using these advances in technology, Hillenbrand still prefers to create the actual pictures with traditional art media.

Hillenbrand has explored the visual possibilities in a diverse selection of stories during his career. Speaking with Ken and Sylvia Marantz, he summed up his approach to illustration and the delight he takes in his work: "'Everything I've learned ends up still coming into play when I create a picture book. Your work should be powerful and lively. If it isn't, it won't work for children. The idea is that it is an adventure, and you become a hero. You see your work; you revise your work; you see it again, and revise it again. . . . Looking at where I've come from, I'm living a dream. It's the dream I'm intended for, I'm sure.'"

Biographical and Critical Sources

PERIODICALS

Booklist, September 15, 1995, Mary Harris Veeder, review of *The House That Drac Built;* August, 1996, Carolyn Phelan, review of *Sam Sunday and the Mystery at the Ocean Beach Hotel,* p. 1909; October 1, 1996, Karen Morgan, review of *Coyote and the Fire Stick: A Pacific Northwest Indian Tale,* p. 345; December 1, 1996, Carolyn Phelan, review of *The Tale of Ali Baba and the Forty Thieves: A Story from the Arabian Nights,* p. 667; September 1, 1997, Kathleen Squires, review of *Counting Crocodiles,* p. 135; April, 1998, Karen Morgan, review of *The Golden Sandal: A Middle Eastern Cinderella,* p. 1326; December 15, 1998, Margery Cuyler, review of *The Biggest, Best Snowman,* p. 754; February 8, 1999, review of *The Last Snake in Ireland: A Story about St. Patrick,* p. 214; October 15, 1999, GraceAnne A. DeCandido, review of *Down by the Station,* p. 448; November 15, 2000, Carolyn

Phelan, review of *Kiss the Cow,* p. 650; July, 2002, Shelle Rosenfeld, review of *Fiddle-I-Fee,* p. 1851; August, 2003, Ilene Cooper, review of *Here We Go Round the Mulberry Bush,* p. 1994; February 1, 2004, Karin Snelson, review of *Please Say Please! Penguin's Guide to Manners,* p. 980; April 1, 2004, Carolyn Phelan, review of *Down on the Farm,* p. 1369; March 1, 2005, Ilene Cooper, review of *The One and Only Declaration of Independence,* p. 1201; September 1, 2005, Gillian Engberg, review of *The Bumpy Little Pumpkin,* p. 143; January 1, 2006, Jennifer Mattson, review of *This Little Piggy and Other Rhymes to Sing and Play,* p. 93; August 1, 2006, Ilene Cooper, review of *Please Play Safe! Penguin's Guide to Playground Safety,* p. 84; December 1, 2006, Julie Cummins, review of *Smash! Mash! Crash! There Goes the Trash!,* p. 53; February 15, 2007, Carolyn Phelan, review of *The Moon Might Be Milk,* p. 76; April 1, 2007, Hazel Rochman, review of *Calendar,* p. 51; June 1, 2007, Jennifer Mattson, review of *Whopper Cake,* p. 87; March 15, 2009, Gillian Engberg, review of *Louie!,* p. 66.

Children's Bookwatch, April 1, 2009, review of *Down on the Farm.*

Horn Book, January-February, 1997, Mary M. Burns, review of *The Tale of Ali Baba and the Forty Thieves,* p. 73; March-April, 1998, Susan P. Bloom, review of *The Golden Sandal,* p. 227; November, 1999, Nancy Vasilakis, review of *Down by the Station,* p. 753; January, 2001, review of *Kiss the Cow,* p. 85; May, 2001, review of *Preschool to the Rescue,* p. 317; July-August, 2002, Kitty Flynn, review of *Fiddle-I-Fee,* pp. 446-447; May-June, 2004, Christine M. Heppermann, review of *Please Say Please!,* p. 310; November-December, 2004, review of *Asleep in the Stable,* p. 659; January-February, 2005, Susan Dove Lempke, review of *One, Two, Three O'Leary,* p. 76; July-August, 2005, Vicky Smith, review of *The Journey of the One and Only Declaration of Independence,* p. 490; May-June, 2006, Kitty Flynn, review of *What a Treasure!,* p. 296; July-August, 2006, Bridget T. McCaffrey, review of *Please Play Safe!,* p. 423.

Kirkus Reviews, March 15, 2002, review of *Fiddle-I-Fee,* p. 413; November 1, 2002, review of *'Twas the Fright before Christmas,* pp. 1625-1626; July 15, 2003, review of *Here We Go Round the Mulberry Bush,* p. 964; February 1, 2004, review of *Down on the Farm,* p. 135; April 1, 2004, review of *Please Say Please!,* p. 327; August 1, 2004, review of *One, Two, Three O'Leary,* p. 740; November 1, 2004, review of *Asleep in the Stable,* p. 1050; July 1, 2005, review of *The Bumpy Little Pumpkin,* p. 733; March 1, 2006, review of *What a Treasure!,* p. 231, and *This Little Piggy and Other Rhymes to Sing and Play,* p. 243; July 1, 2006, review of *Please Play Safe!,* p. 676; August 1, 2006, review of *My Book Box,* p. 787; September 15, 2006, review of *Smash! Mash! Crash! There Goes the Trash!,* p. 963; January 15, 2007, review of *The Moon Might Be Milk,* p. 81; June 15, 2007, review of *Whopper Cake;* July 15, 2008, review of *Baby Dragon,*; February 15, 2009, review of *One Fine Trade;* March 1, 2009, review of *Louie!*

New York Times Book Review, December 8, 2002, review of *'Twas the Fright before Christmas,* p. 76.

Publishers Weekly, September 16, 1996, review of *The Tale of Ali Baba and the Forty Thieves,* p. 82; September 23, 1996, review of *Sam Sunday and the Mystery at the Ocean Beach Hotel,* p. 75; October 21, 1996, review of *Coyote and the Fire Stick,* p. 83; June 30, 1997, review of *Counting Crocodiles,* p. 75; January 26, 1998, review of *The Golden Sandal,* p. 91; August 17, 1998, review of *The Many Troubles of Andy Russell,* p. 73; November 9, 1998, review of *The Biggest, Best Snowman,* p. 75; February 8, 1999, review of *The Last Snake in Ireland,* p. 214; September 20, 1999, review of *Down by the Station,* p. 86; November 27, 2000, review of *Kiss the Cow,* p. 76; March 19, 2001, review of *Preschool to the Rescue,* p. 98; September 10, 2001, review of *Look out, Jack! The Giant Is Back!,* p. 92; February 25, 2002, review of *Fiddle-I-Fee,* pp. 62-63; September 16, 2002, review of *Down by the Station,* p. 71; July 7, 2003, review of *Here We Go Round the Mulberry Bush,* p. 71; March 22, 2004, review of *Down on the Farm,* p. 84; April 19, 2004, review of *Please Say Please!,* p. 59; September 27, 2004, review of *Asleep in the Stable,* p. 61; October 4, 2004, review of *One, Two, Three O'Leary,* p. 86; June 6, 2005, review of *The Journey of the One and Only Declaration of Independence,* p. 64; August 1, 2005, review of *The Bumpy Little Pumpkin,* p. 64; March 6, 2006, review of *What a Treasure!,* p. 73; September 4, 2006, review of *My Book Box,* p. 65; May 28, 2007, review of *Calendar,* p. 60; July 23, 2007, review of *Whopper Cake,* p. 67; August 18, 2008, review of *Baby Dragon,* p. 61.

School Arts, September, 1998, Ken and Sylvia Marantz, "The Dream World of Picture Book Artist Will Hillenbrand," p. 50.

School Library Journal, October, 1996, Joy Fleishhacker, review of *Sam Sunday and the Mystery at the Ocean Beach Hotel,* p. 107, and Patricia Lothrop Green, review of *Coyote and the Fire Stick,* pp. 113-114; December, 1996, Julie Cummins, review of *The Tale of Ali Baba and the Forty Thieves,* p. 114; October, 1997, Lisa Falk, review of *Counting Crocodiles,* pp. 110-111; April, 1998, Donna L. Scanlon, review of *The Golden Sandal,* pp. 117-118; December, 1998, Todd Morning, review of *The Many Troubles of Andy Russell,* p. 75; March, 1999, Jody McCoy, review of *The Last Snake in Ireland,* p. 197; November, 1999, Christy Norris Blanchette, review of *School Trouble for Andy Russell,* p. 108; October, 2000, Lynda Ritterman, review of *Parachuting Hamsters and Andy Russell,* p. 110; December, 2000, Anne Knickerbocker, review of *Kiss the Cow,* p. 124; May, 2001, Marlene Gawron, review of *Preschool to the Rescue,* p. 135; October, 2001, Janie Schomberg, review of *Look Out, Jack! The Giant Is Back!,* p. 104; March, 2002, Helen Foster James, review of *Fiddle-I-Fee,* p. 214; September, 2003, Grace Oliff, review of *Here We Go Round the Mulberry Bush,* p. 199; March, 2004, Wendy Woodfill, review of *Down on the Farm,* p. 172; April, 2004, Janet M. Bair, review of *Please Say Please!,* p. 109; November, 2004, Wanda Meyers-Hines, review of *One, Two, Three O'Leary,* p. 97; June, 2005, Lee Bock, review of *The Journey of the One and Only Declaration of Independence,* p. 186; August, 2005, Kara Schaff Dean, review of *The Bumpy Little Pump-*

kin, p. 87; February, 2006, Judith Constantinides, review of *This Little Piggy and Other Rhymes to Sing and Play,* p. 125; April, 2006, Julie Roach, review of *What a Treasure!,* p. 108; August, 2006, Maura Bresnahan, review of *Please Play Safe!,* p. 78; October, 2006, Julie Roach, review of *My Book Box,* p. 112; November, 2006, Joy Fleishhacker, review of *Smash! Mash! Crash! There Goes the Trash!,* p. 107; June, 2007, Sally R. Dow, review of *The Moon Might Be Milk,* p. 124; July, 2007, Wendy Lukehart, review of *Whopper Cake,* p. 87; August, 2007, Kathleen Whalin, review of *Calendar,* p. 101; September 1, 2008, Mary Jean Smith, review of *Baby Dragon,* p. 145; March 1, 2009, Susan Weitz, review of *Louie!,* p. 114; March 1, 2009, Wendy Lukehart, review of *One Fine Trade,* p. 137.

ONLINE

Curled Up with a Good Kid's Book Web site, http://www.curledupkids.com/ (June 8, 2009), Lois Henderlong, review of *Baby Dragon.*

Harcourt Books Web site, http://www.harcourtbooks.com/ (April 1, 2008), interview with Hillenbrand.

Northern Ohio Society of Children's Book Writers and Illustrators Web site, http://www.nohscbwi.org/ (April 1, 2008), Barbara S. Huff, "Will Hillenbrand."

Reading Tub, http://www.thereadingtub.com/ (June 8, 2009), review of *Louie!*

Will Hillenbrand Home Page, http://www.willhillenbrand.com (June 8, 2009)*.

*   *   *

HITZ, Demi
See DEMI

*   *   *

HOGAN, Mary 1957-

Personal

Born April 27, 1957; married Robert Hogan (a television actor). *Education:* University of California at Berkeley, degree.

Addresses

Home—New York, NY. *Agent*—Laura Langlie, 239 Carroll St., Garden Apt., Brooklyn, NY 11231. *E-mail*—maryhogan@msn.com.

Career

Novelist and freelance magazine writer. *Teen* magazine, former editor.

Member

Writer's Guild.

Mary Hogan (Photograph by David Wilson Barnes. Reproduced by permission.)

Writings

JUVENILE FICTION

The Serious Kiss, HarperCollins (New York, NY), 2005.
Perfect Girl, HarperTempest (New York, NY), 2007.
Pretty Face, HarperTeen (New York, NY), 2008.

"SUSANNA" SERIES; JUVENILE FICTION

Susanna Sees Stars, Delacorte Press (New York, NY), 2006.

Susanna Hits Hollywood, Delacorte Press (New York, NY), 2008.

Susanna Covers the Catwalk, Delacorte Press (New York, NY), 2008.

Susanna Falls in Love . . . in London, Simon & Schuster (London, England), 2009, also published as *Susanna Loves London,* Simon & Schuster Children's (New York, NY), 2009.

OTHER

Also author of nonfiction book, *Straight Talk on Careers.* Wrote episodes for television series *Working It Out* and *Busy Signals.* Contributor to *TV Guide Online.*

Author of articles for *Sassy, Seventeen, Teen, Family Circle, Parenting, New Woman, Woman, First for Women,* and *Fitness.*

Sidelights

Juvenile fiction author Mary Hogan began her career as an editor at *Teen* magazine, a job that has greatly helped her in her work as a young-adult novelist. After years spent as a freelance writer and an occasional writer for television, Hogan turned to writing novels full time. As she told E. Dian Moore for *BookPleasures.com,* "My goal in writing for young adults is to write REAL-LIFE stories from the unique perspective of a kid. And, real life is often funny, tragic, confusing, joyous. Kids really get that."

In *The Serious Kiss* Hogan introduces Libby Madrigal, a high-school freshman. Libby is horrified by her family, and with good reason: her father is an alcoholic, her brother puts cigarettes in his hair, and her mother is very eccentric. To make matters worse, the family relocates to a mobile home park during the middle of Libby's school year, next to a grandmother whom the teen thought was dead. All of these things interfere with Libby's chance of sharing her first serious kiss with a boy. "The plot moves along with many surprising turns that keep readers guessing; there is never a dull moment," wrote Leigh Ann Morlock in *School Library Journal,* and a contributor in *Kirkus Reviews* observed that, as *The Serious Kiss* progresses, "Libby's tone shifts . . . from an overdramatic annoyedness to an open realness."

In Hogan's "Susanna" series readers meet a fifteen year old with an internship at *Scene* magazine, a *People*-like publication. In *Susanna Sees Stars,* the budding journalist has to prove to her coworkers that she is more than just an errand-runner and that she really has a nose for the business. Amanda MacGregor, reviewing the book in *Kliatt,* applauded *Susanna Sees Stars,* stating that "what helps set this book apart from the many like it, is that it's fun and unpredictable, and Susanna is a great character."

Hogan continues her "Susanna" series with *Susanna Hits Hollywood* and *Susanna Covers the Catwalk.* Still interning at *Scene* in *Susanna Covers the Catwalk,* Susanna gets the opportunity to help the magazine cover the biggest event of the year: New York Fashion Week. Despite the great difficulty involved, she manages to sneak backstage at Bryant Park to get exclusive interviews, much as she does at the Academy Awards in *Susanna Hits Hollywood.* Zoë Page, writing in *Bookbag* online, called *Susanna Covers the Catwalk* "an easy, fun read" featuring "slapstick comedy" and "great writing." Page predicted that Hogan's "inspiring lead character" will be "appealing to the ordinary girl."

Perfect Girl follows Ruthie, a teen who is having difficulties with her heartthrob, Perry. Seeking advice, she contacts her Aunt Marty, a glamorous love columnist who gives Ruthie some offbeat but interesting lessons about love. By novel's end, wrote Tina Zubak in *School Library Journal,* "Ruthie realizes that it's the little details that define a relationship and that perfection is irrelevant." A *Kirkus Reviews* contributor remarked that the author "excels at young tenderness, such as Perry's spooning Ruthie's foot."

Pretty Face, another young-adult title, focuses on Southern Californian teen Hayley, who is pretty and smart and also overweight. Although she is attracted to school heartthrob Drew Wyler, Hayley is resigned to the fact that Drew will always see her as just a friend. A summer spent at a "fat camp" in Italy changes everything, however, in a novel that a *Publishers Weekly* critic praised for its heroine's "sharp wit and . . . smart insights."

In an interview in *Bookworm Readers,* Hogan offered advice to young adults looking to one day become authors. "Be brave. Let it all hang out," she noted. "To me, that's the best way to tell a completely unique, ut-

Cover of Hogan's middle-grade novel Susanna Sees Stars, *featuring artwork by Amy Saidens.* (Illustration copyright © 2007 by Amy Saidens. Used by permission of Delacorte Press, an imprint of Random House Children's Books, a division of Random House, Inc.)

terly riveting story." She cautioned, though, that "if you write about real people, change their hair color. For some reason, no one recognizes themselves if you change their hair color. Except my parents, of course, but you can't have everything."

Biographical and Critical Sources

PERIODICALS

Booklist, February 1, 2005, Debbie Carton, review of *The Serious Kiss,* p. 954.
Bookseller, February 18, 2005, review of *The Serious Kiss,* p. 38.
Kirkus Reviews, December 14, 2004, review of *The Serious Kiss,* p. 1202; March 15, 2007, review of *Perfect Girl.*
Kliatt, March, 2007, Myrna Marler, review of *Perfect Girl,* p. 14; September, 2007, Amanda MacGregor, review of *Susanna Sees Stars,* p. 22.
Publishers Weekly, January 17, 2005, review of *The Serious Kiss,* p. 57; March 3, 2008, review of *Pretty Face,* p. 49.
School Library Journal, January, 2005, Leigh Ann Morlock, review of *The Serious Kiss,* p. 130; June, 2007, Tina Zubak, review of *Perfect Girl,* p. 146.
Times Educational Supplement, October 21, 2005, Jo Klaces, review of *The Serious Kiss,* p. 19.

ONLINE

Authors in Schools Web site, http://www.authorsinschools.com/ (March 1, 2008), "Mary Hogan."
Bookbag Web site, http://www.thebookbag.co.uk/ (May 22, 2009), Zoë Page, review of *Susanna Covers the Catwalk.*
Book Pleasures.com, http://www.bookpleasures.com/ (February 28, 2008), E. Dian Moore, interview with Hogan.
Bookworm Readers Web log, http://bookwormbooklovers.blogspot.com/ (May 22, 2009), interview with Hogan.
Mary Hogan Home Page, http://www.maryhogan.com (May 22, 2009).
Simon & Schuster Web site, http://www.simonsays.com/ (March 1, 2008), "Mary Hogan."*

*   *   *

HUNT, Charlotte Dumaresq
See DEMI

*   *   *

HYMAN, Miles 1962-

Personal

Born 1962, in Bennington, VT. *Education:* Studied painting at Buxton School; attended Wesleyan University; attended École des Beaux-Arts (Paris, France).

Addresses

Home and office—Meudon, France. *Agent*—Lindgren & Smith, 630 9th Ave., New York, NY 10036. *E-mail*—mileshyman@mac.com.

Career

Artist, illustrator, and set designer. Has done commercial illustration for Louis Vuitton, Frito-Lay, Bellsouth, Bellagio Casino, Glaxo-Wellcome, McDonald's, Givenchy, Hermès, and Green Mountain Coffee Roasters. Has worked in production design for *Cinéma de Poche* (television), 1991, *Messieurs les Enfants* (film), 1996, and *Peter Pan* (stage musical), 1997. Instructor at Paris Parsons School of Design and University of California, Los Angeles Extension Program. *Exhibitions:* Work has been exhibited at Palais de Tokyo, Paris, France, 1990; Galerie Rohwedder and Galerie Medicis, Paris; Papiers Gras, Geneva, Switzerland; Galeria Maeght, Barcelona, Spain; and Galerie Michael, Beverly Hills, CA.

Awards, Honors

Notable Children's Book selection, *New York Times,* 1995, for *Broadway Chicken* by Jean-Luc Fromental.

Writings

SELF-ILLUSTRATED

ABC (30/40), Futuropolis (Paris, France), 1993.
Ouest, Alain Beaulet (Chatenay-Malabry, France), 1995.

ILLUSTRATOR; FOR CHILDREN

Christine Nöstlinger, *Hanneton, Vole!,* Hachette (Paris, France), 1988.
Hervé Jaouen, *La croix du sud,* Syros (Paris, France), 1988.
Mecka Lind, *Anna et la guerre,* Bayard-Presse (Paris, France), 1989.
Lena Martignol, *L'or bleu,* Hachette (Paris, France), 1989.
Jean-Luc Fromental, *Le carnet noir,* Nathan (Paris, France), 1991.
Tor Seidler, *Terrible Noël,* Bayard-Presse (Paris, France), 1991.
Jack London, *L'appel sauvage* (translation of *Call of the Wild*), Hachette (Paris, France), 1992.
Jan Kuriata, *Berlin Express,* Bayard-Presse (Paris, France), 1992.
Tor Seidler, *Alexandre le dinosaur,* Gallimard (Paris, France), 1992.
Marita Conlon-McKenna, *Les enfants de la faim,* Hachette (Paris, France), 1992.
Leigh Sauerwein, *Le journal de Sarah Templeton,* Gallimard (Paris, France), 1993.
Jean-Luc Fromental, *Le poulet de Broadway,* Gallimard (Paris, France), 1993, translated as *Broadway Chicken,* Hyperion Books for Children (New York, NY), 1995.

Leigh Sauerwein, *The Way Home,* Farrar, Straus & Giroux (New York, NY), 1994.

Daniel Pennac, *Cabot-caboche,* Nathan (Paris, France), 1994.

Jean-Luc Fromental, *Le cochon à l'Oreille coupée,* Le Seuil (Paris, France), 1994.

Nadèjda Garrel, *Dans les forêts de la nuit,* Nathan (Paris, France), 1995.

Brooks Hansen, *The Chess Garden,* Farrar, Straus & Giroux (New York, NY), 1995.

Luis Sepulveda, *Histoire d'une mouette et du chat qui lui apprit à voler,* Le Seuil-Jeunesse (Paris, France), 1996.

Thierry Lenain, *Trouillard!,* Nathan (Paris, France), 1997.

Evelyne Brisou-Pellen, *L'incroyable retour,* Nathan (Paris, France), 1997.

Melvin Burgess, *L'esprit du Tigre,* Gallimard-Jeunesse (Paris, France), 1999.

Claire Mazard, *Maman les p'tits bateaux,* Casterman (Paris, France), 1999.

Berlie Doherty, *Le grand voilier dan les arbes,* Gallimard (Paris, France), 2000.

Satyajit Ray, *Deux aventures de Félouda,* Seuil/Metaillié (Paris, France), 2001.

Shirley Jackson, *Nine Magic Wishes,* Farrar, Straus & Giroux (New York, NY), 2001.

Anne Montange, *Shanti et le Berceau de lune,* Actes Sud Junior (Arles, France), 2002.

Nicky Singer, *Poids-plume,* Gallimard-Jeunesse (Paris, France), 2002.

Anne Jonas, *Légende de la ville d'Ys,* Milan (Toulouse, France), 2003.

Celeste Davidson Mannis, *Julia Morgan Built a Castle,* Viking (New York, NY), 2006.

Charles Perrault, *Le petit poucet,* Gallimard-Jeunesse (Paris, France), 2007.

ILLUSTRATOR

Robin Cook, *Rue de Lappe,* Eden (France), 1987.

Milo Daax, *L'homme à deux têtes,* Futuropolis (Paris, France), 1987.

Michel Ragon, *Milan ville rêvée,* Autrement (Paris, France), 1987.

Iossif Brodski, *Leningrade ville rêvée,* Autrement (Paris, France), 1987.

J. de Decker, *Bruxelles ville rêvée,* Autrement (Paris, France), 1988.

Marc Villard, *Agenda Polar 1989,* Eden (France), 1988.

Marc Villard, *Chroniques ferroviaires,* Futuropolis (Paris, France), 1989.

John Dos Passos, *Manhattan Transfer,* Futuropolis (Paris, France), 1990.

Laurence J. Hyman and Laura Thorpe, editors, *Tales of the Diamond: Selected Gems of Baseball,* Woodford Press (San Francisco, CA), 1991.

Philippe Djian, *Lorsque Lou,* Futuropolis (Paris, France), 1992.

Joseph Conrad, *L'agent secret,* Futuropolis (Paris, France), 1992.

Susan Sontag, *A Place in the World Called Paris,* Chronicle Books (San Francisco, CA), 1994.

H. Turet, *La nuit de la louve,* Bayard Presse (Paris, France), 1995.

Marc Villard, *Pigalle,* Eden (France), 2000.

Dylan Thomas, *Un noël d'enfant au pays de galles,* Denoël Graphic (France), 2005.

John Hollander, editor, *O. Henry,* Sterling Publishing (New York, NY), 2005.

Jean-François Deniau, *Petit Paul et sa mouette Ursule: les pirates de la mer de Chine,* Hachette (Paris, France), 2006.

Jean-Pierre Milovanoff, *Clam la rapide,* Seuil (Paris, France), 2007.

Jim Thompson, *Nuit de fureur,* Casterman (Paris, France), 2008.

Contributor to periodicals, including *Lire, Rolling Stone, l'Evènement du Jeundi, Globe, Troika, Good Housekeeping, Alfred Hitchcock Mystery Magazine, Family Circle, Le Monde, Libération, Cuisines et Vins de France, Courrier International, New Yorker,* and *International Herald Tribune.*

Sidelights

Artist Miles Hyman has illustrated a number of highly regarded works for young readers, including *Nine Magic Wishes* by Shirley Jackson and *Julia Morgan Built a Castle* by Celeste Davidson Mannis. Born in Vermont, Hyman studied art in the United States before heading to Paris, France, to train at the École des Beaux-Arts. He developed his unique style of illustrating while there, and he has lived in France for much of his adult life. In addition to his book illustrations, Hyman has done editorial work for a variety of magazines and publishers and commercial artwork for clients such as Louis Vuitton, Frito-Lay, and the Bellagio Casino.

Broadway Chicken, a work by Jean-Luc Fromental, is the story of Charlie the Chicken, a dancer with a limp who makes a living hoofing it on the street before he is discovered by Sam Z. Fowler, a theatrical agent. Pushed to fame by Fowler, Charlie enjoys his career but worries that his slight limp may be a problem. He ends up getting it fixed, but a limp-free Charlie loses his characteristic charm. In *Booklist* April Judge praised Hyman's illustrations, stating that his "soft, impressionistic paintings framed by white borders help set the nostalgic mood." Though Hyman's page design "verges on the austere for such a showy tale," observed a *Publishers Weekly* contributor, "the oversize format suits this larger-than-life character."

Hyman's grandmother, Jackson, is best known as the author of *The Lottery* and *The Haunting of Hill House,* two famous gothic tales. Her 1963 children's book, *Nine Magic Wishes,* was reissued in 2001 with new illustrations by Hyman. The tale follows a young girl who is given nine wishes by a magician. She asks for an eclectic mix of fanciful items, including an orange pony, a miniature zoo, and a garden full of candy flowers. After eight of her wishes are fulfilled, the youngster chooses to leave the last one for someone else, because her desires are all satisfied. Although Maryann H. Owen, writing in the *School Library Journal,* commented that the artist "has done an adequate

Miles Hyman's illustration projects include Deborah Blumenthal's picture book **Black Diamond and Blake,** *which is based on a true story from racing history.* (Illustration copyright © 2009 by Miles Hyman. Used by permission of Alfred A. Knopf, an imprint of Random House Children's Books, a division of Random House, Inc.)

job of representing the story in his soft-focus, muted color illustrations," *Booklist* contributor GraceAnne A. DeCandido offered a more positive assessment of the work, remarking that "Hyman's carefully rendered images have the rich and glowing texture of pastels and anchor the fanciful text." A *Publishers Weekly* reviewer also applauded the story, stating that "Jackson's poetic scenes and Hyman's visual imagination provide the real wizardry here."

Mannis chronicles the brilliant life and career of a female architect in *Julia Morgan Built a Castle.* Morgan attended the University of California, Berkeley and graduated with a degree in architecture, which was unusual for a woman in 1895. Battling gender discrimination, she then traveled to Paris, where it took her three attempts to gain acceptance at the prestigious École des Beaux-Arts. After finishing her training, Morgan returned to California and spent more than twenty years as the designer of William Randolph Hearst's lavish estate at San Simeon. Bringing to life her work, "Hy-

man's soft but brilliant colors capture light, space and structure wonderfully," noted a critic in *Kirkus Reviews,* and *School Library Journal* contributor Teresa Pfeifer observed that the artist's "luminescent illustrations, created using soft pastels and pencils in a golden-peach palette, appear to glow with the light" of the scenic locales. Jennifer Mattson, writing in *Booklist,* believed that Hyman's illustrations for *Julia Morgan Built a Castle* "capture the grandeur of both Morgan's aspirations and the dramatic landscapes in which she worked."

Biographical and Critical Sources

PERIODICALS

Booklist, March 15, 1994, Hazel Rochman, review of *The Way Home,* p. 1344; December 15, 1995, April Judge, review of *Broadway Chicken,* p. 704; December 15, 2001, GraceAnne A. DeCandido, review of *Nine Magic Wishes,* p. 739; April 15, 2006, Michael Cart, review of *O. Henry,* p. 47; November 15, 2006, Jennifer Mattson, review of *Julia Morgan Built a Castle,* p. 51.

Horn Book, July-August, 1994, Nancy Vasilakis, review of *The Way Home,* p. 460.

Kirkus Reviews, October 1, 2006, review of *Julia Morgan Built a Castle,* p. 1019.

New York Times, November 30, 1995, Christopher Lehmann-Haupt, "A Child's Kingdom of Words and Pictures," review of *Broadway Chicken.*

New York Times Book Review, November 12, 1995, Frank Rich, "Bantam of the Opera," review of *Broadway Chicken.*

Publishers Weekly, October 16, 1995, review of *Broadway Chicken,* p. 61; August 20, 2001, review of *Nine Magic Wishes,* p. 80.

School Library Journal, October, 2001, Maryann H. Owen, review of *Nine Magic Wishes,* p. 122; May, 2006, Rita Soltan, review of *O. Henry,* p. 128; November, 2006, Teresa Pfeifer, review of *Julia Morgan Built a Castle,* p. 121.

Tribune Books (Chicago, IL), November 19, 2006, Mary Harris Russell, review of *Julia Morgan Built a Castle,* p. 7.

ONLINE

Lindgren & Smith Web site, http://www.lindgrensmith.com/ (February 1, 2008), "Miles Hyman."

Miles Hyman Home Page, http://www.mileshyman.com (December 1, 2009).

Miles Hyman Web log, http://www.mileshyman.blogspot.com (December 1, 2009).

J

JABAR, Cynthia

Personal

Female. *Education:* Attended Rhode Island School of Design and University of Iowa. *Hobbies and other interests:* Painting, kayaking.

Addresses

Home—Peaks Island, ME.

Career

Artist and children's book illustrator.

Writings

SELF-ILLUSTRATED

Party Day!, Little, Brown (Boston, MA), 1987.
Alice Ann Gets Ready for School, Joy Street Books (Boston, MA), 1989.
Bored Blue? Think What You Can Do!, Little, Brown (Boston, MA), 1991.
(Compiler) *Shimmy Shake Earthquake: Don't Forget to Dance Poems,* Little, Brown (Boston, MA), 1992.
Wow!: It Sure Is Good to Be You, Houghton Mifflin (Boston, MA), 2006.

ILLUSTRATOR

Jonathan London, *A Koala for Katie: An Adoption Story,* Albert Whitman (Morton Grove, IL), 1993.
Rick Walton, *How Many, How Many, How Many,* Candlewick Press (Cambridge, MA), 1993.
Alyssa Satin Capucilli, *Good Morning, Pond,* Hyperion (New York, NY), 1994.
Lezlie Evans, *Rain Song,* Houghton Mifflin (Boston, MA), 1995.
John Agard and Grace Nichols, *No Hickory No Dickory No Dock: Caribbean Nursery Rhymes,* Candlewick Press (Cambridge, MA), 1995.

Linda Goss, *The Frog Who Wanted to Be a Singer,* Orchard Books (New York, NY), 1995.
Lezlie Evans, *Snow Dance,* Houghton Mifflin (Boston, MA), 1997.
Catherine Dee, *The Girls' Guide to Life: How to Take Charge of the Issues That Affect You,* photographs by Carol Palmer, Little, Brown (Boston, MA), 1997.
Stuart J. Murphy, *The Greatest Gymnast of Them All,* HarperCollins (New York, NY), 1998.
Mary Lee Donovan, *Won't You Come and Play with Me?,* Houghton Mifflin (Boston, MA), 1998.
Mary O'Neill, *The Sound of Day, the Sound of Night,* Dorling Kindersley (New York, NY), 1999.
Harriet Ziefert, *Daddies Are for Catching Fireflies,* Puffin (New York, NY), 1999.
Harriet Ziefert, *Mommies Are for Catching Stars,* Puffin (New York, NY), 1999.
Stuart J. Murphy, *Game Time,* HarperCollins (New York, NY), 2000.
Debra Lee, *Sylvia's Garage,* photographs by Douglas Evans, Wright Group (Bothell, WA), 2001.
Elizabeth Spires, *The Big Meow,* Candlewick Press (Cambridge, MA), 2002.
Stuart J. Murphy, *The Sundae Scoop,* HarperCollins (New York, NY), 2003.
Irene O'Garden, *The Scrubbly-bubbly Car Wash,* HarperCollins (New York, NY), 2003.
Stuart J. Murphy, *Tally O'Malley,* HarperCollins (New York, NY), 2004.
Rachel Field, *Grace for an Island Meal,* Farrar, Straus & Giroux (New York, NY), 2006.
Shirley Parenteau, *One Frog Sang,* Candlewick Press (Cambridge, MA), 2007.

Sidelights

Cynthia Jabar is the author and illustrator of a number of popular works for young readers. Jabar, who studied illustration at the Rhode Island School of Design and literary history at the University of Iowa, published her first self-illustrated title, *Party Day!,* in 1987. In a more-recent work, *Shimmy Shake Earthquake: Don't Forget to Dance Poems,* Jabar collects eighteen poems about dance and rhythm, including verses from Ogden Nash,

Jack Prelutsky, and Langston Hughes. A contributor in *Publishers Weekly* noted that the author-illustrator's "humorously busy drawings make for an irrepressible invitation to the dance." In *Wow!: It Sure Is Good to Be You*, Jabar describes a young girl's special relationship with her distant relatives. According to *School Library Journal* critic Susan Weitz, "This heartfelt yet light-hearted offering is packed with child appeal."

Jabar has also provided the illustrations for works by such authors as Shirley Parentau, Lezlie Evans and Stuart J. Murphy. *No Hickory No Dickory No Dock: Caribbean Nursery Rhymes,* a volume of poems by John Agard and Grace Nichols, places Mother Goose's char-

acters in an exotic setting. Jabar's "scratchboard illustrations capture the island scene with brilliant tropical colors and folk-art exaggeration," noted Hazel Rochman in *Booklist*. A young amphibian pursues his dream against formidable odds in both *One Frog Sang*, by Parentau, and *The Frog Who Wanted to Be a Singer,* a story by Linda Goss. "Jabar's vigorous scratchboard illustrations are a perfect fit" for Goss's story, "portraying a dynamic forest nightlife in vibrant colors," *Booklist* reviewer Linda Perkins wrote. In bringing to life Shirley Parenteau's counting story in *One Frog Sang*, Jabar's illustrations "nicely play up the rural nighttime setting," observed Amanda Moss in *School Library Journal*.

Cynthia Jabar's entertaining paintings add humor to Shirley Parentau's aquatic drama in **One Frog Sang.** (Illustration copyright © 2007 by Cynthia Jabar. Reproduced by permission of Candlewick Press Inc., Somerville, MA.)

Jabar presents a world bound by loving ties in her self-illustrated **Wow! It Sure Is Good to Be You.**

Jabar and Evans have collaborated on a pair of picture books that celebrate nature. In *Rain Song* two youngsters spend a stormy day playing both indoors and outside. "Jabar's trademark smiley-face illustrations pack plenty of action," a *Publishers Weekly* reviewer noted of the book. A pair of sisters enjoys sledding and making snow angels in *Snow Dance*. "The illustrations are bright, cheerful, and full of animated tomfoolery," wrote Lauren Peterson in a review of *Snow Dance* for

Booklist. Mary O'Neill's *The Sound of Day, the Sound of Night* features two poems that depict the activities of a busy young family. Be Astengo, writing in *School Library Journal*, stated that "Jabar's expressionistic style depicts the[se] verse in vibrant, vivacious paintings."

Murphy introduces math concepts in *The Sundae Scoop*, a humorous work that focuses on a school picnic. According to a *Publishers Weekly* reviewer, "Jabar reinforces the lesson with colorful, whimsical drawings of delectable ice-cream scoops." In Murphy's *Tally O'Malley* a family enlivens a long car trip by counting the objects they pass. Jabar's "zippy, flower-power artwork" for this book earned praise from a *Kirkus Reviews* critic.

A filthy red automobile gets a good rinse and polish in Irene O'Garden's *The Scrubbly-bubbly Car Wash,* a work told in verse that also features Jabar's art. "Infused with vivid colors and swirling textures, the stylized artwork has a modern, upbeat look," noted Joy Fleishhacker in her *School Library Journal* review of the illustrator's contribution. In *Grace for an Island Meal,* which features an early twentieth-century poem by Rachel Field, a family enjoys a visit to a island off the coast of Maine. "In the evocative opening scenes, Jabar creates a tangible sense of sea, sun, and wind," noted *Booklist* contributor Carolyn Phelan, and Mary Hazelton wrote in *School Library Journal* that Jabar's "light, cheery illustrations evoke an idyllic day spent exploring and enjoying the wonders of this unique environment."

Biographical and Critical Sources

PERIODICALS

Booklist, May 1, 1995, Hazel Rochman, review of *No Hickory No Dickory No Dock: Caribbean Nursery Rhymes,* p. 1576; April 15, 1006, Linda Perkins, review of *The Frog Who Wanted to Be a Singer,* p. 1440; October 1, 1997, Lauren Peterson, review of *Snow Dance,* p. 336; December 1, 1998, April Judge, review of *The Greatest Gymnast of All,* p. 668; January 1, 2003, Helen Rosenberg, review of *The Sundae Scoop,* p. 899; April 1, 2003, Diane Foote, review of *The Scrubbly-bubbly Car Wash,* p. 1403; September 15, 2003, Ilene Cooper, review of *The Sound of Day, the Sound of Night,* p. 242; April 1, 2006, Carolyn Phelan, review of *Grace for an Island Meal,* p. 44.

Horn Book, July-August, 1997, Marilyn Bousquin, review of *The Girls' Guide to Life: How to Take Charge of the Issues That Affect You,* p. 473.

Kirkus Reviews, November 15, 2002, review of *The Sundae Scoop,* p. 1700; December 15, 2002, review of *The Scrubbly-bubbly Car Wash,* p. 1855; July 1, 2003, review of *The Sound of Day, the Sound of Night,* p. 912; August 1, 2004, review of *Tally O'Malley,* p. 745; May 1, 2006, review of *Grace for an Island Meal,* p. 457; March 15, 2007, review of *One Frog Sang.*

Publishers Weekly, April 27, 1992, review of *Shimmy Shake Earthquake: Don't Forget to Dance Poems,* p. 270; August 16, 1993, review of *A Koala for Katie: An Adoption Story,* p. 101; October 18, 1993, review of *How Many How Many How Many,* p. 71; March 13, 1995, review of *Rain Song,* p. 69; June 5, 1995, review of *No Hickory No Dickory No Dock,* p. 64; March 18, 1996, review of *The Frog Who Wanted to Be a Singer,* p. 69; February 9, 1998, review of *Won't You Come and Play with Me?,* p. 94; February 18, 2002, review of *The Big Meow,* p. 94; August 11, 2003, review of *The Sound of Day, the Sound of Night,* p. 278; March 27, 2006, review of *Grace for an Island Meal,* p. 77.

School Library Journal, January, 2001, Lynda Ritterman, review of *Game Time!,* p. 104; May, 2002, Marianne Saccardi, review of *The Big Meow,* p. 128; March, 2003, Joy Fleishhacker, review of *The Scrubbly-bubbly Car Wash,* p. 200; December, 2003, Be Astengo, review of *The Sound of Day, the Sound of Night,* p. 138; May, 2006, Mary Hazelton, review of *Grace for an Island Meal,* p. 110; June, 2006, Susan Weitz, review of *Wow! It Sure Is Good to Be You!,* p. 119; April, 2007, Amanda Moss, review of *One Frog Sang,* p. 114.

ONLINE

Candlewick Press Web site, http://www.candlewick.com/ (December 1, 2009), "Cynthia Jabar."*

*   *   *

JONES, Patrick 1961-

Personal

Born August 6, 1961, in Flint, MI; son of Vaughn Paul (an auto worker) and Betty Lou (a homemaker) Jones. *Education:* University of Michigan—Flint, B.A. (English and political science; with honors), 1983, A.M.L.S., 1984.

Addresses

Home—Minneapolis, MN. *E-mail*—Patrick@connectingya.com.

Career

Author, trainer, and consultant. Chatham-Effingham-Liberty Library, Savannah, GA, reference librarian, 1985-86; Springfield City Library, Springfield, MA, young-adult specialist, 1986-88; Cuyahoga County Public Library, Cleveland, OH, young-adult manager of Mayfield Regional Library, 1988-91; Allen County Public Library, Fort Wayne, IN, manager of Tecumseh Branch, 1991-96; St. Agnes Academy Library, Houston, TX, assistant librarian, 1996-98; Houston Public Library, youth services coordinator, program manager, and developer of "Power Card Challenge" program, 1998-2000; library consultant and lecturer, 2000—; Hennepin County Library, Minnetonka, MN, outreach services manager, 2002—.

Member

American Library Association, Young Adult Library Service Association, Public Library Association, National Writers Union.

Patrick Jones (Reproduced by permission.)

Awards, Honors

Project of the Year, Texas Library Association, and John Cotton Dana Award, American Library Association (ALA), both 1999, both for "Power Card Challenge" program; Frances Henne Research Award, Young Adult Library Service Association, 2000; Katharine Drexel Award, Catholic Library Association, 2006, for outstanding contribution to the growth of high school librarianship; Scholastic Library Publishing Award, ALA, 2006, for outstanding library service to teens; Great Lakes Book Award finalist, 2006, for *Nailed;* Ohio Buckeye Teen Book Award finalist, 2007, and Quick Picks for Reluctant Readers selection, ALA, both for *Things Change;* Minnesota Book Award finalist, 2008, for *Chasing Tail Lights.*

Writings

Connecting Young Adults and Libraries: A How-to-Do-It Manual, Neal-Schuman (New York, NY), 1992, third edition. 2004.
What's So Scary about R.L. Stine?, Scarecrow Press (Lanham, MD), 1998.
(With Joel Shoemaker) *Do It Right! Best Practices in Customer Service to Young Adults in Schools and Public Libraries,* Neal-Schuman (New York, NY), 2001.

(Editor, with Linda Waddle) *New Directions for Library Services to Young Adults,* American Library Association (Chicago, IL), 2002.
Running a Successful Library Card Campaign Program: A How-to-Do-It Manual, Neal-Schuman (New York, NY), 2002.
(With Patricia Taylor and Kirsten Edwards) *A Core Collection for Young Adults,* Neal-Schuman (New York, NY), 2003.
(With Patricia Taylor and Maureen L. Hartman) *Connecting with Reluctant Teen Readers: Tips, Titles, and Tools,* Neal-Schuman (New York, NY), 2006.

Contributor to books, including *Children's Books and Their Creators,* Houghton-Mifflin (Boston, MA), 1995; *Libraries and Problem Patrons,* American Library Association (Chicago, IL), 1995; *Twentieth-Century Young Adult Authors,* Gale (Detroit, MI), 1996; *Young Adults and Public Libraries,* Greenwood Press (Westport, CT), 1998; *St. James Encyclopedia of Popular Culture,* St. James Press (Detroit, MI), 1999; and *Beacham's Guide to Young-Adult Literature.* Contributor to periodicals, including *ALAN Review, American Libraries, Booklist, Emergency Librarian, Grassroots, Horn Book, Journal of Youth Services in Libraries, Kliatt, RQ, School Library Journal, Today's Librarian, Voice of Youth Advocates,* and *Voices from the Middle.*

YOUNG-ADULT NOVELS

Things Change, Walker & Company (New York, NY), 2004.
Nailed, Walker (New York, NY), 2006.
Chasing Tail Lights, Walker & Company (New York, NY), 2007.
Cheated, Walker & Company (New York, NY), 2008.
Stolen Car, Walker & Company (New York, NY), 2008.
The Tear Collector, Walker & Company (New York, NY), 2009.

Sidelights

Patrick Jones is a library consultant whose specialization in the needs of young-adult readers has made him an expert in the field. In addition to lecturing and publishing articles in a number of journals devoted to the concerns of librarians, Jones has authored several books designed to aid his colleagues in developing teens' interest in reading. He has also published a number of well-received novels for a young-adult teen audience, including *Things Change* and *Nailed.* "The teen years are so full of drama, both real and imagined, that it is a gold mine for stories," the author stated on his home page.

Born and raised in Flint, Michigan, Jones began writing at a young age. "The first article I wrote for publication was when I was twelve years old," he once commented to *SATA.* "It was a profile of Bobo Brazil for a professional wrestling magazine called *In This Corner.* A little over twelve years later I published one of my first professional articles, called 'Wrestling with Magazines for Teenagers,' for the *Voice of Youth Advocates.* In both cases, the reason for writing the article was simple: It was something I wanted to read. Much of my professional writing stems from wanting to find the answer to a question: What was the best young-adult book? What are the best series books for young adults? How do libraries connect young adults with their services? Unable to find the answers already existing, I did the research and wrote the article."

Jones's first published book, *Connecting Young Adults and Libraries: A How-to-Do-It Manual,* presents practical advice and useful resources for public libraries wishing to serve not only college-bound teens but also latchkey students, homeless teens, and those whose circumstances have forced them to leave school early and enter the working world. "Jones not only understands both libraries and teenagers," commented Cathi Dunn MacRae in *Wilson Library Bulletin,* "but he also has a flair for boiling issues down to essentials, listing ideas in absorbable small doses" that can be easily adopted by libraries of many sizes and budgets. Dubbing the book "the definitive soup-to-nuts manual for young adult librarians," *School Library Journal* contributor Bette D. Ammon praised in particular Jones's inclusion of "a plethora of strategies for enticing readers," among them developing book talk and volunteerism programs, creating advisory boards, and addressing confidentiality and censorship issues.

A recipient of numerous awards for his contributions to young-adult librarianship, Jones takes understandable pride in his achievements. As he told Michele Gorman in a *School Library Journal* interview, "When I published the first edition of *Connecting Young Adults and Libraries* that was it. There was nothing that looked at overall services to teens in libraries. There were a couple of books on YA literature, a book on YA programming. Now people really get that serving teens isn't about books—it's about looking holistically at all the different ways we serve teens in libraries."

In *What's So Scary about R.L. Stine?* Jones addresses the concern of many in the field that the proliferation of easy-reading "series" books such as those by Stine—as well as the "Babysitters's Club" books that were popular during the 1980s and 1990s—have diminished the skills of teen readers. Jones "believes that if kids love Stine's books there has to be a legitimate reason," explained Annette Curtis Klause in her review for *Voice of Youth Advocates.* In making his case in support of Stine's work as a prolific author of such series as the "Goosebumps" and "Fear Street" books, Jones "debunks assumptions about what is 'good' reading and emphasizes the importance of books that answer the emotional needs of YA readers," Klause explained. Noting that the book would be worthwhile reading for budding writers considering work in the YA horror genre as well as older Stine aficionados, the critic called Jones's analysis of Stine's successful formula "fascinating and

informative" and his own writing "lively and enthusiastic." Jones's "respect for young people and their reading tastes shines through," concluded Klause of *What's So Scary about R.L. Stine?* In a *School Library Journal* assessment of Jones's book, Molly S. Kinney also voiced approval, noting that the author presents "a powerful argument for appreciating and evaluating Stine's style, popularity, and contribution to young adult literature."

In *Do It Right! Best Practices in Customer Service to Young Adults in Schools and Public Libraries* Jones and coauthor Joel Shoemaker offer practical ideas for working with teen patrons. "Public and school librarians will appreciate this learn-by-example guide that takes a customer service approach to serving young adults," noted *Library Journal* contributor Rachel Quenk. In *Running a Successful Library Card Campaign Program: A How-to-Do-It Manual,* Jones describes popular registration drives at the Houston Public Library and Philadelphia Free Library, among others. In this work he "takes a 'this is how-it-was done' approach, focusing on success stories," Mary Lankford commented in *School Library Journal.* Another coauthored work, *A Core Collection for Young Adults,* includes a bibliography of more than 1,200 titles of interest to adolescent readers.

In 2004 Jones published his debut work of fiction, *Things Change.* In a *Teenlibrarian.com* interview, he stated that the idea for the novel first came to him in 1987, when he was working as a librarian in Springfield, Massachusetts. "I was reading lots of YA lit," the author recalled. "While there was some good stuff, some of it was horrible: preachy, false, and filled with happy endings. I thought I could do better: not because I thought writing YA was easy (if it was so easy it would not have taken me 17 years to publish), but rather that I had a different vision of what a YA book could and should be." Although Jones completed a first draft of a story about a high schooler's troubled relationship, he put it aside for more than a decade, until the members of his online writing group urged him to update the work. "I finally decided in 2000 to get serious about working on *Things Change,* but the process was so different," he remarked. "It wasn't about trying to share information, but an emotional experience."

Things Change focuses on sixteen-year-old Johanna, an intelligent and determined student from a controlling family. After she begins dating Paul, a brash, outgoing senior, he reveals a darker, destructive side to his personality. Although some critics felt that Jones's writing lacks polish, *Things Change* received generally strong reviews. In *Booklist,* Frances Bradburn noted that "readers will easily understand Johanna's excitement and attraction, as well as her need for love and security," and a contributor in *Publishers Weekly* observed that Jones's "psychologically involving first novel gives a frank, up-close look at a textbook case of dating violence."

Nailed also centers on a sixteen-year-old protagonist. Bret Hendricks, a free-spirited but stubborn intellectual from a blue-collar family, struggles to please his father, who disapproves of his son's unconventional approach to life. Bret also finds himself targeted by the athletes at his school, who deride his love of theater and music, and he must face serious consequences for his refusal to conform to society's expectations. In *Nailed,* Jones observed on his home page, "I did want to write about the environment in schools where certain kids . . . are privileged and others, like Bret, are somewhat disenfranchised, not just by the other students, but by the school establishment itself." "This is a raw novel, filled with intolerance and pain," Bradburn stated, and a contributor in *Kirkus Reviews* described *Nailed* as a "surprisingly witty tale about heartbreak, honesty and just holding on." "Through the first-person narrative," a *Publishers Weekly* critic commented, readers see Bret's shortcomings and his struggle to fit in where he feels like an outsider."

Set in the author's economically depressed hometown of Flint, Michigan, *Chasing Tail Lights* concerns a seventeen-year-old girl who harbors a terrible secret. Since the death of her father, Christy feels powerless to change her bleak circumstances, including the sexual trauma she suffers at the hands of her older brother, Ryan. With the help of an understanding teacher, however, Christy learns to take control of her life. "Jones has tackled a lot in this gutsy, difficult-to-read, difficult-to-put-down novel of drugs, poverty, and violence," reported Bradburn. Although a *Publishers Weekly* contributor found the book's narrative overly complicated, the reviewer also stated that young adults "who enjoy problem novels . . . are likely to appreciate Jones's sympathetic depictions of teen culture," and a critic in *Kirkus Reviews* stated of *Chasing Tail Lights* that "the pacing is excellent, building to a tidy ending."

In *Stolen Car,* teenager Danielle is fed up with her mother and her mother's endless string of boyfriends. The latest boyfriend, Carl, is a jobless alcoholic. Danielle seeks solace from her best friend, Ashley. Ashley's family is normal, and her house is a safe haven for Danielle. Danielle's friend Evan also provides solace, although he would rather be her boyfriend than her friend. Instead, Danielle falls for Reid, a boy who has treated her badly on more than one occasion. Praising *Stolen Car* in *Reading Junky* online, a reviewer cited "the multi-layer plot," and added that "Jones knows how to grab his readers on the first page and keep their attention right up until the last word."

Now spending much of his time writing for teens, Jones enjoys making school visits and meeting his readers face-to-face. "The money is nice, although not much, and there's certainly a thrill in seeing a book with your name and picture on it in bookstores and libraries," Jones wrote on his home page. "But it really has been getting direct feedback from teen readers" that "lets you know that something your words and work really made

a difference." "A professor in college once told me that 'writing is a way of knowing,'" he explained to *SATA,* "and I realize that what she meant is when we write, we learn. When we teach, we discover how much we know. All writers, no matter if they write the great American novel or an article for *School Library Journal,* write because they are curious. I suppose as long as I remain curious and ask questions, I'll continue writing and trying to know more."

Biographical and Critical Sources

PERIODICALS

Adolescence, winter, 2002, review of *New Directions for Library Services to Young Adults,* p. 872.

Booklist, August, 1998, Susan Rosenzweig, review of *Connecting Young Adults and Libraries: A How-to-Do-It Manual,* p. 2019; March 1, 2003, Rochelle Glantz, review of *New Directions for Library Services to Young Adults,* p. 1244; September 1, 2003, Rochelle Glantz, review of *A Core Collection for Young Adults,* p. 168; May 1, 2004, Frances Bradburn, review of *Things Change,* p. 1555; February 1, 2005, Maren Ostergard, review of *Connecting Young Adults and Libraries,* p. 998; February 15, 2006, Frances Bradburn, review of *Nailed,* p. 93; March 1, 2007, Kathleen McBroom, review of *Connecting with Reluctant Teen Readers: Tips, Titles, and Tools,* p. 111; September 15, 2007, Frances Bradburn, review of *Chasing Tail Lights,* p. 57.

Book Report, March-April, 1993, Kathleen Morrissey McBroom, review of *Connecting Young Adults and Libraries,* p. 51.

Bulletin of the Center for Children's Books, March, 1999, Deborah Stevenson, review of *What's So Scary about R.L. Stine?,* pp. 261-262.

Journal of Adolescent and Adult Literacy, March, 2000, Shirley A. Proctor, review of *What's So Scary about R.L. Stine?,* p. 583.

Kirkus Reviews, March 15, 2004, review of *Things Change,* p. 271; April 1, 2006, review of *Nailed,* p. 349; July 1, 2007, review of *Chasing Tail Lights.*

Library Journal, October 1, 2001, Rachel Quenk, review of *Do It Right! Best Practices for Serving Young Adults in School and Public Libraries,* p. 150; April 15, 2002, Lyn Hopper, review of *Running a Successful Library Card Campaign: A How-to-Do-It Manual for Librarians,* p. 131; May 15, 2002, Shari Goldsmith, "Hennepin County Library," p. 34.

Publishers Weekly, March 29, 2004, review of *Things Change,* p. 64; April 17, 2006, review of *Nailed,* p. 189; August 27, 2007, review of *Chasing Tail Lights,* p. 92.

School Library Journal, September, 1992, Bette D. Ammon, review of *Connecting Young Adults and Libraries,* p. 152; July, 1999, Molly S. Kinney, review of *What's So Scary about R.L. Stine?,* pp. 117-118; August, 2001, Miranda Doyle, review of *Do It Right!,* p. 214; July, 2002, Mary Lankford, review of *Running a*

Successful Library Card Campaign, p. 147; August, 2003, Marlyn A. Roberts, review of *A Core Collection for Young Adults,* p. 191; May, 2004, Johanna Lewis, review of *Things Change,* p. 150; December, 2004, Kelly Czarnecki, review of *Connecting Young Adults and Libraries,* p. 178; May, 2006, Kelly Czarnecki, review of *Nailed,* p. 131; August, 2006, Michele Gorman, "Mr. Inspiration: Patrick Jones on Knockout Teen Services, Mentoring Librarians, and, Yes, Loving Wrestling Magazines," p. 32; January, 2007, Kathleen A. Nester, review of *Connecting with Reluctant Teen Readers,* p. 168.

Teacher Librarian, November-December, 1998, review of *Connecting Young Adults and Libraries,* p. 38; October, 2002, Carolyn Giambra, review of *Do It Right!,* p. 36; June, 2004, Ken Haycock, review of *A Core Collection for Young Adults,* p. 36.

Voice of Youth Advocates, October, 1997, Susan Rosenzweig, review of *Connecting Young Adults and Libraries,* p. 226; June, 1999, Annette Curtis Klause, review of *What's So Scary about R.L. Stine?,* p. 145.

Wilson Library Bulletin, January, 1993, Cathi Dunn MacRae, review of *Connecting Young Adults and Libraries,* pp. 85-86.

ONLINE

Patrick Jones Home Page, http://www.connectingya.com (June 2, 2009).

Reading Junky Web log, http://readingjunky.blogspot.com/ (February 3, 2009), review of *Stolen Car.*

Teenlibrarian.com, http://www.teenlibrarian.com/ (April 1, 2008), interview with Jones.*

JUBB, Sophie

Personal

Married Ivor Baddiel (an author and scriptwriter); children: one daughter, one son.

Addresses

Home—London, England.

Career

Educator and author.

Writings

(With Ivor Baddiel) *Cock-a-Doodle Quack! Quack!,* illustrated by Ailie Busby, Picture Corgi (London, England), 2006, David Fickling (New York, NY), 2007.

Biographical and Critical Sources

PERIODICALS

Bulletin of the Center for Children's Books, July-August, 2007, Hope Morrision, review of *Cock-a-Doodle Quack! Quack!,* p. 452.

Kirkus Reviews, April 1, 2007, review of *Cock-a-Doodle Quack! Quack!*

Publishers Weekly, April 2, 2007, review of *Cock-a-Doodle Quack! Quack!,* p. 56.

School Library Journal, March, 2007, Rachel G. Payne, review of *Cock-a-Doodle Quack! Quack!,* p. 150.*

K

KAY, Verla 1946-

Personal

Born October 25, 1946, in Watsonville, CA; daughter of Donald (a crop duster) and Norma (a homemaker) Deisenroth; married Terry Kay (a glazier), April 18, 1965; children: Eric, Portia, Donn, Bruce. *Hobbies and other interests:* Boating, fishing, reading, writing, working puzzles, sewing, playing pinochle, Puzzle Pirates and other computer games.

Addresses

Home and office—Tekoa, WA. *Agent*—Curtis Brown Ltd., 10 Astor Pl., New York, NY 10003. *E-mail*— verlakay@aol.com.

Career

Children's writer, 1994—. Worked variously as a teacher's aide, church school teacher, licensed day-care provider, real-estate agent, owner/operator of a laundromat, manager of a condominium complex, sales and district manager of a home-party plan, secretary, receptionist, bookkeeper, traffic manager in radio stations, and desk clerk and night auditor for motels, among other jobs.

Awards, Honors

Best Book of the Year selection, Bank Street College of Education, for *Gold Fever;* International Honor Book designation, Society of School Librarians, 1999, and Notable Social Studies Trade Books for Young People designation, National Council for the Social Studies/ Children's Book Council (NCSS/CBC), 2000, both for *Iron Horses;* Missouri Reading Circle selection, Missouri State Teachers' Association, for *Covered Wagons, Bumpy Trails* and *Orphan Train;* Notable Social Studies Trade Books for Young People designation, NCSS/ CBC, 2002, for *Tattered Sails;* Best Children's Book of the Year selection, Bank Street College of Education, for *Broken Feather;* Amelia Bloomer listee, 2008, for *Rough, Tough Charley.*

Verla Kay (Photograph by Terry Kay. Reproduced by permission.)

Writings

FOR CHILDREN

Gold Fever, illustrated by S.D. Schindler, Putnam (New York, NY), 1999.

Iron Horses, illustrated by Michael McCurdy, Putnam (New York, NY), 1999.

Covered Wagons, Bumpy Trails, illustrated by S.D. Schindler, Putnam (New York, NY), 2000.

Tattered Sails, illustrated by Dan Andreasen, Putnam (New York, NY), 2001.

Broken Feather, illustrated by Stephen Alcorn, Putnam (New York, NY), 2002.

Homespun Sarah, illustrated by Ted Rand, Putnam (New York, NY), 2003.

Orphan Train, illustrated by Ken Stark, Putnam (New York, NY), 2003.

Rough, Tough Charley, illustrated by Adam Gustavson, Tricycle Press (Berkeley, CA), 2007.

Author of short stories published in *Humpty Dumpty's* and *Turtle* magazine.

Sidelights

Verla Kay has written several award-winning books for children that feature her distinctive, sparse rhyming style. Kay began her career as an author while working as a licensed day-care provider. She became so interested in the stories she read to the children she cared for that she decided to try her own hand at writing. In 1989 Kay began taking correspondence courses through the Institute of Children's Literature in Connecticut. She spent a number of years studying her craft and penning stories before her debut work of fiction, *Gold Fever,* was published in 1999.

In *Tattered Sails* Kay explores one family's immigration story from London to Massachusetts in 1635. A *Kirkus Reviews* contributor deemed the book "a magical combination of poetry, history, and art." *Homespun Sarah* details the life of a girl in 1770s Pennsylvania, describing the many chores she must complete in order to make herself a new dress. A *Publishers Weekly* reviewer complimented the author's "signature spare and crisp rhyming verse," and a critic in *Kirkus Reviews* reported that "teachers will love this attractive window on the period, which provides many threads to different aspects of the time."

In *Rough, Tough Charley* Kay tells the story of Charley Parkhurst, one of the fastest stagecoach drivers in the Old West. Charlie, who is revered by his peers, has a reputation for bravery, but after he dies, the undertaker declares that Charley was really a woman disguised as a man. As Kay told Cynthia Leitich Smith on the *Cynsations* Web site, "Charley seems to tell kids, 'You can do anything with your life you want to do, as long as you are willing to sacrifice and work hard for it.' Charley wanted to drive stagecoaches in a day when women were 'just' housewives and mothers. In order to do what she wanted to do, she had to 'become' a man. So she did." Mary Hazelton, writing in *School Library Journal,* praised the effort, noting that Kay's "clipped rhythm is just right for a book about a no-nonsense individual." A critic in *Kirkus Reviews* felt that "this true-life tale of a woman masquerading all her life as a man . . . bears telling," and in *Booklist* Gillian Engberg wrote that Kay "admirably distills the facts with the fewest possible words."

"Writing is the love of my life," Kay once told *SATA,* "which seems amazing to me because as a child, I not only hated to write, but was convinced that I was the world's worst writer. It wasn't until I was in my forties that I finally understood the reason I had such a hard time writing wasn't because I was a bad writer, but because I was a dedicated writer. I needed to revise over and over again before I was satisfied with what I'd written.

"Today I love writing and can't imagine my life without it. I enjoy everything about it, from the initial research on a subject, through the many drafts of a manuscript, to the thrill of a perfectly crafted story. I love all of the 'author' stuff, too—the workshops and speeches to other aspiring writers, the school visits, the book signing events."

Kay remarked to Smith that persistence and education are keys to becoming successful. Asked if she had any advice for aspiring writers, she stated: "Learn! Learn all you can about what makes a good, strong children's story. Learn all you can about the marketing aspect of the business, because you can write the best story in the world, but if you don't know how to get it onto the desk of the editor who will love it, you may find it impossible to sell. And finally, if you truly believe in your story, never give up on it." Helping others to become successful is also a driving force for Kay: "It's my fervent hope and desire to assist other aspiring writers to find their success in this business. That is why I created a Web site with a chat room where writers of children's literature can gather and share information. I would hate someday to make it to the top and find myself totally alone. If I ever get there, I want all my writing friends there, too!"

Biographical and Critical Sources

PERIODICALS

Booklist, January 1, 1999, Lauren Peterson, review of *Gold Fever,* p. 888; June 1, 1999, Hazel Rochman, review of *Iron Horses,* p. 1842; October 15, 2001, Helen Rosenberg, review of *Tattered Sails,* p. 401; November 1, 2002, Susan Dove Lempke, review of *Broken Feather,* p. 500; March 1, 2003, Kay Weisman, review of *Homespun Sarah,* p. 1208; June 1, 2003, Gillian Engberg, review of *Orphan Train,* p. 1785; June 1, 2007, Gillian Engberg, review of *Rough, Tough Charley,* p. 94.

Buffalo News (Buffalo, NY), March 7, 1999, Jean Westmoore, review of *Gold Fever,* p. G5.

Horn Book, March, 1999, Margaret A. Bush, review of *Gold Fever,* p. 192; July, 1999, review of *Iron Horses,* p. 456; January, 2001, review of *Covered Wagons, Bumpy Trails,* p. 84.

Kirkus Reviews, December 15, 1998, review of *Gold Fever,* p. 1798; May 15, 1999, review of *Iron Horses,* p. 802; August 1, 2002, review of *Tattered Sails,* p. 1126;

September 15, 2002, review of *Broken Feather,* p. 1392; March 15, 2003, review of *Homespun Sarah,* p. 470; May 1, 2003, review of *Orphan Train,* p. 678; April 15, 2007, review of *Rough, Tough Charley.*

Publishers Weekly, January 11, 1999, review of *Gold Fever,* p. 71; June 21, 1999, review of *Iron Horses,* p. 67; February 17, 2003, review of *Homespun Sarah,* p. 74; May 7, 2007, review of *Rough, Tough Charley,* p. 58.

School Library Journal, March, 1999, John Sigwald, review of *Gold Fever,* p. 177; July, 1999, Steven Engelfried, review of *Iron Horses,* p. 74; September, 2001, Diane S. Marton, review of Tattered Sails, p. 192; November, 2002, S.K. Joiner, review of *Broken Feather,* p. 145; April, 2005, Nina Lindsay, review of *Gold Fever,* p. 55; August, 2007, Mary Hazelton, review of *Rough, Tough Charley,* p. 100.

Teacher Librarian, December, 1999, Teri Lesesne, "Journeys Real and Imagined: Books to Take Us Places," review of *Iron Horses,* p. 45.

ONLINE

Cynsations Web log, http://cynthialeitichsmith.blogspot. com/ (November 19, 2007), Cynthia Leitich Smith, interview with Kay.

Cynthia Leitich Smith Home Page, http://www. cynthia leitichsmith.com/ (February 1, 2008), Cynthia Leitich Smith, interview with Kay.

Suite 101.com, http://www.suite101.com/ (May 1, 2002), Sue Reichard, "Inspiring Words from Children's Author Verla Kay."

Verla Kay Home Page, http://www.verlakay.com (February 1, 2008).

*   *   *

KELLY, Irene 1957-

Personal

Born August 8, 1957, in Morristown, NJ; daughter of Frank and Ann Kelly; married Jeffrey Nelson (a television producer, writer, and editor), 1986; children: Derek, Lucy. *Education:* New York University, B.A., 1980.

Addresses

Home—Maplewood, NJ. *Agent*—Edite Kroll, 12 Grayhurst Park, Portland, ME 04102. *E-mail*—irenekelly1@ comcast.net.

Career

Author and illustrator. Visiting author/illustrator in schools and presenter of "Creating Books" assemblies and writing workshops, 1998—. *Exhibitions:* Illustrations shown at Children's Museum of the Arts, New York, NY.

Awards, Honors

Children's Choice selection, International Reading Association/Children's Book Council, 1999, for *Ebbie and Flo;* John Burroughs List of Nature Books for Young Readers selection, Society of School Librarians International Honor Book designation, Best Children's Books of the Year Selection, Bank Street College, all 2003, all for *It's a Hummingbird's Life;* John Burroughs List of Nature Books for Young Readers selection, and Outstanding Science Book, National Science Teachers Association, both 2007, both for *It's a Butterfly's Life.*

Writings

SELF-ILLUSTRATED

Ebbie and Flo, Smith & Kraus (Lyme, NH), 1998.
It's a Hummingbird's Life, Holiday House (New York, NY), 2003.
A Small Dog's Big Life: Around the World with Owney, Holiday House (New York, NY), 2005.
It's a Butterfly's Life, Holiday House (New York, NY), 2007.
Birds at Home, Holiday House (New York, NY), 2009.

ILLUSTRATOR

L.E. McCullough, *Stories of the Songs of Christmas,* Smith & Kraus (Lyme, NH), 1997.
Patricia Tunstall, *Note by Note,* Simon & Schuster (New York, NY), 2008.

Sidelights

Irene Kelly's self-illustrated books for children revolve around animal themes. Whether lighthearted fiction such as *Ebbie and Flo* or cheerful nonfiction such as *It's a Butterfly's Life,* Kelly offers lessons on animals and animal behavior that children can relate to and understand.

In *Ebbie and Flo* two Atlantic salmon siblings hatch and begin to grow. Flo, outgoing and exuberant and with a pink striped belly, is interested in adventure, daring, and living life to the fullest. Flo's brother Ebbie is more subdued, even timid, with a yellow-striped belly and a desire to leave life's excitement to someone else. Some might even call the fainthearted little fish a coward. As the two grow and mature, Flo becomes more daring and Ebbie more nervous, all the while migrating further and further out to sea. When Flo bravely swims up to a hungry killer whale and introduces herself, Ebbie must dive deep into himself to find the courage and determination to rescue her before she becomes a whale snack. Afterward, the two return to the freshwater stream where they were spawned to seek mates and begin the ebbing and flowing cycle of life all over again.

Within the story of the two young fish, Kelly provides scientific facts and tidbits about salmon and life in the ocean. A page of Atlantic salmon "Fish Facts" includes information on Ebbie and Flo's real-life counterparts. While claiming that the story works as a whole, *School*

Library Journal critic Patricia Manning found that the pairing of a fictional story with scientific facts "result[s] in a somewhat confusing dichotomy." In contrast, a *Publishers Weekly* critic observed of *Ebbie and Flo* that "the humorously expressive fish and vivid illustrations add up to a thoroughly enjoyable fish story."

With *It's a Hummingbird's Life* Kelly switches her focus to natural facts, avoiding the framework of fiction, offers a profile of ruby-throated hummingbirds, their behaviors, and their activities throughout the seasons in the United States. Kelly's concise descriptions and detailed illustrations impart biological facts and trivia about the tiny but dynamically powerfully hummingbirds. For example, she relates that hummingbirds beat their wings about 2,000 times per minute; that newly hatched hummingbirds must be fed every three minutes; and that hummingbird nests are similar in size to a halved ping-pong ball. Kelly provides facts on topics such as hummingbird mating, rearing of young, feeding, bathing, defining and defending territory, and more. Barbara L. McMullin, writing in *School Library Journal,* called *It's a Hummingbird's Life* "a whimsical look at the traits and tendencies of these fascinating creatures." Kelly

Kelly "does a terrific job of giving readers real-life equivalents to understand the scale of the hummingbird's world," commented Linnea Lannon in *New York Times Book Review.* A *Publishers Weekly* reviewer noted that Kelly's work offers "young bird lovers a close look

into this tiny bird's busy days," while *Booklist* critic Carolyn Phelan called *It's a Hummingbird's Life* a "very decorative book" due to the many illustrations by Kelly that adorn the volume. A *Kirkus Reviews* critic described the book as "sweet, colorful, and fluttery," calling it a "bright little jewel [that] is as cheerful as the bird it depicts."

Kelly examines the life of another winged creature in *It's a Butterfly's Life.* She details the life cycle of a butterfly, from egg to caterpillar to chrysalis to butterfly. A contributor in *Kirkus Reviews* praised the work, asserting that it "proves science nonfiction can be accurate, factual and completely engrossing," and Hazel Rochman remarked in *Booklist* that the book has "simple, informative text and detailed illustrations." Kirsten Cutler, writing in *School Library Journal,* called *It's a Butterfly's Life* "a delightful book to share with children and would be a splendid resource for reports."

In *A Small Dog's Big Life: Around the World with Owney* Kelly looks at the life of a special canine. Owney was a scruffy dog who wandered into a post office in Albany, New York, in 1889. With his winning ways and adventurous spirit, Owney was quickly taken in by the staff and ended up jumping on many mail trains and boats, traveling thousands of miles while helping to deliver the U.S. mail. In 1895, the dog was adopted as the official mascot of the U.S. Postal Service. Kelly tells Owney's tale through fictional letters written to the dog by people who could have known him, and

Irene Kelly pairs her simple, informative text with her naif-style watercolor art in **It's a Hummingbird's Life.** (Copyright © 2003 by Irene Kelly. All rights reserved. Reproduced by permission of Holiday House, Inc.)

Kelly uses art and text to share her fascination with nature in the picture book **Even an Ostrich Needs a Nest.** (Holiday House, 2007. Copyright © 2007 by Irene Kelly. Reproduced by permission.)

also includes maps of the dog's many journeys. Rachael Vilmar, writing in *School Library Journal,* complimented the story, noting that, "overall, this is an effective treatment of a tale that's strange but true. Young dog lovers will be fascinated."

Biographical and Critical Sources

PERIODICALS

Booklist, April 1, 2003, Carolyn Phelan, review of *It's a Hummingbird's Life,* p. 1398; July, 2005, Hazel Rochman, review of *A Small Dog's Big Life: Around the World with Owney,* p. 1929; March 1, 2007, Hazel Rochman, review of *It's a Butterfly's Life,* p. 87.

Horn Book, July-August, 2007, Betty Carter, review of *It's a Butterfly's Life,* p. 413.

Kirkus Reviews, March 1, 2003, review of *It's a Hummingbird's Life,* p. 389; June 1, 2005, review of *A Small Dog's Big Life,* p. 638; April 1, 2007, review of *It's a Butterfly's Life.*

New York Times Book Review, May 18, 2003, Linnea Lannon, review of *It's a Hummingbird's Life.*

Publishers Weekly, May 18, 1998, review of *Ebbie and Flo,* p. 112; March 31, 2003, review of *It's a Hummingbird's Life,* p. 70.

Reading Teacher, October, 1999, review of *Ebbie and Flo,* p. 173.

School Library Journal, October, 1997, Jane Marino, review of *Stories of the Songs of Christmas,* p. 47; June, 1998, Patricia Manning, review of *Ebbie and Flo,* p. 112; June, 2003, Barbara L. McMullin, review of *It's a Hummingbird's Life,* p. 129; August, 2005, Rachael Vilmar, review of *A Small Dog's Big Life,* p. 98; June, 2007, Kirsten Cutler, review of *It's a Butterfly's Life,* p. 135.

Star-Ledger (Newark, NJ), December 10, 1998, "Author to Demystify Book-production Process," p. 2; January

11, 2006, Elizabeth Moore, "This One's a Page-Turner: Kids Have Eye for Bookmaking," p. 19.

ONLINE

Author Illustrators Source Web site, http://www.author-illustr-source.com/ (February 1, 2008), "Irene Kelly."

Irene Kelly Home Page, http://www.irenekellybooks.com (January 10, 2010).

* * *

KENNEDY, Marlane 1962-

Personal

Born November 17, 1962, in Waverly, OH; father a banker/milkman, mother a social worker; married; husband's name Joel (an optometrist); children: Seth, Spencer, Molly (deceased), Hope. *Education:* Graduated from Ohio State University.

Addresses

Home—Wooster, OH. *E-mail*—marlane@marlane kennedy.com.

Career

Writer. Worked in loan servicing at a bank.

Awards, Honors

Children's BookSense Pick, 2007, for *Me and the Pumpkin Queen.*

Writings

Me and the Pumpkin Queen (middle-grade novel), Greenwillow Books (New York, NY), 2007.

The Dog Days of Charlotte Hayes (middle-grade novel), Greenwillow Books (New York, NY), 2009.

Sidelights

Writing stories was a skill that came early to Marlane Kennedy, author of the critically acclaimed middle-grade novel *Me and the Pumpkin Queen.* "My fourth grade teacher, Mrs. Newman, gave me a tremendous boost of confidence in my ability to write," Kennedy stated in an interview on the HarperCollins Web site. "I clearly remember the day she passed out pictures cut from magazines as a writing prompt. I received a picture of a barn and wrote a story about a girl who saved a horse from a barn fire. Mrs. Newman was so pleased with the story that she read it out loud to the class and posted it in a place of honor on the bulletin board. I was thrilled, so happy. Maybe, I thought, I should be an author."

Marlane Kennedy (Reproduced by permission.)

It took many more years before Kennedy's efforts were rewarded with a publication contract. In fact, she attempted seven novels before she sold *Me and the Pumpkin Queen.* "My family has always been great, even though it took me fourteen years to be published," she remarked on the *Class of 2k7* Web site. "My father has been bragging to people for years that he had a daughter that was a children's book author." Kennedy's decision to write for young people was an easy one. "I never outgrew children's books," she stated. "Instead of making the jump to reading adult books, I kept on heading for the middle grade/young adult section of the library. My twenties and thirties have passed and reading books for kids is still a passion of mine."

Me and the Pumpkin Queen centers on an eleven-year-old girl named Mildred who lost her mother to cancer when she was six years old. Now Mildred works on growing a pumpkin big enough to win the prize at the local fair. Through challenges both natural and man-made, she perseveres, but the final weigh-in at the fair reveals an interesting twist. According to Kennedy, *Me and the Pumpkin Queen* is based on a real event that occurs in Circleville, Ohio, each October. In her review of the book, *School Library Journal* contributor Kathryn Kosiorek remarked that Kennedy adds "just the right amount of humor and tension to keep the plot moving along." Christine M. Heppermann, writing in *Horn Book,* observed that the story's "narrative's appeal derives mainly from Mildred's methodically documented gardening," and a *Kirkus Reviews* contributor deemed *Me and the Pumpkin Queen* "a warmhearted and genuine offering that demands little and gives much."

In Kennedy's middle-grade novel *The Dog Days of Charlotte Hayes* twelve-year-old Charlotte is definitely not a dog person. Nonetheless, she finds herself responsible for taking care of the famiy's pet St. Bernard, Beauregard, after the birth of a new baby. Charlotte comes up with numerous schemes to save time or cut corners with regard to her doggie duties, but she eventually comes to care for Beauregard more than she wants to admit. Terry Miller Shannon, reviewing the novel in *Kidsreads.com,* claimed that "Charlotte's story is often funny, but with a poignant undertone that just may cause readers to sniffle as they read to the end." In *Kirkus Reviews* a contributor hoped that Kennedy's "entertaining read will serve to catch the attention of children everywhere living with too-easily neglected pets," while Kathleen Isaacs concluded in *Booklist* that "the familiar family and friendship issues and satisfying resolution make this an agreeable read."

Biographical and Critical Sources

PERIODICALS

Booklist, July 1, 2007, Ilene Cooper, review of *Me and the Pumpkin Queen,* p. 62; February 15, 2009, Kathleen Isaacs, review of *The Dog Days of Charlotte Hayes,* p. 82.
Horn Book, July-August, 2007, Christine M. Heppermann, review of *Me and the Pumpkin Queen,* p. 397.
Kirkus Reviews, June 1, 2007, review of *Me and the Pumpkin Queen;* February 1, 2009, review of *The Dog Days of Charlotte Hayes.*
School Library Journal, August, 2007, Kathryn Kosiorek, review of *Me and the Pumpkin Queen,* p. 82.

ONLINE

Class of 2k7 Web site, http://www.classof2k7.com/ (September 21, 2007), Rose Kent, interview with Kennedy.
HarperCollins Web site, http://www.harpercollins.com/ (February 1, 2008), "Marlane Kennedy."
Kidsreads.com, http://www.kidsreads.com/ (May 26, 2009), Terry Miller Shannon, review of *The Dog Days of Charlotte Hayes.*
Marlane Kennedy Home Page, http://www.marlane kennedy.com (June 1, 2009).

*   *   *

KRISTIANSEN, Teddy 1964-
(Teddy H. Kristiansen)

Personal

Born 1964, in Denmark. *Education:* Studied at Ulrik Hoff's School of Drawing and Painting.

Addresses

Home—Denmark. *E-mail*—mail@teddykristiansen.dk.

Career

Illustrator and animator.

Awards, Honors

Eisner Award for Best Painter/Multimedia Artist, 2005, for *It's a Bird . . . .*

Writings

ILLUSTRATOR

Niels Søndergaard, *Superman og fredsbomben* (title means "Superman and the Peace Bomb"), Interpresse (Denmark), 1990.
James Robinson, *Grendel Tales: Four Devils, One Hell* (originally published in comic-book form in six issues), Dark Horse Comics (Milwaukie, OR), 1994.
(As Teddy H. Kristiansen) Eddie Campbell, *Bacchus,* Dark Horse Comics (Milwaukie, OR), 1995.
Neil Gaiman and Matt Wagner, *Sandman Midnight Theatre,* DC Comics (New York, NY), 1995.
(With others) Neil Gaiman, *The Sandman: The Kindly Ones,* DC Comics (New York, NY), 1996.
(With others) James Robinson, *WitchCraft,* DC Comics (New York, NY), 1996.
Steven T. Seagle, *House of Secrets: Foundation,* DC Comics (New York, NY), 1997.
(With others) Matt Wagner, *Grendel: Black, White, and Red,* Dark Horse Comics (Milwaukie, OR), 1999.
(With others) Neil Gaiman, *Midnight Days,* DC Comics (New York, NY), 1999.
Steven T. Seagle, *House of Secrets: Façade,* DC Comics (New York, NY), 2001.
Steven T. Seagle, *It's a Bird . . .,* Vertigo (New York, NY), 2004.
Neil Gaiman, *M Is for Magic,* HarperCollins (New York, NY), 2007.

Also illustrator of comic books, including *Tarzan: Love, Lies, and the Lost City,* Malibu Comics, 1992; *Grendel: War Child,* Dark Horse Comics, 1993; *Harlan Ellison's Dream Corridor,* Dark Horse Comics, 1995; *Grendel: Devil by the Deed,* Dark Horse Comics, 1997; *Vertigo: Winter's Edge,* DC Comics, 1998; *The Dreaming,* DC Comics, 1999; and *Grendel: Devil Child,* 1999.

OTHER

Author and illustrator of story in "Solo" (comic-book series), issue 8, DC Comics (New York, NY), 2005.

Sidelights

Danish artist Teddy Kristiansen has illustrated dozens of comic books and graphic novels, including the comic-book compilation *Superman og fredsbomben*

("Superman and the Peace Bomb"), the first "Superman" comic to be fully produced outside of the United States, and *It's a Bird . . .,* a critically acclaimed title by Steven T. Seagle. Kristiansen has also provided the artwork for Seagle's "House of Secrets" comic-book series, and he has contributed illustrations to Neil Gaiman's popular "Sandman" comic-book series and Matt Wagner's "Grendel" series.

It's a Bird . . ., Seagle's semi-autobiographical work, focuses on Steve, a comic-book writer who balks at his latest assignment: a work about Superman, an alien and unbelievable character to whom Steve cannot relate. As he struggles with the project, the writer offers a number of meditations on the Superman mythos, examining the character's Nietzchean overtones and the symbolism of his costume. The writer's personal life is also in shambles: Steve must search for his father, who has gone missing, and face the disturbing prospect that he may have inherited Huntington's disease, an incapacitating genetic muscle disorder. "The story unfolds like a one-man play as Seagle takes the reader on a guided tour of his life," observed *Comicreaders.com* reviewer David Brennan.

Kristiansen's illustrations for *It's a Bird . . .* earned the artist a prestigious Eisner Award for his efforts. According to a *Publishers Weekly* contributor, Kristiansen's "inventive ink-and-watercolor artwork" injects the comic with "a crisp, arty look," and Tom Russo noted in *Entertainment Weekly* that the artist's "slender, angular not-quite-caricatures . . . are well matched to the pervading air of restlessness" in Seagle's story. According to *USA Today* reviewer David Colton, "Seagle's writing has the verite of *American Splendor*'s Harvey Pekar; Kristiansen's art is spare and limber; the book's payoff is satisfying and wise."

Kristiansen has also served as both author and illustrator for an issue of the "Solo" comic-book series. Published by DC Comics, the issue collects several works by Seagle and Gaiman, as well as three tales by Kristiansen, including "Love Story," which concerns an obsessive relationship. Reviewing "Love Story" in *Comicreaders.com,* Derek Ash stated: "The whole thing reads like poetry, and Kristiansen's artwork is beautiful . . ., all angles and curves, darkness and gentle shades of aqua, with reds and browns used to punch the eye where it counts." In *Solo* "Kristiansen proves himself to be as talented a storyteller as he is an artist," Ash added, "and his gothic, angular style is put to many different uses in these pages."

Biographical and Critical Sources

PERIODICALS

Booklist, April 1, 2004, Gordon Flagg, review of *It's a Bird . . .,* p. 1358; April 15, 2007, Kathleen Isaacs, review of *M Is for M agic,* p. 38.

Entertainment Weekly, May 14, 2004, Tom Russo, review of *It's a Bird . . .,* p. 76.

Kirkus Reviews, June 1, 2007, review of *M Is for Magic.*

Library Journal, September 1, 2004, Steve Raiteri, review of *It's a Bird . . .,* p. 129.

Magazine of Fantasy and Science Fiction, October-November, 2004, Charles de Lint, review of *It's a Bird . . .,* p. 37.

Publishers Weekly, March 15, 2004, review of *It's a Bird . . .,* p. 57; July 9, 2007, review of *M Is for Magic,* p. 54.

School Library Journal, August, 2007, Beth Wright, review of *M Is for Magic,* p. 116.

USA Today, April 29, 2004, review of *It's a Bird . . .,* p. 4D.

Washington Post Book World, July 25, 2004, Dan Nadel, "Superman 101," review of *It's a Bird . . .,* p. 15.

ONLINE

Comicreaders.com, http://www.comicreaders.com/ (April, 1, 2008), Derek Ash, review of "Solo," number 8, and David Brennan, review of *It's a Bird . . . .*

Lambiek.net, http://lambiek.net/ (April, 1, 2008), "Teddy Kristiansen."

Teddy Kristiansen Web log, http://teddykristiansenblog.blogspot.com (May 1, 2008).

*   *   *

KRISTIANSEN, Teddy H.
See KRISTIANSEN, Teddy

*   *   *

KRUDOP, Walter
See KRUDOP, Walter Lyon

*   *   *

KRUDOP, Walter Lyon 1966-
(Walter Krudop)

Personal

Born 1966, in Elizabeth, NJ; married; wife's name Sara. *Education:* Attended School of Visual Arts, Parsons School of Design, and New York University. *Hobbies and other interests:* Old photographs and movies.

Addresses

Home—New York, NY. *E-mail*—walter@walterkrudop.com.

Career

Illustrator, designer, animator, and author. *Exhibitions:* Work exhibited at Society of Illustrators show, New York, NY.

Awards, Honors

Smithsonian recommended book citation; Africana Award; Notable Book for Children selection, American Library Association; Orbus Pictus Award.

Writings

SELF-ILLUSTRATED

Blue Claws, Atheneum (New York, NY), 1993.
Something Is Growing, Atheneum (New York, NY), 1995.
The Man Who Caught Fish, Farrar, Straus & Giroux (New York, NY), 2000.

ILLUSTRATOR

Jim Aylesworth, *The Good-night Kiss,* Atheneum (New York, NY), 1993.
Gina Willner-Pardo, *What I'll Remember When I Am a Grownup,* Clarion Books (New York, NY), 1994.
Doris Gove, *One Rainy Night,* Atheneum (New York, NY), 1994.
Gina Willner-Pardo, *Hunting Grandma's Treasures,* Clarion Books (New York, NY), 1996.
Jim Aylesworth, *Wake up, Little Children: A Rise-and-shine Rhyme,* Atheneum (New York, NY), 1996.
Claudia Mills, *One Small Lost Sheep,* Farrar, Straus & Giroux (New York, NY), 1997.
Ralph Fletcher, *Ordinary Things: Poems from a Walk in Early Spring,* Atheneum (New York, NY), 1997.
Robert Burleigh, *Black Whiteness: Admiral Byrd Alone in the Antarctic,* Atheneum (New York, NY), 1998.
Louise Peacock, *Crossing the Delaware: A History in Many Voices,* Atheneum (New York, NY), 1998.
(With Eileen Christelow and Jo Ellen McAllister-Stammen) Jim Aylesworth, *Jim Aylesworth's Book of Bedtime Stories,* Atheneum (New York, NY), 1998.
Ralph Fletcher, *Relatively Speaking: Poems about Family,* Orchard Books (New York, NY), 1999.
Tres Seymour, *Our Neighbor Is a Strange, Strange Man,* Orchard Books (New York, NY), 1999.
Christina Kessler, *My Great-grandmother's Gourd,* Orchard Books (New York, NY), 2000.
Kathryn Lasky, *Born in the Breezes: The Seafaring Life of Joshua Slocum,* Orchard Books (New York, NY), 2001.
Louise Peacock, *At Ellis Island: A History in Many Voices,* Atheneum (New York, NY), 2007.

Also creator, under name Walter Lyon, of wordless online story *Milliner's Bliss.*

Sidelights

Walter Lyon Krudop is an award-winning author, illustrator and animator. "When people ask me what I do, I say I tell stories with pictures," he remarked in an essay on the *Design Inspiration* Web site. Krudop published his first children's book, the self-illustrated *Blue Claws,* in 1993, and since then he has provided the artwork for more than a dozen other works, including Robert Burleigh's critically acclaimed *Black Whiteness: Admiral Byrd Alone in the Antarctic* and Kathryn Lasky's well-received *Born in the Breezes: The Seafaring Life of Joshua Slocum.*

Born in Elizabeth, New Jersey, in 1966, Krudop developed an interest in the arts at a young age, taking his first painting lesson when he was eight years old. Even then, he stated in a *Design Inspiration* interview, "I knew I wanted drawing to be part of my job. But it wasn't until I saw Alphonse Mucha's swirling posters that I realized there was something between being a fine artist and a draftsman. Later I realized I could incorporate my love of storytelling and illustrating in children's books and I was hooked." Krudop later studied illustration, design, animation, filmmaking, and screenwriting at the School of Visual Arts, Parsons: The New School for Design, and New York University. He has garnered praise for his evocative impressionistic paintings.

In *Blue Claws,* a semi-autobiographical picture book, Krudop explores the relationship between a young boy and his sometimes-gruff grandfather as they spend the day fishing for crabs. "As if suspended in amber," wrote a *Publishers Weekly* contributor, "scenes from the fondly remembered day quietly capture a very special relationship." "The realism of the art and the text . . . proscribe sentimentality and make the simple shared experience all the more powerful," Nancy Vasilakis remarked in *Horn Book.*

Krudop's next self-illustrated work, *Something Is Growing,* focuses on a young gardener and his unusual plant. "Krudop's superb acrylic paintings surround readers with lush vegetation," noted *Booklist* reviewer Lauren Peterson in a review of the book. Set in ancient Thailand, Krudop's morality tale *The Man Who Caught Fish* concerns a mysterious fisherman and a greedy king who demands more than his fair share of the catch. *School Library Journal* contributor Diane S. Marton applauded the "spare elegant prose" in this story and noted that Krudop's pictures "richly portray the time and setting." According to *Booklist* critic Marta Segal, *The Man Who Caught Fish* "has the beauty and power of a traditional fable."

In *Black Whiteness,* Burleigh chronicles the exploits of explorer Robert Byrd, who spent several months alone in an underground structure in Antarctica. "Krudop's spare but saturated oil paintings perfectly catch the . . . extremes of Byrd's lonely existence," Stephanie Zvirin commented in a *Booklist* appraisal of *Black Whiteness,* and Susan P. Bloom similarly noted in *Horn Book* that the book's "oil and vinyl paintings intensify Byrd's battles to survive."

Krudop has served as the illustrator for two other biographical tales: Tres Seymour's *Our Neighbor Is a Strange, Strange Man* and Lasky's *Born in the Breezes.*

The former concerns Melville Murrell, an eccentric inventor who developed a human-powered aircraft in 1876, decades before the Wright Brothers took flight at Kitty Hawk. Krudop's "puckish gouaches emphasize the contrast between Murrell and his neighbors," remarked a *Publishers Weekly* reviewer. The latter work centers on Joshua Slocum, the first man to circumnavigate the world alone. "The salt breeze seems to flow from Krudop's impressionistic, thickly brushed scenes," noted a *Kirkus Reviews* critic of the book.

Krudop has also provided the artwork for a pair of works by Louise Peacock. In *Crossing the Delaware: A History in Many Voices,* Peacock examines one of the critical battles of the American Revolution. Krudop employs "a wintry palette of blues, grays and browns in his full-page and vignette oil paintings," observed a critic in *Publishers Weekly,* "effectively capturing the broken spirit of the men and Washington's lonely leadership." Peacock describes an Armenian immigrant's journey to the United States in *At Ellis Island: A History in Many Voices.* According to Luann Toth in *School Library Journal,* "Krudop's gouache paintings are evocative and expressive, and archival photographs are sprinkled throughout."

Gina Willner-Pardo and Krudop collaborated on *What I'll Remember When I Am a Grownup,* which centers on a third-grader's reaction to the news that his father and stepmother will be having a baby. "The blurred edges of Krudop's subtle paintings enhance the meditative tone," a contributor stated in *Publishers Weekly.* In *Hunting Grandma's Treasures,* another work by Willner-Pardo, a young boy learns to cope with a devastating loss, and here Krudop's "slightly blurry oil paintings show the close family bonds," as Hazel Rochman remarked in *Booklist.* In Christina Kessler's *My Great-grandmother's Gourd,* a Sudanese woman comes to the rescue after her village's new water pump breaks down. "Krudop's oil illustrations ably extend the story's strong sense of character and place," Gillian Engberg commented in *Booklist,* and Tammy K. Baggett, reviewing the work in *School Library Journal,* wrote that his "impressionistic oil paintings are vivid and detailed, greatly enhancing the story."

Biographical and Critical Sources

PERIODICALS

Booklist, March 15, 1994, Hazel Rochman, review of *One Rainy Night,* p. 1372; April 1, 1994, Mary Harris Veeder, review of *What I'll Remember When I Am a Grownup,* p. 1453; June 1, 1995, Lauren Peterson, review of *Something Is Growing,* p. 1787; February 1, 1996, Hazel Rochman, review of *Hunting Grandma's Treasures,* p. 932; September 1, 1997, Susan Dove Lempke, review of *One Small Lost Sheep,* p. 140; January 1, 1998, Stephanie Zvirin, review of *Black Whiteness: Admiral Byrd Alone in the Antarctic,* p. 798; November 15, 1998, Carolyn Phelan, review of *Crossing the Delaware: A History in Many Voices,* p. 588; February 1, 1999, Hazel Rochman, review of *Our Neighbor Is a Strange, Strange Man,* p. 977; July, 1999, Susan Dove Lempke, review of *Relatively Speaking: Poems about Family,* p. 1940; February 15, 2000, Marta Segal, review of *The Man Who Caught Fish,* p. 1118; January 1, 2001, Gillian Engberg, review of *My Great-grandmother's Gourd,* p. 970; November 1, 2001, Carolyn Phelan, review of *Born in the Breezes: The Seafaring Life of Joshua Slocum,* p. 479; May 1, 2007, Hazel Rochman, review of *At Ellis Island: A History in Many Voices,* p. 92.

Horn Book, July-August, 1993, Nancy Vasilakis, review of *Blue Claws,* p. 445; March-April, 1998, Susan P. Bloom, review of *Black Whiteness,* p. 232.

Kirkus Reviews, October 15, 2001, review of *Born in the Breezes,* p. 1486; June 1, 2007, review of *At Ellis Island.*

Publishers Weekly, March 22, 1993, review of *Blue Claws,* p. 79; February 7, 1994, review of *What I'll Remember When I Am a Grownup,* p. 88; November 9, 1998, review of *Crossing the Delaware,* p. 76; February 22, 1999, review of *Our Neighbor Is a Strange, Strange Man,* p. 95; June 25, 2007, review of *At Ellis Island,* p. 60.

School Arts, November, 1999, Ken Marantz, review of review of *Our Neighbor Is a Strange, Strange Man,* p. 52.

School Library Journal, April, 2000, Diane S. Marton, review of *The Man Who Caught Fish,* p. 107; December, 2000, Tammy K. Baggett, review of *My Great-grandmother's Gourd,* p. 112; November, 2001, Anne Chapman Callaghan, review of *Born in the Breezes,* p. 147; July, 2007, Luann Toth, review of *At Ellis Island,* p. 108.

ONLINE

Design Inspiration Web site, http://designinspiration. blogspot.com/ (August 25, 2007), "Walter Krudop."

Walter Lyon Krudop Home Page, http://walterkrudop.com (December 1, 2009).*

L

LANDY, Derek 1974-

Personal

Born 1974, in Dublin, Ireland; son of a farmer and an English professor. *Education:* Attended Ballyfermot Senior College, 1994. *Hobbies and other interests:* Kenpo karate.

Addresses

Home—Lusk, Ireland.

Career

Writer and screenwriter. Worked on family farm in Lusk, Ireland, 1995-2001; taught karate for ten years.

Awards, Honors

Centurion Book Award, Barefoot Books, 2009, for *Skulduggery Pleasant.*

Writings

"SKULDUGGERY PLEASANT" NOVEL SERIES

Skulduggery Pleasant, HarperCollins (New York, NY), 2007.
Playing with Fire, HarperCollins (New York, NY), 2008.
The Faceless Ones, Bowen Press (New York, NY), 2009.
Scepter of the Ancients, edited by Brenda Bowen, Harper-Collins Childrens Books (New York, NY), 2009.

SCREENPLAYS

Dead Bodies, Distinguished Features, 2003.
Boy Eats Girl, Element Films, 2005.

Adaptations

Skulduggery Pleasant was optioned for film by Warner Bros. Pictures.

Sidelights

An Irish farmer turned screenwriter turned novelist, Derek Landy is the author of *Skulduggery Pleasant,* a supernatural mystery novel for younger readers that features a fire-throwing, wisecracking, skeletal investigator. The idea for the best-selling work, which has drawn comparisons to Eoin Colfer's "Artemis Fowl" novels and J.K. Rowling's "Harry Potter" series, came to the author quite unexpectedly in 2005. "I was over in London dealing with producers; I was in my hotel room and the name Skulduggery just came to me," Landy remarked in an interview on the *Sarah Webb* Web site. "I realised that the name identified the character—Skulduggery. And the Pleasant—well he's urbane and he wears nice suits. There was a difference between this idea and the ideas I was getting for films. It had a life beyond the visual. Something deeper."

Landy was born in Lusk, Ireland, a suburb of Dublin, in 1974. The son of an English professor, he developed an early interest in literature, devouring "Hardy Boys" mysteries, horror novels by Stephen King and Dean Koontz, and comics. Although Landy later studied animation at Ballyfermot Senior College, he left after just one year. "I was good at art, but it turned out I wasn't that good at animation," he admitted to Webb. Returning home to work on his father's farm, Landy devoted his days to tending the fields and his nights to screenwriting. "I must have created havoc around me because I didn't pay attention to anything I was doing," he told *Bookseller* interviewer Caroline Horn. "I would spend eight hours picking cauliflowers and then sit down and write everything that I'd been planning in my head. I remembered everything word for word."

Landy enjoyed modest success as a screenwriter, having two films produced by the Irish Film Board: *Dead Bodies,* a suspense thriller, and *Boy Eats Girl,* a zombie film. When the idea for Skulduggery Pleasant came to him, however, he realized that a screenplay would not suffice. "There was just too much to capture in a script, so I found myself in the unfortunate position of having to write a book, which was not in the plan," Landy remarked in a *Publishers Weekly* interview with Sue Corbett. Despite such initial misgivings, Landy found the experience of writing a novel worthwhile. He told Corbett: "There's a freedom to writing a book, as opposed to writing a script. . . . When you've written a script, there's a lot of . . . *intervention,* from the directors and even the financiers, people who don't necessarily know anything about how to tell a story. So book writing is really freeing."

Skulduggery Pleasant centers on Stephanie Edgley, a plucky twelve year old who inherits a mansion from her uncle Gordon, a famous novelist. When Stephanie is attacked at the estate, the enigmatic Skulduggery Pleasant comes to her rescue. Stephanie soon joins forces with Skulduggery to combat Nefarian Serpine, an evil sorcerer who is determined to gain possession of the legendary Sceptre of the Ancients, an object that will allow him to rule the world. Landy "gives his wonderfully tough, sassy youngster a real workout," a *Kirkus Reviews* critic observed, and a *Publishers Weekly* reviewer commented that "the repartee between the two leads recalls [noted twentieth-century actors Katherine] Hepburn and [Spencer] Tracy in its ongoing, affectionate contest of verbal one-upmanship." Other critics praised Landy's fast-paced action. "Deadly hand-to-hand combat, nasty villains, magical derring-do, and traitorous allies will keep readers turning the pages," remarked *School Library Journal* contributor Eva Mitnick, and Claire E. Gross, writing in *Horn Book,* stated that "the flowing action sequences, detailed mythology, and frequent twists will keep readers engaged." Lindsay Beaumont, reviewing the novel in *Blogcritics,* stated: "A fun and enjoyable read, *Skulduggery Pleasant* has something for everyone. It will also help encourage reluctant readers with its gripping battle scenes, intriguing characters, and creative plot development."

In Landy's *Playing with Fire* thirteen-year-old Stephanie—now called Valkyrie—helps Skulduggery prevent the evil Baron Vengeous from reanimating the Grotesquery, which will signal the return of the Faceless Ones. Beth L. Meister, reviewing the book in *School Library Journal,* called *Playing with Fire* a "humorous" as well as "dark and often-violent novel," and concluded that "fans of the first book will particularly enjoy the new schemes and evil creatures found here." In *Kirkus Reviews,* a writer declared that those who like "their heroes laconic and their action nonstop are in for a wild ride," and Kay Weisman suggested in *Booklist* that both series fans and "fantasy buffs pining for the now-vanquished Voldemort will enjoy this tale of good versus evil."

In the third novel in Landy's "Skulduggery Pleasant" series, *The Faceless Ones,* Skulduggery and Valkyrie are suspicious that the Faceless Ones are responsible for the rolling deaths of Teleporters, but the Sanctuary is not taking the concern seriously. An online contributor, writing in *Bookbag,* called *The Faceless Ones* "a rip-roaring supernatural adventure with a tongue that

visits its cheek regularly. It's irresistible." "The writing . . . is crisp and snappy and deceptively clever," the critic added.

Biographical and Critical Sources

PERIODICALS

Booklist, May 1, 2007, Kay Weisman, review of *Skulduggery Pleasant,* p. 48; June 1, 2008, Kay Weisman, review of *Playing with Fire,* p. 82.

Bookseller, March 2, 2007, Caroline Horn, "For My Next Trick . . . Scriptwriter Derek Landy Is Moving into Children's Books with the Launch of *Skulduggery Pleasant,*" p. 25.

Guardian (London, England), April 7, 2007, Philip Ardagh, review of *Skulduggery Pleasant,* p. 20.

Horn Book, July-August, 2007, Claire E. Gross, review of *Skulduggery Pleasant,* p. 298.

Independent (London, England), December 14, 2008, Leo Taylor, review of *Playing with Fire.*

Independent Weekly (Adelaide, South Australia, Australia), May 21, 2008, Kate Seller-Evans, review of *Skulduggery Pleasant.*

Kirkus Reviews, March 15, 2007, review of *Skulduggery Pleasant;* April 1, 2008, review of *Playing with Fire.*

Observer (London, England), April 8, 2007, "Aaargh, Get off Me, I'm Trying to Save Humanity," review of *Skulduggery Pleasant,* p. 23.

Publishers Weekly, February 5, 2007, review of *Skulduggery Pleasant,* p. 59; February 15, 2007, Sue Corbett, author interview.

School Library Journal, June, 2007, Eva Mitnick, review of *Skulduggery Pleasant,* p. 150; July 1, 2008, Beth L. Meister, review of *Playing with Fire,* p. 103.

Sun (London, England), March 30, 2007, "I'm Ireland's J.K. Rowling," p. 15.

Sunday Times (London, England), March 5, 2007, "E1.5m Deal to Turn Author into a Star," p. 7.

ONLINE

Blogcritics Web site, http://blogcritics.org/ (June 27, 2008), Lindsay Beaumont, review of *Skulduggery Pleasant.*

Bookbag, http://www.thebookbag.co.uk/ (May 27, 2009), Jill Murphy, review of *Skulduggery Pleasant;* review of *The Faceless Ones.*

Sarah Webb Web site, http://www.sarahwebb.info/ (March 1, 2008), Sarah Webb, interview with Landy.

Skulduggery Pleasant Web site, http://www.skulduggery pleasant.com/ (May 27, 2009).*

*   *   *

LASKY, Kathryn 1944-
(Kathryn Lasky Knight, E.L. Swann)

Personal

Born June 24, 1944, in Indianapolis, IN; daughter of Marven (a wine bottler) and Hortense (a social worker) Lasky; married Christopher G. Knight (a photographer

Kathryn Lasky (Photograph by Christopher Knight. Reproduced by permission.)

and filmmaker), May 30, 1971; children: Maxwell, Meribah. *Education:* University of Michigan, B.A., 1966; Wheelock College, M.A., 1977. *Religion:* Jewish. *Hobbies and other interests:* Sailing, skiing, hiking, reading, movies.

Addresses

Home—Cambridge, MA. *E-mail*—Kathryn@kathryn lasky.com.

Career

Writer.

Awards, Honors

Boston Globe/Horn Book Award, 1981, for *The Weaver's Gift;* Notable Books designation, American Library Association (ALA), 1981, for *The Night Journey* and *The Weaver's Gift;* National Jewish Book Award, Jewish Welfare Board Book Council, and Sydney Taylor Book Award, Association of Jewish Libraries, both 1982, both for *The Night Journey;* Notable Book designation, *New York Times,* and Best Books for Young Adults designation, ALA, both 1983, both for *Beyond the Divide;* Newbery Honor Book, and Notable Books designation, both ALA, both 1984, and both for *Sugaring Time;* Best Books for Young Adults designation, ALA, 1984, for *Prank;* Notable Books designation, ALA, 1985, for *Puppeteer;* Best Books for Young Adults designation, ALA, 1986, for *Pageant; Washington Post*/Children's Book Guild Nonfiction Award, 1986, for body of work; "Youth-to-Youth Books" cita-

tion, Pratt Library's Young Adult Advisory Board, 1988, for *The Bone Wars;* Golden Trilobite Award, Paleontological Society, 1990, for *Traces of Life: The Origins of Humankind;* Parenting Reading Magic Award, 1990, for *Dinosaur Dig;* Edgar Allan Poe Award nominee for Best Juvenile Mystery, 1992, for *Double Trouble Squared;* Orbis Pictus award for Outstanding Nonfiction for Children nomination, National Council of Teachers of English, 1992, Notable Books designation, ALA, 1993, and Notable Children's Book in Language Arts, National Council of Teachers of English/Children's Literature Assembly, all for *Surtsey: The Newest Place on Earth;* Sequoyah Young Adult Book Award, 1994, for *Beyond the Burning Time;* Notable Children's Book selection, Library of Congress, for *The Librarian Who Measured the Earth;* Notable Social Studies Trade Book for Young People, National Council for the Social Studies/Children's Book Council (NSCC/CBC), for *A Journey to the New World: The Diary of Remember Patience Whipple, Mayflower, 1620;* National Jewish Book Award and Notable Books designation, ALA, both 1997, both for *Marven of the Great North Woods;* Notable Social Studies Trade Book for Young People, NCSS/CBC, 1997, and Young Adult Choice selection, International Reading Association, both for *True North;* John Burroughs Award for Outstanding Nature Book for Children, and Editor's Choice designation, *Cricket* magazine, both 1998, both for *The Most Beautiful Roof in the World: Exploring the Rainforest Canopy;* Notable Social Studies Trade Book for Young People, NCSS/CBC, for *Dreams in the Golden Country: The Diary of Zipporah Feldman, a Jewish Immigrant Girl;* Western Heritage Award, National Cowboy Hall of Fame, and Edgar Award nominee, both 1999, both for *Alice Rose and Sam;* Notable Social Studies Trade Book for Young People, NCSS/CBC, for *Elizabeth I, Red Rose of the House of Tudor;* Notable Social Studies Trade Book for Young People, NCSS/CBC, for *Marie Antoinette, Princess of Versailles;* Notable Social Studies Trade Book for Young People, NCSS/CBC, for *Christmas after All: The Great Depression Diary of Minnie Swift;* Lupine Award honor book, 2005, Teachers' Choices Award winner, International Reading Association, 2006, and Notable Children's Book of Jewish Content selection, Association of Jewish Libraries, 2006, all for *Broken Song;* John Burroughs Award for Outstanding Nature Book for Children, and Orbis Pictus Honor Book designation for Outstanding Nonfiction for Children, National Council of Teachers of English, both for *John Muir;* recipient of several child-selected awards.

Writings

FOR CHILDREN

(With Lucy Floyd) *Agatha's Alphabet,* Rand McNally (Chicago, IL), 1975.
I Have Four Names for My Grandfather, illustrated with photographs by husband, Christopher G. Knight, Little, Brown (Boston, MA), 1976.

Tugboats Never Sleep, illustrated with photographs by Christopher G. Knight, Little, Brown (Boston, MA), 1977.

Tall Ships, illustrated with photographs by Christopher G. Knight, Scribner (New York, NY), 1978.

My Island Grandma, illustrated by Emily McCully, Warne (New York, NY), 1979, illustrated by Amy Schwartz, Morrow (New York, NY), 1993.

The Weaver's Gift, illustrated with photographs by Christopher G. Knight, Warne (New York, NY), 1981.

Dollmaker: The Eyelight and the Shadow, illustrated with photographs by Christopher G. Knight, Scribner (New York, NY), 1981.

The Night Journey, illustrated by Trina Schart Hyman, Warne (New York, NY), 1981, reprinted, Puffin (New York, NY), 2005.

Jem's Island, illustrated by Ronald Himler, Scribner (New York, NY), 1982.

Sugaring Time, illustrated with photographs by Christopher G. Knight, Macmillan (New York, NY), 1983.

Beyond the Divide, Macmillan (New York, NY), 1983.

(With son, Maxwell B. Knight) *A Baby for Max,* illustrated with photographs by Christopher G. Knight, Scribner (New York, NY), 1984.

Prank, Macmillan (New York, NY), 1984.

Home Free, Macmillan (New York, NY), 1985.

Puppeteer, illustrated with photographs by Christopher G. Knight, Macmillan (New York, NY), 1985.

Pageant, Four Winds Press (New York, NY), 1986.

Sea Swan, illustrated by Catherine Stock, Macmillan (New York, NY), 1988.

The Bone Wars, Morrow (New York, NY), 1988.

Traces of Life: The Origins of Humankind, illustrated by Whitney Powell, Morrow (New York, NY), 1989.

Dinosaur Dig, illustrated with photographs by Christopher G. Knight, Morrow (New York, NY), 1990.

Fourth of July Bear, illustrated by Helen Cogancherry, Morrow (New York, NY), 1991.

Surtsey: The Newest Place on Earth, illustrated with photographs by Christopher G. Knight and Sigurdur Thoraisson, Hyperion (New York, NY), 1992.

Think like an Eagle: At Work with a Wildlife Photographer, illustrated with photographs by Christopher G. Knight and Jack Swedberg, Little, Brown (Boston, MA), 1992.

I Have an Aunt on Marlborough Street, illustrated by Susan Guevara, Macmillan (New York, NY), 1992.

The Solo, illustrated by Bobette McCarthy, Macmillan (New York, NY), 1993.

The Tantrum, illustrated by Bobette McCarthy, Macmillan (New York, NY), 1993.

Monarchs, illustrated with photographs by Christopher G. Knight, Harcourt (San Diego, CA), 1993.

(With daughter, Meribah Knight) *Searching for Laura Ingalls: A Reader's Journey,* illustrated with photographs by Christopher G. Knight, Macmillan (New York, NY), 1993.

Lunch Bunnies, illustrated by Marylin Hafner, Little, Brown (Boston, MA), 1993.

Memoirs of a Bookbat, Harcourt (San Diego, CA), 1994.

Beyond the Burning Time, Blue Sky Press/Scholastic (New York, NY), 1994.

Cloud Eyes, illustrated by Barry Moser, Harcourt (San Diego, CA), 1994.

The Librarian Who Measured the Earth, illustrated by Kevin Hawkes, Little, Brown (Boston, MA), 1994.

Days of the Dead, illustrated by Christopher G. Knight, Hyperion (New York, NY), 1994.

Pond Year, illustrated by Mike Bostok, Candlewick (Cambridge, MA), 1995.

She's Wearing a Dead Bird on Her Head!, illustrated by David Catrow, Hyperion (New York, NY), 1995.

The Gates of the Wind, illustrated by Janet Stevens, Harcourt (San Diego, CA), 1995.

True North: A Novel of the Underground Railroad, Blue Sky Press/Scholastic (New York, NY), 1996.

A Brilliant Streak: The Making of Mark Twain, illustrated by Barry Moser, Harcourt (San Diego, CA), 1996.

The Most Beautiful Roof in the World: Exploring the Rainforest Canopy, illustrated with photographs by Christopher G. Knight, Harcourt (San Diego, CA), 1997.

Marven of the Great North Woods, illustrated by Kevin Hawkes, Harcourt (San Diego, CA), 1997.

Hercules: The Man, the Myth, the Hero, illustrated by Mark Hess, Hyperion (New York, NY), 1997.

Grace the Pirate, illustrated by Karen Lee Schmidt, Hyperion (New York, NY), 1997.

Shadows in the Dawn: The Lemurs of Madagascar, illustrated with photographs by Christopher G. Knight, Harcourt (San Diego, CA), 1998.

Sophie and Rose, illustrated by Wendy Anderson Halperin, Candlewick Press (Cambridge, MA), 1998.

Alice Rose and Sam, Hyperion (New York, NY), 1998.

Show and Tell Bunnies, illustrated by Marylin Hafner, Candlewick Press (Cambridge, MA), 1998.

The Emperor's Old Clothes, illustrated by David Catrow, Harcourt (San Diego, CA), 1999.

Star Split, Hyperion (New York, NY), 1999.

First Painter, illustrated by Rocco Baviera, DK Ink (New York, NY), 2000.

The Journal of Augustus Pelletier: The Lewis and Clark Expedition, Scholastic (New York, NY), 2000.

Lucille's Snowsuit, Crown Publishers (New York, NY), 2000.

Science Fair Bunnies, Candlewick Press (Cambridge, MA), 2000.

Vision of Beauty: The Story of Sarah Breedlove Walker, illustrated by Nneka Bennett, Candlewick Press (Cambridge, MA), 2000.

Born in the Breezes: The Seafaring Life of Joshua Slocum, illustrated by Walter Lyon Krudop, Orchard (New York, NY), 2001.

Interrupted Journey: Saving Endangered Sea Turtles, photographs by Christopher G. Knight, Candlewick (Cambridge, MA), 2001.

Starring Lucille, illustrated by Marylin Hafner, Alfred A. Knopf (New York, NY), 2001.

(With Jane Kamine) *Mommy's Hands,* Hyperion (New York, NY), 2002.

Porkenstein, illustrated by David Jarvis, Blue Sky Press (New York, NY), 2002.

Before I Was Your Mother, Harcourt (San Diego, CA), 2003.

Lucille Camps In, illustrated by Marilyn Hafner, Alfred A. Knopf (New York, NY), 2003.

The Man Who Made Time Travel, Melanie Kroupa Books (New York, NY), 2003.

A Voice of Her Own: The Story of Phillis Wheatley, Slave Poet, Candlewick Press (Cambridge, MA), 2003.

Blood Secret, HarperCollins (New York, NY), 2004.

Charles Darwin, Candlewick Press (Cambridge, MA), 2004.

Humphrey, Albert, and the Flying Machine, illustrated by John Manders, Harcourt (San Diego, CA), 2004.

Love That Baby! A Book about Babies for New Brothers, Sisters, Cousins, and Friends, illustrated by Jennifer Plecas, Candlewick Press (Cambridge, MA), 2004.

Broken Song, Viking (New York, NY), 2005.

Dancing through Fire, Scholastic (New York, NY), 2005.

Tumble Bunnies, illustrated by Marylin Hafner, Candlewick (Cambridge, MA), 2005.

Georgia Rises, illustrated by Ora Eitan, Farrar, Straus & Giroux (New York, NY), 2006.

John Muir: America's First Environmentalist, illustrated by Stan Fellows, Candlewick (Cambridge, MA), 2006.

Pirate Bob, illustrated by David Clark, Candlewick (Cambridge, MA), 2006.

The Last Girls of Pompeii, Viking (New York, NY), 2007.

Yossel's Journey, Farrar, Straus & Giroux (New York, NY), 2008.

One Beetle Too Many: The Extraordinary Adventures of Charles Darwin, illustrated by Matthew Trueman, Candlewick (Cambridge, MA), 2009.

Poodle and Hound, illustrated by Mitch Vane, Charlesbridge (Watertown, MA), 2009.

Two Bad Pilgrims, illustrated by John Manders, Viking (New York, NY), 2009.

Hawksmaid: The Untold Story of Robin Hood and Maid Marian, HarperCollins (New York, NY), 2009.

"STARBUCK TWINS" MYSTERY SERIES; MIDDLE-GRADE FICTION

Double Trouble Squared, Harcourt (San Diego, CA), 1991, reprinted, 2008.

Shadows in the Water, Harcourt (San Diego, CA), 1992, reprinted, 2008.

A Voice in the Wind, Harcourt (San Diego, CA), 1993, reprinted, 2008.

"DEAR AMERICA" SERIES; MIDDLE-GRADE FICTION

A Journey to the New World: The Diary of Remember Patience Whipple, Mayflower, 1620, Scholastic (New York, NY), 1996.

Dreams in the Golden Country: The Diary of Zipporah Feldman, a Jewish Immigrant Girl, Scholastic (New York, NY), 1998.

Christmas after All: The Great Depression Diary of Minnie Swift, Scholastic (New York, NY), 2001.

A Time for Courage: The Suffragette Diary of Kathleen Bowen, Scholastic (New York, NY), 2002.

"ROYAL DIARIES" SERIES; MIDDLE-GRADE FICTION

Elizabeth I, Red Rose of the House of Tudor, Scholastic (New York, NY), 1999.

Marie Antoinette, Princess of Versailles, Scholastic (New York, NY), 2000.

Mary, Queen of Scots, Queen without a Country, Scholastic (New York, NY), 2002.

Jahanara: Princess of Princesses, Scholastic (New York, NY), 2002.

Kazunomiya: Prisoner of Heaven, Scholastic (New York, NY), 2004.

"MY AMERICA" SERIES; MIDDLE-GRADE FICTION

Hope in My Heart: Sophia's Immigrant Diary, Book One, Scholastic (New York, NY), 2003.

Home at Last: Sophia's Immigrant Diary, Book Two, Scholastic (New York, NY), 2003.

An American Spring: Sophia's Immigrant Diary, Book Three, Scholastic (New York, NY), 2004.

"GUARDIANS OF GA'HOOLE" SERIES; MIDDLE-GRADE FICTION

The Capture, Scholastic (New York, NY), 2003.

The Journey, Scholastic (New York, NY), 2003.

The Rescue, Scholastic (New York, NY), 2004.

The Siege, Scholastic (New York, NY), 2004.

The Shattering, Scholastic (New York, NY), 2004.

The Burning, Turtleback, 2004.

The Hatchling, Scholastic (New York, NY), 2005.

The Outcast, Scholastic (New York, NY), 2005.

The First Collier, Scholastic (New York, NY), 2006.

The Coming of Hoole, Scholastic (New York, NY), 2006.

To Be a King, Scholastic (New York, NY), 2006.

The Golden Tree, Scholastic (New York, NY), 2007.

A Guide Book to the Great Tree, Scholastic (New York, NY), 2007.

The River of Wind, Scholastic (New York, NY), 2007.

Exile, Scholastic (New York, NY), 2008.

The War of the Ember, Scholastic (New York, NY), 2008.

"PRINCESS CAMP" SERIES; MIDDLE-GRADE FICTION

Born to Rule, HarperCollins (New York, NY), 2006.

Unicorns? Get Real!, illustrated by Amy Saidens, HarperTrophy (New York, NY), 2007.

"DAUGHTERS OF THE SEA" SERIES; MIDDLE-GRADE FICTION

Daughters of the Sea: Hannah, Scholastic Press (New York, NY), 2009.

FOR ADULTS; AS KATHRYN LASKY KNIGHT, EXCEPT AS NOTED

Atlantic Circle (nonfiction), illustrated with photographs by Christopher G. Knight, Norton (New York, NY), 1985.

Trace Elements (novel), Norton (New York, NY), 1986.

The Widow of Oz (novel), Norton (New York, NY), 1989.

Mortal Words (novel), Simon & Schuster (New York, NY), 1990.

Mumbo Jumbo (novel), Simon & Schuster (New York, NY), 1991.

Dark Swan (novel), St. Martin's Press (New York, NY), 1994.

(Under pseudonym E.L. Swann) *Night Gardening* (mystery novel), Hyperion (New York, NY), 1998.

Contributor to periodicals, including *Horn Book, New York Times Book Review,* and *Sail.*

Adaptations

An animated feature film, *Guardians of Ga'Hoole,* based on the first three books of Lasky's series, was released by Warner Bros., 2010, with screenplay by John Orloff and John Collee, directed by Zack Snyder. *A Journey to the New World: The Diary of Remember Patience Whipple, Mayflower, 1620, Dreams in the Golden Country: The Diary of Zipporah Feldman, a Jewish Immigrant Girl,* and *Elizabeth I, Red Rose of the House of Tudor* were adapted for video. Several of Lasky's works, including *Sugaring Time,* have been adapted as audiobooks.

Sidelights

Called "a remarkably versatile writer" by *Booklist* reviewer Ilene Cooper, Kathryn Lasky is an American author of fiction, nonfiction, and picture books who is noted for her success in several genres. A prolific writer, Lasky is the creator of contemporary fiction, historical fiction, informational books, and picture books that incorporate both fiction and nonfiction elements. Asked to describe the inspiration for her more than one hundred works, Lasky remarked on her home page, "It's as mysterious to me as it is to all of you. I did read someplace that some famous writer (I forget who) said that a writer is not necessarily the smartest person in the room but the most observant. So I think I am just a good observer, and perhaps I see things and wonder about them in odd ways; and this means sometimes making up stories about them."

Lasky has received praise for exploring topics not often covered in books for the young and for explaining them in an accessible, enjoyable manner. Some critics have also complimented her character development—both in her fiction and nonfiction—and her narrative skill, noting that she provides young readers with strong storylines, even in her informational books. They have described her language as clear and concise, with vivid imagery that has sometimes been called poetic. As Cooper remarked, "Few authors are as eloquent as Lasky." In an essay in *Twentieth-Century Young Adult Writers,* Linda Garrett commented that Lasky "has made and continues to make an impact on young-adult literature. Her well-researched books provide a thorough, accurate

picture of whatever theme is being presented. Her use of lyrical language captures the moods as well as facts leaving the reader with [in Lasky's words] 'a sense of joy—indeed celebration' of the world in which they live." Carol Hurst of *Carol Hurst's Children's Literature Newsletter* added: "I'm always impressed when an author can move from one genre to another with competence, but Kathy Lasky does so with such ease and skill that I am more than impressed, I'm awed."

Lasky was a storyteller from an early age and felt destined to become an author. Despite her love of stories, however, she was labeled a reluctant reader. In fact, she simply did not care for the books that were part of her school curriculum, instead preferring works such as *Peter Pan* and *The Wonderful Wizard of Oz.* Lasky first realized that she could pursue a literary career when she was about ten years old. "Mom was the one who told me to be a writer," Lasky stated on her home page. "She said 'Kathy, you love words. And you have such a great imagination. You should be a writer.' My mom always thought I was the best, even when teachers didn't. She thought I was smart when teachers didn't."

Lasky attended a private all-girls school in Indianapolis, which she felt did not particularly suit her; later, she drew on her experiences in the autobiographical novel *Pageant,* a humorous coming-of-age story about Sarah Benjamin, a Jewish teenager in a Christian girls' school who learns what she really wants from life. After finishing high school, Lasky attended the University of Michigan as an English major; after receiving her degree, she became a teacher and began writing seriously in her spare time. In 1971, she married Christopher Knight, whose youthful experiences kayaking and camping with his father and grandfather form the basis for Lasky's novel *Jem's Island.*

In 1975, Lasky published her first book for children, the colorful concept book *Agatha's Alphabet.* The first of several books to be illustrated by her husband, *I Have Four Names for My Grandfather* also introduces one of the author's major themes: intergenerational bonding. Barbara S. Wertheimer, a contributor to *Children's Book Review Service,* noted "the sensitivity and depth of feeling within the text," while Andd Ward wrote in *School Library Journal* that the strength of *I Have Four Names for My Grandfather* "lies in the compatibility of the text with the abundant photographs."

Lasky's first work to win a major award was *The Weaver's Gift,* a photo essay that won the *Boston Globe/ Horn Book* Award for juvenile nonfiction in 1982. In this book, Lasky and Knight spotlight weaver Carolyn Frye, a Vermont woman who raises sheep and converts their wool to finished products; the author and photographer document Frye's hard work and artistry while demonstrating how sheared wool becomes a child's blanket. Writing in *Interracial Books for Children,* Jan M. Goodman related that *The Weaver's Gift* "is a rare find," adding that the text is "extremely well-written

Cover of Lasky's picture book Sophie and Rose, *featuring illustrations by Wendy Anderson Halperin.* (Illustration copyright © 1998 by Wendy Anderson Halperin. Reproduced by permission of Candlewick Press, Inc., Somerville, MA.)

and factual and shows deep appreciation and respect for a woman and her trade." A critic for *Kirkus Reviews* noted that while "there have been other juvenile introductions to this basic sequence, . . . they are dull or feeble in comparison."

In 1981, Lasky published *The Night Journey,* a young-adult novel that is highly respected as a work of Jewish literature. Based on a true story, the novel outlines how

a nine-year-old girl orchestrates her family's escape from religious persecution in czarist Russia. The girl grows up to become Nana Sachie, great-grandmother to thirteen-year-old Rachel, who learns this piece of family history during their afternoons together; Sachie finishes the tale, which is filled with excitement, shortly before her death. Calling *The Night Journey* "a story to cherish," Cooper noted in *Booklist* that it "has so many aspects that each person will come away with his own idea of what makes the book memorable." Peter Kennerley concluded in a review for *School Librarian:* "I believe this to be a satisfying novel, if not without blemish, and I recommend it strongly."

More than twenty years later, Lasky published a companion volume to *The Night Journey,* titled *Broken Song.* The work concerns fifteen-year-old Reuven Bloom, a talented violist who lives in the Pale, an area in Russia that is reserved for Jews. When the Cossacks slaughter his family and friends, Reuven flees to Poland, where he works as a spy for a revolutionary group. *School Library Journal* contributor Renee Steinberg praised Lasky's narrative in *Broken Song*, citing its "rich prose filled with imagery, distinct characterization, and historical research." A critic for *Kirkus Reviews* described Reuven as "a relatable and admirable protagonist."

Sugaring Time, a photo essay also illustrated by Knight, was named a Newbery honor book in 1984. The volume outlines the activities of the Lacey family during the month of March, the period they call "sugaring time," on their Vermont farm. Lasky and Knight portray the hard work—and the pleasure—involved in turning maple sugar into maple syrup while providing young readers with a sense of the seasons and the value of the earth. Alice Naylor, a contributor to *Language Arts,* called Lasky's text "a model of good exposition," while Martha T. Kane wrote in *Appraisal* that "you can almost hear the crunch of snow beneath the horses' feet, the sweet maple sap dripping into the buckets, and the roar of the fire in the sugarhouse. . . . Lasky involves *all* the reader's senses in her memorable description of the collection and processing of maple sap in a small sugarbush in Vermont."

One of Lasky's most critically acclaimed novels for young adults is *Beyond the Divide.* Set in the mid-1800s, the story outlines the journey of fourteen-year-old Meribah Simon, an Amish girl who travels with her father from Pennsylvania to California by wagon train during the Gold Rush. Meribah's trek to California is an ordeal: her father dies after one of his wounds becomes infected; a friend is raped and commits suicide; and Meribah, now left alone, struggles to survive in the wilderness. Rescued by a group of Yahi Indians, Meribah learns to understand them and to appreciate their lifestyle; at the end of the novel, she decides to go back to a fertile valley she had seen from the wagon train and make a life for herself.

Calling *Beyond the Divide* an "elegantly written tour de force," Cooper commented that Lasky has written a "quintessential pioneer story, a piece so textured and rich that readers will remember it long after they've put it down." Dick Abrahamson, reviewing the novel for the *English Journal,* called *Beyond the Divide* "one of the finest historical novels I've read in a long time. It certainly ought to be considered for the Newbery Award." Writing in *Language Arts,* M. Jean Greenlaw concluded that the major strength of the book is that it "is a magnificent story. The westward movement is an integral part of American history and nature, and this book is the most gripping account of that time I have ever read," In *Twentieth-Century Children's Writers,* Linda Garrett added that the novel "is so realistic it would be easy to believe that *Beyond the Divide* is directly from a diary of a young girl going West."

Lasky's *Traces of Life: The Origins of Humankind* is an informational book that outlines the history of evolution. In this work, the author, who has had a longtime interest in paleontology, attempts to determine the moment at which humanity as we know it began to exist. She discusses evolution and the science of paleoanthropology while presenting biographical information about several notable scientists. *Voice of Youth Advocates* contributor Shirley A. Bathgate said that Lasky "combines research and creativity in yet another excellent book," then concluded that "Younger young-adult readers will find the book both easy and fun to read."

One of Lasky's most well-received picture-book biographies is *Marven of the Great North Woods,* a vignette from her father's childhood. As a ten-year-old, Marven Lasky was sent to a logging camp in the Minnesota

Cover of Lasky's historical novel **A Time for Courage,** *part of the "Dear America" fictional diary series.* (Scholastic Inc., 2001. Reproduced by permission of Scholastic, Inc. Photographs courtesy Culver Pictures.)

Lasky introduces readers to one of history's most fascinating, fashionable, and tragic queens in the biography **Marie Antoinette, Princess of Versailles.** (Painting by Tim O'Brien. Copyright © 2000 by Kathryn Lasky. Illustration copyright © 2000 by Scholastic, Inc. Reprinted by permission of Scholastic, Inc.)

north woods to avoid the influenza epidemic that hit his hometown of Duluth in 1918. At first, Marven finds this new world to be foreign—for example, there was no kosher food at the camp—but he adjusts to his situation and forms warm friendships with the lumberjacks, especially Jean Louis, a French Canadian who is the biggest man in the camp. Calling *Marven of the Great North Woods* a story of "courage inspired by familial affection and the unexpected kindness of strangers," a *Publishers Weekly* critic predicted: "Thanks to Lasky's considerable command of language and narrative detail, readers will linger over" the descriptions in the book. Roger Sutton, writing in *Horn Book,* called the work "both invigorating and cozy" and noted that the text, while long for a picture book, is "fully eventful." In her newsletter, Carol Hurst concluded that Lasky "makes the extraordinary adventure possible and [Kevin Hawkes's] paintings combine with her writing to show wonder and tenderness." *Marven of the Great North Woods* won the National Jewish Book Award in 1997.

Lasky has a particular fascination with American author Samuel Langhorne Clemens, who wrote as Mark Twain: the subject of the picture book biography *A Brilliant Streak: The Making of Mark Twain,* Clemens also ap-

pears as a major character in *Alice Rose and Sam,* a story for middle graders. In *A Brilliant Streak,* Lasky recounts Clemens' life until he takes on his famous pseudonym at age thirty. The author details Clemens' Missouri childhood and his experiences as a steamboat pilot, prospector, and reporter as well as a humorist and social commentator; in addition, Lasky provides a sense of how Clemens' life and personality are reflected in his works. This work won several critical compliments. *Booklist* reviewer Stephanie Zvirin predicted that after reading *A Brilliant Streak,* "Children will definitely want to find out more about Clemens," while a contributor to *Kirkus Reviews* concluded that Clemens' "successes are the source of one colorful anecdote after another, which Lasky taps and twirls into an engaging narrative that glimmers with its own brand of brilliance."

Set in Virginia City, Nevada, during the 1860s, *Alice Rose and Sam* describes how twelve-year-old Alice Rose, a newspaperman's daughter, joins forces with reporter Samuel Clemens to solve a murder and expose a plot by a group of Confederate vigilantes called the Society of Seven. Lasky's fictional treatment of Clemens received praise from some reviewers as well. "Ultimately," noted Jennifer A. Fakolt in *School Library Journal,* Alice Rose and Clemens "end up teaching one another valuable lessons about life and truth." Calling the book an "open-throttled page-turner," a critic for *Kirkus Reviews* observed that fans of Karen Cushman's *The Ballad of Lucy Whipple* and Kathleen Karr's *Oh, Those Harper Girls!* "have a plucky new heroine to admire," while a reviewer for *Publishers Weekly* called *Alice Rose and Sam* a "view of American history teeming with adventure and local color." *Alice Rose and Sam* won the Western Heritage Award and was nominated for an Edgar Allan Poe award in 1999.

Another historical figure featured in one of Lasky's books is John Harrison, whose story is told in *The Man Who Made Time Travel.* When the English Parliament offered a multi-million dollar reward in 1707 for anyone who could accurately measure longitude in a way that would aid in sea navigation, Harrison devoted more than three decades of his life to solving the problem. A *Publishers Weekly* reviewer found that "Lasky gets off to a bumpy start," but when the story begins to focus on Harrison, the author's "prose becomes clear and compelling." *Booklist* commentator Carolyn Phelan remarked that "the text makes absorbing reading both for its sidelights on history and for the personal drama portrayal." Some critics noted that the illustrations by Kevin Hawkes add to the book's appeal. In *School Library Journal,* Dona Ratterree wrote that because of Hawkes's artwork, the book's "clear science, and its compelling social commentary, this title is not to be missed." In another biographical work, *John Muir: America's First Environmentalist,* the author looks at the nineteenth-century naturalist and environmental activist who helped found the Sierra Club. Using Muir's own diary entries, Lasky traces his life from his boyhood in Scotland to his explorations in Florida, Alaska, and California. The author "not only outlines the course of his life, but eloquently conveys his motivation," remarked a *Kirkus Reviews* contributor.

Vision of Beauty: The Story of Sarah Breedlove Walker profiles America's first self-made female African-American millionaire. Walker made her fortune in the hair-care products industry and was a civil-rights pioneer. In *Black Issues Book Review,* Merce Robinson and Kelly Ellis praised the book for its inspiring portrayal of Walker. The noted that Lasky demonstrates that Walker's vision was not "beauty for its sake alone, but that the tools of beauty could be used by black women to inspire self-confidence." *Booklist* critic Marta Segal deemed *Vision of Beauty* "engaging," noting that "Walker's feminism and work for civil rights are described in terms that will make sense to young readers." In *A Voice of Her Own: The Story of Phillis Wheatley, Slave Poet,* Lasky examines the life of the first African American woman poet. Born in West Africa, Wheatley was brought to the colonies at the age of seven. Taught to read and write by the wife of her owner, Wheatley gained fame for her collection, *Poems on Various Subjects, Religious and Moral,* published in England in 1773. "The story is remarkable, important and moving," Nicolette Jones wrote in the London *Sunday Times.*

Returning to fiction, Lasky created a series character with Lucille, a piglet who struggles with everyday challenges common to younger readers. Lasky adds humor to the "Lucille" books to keep the tone light and accessible. In *Lucille Camps In,* Lucille is left at home while her father and siblings go on a camping trip, so she decides to camp in her living room. Gillian Engberg, writing in *Booklist,* described the book as "an endearing, realistic story in short sentences and simple language a new reader can handle." In *School Library Journal,* Martha Topol observed that the "family dynamics are great—supportive while allowing for individuality." In *Lucille's Snowsuit,* the pig is delighted that school is canceled because of snow, but then she has difficulty getting into her snowsuit so she can go out and play. Todd Morning remarked in *Booklist* that "the best pages in the book focus on Lucille's struggles to put on her suit."

Regarded by critics as endearing and touching, Lasky's *Mommy's Hands*—coauthored with Jane Kamine—is told by three toddlers who describe why they love their mommy's hands. The story relates the many things mothers do with their hands that amaze and comfort their children. Maryann H. Owen praised the book for its "affectionate tribute to every mother whose gentle touch has helped to mold her child." Similarly, in *Booklist,* GraceAnne A. DeCandido of called the book a "tender and affectionate series of tête-a-têtes." A *Kirkus Reviews* critic commented that the authors approach the story with a "gentle give-and-take," concluding, "Reading this cozy tale is rather like being enveloped by a mother's warm embrace."

Lasky's story of two tail-wagging friends from different sides of the tracks is brought to life in Mitch Vane's watercolor art for **Poodle and Hound.** (Illustration copyright © 2009 by Mitch Vane. Used with permission by Charlesbridge Publishing, Inc. All rights reserved.)

Lasky's "Guardians of Ga'Hoole" fantasy series is about a community of owls in a world that is fictional but is based partly on facts about owls. The first installment, *The Capture,* tells the story of a baby owl, Soren, who is knocked out of his nest too soon. When he is scooped up by another owl and taken to an orphanage, Soren soon realizes that he is in a military training camp where the captives are being brainwashed. Francisca Goldsmith, writing in *Booklist* noted that Lasky's owlish world inspires "big questions about human social psychology and politics along with real owl science." In *Kliatt,* Erin Lukens Darr praised the educational value of the novel, as Lasky uses "a combination of scientific and creative vocabulary," adding that *The Capture,* "would be a good language arts complement to the study of owls." Later volumes, including *The Hatchling, To Be a King,* and *The River of Wind,* follow the continuing adventures of Soren, his allies Nyroc and Coren, and their deadly rivals, the Pure Ones. The fifteen-volume series is augmented with a companion compendium, *A Guide Book to the Great Tree.*

In *The Last Girls of Pompeii* a critically acclaimed work of historical fiction set in B.C.E. 79, Lasky explores ancient Roman society. The novel centers on twelve-year-old Julia, the youngest daughter of the Petreius family, and her slave, Sura. An outcast because of her deformed arm, Julia learns that she will be banished to a temple, and she prepares to flee the city with Sura just as Vesuvius erupts. According to *School Library Journal* contributor Barbara Scotto, the author "effectively uses subtle indications of the impending eruption to increase the suspense and keep readers on the edge of their seats," and a critic for *Kirkus Reviews* described *The Last Girls of Pompeii* as "an intelligent, ruminative work for thoughtful readers."

Lasky's young-adult novel *Blood Secret* concerns Jerry Luna, a high-school freshman who has remained silent since her mother disappeared several years earlier. When Jerry moves in with her great-great-aunt, Constanza de Luna, she discovers a trunk containing mysterious heirlooms that lead the teen to a startling discovery about her family's history. In the work, Lasky addresses "the legacy of persecution, the power of silence, and the deep mysteries of what's passed between generations," remarked Engberg. In a lighter work for young readers, *Tumble Bunnies,* an anxious rabbit named Clyde discovers that it has a gift for acrobatics. "Lasky puts her finger on the day-to-day concerns of her target audience," Joy Fleishhacker stated in a *School Library Journal* of *Tumble Bunnies.*

Illustrated by Matthew Trueman, Lasky's nonfiction work *One Beetle Too Many: The Extraordinary Adventures of Charles Darwin* traces Darwin's life from his childhood and school days to his voyage on the *Beagle,* and also details how he became interested in science and eventually formulated his theory of evolution. She addresses religious controversies over evolution by quoting Darwin on both his doubts about some tenets of Christianity and his reverence for God as nature's creator. She also includes humorous anecdotes about Darwin's aversion to some of the more disgusting aspects of the natural world. *One Beetle Too Many* received praise from *School Library Journal* contributor Ellen Heath, who remarked that Lasky offers "a clear view" of Darwin, "a man troubled by the implications of his observations." Lasky's text is "well-organized" and Trueman's illustrations "exuberant," Heath added. Although a *Kirkus Reviews* critic faulted the book's "confusingly disjointed" story line, a *Publishers Weekly* contributorconcluded that Lasky's "light, conversational prose" in *One Beetle Too Many* makes complicated ideas accessible and provides "a just-right introduction to Charles Darwin."

According to numerous observers, over her career, Lasky has proven herself capable of producing intelligent, entertaining works in a variety of genres. In an article for *Horn Book,* the author related: "I can't stand doing the same thing twice. I don't want to change just for the sake of change. But the whole point of being an artist is to be able to get up every morning and reinvent the world." She also noted in an interview on the Harcourt Books Web site, "I guess what I like most about writing children's books is that I just feel that I can explore not only the world out there but a lot of hidden parts of myself as well. I have always been a person with a very active interior life. I don't need a lot of people around. I don't need to be in groups or go out a lot. I think I am a dedicated explorer of the interior states of not just myself but others."

Biographical and Critical Sources

BOOKS

Twentieth-Century Young-Adult Writers, edited by Laura Standley Berger, Gale (Detroit, MI), 1994.

PERIODICALS

Appraisal, winter, 1984, Martha T. Kane, review of *Sugaring Time,* pp. 34-35.
Audubon, January-February, 2007, Julie Leibach, review of *John Muir: America's First Environmentalist,* pp. 83.
Black Issues Book Review, November, 2000, Merce Robinson and Kelly Ellis, review of *Vision of Beauty: The Story of Sarah Breedlove Walker,* p. 80.
Booklist, July, 1983, Ilene Cooper, review of *Beyond the Divide,* p. 1402; November 15, 1982, Ilene Cooper, review of *Jem's Island,* p. 446; January 15, 1986, Ilene Cooper, review of *Home Free,* pp. 758-759; November 15, 1981, Ilene Cooper, review of *The Night Journey,* pp. 439-440; April, 1998, Stephanie Zvirin, review of *A Brilliant Streak: The Making of Mark Twain,* p. 1317; August 21, 2000, Marta Segal, review of *Vision of Beauty,* p. 2032; September 15, 2000, Todd Morning, review of *Lucille's Snowsuit,* p. 249; June 1, 2002, GraceAnne A. DeCandido, review of *Mommy's Hands,* pp. 1740-1741; March 1, 2003, Carolyn Phelan, review of *The Man Who Made Time Travel,* p. 1196; July, 2003, Gillian Engberg, review of *Lucille Camps In,* p. 1897; September 15, 2003, Francisca Goldsmith, review of *The Capture,* p. 240; October 1, 2004, Carolyn Phelan, review of *Humphrey, Albert, and the Flying Machine,* p. 335, and Gillian Engberg, review of *Blood Secret,* p. 340; January 1, 2005, Hazel Rochman, review of *Broken Song,* p. 859; December 1, 2005, Carolyn Phelan, review of *Dancing through Fire,* p. 49; February 1, 2006, Hazel Rochman, review of *John Muir,* p. 46; July 1, 2006, Gillian Engberg, review of *Pirate Bob,* p. 65; April 15, 2007, Hazel Rochman, review of *The Last Girls of Pompeii,* p. 50.
Bulletin of the Center for Children's Books, November, 1993, Betsy Hearne, review of *Monarchs,* pp. 88-89.
Carol Hurst's Children's Literature Newsletter, winter, 1999, "Featured Author: Kathryn Lasky," p. 4.
Children's Book Review Service, November, 1976, Barbara S. Wertheimer, review of *I Have Four Names for My Grandfather,* p. 22.
English Journal, January, 1984, Dick Abrahamson, "To Start the New Year off Right," pp. 87-89.
Five Owls, February, 1995, Anne Landis, review of *The Librarian Who Measured the Earth,* pp. 61-62.

Horn Book, June, 1983, Karen Jameyson, review of *Sugaring Time,* p. 323; September-October, 1985, Kathryn Lasky, "Reflections on Nonfiction," pp. 527-532; November-December, 1991, Kathryn Lasky, "Creativity in a Boom Industry," pp. 705-711; November-December, 1997, Roger Sutton, review of *Marven of the Great North Woods,* p. 670; March-April, 2005, Peter D. Sieruta, review of *Broken Song,* p. 204; May-June, 2006, Betty Carter, review of *John Muir,* p. 346.

Interracial Books for Children Bulletin, Volume 12, numbers 4-5, 1981, Jan M. Goodman, review of *The Weaver's Gift,* p. 38.

Kirkus Reviews, March 1, 1981, review of *The Weaver's Gift,* p. 286; March 1, 1998, review of *Alice Rose and Sam,* p. 341; April 1, 1998, review of *A Brilliant Streak,* p. 497; March 15, 2002, review of *Mommy's Hands,* pp. 416-417; July 15, 2004, review of *Blood Secret,* p. 689; February 1, 2005, review of *Broken Song,* p. 178; March 15, 2005, review of *Tumble Bunnies,* p. 354; February 1, 2006, review of *John Muir,* p. 133; April 1, 2007, review of *The Last Girls of Pompeii;* December 15, 2008, review of *One Beetle Too Many: The Extraordinary Adventures of Charles Darwin.*

Kliatt, September, 2003, Erin Lukens Darr, review of *The Capture,* p. 26; July, 2004, Claire Rosser, review of *Blood Secret,* p. 8; May, 2007, Claire Rosser, review of *The Last Girls of Pompeii,* p. 15.

Language Arts, January, 1984, M. Jean Greenlaw, review of *Beyond the Divide,* pp. 70-71; September, 1984, Alice Naylor, review of *Sugaring Time,* p. 543.

Publishers Weekly, October 6, 1997, review of *Marven of the Great North Woods,* p. 83; February 16, 1998, review of *Alice Rose and Sam,* p. 212; August 21, 2000, review of *Lucille's Snowsuit,* p. 73; March 17, 2003, review of *The Man Who Made Time Travel,* p. 77; July 7, 2003, review of *The Capture,* p. 72; March 1, 2004, review of *Love That Baby! A Book about Babies for New Brothers, Sisters, Cousins, and Friends,* p. 71; November 1, 2004, review of *Humphrey, Albert, and the Flying Machine,* p. 64; April 24, 2006, review of *Born to Rule,* p. 61; December 15, 2008, review of *One Beetle Too Many,* p. 53.

Quill & Quire, October, 1994, Joanne Schott, "The One Who . . .," p. 46.

School Librarian, June, 1983, Peter Kennerley, review of *The Night Journey,* p. 144.

School Library Journal, November, 1976, Andd Ward, review of *I Have Four Names for My Grandfather,* p. 48; September, 1993, Susan Oliver, review of *Monarchs,* p. 244; May, 1998, Jennifer A. Fakolt, review of *Alice Rose and Sam,* p. 145; July, 2002, Maryann H. Owen, review of *Mommy's Hands,* p. 94; April, 2003, Dona Ratterree, review of *The Man Who Made Time Travel,* p. 184; July, 2003, Martha Topol, review of *Lucille Camps In,* p. 100; February, 2004, Krista Tokarz, review of *Home at Last: Sophia's Immigrant Diary, Book Two,* p. 116; May, 2004, Tim Wadham, review of *The Journey,* p. 152; August, 2004, Sharon Morrison, review of *Blood Secret,* p. 124; October, 2004, Grace Oliff, review of *Humphrey, Albert, and the Flying Machine,* p. 120; March, 2005, Renee Steinberg, review of *Broken Song,* p. 214; April, 2005, Joy Fleishhacker, review of *Tumble Bunnies,* p. 105; June, 2005, Nancy A. Gifford, review of *Kazunomiya: Prisoner of Heaven,* p. 161; October, 2005, Patricia Manning, review of *The Most Beautiful Roof in the World: Exploring the Rainforest Canopy,* p. 64; November, 2005, Christina Stenson-Carey, review of *Dancing through Fire,* p. 138; January, 2006, Walter Minkel, review of *The Hatchling,* p. 136; April, 2006, Margaret Bush, review of *John Muir,* p. 127; May, 2006, Alison Grant, review of *Born to Rule,* p. 92; July, 2006, Kara Schaff Dean, review of *Pirate Bob,* p. 82; August, 2007, Barbara Scotto, review of *The Last Girls of Pompeii,* p. 118; January, 2009, Ellen Heath, review of *One Beetle Too Many,* p. 127.

Sunday Times (London, England), April 13, 2003, Nicolette Jones, review of *A Voice of Her Own: The Story of Phillis Wheatley, Slave Poet,* p. 32.

Voice of Youth Advocates, June, 1990, Shirley A. Bathgate, review of *Traces of Life: The Origins of Humankind,* pp. 126-127.

ONLINE

Harcourt Books Web site, http://www.harcourtbooks.com/ (June 19, 2009), interview with Lasky.

Kathryn Lasky Home Page, http://www.kathrynlasky.com (June 19, 2009).

Scholastic Web site, http://www.scholastic.com/ (June 19, 2009), "Kathryn Lasky."*

* * *

LASKY KNIGHT, Kathryn
See LASKY, Kathryn

* * *

LUTES, Jason 1967-

Personal

Born December 7, 1967, in Philipsburg, NJ. *Education:* Rhode Island School of Design, B.F.A. (illustration), 1991.

Addresses

E-mail—jlutes@earthlink.net.

Career

Cartoonist, comic book artist/writer, and graphic novelist. Creator of comic strip "Jar of Fools," published in *The Stranger.* Fantagraphics, Seattle, WA, worked in production and as assistant to art director, 1992-93; *The Stranger, Seattle,* production staffer and art director, 1993-96. Instructor, Seattle Institute of Fine Art.

Awards, Honors

Xeric Foundation grant, 1995, for self-publication, and Harvey Award nomination for Best Graphic Album of Original Material and Special Award for Excellence in Presentation, all 1996, all for *Jar of Fools;* Harvey Award nominations for Best New Series, Ignatz Award nomination for Outstanding Series, and Good Taste Awards for Best New Series, all 1997, Best Ongoing Serialized Story, 1999, and Eisner Award nomination for Best Continuing Series and for Best Writer/Artist, both 2001, and Best Graphic Album Reprint, 2002, all for *Berlin: City of Stones;* Eisner Award nominations for Best Single Issue, 2002, for *The Fall.*

Writings

Jar of Fools (collected comic strips; originally published in *The Stranger*), Black Eye Productions (Montreal, Quebec, Canada), 1996.

Berlin: City of Stones (graphic novel), Drawn & Quarterly (Montreal, Quebec, Canada), 2001.

(Illustrator) Ed Brubaker, *The Fall,* Drawn & Quarterly (Montreal, Quebec, Canada), 2001.

(With Nick Bertozzi) *Houdini: The Handcuff King* (graphic novel), introduction by Glen David Gold, Hyperion (New York, NY), 2007.

Berlin: City of Smoke (graphic novel; sequel to *Berlin: City of Stones*), Drawn & Quarterly (Montreal, Quebec, Canada), 2008.

Illustrator of *The Secret Three,* by Jake Austen, for *Nickelodeon* and *Catchpenny Comics.*

Lutes's work has also been published in France and Spain.

Sidelights

Jason Lutes is the creator of the acclaimed comic strip "Jar of Fools," about an out-of-work musician and his mentor, as well as of the comics novella *Houdini: The Handcuff King.* Lutes is best known, however, for *Berlin: City of Stones,* a work of historical fiction set in Germany during the 1920s and 1930s. In an interview with Rebecca Bengal on the Public Broadcasting Service Web site, Lutes remarked that "comics is the means of artistic expression that feels most comfortable to me. It's also still a largely uncharted medium with enormous unrealized potential. I like finding new ways to communicate an idea or a feeling, ways that can't be duplicated in other media, so I take great pleasure in the invention and exploration that comics necessitates."

Born in New Jersey, Lutes began copying comic-book illustrations when he was very young, assisted by his mother. "I still have some pages of *Avengers* comics that I copied with terrible Stan Lee dialogue lettered in my mom's handwriting," he explained to Barb Lien in a *Sequential Tart* online interview. When Lutes was eight years old, his family traveled to France, where he was introduced to classic European comics such as "Tintin" and "Asterix." "That early exposure to non-American comics was a big influence on my current style of drawing," Lutes further explained to Lien. Upon returning to the United States, he renewed his interest in comics while he attended schools in Missoula, Montana, and in California. When he enrolled at the Rhode Island School of Design, Lutes vowed to pursue serious art. However, he was drawn back to his first love when he read the "Raw" comics edited by Art Spiegelman and realized the potential of the medium. He began a student comic-book series called "Penny Dreadful Comics" that ran for seven issues, and also edited comics for a newspaper put out by his school's students and those at nearby Brown University.

After graduation Lutes moved to Seattle, Washington, where he worked for Fantagraphics for a year. He was later offered a job at Seattle's alternative paper, *The Stranger.* Lutes was invited to draw a comic strip for them, and he began "Jar of Fools," which he later published as a graphic novel of the same name. The comic appeared one page at a time in *The Stranger,* "and if

Jason Lutes teams up with writer Nick Bertozzi to create the biographical graphic novel **Houdini the Handcuff King.** *(Hyperion, 2007. Reproduced by permission.)*

you didn't follow it on a weekly basis, the individual pages were like comics non-sequitors," Lutes told Darren Schroeder in an interview for *Silver Bullet Comic Books.* Lutes eventually became art director at the paper and worked there for more than two years before pursing a career as a freelance writer and illustrator.

Jar of Fools centers on Al Flosso, former magician extraordinaire, who has decided to leave his boring life at the nursing home behind. With the help of his one-time protégé Ernesto Weiss, a magician who has lost his magic and his work, Al hopes to recover the magic—both literal and figurative—in his life. Weiss is pursued by his own demons, including the memory of the death of his brother, an escape artist, who committed suicide. *Jar of Fools* received considerable praise. *Print* contributor Daniel Nadel called it a "little gem of magic realism in comics form," and Tom de Haven remarked in the *New York Times Book Review* that *Jar of Fools,* is a "lovely" work that explores "the tenacious bond between an alcoholic stage magician and his cranky mentor."

Richard von Busack, writing in *Metroactive* online, also praised *Jar of Fools,* applauding Lutes for his "masterful control of the essence of comics" and his "facility with mute images, poetic dialogue and characterization." "The book was an experiment for me, sort of like a high school project in my ongoing comics education," Lutes told Schroeder. "I think it was well received partly because I set out specifically to tell a story that could be picked up and read by people who did not usually read comics, and partly because the reader could in some way participate in the same process of discovery I went through in its creation."

In 2001 Lutes published *Berlin: City of Stones,* the first volume of a planned trilogy. After completing his work on *Jar of Fools,* he told Bengal, "I knew I wanted to do something that would really challenge my ability as a cartoonist. I was leafing through a magazine one day and saw an advertisement for a book called *Bertolt Brecht's Berlin: A Scrapbook of the Twenties,* accompanied by a short blurb that sparked my interest. Without really knowing much more about the period than what I had seen in *Cabaret* and inferred through *Threepenny Opera,* I decided right then that my next book would be about Berlin in the '20s and '30s, that it would be broad in scope and substantial in length."

Berlin: City of Stones opens in Weimar Germany, the epoch immediately preceding the Nazi's rise to power. The central protagonists are Kurt Severing, a cynical, middle-aged journalist; Marthe Müller, a young art student with whom Severing has an affair; and Gudrun, a factory worker whose marriage suffers when she and her husband lose their jobs. As Jim Feast noted in *American Book Review,* Lutes "uses these two couples to exhibit how the different classes love. The relationship of the mother, Gudrun, with the leftist agitator who befriends her is taken up with getting her a job (in road

building), finding her a cheap lodging, and participating in political rallies. The love affair of Severing and the artist Marthe Müller is given over to artistic activities (such as her sketching him), humourous banter, and their observing of political rallies." "When I set out to write the story," Lutes told Rob Neufeld in the *Asheville Citizen-Times,* "I tried to figure out what resonates. I didn't set out to communicate a message, but rather to explore the lives of characters during a particular time in history. I didn't know what I was going to write until I got there. That's what keeps the story alive."

According to Bradford W. Wright, reviewing *Berlin: City of Stones* for the *Washington Post Book World,* "the real star of the novel is the city itself, rendered in marvelously clean detail from bird's-eye views to cobblestone street level." A *Publishers Weekly* contributor wrote that Lutes "thoughtfully renders" Berlin's "cabarets, parlors, plazas, alleyways, and citizens in a clear, evocative, black-and-white line style." "Lutes' clean drawings have an elegant European flair reminiscent of 'Tintin,' and depict a Berlin with all sorts of inhabitants," wrote Daniel Nadel in *Print.* "It is a satisfying, often moving project. We should be grateful Lutes took up the challenge." A *Kirkus Reviews* writer, noting that Lutes "captures the time and place with an historian's precision and a cinematographer's skill," called *Berlin: City of Stones* "an original project worth watching as it shapes up to something that may be quite magnificent."

Lutes collaborates with illustrator Nick Bertozzi on *Houdini,* a tale about celebrated magician and illusionist Harry Houdini. The work centers on a single event from the performer's life: On May 1, 1908, he made a well-publicized leap from Boston's Harvard Bridge into the frigid Charles River while his hands were bound by handcuffs. As Lutes and Bertozzi describe Houdini's preparations for the daring underwater escape, they offer an intimate look at his private life, including his obsession with fame, his encounters with prejudice, and his devotion to his wife. "Houdini himself comes off as a flawed but respectable man," a contributor in *Publishers Weekly* noted, and a critic in *Kirkus Reviews* described the work as "a glimpse into a life of determination and perseverance." *Houdini* drew praise both for its narrative structure and its illustrations. "Avoiding overt, showy tricks themselves, Lutes and Bertozzi use clean, simple storytelling and crisp, clear black-and-white art" in the work, observed Jesse Karp in *Booklist.* Nancy Kunz, writing in *School Library Journal,* also complimented the drawings, noting that "the tight focus on the action keeps the story moving."

In his interview with Bengal, Lutes stated that his approach to making comics "comes out of my own personal desire and struggle to understand our world, and the complex interactions of people with one another and their environment. My work is an improvised exploration of this complexity, as opposed to a structured, plot-driven narrative. Although my earlier work had a more internal focus, my current approach has evolved naturally from it. The challenge I face now is to keep this non-traditional approach engaging and accessible without compromising its exploratory nature."

Berlin: City of Smoke, the sequel to *Berlin: City of Stones,* was released in 2008, as the second part of a planned trilogy. Given the popularity of the first installment, the sequel was highly anticipated by both graphic artists and fans of graphic novels alike. As Lutes noted in an online *Newsarama* online interview with Michael C. Lorah, "the second book was definitely the hump to get over, and I feel content—well, relatively satisfied, as much as I can—with the way the second volume pulled together. For the first time in a long while, I'm actually excited about what lies ahead." He added: "It has often felt like a chore or a difficult task that I have to face, though by turn it sometimes [is] also exciting and fun. And right now, with 2/3rds behind me, I'm a little bit charged up."

Reviewers praised *Berlin: City of Smoke* for its vivid images and storyline. Andrew Wheeler, writing in *ComicMix* online, stated that "what *Berlin* does is flow—like water, or, given the title of this book, perhaps more like smoke—from one plot thread to another, through the lives of all of the characters, out one side and back to the other. Scenes follow scenes mostly through movie-style transitions—the viewpoint pulls out and then back in somewhere else, or jump-cut during page transitions." *High-Low* online contributor Rob Clough remarked that *Berlin: City of Smoke* "features an interesting premise and setting, a rich array of characters, and a complex storyline rife with room for discussion of all sorts of ideas. None of this would be effective without Lutes' amazing line. He manages to pull off the rare trick of using a line that is distinctive and clear without being overly slick. It's naturalistic but with a slightly rubbery quality that makes each page and each character feel like an organic entity."

Biographical and Critical Sources

PERIODICALS

American Book Review, May, 2001, Jim Feast, review of *Berlin: City of Stones,* p. 3.
Asheville Citizen-Times (Asheville, NC), February 21, 2003, Rob Neufeld, interview with Lutes.

Booklist, March 15, 2007, Jesse Karp, review of *Houdini: The Handcuff King,* p. 58; January 1, 2009, Gordon Flagg, review of *Berlin: City of Smoke,* p. 57.
Kirkus Reviews, May 1, 2001, review of *Berlin: City of Stones,* p. 624; March 15, 2007, review of *Houdini.*
New York Times Book Review, May 31, 1998, Tom de Haven, "Comics," p. 9.
Print, May, 2001, Daniel Nadel, review of *Berlin: City of Stones,* p. 17.
Publishers Weekly, October 22, 2001, review of *Berlin: City of Stones,* p. 56; February 19, 2007, review of *Houdini,* p. 171.
Quill & Quire, August, 1996, Mark Shainblum, review of *Jar of Fools,* p. 26.
School Library Journal, July, 2007, Nancy Kunz, review of *Houdini,* p. 126.
Time, December 8, 2000, Andrew D. Arnold, review of *Berlin: City of Stones.*
Tribune Books (Chicago, IL), April 1, 2007, Mary Harris Russell, review of *Houdini,* p. 7.
Washington Post Book World, August 12, 2001, Bradford W. Wright, review of *Berlin: City of Stones,* p. 9.
World Literature Today, March-April, 2007, Andrew D. Arnold, "Seeing Your Graphic Literature Library," review of *Berlin: City of Stones,* p. 29.

ONLINE

Artbomb.net, http://www.artbomb.net/ (April 1, 2008), Matt Fraction, reviews of *Jar of Fools* and *Berlin: City of Stones;* Warren Ellis, review of *The Fall.*
ComicMix Web site, http://www.comicmix.com/ (November 3, 2008), Andrew Wheeler, review of *Berlin: City of Smoke.*
Drawn & Quarterly Web site, http://www.drawnandquarterly.com/ (April 1, 2008), "Jason Lutes."
High-Low Web site, http://highlowcomics.blogspot.com/ (March 19, 2009), Rob Clough, review of *Berlin: City of Smoke.*
Metroactive.com, http://www.metroactive.com/ (May 9-15, 1996), Richard von Busack, "Fools of Wisdom: Jason Lutes Tells His Stories between the Panels in a Brilliant New Comic Book."
Newsarama.com, http://www.newsarama.com/ (October 1, 2008), Michael C. Lorah, interview with Lutes.
Public Broadcasting Service Web site, http://www.pbs.org/ (June 29, 2006), Rebecca Bengal, "On Cartooning: Jason Lutes."
Silver Bullet Comic Books Web site, http://www.silverbulletcomicbooks.com/ (February 6, 2001), Darren Schroeder, interview with Lutes.

M

MAIZELS, Jennie

Personal

Born in England; married; children: Millie.

Addresses

Home—Brighton, England.

Career

Illustrator and author of children's books.

Writings

SELF-ILLUSTRATED

(With Kate Petty) *The Amazing Pop-up Grammar Book*, Dutton (New York, NY), 1996, published as *The Great Grammar Book*, Bodley Head (London, England), 1996.

(With Kate Petty) *The Amazing Pop-up Multiplication Book*, Dutton (New York, NY), 1998, published as *The Terrific Times Tables Book*, Bodley Head (London, England), 1998.

(With Kate Petty) *The Amazing Pop-up Music Book*, Dutton (New York, NY), 1999, published as *The Magnificent I-Can-Read-Music Book*, Bodley Head (London, England), 1999.

Rory Has a Party, Bloomsbury (London, England), 1999.

Rory Goes in Fancy Dress, Bloomsbury (London, England), 1999.

Journey to Jigsaw Town, David & Charles (London, England), 1999.

Picnic at Jigsaw Town, David & Charles (London, England), 1999.

Party in Jigsaw Forest, David & Charles (London, England), 2000.

Rocket to Jigsaw Planet, David & Charles (London, England), 2000.

(With Kate Petty) *The Amazing Pop-up Geography Book*, Dutton (New York, NY), 2000, published as *The Wonderful World Book*, Bodley Head (London, England), 2000.

(With Kate Petty) *The Super Science Book*, Bodley Head (London, England), 2002.

Finger Food for Babies and Toddlers, Vermilion (London, England), 2003.

(With Kate Petty) *The Global Garden*, Eden Project (London, England), 2005.

Jennie Maizels' Things to Do Book: Over 200 Fun-filled Activities, Games, Jokes, and Song!, Walker (London, England), 2005.

(With Kate Petty) *The Perfect Pop-up Punctuation Book*, Dutton (New York, NY), 2006.

(With Kate Petty) *Earthly Treasure*, Dutton (New York, NY), 2009.

Author's works have been translated into French.

ILLUSTRATOR

Jenny Oldfield, *Live the Dream!*, A. & C. Black (London, England), 2004.

Biographical and Critical Sources

PERIODICALS

Magpies, March, 2000, review of *The Magnificent I-Can-Read-Music Book*, p. 45.

Kirkus Reviews, July 1, 2006, review of *The Perfect Pop-up Punctuation Book*.

Publishers Weekly, October 28, 1996, review of *The Amazing Pop-up Grammar Book*, p. 82; September 14, 1998, review of *The Amazing Pop-up Multiplication Book*, p. 71.

School Library Journal, September, 2006, Lisa Gangemi Kropp, review of *The Perfect Pop-up Punctuation Book*, p. 196.

Time Educational Supplement, October 14, 2005, Gillian Ravenscroft, review of *The Global Garden,* p. 13.*

*   *   *

MANY, Paul 1947-
(Paul A. Many)

Personal

Surname is pronounced "Manny"; born July 8, 1947, in New York, NY; married; children: one daughter. *Ethnicity:* "Caucasian." *Education:* St. John's University, B.A.; Ohio State University, M.A., Ph.D.; Bowling Green State University, M.F.A.

Addresses

Home—Ottawa Hills, OH. *Office*—Department of Communication, University of Toledo, 2801 W. Bancroft St., Toledo, OH 43606. *Agent*—Andrea Brown Literary Agency, P.O. Box 371027, Montara, CA 94037. *E-mail*—Paul.Many@utoledo.edu.

Career

Educator and author. University of Toledo, Toledo, OH, assistant professor, 1980-88, associate professor, 1988-97, professor of communications, 1997—.

Awards, Honors

Los Angeles Times Best Children's Book selection, 2002, for *The Great Pancake Escape;* New York Public Library Books for the Teen Age citations, for *These Are the Rules, My Life, Take Two,* and *Walk away Home.*

Writings

These Are the Rules (young-adult novel), Walker & Company (New York, NY), 1997.
My Life, Take Two (young-adult novel), Walker & Company (New York, NY), 2000.
The Great Pancake Escape (picture book), illustrated by Scott Goto, Walker & Company (New York, NY), 2002.
Walk away Home (young-adult novel), Walker & Company (New York, NY), 2002.
Dad's Bald Head (picture book), illustrated by Kevin O'Malley, Walker & Company (New York, NY), 2007.

Work represented in anthologies, including *Glass Will: Anthology of Toledo Poets,* edited by Joel Lipman, Toledo Poets Center Press (Toledo, OH), 1986; and *Ohio Short Fiction: A Collection of Twenty-two Stories by Ohio Writers,* Northmont Publishing (West Bloomfield, MI), 1995. Contributor of articles, stories, and poems to journals, including *Nebo, Exquisite Corpse, Academe, Toledo Blade, Connecticut Review, Gaslight Review, Light, Michigan Academician,* and *Community College Journalist.*

Author's novels have been published in Danish and Italian.

Sidelights

Paul Many, a professor of communications at the University of Toledo, is also the author of young-adult novels and children's picture books. "Books allow us to see into the private lives of characters in ways that usually are restricted to only a few people we intimately know," the author told a *Teenreads.com* interviewer. "Reading about characters who have gone through grief and loss can be comforting in trying times. Books also organize and make sense of the crazy reality we live in. This is also comforting."

In his debut novel, *These Are the Rules,* Many introduces teenager Colm, who is spending the summer at White Sand Lake. The summer seems to be a series of failures for Colm, who cannot learn to drive a car, win the heart of his crush, or swim across the lake. For most of the summer, Colm remains blind to how conceited his would-be girlfriend Carmella is, and he is also oblivious to the real affection shown by Marlene. However, when Colm most needs a friend Marlene offers her help, and he finally realizes what she means to him. "Readers catch a glimpse of the world according to teenager Colm in this wry account of his trials," wrote the critic for *Publishers Weekly.* Hazel Rochman, reviewing *These Are the Rules* for *Booklist,* concluded that, "laugh-out-loud funny, Many's story is the archetypal YA first-person narrative of the sensitive, bumbling teenager."

My Life, Take Two finds high schooler Neal Thackeray having to finish an overdue film documentary over the summer in order to pass his film class. Losing a job, the criticism of his mother and girlfriend, and the still-fresh loss of his father a few years before had prevent Neal from working on the project. The only person he can talk to is Claire, who has troubles of her own: Because of financial problems, her family may lose their home. Neal must come to terms with what he wants from life before he can resolve his or Claire's problems. Anita L. Burkam, writing in *Horn Book,* called *My Life, Take Two* an "impressively themed novel," and Debbie Carton wrote in *Booklist* that "Neal's voice . . . drives both the plot and the message, realistically reflecting teen angst, humor, and hormones."

Many tells of a teen who leaves his troubled family life in *Walk away Home.* Nick Doran decides to walk across the state to his aunt Wanda's house, but he soon finds that there are troubles there as well. The aging hippies who share his aunt's house are having their rural dwelling encroached upon by a new subdivision. When Nick meets Diana, one of the teenagers in the new neighborhood, he is drawn into helping her. Diana also has reasons to leave home. She has been sexually abused by her father and she is afraid that her younger sisters may be next. Many "tackles teen angst, the desire to prove oneself, and the search for self-understanding knowledgably and convincingly," according to Paula Rohrlick in *Kliatt*. "Nick is a refreshing character," Francisca Goldsmith wrote in *School Library Journal*, "and the happy ending is well deserved by both him and readers."

The inspiration behind Many's picture book *The Great Pancake Escape* came to him while cooking breakfast one morning. As he told Erica Ryan for *University of Toledo News Online*, preparing pancakes "is something I do regularly. It's magic when you take gloppy, gluey stuff and you cook it and it becomes edible." In the story, a magician loses control of the pancakes he is making; they flee the kitchen and lead his children on a merry adventure. Along the way, the magic pancakes disguise themselves as frisbees, manhole covers, and wheels to avoid being found by the hungry children. Finally, Father finds the cookbook and the spell is reversed. A critic in *Kirkus Reviews* called *The Great Pancake Escape* "a rhythmic, rip-roaring romp," and Lauren Peterson noted in *Booklist* that Many's "rhyming text, which appears to float across the page inside tan-colored pancake shapes, is clever and funny."

In *Dad's Bald Head* Pete is startled one morning when his father decides to shave off the remaining bits of his hair and go bald. Despite the reassurances of his parents, Pete has a hard time accepting the change. Rachel G. Payne, reviewing Many's tale in the *School Library Journal* concluded that the "lighthearted story could encourage fathers to explore their own hair loss with their children."

Many once commented: "I have been writing for some thirty years and have written everything from newspaper articles to novels, with academic journal pieces and short fiction and poetry in between. In my current career, I am writing young-adult novels. I think of these as real novels that happen to be for young adults, and I avoid formula in any way. I am interested in archetypes, however—the deep underpinnings that are the unspoken text of many of the stories we tell. I include some of these deep story elements in each of my novels.

"The writer C.S. Lewis has been quoted as saying: 'We read to know we are not alone.' I think that, like many other writers, I write to reaffirm this idea in readers. By telling stories, we write about what is truly in the minds and hearts of people and convince them in ways substantial and trivial that we all share in the same humanity.

"In addition, I believe that life is lived best and we can avoid cynicism and despair by staying alert and aware. Spring does not return each year. Each year brings a new spring; one which, despite surface similarities, the world has not previously experienced. And, although everything in the world may not be beautiful, I don't know of a more beautiful world. It is the obligation of the writer to continually discover ways of bringing this world anew to readers so they, too, may see it as it is."

Biographical and Critical Sources

PERIODICALS

Booklist, May 1, 1997, Hazel Rochman, review of *These Are the Rules*, p. 1489; May 1, 2000, Debbie Carton, review of *My Life, Take Two*, p. 1659; April 1, 2002, Lauren Peterson, review of *The Great Pancake Escape*, p. 1334.

Bulletin of the Center for Children's Books, April, 1997, review of *These Are the Rules*, p. 289; July, 2000, review of *My Life, Take Two*, p. 411; September, 2007, review of *Dad's Bald Head*, p. 38.

Horn Book, September, 2000, Anita L. Burkam, review of *My Life, Take Two*, p. 576; January, 2003, review of *Walk away Home*, p. 78.

Kirkus Reviews, April 1, 2002, review of *The Great Pancake Escape*, p. 495; October 1, 2002, review of *Walk away Home*, p. 1475; April 15, 2007, review of *Dad's Bald Head*.

Kliatt, November, 2002, Paula Rohrlick, review of *Walk away Home*, p. 12.

Library Media Connection, April, 2003, review of *Walk away Home*, p. 76.

Publishers Weekly, April 28, 1997, review of *These Are the Rules*, p. 76; June 29, 1998, review of *These Are the Rules*, p. 61; June 19, 2000, review of *My Life, Take Two*, p. 81; March 11, 2002, review of *The Great Pancake Escape*, p. 72; November 25, 2002, review of *Walk away Home*, p. 69.

School Library Journal, May, 1997, Connie Tyrrell Burns, review of *These Are the Rules*, p. 137; July, 2000, Francisca Goldsmith, review of *My Life, Take Two*, p. 107; March, 2002, Carol L. MacKay, review of *The Great Pancake Escape*, p. 193; September, 2002, Francisca Goldsmith, review of *Walk away Home*, p. 228; June, 2007, Rachel G. Payne, review of *Dad's Bald Head*, p. 115.

Voice of Youth Advocates, August, 1997, review of *These Are the Rules*, p. 187; October, 2000, review of *My Life, Take Two*, p. 268; December, 2002, review of *Walk away Home*, p. 387.

ONLINE

Ohio Authors and Illustrators for Young People Web site, http://school.uaschools.org/ (January 1, 2010), interview with Many.

Paul Many Home Page, http://homepages.utoledo.edu/pmany (January 1, 2010).

Teenreads.com, http://www.teenreads.com/ (February 26, 2002), interview with Many.

University of Toledo News Online, http://utnews.utoledo.edu/ (November 18, 2002), Erica Ryan, "Pancake Idea Sizzles into Children's Book by UT Professor"; (November 6, 2003) Deanna Lytle, "Pancakes Can't Escape This Performance."*

* * *

MANY, Paul A.
See MANY, Paul

MAZELLAN, Ron

Personal

Born in England; married; wife's name Jil (a musician); children: three sons. *Education:* Wheaton College, A.B., 1981; California State University at Fullerton, M.A., 1991.

Addresses

Home—Marion, IN. *Office*—Indiana Wesleyan University, 4201 S. Washington St., Marion, IN 46953. *Agent*—Kirchoff/Wohlberg, 866 United Nations Plaza, Rm. 525, New York, NY 10017.

Career

Graphic designer, illustrator, and educator. Indiana Wesleyan University, Marion, associate professor of art, 1993—.

Awards, Honors

National Jewish Book Awards finalist, for *The Harmonica.*

Illustrator

Q.L. Pearce, *Why Is a Frog Not a Toad?,* Lowell House (Los Angeles, CA), 1992.

Calvin Miller, *My Friend and My King: John's Vision of Our Hope of Heaven,* Chariot Victor Publishing (Colorado Springs, CO), 1999.

Bruce Brager, *Bessie Coleman,* Scholastic, Inc. (New York, NY), 2002.

Cheryl Fawcett and Robert C. Newman, *Kids' Questions about Church and the Future,* Regular Baptist Press (Schaumburg, IL), 2002.

Cheryl Fawcett and Robert C. Newman, *Kids' Questions about Church and Jesus,* Regular Baptist Press (Schaumburg, IL), 2003.

Tony Johnston, *The Harmonica,* Charlesbridge (Watertown, MA), 2004.

Sarah Kovatch, *We Will Walk,* Zaner-Bloser (Columbus, OH), 2005.

Jo Harper and Josephine Harper, *Finding Daddy: A Story of the Great Depression,* Turtle Books (New York, NY), 2005.

Cal Ripken, Jr., *The Longest Season: The Story of the Orioles' 1988 Losing Streak,* Philomel (New York, NY), 2007.

A soldier's welcome home is captured in Ron Mazellan's paintings for Peggy Mercer's picture book There Comes a Soldier. (Handprint Books, 2007. Illustration copyright © 2007 by Peggy Mercer. Reproduced by permission.)

Peggy Mercer, *There Come a Soldier,* Handprint Books (New York, NY), 2007.

Richard Michelson, *A Is for Abraham: A Jewish Family Alphabet,* Sleeping Bear Press (Chelsea, MI), 2008.

Sidelights

Ron Mazellan, an educator, graphic designer, and commercial illustrator, has provided the artwork for such critically acclaimed children's books as *The Harmonica* by Tony Johnston and *The Longest Season: The Story of the Orioles' 1988 Losing Streak* by Cal Ripken, Jr. Inspired by a Holocaust survivor's true story, *The Harmonica* concerns a young Polish boy who learns to play works by Franz Schubert on his harmonica, a gift from his father. When the boy is sent to a concentration camp, he is ordered to play for the murderous commandant, although his music also reaches his fellow prisoners. Mazellan's mixed-media illustrations "communicate the story's pathos while sparing the audience many of the setting's horrors," noted a critic in *Publishers Weekly.*

A young girl searches for her father after their family is torn apart by poverty in *Finding Daddy: A Story of the Great Depression,* a work coauthored by Jo Harper and Josephine Harper. Mazellan's "illustrations, rendered in oil and acrylic, are noteworthy, capturing the transition from happiness to sorrow to hope through the use of color," Suzanne Myers Harold wrote in *School Library Journal.* In another historical work, Peggy Mercer's *There Come a Soldier,* a Georgia sharecropper serves as a paratrooper during World War II. *School Library Journal* contributor Lucinda Snyder Whitehurst praised Mazellan's "cool palette," stating that "the many hues of blue, green, and purple produce a peaceful effect even in the midst of war."

In *The Longest Season,* Baseball Hall-of-Fame shortstop Ripken offers a lesson on perseverance as he recounts the Baltimore Orioles' dismal start to the 1988 season, when they lost their first twenty-one games. According to a *Publishers Weekly* reviewer, "Mazellan's watercolors emit the burnished glow of yesteryear" in his work for *The Longest Season.* His "color-drenched illustrations capture the emotional intensity of the narrative," remarked *School Library Journal* critic Marilyn Taniguchi in another positive appraisal of the book.

Biographical and Critical Sources

PERIODICALS

Booklist, January 1, 2004, Hazel Rochman, review of *The Harmonica,* p. 857; July, 2005, Hazel Rochman, review of *Finding Daddy: A Story of the Great Depression,* p. 1925; November 15, 2007, Hazel Rochman, review of *There Come a Soldier,* p. 44.

Kirkus Reviews, December 15, 2003, review of *The Harmonica,* p. 1451.

Publishers Weekly, January 26, 2004, review of *The Longest Season: The Story of the Orioles' 1988 Losing Streak,* p. 184; November 12, 2007, review of *There Come a Soldier,* p. 55.

School Library Journal, May, 2004, Cris Riedel, review of *The Harmonica,* p. 116; September, 2005, Suzanne Myers Harold, review of *Finding Daddy,* p. 171; May, 2007, Marilyn Taniguchi, review of *The Longest Season,* p. 123; November, 2007, Lucinda Snyder Whitehurst, review of *There Come a Soldier,* p. 96.

USA Today, June 14, 2007, Bob Minzesheimer, review of *The Longest Season,* p. D6.*

* * *

McCULLY, Emily Arnold 1939- (Emily Arnold)

Personal

Born July 1, 1939, in Galesburg, IL; daughter of Wade E. (a writer) and Kathryn (a teacher) Arnold; married George E. McCully (an historian), June 3, 1961 (divorced, 1975); children: Nathaniel, Tad. *Education:* Brown University, B.A., 1961; Columbia University, M.A., 1964. *Hobbies and other interests:* Theater, acting, gardening, cooking, travel, tennis.

Addresses

Home—New York, NY; and Chatham, NY. *Agent*—Harriet Wasserman Literary Agency, Inc., 137 E. 36th St., New York, NY 10016.

Career

Writer. Worked in advertising and as freelance magazine artist, 1961-67; illustrator of children's books, 1966—; writer, 1975—. Teacher at workshops at Brown University, Boston University, St. Clements, Cummington Community of the Arts, and Rockland Center for the Arts.

Member

Authors Guild, Authors League of America, PEN American Center, Society of Children's Book Writers.

Awards, Honors

Gold medal, Philadelphia Art Directors, 1968; Showcase Title citation, Children's Book Council, 1972, for *Hurray for Captain Jane!;* Art Books for Children citation, Brooklyn Museum and New York Public Library, for *MA nDA LA;* Juvenile Award, Council of Wisconsin Writers, 1979, for *Edward Troy and the Witch Cat;* National Endowment for the Arts grant in creative writing, 1980; New York State Council on Arts fiction grant, 1982; American Book Award nomination, 1982, for *A Craving;* Best Books of the Year citation, *School Library Journal,* 1984, Notable Book citation, American

Emily Arnold McCully (Reproduced by permission.)

Library Association (ALA), 1984, Christopher Award, 1985, and inclusion in International Biennale at Bratislava, 1985, all for *Picnic;* Randolph Caldecott Medal, ALA, and Best Illustrated Book designation, *New York Times,* both 1993, both for *Mirette on the High Wire;* Spur Awards nomination, 1998; honorary degree from Brown University, for achievement in literature and illustration, 2002.

Writings

SELF-ILLUSTRATED

Picnic, Harper (New York, NY), 1984, reprinted, HarperCollins (New York, NY), 2003.

First Snow, Harper (New York, NY), 1985, reprinted, HarperCollins (New York, NY), 2004.

The Show Must Go On, Western (New York, NY), 1987.

School, Harper (New York, NY), 1987, reprinted, HarperCollins (New York, NY), 2005.

New Baby, Harper (New York, NY), 1988.

Christmas Gift, Harper (New York, NY), 1988.

You Lucky Duck!, Western (Racine, WI), 1988.

The Grandma Mixup, Harper (New York, NY), 1988.

Zaza's Big Break, HarperCollins (New York, NY), 1989.

The Evil Spell, HarperCollins (New York, NY), 1990.

Grandmas at the Lake, HarperCollins (New York, NY), 1990.

Speak up, Blanche!, HarperCollins (New York, NY), 1991.

Grandmas at Bat, Harper (New York, NY), 1992.

Mirette on the High Wire, Putnam (New York, NY), 1992.

Crossing the New Bridge, Putnam (New York, NY), 1994.

My Real Family, Harcourt Brace (San Diego, CA), 1994.

Little Kit; or, The Industrious Flea Circus Girl, Dial (New York, NY), 1995.

The Pirate Queen, Putnam (New York, NY), 1995.

The Ballot Box Battle, Knopf (New York, NY), 1996.

The Bobbin Girl, Dial (New York, NY), 1996.

Popcorn at the Palace, Browndeer Press/Harcourt Brace (San Diego, CA), 1997.

Starring Mirette and Bellini, Putnam (New York, NY), 1997.

Beautiful Warrior: The Legend of the Nun's Kung Fu, Arthur A. Levine Books (New York, NY), 1998.

An Outlaw Thanksgiving, Dial (New York, NY), 1998.

Mouse Practice, Arthur A. Levine Books (New York, NY), 1999.

Hurry (adapted from *Farewell to the Farivox* by Harry Hartwick), Harcourt Brace (San Diego, CA), 2000.

Mirette and Bellini Cross Niagara Falls, Putnam (New York, NY), 2000.

Monk Camps Out, Arthur A. Levine Books (New York, NY), 2000.

Four Hungry Kittens, Dial (New York, NY), 2001.

The Grandmas Trick-or-Treat, HarperCollins (New York, NY), 2001.

The Orphan Singer, Arthur A. Levine Books (New York, NY), 2001.

The Battle for St. Michael's, HarperCollins (New York, NY), 2002.

Squirrel and John Muir, Farrar, Straus & Giroux (New York, NY), 2005.

Marvelous Mattie: How Margaret E. Knight Became an Inventor, Farrar, Straus & Giroux (New York, NY), 2006.

The Escape of Oney Judge: Martha Washington's Slave Finds Freedom, Farrar, Straus & Giroux (New York, NY), 2007.

Manjiro: The Boy Who Risked His Life for Two Countries, Farrar, Straus & Giroux (New York, NY), 2008.

ILLUSTRATOR

George Panetta, *Sea Beach Express,* Harper (New York, NY), 1966.

Emily Cheney Neville, *The Seventeenth Street Gang,* Harper (New York, NY), 1966.

Marjorie W. Sharmat, *Rex,* Harper (New York, NY), 1967.

Natalie S. Carlson, *Luigi of the Streets,* Harper (New York, NY), 1967.

Liesel M. Skorpen, *That Mean Man,* Harper (New York, NY), 1968.

Barbara Borack, *Gooney,* Harper (New York, NY), 1968.

Seymour Simon, *Animals in Field and Laboratory: Science Project in Animal Behavior,* McGraw (New York, NY), 1968.

Meindert De Jong, *Journey from Peppermint Street,* Harper (New York, NY), 1968.

Barbara K. Wheeler, and Naki Tezel, *The Mouse and the Elephant,* Parents' Magazine Press (New York, NY), 1969.

Jan Wahl, *The Fisherman,* Norton (New York, NY), 1969.

Pierre Gripari, *Tales from the Rue Broca,* translated by Doriane Grutman, Bobbs, Merrill, 1969.

Virginia O. Baron, editor, *Here I Am! An Anthology of Poems Written by Young People in Some of America's Minority Groups,* Dutton (New York, NY), 1969.

Janet Louise Swoboda Lunn, *Twin Spell,* Harper (New York, NY), 1969.

Jane H. Yolen, *Hobo Toad and the Motorcycle Gang,* World Publishing (Cleveland, OH), 1970.

Jeanne B. Hardendorff, *Slip! Slop! Gobble!,* Lippincott (Philadelphia, PA), 1970.

Ruth A. Sonneborn, *Friday Night Is Papa Night,* Viking (New York, NY), 1970.

Mildred Kantrowitz, *Maxie,* Parents' Magazine Press (New York, NY), 1970.

Phyllis M. Hoffman, *Steffie and Me,* Harper (New York, NY), 1970.

Jeanne B. Hardendorff, *The Cat and the Parrot,* Lippincott (Philadelphia, PA), 1970.

Betsy Byars, *Go and Hush the Baby,* Viking (New York, NY), 1971.

Alix Shulman, *Finders Keepers,* Bradbury Press (New York, NY), 1971.

Arnold Adoff, *MA nDA LA,* Harper (New York, NY), 1971.

Sam Reavin, *Hurray for Captain Jane!,* Parents' Magazine Press (New York, NY), 1971.

Helen E. Buckley, *Michael Is Brave,* Lothrop (New York, NY), 1971.

Seymour Simon, *Finding out with Your Senses,* McGraw (New York, NY), 1971.

Louise McNamara, *Henry's Pennies,* F. Watts (New York, NY), 1972.

Arthur Miller, *Jane's Blanket,* Viking (New York, NY), 1972.

Lynn Schoettle, *Grandpa's Long Red Underwear,* Lothrop (New York, NY), 1972.

Lee Bennett Hopkins, *Girls Can Too!,* F. Watts (New York, NY), 1972.

Jane Langton, *The Boyhood of Grace Jones,* Harper (New York, NY), 1972.

Arnold Adoff, *Black Is Brown Is Tan,* Harper (New York, NY), 1973, revised edition, HarperCollins (New York, NY), 2002.

Constance C. Greene, *Isabelle the Itch,* Viking (New York, NY), 1973.

Mildred Kantrowitz, *When Violet Died,* Parents' Magazine Press (New York, NY), 1973.

Mary H. Lystad, *That New Boy,* Crown (New York, NY), 1973.

Thomas Rockwell, *How to Eat Fried Worms,* F. Watts (New York, NY), 1973.

Anne Norris Baldwin, *Jenny's Revenge,* Four Winds Press (New York, NY), 1974.

Jane Langton, *Her Majesty, Grace Jones,* Harper (New York, NY), 1974.

Miska Miles, *Tree House Town,* Little, Brown (Boston, MA), 1974.

Marjorie W. Sharmat, *I Want Mama,* Harper (New York, NY), 1974.

Jean Little, *Stand in the Wind,* Harper (New York, NY), 1975.

Susan Terris, *Amanda the Panda and the Redhead,* Doubleday (New York, NY), 1975.

Sylvia Plath, *The Bed Book,* Harper (New York, NY), 1976.

Ianthe Thomas, *My Street's a Morning Cool Street,* Harper (New York, NY), 1976.

Rita Golden Gelman and Joan Richter, *Professor Coconut and the Thief,* Holt (New York, NY), 1977.

Miranda Hapgood, *Martha's Mad Day,* Crown (New York, NY), 1977.

Elizabeth Winthrop, *That's Mine,* Holiday House (New York, NY), 1977.

Arnold Adoff, *Where Wild Willie,* Harper (New York, NY), 1978.

Betty Baker, *No Help at All,* Greenwillow (New York, NY), 1978.

Betty Baker, *Partners,* Greenwillow (New York, NY), 1978.

Russell Hoban, *The Twenty-Elephant Restaurant,* Atheneum (New York, NY), 1978.

Glory St. John, *What I Did Last Summer,* Atheneum (New York, NY), 1978.

Nancy Willard, *The Highest Hit,* Harcourt (New York, NY), 1978.

Constance C. Greene, *I and Sproggy,* Viking (New York, NY), 1978.

Sarah Sargent, *Edward Troy and the Witch Cat,* Follett (New York, NY), 1978.

Kathryn Lasky, *My Island Grandma,* F. Warne (New York, NY), 1979.

Barbara Williams, *Whatever Happened to Beverly Bigler's Birthday?,* Harcourt (New York, NY), 1979.

Clyde Robert Bulla, *Last Look,* Crowell (New York, NY), 1979.

Mirra Ginsburg, *Ookie-Spooky,* Crown (New York, NY), 1979.

Edith Thacher Hurd, *The Black Dog Who Went into the Woods,* Harper (New York, NY), 1980.

Pat Rhoads Mauser, *How I Found Myself at the Fair,* Atheneum (New York, NY), 1980.

Tobi Tobias, *How We Got Our First Cat,* F. Watts (New York, NY), 1980.

Jane Breskin Zalben, *Oliver and Allison's Week,* Farrar, Straus (New York, NY), 1980.

Brooke M. Varnum, *Play and Sing . . . It's Christmas! A Piano Book of Easy-to-Play Carols,* Macmillan (New York, NY), 1980.

Vicki Kimmel Artis, *Pajama Walking,* Houghton (Boston, MA), 1981.

Alice Schertle, *The April Fool,* Lothrop (New York, NY), 1981.

Kathleen Benson, *Joseph on the Subway Trains,* Addison-Wesley (New York, NY), 1981.

Beatrice Gormley, *Mail-Order Wings,* Dutton (New York, NY), 1981.

Jeannette Everly, *The Seeing Summer,* Lippincott (Philadelphia, PA), 1981.

Charlotte Zolotow, *The New Friend,* Harper (New York, NY), 1981.

Beatrice Gormley, *Fifth Grade Magic,* Dutton (New York, NY), 1982.

Marion M. Markham, *The Halloween Candy Mystery,* Houghton (Boston, MA), 1982.

Edith Thacher Hurd, *I Dance in My Red Pajamas,* Harper (New York, NY), 1982.

Barbara Williams, *Mitzi and the Terrible Tyrannosaurus Rex,* Dutton (New York, NY), 1982.

Barbara Williams, *Mitzi's Honeymoon with Nana Potts,* Dutton (New York, NY), 1983.

Laurie Adams, and Allison Coudert, *Alice and the Boa Constrictor,* Houghton (Boston, MA), 1983.

Corrine Gerson, *Good Dog, Bad Dog,* Macmillan (New York, NY), 1983.

Beatrice Gormley, *Best Friend Insurance,* Dutton (New York, NY), 1983.

Christopher Smart, *For I Will Consider My Cat Jeoffry,* Atheneum (New York, NY), 1984.

Marion M. Markham, *The Christmas Present Mystery,* Houghton (Boston, MA), 1984.

The Playground, Golden Books (New York, NY), 1984.

Barbara Williams, *Mitzi and Frederick the Great,* Dutton (New York, NY), 1984.

Miska Miles, *Gertrude's Pocket,* Peter Smith (New York, NY), 1984.

Charlotte T. Graeber, *The Thing in Kat's Attic,* Dutton (New York, NY), 1985.

Beatrice Gormley, *The Ghastly Glasses,* Dutton (New York, NY), 1985.

Barbara Williams, *Mitzi and the Elephants,* Dutton (New York, NY), 1985.

Mary Stolz, *The Explorer of Barkham Street,* Harper (New York, NY), 1985.

Barbara M. Joosse, *Fourth of July,* Knopf (New York, NY), 1985.

Jane O'Connor, *Lulu and the Witch Baby,* Harper (New York, NY), 1986.

Jane R. Thomas, *Wheels,* Clarion Books (New York, NY), 1986.

Barbara M. Joosse, *Jam Day,* Harper (New York, NY), 1987.

Jane O'Connor, *Lulu Goes to Witch School,* Harper (New York, NY), 1987.

Ruth Shaw Radlauer, *Molly,* Simon & Schuster (New York, NY), 1987.

Ruth Shaw Radlauer, *Molly Goes Hiking,* Simon & Schuster (New York, NY), 1987.

Doreen Rappaport, *The Boston Coffee Party,* Harper (New York, NY), 1987.

Marcia Sewall, *Ridin' That Strawberry Roan,* Puffin Books (New York, NY), 1987.

Beatrice Gormley, *Richard and the Vratch,* Avon (New York, NY), 1988.

Ruth Shaw Radlauer, *Molly Goes to the Library,* Prentice-Hall (New York, NY), 1988.

Ruth Shaw Radlauer, *Breakfast by Molly,* Prentice-Hall (New York, NY), 1988.

Rhoda Josephs, *The Baby Bubble Book,* Grosset & Dunlap (New York, NY), 1988.

Juanita Havill, *It Always Happens to Leona,* Crown (New York, NY), 1989.

Barbara M. Joosse, *Dinah's Mad, Bad Wishes,* HarperCollins (New York, NY), 1989.

Joan W. Bloss, *The Grandpa Days,* Simon & Schuster (New York, NY), 1989.

Beatrice Gormley, *The Magic Mean Machine,* Avon (New York, NY), 1989.

Beatrice Gormley, *More Fifth Grade Magic,* Dutton (New York, NY), 1989.

Lucy Diggs, *Selene Goes Home,* Macmillan (New York, NY), 1989.

Barbara A. Porte, *The Take-along Dog,* Greenwillow Books (New York, NY), 1989.

Achim Broger, *The Day Chubby Became Charles,* translated by Renee Vera Cafiero, HarperCollins (New York, NY), 1990.

Sally Wittman, *Stepbrother Sabotage,* HarperCollins (New York, NY), 1990.

Beatrice Gormley, *Wanted, UFO,* Dutton (New York, NY), 1990.

Juanita Havill, *Leona and Ike,* Crown (New York, NY), 1991.

Phyllis Hoffman, *Meatball,* HarperCollins (New York, NY), 1991.

Beatrice Gormley, *Sky Guys to White Cat,* Dutton (New York, NY), 1991.

Ann Bixby Herold, *The Butterfly Birthday,* Macmillan (New York, NY), 1991.

Marilyn Singer, *In My Tent,* Macmillan (New York, NY), 1992.

Patricia Reilly Giff, *Meet the Lincoln Lions Marching Band,* Dell (New York, NY), 1992.

Patricia Reilly Giff, *Yankee Doodle Drumsticks,* Dell (New York, NY), 1992.

Crescent Dragonwagon, *Annie Flies the Birthday Bike,* Macmillan (New York, NY), 1993.

Ruth Belov Gross, *If You Grew up with George Washington,* Scholastic, Inc. (New York, NY), 1993.

Paula Fox, reteller, *Amzat and His Brothers: Three Italian Tales,* remembered by Floriano Vecchio, Orchard Books (New York, NY), 1993.

Patricia Reilly Giff, *The Great Shamrock Disaster,* Dell (New York, NY), 1993.

Grace Maccarone, *Pizza Party,* Cartwheel Books (New York, NY), 1994.

Donald Hall, *Old Home Day,* Browndeer Press/Harcourt Brace (San Diego, CA), 1996.

Ann M. Martin, *Leo the Magnificent,* Scholastic, Inc. (New York, NY), 1996.

Michael Bedard, *The Divide,* Bantam Doubleday (New York, NY), 1997.

Judy Cox, *Rabbit Pirates: A Tale of the Spinach Main,* Browndeer Press/Harcourt Brace (San Diego, CA), 1999.

Arthur Dorros, *Ten to Go Tango,* HarperCollins (New York, NY), 2000.

Katherine Paterson, *The Field of the Dogs,* HarperCollins (New York, NY), 2001.

Eve Bunting, *Sing a Song of Piglets: A Calendar in Verse,* Clarion (New York, NY), 2002.

Barbara Shook Hazen, *Katie's Wish,* Dial Books (New York, NY), 2003.

Eileen Spinelli, *What Do Angels Wear?,* HarperCollins (New York, NY), 2003.

Doreen Rappaport, *The Secret Seder,* Hyperion (New York, NY), 2003.

Alice Schertle, *One, Two, I Love You,* Chronicle Books (San Francisco, CA), 2004.

Marilyn Singer, *So Many Kinds of Kisses,* Atheneum (New York, NY), 2004.

Eve Bunting, *That's What Leprechauns Do,* Clarion (New York, NY), 2005.

Natalie Kinsey-Warnock, *Noah's Ark,* HarperCollins (New York, NY), 2005.

Jan Karon and Melanie Cecka, *Cynthia Coppersmith's Violet Comes to Stay,* Viking (New York, NY), 2006.

Jan Karon and Melanie Cecka, *Cynthia Coppersmith's Violet Goes to the Country,* Viking (New York, NY), 2007.

Tess Weaver, *Cats Jumped In!,* Clarion (New York, NY), 2007.

Eve Bunting, *The Banshee,* Clarion Books (New York, NY), 2009.

Jane Cutler, *Guttersnipe,* Farrar Straus Giroux (New York, NY), 2009.

OTHER

(Contributor) William Abrahams, editor, *The O. Henry Collection: Best Short Stories,* Doubleday (New York, NY), 1976.

A Craving (novel), Avon (New York, NY), 1982.

Life Drawing, Delacorte (New York, NY), 1986.

Also contributor of short stories to *Massachusetts Review, Dark Horse,* and *Cricket.*

Sidelights

Emily Arnold McCully is a prolific and award-winning illustrator and author of children's books. Since the mid-1960s, she has illustrated over one hundred works by other authors, such as Arnold Adoff's *Black Is Brown Is Tan* and Eve Bunting's *That's What Leprechauns Do,* and has also produced several of her own picture books, including *Picnic* and *Squirrel and John Muir.* McCully's children's books have earned numerous honors: in 1984 she received a Christopher award for her first solo picture book, *Picnic,* and she also illustrated Meindert De Jong's National Book Award-winning *Journey from Peppermint Street.* McCully once commented that she strives for a "spontaneous, sketch-like quality" in her illustrations, and she considers characterization the most important aspect of illustrating books. "It is through the characters that the reader enters the story," she once noted.

Born in Galesburg, Illinois, in 1939, McCully began drawing around age three and within two years was already producing "fairly ambitious drawings of men with trouser cuffs, buttons, and pleats." Soon McCully became concerned with the subjects of her drawings. "To this day, I cannot imagine what my work would look like if I were a painter or sculptor instead of an illustrator," she went on. "The need to be linked to something else, to connect with a subject outside of oneself is, I think, at the heart of the impulse to illustrate, and is still the inspiration for all of my drawing."

As a child, McCully began writing and illustrating her own stories, whose characters were usually boys. "I envied . . . their freedom and action-packed lives," she once commented, "and my stories and art reflected this with lots of excitement and drama, and no pretty little girls sitting around not getting their dresses dirty." Similarly, McCully's reading preferences included adventure stories such as *Treasure Island* and *Robin Hood,* in addition to adventure comic strips which she also admired for the "economy of the dramatic techniques employed." She later became very interested in the works of the "Ashcan" school of eight American artists who were famous for their depictions of everyday life. McCully began copying their work from a book, while discovering her own preference for, as she once noted, "gritty, significant subject matter."

McCully's family moved to Long Island, New York, as a "very conventional" town with "an interesting sense of history, but . . . like a place under glass: there were no blacks, no Jews, no minorities of any stripe," as she once noted. A self-described "maverick" in high school, McCully stood out because of her drawing talents, and was influenced by an art teacher who encouraged her "naturally quick, spontaneous style of execution." Describing herself as the "only remotely left-wing person" among her peers, McCully "felt horribly out of sync and isolated" in her community yet was invigorated by nearby New York City. McCully often visited her father at his work as a documentary writer and producer in New York's Rockefeller Center, and also became fond of the Museum of Modern Art and of sketching people in Union Square Park. "New York City fueled my ambitions for an active life in the arts, theatre and publishing," she once explained. "I had visions of having a glamorous career as an illustrator for the *Saturday Evening Post.*"

Although McCully attended Brown University in Rhode Island with the intention of studying at the Rhode Island School of Design, she instead devoted time to her interests in the theater, reading, and art history. "I was tired of the freakishness that seemed to be part of being an artist," she once observed. "For years, people stood around me as I drew, marveling that I could reproduce someone or something. I threw myself into other activities . . . which I hadn't done before." She married after graduation, and attended Columbia University in New

York where she received a master's degree in art history. She eventually returned to drawing after growing "weary of making so many verbal descriptions of art works." In 1963, she moved to Belgium with her husband, an historian, and again became involved in drawing sketches of people and scenes, and also making collages. As she once noted, "This was very new for me, and I cultivated a freewheeling work style."

McCully once noted that she came to illustrating children's books "in a roundabout way." After returning from Europe, she settled outside of Philadelphia where her husband had a teaching job, and she began doing book review illustrations for the *New York Herald Tribune,* eventually moving into other freelance work. One of McCully's projects, a series of poster advertisements for a radio station, came to the attention of a New York City editor who approached McCully with the idea of illustrating a children's book. "At first, it wasn't easy for me to recapture a child's sensibility," the artist once

observed. "But as I went along, that came more naturally, and then having children of my own certainly helped."

McCully proved to be very successful in her new career; since illustrating her first book in 1966, she has gone on to provide artwork for countless children's books. Along the way she has collaborated with such acclaimed authors as Marjorie W. Sharmat, Mary Stolz, Betsy Byars, Arnold Adoff, and Eve Bunting. Originally published in 1973, Adoff's classic story *Black Is Brown Is Tan* was reprinted almost two decades later with new illustrations by McCully. According to a *Kirkus Reviews* critic, "this fresh rendition still makes a cogent statement" on interracial families. In Bunting's *That's What Leprechauns Do,* a trio of wee folk plays a number of pranks as they haul their pot of gold to the end of a rainbow. "McCully graces this lighthearted story with her characteristically expressive and charming watercolors," wrote Linda L. Walkins in *School Library*

***McCully pairs her adaptation of a traditional story with her detailed art in* Beautiful Warrior.** (Copyright © 1998 by Emily Arnold McCully. Reproduced by permission of Scholastic, Inc.)

McCully's original self-illustrated picture books include the U.S. Civil-War era story **The Escape of Oney Judge.** (Copyright © 2007 by Emily Arnold McCully. Reproduced by permission.)

Journal. McCully's ink-and-watercolor illustrations for *Guttersnipe,* Jane Cutler's book about a young immigrant boy in early-twentieth-century Canada, are filled with small details that convey both the character's emotions and the vitality of his urban neighborhood, wrote *Booklist* reviewer Hazel Rochman.

McCully branched out on her own in 1984 with *Picnic,* a storybook told entirely in watercolor paintings. The tale of a family of mice who go off for a picnic and discover that the youngest mouse has fallen out of their pickup truck, *Picnic* describes both the family's search and the experiences of the little mouse. "The story is . . . about the job of coming back after two separate adventures," she explained to Lael Locke in *Paper: The Monthly Guide to the Berkshires and the Hudson Valley.* "The little mouse who's lost is not utterly miserable—the mouse finds a way of coping with the situation, and I think that's very important." McCully's sequel, *First Snow,* recounts the youngest mouse's fear of sledding down a steep hill. "It's another very simple story, but it's funny and has to do with really essential feelings that little kids have—being afraid of sensations, and then experiencing them and loving it," she told Locke. "That's what's so wonderful about children's books . . . because they can't be terribly complicated, they get at things that are . . . basic and universal."

This sensitivity to children's emotional needs is evident throughout McCully's body of work; critics have expressed particular admiration for her series about a young nineteenth-century French girl, Mirette, who befriends The Great Bellini, a famous tightrope walker,

and helps him regain his lost confidence. *Mirette on the High Wire,* the series' introductory volume, won the Caldecott Medal, and its sequel, *Starring Mirette and Bellini,* was praised for its emotional depth. As a *Publishers Weekly* reviewer put it, McCully "speaks of universal issues—hunger, hopelessness, hard times, freedom—[in ways] that many children will grasp." In a third volume, *Mirette and Bellini Cross Niagara Falls,* Mirette and Bellini take their high-wire act to the famous east-coast landmark. The narrative "is gripping, the friendship theme is well developed, and the watercolor-and-pastel illustrations are breathtaking," remarked *Booklist* contributor Connie Fletcher.

In many other volumes, McCully incorporates rigorous historical research with stories marked by what her publisher, Arthur Levine, identified in a *Horn Book* article as a special "sense of drama." *The Ballot Box Battle* focuses on the struggle for women's suffrage, and *The Bobbin Girl* describes the life of factory girls in early-nineteenth-century New England textile mills. Victorian England is the setting for *Little Kit; or, The Industrious Flea Circus Girl,* a book that a reviewer for *Publishers Weekly* considered "a scrumptious period piece [that] balances treachery with poetic justice in as cozy a manner as any of Dickens's peers." *The Pirate Queen* is based on the adventures of legendary Irish pirate Grania O'Malley, a contemporary of English queen Elizabeth I.

Another bold woman is featured in *Beautiful Warrior: The Legend of the Nun's Kung Fu,* which tells the story of a girl in seventeenth-century China who rejects the circumscribed roles available to women and goes to live in a monastery, where she can devote her life to mastering kung fu. Margaret A. Chang, writing in *School Library Journal,* noted McCully's "fresh interpretation of classic Chinese art" in the double page spreads that "evoke the sweep of Chinese scroll paintings," and concluded that the author-illustrator not only "authentically recreates a period of Chinese history," but also presents "two lively heroines." Deborah Stevenson, in a review of *Beautiful Warrior* for *Bulletin of the Center for Children's Books,* noted that "McCully's control of her unusual story is superb, and she doesn't make the mistake of ignoring the more conventionally appealing aspects in order to focus on high-minded philosophy."

McCully recounts the tale of a gifted vocalist in *The Orphan Singer,* a story set in eighteenth-century Italy. "McCully's swift-moving text and signature compositions, a textured blend of watercolor and tempera, awaken the sights and sounds of Venice's canals," a *Publishers Weekly* critic remarked. In *The Battle for St. Michael's,* a work based on an incident from the War of 1812, nine-year-old Caroline Banning helps her townspeople defend their homes from British soldiers. "McCully does a fine job of making the battle scene exciting without glorifying war or violence," stated a contributor to *Kirkus Reviews.* The unlikely relationship between Floy "Squirrel" Hutchings, a lonely young girl living in the Yosemite Valley, and a famed naturalist is the focus of *Squirrel and John Muir,* another work of historical fiction. According to *Horn Book* reviewer Hilary Breed Van Dusen, McCully's illustrations capture "the warmth and respect between man and child" as well as "the beauty of one of America's natural treasures."

McCully depicts the life of the woman who established the Eastern Paper Bag Company in *Marvelous Mattie: How Margaret E. Knight Became an Inventor.* Knight produced more than ninety inventions during her lifetime, including a foot warmer, a snow sled, and a safety device for textile mills. McCully's "lucid narrative and crisp period illustrations illuminate the early life of an impressive visionary," commented a reviewer in *Publishers Weekly,* and Betty Carter, writing in *Horn Book,* noted that the artist's "delicate pen and ink sketches of Mattie's designs . . . give additional insight into the workings of an inventor's mind." In *The Escape of Oney Judge: Martha Washington's Slave Finds Freedom,* McCully recounts the tale of a young seamstress who was owned by the nation's first president. "McCully doesn't pull many punches," noted a contributor in *Kirkus Reviews,* and *Booklist* writer Ilene Cooper stated that the author "takes a rather sophisticated piece of history and writes it in a way that will draw in children."

Manjiro: The Boy Who Risked His Life for Two Countries tells the true story of a fourteen-year-old Japanese fisherman who was marooned with four others when their small boat was destroyed in a storm in 1841. After six harrowing months they were rescued by an American whaling ship whose captain brought Manjiro home with him to New Bedford, Massachusetts. He sent the boy to school and taught him farming and sea navigation so that he would eventually be able to sail back to Japan. A homecoming, Manjiro knew, would carry extreme risks: Japan had been officially closed to the outside world for more than two hundred years and anyone who left the country and then attempted to reenter it could be put to death. Nevertheless, Manjiro wanted to try. Captain Whitfield helped him obtain funding for the journey, and Manjiro earned several hundred dollars panning for gold in California. After about nine years in the United States, he and two of the other shipwrecked fishermen made the trip back to Japan. There, they were thrown into jail and questioned extensively. Manjiro was able to give Japanese authorities much information about American life, including such new technologies as railroads, drawbridges, and wristwatches. He explained that the United States was interested in trading with Japan and wanted to engage in friendly diplomatic relations. Finally Manjiro was released, and achieved a position of honor as a samurai. His efforts helped to open Japan's doors to the outside world after more than 250 years of isolation.

Reviewers admired the dramatic narrative and realistic watercolor illustrations through which McCully tells Manjiro's story. A writer for *Kirkus Reviews* described the book's text as "historically rich" and a "first-rate introduction" to an historical figure who has received relatively little attention in the history of U.S.-Japanese relations. Barbara Auerbach, writing in *School Library Journal,* admired the concrete details in McCully's illustrations, noting that they convey the contrasts between Japanese and American fishing practices of the period as well as the dangers of life at sea. *Manjiro,* concluded the reviewer, is an "exciting account of a pivotal period in U.S.-Japanese history." McCully includes an appendix of books and Web sites related to her topic, as well as an author's note that explains the context in which Japan pursued its isolationist policy and its subsequent decision to open itself to outside trade.

Renowned as both an illustrator and a writer, McCully divides her time between the two interests. "Picture books offer me a chance to unite two powerful impulses—to write and to draw," she remarked in an essay for the *St. James Guide to Children's Writers.* "Although I was pulled into children's books by a visionary editor, and didn't think of it myself, the field has given me a chance to tell stories in a way that uniquely satisfies this pair of urges." She also once relayed words of advice to aspiring artists and writers: "Don't worry about what other people are doing. Don't try to emulate. Work from what is inside you, crying out—however softly, however timidly—for expression."

Biographical and Critical Sources

BOOKS

Children's Literature Review, Volume 46, Gale (Detroit, MI), 1998.

Pendergast, Sara, and Tom Pendergast, editors, *St. James Guide to Children's Writers,* 5th edition, St. James Press (Detroit, MI), 1999.

Silvey, Anita, editor, *Children's Books and Their Creators,* Houghton Mifflin (Boston, MA), 1995.

Something about the Author Autobiography Series, Volume 7, Gale (Detroit, MI), 1998.

PERIODICALS

Booklist, November 11, 1992, Kathryn Broderick, review of *Mirette on the High Wire,* p. 609; November 15, 2000, Connie Fletcher, review of *Mirette and Bellini Cross Niagara Falls,* p. 638; September 1, 2001, Hazel Rochman, review of *The Grandmas Trick-or-Treat,* p. 121; September 15, 2002, Carolyn Phelan, review of *The Battle for St. Michael's,* p. 235; May 1, 2003, Carolyn Phelan, review of *Picnic,* p. 1605; July, 2004, Hazel Rochman, review of *Squirrel and John Muir,* p. 1849; January 1, 2005, Hazel Rochman, review of *The Secret Seder,* p. 860; February 15, 2006, Gillian

Engberg, review of *Marvelous Mattie: How Margaret E. Knight Became an Inventor,* p. 110; November 15, 2006, Ilene Cooper, review of *The Escape of Oney Judge: Martha Washington's Slave Finds Freedom,* p. 44, and Carolyn Phelan, review of *Cynthia Coppersmith's Violet Comes to Stay,* p. 52; September 1, 2007, Carolyn Phelan, review of *Cynthia Coppersmith's Violet Goes to the Country,* p. 130; September 1, 2008, Carolyn Phelan, review of *Manjiro: The Boy Who Risked His Life for Two Countries,* p. 93; January 1, 2009, Hazel Rochman, review of *Guttersnipe,* p. 90.

Bulletin of Center for Children's Books, March, 1998, Deborah Stevenson, review of *Beautiful Warrior: The Legend of the Nun's Kung Fu,* p. 233.

Horn Book, July-August 1993, Arthur Levine, "Emily Arnold McCully," p. 430; January-February, 2005, Hilary Breed Van Dusen, review of *Squirrel and John Muir,* p. 81; March-April, 2006, Betty Carter, review of *Marvelous Mattie: How Margaret E. Knight Became an Inventor,* p. 206; November 1, 2008, Roger Sutton, review of *Manjiro.*

Instructor, March, 1994, Judy Freeman, review of *Mirette on the High Wire,* p. 79.

Kirkus Reviews, October 15, 1992, review of *Mirette on the High Wire,* p. 1313; March 15, 2002, review of *Black Is Brown Is Tan,* p. 404; August 1, 2002, review of *The Battle for St. Michael's,* p. 1137; March 1, 2003, review of *Picnic,* p. 392; October 1, 2003, review of *What Do Angels Wear?,* p. 1230; January 15, 2007, review of *The Escape of Oney Judge,* p. 78; September 1, 2008, review of *Manjiro.*

Newsday, May 16, 1982, John Gabree, review of *A Craving.*

Paper: The Monthly Guide to the Berkshires and the Hudson Valley, April, 1984, Lael Locke, "Silent Stories, Moving Pictures."

Publishers Weekly, October 26, 1992, review of *Mirette on the High Wire,* p. 70; November 2, 1992, review of *Meet the Lincoln Lions Marching Band,* p. 71; April 12, 1993, review of *Amzat and His Brothers: Three Italian Tales,* p. 64; March 28, 1994, review of *My Real Family,* p. 96; September 5, 1994, review of *Crossing the New Bridge,* p. 109; December 12, 1994, review of *Little Kit; or, The Industrious Flea Circus Girl,* p. 62; October 9, 1995, review of *The Pirate Queen,* p. 85; June 3, 1996, review of *The Bobbin Girl,* p. 83; July 8, 1996, review of *The Ballot Box Battle,* p. 83; August 12, 1996, review of *Old Home Day,* p. 82; February 17, 1997, review of *Starring Mirette and Bellini,* p. 219; June 30, 1997, review of *Popcorn at the Palace,* p. 76; September 22, 1997, review of *The Divide,* p. 80; November 24, 1997, review of *Beautiful Warrior,* p. 73; March 29, 1999, review of *Mouse Practice,* p. 102; August 2, 1999, review of *Rabbit Pirates: A Tale of the Spinach Main,* p. 83; March 6, 2000, review of *Ten to Go Tango,* p. 109; March 13, 2000, review of *Hurry,* p. 84; August 14, 2000, review of *Mirette and Bellini Cross Niagara Falls,* p. 133; January 1, 2001, review of *The Field of the Dogs,* p. 93; February 5, 2001, review of *Four Hungry Kittens,* p. 87; October 22, 2001, review of *The Orphan Singer,* p. 87; August 26, 2002, review of *Katie's Wish,* p. 68; October 4, 2004, review of *One, Two, I Love You,* p. 86; January 9, 2006, review of *Marvelous Mattie,* p. 53.

School Library Journal, October, 1992, Ruth K. MacDonald, review of *Mirette on the High Wire,* p. 92; February, 1998, Margaret A. Chang, review of *Beautiful Warrior,* p. 88; November, 2000, Rosalyn Pierini, review of *Mirette and Bellini Cross Niagara Falls,* p. 126; March, 2001, Wendy Lukehart, review of *Four Hungry Kittens,* p. 214; August, 2002, Carol L. MacKay, review of *Sing a Song of Piglets: A Calendar in Verse,* p. 174; September, 2002, Jessica Snow, review of *The Battle for St. Michael's,* p. 201; January, 2004, Wendy Woodfill, review of *First Snow,* p. 102; September, 2005, Kathy Piehl, review of *Noah's Ark,* p. 175; February, 2006, Linda L. Walkins, review of *That's What Leprechauns Do,* p. 92; October 1, 2008, Barbara Auerbach, review of *Manjiro,* p. 134.

ONLINE

Children's Literature Web site, http://childrenslit.com/ (May 27, 2009), Marilyn Courtot, "Meet Authors and Illustrators: Emily Arnold McCully."*

*   *   *

MILLER, Karen 1949-
(Karen Hokanson Miller)

Personal
Born March 27, 1949; married; children: three sons, one daughter.

Addresses
Home—Burnsville, NC. *E-mail*—karenhokansonmiller@ gmail.com.

Career
Author. Formerly worked as a journalist, school teacher, and bookseller. Elementary-school tutor. Carolina Mountains Literary Festival, children's literature coordinator; former judge for *Writers' Digest* Writing Contest and Rebecca Caudhill Award.

Member
Author's Guild, American Library Association, National Council of Teachers of English, Society of Children's Book Writers and Illustrators, North Carolina Writers's Network.

Writings

Monsters and Water Beasts: Creatures of Fact or Fiction?, illustrated by Sergio Ruzzier, Henry Holt (New York, NY), 2007.

Karen Miller (Reproduced by permission.)

Contributor to periodicals, including *Chicago Tribune* and *National Geographic World.*

Sidelights

A former schoolteacher, Karen Miller drew on her experiences in the classroom to write her first book, *Monsters and Water Beasts: Creatures of Fact or Fiction?* Miller's students used to tell her that they could find nothing good to read, and their disinterest inspired her to produce a book that would capture their interest. Knowing that children have a perennial interest in scary creatures, she set out to provide factual information as

well as entertaining stories about such beasts. Finding monsters that were "real," was an important consideration, Miller explained on her home page.

Monsters and Water Beasts gives accounts of various creatures, from the well-known Bigfoot to such obscure beasts as the Jersey Devil and the sea maiden of Biloxi, Mississippi. The book reports the alleged sightings of these creatures, explains the physical evidence (such as footprints or tracks) that has been linked to them, and discusses the ways in which this information can be interpreted. Miller begins by discussing the 2002 discovery of the giant squid. This enormous creature, she explains, could be what ancient sailors had been talking about when they told stories of encountering gigantic sea serpents. Bringing similar objectivity to accounts of Big Foot, the Big Bird of Texas, the sea serpent of Gloucester, and the Cadborosaurus, among others, Miller considers the evidence for belief in these creatures as well as scientific theories that are skeptical.

Reviewing *Monsters and Water Beasts* in *School Library Journal,* Gloria Koster applauded Miller's extensive research and ability to "blend . . . the logical and the mysterious" in an engaging work for young readers. While a contributor to *Kirkus Reviews* considered other titles on this subject more fully informative, the reviewer praised Miller's "lucid prose and matter-of-fact tone." In a similar vein, *Booklist* contributor Carolyn Phelan gave *Monsters and Water Beasts* high marks for its appealing design and its "even, nonsensational tone."

Biographical and Critical Sources

PERIODICALS

Booklist, May 1, 2007, Carolyn Phelan, review of *Monsters and Water Beasts: Creatures of Fact or Fiction?,* p. 91.
Kirkus Reviews, April 15, 2007, review of *Monsters and Water Beasts.*
School Library Journal, July, 2007, Gloria Koster, review of *Monsters and Water Beasts,* p. 119.

ONLINE

Karen Miller Home Page, http://www.karenhokanson miller.com (June 9, 2009).
Western North Carolina Woman Online, http://wnc-woman. com/ (June 9, 2009), Britt Kaufmann, review of *Monsters and Water Beasts.**

*   *   *

MILLER, Karen Hokanson
See MILLER, Karen

MITCHELL, Susan
See MITCHELL, Susan K.

*   *   *

MITCHELL, Susan K. 1972-
(Susan Mitchell)

Personal

Born April 1, 1972; married Joseph Mitchell; children: Emily, Rachel. *Education:* University of Texas—Austin, B.A., 1993.

Addresses

Home—Houston, TX. *E-mail*—susan@susankmitchell.com.

Career

Writer. Ford Motor Company, worked in finance for seven years; Creative Learning Center, preschool teacher for seven years.

Member

Society of Children's Book Writers and Illustrators.

Awards, Honors

National Parenting Publication Award, 2007, and Teacher's Choice Award, *Learning* magazine, and Mom's Choice Award, both 2008, all for *The Rainforest Grew All Around.*

Writings

FOR CHILDREN

The Rainforest Grew All Around, Sylvan Dell (Mt. Pleasant, SC), 2007.
Stone Pizza, RGU Group (Tempe, AZ), 2007.
Kersplatypus, illustrated by Sherry Rogers, Sylvan Dell (Mt. Pleasant, SC), 2008.
Amusement Park Rides, Gareth Stevens (Pleasantville, NY), 2009.
(Illustrator) Paula Deen, *Paula Deen's Cookbook for the Lunch-box Set,* Simon & Schuster (New York, NY), 2009.

Contributor to *Boy's Quest* magazine.

"TODAY'S SUPERSTARS" BIOGRAPHY SERIES

Will Smith, Gareth Stevens (Milwaukee, WI), 2007.
Tyra Banks, Gareth Stevens (Milwaukee, WI), 2007.
Jessica Simpson, Gareth Stevens (Milwaukee, WI), 2007.

Susan K. Mitchell (Reproduced by permission.)

Jack Black, Gareth Stevens (Milwaukee, WI), 2007.

"MEGASTRUCTURES" NONFICTION SERIES

The Largest Indoor Parks and Malls, Gareth Stevens (Milwaukee, WI), 2007.
The Largest Stadiums, Gareth Stevens (Milwaukee, WI), 2007.
The Longest Bridges, Gareth Stevens (Milwaukee, WI), 2007.
The Longest Tunnels, Gareth Stevens (Milwaukee, WI), 2007.
The Biggest Thrill Rides, Gareth Stevens (Milwaukee, WI), 2007.
The Tallest Buildings, Gareth Stevens (Milwaukee, WI), 2007.

"AMAZING ANIMAL DEFENSES" NONFICTION SERIES

Animals with Awesome Armor: Shells, Scales, and Exoskeletons, Enslow Publishing (Berkeley Heights, NJ), 2008.
Animal Body-part Regenerators: Growing New Heads, Tails, and Legs, Enslow Publishing (Berkeley Heights, NJ), 2008.
Animal Chemical Combat: Poisons, Smells, and Slime, Enslow Publishing (Berkeley Heights, NJ), 2008.
Animals with Crafty Camouflage: Hiding in Plain Sight, Enslow Publishing (Berkeley Heights, NJ), 2008.
Animal Mimics: Look-alikes and Copycats, Enslow Publishing (Berkeley Heights, NJ), 2008.
Animals with Wicked Weapons: Stingers, Barbs, and Quills, Enslow Publishing (Berkeley Heights, NJ), 2008.

Sidelights

Susan K. Mitchell has written several picture books and nonfiction books for young readers. "I'm not one of those children's authors who will tell you she 'grew up writing,'" Mitchell stated on her home page. "Looking back, I didn't even realize that I loved it." Mitchell, who grew up in a small town in rural Texas, added that writing "was something I liked to do, but it never dawned on me that writing was something that I could do for a living."

After graduating from college with a degree in English literature, Mitchell worked in finance for several years before she had children, and she later taught preschool. After penning a letter to the editor of her newspaper, she realized how much she had always enjoyed writing. She began writing children's books and tried for several years to publish them. Finally, after writing a number of books that did not sell, Mitchell found success with *The Rainforest Grew All Around* and *Stone Pizza.* "My goal," she told Valerie Sweeten in the *Houston Chronicle,* "was to be published by the time I turned thirty-five, and I can't believe I did it. I didn't expect to be where I am, but I'm a little pleasantly surprised."

The Rainforest Grew All Around centers on a tall kapok tree and, in a rhyming text, tells of all the different animals, insects, birds, and plants which depend on the tree for life. A critic for *Children's Bookwatch* called the book "beautifully written" and dubbed it "an ideal introduction to rainforest ecology." Kathy Piehl concluded in *School Library Journal* that **The Rainforest Grew All Around serves as a "lively introduction to plants and animals of the Amazon rainforest."**

Kersplatypus, as Mitchell explained in an interview for the *World of Words* Web log, "was born from a single

Mitchell's **The Rainforest Grew All Around** *introduces readers to sloths and other interesting creatures with help from Connie McClennan's art.* (Sylvan Dell Publishing, 2007. Illustration copyright © 2007 by Connie McLennan.)

word." When her two-year-old daughter fell down, the author picked her up and said "Oh baby! Did you go kersplatypus?" Having invented this word on the spot, Mitchell found it so much fun that she used is as the basis for a story about a little platypus looking for where he belongs. He wanders through Australia, his native habitat, encountering several other animals native to this isolated region. The brushtail possum, observing his claws, encourages the platypus to climb trees with them, but the platypus goes falls and goes kersplat. In another discouraging encounter, he meets a kookaburra that thinks the platypus's webbed feet and duck bill make him a type of waterfowl that can take to the air. Again, Platypus goes kersplat. Wallaby thinks that Platypus's fur makes him a kindred species and encourages the creature to hop, but once more Platypus goes kersplat. Finally the confused young animal goes on a traditional Australian walkabout, a journey of discovery and identity.

Many reviewers applauded *Kersplatypus* as a delightful blend of whimsy and factual information about Australian species and their characteristics. A contributor to *Ready Set Read Reviews* online described the book as a "sweet story" that "children will love" and that gently introduces important lessons on diversity. Similarly, *School Library Journal* reviewer Patricia Manning praised the book for its enjoyable approach to classroom topics, concluding that it "will provide a springboard for discussions on friendship and bullying." A writer for *Children's Bookwatch* admired *Kersplatypus* as a "delightful, enthusiastic, and educational" book for young children.

For the "Today's Superstars" series Mitchell has written brief biographies of several performers of interest to young readers, including Will Smith, Tyra Banks, Jessica Simpson, and Jack Black. She is also the author of a six-book series on megastructures, including *The Largest Stadiums, The Longest Bridges,* and *The Tallest Buildings.* These books take a lot of research, but as Mitchell explained to Sweeten: "It's neat to be a temporary expert on a lot of different subjects."

Among the many titles in Mitchell's "Amazing Animal Defenses" series are *Animal Mimics: Look-alikes and Copycats, Animals with Awesome Armor: Shells, Scales, and Exoskeletons, Animal Body-part Regenerators: Growing New Heads, Tails, and Legs,* and *Animal Chemical Combat: Poisons, Smells, and Slime.* In *Animal Chemical Combat* Mitchell discusses the chemical defenses used by monarch butterflies, bombardier beetles, poison dart frogs, and skunks. *Animal Body-part Regenerators* includes material on starfish, salamanders, earthworms, and crayfish. Reviewing *Animal Chemical Combat* in *Science Teacher,* Claudia Fetters observed that the all books in the series "present important concepts in a format that will appeal to reluctant readers." The titles, continued Fetters, combine appealing graphic design with text that is organized in brief, easily digested segments.

Biographical and Critical Sources

PERIODICALS

Booklist, June 1, 2007, Carolyn Phelan, *The Rainforest Grew All Around,* p. 78.

Children's Bookwatch, August, 2007, review of *The Rainforest Grew All Around;* February 1, 2008, review of *Kersplatypus;* December 1, 2008, review of *Animal Mimics: Look-alikes and Copycats.*

Houston Chronicle, July 19, 2007, Valerie Sweeten, "Faces in the Crowd: Mitchell Leaves Classroom for World of Books," p. 2.

Kirkus Reviews, March 15, 2007, review of *The Rainforest Grew All Around.*

Publishers Weekly, February 11, 2008, review of *Kersplatypus,* p. 68.

School Library Journal, August, 2007, Kathy Piehl, review of *The Rainforest Grew All Around,* p. 102; August 1, 2008, Patricia Manning, review of *Kersplatypus,* p. 99.

Science Teacher, January 1, 2009, Claudia Fetters, review of *Animal Chemical Combat: Poisons, Smells, and Slime,* p. 74.

ONLINE

Ready Set Read Reviews Web site, http://readysetread reviews.blogspot.com/ (June 9, 2009), review of *Kersplatypus.*

Susan K. Mitchell Home Page, http:www.susankmitchell.com (June 9, 2009).

Well-Read Child Web log, http://wellreadchild.blogspot.com/ (June 9, 2009), review of *Kersplatypus.*

World of Words Web log, http://marcieaf.blogspot.com/ (June 9, 2009), interview with Mitchell.*

* * *

MORRIS, Carla
(Carla D. Morris)

Personal

Married Steven R. Morris; children: three. *Education:* Brigham Young University, B.A., M.L.S.

Addresses

Home—Springville, UT. *E-mail*—carlam@provo.lib.ut.us.

Career

Writer. Provo City Library, Provo, UT, reference librarian, 1979-90; children's services manager, 1991—Served on Caldecott Medal committee, 2004.

Awards, Honors

2007 Booksense Children's Pick, 2007, and Kansas State Reading Circle Recommendation, 2008, both for *The Boy Who Was Raised by Librarians.*

Writings

(As Carla D. Morris; with husband, Steven R. Morris) *How to Index Your Local Newspaper Using WordPerfect or Miscrosoft Word for Windows,* Libraries Unlimited (Englewood, CO), 1995.

The Boy Who Was Raised by Librarians, illustrations by Brad Sneed, Peachtree Press (Atlanta, GA), 2007.

Sidelights

Carla Morris has been a librarian at the Provo City Library since 1979. During her years there, a teenaged boy worked at the library and was "adopted" by several of the librarians. Because he was living on his own, they helped him with his schoolwork and with learning life skills such as cooking. Eventually, the boy grew up and became a librarian himself. Morris adapted this real-life story for her book *The Boy Who Was Raised by Librarians.* "I'm fascinated by the idea of coming up with a story and having it live on in the minds of children," she told Tad Walch in the *Deseret Morning News.*

Morris's story concerns Melvin, a kindergartner who befriends three reference librarians—Marge, Betty, and Leeola. Not only do they answer all of his many questions, the librarians also help the boy to win a local spelling bee by guiding him to the best research materials. As he grows up, Melvin attends all of the library's programs and works there part-time in high school. When he goes away to college, he keeps in touch with the librarians by letter and phone. Years later, Melvin returns to his old friends—as the new librarian.

The Boy Who Was Raised by Librarians, noted Ilene Cooper in *Booklist,* "effectively shows the solid bond that can develop between librarians and their young patrons," and *School Library Journal* contributor Catherine Threadgill remarked that the author's "enthusiasm for the field permeates her narrative." "Kids should get a kick out of the geeky Melvin," noted a critic in *Kirkus Reviews,* and a reviewer for *Children's Bookwatch* concluded that *The Boy Who Was Raised by Librarians* is a "warmhearted and upbeat children's story."

Biographical and Critical Sources

PERIODICALS

Booklist, May 1, 2007, Ilene Cooper, review of *The Boy Who Was Raised by Librarians,* p. 100.

Children's Bookwatch, May, 2007, review of *The Boy Who Was Raised by Librarians.*

Deseret Morning News, March 27, 2007, Tad Walch, "Provo Librarian's Book Imitates Life."

Kirkus Reviews, March 15, 2007, review of *The Boy Who Was Raised by Librarians.*

School Library Journal, June, 2007, Catherine Threadgill, review of *The Boy Who Was Raised by Librarians,* p. 116.

ONLINE

Provo City Library Web site, http://www.provo.lib.ut.us/ (April 15, 2008), "Carla Morris."

Utah State Library Web site, http://library.utah.gov/ (April 15, 2008), "Carla Morris."*

*   *   *

MORRIS, Carla D.
See MORRIS, Carla

*   *   *

MURPHY, Elizabeth Ann Maureen
See MURPHY, Liz

*   *   *

MURPHY, Liz 1964-
(Elizabeth Ann Maureen Murphy)

Personal

Born November 24, 1964, in Surrey, England; married; children: two sons. *Education:* Attended Kingston Art College.

Addresses

Home—Montclair, NJ.

Career

Writer and illustrator.

Writings

SELF-ILLUSTRATED

ABC Doctor: Staying Healthy from A to Z, Blue Apple Books (Maplewood, NJ), 2007.

A Dictionary of Dance, Blue Apple Books (Maplewood, NJ), 2007.

Who Am I?, Begin Smart Books (Maplewood, NJ), 2008.

ILLUSTRATOR

Bernadette Peters, *Broadway Barks,* Blue Apple Books (Maplewood, NJ), 2008.

Harriet Ziefert, *ABC Dentist: Healthy Teeth from A to Z,* Blue Apple Books (Maplewood, NJ), 2008.

Hugh Martin and Ralph Blane, *Have Yourself a Merry Little Christmas,* Blue Apple Books (Maplewood, NJ), 2009.

Harriet Ziefert, *My Forever Dress,* Blue Apple Books (Maplewood, NJ), 2009.

Sidelights

Liz Murphy, the author and illustrator of several children's books, "has a wonderful whimsical style that is very versatile," according to an online contributor to *Goodnite Moon Kids.* In *ABC Doctor: Staying Healthy from A to Z,* Murphy presents a variety of medical tools, procedures, and physical conditions, such as fever and otoscope, and introduces young readers to the practices of a routine visit to a doctor's office. "Murphy has compiled an interesting array of terms," observed Linda Stasleus in *School Library Journal,* and a critic in *Kirkus Reviews* stated that her "colorful mixed-media illustrations add texture and humor without diminishing the importance of the topics."

In *A Dictionary of Dance,* Murphy offers an overview of the dance world. "This book is a light-hearted but informative hop, skip and a jump through the complex

Liz Murphy creates the colorful art that brings to life Harriet Ziefert's family-centered tale in **The Forever Dress.** (Blue Apple Books, 2009. Illustration copyright © 2009 by Liz Murphy. Reproduced by permission.)

language of dance," the author/illustrator explained in an interview on *Powells.com.* Murphy discusses dance terms such as arabesque, quickstep, and recital, and also explores different types of ethnic dances, including the Chinese dragon dance and the hula. A contributor to *Kirkus Reviews* noted of *A Dictionary of Dance* that this "first look at dance for preschoolers" tackles "a complex subject." "The dynamic and colorful illustrations have real child appeal," Carol Schene commented in a *School Library Journal* review of the same book.

Murphy illustrated actress and singer Bernadette Peters's *Broadway Barks,* a book benefitting the annual adopt-a-thon benefit that Peters founded with fellow actor Mary Tyler Moore as a way to raise awareness about animal shelters in Manhattan. Douglas is an abandoned, scraggly, gray terrier who wanders around New York's Central Park. He laments the fact that there is nobody to love him, feed him, or take care of him. One day he happens to meet Peters, who takes him in a taxi to Shubert Alley where Moore is emceeing a pet-show pageant. There he is cared for and participates in the pageant, doing his best to sing and dance on stage. Eventually he obtains a new little-girl owner and is given the name Kramer. The book includes a two-track CD that serves as a narration of the book by Peters herself and a piano-bar style version of a lullaby that Kramer's owner would sing to him.

Although a *Publishers Weekly* contributor maintained that *Broadway Barks* has an "appeal [that] . . . rests chiefly on the good intentions of its creators," Kathy Krasniewicz observed in *School Library Journal* that "Murphy's bright mixed-media cartoon illustrations" are a bright spot: she uses "snips of measuring tape, telegrams, and pieces of printed matter" to create the story's Manhattan backdrop. In *Kirkus Reviews,* a critic decided that "the story is simple but humorous, artfully complemented by Murphy's delightful mixed-media illustrations."

Harriet Ziefert's *ABC Dentist: Healthy Teeth from A to Z,* illustrated by Murphy, is similar to *ABC Doctor,* in this case providing an art-filled explanation of dental check-ups. Here Murphy uses her illustration techniques to give children an education about the teeth and gums, as well as of the tools and sights that they will see at the dentist's office. Ziefert's story also reassures children that a visit to the dentist or hygienist will not hurt as much as they think. Nancy Baumann, writing in *School Library Journal,* noted that *ABC Dentist* features "colorful illustrations and diagrams" that provide a realistic picture" of a typical trip to the dentist.

Biographical and Critical Sources

PERIODICALS

Booklist, April 1, 2007, Jennifer Mattson, review of *ABC Doctor: Staying Healthy from A to Z,* p. 58; November 15, 2008, Abby Nolan, review of *ABC Dentist: Healthy Teeth from A to Z,* p. 47.
Kirkus Reviews, March 15, 2007, review of *ABC Doctor;* August 15, 2007, review of *A Dictionary of Dance;* May 15, 2008, review of *Broadway Barks.*
Publishers Weekly, September 3, 2007, review of *A Dictionary of Dance,* p. 61; May 5, 2008, review of *Broadway Barks,* p. 61.
School Library Journal, April, 2007, Linda Stasleus, review of *ABC Doctor,* p. 124; September, 2007, Carol Schene, review of *A Dictionary of Dance,* p. 185; August 1, 2008, Kathy Krasniewicz, review of *Broadway Barks,* p. 100; November 1, 2008, Nancy Baumann, review of *ABC Dentist,* p. 113.

ONLINE

Goodnite Moon Kids Web site, http://www.goodnitemoon kids.com/ (May 27, 2009), "Liz Murphy."
Powells.com, http://www.powells.com/ (March 10, 2008), interview with Murphy.*

N-O

NANCE, Andrew

Personal

Born in TX; married; children: Will, Jamie.

Addresses

Home—St. Augustine, FL. *E-mail*—andrewnance@ hholt.com.

Career

Writer and broadcaster. Radio talk-show host, 1976-2001.

Writings

Daemon Hall (juvenile novel), illustrated by Coleman Polhemus, Henry Holt (New York, NY), 2007.

Sidelights

Andrew Nance turned to writing full time only after retiring from a quarter-century career as a radio talk-show host. As Nance explained on the Daemon Hall Web site, "I took the long road rather than the interstate" to publication. By this he meant not only that he did not start writing until finishing his first career, but also that his debut novel, *Daemon Hall,* took six years from inception to publication.

Daemon Hall began life as a series of short stories that were inspired, in part, by the work of horror writers such as Stephen King. With additional help from one of his sons, who was ten at the time, Nance came up with the idea of gathering a group of kids in a spooky house and giving all but one of them a candle. Each would then tell a scary story, after which a candle would be blown out. This would continue until the last story, which had to be told in the dark. Initially, the short stories in Nance's book were each told from the point of view of a different character. As Nance noted: "I didn't want to patronize young adult readers with a horror-lite novel, so I don't hold any punches. It's a dark and suspenseful book." Failing to find an agent for the work, Nance finally succeeded in attracting the attention of one editor who wanted him to turn the story collection into a novel. When that publisher ceased publication of young-adult titles, Henry Holt agreed to publish *Daemon Hall*.

Daemon Hall tells the tale of famous horror author Ian Tremblin, who initiates a writing contest for his young readers. The winner will get a book contract, and when Tremblin selects his five finalists, among them Wade Reilly, the main character of the book. Tremblin gathers these five for one night in Daemon Hall, a mansion that local people say is haunted. The contestants will tell stories all night, putting out one of the nine candles they are given after each tale, and in the morning Tremblin will pick the winner. However, the candles are the only form of light in the mansion, and as they are extinguished, Daemon Hall gets gloomier and scarier. Ultimately, the five young writers realize that they are not simply telling horror stories: they are actually experiencing them.

According to a *Children's Bookwatch* contributor, *Daemon Hall* is a "tense thriller," and *Booklist* contributor Ed Sullivan predicted that youngsters "looking for creepy chills and thrills will find plenty of satisfaction in this fast-paced book." Donna Rosenblum, writing in *School Library Journal,* wrote that although Nance's characters are not entirely convincing, his "gripping page-turner . . . will keep readers on the edge of their seats," and a *Kirkus Reviews* critic termed *Daemon Hall* a "gentle horror tale."

As Nance told *Cynsations* online interview Cynthia Leitich Smith, he regrets taking so long to discover his new career as a writer. "My dad always told me I could do whatever I wanted," he explained, "but deep down I didn't believe him. I didn't realize he was right until just a few years ago. So maybe it was a delayed start, but I'm finally pursuing my dream. I hope any teens who read this will take it as a lesson to follow their passion."

Biographical and Critical Sources

PERIODICALS

Booklist, July 1, 2007, Ed Sullivan, review of *Daemon Hall,* p. 48.

Bulletin of the Center for Children's Books, June, 2007, Cindy Welch, review of *Daemon Hall,* p. 433.

Children's Bookwatch, August, 2007, review of *Daemon Hall.*

Kirkus Reviews, June 1, 2007, review of *Daemon Hall.*

School Library Journal, December, 2007, Donna Rosenblum, review of *Daemon Hall,* p. 138.

Voice of Youth Advocates, April, 2007, Laura Panter, review of *Daemon Hall,* p. 68.

ONLINE

Cynsations Web site, http://www.cynthialeitichsmith. blogspot.com/ (August 16, 2007), Cynthia Leitich Smith, interview with Nance.

Daemon Hall Web site, http://www.daemonhall.com (January 1, 2010).*

*   *   *

NIX, Garth 1963-

Personal

Born 1963, in Melbourne, Victoria, Australia; married, 2000; wife's name Anna; children: two sons. *Education:* University of Canberra, B.A., 1986. *Hobbies and other interests:* Traveling, fishing, bodysurfing, book collecting, reading, films.

Addresses

Home—Sydney, New South Wales, Australia. *E-mail*—garthnix@ozemail.com.au.

Career

Author, editor, publicist, public-relations consultant, and agent. Worked for Australian government; worked in a bookshop in Sydney, New South Wales, Australia; senior editor for multinational publisher; Gotley Nix Evans Pty. Ltd., Sydney, marketing communications consultant, 1996-98; Curtis Brown (literary agent), Australia, part-time agent, 1999-2002. *Military service:* Served four years in Australian Army Reserve.

Awards, Honors

Aurelis Awards for Best Fantasy Novel and Best YA Novel, both 1995, Notable Book designation and Best Book for Young Adults designation, both American Li-

Garth Nix (Photograph by Robert McFarlane. Reproduced by permission.)

brary Association (ALA), Recommended Fantasy Novel designation, *Locus* magazine, and Books for the Teen Age designation, New York Public Library, all 1997, Popular Paperbacks for Young Adults selection, ALA, 2003, and six state-award shortlists, all for *Sabriel;* Outstanding Titles selection, *Voice of Youth Advocates,* 1996, for *Sabriel,* and 1997, for *Shade's Children;* Aurealis Award shortlist, 1997, Best Book for Young Adults designation, ALA, Pick of the Lists choice, American Bookseller Association, Notable Book designation, Children's Book Council of Australia, Heartland Prize shortlist, Pacific Northwest Reader's Choice Awards, South Carolina Reader's Choice Awards, Evergreen YA Award, Garden State Young Reader's Awards, and Popular Paperbacks for Young Adults selection, ALA, all 2004, all for *Shade's Children;* Adelaide Festival Award for Children's Literature, Best Book for Young Adults designation, ALA, Recommended Reading Fantasy Novel choice, *Locus* magazine, Young-Adult and Fantasy Novel shortlist, Aurealis Awards, and Australian Science Fiction Achievement Award shortlist, all 2002, all for *Lirael: Daughter of the Clayr.*

Writings

FOR CHILDREN; EASY READERS

Bill the Inventor (also see below), illustrated by Nan Bodsworth, Koala Books (Sydney, New South Wales, Australia), 1998.

Blackbread the Pirate (also see below), Koala Books (Sydney, New South Wales, Australia), 1999.

Serena and the Sea Serpent (also see below), illustrated by Stephen Michael King, Puffin (New York, NY), 2001.

One Beastly Beast: Two Aliens, Three Inventors, Four Fantastic Tales (includes *Bill the Inventor, Blackbread the Pirate,* and *Serena and the Sea Serpent*), illustrated by Brian Biggs, HarperCollins (New York, NY), 2005.

"VERY CLEVER BABY" SERIES

Very Clever Baby's First Reader: A Simple Reader for Your Child Featuring Freddy the Fish and Easy Words, Nix Books (Sydney, New South Wales, Australia), 1988.

Very Clever Baby's Ben Hur: Starring Freddy the Fish as Charlton Heston, Nix Books (Sydney, New South Wales, Australia), 1988.

Very Clever Baby's Guide to the Greenhouse Effect, Nix Books (Sydney, New South Wales, Australia), 1992.

Very Clever Baby's First Christmas, Text Publishing Co. (Melbourne, New South Wales, Australia), 1998.

"OLD KINGDOM" TRILOGY; FOR YOUNG ADULTS

Sabriel, HarperCollins (New York, NY), 1995.

Lirael: Daughter of the Clayr, HarperCollins (New York, NY), 2001.

Abhorsen, HarperCollins (New York, NY), 2003.

The Abhorsen Trilogy (omnibus; box set), HarperCollins (New York, NY), 2005, published in one volume as *The Abhorsen Chronicles,* HarperCollins (New York, NY), 2009.

"SEVENTH TOWER" NOVEL SERIES

The Fall, Scholastic, Inc. (New York, NY), 2000.

Castle, Scholastic, Inc. (New York, NY), 2000.

Aenir, Scholastic, Inc. (New York, NY), 2001.

Above the Veil, Scholastic, Inc. (New York, NY), 2001.

Into Battle, Scholastic, Inc. (New York, NY), 2001.

The Violet Keystone, Scholastic, Inc. (New York, NY), 2001.

"KEYS TO THE KINGDOM" NOVEL SERIES

Mister Monday, Scholastic, Inc. (New York, NY), 2004.

Grim Tuesday, Scholastic, Inc. (New York, NY), 2004.

Drowned Wednesday, Scholastic, Inc. (New York, NY), 2005.

Sir Thursday, Scholastic, Inc. (New York, NY), 2006.

Lady Friday, Scholastic, Inc. (New York, NY), 2006.

Superior Saturday, Scholastic, Inc. (New York, NY), 2008.

OTHER

The Ragwitch, Pan Books (Sydney, New South Wales, Australia), 1990, Tor (New York, NY), 1995.

Shade's Children, HarperCollins (New York, NY), 1997.

The Calusari ("X Files" series), HarperCollins (New York, NY), 1997.

Across the Wall: Tales of the Abhorsen and Other Stories, Eos (New York, NY), 2005.

Work represented in anthologies, including *Fantastic Worlds,* 1999; *A Wolf a the Door,* 2000; and *The Year's Best Science Fiction and Fantasy for Teens,* edited by Jane Yolen and Patrick Nielsen Hayden, Tor (New York, NY), 2005. Also author of short stories; coauthor of shows for dinner theater.

Adaptations

Several of Nix's titles have been adapted as audiobooks.

Sidelights

The author of dozens of books for children and young adults, Australian writer Garth Nix is best known for his fantasy novels in the "Old Kingdom" trilogy, which includes *Sabriel, Lirael: Daughter of the Clayr,* and *Abhorsen.* Writing for a slightly younger audience, he has also penned the six-novel cycle published as the "Seventh Tower" series as well as the ongoing "Keys to the Kingdom" fantasy saga.

Nix is known for his engaging and finely detailed fiction. He told Kelly Milner Halls for *Teenreads* online about the need for fantasy and magic in his own life and how it helps to fuel his popular fiction. "Like most fantasy authors, I would love to have magic in this world," Nix explained. "It would be great to be able to fly, or summon a complete restaurant meal on a white tablecloth to a deserted beach, or to take the shape of an animal. But I wouldn't want the downside of most fantasy books—the enemies, evil creatures, and threats to the whole world—and my sense of balance indicates that you can't have the good without the bad." Nix has also explained the genesis of his novels on his home page: "Most of my books seem to stem from a single image or thought that lodges in my brain and slowly grows into something that needs to be expressed. That thought may be a 'what if?' or perhaps just an image. . . . Typically I seem to think about a book for a year or so before I actually start writing."

Born in 1963, in Melbourne, Victoria, Australia, Nix grew up in Canberra with an older and a younger brother. His father worked in science, while his mother was an artist, working with papermaking. Both parents wrote and read widely, so Nix had a firm foundation for his own future work. In fact, as Nix has noted, his mother was reading J.R.R. Tolkien's "Lord of the Rings" trilogy when she was pregnant with him, "so I absorbed this master work of fantasy *in utero,* as it were."

"I went all through school in Canberra," Nix remarked in an autobiographical sketch on his home page, "but as with many authors, much of my education came from books. . . . My apprenticeship as an author began with reading." Early on he encountered the works of Ursula Le Guin, Robert Heinlein, Robert Louis Stevenson, John Masefield, Mary Stewart, Isaac Asimov, Madeleine L'Engle, and a variety of other fantasy and science fiction authors. He would much rather read a book than do his homework, but did well in school. "I was a smart and smart-mouthed kid," he remarked on his home page, "but I got on pretty well with everyone, probably because my best friend was always the school captain in every school and he was friends with everybody."

At age seventeen, Nix considered a career as an army officer, so he joined the Australian Army Reserve, serving for one weekend a month and one month per year in training. However, he discovered that he did not want to make the military his career, but enjoyed the part-time soldiering enough to stick with it, learning how to build bridges and then blow them up. He was also going to the University of Canberra during these years, and worked a paper-shuffling job with the Australian government for a year. He saved enough money to go traveling for six months, hitting the roads in England. It was during this time away from Australia that he began writing, composing the short story "Sam, Cars and the Cuckoo" while on the road. He not only learned of its sale when he returned to Australia and was contacted for reprint rights.

Cover of Nix's debut middle-grade novel The Ragwitch, *which recounts the amazing adventures of two siblings who fall under the power of a maniacal toy.* (Copyright © 1990 by Garth Nix. Reproduced by permission of St. Martin's Press.)

With this success, Nix decided he could become a professional writer. To that end, he earned a bachelor's degree in professional writing from the University of Canberra, and immediately took a job at Dalton's Bookshop in Canberra. "I now believe that anyone who works in publishing should spend at least three months in a bookshop, where the final product ends up," he once commented. Nix spent six months at the job, and then went into publishing, working as a sales representative, publicist, and editor to gain knowledge of all ends of the publishing and writing industry. During the six years he spent in publishing, he also became a published novelist.

Nix's earliest publications were far from fantasy, although they do include elements of the fantastical. His self-published "Very Clever Baby" books are parodies, pling fun at an easy readers and the movie *Ben Hur.* "They're little books that I first made back in 1988 as presents for some friends expecting babies, on the basis that all parents think their babies are geniuses," Nix explained to Claire E. White on *Writers Write.* Greeting-card sized, the little books are intended for adults rather than children.

If the "Very Clever Baby Books" were intended as a joke, there was nothing joke-like about Nix's first published novel, *The Ragwitch,* which he had worked on as part of his degree requirement. Published in Australia in 1990, the novel tells the story of Paul and his sister Julia who are exploring a prehistoric garbage dump. There they find a nest that contains a rag doll that has the power to enslave others; and Julia becomes its first victim. Paul must then go into a bizarre fantasy world in order to save his sister. Reviewing this first novel, Ann Tolman wrote in *Australian Bookseller and Publisher* that Nix "skillfully relates a magical tale which begins in a nice and easy way, but soon develops into a compelling and involving story of a journey through evil times." Tolman further noted that the book provides "good adult mystic escapism with considerable imaginative experiences for the reader." Similarly, Laurie Copping, writing in the *Canberra Times,* called *The Ragwitch* an "engrossing novel which should be enjoyed by true lovers of high fantasy."

Nix traveled in Turkey, Syria, Jordan, Iran, and Pakistan in 1993. During the trip, be began his next novel, *Sabriel,* finishing it upon his return to Australia. Also on his return, he left publishing for the public relations firm he helped to establish. The first volume in an eventual trilogy, *Sabriel* was described as "a vividly imagined fantasy" by *School Library Journal* contributor John Peters. Sabriel, a young woman, has been trained by her father, Abhorsen, a necromancer who, unlike others of his trade, puts uneasy souls to rest instead of calling them to life. Sabriel is in her last year of boarding school when she receives Abhorsen's necromancing tools and sword and realizes that her father's life is in danger—he has left the Land of the Living. Sabriel leaves the safety of her school to return to the Old

Kingdom, which her father was supposed to protect, in order to rescue him. As she travels to the world beyond the Land of the Living to the Gates of Death, she is joined by Mogget, a powerful being in the form of a cat, and the prince Touchstone. With their help, Sabriel battles her way past monsters, beasts, and evil spirits until she reaches her father, "only to lose him permanently in the opening rounds of a vicious, wild climax," as Peters explained.

According to Peters, *Sabriel* "is guaranteed to keep readers up way past their bedtime." "Rich, complex, involving, hard to put down," according to a *Publishers Weekly* critic, the novel "is excellent high fantasy." *Booklist* reviewer Sally Estes compared the novel favorably to English writer Philip Pullman's fantasy *The Golden Compass,* stating that Nix's storyline "charges along at a gallop, imbued with an encompassing sense of looming disaster." Writing in *Horn Book,* Ann A. Flowers commented that Nix's "story is remarkable for the level of originality of the fantastic elements . . . and for the subtle presentation, which leaves readers to explore for themselves the complex structure and significance of the magic elements." According to a critic for *Voice of Youth Advocates, Sabriel* is "one of the best fantasies of this or any other year."

Nix's novel, *Shade's Children* is science fiction. Nonetheless, wrote a *Publishers Weekly* critic, the book "tells essentially the same story" as *Sabriel,* with its "desperate quest by a talented few." In *Shade's Children* a psychic young boy, Gold-Eye, runs to escape the evil Overlords who use the body parts of children for their own insidious purposes. The novel is set in a future time when the earth has been taken over by terrible aliens that have destroyed all humans over age fourteen; the only adult presence is Shade, a computer-generated hologram. Gold-Eye joins a group of teenagers who, working from Shade's submarine base, fight the Overlords. In addition to battling the aliens, these young people must deal with betrayal and with losing half their group; however, they learn about their special talents and achieve victory through their sacrifices.

A *Publishers Weekly* reviewer concluded that, while *Shade's Children* "lacks some of the emotional depth of Nix's first work, it will draw (and keep) fans of the genre." According to a critic in *Kirkus Reviews,* the book "combines plenty of comic-book action in a sci-fi setting to produce an exciting read. . . . [An] action-adventure with uncommon appeal outside the genre." Flowers praised Nix's characterization of his young protagonists, adding that "the author leaves the reader to draw many conclusions from scattered evidence, hence capturing and holding the audience's attention all the way to the bittersweet ending." Donna L. Scanlon, writing in *Voice of Youth Advocates,* had further praise for the title, noting that through "a fast-paced combination of narrative, transcripts, chilling statistical reports, and shifting points of view, Nix depicts a chilling future." For Scanlon, Nix's grim futuristic view is also

Cover of Nix's novel Aenir, *part of his "Seventh Tower" series featuring artwork by Larry Rostant.* (Illustration copyright © 2001 by Scholastic, Inc. Reproduced by permission of Scholastic, Inc.)

"laced with hope," while *Reading Time* contributor Kevin Steinberger deemed *Shade's Children* "one of the best adolescent reads of the year."

Following the publication of *Shade's Children,* Nix left his public relations firm to devote his time to writing, and also met the woman who would become his wife. After writing *The Calusari,* a novelization of an episode from the television series, *The X-Files,* he set to work to complete *Lirael,* the next novel in the "Old Kingdom" series, as well as several easy readers for young children: *Bill the Inventor, Blackbread the Pirate,* and *Serena and the Sea Serpent.* Russ Merrin, reviewing *Blackbread the Pirate* in *Magpies,* described it as "utterly delightful nonsense." *Serena and the Sea Serpent,* about a little girl who saves a town from a misunderstood vegetarian sea serpent, was hailed as a "great story," according to another *Magpies* contributor. These stories would be re-illustrated by Brian Bigs and included in *One Beastly Beast: Two Aliens, Three Inventors, Four Fantastic Tales,* described as "a quartet of wacky yarns set in fantasy-laced worlds and topped off with plenty of wordplay" by a *Publishers Weekly* contributor. A *Kirkus Reviews* contributor described the stories as "thoroughly ridiculous and hugely enjoyable."

Lirael takes place fourteen years after the action in *Sabriel,* and the Old Kingdom is still facing dangers, this time from an evil necromancer who wants to free a terribly evil being. Here Nix focuses on a group of clairvoyant women, the Clayr, who are gifted with what is called the "Sight." One of these, Lirael, does not have such powers, partly due to the mystery of her birth. Turning fourteen, she fears that she will never gain the Sight and become an adult. Yet she does have magic powers, and in the company of the Disreputable Dog, she is able to complete a quest that wins her the trust of her fellow Clayr. When they thus entrust her with an even-more-dangerous and seemingly impossible mission, Prince Sameth, son of King Touchstone and Sabriel, fears he is not fit to perform the duties of office after battling with the evil necromancer, Hedge. Sameth and Lirael ultimately team up to battle the evil force attacking the Old Kingdom in a book "outstanding" for its "imaginative magical descriptions, plot intrigues, and adventure sequences," according to *Horn Book* contributor Anita L. Burkam.

Beth Wright, reviewing *Lirael* for *School Library Journal,* praised Nix's novel for its "fast-paced plot" as well as for the intricacy of the "haunting and unusual, exhaustively and flawlessly conceived connections among . . . rulers and guardians, and the magic that infuses them all." In *Booklist* Sally Estes also lauded the book, noting that "the characterizations are appealing," and that Nix "not only maintains the intricate world he created for the earlier book but also continues the frenetic pace of the action and the level of violence." Janice M. Del Negro, writing in *Bulletin of the Center for Children's Books,* commended the author for creating a book "filled with hair-raising escapes, desperate flights, relentless pursuits, and magical duels, described in sensual language that makes the scenes live." A reviewer for *Publishers Weekly* likewise found Nix's creation of the Old Kingdom "entrancing and complicated."

The third installment in the "Old Kingdom" series, *Abhorsen,* find Sameth and Lirael continuing to do battle with the forces of the dead, brought together by the evil Hedge. Again Disreputable Dog and Mogget are on hand to help out their respective companions. Lirael is now Abhorsen-in-waiting and must travel into death to foil plans to release the Destroyer from an age-old prison. Secrets are revealed and ends tied up in this concluding novel of the trilogy, a book at once "breathtaking, bittersweet, and utterly unforgettable," as a critic for *Kirkus Reviews* described it. A reviewer for *Publishers Weekly* was also impressed by Nix's achievement, calling *Abhorsen* a "riveting continuation" of the saga as well as an "allegory regarding war and peace and a testament to friendship." Estes, writing in *Booklist,* similarly held that the "tension throughout the story is palatable" and the conclusion is "satisfying." In the opinion of London *Times* contributor Amanda Craig, "the evocative prose and strong sense of character lift *Abhorsen* into a thrillingly complex, metaphysical adventure that oozes menace and mystery."

A tie-in to Nix's "Old Kingdom" books, *Across the Wall: Tales of the Abhorsen and Other Stories* collects twelve tales of horror, science fiction, and fantasy, as well as a novella set in the Old Kingdom. The selections range from Nix's take on an Arthurian legend to a choose-your-own-adventure story to a retelling of "Hansel and Gretel." Readers will "find a nice range of writing from one of the leading fantasy writers at work today," a critic in *Kirkus Reviews* remarked of *Across the Wall*

In between completing the "Old Kingdom" series, Nix also busied himself working on a six-part series for Scholastic Press and Lucas Films, "The Seventh Tower," a children's fantasy series featuring young Tal, a Chosen one of Orange Order from the Castle of the Seven Towers and his adventures in search of the Sunstones which he needs to save not only his family but his future. Tal's world is in the dark, literally; the sun only shines above the mysterious Veil, high above in the atmosphere over the Seven Towers. Tal's father disappears in the first book of the series, *The Fall,* on the very day that Tal is ascending to the throne. His missing father is in possession of the Sunstone, which Tal needs for the ascension. Without the Sunstone, Tal cannot bind himself to a Shadowspirit, and failing that, he will lose not only his Chosen status, but also will not be able to find a cure for his mother's illness. Joining Tal in his search for this talisman is the young woman, Milla. Reviewing the fourth book in the series, *Above the Veil,* in *Publishers Weekly,* a critic praised Nix's creation of a "very complex world," and predicted that series fans will enjoy the book's "exciting chase scenes, and stunning revelations."

Beginning in 2004, Nix turned his attention to a planned seven-volume series titled "Keys to the Kingdom." The saga center on the exploits of Arthur Penhaligon, a severely asthmatic seventh grader who gains possession of a mysterious atlas as well as a powerful key shaped like the minute hand of a clock. When a sleeping sickness descends upon his world, Arthur enters the magical realm of the House where he learns that he is the rightful heir to a vital will left by the Architect of creation. In *Mister Monday,* the first work in the series, Arthur finds himself pursued by the Fetchers, a terrifying group under the control of Mister Monday, one of the Morrow Days who refuse to honor the Architect's wishes. "Nix conveys beautifully the feeling of pursuing a desperate quest against the backdrop of a surreal universe where we don't understand the rules," wrote Anne Johnstone in the Glasgow *Herald.* "Not just the stuff of nightmare but an epigram for every adolescent attempting to find a place in the adult world."

In *Grim Tuesday,* Arthur is summoned to battle his second foe, a nasty, greedy individual who holds claim to the second fragment of the will and the second key. According to *School Library Journal* reviewer Susan L. Rogers, Arthur's "adventures are absorbing and entertaining, with worthy characters and thought-provoking situations." Arthur takes to the high seas to combat his next foe, a Morrow Day who has transformed into a gigantic whale, in *Drowned Wednesday,* "another great entry with a cliff-hanger ending," according to Karyn N. Silverman in *School Library Journal.* In *Sir Thursday,* Arthur is drafted into the army of the titular character and joins a war against the Nithlings. In the opinion of *Kliatt* contributor Deirdre Root, "fans will devour" this fourth work in the series. *Lady Friday* concerns Arthur's struggles to obtain the fifth key from the evil Morrow Day who has kidnapped one of his allies. "As always," commented Cheri Dobbs in *School Library Journal,* "Nix's writing is witty and the plays on words are entertaining."

The sixth volume in the "Keys to the Kingdom" series, *Superior Saturday,* finds Arthur in search of the sixth key while attempting to conceal his identity, his powers, and his journey to immortality. Now in possession of the fifth part of the will and five keys, he seeks the next, which is in the possession of Superior Saturday, who is not only a trustee of the will but also the oldest and most powerful of the sorcerers of the House. As he increasingly relies on his powers, Arthur finds himself becoming more of a Denizen of the world he inhabits and unable to return to the real world. He must continue, however, if he is to save that world, including his own home city, which has been touched by plague.

In reviewing *Superior Saturday* for *Kidsreads.com,* Sarah Sawtelle wrote that "Arthur has gone from a reluctant young hero to a determined, (almost) fearless young leader." Thomas Murphy, reviewing the novel in *Aussie Reviews* online, commented that, as with the earlier books in this series, "there is plenty of action, loads of twists and turns and a great range of characters both quirky and gruesome."

In his books for young readers, Nix creates amazing and intricate worlds, a cast of characters that stick in the imagination, and lessons of friendship and loyalty that resonate. According to K.V. Johansen, writing in *Resource Links,* "Nix's ability to create unique and vividly detailed secondary worlds, interesting, engaging characters both strong and vulnerable, and plots in which neither tension nor balance between desperate struggle and hope of success is lost, along with an excellent prose style, makes him stand out among today's fantasy writers for young people."

Biographical and Critical Sources

BOOKS

Children's Literature Review, Volume 68, Gale (Detroit, MI), 2001.
St. James Guide to Young-Adult Writers, 2nd edition, edited by Tom Pendergast and Sara Pendergast, St. James Press (Detroit, MI), 1999.

PERIODICALS

Austin American-Statesman, July 21, 2005, Jeff Salamon, "Fantasy Author Speaks for a Spell about His Magic," p. E1.
Australian Bookseller and Publisher, November, 1990, Ann Tolman, review of *The Ragwitch.*
Booklist, October 1, 1996, Sally Estes, review of *Sabriel,* p. 350; April 15, 2001, Sally Estes, review of *Lirael: Daughter of the Clayr,* p. 1557; July, 2001, Jennifer Hubert, review of *Shade's Children,* p. 1999; January 1, 2003, Sally Estes, review of *Abhorsen,* p. 871; June 1, 2005, Jennifer Mattson, review of *Across the Wall: Tales of the Abhorsen and Other Stories,* p. 1787; July, 2005, Jennifer Mattson, review of *Drowned Wednesday,* p. 1926; February 15, 2006, Carolyn Phelan, review of *Sir Thursday,* p. 92; July 1, 2007, Carolyn Phelan, review of *One Beastly Beast: Two Aliens, Three Inventors, Four Fantastic Tales,* p. 62; November 15, 2008, Carolyn Phelan, review of *Superior Saturday,* p. 40.
Bulletin of the Center for Children's Books, May, 2001, Janice M. Del Negro, review of *Lirael,* pp. 348-349.
Canberra Times, June 2, 1991, Laurie Copping, review of *The Ragwitch.*
Children's Bookwatch, September, 2008, review of *Superior Saturday.*
Herald (Glasgow, Scotland), January 31, 2004, Anne Johnstone, "Welcome to Their Worlds; Fuelled by Fantasy, Garth Nix and Christopher Paolini Now Join the Genre's Big Guns," p. 6.
Horn Book, January-February, 1997, Ann A. Flowers, review of *Sabriel,* pp. 64-65; September-October, 1997, Ann A. Flowers, review of *Shade's Children,* pp. 576-77; July-August, 2001, Anita L. Burkam, review of *Lirael,* p. 459.
Journal of Adolescent & Adult Literacy, October, 2004, Amy Fiske, review of *Grim Tuesday,* p. 178.
Kirkus Reviews, August 15, 1997, review of *Shade's Children,* pp. 1309-1310; December 15, 2002, review of *Abhorsen,* pp. 1854-1855; June 15, 2005, review of *Across the Wall,* p. 688; August 1, 2007, review of *One Beastly Beast.*
Kliatt, January, 1998, Lesley S.J. Farmer, review of *Sabriel,* p. 17; January, 2004, Deirdre Root, review of *Mister Monday,* p. 24; July, 2004, Deirdre Root, review of *Grim Tuesday,* p. 32; January, 2005, Donna Scanlon, review of *Abhorsen,* p. 20; March, 2006, Deirdre Root, review of *Sir Thursday,* p. 16.
Magpies, September, 1998, Annette Dale Meiklejohn, review of *Bill the Inventor,* p. 33; September, 1999, Russ Merrin, review of *Blackbread the Pirate,* p. 28; March, 2001, review of *Serena and the Sea Serpent,* p. 29.
Publishers Weekly, October 21, 1996, review of *Sabriel,* p. 84; June 16, 1997, review of *Shade's Children,* p. 60; March 19, 2001, review of *Lirael,* p. 101; March 18, 2002, John F. Baker, "Garth Nix," p. 16; May 27, 2002, review of *Lirael,* p. 62; November 25, 2002, review of *Abhorsen,* p. 70; February 16, 2004, review of *Grim Tuesday,* p. 175; July 18, 2005, review of *Across the Wall,* p. 208; August 6, 2007, review of *One Beastly Beast,* p. 189.

Reading Time, November, 1997, Kevin Steinberger, review of *Shade's Children,* p. 35.

Resource Links, December, 2003, K.V. Johansen, "The Twenty-first Century: J.K. Rowling, Neil Gaiman, Garth Nix," p. 30.

School Library Journal, September, 1996, John Peters, review of *Sabriel,* p. 228; May, 1998, review of *Shade's Children,* p. 52; May, 2001, Beth Wright, review of *Lirael,* p. 157; September, 2001, John Peters, review of *Above the Veil,* p. 231; February, 2003, Sharon Rawlins, review of *Abhorsen,* p. 146; December, 2003, Ginny Collier, review of *Mister Monday,* p. 158; August, 2004, Susan L. Rogers, review of *Grim Tuesday,* p. 127; July, 2005, Karyn N. Silverman, review of *Drowned Wednesday,* p. 106; November, 2005, Carolyn Lehman, review of *Across the Wall,* p. 144; March, 2006, Richard J. Snyder, review of *Sir Thursday,* p. 228; June, 2007, Cheri Dobbs, review of *Lady Friday,* p. 156; September, 2007, Elaine E. Knight, review of *One Beastly Beast,* p. 173.

Times (London, England), May 1, 2004, review of *Abhorsen,* p. 17.

Voice of Youth Advocates, June, 1997, review of *Sabriel;* February, 1998, Suzann Manczuk and Ray Barber, review of *Shade's Children,* p. 366; June, 1998, Donna M. Scanlon, review of *Shade's Children,* p. 132.

ONLINE

Aussie Reviews Online, http://www.aussiereviews.com/ (May 29, 2009), Thomas Murphy, review of *Superior Saturday.*

Garth Nix Home Page, http://www.garthnix.com (May 29, 2009).

Jubilee Books Web site, http://www.jubileebooks.co.uk/jubilee/magazine (September 1, 2002), Joseph Pike, interview with Nix.

Kidsreads.com, http://www.kidsreads.com/ (May 29, 2009), Sarah Sawtelle, review of *Superior Saturday.*

Teenreads.com, http://www.teenreads.com/ (March 10, 2008), Kelly Milner Halls, interview with Nix.

Trades Online, http://www.the-trades.com/ (June 25, 2008), R.J. Carter, review of *Superior Saturday.*

Writers Write Web site, http://www.writerswrite.com/ (July-August, 2000), Claire E. White, interview with Nix.*

*   *   *

ORMEROD, Jan 1946-
(Janette Louise Ormerod)

Personal

Born September 23, 1946, in Bunbury, Western Australia, Australia; daughter of Jack and Thelma Hendry; married Paul Ormerod (an information scientist), January 21, 1971 (divorced, 1991); children: Sophie, Laura. *Education:* Western Australian Institute of Technology, associateship (graphic design), 1966, (art teaching), 1973; Claremont Teachers College, teacher's certificate, 1967.

Addresses

Home—Uppingham, England. *Agent*—Laura Cecil, 17 Alwyne Villas, London N1 2HG, England.

Career

Author and illustrator of children's books. Western Australian Education Department, Bunbury, art teacher, 1968-72; Mt. Lawley College of Advanced Education, Perth, Western Australia, lecturer in art education, 1973-75; Western Australian Institute of Technology, Perth, part-time lecturer in drawing and basic design, 1976-79.

Member

Society of Authors.

Awards, Honors

Kate Greenaway Medal commendations, 1982, for *Sunshine,* and 1986, for *Happy Christmas, Gemma;* Mother Goose Award, and Australian Picture Book of the Year Award, Children's Book Council of Australia (CBCA), both 1982, both for *Sunshine;* Notable Book citations, American Library Association (ALA), 1981, for *Sunshine,* 1982, for *Moonlight,* 1985, for *Dad's Back, Messy Baby, Sleeping,* and *Reading,* 1986, for *The Story of Chicken Licken,* and 1987, for *Bend and Stretch, Making Friends, Mom's Home,* and *This Little Nose;* Australian Honor Book designation, International Board on Books for Young People, 2006, for *Lizzie Nonsense;* Western Australian Premier's Award shortlist and Picture Book of the Year shortlist, CBCA, both 2007, both for *The Water Witcher.*

Writings

SELF-ILLUSTRATED; FOR CHILDREN

Sunshine, Lothrop (New York, NY), 1981, revised edition, Frances Lincoln (London, England), 2005.

Moonlight, Lothrop (New York, NY), 1981, revised edition, Frances Lincoln (London, England), 2005.

Be Brave, Billy, Dent (London, England), 1983.

101 Things to Do with a Baby, Lothrop (New York, NY), 1984.

(Reteller) *The Story of Chicken Licken,* Walker (London, England), 1985, Lothrop (New York, NY), 1986.

Young Joe, Lothrop (New York, NY), 1986.

Silly Goose, Lothrop (New York, NY), 1986.

Our Ollie, Lothrop (New York, NY), 1986.

Just like Me, Lothrop (New York, NY), 1986.

Gemma's First Christmas, Lothrop (New York, NY), 1987.

The Saucepan Game, Lothrop (New York, NY), 1989.

Kitten Day, Lothrop (New York, NY), 1989.

(Reteller, with David Lloyd) *The Frog Prince,* Lothrop (New York, NY), 1990.

When We Went to the Zoo, Lothrop (New York, NY), 1991.

Come Back, Kittens, Lothrop (New York, NY), 1992.

Come Back, Puppies, Lothrop (New York, NY), 1992.

Joe Can Count, Mulberry Books (New York, NY), 1993.

Midnight Pillow Fight, Candlewick Press (Cambridge, MA), 1993.

Ms. McDonald Has a Class, Clarion (New York, NY), 1996.

Who's Whose?, Lothrop (New York, NY), 1998.

Emily Dances: A Novelty Action Book, Tupelo Books (New York, NY), 1999.

Ben Goes Swimming: A Novelty Action Book, HarperCollins (New York, NY), 1999.

Miss Mouse's Day, HarperCollins (New York, NY), 2001.

Miss Mouse Takes Off, HarperCollins (New York, NY), 2001.

Ten in a Bed, Dorling Kindersley (New York, NY), 2001.

Hat Off, Baby!, Barron's (Hauppage, NY), 2002.

Kiss It Better, Walker (London, England), 2003.

Toys' Teatime, Walker (London, England), 2003.

Lizzie Nonsense, Little Hare (Surry Hills, New South Wales, Australia), 2004, published as *Lizzie Nonsense: A Story of Pioneer Days,* Clarion (New York, NY), 2005.

When an Elephant Comes to School, Frances Lincoln (London, England), 2004, Orchard Books (New York, NY), 2005.

Ballet Sisters: The Duckling and the Swan, Scholastic, Inc. (New York, NY), 2007.

The Water Witcher, Little Hare (Surry Hills, New South Wales, Australia), 2007.

Ballet Sisters: The Newest Dancer, Scholastic, Inc. (New York, NY), 2008.

"JAN ORMEROD BABY BOOK" SERIES; SELF-ILLUSTRATED

Sleeping, Lothrop (New York, NY), 1985.

Reading, Lothrop (New York, NY), 1985.

Dad's Back, Lothrop (New York, NY), 1985.

Messy Baby, Lothrop (New York, NY), 1985.

Jan Ormerod's Baby Books, Lothrop (New York, NY), 1986.

Jan Ormerod's Little Ones, Lothrop (New York, NY), 1987.

"JAN ORMEROD NEW BABY BOOK" SERIES; SELF-ILLUSTRATED

Bend and Stretch, Lothrop (New York, NY), 1987.

Making Friends, Lothrop (New York, NY), 1987.

This Little Nose, Lothrop (New York, NY), 1987.

Mom's Home, Lothrop (New York, NY), 1987.

To Baby with Love, Lothrop (New York, NY), 1994.

Rock-a-Baby, Dutton (New York, NY), 1998.

FOR CHILDREN

If You're Happy and You Know It!, illustrated by Lindsey Gardiner, Star Bright Books (New York, NY), 2003.

Emily and Albert, illustrated by David Slonim, Chronicle Books (San Francisco, CA), 2004.

Doing the Animal Bop, illustrated by Lindsey Gardiner, Oxford University Press (Oxford, England), 2005.

Whoosh around the Mulberry Bush, illustrated by Lindsey Gardiner, Oxford University Press (Oxford, England), 2007.

Molly and Her Dad, illustrated by Carol Thompson, Roaring Brook Press (New York, NY), 2008.

ILLUSTRATOR

Jan Mark, *Hairs in the Palm of the Hand,* Kestrel (Harmondsworth, England), 1981.

Margaret Mahy, *The Chewing-Gum Rescue and Other Stories,* Dent (London, England), 1982.

Pat Thompson, compiler, *Rhymes around the Day,* Lothrop (New York, NY), 1983.

Karin Lorentzen, *Lanky Longlegs,* translated by Joan Tate, Atheneum (New York, NY), 1983.

Sarah Hayes, *Happy Christmas, Gemma,* Lothrop (New York, NY), 1986.

James M. Barrie, *Peter Pan,* Viking (New York, NY), 1987.

Sarah Hayes, *Eat up, Gemma,* Lothrop (New York, NY), 1988, reprinted, Walker (London, England), 2007.

Sarah Hayes, *Stamp Your Feet,* Lothrop (New York, NY), 1988.

Vivian French, *One Ballerina Two,* Lothrop (New York, NY), 1991.

Michelle Magorian, *Jump!,* Walker (London, England), 1992.

Jan Mark, *The Snow Maze,* Walker (London, England), 1992.

Enid Richemont, *The Magic Skateboard,* Candlewick Press (Cambridge, MA), 1992.

Elizabeth Clark, *Father Christmas and the Donkey,* Viking (New York, NY), 1993.

Helen E. Buckley, *Grandfather and I,* Lothrop (New York, NY), 1994.

Helen E. Buckley, *Grandmother and I,* Lothrop (New York, NY), 1994.

Norman Silver, *Cloud Nine,* Clarion (New York, NY), 1995.

Jack Bushnell, *Sky Dancer,* Lothrop (New York, NY), 1996.

Mary Hoffman, reteller, *A Twist in the Tail: Animal Stories from around the World,* Holt (New York, NY), 1998.

Helen Elizabeth Buckley, *Where Did Josie Go?,* Lothrop (New York, NY), 1999.

Robie H. Harris, *Goodbye Mousie,* Margaret K. McElderry (New York, NY), 2001.

Meredith Hooper, *Ponko and the South Pole,* Frances Lincoln (London, England), 2002.

Robie H. Harris, *I Am Not Going to School Today!,* Margaret K. McElderry (New York, NY), 2003.

Linda Ashman, *Mama's Day,* Simon & Schuster (New York, NY), 2006.

Katherine Applegate, *The Buffalo Storm,* Clarion (New York, NY), 2007.

Stephanie Calmenson, *May I Pet Your Dog? The How-to Guide for Kids Meeting Dogs (and Dogs Meeting Kids),* Clarion (New York, NY), 2007.

Sidelights

Australian-born author and illustrator Jan Ormerod has established herself as a sensitive and skillful creator of children's picture books, including such award-winning titles as *Sunshine* and *Lizzie Nonsense*. Often wordless or of minimal text, Ormerod's works are characterized by detailed watercolor illustrations that frequently depict warm domestic scenes. When assessing her work, reviewers have pointed to Ormerod's ability to render everyday events with both insight and gentle humor, a quality that makes her books appealing to both children and their parents. Her work has also been popular with critics; in a *Washington Post Book World* article, Michael Dirda judged Ormerod to be "a contemporary master of the board book."

Ormerod's family life inspired her successful career in children's literature. Her husband, Paul, worked as a children's librarian at the time the couple's first child, Sophie, was born. Sophie's interest in the books her father brought home for her encouraged Ormerod, then an art teacher, to begin creating picture books of her own. Confident of realizing some success in this venture, she and her husband decided to quit their jobs and move from Australia to London, England, home of a number of publishing companies. Ormerod drew on her training in graphic design to create a portfolio and submitted her illustrations to various London publishing houses. Her efforts resulted in the publication of *Sunshine* in 1981.

In *Sunshine* Ormerod's colorful, naturalistic illustrations depict a little girl's morning routine. Using cartoon-like panels to separate scenes from one another, Ormerod wordlessly presents the little girl (modeled after her daughter, Sophie) waking up, prodding her lethargic parents out of bed, getting dressed, eating breakfast, and going to school. Scenes such as the father distractedly allowing the breakfast toast to burn as he reads the newspaper provide comic relief. The companion book to *Sunshine, Moonlight* uses the same format to describe the end of the little girl's day: she eats dinner, takes a bath, listens to a story, and eventually goes to bed. Despite the absence of words in both books, Michele Landsberg stated in *Reading for the Love of It: Best Books for Young Readers,* that "the drama of nuance and character are fully present." In *Books for Your Children* Margaret Carter described Ormerod's illustrations as "gentle, tolerant, tender, observant and shrewd," and in *Growing Point,* Margery Fisher declared, "Domestic truth is achieved by pictures alone in *Moonlight,* and with complete success."

Several of Ormerod's books focus on small slices of day-to-day family life. In *Be Brave, Billy,* for instance, a little boy comes to terms with everyday anxieties, and in *101 Things to Do with a Baby* a young girl discovers a variety of activities that can be done with her new sibling. Reviewers praised these titles, assessing that Ormerod sensitively depicts the fears, jealousies, and triumphs of young children. Her illustrations in *101 Things to Do with a Baby* were deemed "magnificent" by Joe McGinniss in the *New York Times Book Review,* the critic adding that the pictures evoke "both the tenderness and tumult with which each day in a two-sibling household is filled."

Ormerod's two series of books for very young children also revolve around the home and family ties. The "Jan Ormerod Baby Book" series—highlighting a father and infant's affectionate relationship—includes *Reading* and *Dad's Back.* In *Reading* and *Sleeping* the baby attempts to become the center of the father's attention. Father cleans house in *Messy Baby,* while the child follows behind and undoes his handiwork. In *Dad's Back,* the father's return from an errand gives the child an opportunity to play with his keys, gloves, and scarf. Robert Wool, writing in the *New York Times Book Review,* noted that Ormerod effectively brings the father and baby's relationship to life "with a novelist's eye for detail and a painter's grasp of nuance." The reviewer added that Ormerod's "marvelous, soft, figurative drawings [make] you smile with recognition."

The "Jan Ormerod New Baby Book" series also focuses on a family relationship—this time between a pregnant mother and her infant—and includes *Bend and Stretch* and *This Little Nose.* In these books Mom exercises with baby underfoot, makes a doll for baby, and brings home a shopping bag full of items for the infant to explore. Critics judged that this series reflects Ormerod's familiarity with and understanding of parents and infants. In a *Horn Book* review Karen Jameyson declared that in "Ormerod's hands the most ordinary chunks of everyday life are given vivid shape and substance."

In a departure from her typical home settings, Ormerod uses minimal text and bright illustration panels to describe a family outing in *When We Went to the Zoo.* The reader follows two children and their father as they visit creatures such as gibbons, pelicans, elephants, otters, toucans, and orangutans. Near the zoo's exit the family notices a pair of sparrows building a nest and decides that "in the end we liked that best, spying the sparrows and their nest." Observant readers will have noticed the sparrows earlier, as they appear in the illustrations throughout the family's tour. Critics commented that drawing attention to the sparrows in a zoo of exotic animals reflects Ormerod's ability bring charm to the commonplace.

Ormerod collaborated with David Lloyd in Lloyd's retelling of the classic fairy tale *The Frog Prince,* which Ormerod illustrated using double-page spreads and decorative borders. In Ormerod and Lloyd's version, a princess loses her ball in a pond and promises a frog her love if he finds it for her. Once the frog retrieves the ball, however, the princess takes it and runs home, hoping the frog will forget her promise. The persistent frog follows her, and the princess is forced to keep her promise by letting the frog sit on her lap, eat with her, and sleep on her pillow. After sleeping on her pillow for three nights, the frog transforms into a prince and, "as in all the best deep, dark, and royal stories," the narrator states, "they lived happily ever after."

Inspired by the life of Ormerod's grandmother, *Lizzie Nonsense: A Story of Pioneer Days* illustrates the isolation of the Australian bush. With her father gone for weeks, young Lizzie must help her mother tend the garden, gather firewood, and mend clothes. "The text is simple yet evocative, emphasizing the parent-child relationship," *School Library Journal* reviewer Grace Oliff commented. According to London *Sunday Times* contributor Nick Robinson, Ormerod's drawings "convey dazzling sunshine, autumnal softness, interiors lit by oil lamps, and faces and bodies that express" a variety of emotions, and *Booklist* reviewer Gillian Engberg similarly noted that her "ethereal watercolor illustrations . . . powerfully evoke the history, the heat, the dust, and the brave, strong family."

In a humorous tale, *When an Elephant Comes to School,* a shy new student gets acclimated to his classroom. "Some of the pictures have the effect of collage; the elephant especially has some heft," wrote Ilene Cooper in *Booklist,* and Oliff remarked that Ormerod's "illustrations have clean lines and cheery colors." An older sibling learns to tolerate her admiring but feisty younger sister in *Ballet Sisters: The Duckling and the Swan,* an easy reader by Ormerod. Older sister Bonnie, slightly bossy but loving, is the graceful swan who takes ballet lessons and enjoys impressing her sibling with her beautiful costumes and movements. Sylvie, too young for dance lessons, is the more clumsy duckling, and waits in the wings for her turn to shine. She chafes at the younger-sister role that keeps her on the sidelines and gets into mild trouble when she tries too hard to emulate her sister. "The words and pictures work well together," Rachael Vilmar observed in *School Library Journal,* and Jennifer M. Brabander, writing in *Horn Book,* stated that "Ormerod's familiar clean line drawings, humorous and expressive, will help readers keep pace with this dancing duo."

A sequel to *Ballet Sisters: The Duckling and the Swan,* *Ballet Sisters: The Newest Dancer* focuses on Sylvie's being recognized as a budding talent in her own right. Sylvie is not old enough to start taking ballet classes, and the book follows her adventures as she meets her new teacher, enjoys a "not-birthday" party where she receives ballet clothing as presents, and attends her first real class. Back at home afterward, she and Bonnie play dress-up and dance together. Cooper, writing in *Booklist,* deemed this second story "delightful," and *School Library Journal* reviewer Catherine Callegari praised *Ballet Sisters: The Newest Dancer* for its effective combination of text and illustration.

The somber subject of divorce is given respectful and sympathetic treatment in Ormerod's picture book *Molly and Her Dad,* a book illustrated by Carol Thompson. Molly, who lives with her mother, scarcely knows her father, who lives so far away that frequent visits are not possible. The girl creates dramatic fantasies about him, imagining that he is an astronaut, a famous artist, or an explorer in the jungle. When her mother has to be out of town, however, Molly gets to spend some extended time with her real father, who flies in to care for her. Though the adjustment between Molly's idealized father and her real one is a bit of a challenge at first, the girl soon warms to the outgoing man who calls her silly names and loves cooking her spicy meal. And, when Papa visits Molly's school and entertains her classmates with his storytelling skills, Molly comes to see that, as her teacher says, he and she are like "two peas in a pod." Reviewers hailed the book as a sensitive but upbeat look at divorce from a child's perspective. Gillian Engberg, writing in *Booklist,* admired the author's reassuring tone, as did *School Library Journal* contributor Wendy Lukehart, who observed that "the story is warm and tender, and oh so satisfying." Calling *Molly and Her Dad* a "delightful" work, a writer for *Kirkus Reviews* observed that "Ormerod's spare text deftly captures Molly's child-centered concerns" and results in a book that is a "genuine celebration" of life in a nontraditional family.

In addition to her own work, Ormerod has illustrated a number of books by children's authors, among them *Hairs in the Palm of the Hand* by Jan Mark, *Peter Pan* by James M. Barrie, and *One Ballerina Two* by Vivian French. According to Michael Patrick Hearn writing in the *New York Times Book Review,* Ormerod "is a keen observer of the intimate details of childhood. . . . She can make the mundane beautiful with her extraordinary figure studies. . . . She can take the simplest subject . . . and weave it into an engrossing picture book."

Mary M. Burns, a reviewer in *Horn Book,* noted that Ormerod's illustrations in Mary Hoffman's *A Twist in the Tail: Animal Stories from around the World* "provide opportunities to extend the text without interrupting the pace." Joy Fleishhacker, writing in *School Library Journal,* noted that Ormerod's illustrations in *Goodbye Mousie* by Robie H. Harris include "pleasing buff-colored backgrounds" and "black-pencil line and watercolor washes echo the emotional nuances" of the book. A critic in *Publishers Weekly* also praise the book which describes a child's first experience with the death of a pet, stated that "the artist's fluid pencil lines underscore the vulnerability of the boy and the poignancy of his story."

Filled with unanswered questions about the first day of school, a jittery youngster refuses to leave home in *I Am Not Going to School Today!,* another collaboration between Ormerod and Harris. "Ormerod's colorful, expressive illustrations capture a child's anxiety and the warmth of family with equal success," Karin Snelson noted of the work in *Booklist.* Linda Ashman's *Mama's Day* depicts the many ways that mothers share their love for their infants. According to a *Kirkus Reviews* critic, "the pencil-and-wash pictures" for this book "are in Ormerod's rosy crystalline style." In *Booklist* Jennifer Mattson stated that "Ashman's skillful verse and

Ormerod's cozy ink-and-gouache artwork improve upon many other picture-book fulminations on mother love." "Together, the eloquent simplicity of the words and the understated warmth of the pictures exude a cozy contemplativeness," observed a reviewer in *Publishers Weekly.*

The Buffalo Storm, a work by Katherine Applegate, follows a pioneer family as it travels across the plains to Oregon. When young Hallie, who is frightened of storms, discovers a trapped buffalo calf and hears a rumble of thunder in the distance, she must overcome her fears to free the animal. Ormerod's "textured watercolors and pastels employ billowy swaths of color to suggest the vastness of the setting," a *Publishers Weekly* remarked, and Engberg stated that the artist's "dramatic, double-page spreads of thickly outlined figures are set against richly textured landscapes energized with flashes of neon color."

"My task as a visual storyteller is to observe, record, and edit," Ormerod stated in an essay on the Harper-Collins Web site. "Telling a story with words and pictures is a little like watching a movie, then selecting the evocative moment like a still taken from a film."

Biographical and Critical Sources

BOOKS

Children's Literature Review, Volume 20, Gale (Detroit, MI), 1990.

Landsberg, Michele, *Reading for the Love of It: Best Books for Young Readers,* Prentice Hall, 1987.

Ormerod, Jan, *When We Went to the Zoo,* Lothrop (New York, NY), 1991.

Ormerod, Jan, and David Lloyd, retellers, *The Frog Prince,* Lothrop (New York, NY), 1990.

PERIODICALS

Booklist, June 1, 2001, Carolyn Phelan, review of *Miss Mouse Takes Off,* p. 1894; September 1, 2001, Ilene Cooper, review of *Goodbye Mousie,* p. 114; August, 2003, Karin Snelson, review of *I Am Not Going to School Today!,* p. 1992; June 1, 2004, Hazel Rochman, review of *Emily and Albert,* p. 1744; June 1, 2005, Ilene Cooper, review of *When an Elephant Comes to School,* p. 1823; September 15, 2005, Gillian Engberg, review of *Lizzie Nonsense: A Story of Pioneer Days,* p. 75; March 15, 2006, Jennifer Mattson, review of *Mama's Day,* p. 52; December 1, 2006, Ilene Cooper, review of *Ballet Sisters: The Duckling and the Swan,* p. 53; December 1, 2007, Gillian Engberg, review of *The Buffalo Storm,* p. 45; February 15, 2008, Ilene Cooper, review of *Ballet Sisters: The Newest Dancer,* p. 87; January 1, 2009, Gillian Engberg, review of *Molly and Her Dad,* p. 92.

Books for Your Children, autumn-winter, 1983, Margaret Carter, "Cover Artist—Jan Ormerod," p. 7.

Growing Point, July, 1982, Margery Fisher, review of *Moonlight,* p. 3917.

Guardian (London, England), June 13, 2001, review of *Miss Mouse's Day,* p. 11.

Horn Book, March-April, 1988, Karen Jameyson, review of *Bend and Stretch,* p. 193; November, 1998, Mary M. Burns, review of *A Twist in the Tail: Animal Stories from around the World,* p. 746; July-August, 2007, Jennifer M. Brabander, review of *Ballet Sisters: The Duckling and the Swan,* p. 400, and Roger Sutton, review of *May I Pet Your Dog? The How-to Guide for Kids Meeting Dogs (and Dogs Meeting Kids),* p. 410.

Kirkus Reviews, January 15, 2003, review of *If You're Happy and You Know It!,* p. 145; March 15, 2006, review of *Mama's Day,* p. 286; February 1, 2007, review of *Ballet Sisters: The Duckling and the Swan,* p. 127; February 15, 2008, review of *Ballet Sisters,;* July 1, 2008, review of *Molly and Her Dad.*

New York Times Book Review, November, 11, 1984, Joe McGinniss, "How to Survive a Sibling," p. 48; March 24, 1985, Robert Wool, reviews of *Messy Baby, Reading, Dad's Back,* and *Sleeping,* p. 35; August 19, 1990, Michael Patrick Hearn, review of *The Frog Prince,* p. 29; August 14, 2005, review of *When an Elephant Comes to School.*

Publishers Weekly, July 30, 2001, review of *Goodbye Mousie,* p. 83; January 27, 2003, review of *If You're Happy and You Know It!,* p. 258; May 24, 2004, review of *Emily and Albert,* p. 61; April 3, 2006, review of *Mama's Day,* p. 71; October 15, 2007, review of *The Buffalo Storm,* p. 60.

School Library Journal, September, 2001, Joy Fleishhacker, review of *Goodbye Mousie,* p. 190; July, 2003, Joy Fleishhacker, review of *I Am Not Going to School Today!,* p. 98; August, 2005, Grace Oliff, review of *When an Elephant Comes to School,* p. 103; September, 2005, Grace Oliff, review of *Lizzie Nonsense,* p. 183; January, 2007, Rachel Vilmar, review of *Ballet Sisters: The Duckling and the Swan,* p. 100; May 1, 2008, Catherine Callegari, review of *Ballet Sisters,* p. 104; September 1, 2008, Wendy Lukehart, review of *Molly and Her Dad,* p. 156.

Times (London, England), September 26, 2004, Nick Robinson, review of *Lizzie Nonsense,* p. 54.

Washington Post Book World, June 8, 1986, Michael Dirda, "Books for Beach Bag and Knapsack," p. 10.

ONLINE

HarperCollins Web site, http://www.harpercollins.com/ (June 2, 2009), "Jan Ormerod."

Laura Cecil Web site, http://www.lauracecil.co.uk/ (June 2, 2009), "Jan Ormerod."

Walker Books Web site, http://www.walkerbooks.co.uk/ (June 2, 2009), "Jan Ormerod."*

*   *   *

ORMEROD, Janette Louise
See ORMEROD, Jan

P

PAROS, Jennifer

Personal

Married; children: two sons. *Education:* Graduated from Evergreen State College, 1986.

Addresses

Home—Seattle, WA.

Career

Author and illustrator.

Member

Pacific Northwest Writers Association.

Writings

(Self-illustrated) *Violet Bing and the Grand House,* Viking (New York, NY), 2007.

Contributor to online magazine *Author.*

Sidelights

Jennifer Paros is the author and illustrator of *Violet Bing and the Grand House,* "a sly story, written and illustrated with fulsome charm," according to *Booklist* contributor GraceAnne A. DeCandido. Originally planned as a picture book for young readers, *Violet Bing and the Grand House* evolved into a chapter book over a period of six years. Paros's story concerns a finicky seven year old who refuses to accompany her family on vacation. Violet's parents arrange for her to stay at the home of Great-Aunt Astrid, who lives in a spacious mansion known as the Grand House. During her stay, Violet lets down her guard, making a new friend,

Magnolia Greene Gold, and discovering a secret passage in her great-aunt's home. "Violet is utterly credible as a kid who's . . . starting to sense the possibility that she's missing out," observed Deborah Stevenson in the

Jennifer Paros tells a quirky tale in her self-illustrated story **Violet Bing and the Grand House.** (Viking 2007. Reproduced by permission.)

Bulletin of the Center for Children's Books, the critic adding that readers will "warm to this tenderly jocular but understanding literary exploration of a kid who considers stasis her best friend."

Other reviewers praised Paros's blend of text and art. According to *School Library Journal* critic Elizabeth Bird, "the author's pen-and-ink illustrations complement this fine, subtle early chapter book perfectly," and a contributor in *Kirkus Reviews* similarly noted that the book's "delightful sketches . . . are the perfect light touch this endearing story deserves." Reviewing *Violet Bing and the Grand House* in the *Washington Post Book World,* Elizabeth Ward concluded that Paros's "line drawings are as funny and tart as Violet's own voice."

Biographical and Critical Sources

PERIODICALS

Booklist, March 15, 2007, GraceAnne A. DeCandido, review of *Violet Bing and the Grand House,* p. 54.

Bulletin of the Center for Children's Books, June, 2007, Deborah Stevenson, review of *Violet Bing and the Grand House,* p. 399.

Kirkus Reviews, March 15, 2007, review of *Violet Bing and the Grand House.*

School Library Journal, August, 2007, Elizabeth Bird, review of *Violet Bing and the Grand House,* p. 88.

Washington Post Book World, June 3, 2007, Elizabeth Ward, review of *Violet Bing and the Grand House,* p. 12.

ONLINE

Westerly Sun Online, http://www.thewesterlysun.com/ (December 20, 2007), David Smith, "Matunuck Students Meet Creator of Violet Bing."*

*   *   *

PEACOCK, Louise

Personal

Female; children: one son. *Education:* Ph.D. (Medieval studies).

Addresses

Home—Haslett, MI. *Agent*—Jean V. Naggar Literary Agency, Inc., 216 E. 75th St., New York, NY 10021. *E-mail*—jvnla@jvnla.com.

Career

Writer.

Writings

Crossing the Delaware: A History in Many Voices, illustrated by Walter Lyon Krudop, Atheneum Books for Young Readers (New York, NY), 1998.

At Ellis Island: A History in Many Voices, illustrated by Walter Lyon Krudop, Atheneum Books for Young Readers (New York, NY), 2007.

Sidelights

Louise Peacock has a passion for history, and in addition to earning a Ph.D. in Medieval studies, her interest has inspired her to write books for children. *Crossing the Delaware: A History in Many Voices* recounts George Washington's crossing of the Delaware River during the American Revolution, and *At Ellis Island: A History in Many Voices* describes how immigrants came to America through the Ellis Island immigrant-processing facility. In both titles, Peacock tells her story through the voices of several different characters.

In *Crossing the Delaware* Peacock combines her own narrative with the words of a fictional American solder named Henry and the words of actual participants in the event. A critic for *Publishers Weekly* believed that "the mix of viewpoints offers a well-balanced view. . . . The authentic historic voices deliver the most impact, but the other narrative streams place them in context." Carolyn Phelan, writing in *Booklist,* described *Crossing the Delaware* as "a fresh look at a pivotal event in American history."

At Ellis Island tells the story of the many millions of immigrants who entered the United States through Ellis Island. For many years, all arriving immigrant ships from Europe dropped their passengers off at Ellis Island in New York City harbor. The new arrivals were checked for disease and provided with identity papers before being allowed into the country. Peacock presents the words of a young girl who visits Ellis Island to see where her great-great-grandmother arrived in America. At the same time, a parallel story is told about a young Armenian girl who arrives at Ellis Island in the early twentieth century. Added throughout the book are actual letters and diary excerpts from immigrants who tell their own stories of coming to America. Hazel Rochman in *Booklist* believed that "many readers will find connections with their own family stories." A *Publishers Weekly* reviewer concluded that "Peacock has seamlessly stitched together fact and fiction and presented a composite picture of courage and hope."

Biographical and Critical Sources

PERIODICALS

Booklist, November 15, 1998, Carolyn Phelan, review of *Crossing the Delaware: A History in Many Voices,* p. 588; May 1, 2007, Hazel Rochman, review of *At Ellis Island: A History in Many Voices,* p. 92.

Kirkus Reviews, June 1, 2007, review of *At Ellis Island.*

Publishers Weekly, November 9, 1998, review of *Crossing the Delaware,* p. 76; June 25, 2007, review of *At Ellis Island,* p. 60.

School Library Journal, October, 1998, Steven Engelfried, review of *Crossing the Delaware,* p. 158; July, 2007, Luann Toth, review of *At Ellis Island,* p. 108.

ONLINE

Jean V. Naggar Literary Agency Web site, http://www.jvnla.com/ (April 14, 2008), "Louise Peacock."*

*   *   *

PINKWATER, Daniel 1941-
(D. Manus Pinkwater, Daniel M. Pinkwater, Daniel Manus Pinkwater, Manus Pinkwater)

Personal

Born November 15, 1941, in Memphis, TN; son of Philip (a ragman and entrepreneur) and Fay (a chorus girl) Pinkwater; married Jill Miriam Schutz (an author and illustrator), October 12, 1969. *Education:* Bard College, B.A., 1964. Studied sculpture privately with David Nyvall. Also studied at Art Institute of Chicago, Harvard University, University of Liverpool, and University College, Nairobi, Kenya. *Politics:* Republican. *Religion:* "Taoist."

Addresses

Home—Hyde Park, NY. *Agent*—Jennifer Laughran, Andrea Brown Literary Agency; JennL@andreabrownlit.com.

Career

Author and illustrator of children's books, and radio commentator. *All Things Considered,* National Public Radio (NPR), regular commentator, 1987—. Host of *Chinwag Theater,* and book reviewer on *Weekend Edition Saturday,* NPR.

Member

American Federation of Theater and Radio Artists.

Awards, Honors

American Library Association Notable Book designation, 1976, for *Lizard Music; New York Times* Outstanding Book designation, 1978, for *The Last Guru;* Children's Choice designation, International Reading Association/Children's Book Council (IRA/CBC), 1981, for *The Wuggie Norple Story;* Parents' Choice Award (literature), 1982, for *Roger's Umbrella;* Emphasis on Reading Award (grades K-1), 1983-84, for *The Big Orange Splot;* Charles Flint Kellogg Medal, Bard College, 1999; Children's Choice designation, IRA/CBC, 2000, for *Ice Cream Larry.*

Daniel Pinkwater (Photograph by Kathy McLaughlin. Reproduced by permission.)

Writings

FOR CHILDREN; AS MANUS PINKWATER

The Terrible Roar, Knopf (New York, NY), 1970.
(Self-illustrated) *Bear's Picture,* Holt (New York, NY), 1972, published under name Daniel Pinkwater, with illustrations by D.B. Johnson, Houghton Mifflin (Boston, MA), 2008.
Fat Elliot and the Gorilla, Four Winds (New York, NY), 1974.
Three Big Hogs, Seabury (New York, NY), 1975.
Wingman, 1975.
(Self-illustrated) *Blue Moose,* (also see below), Dodd (New York, NY), 1975.
Around Fred's Bed, illustrated by Robert Mertens, Prentice-Hall (Englewood Cliffs, NJ), 1976.

FOR CHILDREN; SELF-ILLUSTRATED

(As Daniel Manus Pinkwater) *Wizard Crystal,* Dodd (New York, NY), 1973.
(As Daniel Manus Pinkwater) *Magic Camera,* Dodd (New York, NY), 1974.
(As Daniel Manus Pinkwater) *Lizard Music* (also see below), Dodd (New York, NY), 1976.
(As Daniel Manus Pinkwater) *The Blue Thing,* Prentice-Hall (Englewood Cliffs, NJ), 1977.
(As Daniel Manus Pinkwater) *The Big Orange Splot,* Hastings House (New York, NY), 1977.

(As Daniel Manus Pinkwater) *Fat Men from Space,* Dodd (New York, NY), 1977.

(As D. Manus Pinkwater) *The Hoboken Chicken Emergency,* Prentice-Hall (Englewood Cliffs, NJ), 1977, published with illustrations by Tony Auth, Atheneum (New York, NY), 2007.

(As Daniel M. Pinkwater) *The Last Guru* (also see below), Dodd (New York, NY), 1978.

(As Daniel M. Pinkwater) *Return of the Moose* (also see below), Dodd (New York, NY), 1979.

(As Daniel M. Pinkwater) *Pickle Creature,* Four Winds (New York, NY), 1979.

The Magic Moscow, Four Winds (New York, NY), 1980.

Tooth-Gnasher Superflash, Four Winds (New York, NY), 1981.

Attila the Pun: A Magic Moscow Book, Four Winds (New York, NY), 1981.

I Was a Second Grade Werewolf, Dutton (New York, NY), 1983.

Ducks!, Little, Brown (Boston, MA), 1984.

Devil in the Drain, Dutton (New York, NY), 1984.

The Moosepire (also see below), Little, Brown (Boston, MA), 1986.

The Muffin Fiend, Lothrop (New York, NY), 1986.

The Frankenbagel Monster, Dutton (New York, NY), 1986.

Aunt Lulu, Macmillan (New York, NY), 1988.

Guys from Space, Macmillan (New York, NY), 1989.

Uncle Melvin, Macmillan (New York, NY), 1989.

Doodle Flute, Macmillan (New York, NY), 1991.

Wempires, Macmillan (New York, NY), 1991.

The Phantom of the Lunch Wagon, Macmillan (New York, NY), 1992.

I Was a Class Two Werewolf, 1992.

Author's Day, Macmillan (New York, NY), 1993.

Blue Moose and Return of the Moose, Bullseye Books (New York, NY), 1993.

Ned Feldman: Space Pirate, Macmillan (New York, NY), 1994.

Once upon a Blue Moose (contains *Blue Moose, Return of the Moose,* and *The Moospire*), Yearling (New York, NY), 2006.

FOR CHILDREN

(As D. Manus Pinkwater; with wife, Jill Pinkwater) *Superpuppy: How to Choose, Raise, and Train the Best Possible Dog for You* (nonfiction), illustrated by Jill Pinkwater, Seabury (New York, NY), 1977, revised edition, Clarion Books (New York, NY), 2002.

(As Daniel M. Pinkwater) *Alan Mendelsohn, the Boy from Mars,* (also see below), Dutton (New York, NY), 1979.

(As Daniel M. Pinkwater) *Yobgorgle: Mystery Monster of Lake Ontario,* Clarion (New York, NY), 1979, revised edition, Bantam (New York, NY), 1981.

(With Luqman Keele) *Java Jack,* Crowell (New York, NY), 1980.

The Wuggie Norple Story, illustrated by Tomie dePaola, Four Winds (New York, NY), 1980.

The Worms of Kukumlima, Dutton (New York, NY), 1981.

Slaves of Spiegel: A Magic Moscow Story (also see below), Four Winds (New York, NY), 1982.

Young Adult Novel (also see below), Crowell (New York, NY), 1982.

Roger's Umbrella, illustrated by James Marshall, Dutton (New York, NY), 1982.

The Snarkout Boys and the Avocado of Death (also see below), Lothrop (New York, NY), 1982.

The Snarkout Boys and the Baconburg Horror, Lothrop (New York, NY), 1984.

Jolly Roger: A Dog of Hoboken, Lothrop (New York, NY), 1985.

Borgel, Macmillan (New York, NY), 1990.

Spaceburger: A Kevin Spoon and Mason Mintz Story, Macmillan (New York, NY), 1993.

The Time Tourists, Armada (London, England), 1993.

Mush: A Dog from Space, illustrated by Jill Pinkwater, Atheneum (New York, NY), 1995.

Wallpaper from Space, illustrated by Jill Pinkwater, Atheneum (New York, NY), 1996.

Goose Night, Random House (New York, NY), 1996.

Five Novels (includes *Alan Mendelsohn, The Boy from Mars, Slaves of Spiegel, The Snarkout Boys and the Avocado of Death, The Last Guru,* and *Young Adult Novel*), Farrar, Straus (New York, NY), 1997.

Magic Goose, Scholastic, Inc. (New York, NY), 1997.

Second Grade Ape, illustrated by Jill Pinkwater, Scholastic, Inc. (New York, NY), 1997.

At the Hotel Larry, illustrated by Jill Pinkwater, Marshall Cavendish (New York, NY), 1998.

Bongo Larry, illustrated by Jill Pinkwater, Marshall Cavendish (New York, NY), 1998.

The Education of Robert Nifkin, Farrar, Straus (New York, NY), 1998.

Rainy Morning, illustrated by Jill Pinkwater, Atheneum (New York, NY), 1998.

Wolf Christmas, illustrated by Jill Pinkwater, Marshall Cavendish (New York, NY), 1998.

Big Bob and the Thanksgiving Potatoes, illustrated by Jill Pinkwater, Scholastic, Inc. (New York, NY), 1998.

Young Larry, illustrated by Jill Pinkwater, Marshall Cavendish (New York, NY), 1998.

Ice Cream Larry, illustrated by Jill Pinkwater, Marshall Cavendish (New York, NY), 1999.

Big Bob and the Winter Holiday Potato, illustrated by Jill Pinkwater, Scholastic, Inc. (New York, NY), 1999.

Big Bob and the Halloween Potatoes, illustrated by Jill Pinkwater, Scholastic, Inc. (New York, NY), 1999.

Big Bob and the Magic Valentine's Day Potato, illustrated by Jill Pinkwater, Scholastic, Inc. (New York, NY), 1999.

The Lunchroom of Doom, illustrated by Jill Pinkwater, Atheneum (New York, NY), 2000.

The Magic Pretzel, Atheneum (New York, NY), 2000.

Four Fantastic Novels (includes *Borgel, Yobgorgle: Mystery Monster of Lake Ontario, The Worms of Kukumlima,* and *The Snarkout Boys and the Baconburg Horror*), Aladdin (New York, NY), 2000.

Fat Camp Commandos, Scholastic, Inc. (New York, NY), 2001.

Cone Kong: The Scary Ice Cream Giant, illustrated by Jill Pinkwater, Scholastic, Inc. (New York, NY), 2001.

The Werewolf Club Meets Dorkula, illustrated by Jill Pinkwater, Atheneum (New York, NY), 2001.

The Werewolf Club Meets the Hound of the Basketballs, Atheneum (New York, NY), 2001.

Irving and Muktuk: Two Bad Bears, illustrated by Jill Pinkwater, Houghton Mifflin (Boston, MA), 2001.

Uncle Boris in the Yukon and Other Shaggy Dog Stories, illustrated by Jill Pinkwater, Simon & Schuster (New York, NY), 2001.

The Werewolf Club Meets Oliver Twit, Atheneum (New York, NY), 2002.

Music and Dance, San Val, 2002.

Fat Camp Commandos Go West, illustrated by Andy Rash, Scholastic, Inc. (New York, NY), 2002.

Mush's Jazz Adventure, illustrated by Jill Pinkwater, Aladdin (New York, NY), 2002.

The Picture of Morty and Ray, illustrated by Jack E. Davis, HarperCollins (New York, NY), 2003.

Bad Bears in the Big City, illustrated by Jill Pinkwater, Houghton Mifflin (Boston, MA), 2003.

Looking for Bobowicz: A Hoboken Chicken Story, illustrated by Jill Pinkwater, HarperCollins (New York, NY), 2004.

Bad Bears and a Bunny, illustrated by Jill Pinkwater, Houghton Mifflin (Boston, MA), 2005.

The Artsy Smartsy Club, illustrated by Jill Pinkwater, HarperCollins (New York, NY), 2005.

Bad Bear Detectives, illustrated by Jill Pinkwater, Houghton Mifflin (Boston, MA), 2006.

Dancing Larry, illustrated by Jill Pinkwater, Marshall Cavendish (New York, NY), 2006.

Sleepover Larry, illustrated by Jill Pinkwater, Marshall Cavendish (New York, NY), 2006.

Bad Bears Go Visiting, illustrated by Jill Pinkwater, Houghton Mifflin (Boston, MA), 2007.

The Neddiad: How Neddie Took the Train, Went to Hollywood, and Saved Civilization, illustrated by Calef Brown, Houghton Mifflin (Boston, MA), 2007.

Yo-Yo Man, illustrated by Jack E. Davis, HarperCollins (New York, NY), 2007.

The Yggyssey: How Iggy Wondered What Happened to All the Ghosts, Found out Where They Went, and Went There, Houghton Mifflin (Boston, MA), 2009.

OTHER

Young Adults (fiction; portion adapted from *Young Adult Novel*), Tor (New York, NY), 1985.

Fish Whistle: Commentaries, Uncommentaries, and Vulgar Excesses (essays; also see below), Addison-Wesley (Reading, MA), 1990.

Chicago Days, Hoboken Nights (autobiographical essays; also see below) Addison-Wesley (Reading, MA), 1991.

(Adaptor with Christina Calrit) *Lizard Music* (musical; based on the novel), music by Douglas Wood, produced by Lifeline Theatre, Chicago, IL, 1992.

The Afterlife Diet (novel), Random House (New York, NY), 1995.

Hoboken Fish and Chicago Whistle (contains *Fish Whistle* and *Chicago Days, Hoboken Nights*), Xlibris (Princeton, NJ), 1999.

Author of *Comic Cosmic Novel* and *I Snarked with a Zombie,* for Lothrop. Contributor to books, including *The Year's Best Fantasy Second Annual Collection,* 1989, and *It's Fine to Be Nine,* 2000. Contributor of articles, reviews, and illustrations to periodicals, such as *Cricket, Gnomon, Island Review, Liberation, New York Times, Smithsonian, Washington Post,* and *Zen Notes.*

Adaptations

Wingman was made into a cassette by Listening Library, 1981; *Blue Moose* was produced as a videocassette by Positive Images, 1982; *The Hoboken Chicken Emergency* was adapted for television by the Public Broadcasting System (PBS), 1984; *I Was a Second Grade Werewolf* was made into a cassette by Live Oak Media, 1986; *Fish Whistle* was released as a sound recording by Bantam Audio, 1990; *Chicago Days, Hoboken Nights* was released as an audiobook, narrated by Pinkwater, by Dove Audio, 1991.

Sidelights

Daniel Pinkwater is a prolific and popular author and illustrator who is celebrated as an original, imaginative, and versatile contributor to literature for children and young adults. Renowned as a humorist and satirist, Pinkwater creates unusual books that characteristically point out the absurdity of reality, especially as related to contemporary society, while presenting young readers with both solid morals and plenty of laughs. The author is well known for his irreverent—some say anarchic—sensibility as well as for the droll wit he uses to skewer his targets. Often parodying genre fiction such as the detective story, the horror story, the adventure tale, and the science-fiction and young adult "problem" novel, Pinkwater typically features ordinary characters—often boys from Rochester, New York, and Hoboken, New Jersey—who are placed in incredible, improbable situations. Their fantastic, often frenetic adventures lead these boys and girls to meet an array of odd creatures, both human and otherwise.

Pinkwater fills his works with puns, nonsense words, one-liners, vivid imagery, and allusions to other books (some of them his own), food, and popular culture. The author generally uses a deadpan tone that belies the outlandishness and wild humor of his stories. Pinkwater, who often includes surprise twists at the end of his stories, is often noted for his playfulness and exuberance as well as for the color and vitality of his characterizations. According to a contributor in the *St. James Guide to Young-Adult Writers,* Pinkwater's books "crackle with antic energy. In a prose style marked by humor and a fondness for puns, he celebrates the eruption of the fantastic into everyday life. Although many of his books can be classified as science fiction or fantasy, his secondary worlds or alternate universes do not quite fit the standard paradigms for those genres because of the irreverent sensibility which informs them."

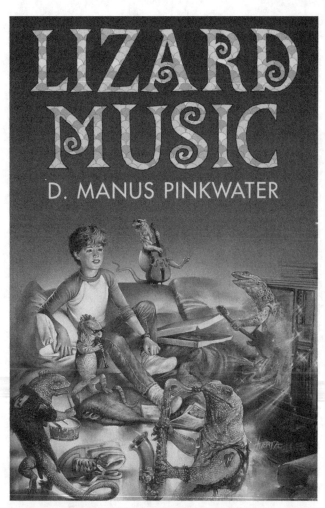

Published under the name D. Manus Pinkwater, Pinkwater's middle-grade novel **Lizard Music** *features artwork by Catherine Huerta.* (Cover art copyright © by Catherine Huerta. Used by permission of Yearling, an imprint of Random House Children's Books, a division of Random House, Inc.)

As an artist, Pinkwater usually creates his illustrations in a deceptively simple, cartoonlike style—black and white drawings, often outlined with heavy lines and filled with bright colors—that is credited with complementing the energetic quality of his texts. In some of his more recent works, the artist has used colorful computer graphics. Many critics consider Pinkwater to be a masterful humorist whose stories are both inspired nonsense and accurate assessments of modern life, making the author especially popular with young people. Called "one of the star authors in the junior high stable" by Susan B. Madden in *Voice of Youth Advocates,* Pinkwater was described by *New York Times Book Review* contributor Peter Andrews as "a children's author who does not treat his audience as if they are little darlings."

Pinkwater's books are filled with references to his own life. Born in Memphis, Tennessee, he moved to Chicago when he was two years old. His family stayed there until Pinkwater was eight; after moving to Los Angeles, he came back to Chicago as a teenager. Writing in his collection of autobiographical essays titled *Chicago Days, Hoboken Nights,* he said, "I regarded

Chicago, and that first large apartment, as home. I used to dream of living there, and frequently imagine it as the setting for works of fiction I write."

Pinkwater began writing and drawing at an early age; while living in Los Angeles, he found a store that sold art supplies, which fascinated him. He remembers writing one-page parodies in the fifth grade, enjoying grammar and logic exercises, and being inspired by *Mad Magazine.* In school, Pinkwater used to write funny notes to pass around the classroom and get his friends to laugh out loud, thus getting them into trouble. When he won a short-story contest and was given a subscription to *National Geographic,* he had a revelation: in an interview with Deborah Kovacs and James Preller for *Meet the Authors and Illustrators,* he stated, "That's how I first learned that you could get things by writing."

After graduating from high school, Pinkwater enrolled at Bard College in New York's Hudson River Valley. Initially, Pinkwater majored in English, philosophy, history, drama, and religion. However, when his father threatened to take him out of school, Pinkwater switched his major to art. When he went to his sculpture teacher, the instructor told Pinkwater that he might as well start getting some experience; consequently, the new student was made to teach all three sections of Sculpture 101. "This began," Pinkwater wrote, "my formal education as an artist."

In order to complete a research project, Pinkwater took a job as an intern in a sculpture foundry; Navin Diebold, a sculptor whom he met at the foundry, agreed to take him on as an apprentice. The author wrote, "I began as the pupil of Navin Diebold, the product of whose teaching I am, for better or worse, to this day." Pinkwater studied with Diebold—his pseudonym for David Nyvall—for three years. In his senior year at Bard, Pinkwater was given his own studio, where he worked on his senior project, a series of woodblock prints. At the end of their sessions, Nyvall told Pinkwater that he would never be a sculptor; instead, Nyvall told his student that he would be a writer.

After leaving Bard College, Pinkwater went to New York City to make his name as—despite his teacher's prediction—an artist. Before departing, he had three shows; the most successful one was in a saloon. He eventually moved to Hoboken, New Jersey, a picturesque town across from New York City that was filled with colorful characters. Hoboken, which was to become Pinkwater's home for the next dozen years, also became, as he noted in *Chicago Days, Hoboken Nights,* "my spiritual home for the rest of my life."

While working on his art, Pinkwater took extensive courses in art therapy, then worked as an art teacher in settlement houses and youth centers around New York City and New Jersey. He also traveled to Africa, joining an artists' cooperative in which he was the only member who was not from the Chagga tribe. In 1969 he married Jill Schutz, a teacher, writer, and artist who, as Jill Pinkwater, has created works of her own and has illustrated many of her husband's books.

While trying to sell his sculptures and prints, Pinkwater met a children's book editor who was looking for pictures to go with a book of African folktales she was editing. Learning that Pinkwater had recently returned from Africa, the editor suggested that he might like to try illustrating the story. After going to his studio, the editor went even further. She told Pinkwater that he should try writing and illustrating his own book. That effort, *The Terrible Roar,* was published in 1970 under the name Manus Pinkwater. The author remarked in the *Something about the Author Autobiography Series,* "I knew at once that I had found my calling."

Over the next several years Pinkwater published a number of well-received picture books, including *Blue*

Moose. In 1976 he produced *Lizard Music,* a fantasy that is considered among his best works. Eleven-year-old Victor sees a movie on late-night television about pods invading the earth; then, he sees pod people on a talk show as well as a lizard band on television playing incredibly beautiful music. After this, he starts seeing lizards everywhere. Next, Victor meets the Chicken Man, an old black man with a performing chicken named Claudia. The Chicken Man takes Victor to an invisible island inhabited by friendly lizards; here, Claudia hatches the egg that, according to legend, will lead the lizards in conquering the pods. A critic in *Kirkus Reviews* stated that *Lizard Music* is "that rarity, a children's fantasy that is truly contemporary in sensibility as well as setting. It's funny, [and] properly paranoid, shot through with bad puns and sweet absurdities."

With *Alan Mendelsohn, the Boy from Mars,* a book published in 1979, Pinkwater created one of his most

One of Pinkwater's most beloved picture books, **The Big Orange Splot,** *illustrates the importance of self-expression.* (Illustration copyright © 1977 by Daniel Manus Pinkwater. Reproduced with permission of Scholastic, Inc.)

highly regarded titles. When Leonard Neeble moves from the city to the suburbs and begins attending Bat Masterson Junior High, he is snubbed by the snobbish faculty and students. Leonard finds friendship with Alan Mendelsohn, a fellow classmate who claims to be a Martian. Leonard and Alan discover the Bermuda Triangle Chili Parlor, where they meet Samuel Klugarsh, a used-book dealer who has developed a cabalistic mind-control system, and Clarence Yojimbo, a Venusian who leads them to the existential plane of Waka-Waka. At the end of the novel, Alan returns to Mars and Leonard returns to school better able to make friends with other students who have been dismissed by the snobs. Ann S. Haskell, a contributor to the *New York Times Book Review* called *Alan Mendelsohn* Pinkwater's "most ambitious book to date . . . that is, in spots, reminiscent of E. Nesbit, and everywhere vintage Pinkwater."

In 1982, Pinkwater created a send-up of young-adult novels—called, appropriately enough, *Young Adult Novel*—that remains one of his most popular books. In the first four pages of this short novel, the author introduces Kevin Shapiro, a gay, alcoholic, thirteen year old who supports himself by stealing and selling drugs. Kevin's mother is locked away in a madhouse, his father is severely mentally impaired, and his sister is a prostitute. Readers of *Young Adult Novel* learn that Kevin is the hero of a story by the Wild Dada Ducks, a group of five high-school friends who have modeled themselves on the Dada movement of twentieth-century artists and writers. When the Ducks find that there really is a Kevin Shapiro at their school, they turn the boy—an antisocial nerd—into president of the student body. Shapiro retaliates by forming an alternate group, the Fanatical Praetorians, who provide a comeuppance for the Wild Dada Ducks. Susan B. Madden, a *Voice of Youth Advocates* reviewer, concluded that of all Pinkwater's books, this "particular wonderfully titled piece of nonsense is the best of all. . . . As is typical with Pinkwater, the wit pinpoints some very real adolescent concerns and feelings."

Uncle Melvin, a picture book published in 1989, is considered by critics to be one of Pinkwater's most touching works. Uncle Melvin is mentally ill, spending his days with little Charles and his family and his nights in what he calls the "Looney Bin." Melvin sends messages to flying saucers and thinks that the president of the United States is a lizard. When he claims that he can start the rain and make rainbows, Melvin tests his family's limits. However, when he makes good on his claim, Charles becomes, in the words of Susan Perren in *Quill & Quire,* "an apostle for life." "With a few deft squiggles of the pen, a generous rainbow palette of colour, and the right number of well-chosen words," Perren added, "Daniel Pinkwater's Uncle Melvin gives the young an amusing and intriguing portrait of a family's 'crazy' relative and, indirectly, that family's capacity to hold that relative within its boundaries."

The Education of Robert Nifkin, a young-adult novel, is one of Pinkwater's directly autobiographical works. Ostensibly written by its title character as a college application essay, the book describes how Robert, a friendless, overweight boy living in Chicago during the late 1950s, learns to survive high school and begin to find himself. In *Horn Book* critic Ann A. Flowers commented, "If the book weren't so funny, it could almost be a prescription for an interesting education. . . . This book will find its way to the hearts of individualists everywhere."

Turning his hand to series fiction in the "Werewolf Club" chapter books, Pinkwater recounts the adventures of a group of children at Watson Elementary School who just happen to be able to change themselves into werewolves. In the first book of the series, *The Magic Pretzel,* members of the Werewolf Club try to save their sponsor, caught in the wolf stage of shape-changing, by tracking down a Magic Pretzel which can lift the curse. *Booklist* critic Carolyn Phelan noted that, if the premise of the series "seems a little wacky, the story's details are sometimes downright bonkers, and Pinkwater's fans wouldn't have it any other way."

In the club's second outing, *The Lunchroom of Doom,* one of the members is banned from the school cafeteria after having a food fight with himself. Thereafter the

Cover of Pinkwater's adventure-filled romp Fat Camp Commandos, *featuring cartoon art by Andy Rash.* (Illustration copyright © 2001 by Andy Rash. Reproduced by permission of Scholastic, Inc.)

Werewolf Club takes its lunch downtown at Honest Tom's Tibetan-American Lunchroom, where the patrons make the Watson Elementary School students look tame by comparison. Betsy Barnett, writing in *School Library Journal,* called the work "another winning chapter book" that will appeal to young readers' "warped sense of humor."

In *The Werewolf Club Meets Dorkula* a vampire rears its ugly head in the form of Count Henry Dorkula, sucking the life out of all the fresh fruits and vegetables in town. "This is goofy, fast-paced, easy-reading," wrote *Booklist* critic Todd Morning. A fourth offering in the series, *The Werewolf Club Meets the Hound of the Basketballs,* concerns the group's effort to locate an annoying dog that wanders the grounds of stately Basketball Hall.

An intelligent, extraterrestrial canine is the subject of *Mush: A Dog from Space* and *Mush's Jazz Adventure.* In *Mush,* young Kelly discovers the title character, a talking mushamute from the planet Growf-Woof-Woof, while walking through the woods. Though Kelly's parents forbid her from owning a pet, they quickly change their minds after the alien helps Kelly prepare a gourmet meal. In *Mush's Jazz Adventure,* Kelly learns how her friend crash-landed on Earth, formed a traveling band, and foiled a robbery. *Mush's Jazz Adventure* "is fast-paced and funny and full of total improbabilities," wrote Sally R. Dow in *School Library Journal.*

More off-beat humor is presented in *Fat Camp Commandos,* in which Ralph and Sylvia are shipped off to Camp Noo Yoo, run by their gym instructor, Dick Tator, to make them slim down. Soon, however, they skip camp and make it back to their hometown where they begin a campaign to fight prejudice against fat people. "This short chapter book is a good adventure with some laugh-out-loud moments," wrote *Booklist* reviewer Carolyn Phelan, "an unapologetic acceptance of fat." Ralph and Sylvia return in *Fat Camp Commandos Go West,* wherein the pair helps their friend Mavis unite two feuding factions—health freaks and ranchers—in the town of Horny Toad. According to *School Library Journal* contributor Marilyn Ackerman, Pinkwater's "story has an overall message of tolerance and acceptance."

Polar bears of a different stripe take center stage in *Irving and Muktuk: Two Bad Bears,* about a pair of critters running a muffin swindle during a New Year's Day celebration. Karen J. Tannenbaum, writing in *School Library Journal,* commended the book as "cleverly written" and "a great read-aloud." A sequel, *Bad Bears in the Big City,* finds Irving and Muktuk sentenced to a zoo in New Jersey as punishment for their scam. It is not long, however, before the duo escapes and sneaks into the muffin factory next door. "Pinkwater's many fans will enjoy the further adventures of these mischievous creatures," noted Donna Cardon in *School Library Journal.* In *Bad Bears and a Bunny,* Irving and Muktuk have a run-in with a temperamental rabbit. Ilene Cooper, reviewing the work in *Booklist,* praised the author's "droll, understated text." Suspected of pilfering a shipment of Italian designer muffins, Irving and Muktuk search for clues to the real culprit's identity in *Bad Bear Detectives,* a "charming mystery will have kids guessing," according to Wanda Meyers-Hines in *School Library Journal.* In *Bad Bears Go Visiting,* the pair drops in on an unsuspecting family. According to *Horn Book* critic Vicky Smith, "the Irving and Muktuk books are a refreshing antidote to the pervasive sweetness of so much of children's literature."

In 2004, some twenty-five years after the publication of *The Hoboken Chicken Emergency,* Pinkwater's classic tale concerning Arthur Bobowicz and Henrietta, his 266-pound pet chicken, Pinkwater completed a sequel. In *Looking for Bobowicz: A Hoboken Chicken Story* Ivan Itch and his companions Bruno Ugg and Loretta Fisehetti search for the mysterious figure who stole Ivan's bike and comic books, with the evidence pointing straight to Henrietta. "This loosely plotted comic mystery features dialogue straight from the Borscht Belt," noted Peter D. Sieruta in *Horn Book.* In a follow-up, *The Artsy Smartsy Club,* the three youngsters pick up some pointers from legendary Hoboken sidewalk-chalk artist Lucy Casserole, then travel to New York City's Metropolitan Museum of Art with Henrietta as their chaperone. According to *School Library Journal* critic Alison Follos, *The Artsy Smartsy Club* contains "just the right ingredients to make it a hit with kids: fanciful fiction plunked into the middle of madcap reality."

In 2007 Pinkwater took the unusual step of serializing a novel online. Unhappy with the way his previous works had been promoted, the author released *The Neddiad: How Neddie Took the Train, Went to Hollywood, and Saved Civilization* on its own Web site, one chapter at a time, free of charge. "I didn't want to wait two years to have nobody read it," the author told Nina Shengold in a *Chronogram* online interview. "I wanted to have nobody read it now." Set in the late 1940s, *The Neddiad* centers on Neddie Wentworthstein, whose eccentric father has decided to move the family from Chicago to Los Angeles. During the trip west, a shaman named Melvin hands Neddie a small carved turtle that possesses incredible powers. Unfortunately for Neddie, the sinister Sandor Eucalyptus wants the turtle for his own and follows the Wentworthsteins across the country. In the opinion of *Kliatt* contributor Paula Rohrlick, Pinkwater's "amiable, old-fashioned adventure saga . . . is a lot of fun to read, full of unexpected plot twists, LA atmosphere, and goofy names." Though the novel won't satisfy hard-core mystery fans, observed *Horn Book* reviewer Christine M. Heppermann, readers "who do get drawn into Pinkwater's portrait of old Hollywood, embellished with loopy supernatural intrigue, will devour it like a double-chocolate doughnut."

Set about two years after *The Neddiad, The Yggyssey: How Iggy Wondered What Happened to All the Ghosts,*

Found out Where They Went, and Went There is narrated by Neddie's friend Yggdrasil Birnbaum, who is called Iggy, although she does not like the nickname. Yggdrasil, along with Neddie and their friend Seamus, becomes involved in an unusual ghost story. Neddie and Seamus go to a strict military academy, but Yggdrasil is educated at the Harmonious Reality School, a very undemanding, progressive school. Yggdrasil spends a lot of her free time visiting with various interesting ghosts that inhabit the Hermione, a Los Angeles apartment building where the girl lives with her parents. The building, which was once a grand hotel, has so many ghosts in residence that they have their own apartment. The otherworldly tenants include a prehistoric woman who died in the La Brea tar pits, silent film star Rudolph Valentino, and a rabbit named Chase. When the ghosts of Valentino and Harry Houdini disappear, Yggdrasil becomes concerned, and in an attempt to find them, she follows Chase down a hole that leads to a place called Underland. As Iggy and her friends travel through Underland in search of their missing spirits, they take the reader along on a whimsical trip through many classic children's stories, presented with a humorous twist in sixty-nine chapters.

Cover of Pinkwater's middle-grade novel The Yggyssey, *a humorous update on Homer's Odyssey.* (Jacket art copyright 2008 © by Calef Brown. Reprinted by permission of Houghton Mifflin Harcourt Publishing Company. All rights reserved.)

The Yggyssey is "awash in jolly nostalgia" for 1940s Los Angeles, according to Larry Doyle in a review for *New York Times Book Review Online.* Doyle thought the episodic story provided readers with "fun all along the way." Eva Mitnick, reviewing *The Yggyssey* for *School Library Journal,* called the setting "authentically and delightfully kooky." Pinkwater's command of the many different cultural references he makes was praised by Sarah Ellis in her *Horn Book* review, and she called *The Yggyssey* a "wacky, allusive, hilarious, indefatigable adventure." Noting Pinkwater's long-term, solid, yet low-key success, Doyle commented about *The Yggyssey*: "The latest Pinkwater is nothing special, only the usual wonderful." Reviewing the book for *Kidsreads.com,* Norah Piehl commented: "What's most enjoyable about Pinkwater's novels is the fun he seems to have creating them, ensuring that readers will gleefuly go along for the ride."

In addition to his success has an author, since 1987 Pinkwater has enjoyed a second career as a radio commentator. Appearing on the National Public Radio program *All Things Considered,* he has become a well-known figure among radio audiences. In addition, Pinkwater created and co-hosted *Chinwag Theater,* a program for young people, and reviewed books for *Weekend Edition Saturday* with Scott Simon. His radio commentaries have been collected in the volumes *Fish Whistle: Commentaries, Uncommentaries, and Vulgar Excesses* and *Chicago Days, Hoboken Nights,* the second a collection of autobiographical essays. Although directed to adults, *Chicago Days, Hoboken Nights* is often enjoyed by young readers. The volume, which recounts Pinkwater's childhood through his becoming a writer, was described by *School Library Journal* contributor Judy McAloon as "great reading" by a "superb storyteller."

Discussing the intent of his literary efforts, Pinkwater once commented: "I want my readers to feel encouraged and *snarky,* because basically they are kids taking on a hostile and/or indifferent world. My books are about finding favoring signs in the world, about discovering riches—things which are not dead. My stories are about people prevailing." In an online interview for *Seven Impossible Interviews before Breakfast,* Pinkwater commented: "I have had many adventures, including being stranded at night in the Serengeti, living on the slopes of Kilimanjaro, meeting many remarkable people, being in the right place at the right time over and over . . . and none of these are as much fun as writing." Asked about the writing process, he further noted: "Like everyone else I have sixty ideas a minute. The trick is to pick the ones that are least lousy out of the flow, and what to do with them once you've picked."

Biographical and Critical Sources

BOOKS

Children's Books and Their Creators, edited by Anita Silvey, Houghton Mifflin (Boston, MA), 1995.

Children's Literature Review, Volume 4, Gale (Detroit, MI), 1982.

Contemporary Literary Criticism, Volume 35, Gale (Detroit, MI), 1985.

Hogan, Walter, *The Agony and the Eggplant,* Scarecrow Press (Lanham, MD), 2001.

Landsberg, Michele, *Reading for the Love of It,* Prentice-Hall (Englewood Cliffs, NJ), 1987.

Meet the Authors and Illustrators, Volume II, Scholastic, Inc. (New York, NY), 1993.

Pinkwater, Daniel, *Chicago Days, Hoboken Nights,* Addison-Wesley (Reading, MA), 1991.

St. James Guide to Young-Adult Writers, St. James Press (Detroit, MI), 1999.

Something about the Author Autobiography Series, Volume 3, Gale (Detroit, MI), 1987.

Twentieth-Century Children's Writers, 3rd edition, St. James Press (Detroit, MI), 1989.

PERIODICALS

Albany Times Union (Albany, NY), December 8, 1991, Donna Liquori, "Writer Leans toward the Light Side," p. C10; November 29, 1998, Doug Blackburn, "In The Pink: *All Things Considered* Personality Charms Airwaves, Kids' Imaginations," p. G1; October 1, 2006, Kathy Ceceri, "Children's Novel Hits Internet Chapter by Chapter," p. I1.

Booklist, April 1, 1974, review of *Magic Camera,* p. 878; April 1, 1982, Stephanie Zvirin, review of *Young Adult Novel,* p. 1014; October 15, 1991, Donna Seaman, review of *Chicago Days, Hoboken Nights,* p. 399; June 1, 1998, Stephanie Zvirin, review of *The Education of Robert Nifkin,* p. 1749; July, 1998, Kathleen Squires, review of *Bongo Larry,* pp. 1187-1888; April 1, 1999, Susan Dove Lempke, review of *Ice Cream Larry,* p. 1422; July, 2000, Carolyn Phelan, review of *The Magic Pretzel,* p. 2030; April 15, 2001, Carolyn Phelan, review of *Fat Camp Commandos,* p. 1553; September 15, 2001, Connie Fletcher, review of *Irving and Muktuk: Two Bad Bears,* p. 233, and Todd Morning, review of *The Werewolf Club Meets Dorkula,* p. 223; November 1, 2001, Donna Seaman, review of *Uncle Boris in the Yukon and Other Shaggy Dog Stories,* p. 456; June 1, 2002, Carolyn Phelan, review of *Fat Camp Commandos Go West,* p. 1724; September 15, 2003, Terry Glover, review of *The Picture of Morty and Ray,* p. 248; March 1, 2004, Todd Morning, review of *Bad Bears in the Big City,* p. 1198; February 15, 2005, Ilene Cooper, review of *Bad Bears and a Bunny,* p. 1085; May 1, 2005, Todd Morning, review of *The Artsy Smartsy Club,* p. 1584; March 15, 2006, Carolyn Phelan, review of *Dancing Larry,* p. 53; July 1, 2006, Hazel Rochman, review of *Bad Bear Detectives,* p. 67; April 1, 2007, Julie Cummins, review of *Bad Bears Go Visiting,* p. 60; February 1, 2008, Julie Cummins, review of *Bear's Picture,* p. 44; February 15, 2009, Todd Morning, review of *The Yggyssey: How Iggy Wondered What Happened to All the Ghosts, Found out Where They Went, and Went There,* p. 73.

Bulletin of the Center for Children's Books, September, 1979, Zena Sutherland, review of *Alan Mendelsohn,* the Boy from Mars, p. 54; November, 1989, Robert Strang, review of *Uncle Melvin,* pp. 69-70; July-August, 1998, Deborah Stevenson, review of *The Education of Robert Nifkin,* p. 408.

Horn Book, July-August, 1998, Ann A. Flowers, review of *The Education of Robert Nifkin,* pp. 495-496; May-June, 2004, Peter D. Sieruta, review of *Looking for Bobowicz: A Hoboken Chicken Story,* p. 336; March-April, 2007, Vicky Smith, review of *Bad Bears Go Visiting,* p. 188; May-June, 2007, Christine M. Heppermann, review of *The Neddiad: How Neddie Took the Train, Went to Hollywood, and Saved Civilization,* p. 288; March 1, 2009, Sarah Ellis, review of *The Yggyssey.*

Kirkus Reviews, June 15, 1975, review of *Blue Moose,* p. 661; July 15, 1977, review of *Superpuppy: How to Choose, Raise, and Train the Best Possible Dog for You,* p. 731; April 15, 1998, review of *The Education of Robert Nifkin,* p. 585; August 15, 2001, review of *Irving and Muktuk,* p. 1220; November 1, 2002, review of *Mush's Jazz Adventure,* p. 1612; July 1, 2003, review of *The Picture of Morty and Ray,* p. 913; February 15, 2004, review of *Bad Bears in the Big City,* p. 183; March 15, 2005, review of *Bad Bears and a Bunny,* p. 356; May 1, 2005, review of *The Artsy Smartsy Club,* p. 544; February 15, 2006, review of *Dancing Larry,* p. 189; July 1, 2006, review of *Bad Bear Detectives,* p. 680; March 15, 2007, review of *Bad Bears Go Visiting;* August 15, 2007, review of *Sleepover Larry;* March 15, 2008, review of *Bear's Picture,;* January 1, 2009, review of *The Yggyssey.*

Kliatt, September, 1981, Fran Lantz, review of *Alan Mendelsohn, the Boy from Mars,* p. 14; July, 1998, Paula Rohrlick, review of *The Education of Robert Nifkin;* March, 2007, Paula Rohrlick, review of *The Neddiad,* p. 18.

New York Times Book Review, April 29, 1979, Ann S. Haskell, "The Fantastic Mr. Pinkwater," pp. 32, 43; April 25, 1987, Peter Andrews, review of *Slaves of Spiegel: A Magic Moscow Story,* p. 51.

Publishers Weekly, February 26, 1973, review of *Wizard Crystal,* p. 123; June 9, 1975, review of *Blue Moose,* p. 63; August 1, 1976, review of *Lizard Music,* p. 846; October 18, 1976, review of *Lizard Music,* p. 64; August 1, 1977, review of *Superpuppy* p. 115; July 7, 1997, review of *At the Hotel Larry,* p. 70; March 23, 1998, review of *The Education of Robert Nifkin,* p. 101; February 22, 1999, review of *Rainy Morning,* p. 94; August 21, 2000, "Pinkwater Undammed," p. 75; May 21, 2001, review of *Fat Camp Commandos,* p. 108; October 15, 2001, review of *Uncle Boris in the Yukon and Other Shaggy Dog Stories,* p. 60; June 30, 2003, review of *The Picture of Morty and Ray,* pp. 78-79; July 7, 2003, review of *Fat Camp Commandos Go West,* p. 74; September 8, 2003, review of *Irving and Muktuk,* p. 79; January 29, 2007, review of *The Neddiad,* p. 72; July 23 2007, review of *Yo-Yo Man,* p. 67; January 21, 2008, review of *Bear's Picture,* p. 169; January 26, 2009, review of *The Yggyssey,* p. 119.

Quill & Quire, January, 1990, Susan Perren, review of *Uncle Melvin,* p. 18.

School Library Journal, March, 1971, Ann D. Schweibish, review of *The Terrible Roar,* p. 123; January, 1990, Anna Biagioni Hart, review of *Uncle Melvin,* p. 88; April, 1992, Judy McAloon, review of *Chicago Days, Hoboken Nights,* p. 168; May, 2001, Betsy Barnett, review of *The Lunchroom of Doom,* p. 131; Elizabeth Maggio, review of *Fat Camp Commandos,* p. 158; September, 2001, Karen J. Tannenbaum, review of *Irving and Muktuk,* p. 203; February, 2002, Kate Kohlbeck, review of *The Werewolf Club Meets the Hound of the Basketballs,* p. 110; June, 2002, Marilyn Ackerman, review of *Fat Camp Commandos Go West,* p. 108; October, 2002, Wendy S. Carroll, review of *Mush: A Dog from Space,* p. 125; February, 2003, Sally R. Dow, review of *Mush's Jazz Adventure,* p. 120; September, 2003, Steven Engelfried, review of *The Picture of Morty and Ray,* p. 187; April, 2004, Donna Cardon, review of *Bad Bears in the Big City,* p. 120; July, 2004, James K. Irwin, review of *Looking for Bobowicz,* pp. 110-111; March, 2005, Kelley Rae Unger, review of *Bad Bears and a Bunny,* p. 186; May, 2005, Alison Follos, review of *The Artsy Smartsy Club,* p. 138; June, 2006, Andrea Tarr, review of *Dancing Larry,* p. 125; August, 2006, Wanda Meyers-Hines, review of *Bad Bear Detectives,* p. 94; April, 2007, Mara Alpert, review of *The Neddiad,* p. 146; September, 2007, Marge Loch-Wouters, review of *Yo-Yo Man,* p. 174; November, 2007, Martha Simpson, review of *Sleepover Larry,* p. 98; April 1, 2008, Marianne Saccardi, review of *Bear's Picture,* p. 119; October 1, 2008, review of *Bear's Picture,* p. 28; February 1, 2009, Eva Mitnick, review of *The Yggyssey,* p. 108.

Voice of Youth Advocates, June, 1982, Susan B. Madden, review of *Young Adult Novel,* p. 36; August, 1986, Susan B. Madden, review of *The Snarkout Boys and the Baconburg Horror,* p. 144.

Wilson Library Bulletin, March, 1982, Patty Campbell, review of *Young Adult Novel,* p. 533.

ONLINE

Chronogram Web site, http://www.chronogram.com/ (June 19, 2009), Nina Shengold, "The Gospel according to Pinkwater."

Daniel Pinkwater Home Page, http://www.pinkwater.com (June 19, 2009).

Kidsreads.com, http://www.kidsreads.com/ (June 19, 2009), Noah Piehl, review of *The Yggyssey.*

New York Times Book Review Online, http://www.nytimes.com/ (June 19, 2009), Larry Doyle, review of *The Yggyssey.*

Salon.com, http://www.salon.com/ (June 19, 2009), Paul LaFarge, "Welcome to Planet Pinkwater."

Seven Impossible Interviews before Breakfast, http://blaine.org/ (June 19, 2009), interview with Pinkwater.

Yggyssey Web site, http://www.theyggyssey.com/ (June 19, 2009).*

*   *   *

PINKWATER, Daniel M.
See PINKWATER, Daniel

PINKWATER, Daniel Manus
See PINKWATER, Daniel

*   *   *

PINKWATER, D. Manus
See PINKWATER, Daniel

*   *   *

PINKWATER, Manus
See PINKWATER, Daniel

*   *   *

POLHEMUS, Coleman

Personal

Born in AL.

Addresses

Home—Australia. *Agent*—Eunice McMullen Children's Literary Agency, Low Ibbotsholme Cottage, Off Bridge Ln., Troutbeck Bridge, Windermere, Cumbria LA23 1HU, England.

Career

Artist, author, and illustrator.

Writings

SELF-ILLUSTRATED

The Crocodile Blues, Candlewick Press (Cambridge, MA), 2007.

ILLUSTRATOR

Andrew Nance, *Daemon Hall,* Holt (New York, NY), 2007.

Sidelights

Coleman Polhemus is an American-born artist living in Australia. His first illustration project, Andrew Nance's horror story *Daemon Hall,* finds famed horror writer Ian Tremblin inviting five aspiring young writers to spend the night with him in a haunted mansion. Members of the group, which includes panic-stricken Wade and Goth girl Chelsea, experience a number of strange and frightening events during the evening. Polhemus's artwork drew praise from *Daemon Hall*'s creator.

"When . . . my editor . . . sent me copies of his illustrations, I remember sitting at my kitchen table and laughing like I'd won the lottery or something," Nance stated in an interview on the *Daemon Hall* Web site. Polhemus's "depiction of Chelsea was totally different from what I had in mind," Nance added. "Yet, I could tell by how lovely he made her, that maybe he'd become as fond of her as I had."

In *The Crocodile Blues,* Polhemus's nearly wordless picture book, a dapper gent and his pet cockatoo come into possession of a small egg. After the egg hatches and a crocodile emerges from the shell, the man and his bird make a quick exit from his apartment. They later receive an invitation to return to the building, only to find that it has been turned into a nightclub. "Youngsters will laugh at both the story line and the characters depicted in this zany book," noted *School Library Journal* reviewer Clare A. Dombrowski, and a contributor in *Publishers Weekly* praised Polhemus's "high-contrast, silkscreen-style digital imagery, in saturated shades of gray, royal blue and electric yellow on white."

Coleman Polhemus tells an almost wordless story that focuses on two unusual friends in his graphic illustrations for the picture book **The Crocodile Blues.** (Copyright © 2007 by Coleman Poehemus. Reproduced by permission of Candlewick Press Inc., Somerville, MA.)

Biographical and Critical Sources

PERIODICALS

Booklist, July 1, 2007, Ed Sullivan, review of *Daemon Hall,* p. 48.

Kirkus Reviews, June 1, 2007, review of *Daemon Hall;* August 15, 2007, review of *The Crocodile Blues.*

Publishers Weekly, September 24, 2007, review of *The Crocodile Blues,* p. 70.

School Library Journal, November, 2007, Clare A. Dombrowski, review of *The Crocodile Blues,* p. 98; December, 2007, Donna Rosenblum, review of *Daemon Hall,* p. 138.

ONLINE

Daemon Hall Web site, http://www.daemonhall.com/ (March 10, 2008), "Q&A with Andrew Nance."*

R

RIGGENBACH, Holly
See BLACK, Holly

* * *

ROMANO, Christy
See ROMANO, Christy Carlson

* * *

ROMANO, Christy Carlson 1984-
(Christy Romano)

Personal

Born March 20, 1984, in Milford, CT. *Education:* Professional Children's School, degree; attended School of American Ballet; attended Barnard College, Columbia University; studied acting at Beverly Hills Playhouse.

Addresses

Home—Los Angeles, CA. *Agent*—Geoff Cheddy, Brillstein Entertainment Partners, 9150 Wilshire Blvd., Ste. 350, Beverly Hills, CA 90212; April Lim, Global Artists Agency, 6253 Hollywood Blvd., Ste. No. 1508, Los Angeles, CA 90028.

Career

Actor, dancer, singer, and author. Actor in television series, including *Even Stevens,* Disney Channel, 1999-2003, and *Kim Possible* (animated), Disney Channel, 2002—. Actor in television films, including *Cadet Kelly,* Disney Channel, 2002, and *The Even Stevens Movie,* Disney Channel, 2003. Actor in films, including *Henry Fool,* 1997; (as Christy Romano) *Looking for an Echo,* 2000; and *The Cutting Edge 2: Going for the Gold,* 2006. Actor on stage, including in *Parade,* 1998-99, and *Beauty and the Beast,* 2004. Singer on recordings, including solo album *Christy Carlson Romano: Great-est Disney TV and Film Hits,* Disney Records; and on soundtracks, including *Everyone Says I Love You.* Voice artist, recording audio books for Hyperion Books and Random House Audio. Former congressional intern for U.S. Senator Christopher Dodd (D-CT).

Member

American Federation of Television and Radio Artists, Actors' Equity Association, Screen Actors Guild.

Awards, Honors

Emmy Award nomination for Outstanding Performer in an Animated Program, 2002, for *Kim Possible;* Books for the Teen Age selection, New York Public Library, 2007, for *Grace's Turn;* awarded key to City of Milford, CT, and February 22nd declared Christy Carlson Romano Day; Connecticut Finest Award.

Writings

Grace's Turn, Hyperion (New York, NY), 2006.

Sidelights

Stage, screen, and television star Christy Carlson Romano is perhaps best known as the voice of the title character in *Kim Possible,* a popular animated television program on the Disney Channel about a high-school cheerleader and straight-A student who spends her free time saving the world from evil-doers. In addition, Romano has played the irrepressible Ren Stevens in the Disney Channel comedy series *Even Stevens,* and she also starred as Belle in the Broadway musical *Beauty and the Beast.* In 2006 Romano added to her list of achievements by writing the young-adult novel *Grace's Turn,* a semi-autobiographical tale about a high-school student who lands a role in a Broadway play.

Raised in Connecticut, Romano began working as an entertainer at age six, making her theater debut in an Atlanta production of the hit musical *Annie.* She later toured with *The Will Rogers Follies* and *The Sound of Music,* and she made her Broadway debut at age fourteen in *Parade.* In addition, Romano has appeared in television films and in motion pictures such as Woody Allen's *Everyone Says I Love You.* A gifted singer, she has also contributed to soundtrack recordings. "I'm a firm believer that if you're a hard worker and a good worker, that people will cast you again and again and again," Romano told *Broadway Buzz* interviewer Lara De Meo. "That's just the way this business works."

Grace's Turn, Romano's debut novel, centers on Grace di Giovanni, a high-school junior who is determined to pursue her dreams of becoming an actress. The school year gets off to a promising start when Grace earns the lead in her school's production of *Grease,* which is staged by an award-winning Broadway director. After Grace is invited to audition for an actual Broadway production and earns a spot in the show, she struggles to maintain her relationships with best-friend Emily and her new boyfriend, star quarterback Hunter Wells. *Grace's Turn* garnered a number of positive reviews. Debbie Stewart Hoskins, writing in *School Library Journal,* praised the novel's authenticity, stating that Grace's "family interactions are portrayed with affectionate humor, and they are realistic, as are the audition scenes." According to a contributor in *Kirkus Reviews,* "Romano writes with fluid ease, rendering the book accessible and interesting."

Asked if she had any advice for youngsters interested in pursuing a career in show business, Romano told *Savvy Miss* online contributor Carita Rizzo: "I would tell them to be realistic. This business is amazing and glamorous and *everything that people say.* But then again it's everything that people say. Take it a day at a time because for every win you're going to get ten failures. And be committed. Make sure that this is what you want and go for it. I really am a firm believer that anything is possible."

Biographical and Critical Sources

PERIODICALS

Atlanta Journal-Constitution, January 10, 2005, Mary Beth Bishop, "*Kim Possible* Star Shows Many Talents," p. D4.
Kirkus Reviews, July 15, 2006, review of *Grace's Turn,* p. 729.
School Library Journal, November, 2006, Debbie Stewart Hoskins, review of *Grace's Turn,* p. 148.
Women's Wear Daily, September 11, 2003, Julee Greenberg, "Anything's Possible," p. 14.

ONLINE

Broadway.com, http://www.broadway.com/ (August 16, 2004), Lara De Meo, "Broadway Buzz Q & A: Christy Carlson Romano."

Christy Carlson Romano Home Page, http://christycarlson romano.com (March 10, 2008).
Saavy Miss Web site, http://www.savvymiss.com/ (March 10, 2008), Carita Rizzo, "Ambitious Women: Christy Carlson Romano."*

*   *   *

RUDDELL, Deborah 1949-

Personal

Born 1949, in IN; married; husband's name Brian. *Education:* University of Illinois at Urbana-Champaign, B.A., 1971.

Addresses

Home—Peoria, IL. *E-mail*—druddell@deborahruddell. com.

Career

Writer and poet. Graphic designer and newsletter editor for Peoria Public Schools, Peoria, IL, and as an art teacher and freelance artist.

Member

Society of Children's Writers and Illustrators.

Writings

Today at the Bluebird Café: A Branchful of Birds, illustrated by Joan Rankin, Margaret K. McElderry Books (New York, NY), 2007.
A Whiff of Pine, a Hint of Skunk: A Forest of Poems, illustrated by Joan Rankin, Margaret K. McElderry Books (New York, NY), 2009.

Contributor of a short story to *Highlights for Children.*

Sidelights

One of five children raised in a small Illinois town, writer and poet Deborah Ruddell credits her upbringing with helping her develop a sensitivity to the arts and letters. As an adult, Ruddell worked as a freelance artist and an art teacher, and she enjoyed a career in public relations at a public school. After seeing her children graduate from college, Ruddell turned to her first love: writing. Her books for children include *Today at the Bluebird Café: A Branchful of Birds* and *A Whiff of Pine, a Hint of Skunk: A Forest of Poems.*

Ruddell began writing poetry in 1998, taking her time to develop her craft and finding inspiration in many areas, including the world of nature. She studied other children's poets, learning from those writers, and also gained feedback as part of a local critique group. In ad-

Deborah Ruddell (Photograph by Ava Tramer. Reproduced by permission.)

dition, Ruddell joined the Society of Children's Writers and Illustrators, which holds an annual conference in Los Angeles. she attended this conference in 2003 with twenty-two polished poems in hand, all dealing with the subject of birds, and she also had illustrations for a picture-book project that had been done by her sister, Robin Luebs. At the conference, she was paired with a professional poet who took a genuine interest in Ruddell's work, passing it on to an agent who in turn managed to sell it to a publisher within only a few weeks.

The resulting children's book, *Today at the Bluebird Café,* is a collection of poems geared for elementary-age readers from kindergarten through fifth grade. The verses relate incidents in the lives of a hummingbird, a toucan, an owl, a crow, and a puffin, among other birds, each poem illustrated by the South African artist Joan Rankin. *Horn Book* contributor Joanna Rudge Long found much to like in this debut collection, observing that Ruddell's "rhymes are neat, her scansion [rhythm or beat] impeccable." Similarly, *Booklist* reviewer Gillian Engberg thought that "the best poems are funny, thoughtful, and lyrical," while *School Library Journal* contributor Grace Oliff noted that "all of the poems contain clever imagery and scan well." A *Publishers Weekly* critic also enjoyed *Today at the Bluebird Café,* writing that Ruddell's picture book "demonstrates a passion for winged creatures that readers may well find both palpable and infectious."

Another collaboration with Rankin, *A Whiff of Pine, a Hint of Skunk,* focuses on animals and nature and conveys zoological facts in a way children can relate to.

Writing on her home page, Ruddell revealed that she finds inspiration for writing children's poetry by remembering the days of her youth, adding that "I especially remember the things that made me laugh." Gillian Engberg, reviewing the picture book for *Booklist,* wrote that, "both lighthearted and substantive, this is a good choice for cross-curricular sharing," and a contributor to *Kirkus Reviews* called *A Whiff of Pine, a Hint of Skunk* "an excellent collection with broad age appeal."

Ruddell once commented: "Being a writer for children is a great privilege. I love talking to kids about my work and about what it's like being a writer: the fun of letting my imagination run wild; the hard, sometimes lonely, work of sitting in a quiet room and putting my ideas on a blank page; how it feels when I make myself laugh; the satisfaction that comes with revising until every word is just right; the joy of holding my own book in my hands; and the thrill of hearing from a reader who liked the book."

Biographical and Critical Sources

PERIODICALS

Booklist, January 1, 2007, Gillian Engberg, review of *Today at the Bluebird Café: A Branchful of Birds,* p. 110; March 15, 2009, Gillian Engberg, review of *A Whiff of Pine, a Hint of Skunk: A Forest of Poems,* p. 64.

Horn Book, May-June, 2007, Joanna Rudge Long, review of *Today at the Bluebird Café,* p. 297.

Kirkus Reviews, January 15, 2009, review of *A Whiff of Pine, a Hint of Skunk.*

Publishers Weekly, December 11, 2006, review of *Today at the Bluebird Café,* p. 68.

School Library Journal, February, 2007, Grace Oliff, review of *Today at the Bluebird Café,* p. 112.

ONLINE

BookLoons.com, http://www.bookloons.com/ (May 27, 2009), Hilary Daninhirsch, review of *A Whiff of Pine, a Hint of Skunk.*

Deborah Ruddell Home Page, http://www.deborahruddell.com (May 27, 2009).

Society of Children's Book Writers and Illustrators Illinois Chapter Web site, http://www.scbwi-illinois.org/ (March 28, 2008), "Deborah Ruddell."

*   *   *

RUZZIER, Sergio 1966-

Personal

Born 1966, in Milan, Italy; children: Viola.

Sergio Ruzzier (Photograph by Karen Devine. Reproduced by permission.)

Addresses

Home—New York, NY. *Office*—684 6th Ave., Ste. 3, New York, NY 11215. *E-mail*—sergio@ruzzier.com.

Career

Illustrator, 1986—. Creator of comic strips for *Linus* magazine, 1989-93, and *Lupo Alberto* magazine; writer. School of Visual Arts, New York, NY, instructor, 2004—; Parsons: The New School for Design, New York, NY, instructor. *Exhibitions:* Solo exhibitions at Galleria Derbylius, Milan, Italy, 1993, Galleria Nuages, Milan, 1999, Galleria Affiche, Milan, 2002-03, and Galleria Hoepli, Milan, 2002. Works included in group shows in the United States and Italy.

Awards, Honors

Awards from Society of Illustrators, Society of Publication Designers, *American Illustration,* and *Communication Arts;* Book of the Year selection, *Los Trabajos Prácticos,* for *Gli Uccelli—The Birds;* Parents' Choice Gold Award, 2004, for *Why Mole Shouted and Other Stories;* Parents' Choice Gold Award, 2005, for *The Room of Wonders.*

Writings

SELF-ILLUSTRATED

Un cane insonne e altri animali (title means "A Sleepless Dog and Other Animals"), Nuages (Milan, Italy), 1999.

La culla vuota—The Empty Cradle, Cane Andaluso (Milan, Italy), 1999.
Gli Uccelli—The Birds, Despina (Milan, Italy), 2002.
The Little Giant, Laura Geringer Books (New York, NY), 2004.
The Room of Wonders, Farrar, Straus & Giroux (New York, NY), 2005.
Amandina, Roaring Brook Press (New York, NY), 2008.

Contributor to books, including *Guys Write for Guys Read,* edited by Jon Scieszka, Viking (New York, NY), 2005.

ILLUSTRATOR

Kenneth C. Davis, *Don't Know Much about Space,* HarperCollins (New York, NY), 2001.
Karla Kuskin, *Moon, Have You Met My Mother? The Collected Poems of Karla Kuskin,* Laura Geringer Books (New York, NY), 2003.
Lore Segal, *Why Mole Shouted and Other Stories,* Farrar, Straus & Giroux (New York, NY), 2004.
Lore Segal, *More Mole Stories and Little Gopher, Too,* Farrar, Straus & Giroux (New York, NY), 2005.
Kenneth C. Davis, *Don't Know Much about World Myths,* HarperCollins (New York, NY), 2005.
Emily Jenkins, *Love You When You Whine,* Farrar, Straus & Giroux (New York, NY), 2006.
Karen Miller, *Monsters and Water Beasts: Creatures of Fact or Fiction?,* Holt (New York, NY), 2007.

Contributor of illustrations to periodicals, including *New York Times, Wall Street Journal, New Yorker, Boston Globe,* and *Atlantic Monthly.*

Sidelights

The work of award-winning author and illustrator Sergio Ruzzier has been described as "very adult and sophisticated" yet "still adaptable to children's sensitivity," according to Veronique Alaimo on the USItalia Web site. Ruzzier's first self-illustrated picture book, *Un cane insonne e altri animali,* was published in Italy in 1999, and since that time he has made highly praised artistic contributions to a number of titles for children, including *Moon, Have You Met My Mother? The Collected Poems of Karla Kuskin* and Lore Segal's *Why Mole Shouted and Other Stories.* In addition, Ruzzier has continued to create original self-illustrated works, such as *The Little Giant* and *The Room of Wonders,* and his work has been compared to that of noted illustrator Maurice Sendak due to his subtle use of color and his sketchy yet exacting line drawings.

Ruzzier, who was born in Milan, Italy, began his career in illustration in 1986. His comic strips appeared in *Linus,* a popular Italian magazine, from 1989 to 1993, as well as in *Lupo Alberto* magazine. In 1995 Ruzzier moved to New York City, where he began contributing illustrations to books and periodicals, including the *Wall Street Journal,* the *New Yorker,* and the *Atlantic*

Monthly. In addition to his work as an artist, Ruzzier also teaches at Parsons: The New School for Design as well as at New York City's School of Visual Arts. His work has appeared in shows in both the United States and Italy, and he has received awards from the Society of Illustrators and the Society of Publication Designers.

In 2001 Ruzzier provided the illustrations for *Don't Know Much about Space,* a nonfiction work for children by Kenneth C. Davis, whose "Don't Know Much About" series was already a hit with adult readers. Using a question-and-answer format, *Don't Know Much*

about Space presents information about the solar system, black holes, famous astronomers, and the history of the universe. In *School Library Journal,* John Peters noted that Ruzzier's "sophisticated but still decorative art for the book is supplemented by several photos and photo-realist paintings." Davis and Ruzzier have also collaborated on *Don't Know Much about World Myths.*

Ruzzier's illustrations have also graced the pages of *Moon, Have You Met My Mother?,* an anthology by celebrated children's poet Karla Kuskin. In the collection, which spans more than forty years of the poet's career,

Ruzzier's illustration projects include bringing to life Lore Segal's quirky picture book **Why Mole Shouted.** (Illustration copyright © 2004 by Sergio Ruzzier. Reprinted by permission of Farrar, Straus & Giroux, LLC.)

Kuskin reflects on a variety of subjects, including the seasons, magic, animals, and childhood experiences, in such works as "Buggity, Buggity, Bug," "A Wizard Has a Lizard," "There Is a Me Inside of Me," "Pigeon Is a Pretty Word," and the title poem. "The compositions have a thoughtful yet unfussy feel, as if dashed off in moments of informal inspiration, and they are nicely complemented by Sergio Ruzzier's simple, loopy line illustrations," remarked Christine Leahy in the *New York Times Book Review*. Ruzzier's efforts also drew praise from other critics. "The book's handsome design resembles a Shel Silverstein collection with small ink drawings—subtle, funny, and wild—on spacious cream-colored pages," remarked *Booklist* reviewer Gillian Engberg. A *Publishers Weekly* critic wrote that "Ruzzier's line illustrations resemble some of Sendak's early drawings, with just the right blend of sophistication and levity," and *School Library Journal* contributor Margaret Bush noted that the illustrator's "small cartoon sketches . . . echo the often humorous tone of the poetry."

Ruzzier's self-illustrated book *The Little Giant* concerns Angelino De Grandi, an undersized giant who is shunned by his community and decides to leave home. During his travels Angelino finds his twin in Osvaldo Curti, an oversized dwarf who is similarly ostracized by his people. The two become fast friends, and when their tribes go to war, they work together to settle the conflict. According to a critic in *Publishers Weekly*, in his watercolor illustrations, Ruzzier "depicts Angelino and Osvaldo as folkloric figures in an all-male realm, who live in a desert painted in muted greens, soft blues, and sandstone yellows and reds." *Booklist* critic Jennifer Mattson recommends that *The Little Giant* for older readers "who will embrace the messages of peace, acceptance, and brotherly love."

Discussing the similarities between Angelino's search for an identity and his own, Ruzzier told Alaimo: "I left Italy because I needed a change, to find satisfaction in my work. Somehow it seems easier to reinvent oneself far away from the judging eyes of those who have known you all your life long and also in a city like New York where everything different is embraced with a certain enthusiasm. That constant influx of new ideas and new stimuli is what I find fascinating about this city and what allows me a greater freedom in my work."

Ruzzier has also provided the artwork for Segal's *Why Mole Shouted and Other Stories,* "a sly, solemn, slightly silly and utterly charming book," according to Lawrence Downes in the *New York Times Book Review.* In her collection of four humorous tales, Segal explores the tender relationship between Grandmother Mole and her young grandson. The opening story centers on Mole's inability to find his perpetually misplaced glasses, a problem Grandmother handles with patience. In the second, the elderly mole scolds her grandson for not dressing warmly enough, but when she comes down with a cold, the youngster helps nurse her back to health. The

title story concerns Mole's need for reassurance, and the final tale follows Grandmother's efforts to answer her grandson's seemingly never-ending stream of questions. "Ruzzier's vignettes in muted hues complement the narrative with subtle nuances," observed a *Publishers Weekly* contributor, and Linda M. Kenton noted in *School Library Journal* that the artist's "earth-tone palette echoes the characters' underground world." According to a critic in *Kirkus Reviews,* "Ruzzier applies muted earth-tones to intimate, distinct illustrations illuminating the reassuring love" the characters have for each other.

In a companion volume, *More Mole Stories and Little Gopher, Too,* Segal offers four additional tales about Mole and his grandmother. Mole has trouble resisting the chocolate chip cookies his grandma has baked for dessert in one episode, and he will not share with Little Gopher, a playmate, in another. Mole also keeps an entire bag of pretzels to himself, and he attempts to interrupt Grandmother's phone conversation when he wants her undivided attention. "Intimate earth-tone watercolor illustrations convey Little Mole's behavior and a love and loyalty" between the characters, noted a *Kirkus Reviews* contributor. Hazel Rochman, writing in *Booklist,* praised Ruzzier's "small, emotional line-and-watercolor pictures," and *Horn Book* reviewer Deirdre F. Baker commented that the artist's "portrait of the moles as lovable grotesques . . . complete this triumphant mix of homey charm and otherworldly weirdness."

Another self-illustrated title, *The Room of Wonders,* was described as "a thought-provoking parable for old and young alike" by *Booklist* critic Gillian Engberg. Pius Pelosi, an adventurous pack rat, spends his days roaming the land searching for all manner of unusual and interesting objects, including twigs, feathers, leaves, buttons, and shells. Pius displays the massive collection in his Room of Wonders, and he draws visitors from near and far who marvel at his curiosities. When his guests criticize one particular object—an ordinary, uninspiring gray pebble that was Pius's first prized item—the pack rat becomes depressed, tosses the pebble into the river, and gives away his remaining treasures. Later, an unexpected find rekindles his passion for collecting. "Ruzzier's characters' overlarge eyes and elongated noses seem ideally suited to this tale about inquisitiveness, and subtle humor comes through in the text," a contributor remarked in *Publishers Weekly,* and Maura Bresnahan, critiquing the work in *School Library Journal,* wrote that "Ruzzier's gently told story is perfectly pitched for the picture-book crowd."

Ruzzier collaborates with Emily Jenkins on the picture book *Love You When You Whine,* in which a harried but caring mother cat presents a comforting message to her rambunctious preschooler. Despite the tot's outrageous antics, such as pouring cereal food on the floor, unfolding the laundry, throwing a tantrum in public, spreading jelly on the computer, and placing crayons in the dryer, her mother's affections never waver. "Ruzzier's inti-

Ruzzier's self-illustrated Amandina *introduces a budding actress with a passion for performing.* (Copyright © 2008 by Sergio Ruzzier. Reprinted by arrangement with Henry Holt & Company, LLC.)

mate, warm-hued paintings spotlight each behavior and add lots of humor," Joy Fleishhacker reported in *School Library Journal*. A critic in *Kirkus Reviews* applauded the artist's "humorous, slightly surreal watercolor illustrations featuring a very naughty little creature gleefully acting out," and Christine Heppermann, writing in *Horn Book*, also cited the artist's "comical, understated" pictures of the energetic youngster. A *Publishers Weekly* contributor offered praise for the combination of Ruzzier's illustrations and Jenkins's narrative, stating that "the quirky art and missing first-person pronoun confer a subtly avant-garde quality" to the story.

A collaboration with Karen Miller resulted in *Monsters and Water Beasts: Creatures of Fact or Fiction?* Here Miller explores the myths and legends surrounding a host of fantastical beings, including Bigfoot, Mothman, the Jersey Devil, the Big Bird of Texas, hoop snakes, the sea maiden of Biloxi, the sea serpent of Gloucester, and the Cadborosaurus in British Columbia. Noting the book's engaging design, *Booklist* contributor Carolyn Phelan added that *Monsters and Water Beasts* "depict[s] the creatures as kindly rather than terrifying, echoing the even, nonsensical tone" of Miller's narrative.

An original, self-illustrated picture book, *Amandina* introduces a shy dog who loves the theatre and wants to share her love with others. According to a *Publishers Weekly* critic, in *Amandina* Ruzzier shows "magical insight into the imagination of" children and "the mood he casts will resonate, particularly with introspective readers." A *Kirkus Reviews* contributor admired the author/illustrator's "quiet, precise, whimsical" watercolor art for the book, describing *Amandina* as "a subdued but charming tribute to determination and perseverance." In the *Boston Globe*, Liz Rosenberg noted Ruzzier's creative nods to both "commedia dell'arte and Punch and Judy"; In *Amandina* the artist creates a picture book that "is thrillingly odd, and oddly haunting," Rosenbergc concluded.

Biographical and Critical Sources

PERIODICALS

Booklist, April 1, 2003, Gillian Engberg, review of *Moon, Have You Met My Mother? The Collected Poems of*

Karla Kuskin, p. 1408; March 15, 2004, Jennifer Mattson, review of *The Little Giant,* p. 1310; May 1, 2004, Hazel Rochman, review of *Why Mole Shouted and Other Stories,* p. 1564; March 1, 2005, Hazel Rochman, review of *More Mole Stories and Little Gopher, Too,* p. 1206; February 15, 2006, Gillian Engberg, review of *The Room of Wonders,* p. 104; May 1, 2007, Carolyn Phelan, review of *Monsters and Water Beasts: Creatures of Fact or Fiction?,* p. 91.

Boston Globe, December 21, 2008, Liz Rosenberg, review of *Amandina.*

Horn Book, March-April, 2005, Deirdre F. Baker, review of *More Mole Stories and Little Gopher, Too,* p. 194; September-October, 2006, Christine M. Heppermann, review of *Love You When You Whine,* p. 567.

Kirkus Reviews, February 1, 2003, review of *Moon, Have You Met My Mother?,* p. 234; January 15, 2004, review of *The Little Giant,* p. 88; April 1, 2004, review of *Why Mole Shouted and Other Stories,* p. 337; April 1, 2005, review of *More Mole Stories and Little Gopher, Too,* p. 425; April 15, 2006, review of *The Room of Wonders,* p. 415; August 1, 2006, review of *Love You When You Whine,* p. 788; August 1, 2008, review of *Amandina.*

New York Times Book Review, May 18, 2003, Christine Leahy, review of *Moon, Have You Met My Mother?;* May 16, 2004, Lawrence Downes, review of *Why Mole Shouted and Other Stories.*

Publishers Weekly, July 23, 2001, review of *Don't Know Much about Space,* p. 78; January 13, 2003, review of *Moon, Have You Met My Mother?,* p. 62; March 22, 2004, reviews of *The Little Giant* and *Why Mole Shouted and Other Stories,* p. 85; May 29, 2006, review of *The Room of Wonders,* p. 58; July 24, 2006, review of *Love You When You Whine,* p. 56; September 29, 2008, review of *Amandina,* p. 81.

School Library Journal, August, 2001, John Peters, review of *Don't Know Much about Space,* p. 194; February, 2003, Margaret Bush, review of *Moon, Have You Met My Mother?,* p. 162; March, 2004, Marianne Saccardi, review of *The Little Giant,* p. 180; April, 2004, Linda M. Kenton, review of *Why Mole Shouted and Other Stories,* p. 124; April, 2005, Marianne Saccardi, review of *More Mole Stories and Little Gopher, Too,* p. 112; May, 2006, Maura Bresnahan, review of *The Room of Wonders,* p. 103; October, 2006, Joy Fleishhacker, review of *Love You When You Whine,* p. 113; July, 2007, Gloria Koster, review of *Monsters and Water Beasts,* p. 119; October 1, 2008, Linda Ludke, review of *Amandina,* p. 122.

ONLINE

Sergio Ruzzier Home Page, http://www.ruzzier.com (May 28, 2009).

USItalia Web site, http://www.usitalia.info/ (March 14, 2004), Veronique Alaimo, "Sergio Ruzzier's *Little Giant.*"

S

SELZNICK, Brian 1966-

Personal

Born July 14, 1966, in NJ; son of Roger (an accountant) and Lynn (a homemaker) Selznick; partner of David Serlin. *Education:* Rhode Island School of Design, B.F.A., 1988. *Politics:* Democrat. *Religion:* Jewish. *Hobbies and other interests:* Movies, puppetry, travel.

Addresses

Home—Brooklyn, NY; and San Diego, CA.

Career

Eeyore's Books for Children, New York, NY, bookseller and painter of window displays, 1988-91; writer and illustrator of children's books, 1991—.

Awards, Honors

Texas Bluebonnet Award, and Rhode Island Children's Book Award, both 1993, both for *The Houdini Box;* Christopher Award (with Andrew Clements), 1996, for *Frindle;* American Library Association Notable Children's Book designation, and Book Sense Honor Book citation, both 1999, both for *Amelia and Eleanor Go for a Ride;* Orbis Pictus Honor Book designation, and Caldecott Honor, both 2002, both for *The Dinosaurs of Waterhouse Hawkins* by Barbara Kerley; Orbis Pictus Award, 2003, for *When Marion Sang* by Pam Muñoz Ryan; *New York Times* Best Illustrated Books selection, and Robert F. Sibert Informational Book Award Honor Book designation, both 2004, both for *Walt Whitman* by Barbara Kerley; Quill Award, *New York Times* Best Illustrated Books selection, and National Book Award Young People's Literature finalist, all 2007, and Caldecott Medal, 2008, all for *The Invention of Hugo Cabret.*

Writings

SELF-ILLUSTRATED

The Houdini Box, Knopf (New York, NY), 1991, reprinted, 2001.

The Robot King, Laura Geringer Books (New York, NY), 1995.
The Boy of a Thousand Faces, Laura Geringer Books (New York, NY), 2000.
The Invention of Hugo Cabret, Scholastic, Inc. (New York, NY), 2007.

ILLUSTRATOR

Pam Conrad, *Dollface Has a Party!,* HarperCollins (New York, NY), 1994.
Pam Conrad, *Our House: The Stories of Leavittown,* Scholastic, Inc. (New York, NY), 1995, tenth anniversary edition, 2005.
Andrew Clements, *Frindle,* Simon & Schuster (New York, NY), 1996.
Norma Farber, *The Boy Who Longed for a Lift,* Laura Geringer Books (New York, NY), 1997.
Pam Muñoz Ryan, *Riding Freedom,* Scholastic, Inc. (New York, NY), 1998.
Pam Muñoz Ryan, *Amelia and Eleanor Go for a Ride,* Scholastic, Inc. (New York, NY), 1999.
Laura Godwin, *Barnyard Prayers,* Hyperion (New York, NY), 2000.
Ann M. Martin and Laura Godwin, *The Doll People,* Hyperion (New York, NY), 2000.
Barbara Kerley, *The Dinosaurs of Waterhouse Hawkins: An Illuminating History of Mr. Waterhouse Hawkins, Artist and Lecturer,* Scholastic, Inc. (New York, NY), 2001.
Andrew Clements, *The School Story,* Simon & Schuster (New York, NY), 2001.
Pam Muñoz Ryan, *When Marian Sang: The True Recital of Marian Anderson: The Voice of a Century,* Scholastic, Inc. (New York, NY), 2002.
Rosemary Wells, *Wingwalker,* Hyperion (New York, NY), 2002.
Ann M. Martin and Laura Godwin, *The Meanest Doll in the World,* Hyperion (New York, NY), 2003.
Tor Seidler, *The Dulcimer Boy,* new edition, Laura Geringer Books (New York, NY), 2003.
Barbara Kerley, *Walt Whitman: Words for America,* Scholastic, Inc. (New York, NY), 2004.

Andrew Clements, *Lunch Money,* Simon & Schuster (New York, NY), 2005.

David Levithan, *Marly's Ghost: A Remix of Charles Dickens's A Christmas Carol,* Dial (New York, NY), 2006.

Laura Godwin and Ann M. Martin, *The Runaway Dolls,* Hyperion (New York, NY), 2008.

Contributor of illustrations to periodicals, including *Cricket* and *Spider.*

Adaptations

The Invention of Hugo Cabret has been adapted as an audiobook and has been optioned for film by Warner Brothers.

Sidelights

In addition to creating artwork for texts by a variety of children's authors, Brian Selznick became known as an author in his own right when his first original picture book, *The Houdini Box,* earned a burst of recognition and popularity that is rare in children's book-publishing. Reviewers responded enthusiastically to Selznick's de-

Selznick collaborates with popular middle-grade writer Andrew Clements on novels that include the award-winning **Frindle.** (Aladdin Paperbacks, 1996. Illustration copyright © 1996 by Brian Selznick. All rights reserved. Reproduced by permission of illustrator.)

but work, applauding his evocative pencil illustrations, smooth prose style, and ability to mix mystery and fantasy in an engaging story. His more recent self-illustrated works, which include *The Robot King* and *The Boy of a Thousand Faces,* have elicited similar praise, with Barbara Buckley noting in a *School Library Journal* review of *The Boy of a Thousand Faces* that "Selznick has his finger on the pulse of kids and what they love." In 2007 he published his most widely praised title, *The Invention of Hugo Cabret.* With this effort, observed London *Guardian* contributor Joanna Carey, "Selznick seems to have invented a new kind of book. It's at once a picture book, a graphic novel, a rattling good yarn and an engaging celebration of the early days of the cinema."

Although he published *The Houdini Box* at age twenty-three, Selznick did not originally plan on a career in juvenile literature, as he once explained to *SATA.* After graduating from the Rhode Island School of Design (RISD) in 1988, he wanted to design theater sets, but when he did not get into the graduate theater program he wanted, he decided to rethink his career plans. As Selznick recalled to *SATA,* during this time he realized: "What I love to do most of all is draw. I always loved children's books, so I thought, why am I fighting this? This is the most natural, obvious thing for me to do."

While casting about for ideas for illustrations he could send to book editors as part of a portfolio, Selznick recalled a story he had written as part of a school project at RISD. "One week we got an assignment to do something about Houdini," he explained, "and I was really excited about that because when I was a kid Houdini was a hero of mine." This Houdini project consists of a series of seven Plexiglas panels that assemble into a folding screen, creating a three-dimensional display roughly the shape of a box. Each of the panels is painted with parts of a scene; when viewers look through the transparent structure they are presented with a complete picture of famous escape artist Harry Houdini performing his famous Chinese water torture escape. Selznick had been so caught up in the project that he went one step further and came up with a story, writing it on the back of the painted parts of each panel. "It's the exact same story that's in *The Houdini Box,*" explained the author/illustrator, "except in a much shorter version."

Selznick made black-and-white drawings of several scenes from his story about Houdini and sent them off to children's book editors, and the entire idea was accepted for picture-book publication at Knopf. Selznick refined his text and added additional art, and the finished book appeared in 1991. *The Houdini Box* features ten-year-old Victor, who receives a box from Harry Houdini's widow that may or may not contain all the great magician's secrets, but the box is locked. When Victor notices that the initials on the box are E.W. and not H.H., he thinks: "This wasn't Houdini's box at all!" In his sadness and disappointment, Victor takes the box and buries it "forever at the bottom of his closet." It is

Selznick's detailed art brings to life Pam Muñoz Ryan's entertaining story in **Riding Freedom.** (Scholastic Press, a division of Scholastic Inc., 1999. Illustration copyright © 1998 by Brian Selznick. Reproduced by permission.)

not until many years later, after Victor is grown and married and has a young son of his own, that he learns Houdini's real name was Ehrich Weiss, the E.W. on the long-forgotten box. That night, after his wife and child are asleep, Victor creeps up to the attic to find the box. The lock has rusted through, and it opens easily, revealing to Victor the secrets hidden for so long.

According to a *Publishers Weekly* reviewer, *The Houdini Box* expresses "the importance of faith and the ability to believe in the impossible," and the story's illustrations "bring added vitality to a captivating plot." Selznick's "strong, rhythmic prose is great for reading aloud," wrote Hazel Rochman in a review for *Booklist,* the critic also lauding the way the full-page drawings "with close cross-hatching show a dreamy, determined Victor."

When *The Houdini Box* was released, the newly published author/illustrator was working at Eeyore's Bookstore in New York City, where he sold books and painted window displays. Through one of his customers, writer and HarperCollins editor Laura Geringer, he received his next illustration project: creating art for Pam Conrad's *Dollface Has a Party!* When Conrad

wrote the book, it was originally intended to teach English to Japanese students, and she imagined a small Japanese doll as the main character. To Selznick, however, "Dollface" sounded "like a gangster's moll from those old black-and-white gangster movies," as he remarked in his interview. He based the character of Dollface on a doll from the 1920s that he found in a flea market. At the time, she was wearing a 1970s-era pink pants suit, and since she was bald, Selznick gave her a pink bouffant hairdo made of yarn to match. "She is always looking at the world through this one arched eyebrow," Selznick commented. Conrad had envisioned a quiet little book, but when she saw Selznick's bright and wry drawings, he reported that her response was, "You made it really *Broadway!*"

Selznick has continued to produce both original picture books and illustrations for the works of others. His self-illustrated *The Robot King* was inspired by a radio announcer's discussion of a piece of music. "I was only paying half-attention," the author/illustrator recalled, "and it seemed like he said, 'That was "Waltz of the Robots."'" The phrase stayed with him, and he made a note in his journal, "Why would a robot dance?" The answer he came up with is "because his heart is a music box," and three years later Selznick completed work on the story that makes sense of the phrase. In his tale a brother and sister build a robot from odds and ends they find in their house, and for the heart they use a music box that belonged to their late mother. When the music box is wound up, the robot comes magically to life. The newly animated robot begins to animate other objects in the house, and then takes the children to a magical fairgrounds until the children find their father and return home.

The Robot King "has the flavor of a Victorian fairy tale," remarked Deborah Stevenson in the *Bulletin of the Center for Children's Books,* "with electricity and technology forces of silent and incalculable magic and the sensibility more significant than the plotting." Jane Gardner Connor praised the artwork accompanying Selznick's original story, writing in *School Library Journal* that the author/illustrator's illustrations "do a good job of reflecting the somber, detached mood of the story."

The Boy of a Thousand Faces introduces readers to a ten year old who is in love with monsters. With a birthday on Halloween, Alonzo King is a loyal fan of *Monsters at Midnight,* a television program that reruns old horror movies selected by its host, the mysterious Mr. Shadows. Inspired by famous film actor Lon Chaney, Alonzo learns to make up his own face in a multitude of scary guises, and he sends a photograph of his scariest face to Mr. Shadows. Before his idol can reply, Alonzo finds himself with more important concerns: Halloween is approaching and it seems to have summoned forth a creature called the Beast, which is lurking around town. In *Booklist* Michael Cart cited Selznick's "engaging story and . . . witty, eye-popping, black-and-white illustrations" for *The Boy of a Thousand Faces* while Buckley praised the book's "realistic pencil drawings" in her *School Library Journal* review as "expressive and suited to the story's mood." In *Publishers Weekly* a reviewer called *The Boy of a Thousand Faces* an "offbeat tale" in which Selznick's "characteristically detailed and moodily lit" art echoes the old films so loved by the story's young hero.

Containing over 300 color illustrations, Selznick's original picture book *The Invention of Hugo Cabret* was a finalist for the National Book Award in young people's literature and the recipient of a Caldecott medal. Set in the 1930s, the book concerns twelve-year-old Hugo, an orphan living inside the walls of a Parisian train station who becomes obsessed with completing a broken automaton. Hugo steals mechanical parts from the station's toy shop, and he soon becomes involved with the elderly shop owner and his goddaughter, Isabelle. Together, the youngsters slowly peel back the mystery of the shop owner's identity, that of pioneering French filmmaker Georges Méliès. "Méliès began his career as a magician, and he always filmed his movies as if they were stage productions an audience would sit and watch," Selnick noted in an interview on the Scholastic Web site. "He was a great artist who lost everything

A famous poet is brought to life in Selznick's art for Barbara Kerley's **Walt Whitman: Words for America.** (Illustration copyright © 2004 by Brian Selznick. Reprinted by permission of Scholastic, Inc.)

and was rediscovered at the end of his life and celebrated once again. His use of magic, his belief in the power of imagination, and the joy he experienced as he created his art seemed to me the kinds of things that kids would understand."

In addition to awards, *The Invention of Hugo Cabret* garnered positive reviews. "The interplay between the illustrations (including several stills from Méliès's frequently surreal films and others from the era) and text is complete genius, especially in the way Selznick moves from one to the other," noted *Horn Book* critic Roger Sutton. "The story is an engaging meditation on fantasy, inventiveness, and a thrilling mystery in its own right," Ian Beck remarked in the London *Times.* "Selznick should be applauded," the critic added, "not only for extending the form of the illustrated book, but also for mining such a rich and neglected seam for his storytelling." According to Neal Wyatt, writing in *Library Journal,* the work "is an amazing and groundbreaking achievement, compelling us to read each illustration visually in order for the story to progress." In an interview with Rita Williams-Garcia on the National Book Foundation Web site, Selznick commented, *The Invention of Hugo Cabret* "is ABOUT bookmaking and what can happen between the covers of a book." He

Patrick Jennings' middle-grade novel **The Beastly Arms** *features artwork by Selznick.* (Cover illustration copyright © 2003 by Brian Selznick. Reproduced by permission of Scholastic, Inc.)

continued, "I wanted the reader to be reminded with every turn of the page that they are an important part, perhaps the most important part, of the story. It is the reader that moves the story forward."

In his work as an illustrator, Selznick has created art for several authors, including Pam Muñoz Ryan, Clements, Ann M. Martin, Tor Seidler, and Rosemary Wells. One of his favorite illustration projects, Barbara Kerley's *The Dinosaurs of Waterhouse Hawkins: An Illuminating History of Mr. Waterhouse Hawkins, Artist and Lecturer,* drew on his early love of dinosaurs and his interest in history in its story of sculptor Benjamin Waterhouse Hawkins, who worked with scientist Richard Owen and in 1853 unveiled the first life-sized models of dinosaurs ever made. "There is a sly abundance of Victorian humbug in Selznick's pictures," noted *New York Times Book Review* critic Lawrence Downes, "especially when he allows Hawkins himself to introduce the story, lifting up a velvet curtain to invite the reader to the title page, which is executed with splashy lettering that evokes antique circus posters."

Another collaboration with Kerley resulted in the award-winning picture-book biography *Walt Whitman: Words for America,* which focuses on the former poet laureate's love of the common man and his inspiring work during the U.S. Civil War. Calling the book "delightfully old fashioned in design," *School Library Journal* contributor Marilyn Taniguchi deemed *Walt Whitman* "an exuberant picture book" wherein Selznick's "brilliantly inventive paintings add vibrant testimonial to the nuanced text." According to *New York Times Book Review* contributor Abby McGanney Nolan, Selznick "uses extensive research to inform his work. His illustrations for the Civil War section are full of emotion and details. There's the unfinished Capitol dome in the background as Lincoln, by day, and Whitman, by night, both brooding about the war, pass along the same street. There are two sets of illustrations Selznick has modeled on Civil War-era daguerreotypes, the first of soldiers going off to war, the second of injured soldiers who hold chalkboards of their names while displaying their wounds." Jennifer Mattson, reviewing the work for *Booklist,* similarly noted the illustrator's "keen passion for research," and deemed *Walt Whitman* a "sophisticated offering." In *Publishers Weekly* a reviewer concluded that the biography's "talented collaborators' affection and admiration for their subject" creates an "enthusiasm [that] is convincing and contagious."

Selznick's nostalgia-inspired art enhances Muñoz Ryan's *Amelia and Eleanor Go for a Ride* and *When Marian Sang: The True Recital of Marian Anderson,* two books that are based on actual events. In *Amelia and Eleanor Go for a Ride* Selznick illustrates Ryan's account of the time U.S. First Lady Eleanor Roosevelt joined aviatrix Amelia Earhart in a plane ride over Washington, DC. Noting that Selznick's pencil drawings reflect the stylized art of the 1930s, when Roosevelt actually took to the skies, Ilene Cooper wrote in *Booklist*

that both author and illustrator "clearly did their research" to create a story of "two strong women—real pioneers." *Horn Book* reviewer Roger Sutton cited Selznick's art in *When Marian Sang* as "impressive in sweep and scale." "In harmony with the deeply moving text by Ryan," commented Ellen Feldman in the *New York Times Book Review,* "Selznick's warm, earth-hued illustrations are emotionally powerful. The first page, a view of a handful of people trickling into an empty opera house, shimmers with the promise of opening night." Referencing the nostalgic quality of the sepia-toned paintings, a *Kirkus Reviews* writer stated that the illustrator's "carefully researched" acrylic paintings depicting African-American opera singer Marian Anderson's performance on the steps of the Lincoln Memorial after being denied entrance into Constitution Hall "a bravura performance."

According to a *Publishers Weekly* critic, Selznick's "detailed illustrations" for Martin and Laura Godwin's *The Doll People* and its sequel, *The Meanest Doll in the World,* capture the "diverse moods and perspectives" in the two doll families at the center of the series. In Kate Palmer's bedroom live two doll families that are some-

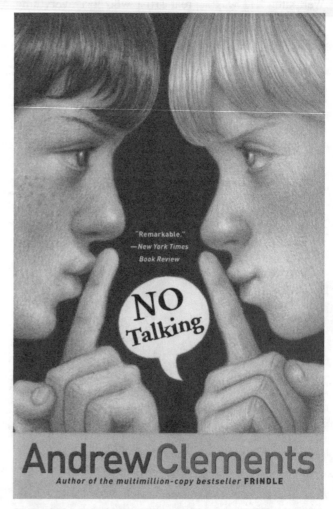

Cover of Clements' middle-grade school story No Talking, *featuring cover art by Selznick.* (Aladdin, 2007. Cover illustration © 2007 by Brian Selznick. Reproduced by permission.)

times at odds: the century-old pedigreed Doll family and the mass-produced plastic Funcraft family. While often forced to interact in play, the two families, including main characters Anabelle Doll and Tiffany Funcraft, are sometimes at odds due to their differences but they band together to solve a mystery. In *The Meanest Doll in the World,* Anabelle and Tiffany join forces again when they meet up with the vengeful Princess Mimi, the doll of the title, and attempt to stop Mimi's efforts to take control of all dolls. Praising Selznick's imaginative, humor-filled illustrations in *The Meanest Doll in the World,* *Horn Book* reviewer Martha V. Parravano wrote that, "in their wit and profusion," the artist's detailed pencil illustration combine all the story's subplots "together in one appealing package." Selznick's "clever title-page progression . . . is not to be missed," wrote *Booklist* reviewer Karin Snelson, and his illustrations are "winningly expressive," while Katherine Devin wrote in *School Library Journal* that "witty illustrations" in *The Meanest Doll in the World* "do a fabulous job of extending the story."

Other books that showcase Selznick's talent for capturing moments of history through his detailed illustration include *Our House: The Stories of Leavittown,* an award-winning volume by Pam Conrad that collects six short stories set in the small Long Island suburb at the start of the baby boom following World War II. In *Horn Book,* Mary M. Burns cited Selznick's "elegant pen-and-ink drawings" for enhancing Conrad's "finely crafted" collection. His paintings for Rosemary Wells' *Wingwalker* bring what a *Kirkus Reviews* writer deemed a "quiet gravity" to the story of a young boy's experiences up in the air with a stunt pilot in 1930s Oklahoma. Writing that Selznick "has a lock on the iconography of history as it intersects with dreams," the *Kirkus Reviews* writer praised his paintings as "full of sky, airplanes, and upward-looking faces" and bringing a sense of optimism to Wells' Depression-era story. According to Linda Phillips Ashour, writing in the *New York Times Book Review,* "the fluid chapters and warm illustrations of *Wingwalker* create a vision of an expanding world in a difficult time."

Asked if he had any advice for budding illustrators, Selznick noted on the Scholastic Web site: "I think the most important thing you can do is to keep drawing no matter what. And to not be afraid of drawing whatever interests you. If there is something that you want to draw, to make, then I think you should pursue it and not let anybody tell you that you can't do it."

Biographical and Critical Sources

BOOKS

Selznick, Brian, *The Houdini Box,* Knopf (New York, NY), 1991.

PERIODICALS

Booklist, June 1, 1991, Hazel Rochman, review of *The Houdini Box,* p. 1875; January 1, 1996, Linda Perkins, review of *Our House: The Story of Levittown,* p. 833; May 15, 1997, Michael Cart, review of *The Boy Who Longed for a Lift,* p. 1579; October 15, 1999, Ilene Cooper, review of *Amelia and Eleanor Go for a Ride: Based on a True Story,* p. 447; September 15, 2000, Michael Cart, review of *The Boy of a Thousand Faces,* p. 244; October 15, 2003, review of *The Meanest Doll in the World,* p. 412; November 15, 2004, Jennifer Mattson, review of *Walt Whitman: Words for America,* p. 575; January 1, 2007, Jennifer Mattson, review of *The Invention of Hugo Cabret,* p. 97.

Bulletin of the Center for Children's Books, June, 1991, Roger Sutton, review of *The Houdini Box,* p. 250; October, 1995, Deborah, Stevenson, review of *The Robot King,* p. 69.

Christian Science Monitor, March 27, 2007, Jenny Sawyer, review of *The Invention of Hugo Cabret,* p. 14.

Guardian (London, England), January 12, 2008, Joanna Carey, "A Subtle World in Black and White," p. 20.

Horn Book, November-December, 1995, Mary M. Burns, review of *Our House* p. 740; May-June, 1997, Martha V. Parravano, review of *The Boy Who Longed for a Lift,* p. 305; July, 2001, Roger Sutton, review of *The School Story,* p. 448; July-August, 2002, Christine M. Heppermann, review of *Wingwalker,* p. 474; November-December, 2002, Roger Sutton, review of *When Marian Sang,* p. 780; November-December, 2003, Martha V. Parravano, review of *The Meanest Doll in the World,* p. 751; November-December, 2004, Kathleen Isaacs, review of *Walt Whitman,* p. 729; March-April, 2007, Roger Sutton, review of *The Invention of Hugo Cabret,* p. 173.

Independent on Sunday (London, England), December 2, 2007, "A Life in Pictures," p. 42.

Journal of Adolescent & Adult Literacy, October, 2007, Judith A. Hayn, review of *The Invention of Hugo Cabret,* p. 189.

Kirkus Reviews, April 15, 2002, review of *Wingwalker,* p. 581; September 1, 2002, review of *When Marian Sang,* p. 1319; September 15, 2004, review of *Walt Whitman,* p. 915; August 1, 2003, review of *The Meanest Doll in the World,* p. 1020; January 15, 2007, review of *The Adventures of Hugo Cabret,* p. 81.

Library Journal, July 1, 2007, Neal Wyatt, review of *The Adventures of Hugo Cabret,* p. 136.

New York Times, January 26, 2008, Motoko Rich, "Reads like a Book, Looks like a Film," p. B7.

New York Times Book Review, November 18, 2001, Lawrence Downes, review of *The Dinosaurs of Waterhouse Hawkins: An Illuminating History of Mr. Waterhouse Hawkins, Artist and Lecturer,* p. 40; April 21, 2002, Linda Phillips Ashour, review of *Wingwalker,* p. 25; February 9, 2003, Ellen Feldman, review of *When Marian Sang,* p. 20; November 14, 2004, Abby McGanney Nolan, review of *Walt Whitman,* p. 36.

Publishers Weekly, May 3, 1991, review of *The Houdini Box,* p. 72; September 20, 1999, review of *Riding Freedom,* p. 90; December 20, 1999, review of *Barn-*

yard Prayers, p. 78; August 14, 2000, review of *The Boy of a Thousand Faces,* p. 356; May 28, 2001, review of *The School Story,* p. 88; January 2, 2006, review of *Marly's Ghost: A Remix of Charles Dickens's A Christmas Carol,* p. 63; March 25, 2002, review of *Wingwalker,* p. 65; August 11, 2003, review of *The Meanest Doll in the World,* p. 280; November 10, 2003, review of *The Meanest Doll in the World,* p. 37; October 18, 2004, review of *Walt Whitman,* p. 64; January 1, 2007, review of *The Invention of Hugo Cabret,* p. 50; February 19, 2007, Sue Corbett, "Drawn to Cinema: A Visual Story about the Roots of French Film," p. 64.

School Library Journal, October, 1995, Jane Gardner Connor, review of *The Robot King,* pp. 139-140; September, 2000, Barbara Buckley, review of *The Boy of a Thousand Faces,* p. 209; June, 2001, Terrie Dorio, review of *The School Story,* p. 144; May, 2002, Heide Piehler, review of *Wingwalker,* p. 162; November, 2002, Wendy Lukehart, review of *When Marian Sang,* p. 147; November 2004, Marilyn Taniguchi, review of *Walt Whitman,* p. 166; August, 2005, Carol L. MacKay, review of *Lunch Money,* p. 122; March, 2007, Wendy Lukehart, review of *The Invention of Hugo Cabret,* p. 218.

Sunday Times (London, England), October 14, 2007, Nicolette Jones, review of *The Invention of Hugo Cabret,* p. 56.

Times (London, England), October 6, 2007, Ian Beck, "A Moving Picture Show," review of *The Invention of Hugo Cabret,* p. 15.

USA Today, March 13, 2007, Bob Minzesheimer, "There's a Film behind His *Invention,*" p. 7D.

ONLINE

BookSense.com, http://www.booksense.com/people/ (March 10, 2008), Gavin J. Grant, "Very Interesting People: Brian Selznick."

Children's Book Council Web site, http://www.cbcbooks.org/cbcmagazine/ (March 10, 2008), Brian Selznick, "The Fine Art of Collaboration."

Children's Book Guild of Washington, DC, Web site, http://www.childrensbookguild.org/ (June 7, 2006), Margaret Blair, "Brian Selznick, Following His 'Gut Instinct.'"

Invention of Hugo Cabret Web site, http://www.theinventionofhugocabret.com/ (March 10, 2008).

National Book Foundation Web site, http://www.nationalbook.org/ (March 10, 2008), Rita Williams-Garcia, interview with Selznick.

Publishers Weekly Online, http://www.publishersweekly.com/ (January 4, 2007), Sue Corbett, interview with Selznick.

Scholastic Web site, http://www.scholastic.com/kids/ (March 1, 2007), "Brian Selznick Gives Us the Inside Story on *The Invention of Hugo Cabret.*"

Invention of Hugo Cabret Web site, http://www.theinventionofhugocabret.com/ (March 10, 2008).*

SMITH, Kirsten 1970-

Personal

Born August 12, 1970, in Port Ludlow, WA. *Education:* Occidental College, degree, 1992; attended New York University.

Addresses

Home—Los Angeles, CA. *E-mail*—kiwi@kiwilovesyou.com.

Career

Screenwriter, poet, and novelist. CineTel Films, Los Angeles, CA, former director of development; postproduction supervisor for films *Poison Ivy II,* 1996, and *Carried Away,* 1996; story editor for *Getting Personal* (television series), Fox, 1998. Writer-in-residence at MacDowell Colony.

Awards, Honors

Breadloaf Writer's fellowship, 1993; Pablo Neruda Prize for Poetry.

Writings

SCREENPLAYS

(With Karen McCullah Lutz) *Ten Things I Hate about You,* Touchstone Pictures, 1999.

(With Karen McCullah Lutz) *Legally Blonde* (based on the novel by Amanda Brown), Metro-Goldwyn-Mayer, 2001.

(With others) *Ella Enchanted* (based on the novel by Gail Carson Levine), Miramax, 2004.

(With Karen McCullah Lutz, Ewan Leslie, and Jack Leslie) *She's the Man,* Dreamworks, 2006.

(With Karen McCullah Lutz; and producer) *The House Bunny,* Columbia Pictures, 2008.

Contributor of poetry to *Poison Ivy II,* 1996.

OTHER

The Geography of Girlhood (young-adult novel), Little, Brown (New York, NY), 2006.

Contributor of poetry to literary magazines, including *Gettysburg Review, Witness, Massachusetts Review,* and *Prairie Schooner.*

Sidelights

Screenwriter Kirsten Smith has a number of popular films to her credit, including *Ten Things I Hate about You, Legally Blonde,* and *Ella Enchanted.* Smith is also an accomplished poet; her work has appeared in such publications as the *Gettysburg Review,* the *Massachusetts Review,* and *Prairie Schooner.* In 2006 she published her debut work of young-adult fiction, *The Geography of Girlhood,* a tale told in verse.

Born in 1970, Smith was raised in Port Ludlow, Washington. While attending Occidental College, she began writing poetry, and her first poem was published when she was nineteen. Smith has studied under such celebrated writers as Amy Hempel, Robert Pinsky, Lucille Clifton, and Marilynne Robinson, and she noted that her verse has been influenced by Sharon Olds, Sylvia Plath, Anne Sexton, and Amy Gerstler. Smith has received a number of honors for her work, including the Pablo Neruda Prize for Poetry.

In her screenwriting career, Smith has enjoyed an enduring partnership with creative colleague Karen McCullah Lutz. While working at CineTel Films, a small, independent film company, Smith came across a screenplay written by Lutz. When Lutz later visited Los Angeles, the women hit it off immediately and began scribbling their first script on a set of cocktail napkins. They have since collaborated on more than a dozen screen-

Cover of Kirsten Smith's middle-grade novel The Geography of Girlhood, *a coming-of-age story narrated by a high-school freshman.* (Copyright © 2006. Reproduced by permission of Little, Brown & Company.)

plays, five of which have become major motion pictures. In a *Moviemaker* online interview with Jennifer M. Wood, Smith commented: "Over the years, we've refined our process so that the first step is to create a very detailed outline (say 10-15 pages) of the story (often this is in collaboration with the producer or studio). Then we divide up scenes and go away and write sections of the script separately of one another." Subsequent revisions to the script are a joint effort; Smith and Lutz sometimes rewrite a screenplay ten times before they consider it finished. "Then we turn it into the producer and we start all over again," Smith joked.

Smith and Lutz had their first big-screen success with 1999's *Ten Things I Hate about You,* "an exuberant and surprisingly sweet adolescent take on [William Shakespeare's] *The Taming of the Shrew,*" remarked *Salon.com* critic Mary Elizabeth Williams. Set at stately Padua High School, the film centers on the unlikely relationship between Katarina "Kat" Stratford, a fiercely intelligent and strong-willed feminist, and Patrick Verona, the rough-edged newcomer who courts her. Although Stephen Holden, writing in the *New York Times,* stated that elements of the plot felt "forced," the critic also noted that, compared to similar films, *Ten Things I Hate about You* "tries the hardest . . . to season its screenplay with authentic Shakespearean touches. Students in a writing class at Padua High School . . . are asked to create sonnets. There is an Elizabethan-theme prom that inspires some fancy hairdos and fetching costumes. And every now and then the banter among the characters incorporates actual Shakespearean quotations." Williams offered a positive assessment of the movie, calling it "a classic comedy of misunderstandings, false starts and, eventually, true love—all tempered with the very 20th century point of view that if the guy is strong enough, the girl doesn't need to be weak." Williams also applauded "the film's sharp wit and tender heart" and noted that *Ten Things I Hate about You* "offers genuine and consistent laughs as it treads through the adolescent milieus of frog dissection, keg parties and French lessons."

Smith and Lutz have also combined their talents on the script for *Legally Blonde,* a 2001 film based on the novel of the same name by Amanda Brown. Starring Reese Witherspoon as a fashion-obsessed sorority sister who seeks to impress her ex-boyfriend by gaining admittance to Harvard Law School, the film was a box-office smash, raking in more than twenty million dollars over its opening weekend. While *Variety* critic Todd McCarthy found the screenplay to be "nicely structured and populated by some good characters," Stephanie Zacharek stated in *Salon.com* that *Legally Blonde* "ambles along amiably enough, and there's a heartbeat of intelligence pulsing beneath" Lutz and Smith's script.

Smith and Lutz have also contributed to the screenplay for *Ella Enchanted,* a 2004 film based on the popular novel by Gail Carson Levine. Writing in the *Chicago Sun-Times,* Roger Ebert described *Ella Enchanted* as "a high-spirited charmer, a fantasy that sparkles with delights," and Ruthe Stein commented in the *San Francisco Chronicle* that the movie "is artful enough to intrigue adults and far more original than other versions of Cinderella portrayed onscreen with alarming regularity." Noting that Smith and Lutz collaborated with three other screenwriters, Stein remarked, "So many hands usually kill creativity, but in this case, they appear to have sparked it. Either that or *Ella Enchanted* is under a magical spell of its own."

The 2006 film *She's the Man,* an adaptation of Shakespeare's *Twelfth Night,* was penned by the team of Smith and Lutz, with help from two other writers. *She's the Man* stars Amanda Bynes as Viola Hastings, a star soccer player who is incensed when her school cuts the girls' soccer program. When her twin brother leaves his new prep school and runs off to England to pursue a musical career, Viola takes his place, joining the soccer team and, unfortunately, falling in love with her new roommate, Duke. According to *Los Angeles Times* reviewer Carina Chocano, the movie "is so good-natured, and its cast seems to enjoy itself so thoroughly, that the total annihilation of disbelief it requires winds up feeling like a reasonable enough request." Allison Benedikt, reviewing *She's the Man* for the *Chicago Tribune,* applauded the efforts of Smith and her collaborators, stating they "have a good feel for this material, indulging our collective teenage fantasies and providing all the right payoffs at almost all the right moments."

In addition to her film work, Smith is also the author of the young-adult novel *The Geography of Girlhood,* a coming-of-age story told through free-verse poems. The work centers on Penny Morrow, a shy, sensitive teen who lives in a small town with her father and older sister. As she enters high school, Penny begins a poignant, at times difficult journey toward adulthood. Along the way, she experiences her first kiss, watches her best friend battle mental illness, runs away with her sister's ex-boyfriend, and comes to terms with the legacy of her mother, who left the family when Penny was just six years old. "*The Geography of Girlhood* is strongest in the way it conveys the drift of adolescence, its searching quality," observed Barbara Feinberg in the *New York Times Book Review.* "These are gifts from Smith's poetic nature." *Kliatt* contributor Michele Winship also praised the work, stating that the author "writes with honesty when her lyric poetry describes Penny's pain and exhilaration, confusion and loss," and in *School Library Journal* Renee Steinberg noted that "it is the clarity, the keen understanding, and the apt metaphors that make Penny's voice so memorable." "Penny Morrow is the latest in a long line of female protagonists whose reflections on growing up get it just right," David M. Pegram remarked in his review of *The Geography of Girlhood* for the *Journal of Adolescent & Adult Literacy.* "Her words are both cerebral and visceral—we are left with something to think about, as well as feel."

Smith continues to write poetry and hopes to complete more books. As she told Wood, "Once you become a screenwriter or producer, the world becomes a giant supermarket of movie ideas. It becomes difficult not to see something as a movie idea. I think that's why it's important for screenwriters to write in different forms—prose, poetry, nonfiction, etc.—so your mind isn't always focused on movies. Otherwise, it becomes too difficult to step back and evaluate your own work as a human and not just as a screenwriter."

Biographical and Critical Sources

PERIODICALS

Booklist, February 1, 2006, Cindy Dobrez, review of *The Geography of Girlhood,* p. 45.
Bulletin of the Center for Children's Books, May, 2006, Karen Coats, review of *The Geography of Girlhood,* p. 423.
Chicago Tribune, September 4, 2007, Allison Benedikt, review of *She's the Man.*
Journal of Adolescent & Adult Literacy, April, 2007, David M. Pegram, review of *The Geography of Girlhood,* p. 609.
Kirkus Reviews, March 1, 2006, review of *The Geography of Girlhood,* p. 240.
Kliatt, March, 2006, Michele Winship, review of *The Geography of Girlhood,* p. 16.
Los Angeles Times, March 17, 2006, Carina Chocano, review of *She's the Man.*
New York Times, March, 31, 1999, Stephen Holden, review of *Ten Things I Hate about You;* July 13, 2001, A.O. Scott, review of *Legally Blonde,* p. E20.
New York Times Book Review, June 4, 2006, Barbara Feinberg, review of *The Geography of Girlhood,* p. 26.
Rolling Stone, August 2, 2001, Peter Travers, review of *Legally Blonde.*
San Francisco Chronicle, April 9, 2004, Ruthe Stein, *Ella Enchanted* Is Not Your Grandmother's Cinderella."
School Library Journal, May, 2006, Renee Steinberg, review of *The Geography of Girlhood,* p. 136.
Variety, July 9, 2001, Todd McCarthy, review of *Legally Blonde,* p. 19; April 5, 2004, David Rooney, review of *Ella Enchanted,* p. 42; March 13, 2006, Robert Koehler, review of *She's the Man,* p. 35.
Voice of Youth Advocates, December, 2006, Kelly Czarnecki, review of *The Geography of Girlhood,* p. 434.

ONLINE

Kirsten Smith Home Page, http://www.kiwilovesyou.com (April 1, 2008).
Kirsten Smith Web log, http://www.kiwilovesyou.com/wordpress (April 1, 2008).
Moviemaker Online, http://www.moviemaker.com/ (February 3, 2007), Jennifer M. Wood, "The Art of Collaboration."
Roger Ebert Web site, http://rogerebert.suntimes.com/ (April 9, 2004), review of *Ella Enchanted.*
Salon.com, http://www.salon.com/ (April 1, 1999), Mary Elizabeth Williams, review of *Ten Things I Hate about You;* (July 13, 2001) Stephanie Zacharek, review of *Legally Blonde.*

Young Adult (& Kids) Books Central Online, http://www.yabookscentral.com/ (March 1, 2006), interview with Smith.

*   *   *

SPEIR, Nancy 1958-

Personal
Born April 25, 1958.

Addresses
Home—Santa Rosa, CA. *E-mail*—nancyspeir@comcast.net.

Career
Illustrator, artist, and designer. Sculptor and fine-art painter; creator of art for cards. *Exhibitions:* Paintings have been exhibited in galleries in New York, NY, San Francisco, CA, and Sacramento, CA.

Awards, Honors
Awards from Communication Arts and Society of Illustrators.

Illustrator
Laurence Schorsch, *Mr. Boffin,* Checkerboard (New York, NY), 1993.

Alice B. McGinty, *Eliza's Kindergarten Surprise,* Marshall Cavendish (New York, NY), 2007.

Patricia Hubbell, *My First Airplane Ride,* Marshall Cavendish (New York, NY), 2008.

Patricia Hubbell, *Teacher! Sharing, Helping, Caring,* Marshall Cavendish (New York, NY), 2009.

Sidelights
Nancy Speir is an award-winning American illustrator, artist, and designer who has worked as a sculptor, a fine-art painter, and an artist for greeting cards. Her first children's book project, illustrating *Mr. Boffin* by Laurence Schorsch, was published in 1993. In the story, grumpy Mr. Boffin hates cats and is dismayed when he finds a stray cat sitting in his favorite chair. Although he tried to get rid of it, the cat keeps coming back, but when it leaves to return no more Mr. Boffin realizes that he misses it. Speir's "green-eyed kitty is a show-stealer," commented a *Publishers Weekly* writer, calling *Mr. Boffin* a "vibrant book [that] offers a diverting take on a familiar refrain."

Another illustration project, Alice B. McGinty's *Eliza's Kindergarten Surprise,* is a first-day-of-school story that finds Eliza homesick and missing her mother. In *Booklist* Gillian Engberg wrote that Speir's "cartoonlike illustrations balance scenes showing Eliza's anguish with brightly colored views of a welcoming classroom." Barbara Auerbach, writing in *School Library Journal,* cited the artist's "bright acrylic cartoons," and a *Kirkus Reviews* contributor noted that "the simplicity of [Speir's] illustrations allows readers to connect with Eliza's changing emotions."

In *My First Airplane Ride* Patricia Hubbell's story follows a little boy on his first trip aloft, including arriving at the airport, checking in, going through the security screening, waiting at the gate, and settling in his seat on the plane. Lynn K. Vanca, reviewing the book in *School Library Journal,* pointed out the "noticeable details in Speir's acrylic spreads" for Hubbell's story and called *My First Airplane Ride* "a worthy choice to share with children new to" flying. A contributor to *Kirkus Reviews* predicted that Hubbell's story will provide a "solid grounding for those about to leave the ground behind," in part because Speir's illustrations will help young readers become "familiar with the interiors of an airport" before they set foot inside one. *Booklist* contributor Carolyn Phelan stated that, "colorful and reassuring, [*My First Airplane Ride*] . . . is a good, practical choice for pre-travel reading."

Biographical and Critical Sources

PERIODICALS

Booklist, August, 2007, Gillian Engberg, review of *Eliza's Kindergarten Surprise,* p. 82; September 1, 2008, Carolyn Phelan, review of *My First Airplane Ride,* p. 106.

Kirkus Reviews, June 15, 2007, review of *Eliza's Kindergarten Surprise;* September 1, 2008, review of *My First Airplane Ride.*

Publishers Weekly, January 11, 1993, review of *Mr. Boffin,* p. 63; June 18, 2007, review of *Eliza's Kindergarten Surprise,* p. 53.

School Library Journal, June 1, 2007, Barbara Auerbach, review of *Eliza's Kindergarten Surprise,* p. 115; November 1, 2008, Lynn K. Vanca, review of *My First Airplane Ride,* p. 90.

ONLINE

LJ Artworks Web site, http://ljartworks.com/ (April 10, 2008), "Nancy Speir."

Nancy Speir Home Page, http://www.nancyspeirillustration.com (May 28, 2009).*

*   *   *

STEAD, Judy

Personal
Female. *Education:* East Carolina University, B.A.; attended Boston Museum School and Massachusetts College of Art.

Addresses

Home—Charlotte, NC. *E-mail*—jam@judystead.com.

Career

Illustrator, designer, educator, and art director.

Awards, Honors

Bookbuilders of Boston honor; Art Director's Club honor.

Illustrator

Cecile Schoberle, *The Princess and Her Best Friend,* Little Simon (New York, NY), 2005.

Mister Sun (with CD), Kindermusik International (Greensboro, NC), 2006.

Bob Raczka, *Who Loves the Fall?,* Albert Whitman (Morton Grove, IL), 2007.

Fran Posner, *Halloween Makes Me Batty!,* Golden Books (New York, NY), 2007.

Bob Raczka, *Spring Things,* Albert Whitman (Morton Grove, IL), 2007.

Sheila Bair, *Isabel's Car Wash,* Albert Whitman (Morton Grove, IL), 2008.

Debra Shirley, *Best Friend on Wheels,* Albert Whitman (Morton Grove, IL), 2008.

Bob Raczka, *Snowy, Blowy Winter,* Albert Whitman (Morton Grove, IL), 2008.

Sonali Fry, *Make Me a Princess! A Mix-and-Match Dress-up Book,* Little Simon (New York, NY), 2008.

Bob Raczka, *Summer Wonders,* Albert Whitman & Co. (Morton Grove, IL), 2009.

The Twelve Days of Christmas in North Carolina, Sterling (New York, NY), 2009.

Sidelights

Judy Stead is an American illustrator, designer, educator, and art director. She graduated from East Carolina University with a bachelor of arts degree in English literature and art and went on to attend the Boston Museum School and Massachusetts College of Art. In 2005 Stead began collaborating with children's book authors and provided the illustrations for her first picture-book project, Cecile Schoberle's *The Princess and Her Best Friend.*

Another book featuring Stead's art, Bob Raczka's *Spring Things,* rhymes out all the sights and fun activities there are to do as winter ends and spring begins. A contributor in *Kirkus Reviews* described Raczka's text as "catchy" and Stead's illustrations as "pleasant," and suggested of *Spring Things* that "the pictures might stimulate creative play."

Another collaboration with Raczka, *Who Loves the Fall?,* covers the range of activities that are fun to do during the fall season, including leaf raking, apple picking, and pie baking. "The brightly colored, well-designed illustrations pulsate with energy, movement, and charm," remarked Barbara Katz in *School Library Journal.* A contributor writing in *Kirkus Reviews* deemed Stead's illustrations both "stylized" and "colorful" and called the book "a vivid and lively introduction to the season that preschoolers will particularly enjoy."

Raczka and Stead's other picture-book projects including *Snowy, Blowy Winter* and *Summer Wonders.* The first book demonstrates the fun on cold-weather activities, such as shoveling sidewalks and making snow angels. "The text is simple and bouncy, and the cartoon illustrations are bright, clear, and inclusive," wrote Rachel Vilmar in *School Library Journal,* and a *Kirkus Reviews* writer observed that "Stead's illustrations provide a narrative" and called the book "a solid choice." Reviewing *Summer Wonders,* which shows the fun outdoors activities available during the summer months, Phelan commented that "Stead's expressive paintings . . . interpret the words in a series of lively, colorful pictures."

Biographical and Critical Sources

PERIODICALS

Booklist, February 15, 2007, Carolyn Phelan, review of *Spring Things,* p. 86; March 15, 2009, Carolyn Phelan, review of *Summer Wonders,* p. 67.

Kirkus Reviews, January 15, 2007, review of *Spring Things,* p. 80; August 15, 2007, review of *Who Loves the Fall?;* September 15, 2008, review of *Snowy, Blowy Winter.*

Publishers Weekly, March 24, 2008, review of *Best Friend on Wheels,* p. 70.

School Library Journal, March 1, 2007, June Wolfe, review of *Spring Things,* p. 184; September 1, 2007, Barbara Katz, review of *Who Loves the Fall?,* p. 174; May 1, 2008, Carolyn Janssen, review of *Best Friend on Wheels,* p. 108; December 1, 2008, Rachael Vilmar, review of *Snowy, Blowy Winter,* p. 100.

ONLINE

Del Mar Day Web site, http://www.delmarday.com/ (April 15, 2008), "Judy Stead."

Judy Stead Home Page, http://judystead.com (May 28, 2009).*

*   *   *

STORK, Francisco
See STORK, Francisco X.

STORK, Francisco X. 1953-
(Francisco Xavier Arguelles, Francisco Stork)

Personal

Born Francisco Xavier Arguelles, 1953, in Monterrey, Mexico; immigrated to United States, c. 1962; son of Charles Stork (stepfather) and Ruth Arguelles; married Jill Syverson (an educator); children: Nicholas, Anna. *Education:* Spring Hill College, B.A.; attended Harvard University; Columbia University, J.D., 1982.

Addresses

Home—MA. *Office*—MassHousing, One Beacon St., Boston, MA 02108. *Agent*—Faye Bender Literary Agency, 337 W. 76th St., Ste. E1, New York, NY 10023. *E-mail*—fstork@masshousing.com.

Career

Lawyer and writer. MassHousing (housing bank), Boston, MA, attorney.

Awards, Honors

Danforth fellowship; Chicano/Latino Literary Prize, 2000, for *The Way of the Jaguar;* Americas Award Commended Title, and Books for the Teen Age selection, New York Public Library, both 2007, both for *Behind the Eyes.*

Writings

The Way of the Jaguar, Bilingual Press (Tempe, AZ), 2000.
Behind the Eyes, Dutton (New York, NY), 2006.
Marcelo in the Real World, Arthur A. Levine Books/ Scholastic (New York, NY), 2009.

Sidelights

Francisco X. Stork is the author of the young-adult novels *Marcelo in the Real World* and *Behind the Eyes,* the latter praised for its "spare prose and unflinching dialogue" by a critic in *Kirkus Reviews.* "My characters are all Mexican-Americans," Stork explained in an interview for *Teenreads.com.* "That's the 'social' piece of my writing. I want everyone to see and appreciate the richness of my culture. A richness hidden sometimes by the stories about gangs and people coming over to take away jobs, by the negative images they see and read about. I want my children to be proud of being Americans and of their heritage."

Born in Mexico and raised in Texas, Stork earned a scholarship that enabled him to attend college and train as an attorney. Writing fiction allows him to use his imagination in a way his work as an attorney does not, as he explained to *Boston Globe* contributor Johnny

Diaz. "It's a way of self-discovery, too, because you learn things about yourself and about the world," Stork told Diazo. "Writing has a way of at least making you confront the important things in life."

Stork published his debut novel, *The Way of the Jaguar,* in 2000. Told in the form of diary entries, the work concerns death-row inmate Ismael Díaz, a former real-estate attorney whose search for his long-lost love in Mexico ends in tragedy. Set in El Paso and based on Stork's own experiences growing up, *Behind the Eyes* centers on sixteen-year-old Hector Robles, a studious Chicano youth whose older brother is murdered by the leader of a neighborhood gang. Seeking revenge, a grief-stricken Hector commits a violent act, placing himself in danger. He agrees to attend a juvenile detention facility for teens in San Antonio, where he begins to confront his troubled past. Soon, though, Hector's life is once again threatened as he learns that he has become a target for murder even behind the institution's walls.

Reviewing *Behind the Eyes* in *Booklist,* Hazel Rochman stated that "the diverse characters are powerfully drawn, as is the elemental immigrant family story." Claire

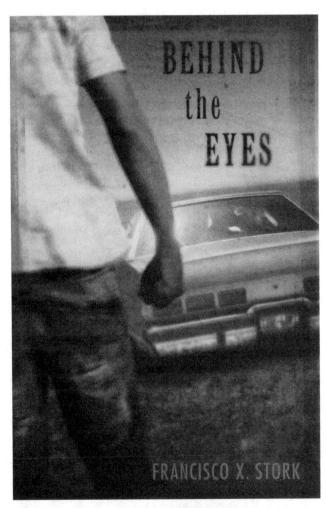

Cover of Francisco X. Stork's novel **Behind the Eyes,** *which focuses on a teen whose violent act has troubling consequences.* (Dutton, 2006. Copyright © 2006 by Francisco X. Stork. Reproduced by permission.)

Rosser, reviewing Stork's young-adult novel in *Kliatt,* similarly noted that the book's "characters are sympathetic, and the complexities of the culture are delineated, with no stereotypes to take away from the story." According to a contributor in *Kirkus Reviews, Behind the Eyes* "ultimately functions effectively as both cautionary tale and success story."

In *Marcelo in the Real World* seventeen-year-old Marcelo Sandoval displays symptoms similar to that of Asperger's syndrome, a form of autism in which social interaction is exceptionally difficult. Marcelo works with ponies at a therapeutic riding stable but is thrust into a far more hectic environment when his father hires him to work at his legal firm in the mailroom. Jonathan Hunt, reviewing the novel in *Horn Book,* predicted that Marcelo's "inspiring, brave journey into the real world will likely engender a fierce protective instinct in readers . . . as the plot winds to its sweet, satisfying denouement." In *Booklist* Ilene Cooper described *Marcelo in the Real World* as "shot with spiritualism, laced with love, and fraught with conundrums," while a *Publishers Weekly* contributor observed that "artfully crafted characters form the heart of Stork's . . . judicious novel." A *Kirkus Reviews* contributor also praised the book, writing that in *Marcelo in the Real World* "Stork delivers a powerful tale" that is "rich in emotional nuance," while *School Library Journal* critic Wendy Smith-D'Arezzo concluded that "the dilemmas that Marcelo faces are told in a compelling fashion, which helps to keep readers engaged."

Stork plans to write more works for a young-adult audience. "Many young people think about the most important issues of life," he told a *Teenreadstoo.com* interviewer. "They feel these issues (about fairness about beauty and evil and suffering and love and the meaning of life and death) in a way that many adults don't. I want to write for young people about the important questions of existence in a way that they enjoy reading about them."

Biographical and Critical Sources

PERIODICALS

Booklist, September 1, 2006, Hazel Rochman, review of *Behind the Eyes,* p. 112; April 1, 2009, Ilene Cooper, review of *Marcelo in the Real World,* p. 38.
Boston Globe, April 9, 2005, Johnny Diaz, "6 Days, 48 Writers, 1 Mission."
Horn Book, March 1, 2009, Jonathan Hunt, review of *Marcelo in the Real World.*
Kirkus Reviews, June 1, 2006, review of *Behind the Eyes,* p. 58; January 15, 2009, review of *Marcelo in the Real World.*
Kliatt, May, 2006, Claire Rosser, review of *Behind the Eyes,* p. 16.
Publishers Weekly, April 24, 2000, review of *The Way of the Jaguar,* p. 61; April 2, 2009, Donna Freitas, interview with Stork; January 5, 2009, review of *Marcelo in the Real World,* p. 51.
School Library Journal, October, 2006, Morgan Johnson-Doyle, review of *Behind the Eyes,* p. 174; March 1, 2009, Wendy Smith-D'Arezzo, review of *Marcelo in the Real World,* p. 156; March 1, 2009, Rick Margolis, interview with Stork, p. 29.

ONLINE

Francisco Stork Home Page, http://www.franciscostork. com (May 29, 2009).
Teenreads.com, http://www.teenreads.com/ (March 31, 2009), interview with Stork; (May 29, 2009) Alexis Burling, review of *Marcelo in the Real World.*
Teenreadstoo.com, http://www.teensreadtoo.com/ (March 10, 2008), interview with Stork.*

*   *   *

SWANN, E.L.
See LASKY, Kathryn

T

TAYLOR, Peter Lane

Personal

Born in Chestnut Hill, PA; father a tax lawyer, mother a teacher. *Education:* Graduated from Middlebury College.

Addresses

Home—Chestnut Hill, PA.

Career

Explorer, photographer, journalist, and documentary film producer. Has worked on a coral reef conservation project in Key West, FL; Writer and associate producer for *Florida Springs Web Expedition* project.

Awards, Honors

Sydney Taylor Honor Book, Association of Jewish Libraries, 2008, for *The Secret of Priest's Grotto.*

Writings

Science at the Extreme: Scientists on the Cutting Edge of Discovery, McGraw-Hill (New York, NY), 2001.
(With Christos Nicola) *The Secret of Priest's Grotto: A Holocaust Survival Story,* Kar-Ben Publishing (Minneapolis, MN), 2007.

Contributor of articles to natural history and conservation publications, including *National Geographic.*

Adaptations

Science at the Extreme was adapted for television, Learning Channel, 2001.

Sidelights

Peter Lane Taylor is a journalist and photographer who writes widely about science, adventure sports, and natural history. His research has taken him to the coast of South Africa, where he encountered a great white shark; to a glacier in Switzerland, where he descended to the bottom of an ice shaft; and to Southern Mexico, where he suffered third-degree acid burns while exploring a sulfur cave. His work has appeared in *National Geographic,* and he has published two books, *Science at the Extreme: Scientists on the Cutting Edge of Discovery* and *The Secret of Priest's Grotto: A Holocaust Survival Story,* coauthored with Christos Nicola.

After majoring in environmental science and creative writing at Middlebury College, Taylor worked on a coral reef project in Florida and later became a freelance writer and photographer, penning stories for adventure magazines and nature publications. He decided to combine his two passions and began work on *Science at the Extreme.* "I got this flash that I could find people who were doing conservation and exploration," he told Eils Lotozo in the *Philadelphia Inquirer.* Taylor eventually interviewed more than one hundred scientists for the book, although some were skeptical of his intentions. "They all had a fear of being regarded as yahoos, as people who risk their lives for adventure, or publicity or adrenaline," Taylor related to Lotozo. "They were fearful of me recasting their work as circus science."

In *Science at the Extreme,* Taylor profiles nine scientists who conduct their work in some of the most inhospitable environments on the planet. He examines the efforts of George Irvine, who studies northern Florida's underwater caves; Giovanni Badino, a physicist who explores European glaciers; and Steve Sillett, who scales California's gigantic redwoods to study biodiversity. "When people think of science today, they think of genome mapping, or the Hubble telescope, or cancer research," Taylor told Lotozo. "I wanted to reestablish the profile of field science. I wanted to show people scientists who were not lab-locked dorks laboring over equations. Science is about passion. What they do is incredibly exciting, and it's world-changing work."

Science at the Extreme received strong reviews. "Mixing eloquent prose with breathtaking photographs of his subjects in their chosen environments," wrote *Natural*

History reviewer Steven N. Austad, "Taylor produces a book you won't soon forget." *Entertainment Weekly* contributor Daneet Steffens stated that the author makes his subjects' "outrageous expeditions breathtakingly vivid."

In *The Secret of Priest's Grotto* Taylor and Nicola recount the true story of the dozens of Ukrainian Jews who escaped invading Nazi troops by hiding in an expansive complex of gypsum caves for almost a year. In 1942, Zaida and Esther Stermer, their six children, and several relatives and neighbors retreated to Popowa Yama, or Priest's Grotto, a massive underground labyrinth. Decades later, Nicola, a veteran caver, discovered signs of human habitation while exploring the area. He later tracked down a number of the people who survived World War II in these caves and who related their story. A critic in *Kirkus Reviews* remarked that *The Secret of Priest's Grotto* "makes riveting reading," and a *Publishers Weekly* critic commented that, "at once sobering and uplifting, [*The Secret of Priest's Grotto*] . . . is an astounding story of survival, powerfully told."

Biographical and Critical Sources

PERIODICALS

Booklist, March 1, 2007, Hazel Rochman, review of *The Secret of Priest's Grotto: A Holocaust Survival Story,* p. 72.

Entertainment Weekly, October 20, 2000, Daneet Stevens, review of *Science at the Extreme: Scientists on the Cutting Edge of Discovery,* p. 72.

Horn Book, July-August, 2007, Elissa Gershowitz, review of *The Secret of Priest's Grotto,* p. 415.

Kirkus Reviews, March 15, 2007, review of *The Secret of Priest's Grotto.*

Natural History, October, 2000, Steven N. Austad, review of *Science at the Extreme,* p. 88.

Philadelphia Inquirer, January 3, 2001, Eils Lotozo, "Photographer's Passion for Science Portrayed in Print."

Publishers Weekly, April 16, 2007, review of *The Secret of Priest's Grotto,* p. 53.

School Library Journal, April, 2007, Heidi Estrin, review of *The Secret of Priest's Grotto,* p. 165.

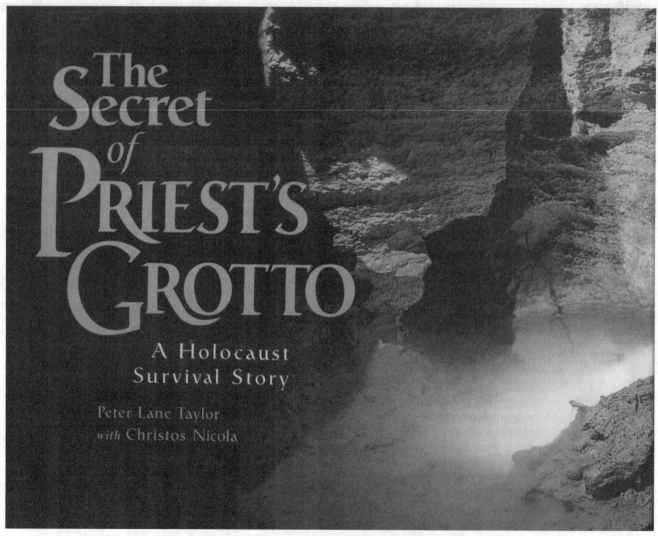

Cover of Peter Lane Taylor's **The Secrets of Priest's Grotto,** *a Holocaust story coauthored with Christos Nicola.* (Kar-Ben, 2007. Reproduced by permission.)

Science News, September 14, 2002, review of *Science at the Extreme,* p. 175.*

* * *

THOMAS, Joyce Carol 1938-

Personal

Born May 25, 1938, in Ponca City, OK; daughter of Floyd David (a bricklayer) and Leona (a housekeeper and hair stylist) Haynes; married Gettis L. Withers (a chemist), May 31, 1959 (divorced, 1968); married Roy T. Thomas, Jr., (a professor), September 7, 1968 (divorced, 1979); children: Monica Pecot, Gregory Withers, Michael Withers, Roy T. Thomas III. *Education:* Attended San Francisco City College, 1957-58, and University of San Francisco, 1957-58; College of San Mateo, A.A., 1964; San Jose State College (now University), B.A., 1966; Stanford University, M.A., 1967.

Addresses

Home—Berkeley, CA. *Agent*—Anna Ghosh, Scovil-Chichak-Galen Literary Agency, Inc., 276 5th Ave., Ste. 708, New York, NY 10001. *E-mail*—jctauthor@aol.com.

Career

Writer, poet, novelist, playwright, educator, and motivational speaker. Telephone operator in San Francisco, CA, 1957-58; Ravenwood School District, East Palo Alto, CA, teacher of French and Spanish, 1968-70; San Jose State College (now University), San Jose, CA, assistant professor of black studies, 1969-72; Contra Costa College, San Pablo, CA, teacher of drama and English, 1973-75; St. Mary's College, Moraga, CA, professor of English, 1975-77; San Jose State University, San Jose, reading program director, 1979-82, associate professor of English, 1982-83; University of Tennessee, Knoxville, associate professor, 1989-92, professor of English, 1992-95. Visiting associate professor of English at Purdue University, 1983.

Member

Dramatists Guild, Authors Guild, Authors League of America.

Awards, Honors

Danforth graduate fellow, University of California at Berkeley, 1973-75; Stanford University scholar, 1979-80, and Djerassi fellow, 1982, 1983; *New York Times* outstanding book of the year citation, American Library Association (ALA) best book citation, and Before Columbus American Book Award, Before Columbus Foundation, all 1982, and American Book Award for children's fiction, Association of American Publishers, and National Book Award, both 1983, all for *Marked by*

Joyce Carol Thomas (Reproduced by permission.)

Fire; Coretta Scott King Award, ALA, 1984, for *Bright Shadow;* named Outstanding Woman of the Twentieth Century, Sigma Gamma Rho, 1986; Pick of the Lists, American Booksellers, 1986, for *The Golden Pasture;* Arkansas Traveler Award, 1987; Oklahoma Senate and House of Representatives citations, 1989; Chancellor's Award for Research and Creativity, University of Tennessee, and Selected Title for Children and Young Adults, National Conference of Christians and Jews, both 1991, both for *A Gathering of Flowers;* Proclamation, City of Berkeley, 1992, for *When the Nightingale Sings;* 100 Children's Books listee, New York Public Library, 1993, Coretta Scott King Honor Book designation, ALA, Notable Children's Books designation, National Council of Teachers of English, and Mirrors and Windows: Seeing the Human Family Award, National Conference of Christians and Jews, all 1994, all for *Brown Honey in Broomwheat Tea;* Poet Laureate Award, Oklahoma State University Center for Poets and Writers, 1996-2000; Oklahoma Governor's Award, 1998; Celebrated Storyteller Award, *People* magazine, 1999, for *Gingerbread Days;* Notable Children's Book designation, ALA, Notable Children's Trade Book in Social Studies designation, National Council for the Social Studies/Children's Book Council, Teacher's Choice Award, International Reading Association, and Coretta Scott King Illustrator Honor Book designation, all 1999, all for *I Have Heard of a Land;* Parents' Choice Award, 2000, and Oklahoma Book Award, 2001, both for *Hush Songs;* Arrell Gibson Lifetime Achievement Award, Oklahoma Center for the Book, 2001, for body of work;

Parents' Choice Award, 2004, for *What's the Hurry, Fox? and Other Animal Stories;* Coretta Scott King Award, 2009, for *The Blacker the Berry;* Oklahoma Lifetime Achievement Award.

Writings

YOUNG-ADULT NOVELS

Marked by Fire, Avon (New York, NY), 1982, reprinted, Jump at the Sun (New York, NY), 2007.

Bright Shadow (sequel to *Marked by Fire*), Avon (New York, NY), 1983.

Water Girl, Avon (New York, NY), 1986.

The Golden Pasture, Scholastic (New York, NY), 1986.

Journey, Scholastic (New York, NY), 1988.

When the Nightingale Sings, HarperCollins (New York, NY), 1992.

House of Light (sequel to *Bright Shadow*), Hyperion (New York, NY), 2001.

Abide with Me, Hyperion (New York, NY), 2001.

FOR CHILDREN

Cherish Me (picture book), illustrated by Nneka Bennett, HarperCollins (New York, NY), 1998.

You Are My Perfect Baby (board book), illustrated by Nneka Bennett, HarperCollins (New York, NY), 1999.

The Bowlegged Rooster and Other Tales That Signify, HarperCollins (New York, NY), 2000.

Hush Songs: African American Lullabies, illustrated by Brenda Joysmith, Jump at the Sun (New York, NY), 2000.

Joy! (board book), illustrated by Pamela Johnson, Hyperion (New York, NY), 2001.

Angel's Lullaby (board book), illustrated by Pamela Johnson, Hyperion (New York, NY), 2001.

The Gospel Cinderella (picture book), illustrated by David Diaz, HarperCollins (New York, NY), 2004.

(Adaptor) Zora Neale Hurston, *The Skull Talks Back and Other Haunting Tales,* illustrated by Leonard Jenkins, HarperCollins (New York, NY), 2004.

(Adaptor) Zora Neale Hurston, *What's the Hurry, Fox? and Other Animal Stories,* illustrated by Bryan Collier, HarperCollins (New York, NY), 2004.

(Adaptor) Zora Neale Hurston, *The Six Fools,* illustrated by Ann Tanksley, HarperCollins (New York, NY), 2006.

(Adaptor) Zora Neale Hurston, *The Three Witches,* illustrated by Faith Ringgold, HarperCollins (New York, NY), 2006.

Shouting!, illustrated by Annie Lee, HarperCollins (New York, NY), 2007.

POETRY

Bittersweet, Firesign Press (San Jose, CA), 1973.

Crystal Breezes, Firesign Press (San Jose, CA), 1974.

Blessing, Jocato Press (Berkeley, CA), 1975.

Black Child, illustrated by Tom Feelings, Zamani Productions (New York, NY), 1981.

Inside the Rainbow, Zikawana Press (Palo Alto, CA), 1982.

Brown Honey in Broomwheat Tea, illustrated by Floyd Cooper, HarperCollins (New York, NY), 1993.

Gingerbread Days, illustrated by Floyd Cooper, HarperCollins (New York, NY), 1995.

The Blacker the Berry, illustrated by Brenda Joysmith, HarperCollins (New York, NY), 1997, illustrated by Floyd Cooper, HarperCollins (New York, NY), 2008.

I Have Heard of a Land, illustrated by Floyd Cooper, HarperCollins (New York, NY), 1998.

A Mother's Heart, a Daughter's Love, HarperCollins (New York, NY), 2001.

Crowning Glory, illustrated by Brenda Joysmith, HarperCollins (New York, NY), 2002.

PLAYS

(And producer) *A Song in the Sky* (two-act), produced in San Francisco, CA, 1976.

Look! What a Wonder! (two-act), produced in Berkeley, CA, 1976.

(And producer) *Magnolia* (two-act), produced in San Francisco, CA, 1977.

(And producer) *Ambrosia* (two-act), produced in San Francisco, CA, 1978.

Gospel Roots (two-act), produced in Carson, CA, 1981.

I Have Heard of a Land, produced in Oklahoma City, OK, 1989.

When the Nightingale Sings, produced in Knoxville, TN, 1991.

(And director) *A Mother's Heart* (two-act), produced in San Francisco, CA, 2001.

OTHER

(Editor and contributor) *A Gathering of Flowers: Stories about Being Young in America* (includes "Young Reverend Zelma Lee Moses"), HarperCollins (New York, NY), 1990.

(Editor and contributor) *Linda Brown, You Are Not Alone: The Brown v. Board of Education Decision,* illustrated by Curtis James, Jump at the Sun (New York, NY), 2003.

Contributor of short story, "Handling Snakes," to *I Believe in Water,* edited by Marilyn Singer, HarperCollins (New York, NY), 2000. Contributor to periodicals, including *American Poetry Review, Black Scholar, Calafia, Drum Voices, Giant Talk,* and *Yardbird Reader.* Editor of *Ambrosia* (women's newsletter), 1980.

Adaptations

Marked by Fire was adapted as the stage musical *Abyssinia,* produced at Goodspeed Opera House, East Haddam, CT.

Sidelights

Joyce Carol Thomas is a celebrated author of young-adult novels, poetry, and picture books, as well as of drama, fiction, and poetry for adults. The winner of the

American Book Award for her first novel, *Marked by Fire,* and the Coretta Scott King Award for her second, *Bright Shadow,* Thomas hit the ground running with her writing career and has never looked back. Using her own unique rural background of Oklahoma and California, she introduces readers to an often lyrical world of childhood—portraying not only its joys but also its gross injustices—that resonates across racial lines. According to Charles P. Toombs, writing in the *Dictionary of Literary Biography,* Thomas's "poetry and fiction celebrate the human experience in multifarious ways. She is able to do what great writers have always been able to do: tell a good story."

In her plays, poetry, and fiction, Thomas conjures up stories of African-American heritage, family history, and universal truths. Her language is a compilation of the sounds, imagery, and rhythms of her Oklahoma roots, church-going days, and California connections where she worked side-by-side with Hispanics in the fields. In the words of Darwin L. Henderson and Anthony L. Manna, writing for the *African American Review,* Thomas's "modes of perceiving the world—the poet's spare, sharp-edged wonder; the playwright's cunning orchestration of incident and character; and the novelist's urge to bring us smack-face against life's pain, joy, and recoveries—she evokes dilemmas and struggles which open the way to a better sense of self and often to a glorious personal epiphany." Henderson and Manna added, "Rich in ambiguity and mystery, and steeped in mythical and religious tropes and metaphors, her writing resonates with a wonderfully bracing music."

Thomas grew up in Ponca City, Oklahoma, a small, dusty town where she lived across from the school. She has set several of her novels in her hometown, including *Marked by Fire, Bright Shadow, The Golden Pasture,* and *House of Light.* When Thomas was ten years old, the family moved to rural Tracy, California. There she learned to milk cows, fish for minnows, and harvest tomatoes and grapes. Thomas spent long summers harvesting crops, working beside many Mexicans, and she began a long-lasting fascination with their language. From 1973 to 1978, Thomas wrote poetry and plays for adults, taught in various colleges and universities, and traveled to conferences and festivals all over the world, including Lagos, Nigeria. In 1982 her career took a turn when her young-adult novel *Marked by Fire* was published.

Steeped in the setting and traditions of Ponca City, *Marked by Fire* focuses on Abyssinia Jackson, a girl who was born in a cotton field during harvest time. The title refers to the fact that she received a burn on her face from a brush fire during her birth, and she is "marked for unbearable pain and unspeakable joy," according to a local healer. Abyssinia shows a remarkable talent for singing until she is raped by a member of her church. The story of how she heals from this tragedy fills the rest of the novel.

Marked by Fire was critically acclaimed and placed on required reading lists at many high schools and universities. Writing for *Black Scholar,* Dorothy Randall-Tsuruta noted that Thomas's "poetic tone gives this work what scents give the roses already so pleasing in color." Reviewing this debut novel for *School Library Journal,* Hazel Rochman felt that while the "lack of a fast-paced narrative line and the mythical overtones may present obstacles to some readers, many will be moved" by the story of Abyssinia. *Best Sellers* contributor Wendell Wray noted that Thomas "captures the flavor of black folk life in Oklahoma," and further observed that though she "has set for herself a challenging task . . . Thomas' book works." Commenting about her stormy novel, Thomas once stated: "As a writer I work to create books filled with conflict. . . . I address this quest in part by matching the pitiful absurdities and heady contradictions of life itself, in part by leading the heroine to twin fountains of magic and the macabre, and evoking the holy and the horrible in the same breath. Nor is it ever enough to match these. Through the character of Abyssinia, I strive for what is beyond these, seeking to find newer worlds."

Bright Shadow, a sequel to *Marked by Fire,* was published in 1983. In this work, Abyssinia goes to college and ends up falling in love with Carl Lee Jefferson. The couple work through many problems in order to find their own kind of love. The winner of the Coretta Scott King Award, *Bright Shadow* was called a "love story" and "appealing" by Zena Sutherland, writing in the *Bulletin of the Center for Children's Books.* However, as with many of Thomas's books, some critics faulted her for the use of overly epic language. Sutherland, for one, felt that "the often-ornate phraseology" sometimes weakens the story.

Several of Thomas's books revisit the popular characters from her first two books, among them *The Golden Pasture,* which journeys back to Carl Lee's earlier life on his grandfather's ranch, and *Water Girl,* which tells the story of Abyssinia's teenage daughter Amber, who was given up for adoption as an infant. Amber only learns of her biological mother when, after an earthquake, she finds an old letter that speaks of the adoption. Reviewing *The Golden Pasture* for *Publishers Weekly,* a contributor called the book "a spirited, lyrical tale with a memorable cast of characters."

With *Journey,* her fifth novel, Thomas charted a new literary course by mixing fantasy and mystery to come up with a story of crime and family history. Meggie Alexander, "blessed" at birth by a tarantula, has uncommon powers. Reaching adolescence, she investigates the disappearance of several of her friends in the woods, discovering that some of them have been murdered. Meggie herself is soon kidnapped and thrust into horrible danger. Less well received than many of Thomas's other novels, *Journey* did earn accolades from a writer for *Kirkus Reviews* who felt that the author "dramatically juxtaposes her story's horror with the joy of existence." Other reviewers, such as Starr LaTronica of *School Library Journal,* were less enthusiastic. "This discordant mixture of fantasy and mystery . . . never blend[s] successfully," LaTronica wrote.

With *When the Nightingale Sings* Thomas creates a sort of Cinderella story about young Marigold who is discovered in a swamp and lives with her foster mother, Ruby, and twin stepsisters. As in the original fairy tale, the family treats the young girl as a servant rather than a relative. Finally, Marigold turns her attentions away from her abusive foster family and to the local Baptist church, where she finds salvation in music and gospel songs. Writing in the *St. James Guide to Young-Adult Writers,* a contributor noted that Thomas's use of language "is exquisite; this craftsmanship provides words that are of music, voice, and song. Her characters are often musical, and the church—the gospel music, rhythm, movement, and harmony—provides not only a backdrop, but a language that expresses the spirit of the community."

Thomas's first adult novel, *House of Light,* furthers the story of Abyssinia Jackson begun in *Marked by Fire* and continued in *Bright Shadow.* Now a doctor and

Cover of Thomas's award-winning adult novel House of Light, *part of her series focusing on Abyssinia Jackson.* (Hyperion, 2001. Jacket photograph © Nonstock/P. Kelly. Reproduced by permission of the photographer.)

healer, Abby Jackson-Jefferson is also the main narrator of these tales which relate the lives of patients in Ponca City, Oklahoma. Reviewing the title for *Booklist,* Hazel Rochman predicted that *House of Light* "is sure to be popular for the lively dialogue, the sense of community, and yes, the hopeful message." A *Publishers Weekly* contributor called the book "moving" but "marred only by unsubtle repetition, a rhetorical device Thomas relies on too frequently." However, a *Kirkus Reviews* contributor offered a different opinion of *House of Light,* writing that "lyrical, earthy prose gives this deceptively simple story depth and richness."

Much of Thomas's talent, energy, and output have been focused on poetry for young readers and on picture books for the very young. Teaming up with illustrator Floyd Cooper, she has created a number of poetry books aimed at the five-to-nine-year-old reading audience. In her award-winning *Brown Honey in Broomwheat Tea,* Thomas gathers a dozen poems dealing with the family, home, and the African-American experience in a "highly readable and attractive picture book," according to a reviewer for *Booklist.* A *Publishers Weekly* contributor called the poems "lyrical" evocations of the African-American heritage. The title poem recalls Thomas's own childhood when broomwheat tea was used as an elixir for anything that ailed the young girl.

Thomas and Cooper again teamed up for *Gingerbread Days,* a picture book containing a dozen poems that "celebrate . . . the passage of a year within the circle of an extended African American family," as Meg Stackpole noted in a review for *School Library Journal.* "Like food stored away for winter, this rich harvest of poems contains enough sustenance to last throughout the year," wrote a *Publishers Weekly* contributor of the same book. "Thomas's simple but touching language describes a hopeful world . . . where love is as wonderful as gingerbread, warm and spicy from the oven," the same reviewer observed. Writing for *Horn Book,* Martha V. Parravano noted that *Gingerbread Days* is a "worthy companion" to *Brown Honey in Broomwheat Tea,* and is "made even stronger by Floyd Cooper's glowing, golden illustrations."

I Have Heard of a Land continues the Thomas-Cooper collaboration, and its poems celebrate the role of African-American women pioneers in the nineteenth-century frontier, largely in Oklahoma. A writer for *Publishers Weekly* called *I Have Heard of a Land* a "moving poetic account of a brave black woman," while *Booklist* contributor Ilene Cooper dubbed it a "lyrical tribute to the pioneer spirit."

Another Cooper-Thomas collaboration, *The Blacker the Berry,* was published in two illustrated editions, the second earning a Coretta Scott King Award for Cooper's illustrations. The book includes twelve poems, with titles such as "Golden Goodness," "Cranberry Red," and "Biscuit Brown," that focus on a celebration of blackness by showing the beauty and diversity repre-

sented by the diversity among children of color. Noting that the collection "encourage[s] African-American children to embrace the skin they're in," Susan Dove Lempke added in *Horn Book* that Thomas's poems apply to children of all races, even those attempting to understand their biracial identity. Praising Thomas's "evocative, colorful poetry," a *Kirkus Reviews* contributor called *The Blacker the Berry* "an essential picture book that helps young children understand and appreciate differences," while Teresa Pfeifer observed in *School Library Journal* that the poetry collection "makes the complexities of a layered heritage visible and the many skin shades celebrated."

In *Crowning Glory,* featuring artwork by Brenda Joysmith, Thomas extols the beauty and tradition of braids, curls, and dreadlocks by focusing on an African-American family. "Children from many cultures and backgrounds will appreciate the portraits," wrote Cynthia Turnquist in *Booklist,* and a contributor to *Kirkus Reviews* stated that "each poem is also a tiny moment in time conveyed in simple, conversational language."

Thomas has worked with illustrator Nneka Bennett on two books for very young children: *Cherish Me* and *You Are My Perfect Baby.* Reviewing the first title in *Booklist,* Kathy Broderick called Thomas's poetic text "compelling" and described the book as a "winning offering." Another title for the very young, *Hush Songs: African-American Lullabies* is designed for adults to sing to babies and preschoolers and collects ten lullabies, including three written by Thomas. Claiming that "the songs themselves are timeless," *Booklist* contributor Rochman wrote that the lullabies "touch all of us."

With *A Mother's Heart, A Daughter's Love* Thomas honors the bond between two family members with poems from the point of view of each. "The dual voices illuminate the emotion in each scene," noted *Booklist* contributor Gillian Engberg. In *The Bowlegged Rooster, and Other Tales That Signify,* the author serves up five short stories for young readers featuring Papa Rooster and his chick, all set in Possum Neck, Mississippi. "Although the plots are not always terrifically involving," wrote Steven Engelfried in *School Library Journal,* "the animals' personalities and the bustling atmosphere of the barnyard make these tales appealing." Shelley Townsend-Hudson, writing for *Booklist,* maintained that the tales in *The Bowlegged Rooster and Other Tales That Signify,* are "a joy to hear as well as to read."

In the picture book *Shouting!,* Thomas explores an exuberant form of holy dancing seen in some African American churches. "This magnificent book is not religious in tone," observed *School Library Journal* critic Mary Hazelton, "but more a reflection of a deep cultural connection to African roots."

As she did in *When the Nightingale Sings,* Thomas offers a Southern spin on a familiar tale in *The Gospel Cinderella.* After the daughter of Queen Mother Rhythm is swept downstream by a hurricane, the infant is found by Crooked Foster Mother, who places her in the service of her cruel twins, Hennie and Minnie. When Queen Mother Rhythm needs a new singer to lead her choir, she holds auditions at the Great Gospel Convention, where a mystery soloist astonishes everyone with her lovely voice before disappearing into the swampland. "This unique twist on a classic subtly emphasizes the roots of gospel music, as a respite from hardship and sorrow," a *Publishers Weekly* contributor stated. "To clothe our Gospel Cinderella with a steadfast sense of fairness and faith, I remembered what I loved about fairy tales and gospel music," Thomas remarked in discussing *The Gospel Cinderella* for the HarperCollins Web site. "Cinderella's singing soul is her light in darkness. In our Gospel Cinderella's saddest moments she finds solace and joy in singing gospel."

In addition to creating original stories, Thomas has adapted several works by celebrated writer Zora Neale Hurston, a pioneering figure in African-American literature. In *What's the Hurry, Fox? and Other Animal Stories* she retells nine pourquoi tales, including "Why the Waves Have Whitecaps" and "Why the Dog Hates the Cat." "Originally transcribed in dialect, their regional flavor has been toned down, but not completely erased," observed a *Kirkus Reviews* critic of the chosen tales. *The Six Fools,* a tale first published in Hurston's *Every Tongue Got to Confess,* concerns a young man who leaves his silly wife and family only to discover that absurdity exists throughout the world. Thomas's adaptation "is wonderful in voice: rich, hilarious, and satisfying," announced *School Library Journal* reviewer Nina Lindsay. According to Rochman, young readers will "love the uproar and the nonsense." In *The Three Witches,* a second tale from Hurston's folktale collection, a pair of siblings are chased up a tree by a trio of hideous crones. A *Publishers Weekly* contributor deemed the work "nerve-wracking and comic," and Lindsay called the author's retelling "careful and clever—she doesn't leave out anything, and elaborates only by drawing engaging dialogue out of the more straightforward original narrative."

To commemorate the fiftieth anniversary of the landmark U.S. Supreme Court ruling that desegregated public schools, Thomas served as editor of *Linda Brown, You Are Not Alone: The Brown v. Board of Education Decision,* a collection of stories, poems, and essays by such noted authors as Eloise Greenfield, Ishmael Reed, and Lois Lowry. Thomas also contributed a poem to the anthology. According to a contributor to *Publishers Weekly,* the authors "collectively lay bare the profound, complex consequences of the decision," and Rona Marech, writing for the *San Francisco Chronicle,* called *Linda Brown, You Are Not Alone* a "sophisticated collection that doesn't shy away from the cruelty of segregation or the mixed legacy of the Brown decision." About her decision to include sometimes painful personal reminiscences, Thomas remarked to Marech: "This is part of what we were and still are in some ways. There's pain and joy in every contribution. . . . In literature, if you don't have those components something is not quite true."

"If I had to give advice to young people," Thomas commented in an essay for *Something about the Author Autobiography Series* (SAAS), "it would be that whatever your career choice, prepare yourself to do it well. Quality takes talent and time. Believe in your dreams. Have faith in yourself. Keep working and enjoying today even as you reach for tomorrow. If you choose to write, value your experiences. And color them in the indelible ink of your own background."

"I work for authenticity of voice, fidelity to detail, and naturalness of developments," Thomas also commented. "I treasure and value the experiences that include us all as people. I don't pay any attention to boundaries."

Biographical and Critical Sources

BOOKS

Children's Literature Review, Volume 19, Gale (Detroit, MI), 1990.

Contemporary Literary Criticism, Volume 35, Gale (Detroit, MI), 1985.

Dictionary of Literary Biography, Volume 33: *Afro-American Fiction Writers after 1955,* Gale (Detroit, MI), 1984.

St. James Guide to Young-Adult Writers, 2nd edition, edited by Tom Pendergast and Sara Pendergast, St. James Press (Detroit, MI), 1999.

Something about the Author Autobiography Series, Volume 7, Gale (Detroit, MI), 1989.

PERIODICALS

African American Review, spring, 1998, Darwin L. Henderson and Anthony L. Manna, "Evoking the 'Holy and the Horrible': Conversations with Joyce Carol Thomas," p. 139.

Best Sellers, June, 1982, Wendell Wray, review of *Marked by Fire,* pp. 123-124.

Black Issues Book Review, May, 2001, Althea Gamble, review of *House of Light,* p. 23.

Black Scholar, summer, 1982, Dorothy Randall-Tsuruta, review of *Marked by Fire,* p. 48.

Booklist, February 15, 1994, review of *Brown Honey in Broomwheat Tea,* p. 1081; September 15, 1995, Susan Dove Lempke, review of *Gingerbread Days,* p. 176; February 15, 1998, Ilene Cooper, review of *I Have Heard of a Land,* p. 1009; January 1, 1999, Kathy Broderick, review of *Cherish Me,* p. 891; October 1, 2000, Shelley Townsend-Hudson, review of *The Bowlegged Rooster and Other Tales That Signify,* p. 342; December 15, 2000, Hazel Rochman, review of *Hush Songs: African-American Lullabies,* p. 823; February 15, 2001, Hazel Rochman, review of *House of Light,* p. 1101; March 15, 2001, Gillian Engberg, review of *A Mother's Heart, A Daughter's Love,* p. 1392; September 15, 2002, Cynthia Turnquest, review of *Crowning Glory,* p. 238; December 1, 2003, Gillian Engberg, review of *Linda Brown, You Are Not Alone: The Brown v. Board of Education Decision,* p. 658; February 15, 2004, Michael Cart, "Carte Blanche: Fifty Years after Brown v. Board of Education," p. 1052, and Ilene Cooper, review of *The Gospel Cinderella,* p. 1078; May 15, 2004, Hazel Rochman, review of *What's the Hurry, Fox? and Other Animal Stories,* p. 1622; February 1, 2006, Hazel Rochman, review of *The Six Fools,* p. 68; June 1, 2006, Hazel Rochman, review of *The Three Witches,* p. 78; February 1, 2007, Ilene Cooper, review of *Shouting!,* p. 60; May 15, 2008, Hazel Rochman, review of *The Blacker the Berry,* p. 46.

Bulletin of the Center for Children's Books, February, 1984, Zena Sutherland, review of *Bright Shadow,* p. 119.

Essence, December, 2006, "Child's Play," review of *The Three Witches,* p. 88.

Horn Book, March-April, 1996, Martha V. Parravano, review of *Gingerbread Days,* pp. 219-220; September-October, 2008, Susan Dove Lempke, review of *The Blacker the Berry.*

Kirkus Reviews, September 15, 1988, review of *Journey,* p. 1410; February 1, 2001, review of *House of Light;*

May 15, 2002, review of *Crowning Glory,* p. 742; November 15, 2003, review of *Linda Brown, You Are Not Alone,* p. 1364; April 1, 2004, review of *What's the Hurry, Fox? and Other Animal Stories,* p. 331; April 15, 2004, review of *The Gospel Cinderella,* p. 402; January 15, 2007, review of *Shouting!,* p. 82; June 15, 2008, review of *The Blacker the Berry.*

Publishers Weekly, July 25, 1986, review of *The Golden Pasture,* p. 191; September 25, 1995, review of *Gingerbread Days,* p. 57; January 8, 1996, review of *Brown Honey in Broomwheat Tea,* p. 70; April 6, 1998, review of *I Have Heard of a Land,* p. 77; February 19, 2001, review of *House of Light,* p. 69; May 6, 2002, review of *Crowning Glory,* p. 57; December 8, 2003, review of *Linda Brown, You Are Not Alone,* p. 62; May 24, 2004, review of *The Gospel Cinderella,* p. 62; August 14, 2006, review of *The Three Witches,* p. 205; January 29, 2007, review of *Shouting!,* p. 74.

San Francisco Chronicle, May 17, 2004, Rona Marech, "*Brown vs. Board of Education:* Fifty Years Later; Authors Reflect on How Ruling Affected Their Young Lives," p. E1.

School Library Journal, March, 1982, Hazel Rochman, review of *Marked by Fire,* p. 162; October, 1988, Starr LaTronica, review of *Journey,* p. 165; January, 1996, Meg Stackpole, review of *Gingerbread Days,* p. 107; August, 1999, p. 132; November, 2000, Steven Engelfried, review of *The Bowlegged Rooster and Other Tales That Signify,* p. 135; February, 2002, Bina Williams, review of *Joy!,* p. 114; June, 2002, Barbara Buckley, review of *Crowning Glory,* p. 126; January, 2004, Kelly Czarnecki, review of *Linda Brown, You Are Not Alone,* p. 161; April, 2004, Mary N. Oluonye, review of *What's the Hurry, Fox? and Other Animal Stories,* p. 144; May, 2004, Mary N. Oluonye, review of *The Gospel Cinderella,* p. 136; January, 2006, Nina Lindsay, review of *The Six Fools,* p. 119; August, 2006, Nina Lindsay, review of *The Three Witches,* p. 105; March, 2007, Mary Hazelton, review of *Shouting!,* p. 186; August, 2008, Teresa Pfeifer, review of *The Blacker the Berry,* p. 114.

ONLINE

HarperCollins Web site, http://www.harpercollins.com/ (April 1, 2008), interview with Thomas.

Joyce Carol Thomas Home Page, http://www.joycecarolthomas.com (December 15, 2009).

KidsGrowth.com, http://www.kidsgrowth.com/ (May 31, 2009), review of *The Blacker the Berry.**

* * *

TILDES, Phyllis Limbacher 1945-

Personal

Born March 23, 1945, in Stratford, CT. *Education:* Rhode Island School of Design, B.F.A. *Hobbies and other interests:* Birdwatching, gardening, writing.

Addresses

Home—Savannah, GA.

Career

Author and illustrator. Freelance graphic designer for over twenty-five years. Dartmouth College, Hanover, NH, assistant art director at Hopkins Center for the Arts; former designer for Hallmark Cards.

Writings

SELF-ILLUSTRATED

Counting on Calico, Charlesbridge (Watertown, MA), 1995.
Calico Picks a Puppy, Charlesbridge (Watertown, MA), 1996.
Animals Black and White, Charlesbridge (Watertown, MA), 1996.
Gifts, Charlesbridge (Watertown, MA), 1997.
Animals Brightly Colored, Charlesbridge (Watertown, MA), 1998.
The Magic Babushka: An Original Russian Tale, Charlesbridge (Watertown, MA), 1998.
Baby Animals Black and White, Charlesbridge (Watertown, MA), 1998.
Calico's Cousins: Cats from around the World, Charlesbridge (Watertown, MA), 1999.
Animals in Camouflage, Charlesbridge (Watertown, MA), 2000.
Baby Face, Charlesbridge (Watertown, MA), 2001.
Billy's Big-Boy Bed, Charlesbridge (Watertown, MA), 2002.
Calico's Curious Kittens, Charlesbridge (Watertown, MA), 2003.
Eye Guess: A Foldout Guessing Game, Charlesbridge (Watertown, MA), 2005.
The Garden Wall, Charlesbridge (Watertown, MA), 2006.

Baby Face has been translated into Spanish.

ILLUSTRATOR

Jacqueline Farmer, *Pumpkins,* Charlesbridge (Watertown, MA), 2004.
Jacqueline Farmer, *Apples,* Charlesbridge (Watertown, MA), 2007.

Pumpkins has been translated into Spanish.

Sidelights

Phyllis Limbacher Tildes is the author and illustrator of more than a dozen books for young readers, including *Calico's Curious Kittens* and *Eye Guess: A Foldout Guessing Game.* Tildes demonstrated a talent for art at a young age, completing her first drawing at the age of two, according to the Charlesbridge Web site. She also

developed a love for literature, spending hours at the local library studying works by such celebrated nineteenth-century "Golden Age" illustrators as Arthur Rackham and Beatrix Potter. After graduating from high school, Tildes earned a bachelor's degree from the Rhode Island School of Design before working as an art director for the Hopkins Art Center at Dartmouth College and a designer for Hallmark Cards. She then spent more than twenty-five years as a freelance graphic designer, publishing her first self-illustrated children's book, *Counting on Calico,* in 1995.

In *Counting on Calico* youngsters develop their counting skills and learn about feline anatomy and behavior at the same time. As Calico the cat and her kittens play with paper bags, watch birds, and groom themselves, a tiny mouse points out the number of paw prints the cat family leaves behind as well as the colorful patterns distinguishing the fur of each kitten. Carolyn Phelan, writing in *Booklist,* observed that *Counting on Calico* would make a good real-aloud and noted the "softly shaded colors" of the illustrations.

In *Calico Picks a Puppy* the title character introduces a variety of dog breeds, including spaniels, setters, and huskies. Tildes's "brief and lighthearted yet informative text" garnered praise from *Booklist* contributor Ellen Mandel. *Calico's Cousins: Cats from around the World,*

Jacqueline Farmer's seasonal picture book **Pumpkins features artwork by Phyllis Limbacher Tildes.** (Illustration copyright © 2004 by Phyllis Limbacher Tildes. Used with permission by Charlesbridge Publishing, Inc. All rights reserved.)

a companion work, focuses on various breeds of cats, including Persians, Angoras, and Norwegian Forest cats. "Tildes draws cats beautifully, and here she has an opportunity to show off that talent," Ilene Cooper remarked in *Booklist*. Calico's rambunctious youngsters are the subject of *Calico's Curious Kittens*. "The brightly hued, detailed landscapes contain plenty of sly feline humor to tickle little fancies," a critic in *Kirkus Reviews* stated, and Cooper similarly noted that Tildes's "watercolors capture all the friskiness and charm of kittens on the loose."

Tildes addresses a milestone in a child's life in *Billy's Big-Boy Bed*. Although little Billy has already picked out a roomy new bed at the furniture store, he is reluctant to leave his crib, which houses his collection of teddy bears. With his parents' help, the toddler gradually adapts to the unfamiliar sleeping arrangement. "Drawn with a loving hand, the watercolor illustrations are gentle and realistic; Billy's expressive face is adorable," a *Kirkus Reviews* critic observed, and Maryann H. Owen, writing in *School Library Journal*, stated that Tildes's illustrations, "worked in cheerful primary colors, tell the story well even without the words."

Tildes examines how animals blend in with their environment in *Animals in Camouflage*. Here readers are provided with clues to the identities of seven creatures and then search a brightly colored illustration of their habitats to locate the critters. A polar bear, crab spider, and great horned owl are among the animals featured. *Booklist* contributor Todd Morning praised the "well-rendered gouache paintings" in the book and called *Animals in Camouflage* "an entertaining package." According to *School Library Journal* critic Patricia Manning, *Animals in Camouflage* "deserves a place in quality collections of natural history." In *Eye Guess* young readers are again given the opportunity to play detec-

tive, and "the gouache paintings energize the information in this book of fact-filled fun," according to *Booklist* reviewer Connie Fletcher.

Biographical and Critical Sources

PERIODICALS

Booklist, June 1, 1995, Carolyn Phelan, review of *Counting on Calico,* p. 1780; November 1, 1996, Ellen Mandel, review of *Calico Picks a Puppy,* p. 505; February 1, 1998, Ilene Cooper, review of *Calico's Cousins: Cats from around the World,* p. 978; January 1, 2000, Todd Morning, review of *Animals in Camouflage,* p. 934; February 1, 2003, Ilene Cooper, review of *Calico's Curious Kittens,* p. 1002; August, 2004, Carolyn Phelan, review of *Pumpkins,* p. 1938; September 1, 2005, Connie Fletcher, review of *Eye Guess: A Fold-out Guessing Game,* p. 138; June 1, 2007, Gillian Engberg, review of *Apples,* p. 64.

Kirkus Reviews, January 15, 2002, review of *Billy's Big-Boy Bed,* p. 111; February 1, 2003, review of *Calico's Curious Kittens,* p. 240; June 15, 2007, review of *Apples.*

School Library Journal, April, 2000, Patricia Manning, review of *Animals in Camouflage,* p. 127; October, 2001, JoAnn Jonas, review of *Baby Face,* p. 132; March, 2002, Maryann H. Owen, review of *Billy's Big-Boy Bed,* p. 204; February, 2003, Gay Lynn Van Vleck, review of *Calico's Curious Kittens,* p. 124; July, 2004, Marge Loch-Wouters, review of *Pumpkins,* p. 93; September, 2007, Grace Oliff, review of *Apples,* p. 182.

ONLINE

Charlesbridge Web site, http://www.charlesbridge.com/ (March 10, 2008), "Phyllis Limbacher."*

U-W

ULLMAN, Barb Bentler

Personal
Married; husband's name Jim; children: two daughters.

Addresses
Home—WA. *E-mail*—barb.ullman@gmail.com.

Career
Writer and artist.

Writings
The Fairies of Nutfolk Wood, Katherine Tegen Books (New York, NY), 2006.

Sidelights
Barb Bentler Ullman worked as an artist for many years, showing her works at local galleries and art fairs before she decided to write a book. Then in her forties, Ullman set to work, even though her time was limited. Writing a single page each day, she eventually produced her first middle-grade novel, *The Fairies of Nutfolk Wood.*

The Fairies of Nutfolk Wood describes a girl's encounter with the tiny people who live in a nearby woods. Willa, whose parents are divorced, lives with her mother in a trailer in the woods. Willa has been worn thin and weak by the emotional turmoil of the divorce. However, her elderly neighbor Hazel, who takes care of the youngster during the day, gives Willa chores to do that help the girl regain her strength. Along with her growing strength, Willa finds that there are fairyfolk living in the woods, tiny people that only she and Hazel can see.

Reviewing *The Fairies of Nutfolk Wood* for *Booklist,* Carolyn Phelan called it "a convincing first-person narrative with the wholesome appeal of fresh-baked bread,"

and a *Kirkus Reviews* critic praised Ullman's inclusion of moments of "sweet imagery and deft characterization." Eva Mitnick, writing in *School Library Journal,* highlighted Willa's relationship with Hazel and "her efforts to deal with her parents' divorce" as among the strongest aspects of *The Fairies of Nutfolk Wood,* stating of the novel that "there are enough satisfying moments to hold readers."

Biographical and Critical Sources

PERIODICALS

Booklist, May 15, 2006, Carolyn Phelan, review of *The Fairies of Nutfolk Wood,* p. 59.
Kirkus Reviews, May 15, 2006, review of *The Fairies of Nutfolk Wood,* p. 525.
Northlake News & The Valley View (Woodinville, WA), August 21, 2006, Riley Mizell, "Artist Turned Writer Creates a Book, One Page at a Time."
School Library Journal, July, 2006, Eva Mitnick, review of *The Fairies of Nutfolk Wood,* p. 113.

ONLINE

Barb Bentler Ullman Home Page, http://barb.bentler.us (April 14, 2008).*

* * *

ULRIKSEN, Mark 1957-

Personal
Born 1957, in San Francisco, CA; married; children: two daughters. *Education:* Chico State University, B.A., 1980; attended University of Massachusetts.

Addresses
Home—San Francisco, CA. *E-mail*—mark@markulriksen.com.

Career

Artist and illustrator. Northeastern University, Boston, MA, graphic designer, 1980-82; worked in graphic design field until 1985; *San Francisco Focus* (magazine), San Francisco, CA, associate art director, then head art director, 1986-93; freelance illustrator and fine artist, specializing in family portraits and dog portraits, 1994—. *Exhibitions:* Work has been exhibited at Meyerovich Gallery, San Francisco, CA, and housed in permanent collections at Smithsonian American Art Museum, Washington, DC, Library of Congress, and Museum of Contemporary Art, Rome, Italy.

Awards, Honors

Silver Medal, Society of Illustrators, 2002; Gold Medal, Society of Illustrators, 2003; Best News Cover designation, American Society of Magazine Editors, 2006, for *New Yorker* cover; honors from numerous juried competitions.

Illustrator

Ann Fiery, *The Completely and Totally True Book of Urban Legends,* Running Press (Philadelphia, PA), 2001.
Elizabeth Winthrop, *Dog Show,* Holt (New York, NY), 2004.
Elizabeth Winthrop, *The Biggest Parade,* Holt (New York, NY), 2006.

Contributor to periodicals, including *New Yorker, Rolling Stone, Vibe, Gentleman's Quarterly, Entertainment Weekly, Time, Newsweek,* and *New York Times.* Work included in *Covering the New Yorker: Cutting-Edge Covers from a Literary Institution,* Abbeville Press, 2000. Illustrator of book covers.

Sidelights

Mark Ulriksen is an award-winning artist whose acrylic paintings have appeared in such publications as *Rolling Stone, Entertainment Weekly,* and *Time.* Since 1993 he has been a regular contributor to the *New Yorker,* and his work has graced numerous covers for that magazine. In addition to his magazine work, Ulriksen has also created illustrations for the picture books, *Dog Show* and *The Biggest Parade,* both with a text by Elizabeth Winthrop. "There's a lot of freedom in kid's books," Ulriksen told *BrooWaha San Francisco* online contributor Ed Attanasio. "I want to explore that avenue more, because I enjoy being a storyteller."

Born in San Francisco, California, in 1957, Ulriksen graduated from Chico State University and worked in graphic design for several years before landing a job with *San Francisco Focus* magazine. He became a full-time painter and illustrator in 1994. His work soon caught the attention of then-*New Yorker* art director Françoise Mouly, who asked him to create a cover image of Hillary Clinton that earned national recognition. Ulriksen's work for the *New Yorker* often satirizes political figures; in 2006 he received an award from the American Society of Magazine Editors for a cover portraying U.S. president George W. Bush and vice president Dick Cheney as cowboys.

In 2004 Ulriksen provided the artwork for his first children's book, *Dog Show.* Winthrop's story centers on a laid-back basset hound named Fred and his ambitious owner, Harvey. Determined to win a blue ribbon at the Bonesport Dog Show, Harvey enters Fred in every conceivable category, including "Dogs with Spots" and "Dogs Who Can't Stand Still," yet the pair keep coming up empty-handed. Harvey realizes they have one last chance to score top prize: the "Dogs in Costumes" competition. Although Harvey offers a unique twist on an old favorite, dressing himself as a lion and Fred as a lion tamer, the performance only earns an honorable mention. As a dejected Harvey prepares to leave the show with his droopy-faced canine, the judges spot an opportunity to create an entirely new category, one that brightens Harvey's day. Ulriksen's "colorful and quirky acrylic illustrations set the pace" for *Dog Show,* according to *School Library Journal* contributor Carol Ann Wilson, and a *Publishers Weekly* critic asserted that the

Mark Ulriksen's illustration projects include creating the cover art for Maurice Gee's young-adult novel The Fat Man. (Simon & Schuster Books for Young Readers, 1997. Illustration © 1997 by Mark Ulriksen. Reproduced by permission of the illustrator.)

"dry wit" in Winthrop's story is matched by Ulriksen's "droll, kickily colored acrylic paintings of man and his best friend."

Ulriksen and Winthrop also team up on *The Biggest Parade,* a follow-up to *Dog Show.* When the mayor of Bonesport asks Harvey to plan a parade for the town's 250th anniversary, the energetic dog owner decides to place Fred in a starring role. The reluctant basset hound balks at the honor, however, remembering past parades when people used his tail as a flagpole and blew horns in his ear. After Harvey realizes that he has enlisted the entire town to march in the parade, however, he finds the perfect job for Fred to tackle during the celebration. Ulriksen's "chunky acrylics add tons of fun to the text," Ilene Cooper noted in *Booklist,* and a critic in *Kirkus Reviews* stated that "readers will pore over the crowd illustrations, laughing at all of the antics." Ulriksen "is a stylish, ironic painter," observed a contributor in *Publishers Weekly,* "but he's clearly put a lot of heart into his work here, too."

Biographical and Critical Sources

PERIODICALS

Booklist, September 1, 2006, Ilene Cooper, review of *The Biggest Parade,* p. 142.
Communication Arts, May-June, 1997, "Mark Ulriksen."
Kirkus Reviews, August 15, 2004, review of *Dog Show,* p. 815.
Publishers Weekly, August 30, 2004, review of *Dog Show,* p. 55; July 31, 2006, review of *The Biggest Parade,* p. 74.
San Francisco Chronicle, April 14, 2001, Jesse Hamlin, "Artist's Work the Talk of the Town," p. B1; March 28, 2004, Sam Whiting, "Outstanding in His Field; One Artist's Pac Bell Park Rendering Went on to Fame and Infamy," p. 12; September 17, 2006, Heidi Benson, "Catching Up: Some Diamonds Really Are Forever."
School Library Journal, October, 2004, Carol Ann Wilson, review of *Dog Show,* p. 136; October, 2006, Susan E. Murray, review of *The Biggest Parade,* p. 131.

ONLINE

Arion Press Web site, http://www.arionpress.com/ (April 1, 2008), "Mark Ulriksen."
BrooWaha San Francisco Web site, http://www.broowaha. com/ (March 3, 2007), Ed Attanasio, "Mark Ulriksen: A Local SF Artist Makes Good."
Mark Ulriksen Home Page, http://www.markulriksen.com (December 19, 2009).
Trafta.com, http://www.trafta.com/ (April 1, 2008), "Mark Ulriksen."*

*   *   *

VEGA, Diego
See ADKINS, Jan

VIECELI, Emma 1979-

Personal

Born June 13, 1979, in Basildon, Essex, England. *Hobbies and other interests:* Singing and composing songs, writing, playing RPG's.

Addresses

Home—Cambridge, England. *E-mail*—emma.vieceli@ gmail.com.

Career

Artist, comics illustrator, and book illustrator. Sweatdrop Studios (manga collective), England, administrative member.

Awards, Honors

Rising Stars of Manga designation, Tokyopop publishers.

Writings

(Illustrator) William Shakespeare, *Hamlet,* text adapted by Richard Appignanesi, Amulet Books (New York, NY), 2007.
(Illustrator) William Shakespeare, *Much Ado about Nothing,* text adapted by Richard Appignanesi, Amulet Books (New York, NY), 2009.

Emma Vieceli (Reproduced by permission.)

Author and illustrator of comic series "Violet," published in London *Guardian* and *DFC*. Author and illustrator (with Andrew Ruddick) of "Dragon Heir" series of manga comics, Sweatdrop Studios. Contributor of illustrations to story "Run Hikaru Run" by Sarah Winningham, published in *Princess Ai: Rumours from the Other Side,* Tokyopop, 2008. Contributor to manga anthologies, including *Cold Sweat & Tears* and *Sugardrops,* both Sweatdrop Studios, and *Comic Book Tattoo,* Image Comics, 2008.

Sidelights

British illustrator Emma Vieceli is a professional "manga" artist whose work features the whimsical style that is characteristic of these Japanese-styled comics and print cartoons. Vieceli and a score of other British artists work as the Sweatdrop Studios collective and are dedicated to creating manga-style comics. In an interview for *Comic Bits Online,* she reported that she has been an ardent comic-book fan since her youth. "I was obsessed in particular with an Italian comic series called 'Dylan Dog,'" Vieceli recalled. "Otherwise, I had the usual comic fandoms for a child: 'Beano,' 'Garfield,' 'B.C,' 'Peanuts' . . . and later on I started to discover the Marvel, DC and '2000AD' worlds. . . . When I was eleven, someone let me borrow their copy of Ranma. . . . It was my first true manga experience and it stayed with me." Vieceli further noted, "I'm happy to say that I love all comics, no matter where they hail from. I wish we could lose categorisation really and just divide comics by genre instead . . . one day maybe."

Vieceli began drawing and creating her own comics story lines from an early age, at first copying the comics she loved and soon creating her own distinctive style and storylines. She noted this extreme form of self-education in her interview: "I always drew. I mean, I'd find a way of covering my workbooks and anything I could find with character art, but no, no education in it. My experience has come largely from being a fan and then from joining Sweatdrop and learning as I went, with lots of support and encouragement from other members."

Considered a rising star within the British manga scene, Vieceli has produced work for publishers including Los Angeles-based Tokyopop and *Neo* magazine. In 2007, working with editor Richard Appignanesi, Vieceli produced a 200-page graphic-novel adaptation of William Shakespeare's *Hamlet,* the first of several versions of the well-known Elizabethan dramas that employ the words of Shakespeare, but in an abridged form. As the illustrator told a *Comic Bits Online* interviewer, "I worked hard on trying to not disagree with, nor over-promote the vast amount of subtexts and theories behind *Hamlet*. After all, it's a story that has been prodded over and over. It's a human story through and through, and half of the battle for me was getting that across. Double meanings and unspoken thoughts—it was tricky!"

Vieceli creates the cartoon art that brings to life Richard Appignanesi's text in the graphic novel adaptation of Shakespeare's famous play **Much Ado about Nothing.** (Amulet, 2009. Reproduced by permission.)

Discussing *Hamlet,* a *Kirkus Reviews* critic felt that Vieceli's adaptation helps to make the play more accessible to new generations. "Refreshingly clear, this adaptation is recommended for all libraries serving teens," the critic concluded. Writing in the London *Guardian,* Craig Taylor also praised the "manganized" adaptation, stating that Vieceli's *Hamlet* "highlight[s] just how much action can be drawn from a play about indecision." A similar opinion was voiced by E. Borley, writing for the British Broadcasting Corporation Web site, who predicted that the "average bored teenager may just pick up" the work "with a tiny burst of rarely seen enthusiasm." Other manga versions of Shakespearean dramas include the comedy *Much Ado about Nothing.*

Biographical and Critical Sources

PERIODICALS

Guardian (London, England), February 10, 2007, Craig Taylor, review of *Hamlet,* p. 19.

Kirkus Reviews, March 15, 2007, review of *Hamlet.*

ONLINE

British Broadcasting Corporation Web site, http://www.
bbc.co.uk/ (September 3, 2007), E. Borley, "Manga
Hamlet by The Bard?"
Comic Bits Web site, http://www.comicbitsonline.com/
(August 1, 2007), interview with Vieceli.
Comic Space Web site, http://www.comicspace.com/ (April
9, 2008), "Emma Vieceli."
Emma Vieceli Home Page, http://emma.sweatdrop.com
(January 10, 2010).
Emma Vieceli Web log, http://emmav.livejournal.com
(January 10, 2010).
Sweatdrop Studios Web site, http://www.sweatdrop.com/
(April 9, 2008), "Emma Vieceli."*

* * *

WARGIN, Kathy-jo 1964-

Personal

Born December 20, 1964, in Tower, MN; married Ed
Wargin (a photographer); children: Jake.

Addresses

Home—Petosky, MI.

Career

Writer. The Wargin Company, Petosky, MI, co-owner,
with husband, Ed Wargin; teacher at Bear River Writers
Workshop.

Awards, Honors

Official Children's Book of Michigan designation,
Michigan House of Representatives, 1998, and Chil-
dren's Choice Award for Best Picture Book, Capital
Area District Library, both for *The Legend of Sleeping
Bear;* Children's Book of the Year Award, Great Lakes
Booksellers Association, 1999, for *The Legend of
Mackinac Island;* Children's Choice Award, Interna-
tional Reading Association (IRA), 2001, for *The Leg-
end of the Loon;* Teacher's Choice Award, IRA, for *Win
One for the Gipper.*

Writings

Scenic Driving Michigan, photographs by Ed Wargin, Falcon Press (Helena, MT), 1997.
The Legend of Sleeping Bear, illustrated by Gijsbert van
Frankenhuyzen, Sleeping Bear Press (Chelsea, MI),
1998.
Michigan: The Spirit of the Land, photographs by Ed Wargin, Voyageur Press (Stillwater, MN), 1999.

The Legend of Mackinac Island, illustrated by Gijsbert van
Frankenhuyzen, Sleeping Bear Press (Chelsea, MI),
1999.
The Michigan Counting Book, illustrated by Michael Glenn
Monroe, Sleeping Bear Press (Chelsea, MI), 2000.
The Legend of the Loon, illustrated by Gijsbert van Fran-
kenhuyzen, Sleeping Bear Press (Chelsea, MI), 2000.
The Great Lakes Cottage Book, photographs by Ed War-
gin, Sleeping Bear Press (Chelsea, MI), 2000.
L Is for Lincoln: An Illinois Alphabet, illustrated by Gijs-
bert van Frankenhuyzen, Sleeping Bear Press (Chelsea,
MI), 2000.
The Legend of the Lady's Slipper, illustrated by Gijsbert
van Frankenhuyzen, Sleeping Bear Press (Chelsea,
MI), 2001.
The Michigan Reader for Boys and Girls, illustrated by
K.L. Darnell, Sleeping Bear Press (Chelsea, MI),
2001.
The Legend of the Voyageur, illustrated by Gijsbert van
Frankenhuyzen, Sleeping Bear Press (Chelsea, MI),
2002.
The American Reader, illustrated by Kathryn L. Darnell,
Sleeping Bear Press (Chelsea, MI), 2002.
The Legend of Leelanau, illustrated by Gijsbert van Fran-
kenhuyzen, Sleeping Bear Press (Chelsea, MI), 2003.
The Edmund Fitzgerald: Song of the Bell, illustrated by
Gijsbert van Frankenhuyzen, Sleeping Bear Press
(Chelsea, MI), 2003.
V Is for Viking: A Minnesota Alphabet, illustrated by Karen
Latham and Rebecca Latham, Sleeping Bear Press
(Chelsea, MI), 2003.
M Is for Melody: A Wisconsin Alphabet, illustrated by
Katherine Larson, Sleeping Bear Press (Chelsea, MI),
2003.
The Legend of the Petosky Stone, illustrated by Gijsbert
van Frankenhuyzen, Sleeping Bear Press (Chelsea,
MI), 2004.
B Is for Badger: A Music Alphabet, illustrated by Renée
Graef, Sleeping Bear Press (Chelsea, MI), 2004.
Win One for the Gipper: America's Football Hero, illus-
trated by Bruce Langton, Sleeping Bear Press
(Chelsea, MI), 2004.
Once upon a Christmas Eve, illustrated by Bruce Langton,
Mitten Press (Ann Arbor, MI), 2005.
A Mother's Wish, illustrated by Irena Roman, HarperCol-
lins (New York, NY), 2006.
The Legend of Old Abe, a Civil War Eagle, illustrated by
Laurie Caple, Sleeping Bear Press (Chelsea, MI),
2006.
The Legend of Minnesota, illustrated by David Geister,
Sleeping Bear Press (Chelsea, MI), 2006.
Minn from Minnesota, illustrated by Karen Busch Holman,
Mitten Press (Ann Arbor, MI), 2006.
Mitt the Michigan Mouse, illustrated by Karen Busch Hol-
man, Mitten Press (Ann Arbor, MI), 2006.
Prairie Numbers: An Illinois Number Book, illustrated by
Kathy O'Malley, Sleeping Bear Press (Chelsea, MI),
2006.
The American Reader, illustrated by K.L. Darnell, Sleep-
ing Bear Press (Chelsea, MI), 2006.
The Legend of Wisconsin, illustrated by David Geister,
Sleeping Bear Press (Chelsea, MI), 2007.
The Voyageur's Paddle, illustrated by David Geister,
Sleeping Bear Press (Chelsea, MI), 2007.

Look and See Michigan with Me, photographs by Ed Wargin, Sleeping Bear Press (Chelsea, MI), 2007.

Mitt and Minn at the Wisconsin Cheese Jamboree, illustrated by Karen Busch Holman, Mitten Press (Ann Arbor, MI), 2007.

(Reteller) *The Frog Prince,* illustrated by Anne Yvonne Gilbert, Mitten Press (Ann Arbor, MI), 2007.

Mitt and Minn's Illinois Adventure, illustrated by Karen Busch Holman, Mitten Press (Ann Arbor, MI), 2007.

North Star Numbers: A Minnesota Numbers Book, illustrated by Laurie Caple, Sleeping Bear Press (Chelsea, MI), 2008.

P Is for Pumpkin, illustrated by YaWen Ariel Pang, Zonderkidz (Grand Rapids, MI), 2008.

Mary's First Thanksgiving: An Inspirational Story of Gratefulness, illustrated by Robert Papp, Zonderkidz (Grand Rapids, MI), 2008.

I Spy with My Little Eye: Minnesota, photographs by Ed Wargin, Sleeping Bear Press (Chelsea, MI), 2008.

The Man behind the Peace Prize: Alfred Nobel, illustrated by Zachary Pullen, Sleeping Bear Press (Chelsea, MI), 2009.

Moose on the Loose, illustrated by John Bendall-Brunello, Sleeping Bear Press (Chelsea, MI), 2009.

K Is for Kites, illustrated by Kim Gatto, Zonderkidz (Grand Rapids, MI), 2009.

Contributor of poems to *M Is for Mitten: A Michigan Alphabet,* by Annie Appleford, illustrated by Michael G. Monroe, Sleeping Bear Press (Chelsea, MI), 1999. Work included in *Voices of Michigan, Vol. II: An Anthology of Michigan Authors,* edited by Jane Winston, Mackinac Jane's Publishing Company (Warner Robbins, GA), 2000.

Sidelights

Northern Michigan resident Kathy-jo Wargin has found a niche writing about the natural beauty, Native-American legends, and history of the Great Lakes region. She has written picture-book versions of legends focusing on such animals as bears, loons, and turtles as well as about such places as Mackinac Island, the Leelanau Peninsula, and Lake Superior, the watery grave of the ore carrier *Edmund Fitzgerald.* "I like to retell old legends because of the wonderful messages they offer," she told Julia Durango of the Ottawa, Illinois, *Daily Times.* "I also believe it's important we keep history alive by remembering the stories passed down for generations through the oral tradition."

Nature and music have long been a part of Wargin's life. Born in Tower, Minnesota, she grew up in Grand Rapids, Michigan, and later studied music at the University of Minnesota in Duluth. She parlayed her interest in the music of instruments into the music of words in her picture books. After teaming up with her husband, photographer Ed Wargin, to create *Scenic Driving Michigan,* she authored *The Legend of Sleeping Bear,* which was the first children's book produced by Michigan-based Sleeping Bear Press. In it, Wargin retells a Native-American tale about the great sleeping bear whose cubs are tranformed into the Manitou Is-

Kathy-jo Wargin's **The Michigan Reader** *features a collection of stories about the mitten-shaped state that are brought to life in K.L. Darnell's art.* (Sleeping Bear Press, 2001. Illustration © 2001 by K.L. Darnell. Reproduced by permission.)

lands of Lake Michigan, located west of the Leelanau Peninsula. The author first heard the legend in 1995, three years before the book saw publication. "I fell in love with it," she told Amy Woods in the Minneapolis *Star Tribune.* "It echoed in my heart." "*The Legend of Sleeping Bear* is both charming and charmed," Woods remarked, going on to praise Wargin's "simple, poignant, poetic" narrative.

The Legend of Sleeping Bear was the first book to pair Wargin's text with illustrations by Gijsbert van Frankenhuyzen. A Dutch artist who came to the United States to enjoy the nation's natural beauty, van Frankenhuyzen served as an art director for *Michigan Natural Resources* magazine before embarking on an illustration career. With more than 200,000 copies sold, *The Legend of Sleeping Bear* has become a mainstay of Sleeping Bear Press and was named the Official Children's Book of Michigan in 1998.

Following up on her initial success, Wargin has written about several other Michigan legends in books such as *The Legend of Mackinac Island.* Pronounced "mak-uh-naw," Mackinac Island lies east of St. Ignace in the Straits of Mackinac and has long played a role in Michigan history. In Wargin's retelling of a Native-American creation tale, the painted turtle Makinauk and his animal friends discover land in an ancient time when all the Earth was covered with water. In _The Legend of the Lady's Slipper,_ which Cathy Collison praised in the _Detroit Free Press_ as a "lovely story," Wargin recounts the tale of young Running Flower, who must make a desperate dash through the forest in an attempt to save the people of her village.

The Legend of Leelanau finds young Leelinau entering the forbidden Spirit Wood, where she is lured into perpetual childhood by playing with the tiny sprites called the Pukwudijinees. In _Kirkus Reviews,_ a critic praised Wargin's version of the Leelanau legend, calling it "a fluid retelling that even young listeners will compre-

hend and older readers will enjoy." The son of an Odawa princess and a French fur trader becomes a skilled hunter in _The Legend of the Petosky Stone,_ a profile of Chief Ignatius Petosegay. The narrative of this book "flows well" in _The Legend of the Petosky Stone,_ noted _School Library Journal_ critic Sean George, the critic adding that Wargin's picture book "is sure to be scooped up by local legend lovers."

Wargin rejoins van Frankenhuyzen to create _The Edmund Fitzgerald: Song of the Bell,_ a picture book focusing on the 1975 sinking of an ore freighter. All twenty-nine crew members drowned, and the tragic event was commemorated by Gordon Lightfoot in his

Wargin's collaboration with artist Gijsbert van Frankenhuyzen include the picture book **Legend of the Lady's Slipper.** (Sleeping Bear Press, 2001. Illustration © 2001 by Gijsbert van Frankenhuyzen. Reproduced by permission of the illustrator.)

Wargin's alphabetical tour of the northern mid-western United States includes the picture book B Is for Badger: A Wisconsin Alphabet, *featuring artwork by Renee Graef.* (Sleeping Bear Press, 2008. Illustration copyright © 2004 by Renee Graef. Reproduced by permission of the author's agent.)

1976 song, "The Wreck of the Edmund Fitzgerald." Wargin combines rhymed couplets and prose, "a device that works fairly well, as the book both tells the tale and laments" the men who died, observed *Booklist* critic Carolyn Phelan.

Expanding her focus from the northern midwest, Wargin has also published a retelling of *The Frog Prince,* a classic tale by the Brothers Grimm. A critic in *Kirkus Reviews* described her work here as "a very pretty rendering of this difficult story," and Debbie Carton observed in *Booklist* that Wargin's revisions to the text "make it more palatable for younger audiences." In *A Mother's Wish,* an original story, a mother and her young daughter wish upon a butterfly; years later they learn that their dreams have come true. *A Mother's Wish* was deemed "a gentle tale of familial love that is good for individual sharing" by *School Library Journal* contributor Catherine Callegari.

The eclectic Wargin has also written chapter books featuring two plucky mice. Brought to life in illustrations by Karen Busch Hollman, the duo are introduced in

Mitt the Michigan Mouse and their adventures continue in *Minn from Minnesota, Mitt and Minn at the Wisconsin Cheese Jamboree,* and *Mitt and Minn's Illinois Adventure.*

Wargin turns to biography in both *Win One for the Gipper: America's Football Hero* and *The Man behind the Peace Prize: Alfred Nobel.* In *Win One for the Gipper* she offers a biography of George Gipp, a gifted athlete at the University of Notre Dame whose deathbed request to legendary coach Knute Rockne inspired his alma mater's gridiron team to a stunning victory over unbeaten Army. A *Publishers Weekly* reviewer praised Wargin's "crisp portrait" as one that "also imparts a sense of Gipp's likable off-field persona." *The Man behind the Peace Prize* relates the story of Nobel, who was both the inventory of dynamite and the endower of the international award that now bears his name. Wargin covers the major points in Nobel's life, including his early love of reading and general tinkering and the discovery of the volatility of nitroglycerin and the blast at his factory that killed one of his brothers. "Throughout, Wargin depicts a melancholy but committed pacifist," noted a contributor for *Kirkus Reviews.*

Wargin is also the author of a number of alphabet books. Some take their themes from various states, such as *V Is for Viking: A Minnesota Alphabet* and *M Is for Melody: A Wisconsin Alphabet,* or music, as in *B Is for Badger: A Music Alphabet.* Still others focus on religious themes, as in *P Is for Pumpkin* and *K Is for Kites.* Reviewing Wargin's *P Is for Pumpkin* in *School Library Journal,* Lee Bock described it as "a sweet, gentle book for family and church settings." Here Wargin shows the presence of spirituality and of God in domestic and seasonal scenes, concentrating on autumnal festivities and activities. For example, the grinning jack-o'-lantern shines with light from God, and the brilliant colors of fall trees and fields are a reflection of the same light. A contributor for *Kirkus Reviews* explained of the same work that "the traditional alphabet-book format combines with rhyming couplets that relate Christian concepts to aspects of the fall season."

Biographical and Critical Sources

PERIODICALS

Booklist, January 1, 2004, Carolyn Phelan, review of *The Edmund Fitzgerald: Song of the Bell,* p. 852; June 1, 2007, Debbie Carton, review of *The Frog Prince,* p. 76.

Buffalo News, December 21, 2003, Jean Westmoore, review of *The Edmund Fitzgerald,* p. F5.

Capital Times (Madison, WI), Debra Carr-Elsing, "*B Is for Badger* Alphabet Book Tells Young Readers about State Treasures," p. 1B.

Children's Bookwatch, December, 2006, review of *Mitt the Michigan Mouse;* April, 2007, review of *The Frog Prince.*

Daily Times (Ottawa, IL), February 20, 2001, Julia Durango, "Kathy-jo Wargin's Illinois Alphabet."

Detroit Free Press, June 10, 2001, Cathy Collison, review of *The Legend of the Lady's Slipper,* p. 5; October 21, 2001, Janis Campbell, review of *The Michigan Reader for Boys and Girls,* p. 5; May 26, 2006, Michele Siuda Jacques, reviews of *Mitt the Michigan Mouse, Minn from Minnesota,* and *A Mother's Wish;* June 1, 2007, Michele Siuda Jacques, review of *Look and See Michigan with Me.*

Kirkus Reviews, April 15, 2003, review of *The Legend of Leelanau,* p. 613; March 15, 2007, review of *The Frog Prince;* July 15, 2008, review of *P Is for Pumpkin,;* August 15, 2008, review of *Mary's First Thanksgiving: An Inspirational Story of Gratefulness;* January 1, 2009, review of *The Man behind the Peace Prize: Alfred Nobel.*

Plain Dealer (Cleveland, OH), November 9, 2003, Cheryl Stritzel McCarthy, "Pictures and Text Give Life to History," review of *The Edmund Fitzgerald.*

Publishers Weekly, November 17, 2003, review of *The Edmund Fitzgerald,* p. 64; November 29, 2004, review of *Win One for the Gipper: America's Football Hero,* p. 40.

Reading Teacher, November, 2005, Jesus Cortez, review of *Win One for the Gipper,* p. 276.

Reviewer's Bookwatch, December, 2004, Kimberly Hutmacher, review of *Win One for the Gipper.*

School Library Journal, February, 2004, Debbie Stewart, review of *The Edmund Fitzgerald,* p. 140; January, 2005, Blair Christolon, review of *Win One for the Gipper,* p. 116; February, 2005, Jane Marino, review of *M Is for Melody: A Wisconsin Alphabet,* p. 130; March, 2005, Sean George, review of *The Legend of the Petosky Stone,* p. 189; May, 2006, Catherine Callegari, review of *A Mother's Wish,* p. 106; October 1, 2008, Lisa Egly Lehmuller, review of *Mary's First Thanksgiving,* p. 128; January 1, 2009, Lee Bock, review of *P Is for Pumpkin,* p. 87.

Small Press Bookwatch, December, 2005, review of *Once upon a Christmas Eve;* November, 2006, review of *Minn from Minnesota.*

Star Tribune (Minneapolis, MN), August 2, 1998, Amy Woods, "*Sleeping Bear* Awakens Praise in Michigan Story Tells Indian Legend of Manitou Islands' Origin," p. F19.

Tribune Books (Chicago, IL), January 7, 2001, Mary Harris Russell, review of *L Is for Lincoln: An Illinois Alphabet,* p. 5.

ONLINE

Mitten Press Web site, http://www.mittenpress.com/ (June 19, 2009), "Kathy-jo Wargin."

Sleeping Bear Press Web site, http://www.sleepingbear press.com/ (June 19, 2009), "Kathy-jo Wargin."

Zondervan Web site, http://www.zondervan.com/ (June 19, 2009), "Kathy-jo Wargin."*

*   *   *

WILKINSON, Carole 1950-

Personal

Born 1950, in Derby, England; immigrated to Australia; married; children: one daughter.

Addresses

Home—Clifton Hill, Victoria, Australia. *E-mail*—mail@ carolewilkinson.com.au.

Career

Writer. Former laboratory assistant.

Awards, Honors

Children's Book Council of Australia (CBCA) Notable Book designation, 2002, for *Ramose and the Tomb Robbers,* 2003, for *Black Snake,* 2008, for *The Dragon*

Carole Wilkinson (Reproduced by permission.)

Companion; Aurealis Award, 2003, CBCA Award, and Queensland Premier's Literary Award, both 2004, and Kids Own Australian Literary Award, and Kalbacher Klapperschlange Award (Germany), both 2006, all for *Dragon Keeper;* West Australian Young Book Readers Award, 2006, for *Garden of the Purple Dragon;* Arealis Award nomination, 2007, and CBCA Award nomination, Patricia Wrightson Award nomination, and Australian Book Industry Award, all 2008, all for *Dragon Moon;* CBCA Award nomination, 2008, for *Ned Kelly's Jerilderie Letter.*

Writings

"DRAGON KEEPER" SERIES

Dragon Keeper, Black Dog Books (Fitzroy, Victoria, Australia), 2003, Hyperion Books for Children (New York, NY), 2005.

Garden of the Purple Dragon, Black Dog Books (Fitzroy, Victoria, Australia), 2005, Hyperion Books for Children (New York, NY), 2007.

Dragon Moon, Black Dog Books (Fitzroy, Victoria, Australia), 2007, Hyperion Books for Children (New York, NY), 2008.

Dragon Dawn, Black Dog Books (Fitzroy, Victoria, Australia), 2008.

"RAMOSE" SERIES

Prince in Exile, Black Dog Books (Fitzroy, Victoria, Australia), 2001.

Ramose and the Tomb Robbers, Black Dog Books (Fitzroy, Victoria, Australia), 2001, Southwood (London, England), 2003.

Sting of the Scorpion, Black Dog Books (Fitzroy, Victoria, Australia), 2001, Catnip (London, England), 2006.

The Wrath of Ra, Black Dog Books (Fitzroy, Victoria, Australia), 2002.

Ascent to the Sun, Catnip (London, England), 2007.

Fury of the Gods, Catnip (London, England), 2007.

NOVELS

Watery Grave, Horwitz Martin (St. Leonards, New South Wales, Australia), 1999, Sundance (Littleton, MA), 2000.

Out of Orbit, Horwitz Martin (St. Leonards, New South Wales, Australia), 1999, Sundance (Littleton, MA), 2000.

Bertrand's Quest, Horwitz Martin (St. Leonards, New South Wales, Australia), 2000, Sundance (Littleton, MA), 2001.

A Knight's Journey, Sundance (Littleton, MA), 2001.

OTHER

Stagefright, Pearson (Frenchs Forest, New South Wales, Australia), 1996.

Deepwater, Horwitz Martin (St. Leonards, New South Wales, Australia), 1999, Sundance (Littleton, MA), 2000.

Who Shot the Movies? (nonfiction), Horwitz Martin (St. Leonards, New South Wales, Australia), 2000.

Knights' Progress, Horwitz Martin (St. Leonards, New South Wales, Australia), 2000.

Wheels Around, Horwitz Martin (St. Leonards, New South Wales, Australia), 2001.

Black Snake: The Daring of Ned Kelly, Black Dog Books (Fitzroy, Victoria, Australia), 2002.

Fire in the Belly: The Inside Story of the Modern Olympics (nonfiction), Black Dog Books (Fitzroy, Victoria, Australia), 2004.

Alexander the Great: Reckless Conqueror, Black Dog Books (Fitzroy, Victoria, Australia), 2004.

Ned Kelly's Jerilderie Letter, Black Dog Books (Fitzroy, Victoria, Australia), 2007.

The Dragon Companion: An Encyclopedia, Black Dog Books (Fitzroy, Victoria, Australia), 2007.

Hatshepsut: The Lost Pharaoh of Egypt, Black Dog Books (Fitzroy, Victoria, Australia), 2008.

Sidelights

Carole Wilkinson was born in Derby, England, and moved with her family to Australia when she was twelve years old. She worked for many years as a laboratory assistant. Though she enjoyed the work, Wilkinson recounted on her home page, "I always had this niggling feeling that it wasn't what I was meant to be doing. One day I realised what I've always wanted to be—a writer!" Wilkinson began by writing educational books, but in 2000 she turned to trade fiction. Her "Ramose" series is set in ancient Egypt and features a prince of the royal family, and her "Dragon Keeper" series has brought the author worldwide attention.

Set in ancient China, *Dragon Keeper* is the first novel in Wilkinson's series and follows the adventures of the slave girl Ping. Sold by her parents to the Imperial

Dragon Keeper when she was a young girl, Ping helps to take care of the two remaining dragons owned by the emperor. When one of the dragons dies and the remaining elderly dragon, Long Danzi, is threatened, Ping steals away with him, chased by a necromancer who needs dragon parts for his evil spell. To make matters worse, Ping is accused of being a sorceress. She and Long Danzi also carry with them the mysterious purple dragon stone, which Ping later learns is a dragon egg, on their journey across China to the sea. Sally Estes, writing in *Booklist,* found that "the relationship between the child and the beast stands at the heart of this compelling adventure," and Margaret A. Chang noted in *School Library Journal* that "the dramatic plot and competently crafted writing make this a good choice for voracious readers of fantasy," especially fans of Anne McCaffrey's work.

Ping's story continues in *Garden of the Purple Dragon,* which finds her hiding on a remote sacred mountain with a baby dragon named Kai. When the necromancer discovers her whereabouts, she and the dragon must leave the mountain. She is soon captured by the emperor's guards. Arriving at the palace, Ping at first believes that the emperor will protect her, but he wants an immortality serum that can only be concocted with dragon's blood and scales. Estes found *Garden of the Purple Dragon* to be "as exciting as its predecessor." "Ping is an appealingly feisty heroine," Quinby Frank wrote in the *School Library Journal,* "and the author paints a vivid picture of life in the Imperial Ming Yang Lodge." Amanda Craig, writing in the London *Times,* stated that "Ping's self-doubt, her courage, honesty, humility and absolute devotion to her charge make her a delight as she proves herself the true dragonkeeper once again."

Wilkinson continues her series in *Dragon Moon.* Ping has now matured into a reliable dragon keeper for Kai as they near the end of their quest to find a safe haven for Kai to live away from humans and find any remaining dragons. Cindy Dobrez, reviewing this novel in *Booklist,* commented that the "humor" as well as the "human-dragon friendship will appeal to young fantasy readers." June H. Keuhn, writing in *School Library Journal,* noted that *Dragon Moon* "offers an unusual combination of fantasy and ancient Chinese culture," while a *Kirkus Reviews* contributor predicted that "dracophiles will enjoy watching the puppylike Kai at least begin . . . to come into his own."

Dragon Dawn functions as a prequel to *Dragon Keeper* and opens with the tale of the thousand-year-young dragon Danzi. Mourning the loss of his dragon keeper, Chem-mo, Danzi migrates to stay ahead of soldiers encroaching on his lands. Along the way he meets the trickster Bingwen, who can read his thoughts. Danzi does not trust Bingwen, but he finds out too late that the fate of the two are intertwined. Sally Murphy, writing in *Aussie Reviews* online, called *Dragon Dawn* "delightful," adding that "this is a wonderful fantasy story, allowing fans to enjoy more of Danzi's adventures and his life."

Asked by Craig who the character of Ping is based on, Wilkinson admitted that her "Dragon Keeper" books have an autobiographical element. "There's a lot of me in Ping," she explained. "When I was at school, I was a very average kid. I wanted Ping to inspire young people who are like me, who aren't the kids at the top of the class or terrific at sports or gifted musicians. They may not believe they have any skills that are out of the ordinary, but I hope they will be encouraged to search inside themselves, find their talents and work hard to refine them."

Biographical and Critical Sources

PERIODICALS

Booklist, April 15, 2005, Sally Estes, review of *Dragon Keeper,* p. 1471; May 15, 2006, November 1, 2007, Sally Estes, review of *Garden of the Purple Dragon,* p. 48; May 15, 2008, Cindy Dobrez, review of *Dragon Moon,* p. 56.
Buffalo News (Buffalo, NY), June 15, 2005, Jean West-moore, review of *Dragon Keeper,* p. N12.
Kirkus Reviews, April 1, 2005, review of *Dragon Keeper,* p. 428; June 1, 2007, review of *Garden of the Purple Dragon;* April 15, 2008, review of *Dragon Moon.*
School Library Journal, May, 2005, Margaret A. Chang, review of *Dragon Keeper,* p. 142; September, 2007, Quinby Frank, review of *Garden of the Purple Dragon,* p. 210; June 1, 2008, June H. Keuhn, review of *Dragon Moon,* p. 152.
Times (London, England), March 18, 2006, Amanda Craig, review of *Dragon Keeper,* p. 17; November 25, 2006, Amanda Craig, review of *Dragon Keeper,* p. 8; February 24, 2007, Amanda Craig, review of *Garden of the Purple Dragon,* p. 15; February 2, 2008, Amanda Craig, interview with Wilkinson, p. 10.

ONLINE

Aussie Reviews Web site, http://www.aussiereviews.com.au/ (May 29, 2009), Sally Murphy, review of *Dragon Dawn.*
Black Dog Books Web site, http://www.bdb.com.au/ (April 22, 2008), "Carole Wilkinson."
Carole Wilkinson Home Page, http://www.carolewilkinson.com.au (December 15, 2009).
Victoria Department of Education and Early Childhood Education Web site, http://www.education.vic.gov.au/ (May 29, 2009), interview with Wilkinson.*

*   *   *

WISEMAN, Eva 1947-

Personal

Born 1947, in Hungary; immigrated to Canada; married; children: two.

Addresses

Home—Winnipeg, Manitoba, Canada. *E-mail*—evak wiseman@gmail.com.

Career

Writer. Former journalist with *Winnipeg Free Press* and *Winnipeg Tribune,* both Winnipeg, Manitoba, Canada; teacher of adult English as a second language.

Member

Canadian Society of Children's Authors, Illustrators, and Performers, Manitoba Writers Guild, Winnipeg Children's Literature Round Table.

Awards, Honors

Blue Heron Book Award finalist, Manitoba Young Readers Choice Award finalist, McNally Robinson Book for Young People Award finalist, Our Choice designation, Canadian Children's Book Centre (CCBC), Sydney Taylor Book Award nomination, Association of Jewish Libraries, Geoffrey Bilson Award for Historical Fiction honour book designation, and Ruth Schwartz Award finalist, all 1997, and New York Public Library Best Books for the Teen Age listee, 1998, all for *A Place Not Home;* Rocky Mountain Book Award finalist, CCBC Our Choice designation, and McNally Robinson Book for Young People Award, all 2002, and New York Public Library Best Books for the Teen Age listee, 2003, all for *My Canary Yellow Star;* CCBC Our Choice designation McNally Robinson Book for Young People Award, and Manitoba Young Readers Choice selection, all 2005, all for *No One Must Know;* Governor General's Literary Award nomination, 2007, and McNally Robinson Book for Young People Award finalist, and Geoffrey Bilson Award for Historical Fiction for Young People, all for *Kanada.*

Writings

A Place Not Home, Stoddart Kids (Buffalo, NY), 1996.

My Canary Yellow Star, Tundra Books (Plattsburgh, NY), 2002.

No One Must Know, Tundra Books (Plattsburgh, NY), 2004.

Kanada, Tundra Books (Plattsburgh, NY), 2006.

Puppet, Tundra Books (Plattsburgh, NY), 2009.

Author's books have been translated into French, Dutch, and Italian.

Sidelights

Eva Wiseman was born in Hungary and moved with her family to Canada when she was a child. Her parents were survivors of the Auschwitz concentration camp where many Jewish people were executed by the Nazis during World War II, and this family legacy has shaped much of Wiseman's fiction. As a girl, Wiseman showed an interest in writing and she began working for the *Winnipeg Free Press* while she was still a teenager. After a career as a journalist and teacher, she started writing novels for young people.

Wiseman's first novel, *A Place Not Home,* takes place in Budapest, Hungary, in 1956. Hungary's communist dictatorship is anti-Semitic, and the country's secret police make life difficult for thirteen-year-old Nelly Adler and her family. When a revolution against the government breaks out, the Adler family takes advantage of the momentary freedom to escape Hungary and cross the border into neighboring Austria. They become refugees, living for a time in a makeshift camp set up for those who have fled the communists. Eventually they travel to a new life in Canada, where Nelly begins school in Montreal and faces fresh problems as an outsider. "Nelly is a resourceful, brave and spunky heroine to whom young people can relate," Helen Norrie wrote in a review of *A Place Not Home* for the *Canadian Review of Materials.* According to a *Resource Links* critic, Wiseman has produced "a very successful first novel which deserves wide readership," and Maureen Griffin described the work in *Kliatt* as a "sensitive, timely and enouraging story."

My Canary Yellow Star, Wiseman's second novel, is also set in Hungary, this time during World War II. After the city is invaded by the Nazis, fourteen-year-old Marta Weisz, the daughter of a Jewish doctor, watches as her life changes dramatically. The Jewish residents of Budapest are set apart and must wear a yellow star on their clothing to identify themselves. Former friends now shun them, and soldiers shoot anyone seen out of doors after curfew. When Marta hears that Swedish passports may be available for those wishing to flee Budapest, she is determined to get some for her family. Because it is based in part on the story of real-life Swedish diplomat Raoul Wallenberg, who saved some 100,000 Hungarian Jews by issuing them passports, *My Canary Yellow Star* "would be best used as part of a history curriculum," according to Rebecca Rabinowitz in *Kliatt.* Jean Franklin wrote in *Booklist* that Wiseman "capably conveys the gradually building terror Jews in Budapest endured and the way some fought back."

In *No One Must Know* Wiseman focuses her attention on her adopted home of Canada, depicting the anti-Semitism that lurked just beneath the surface in some areas of the country. The novel tells of Alexandra, a Jewish girl whose family has moved to Canada to escape the horrors of World-War-II Europe. Her parents hide the family's Jewish heritage from their new neighbors, fearful that they may be discriminated against. Instead, they raise Alexandra as a Roman Catholic and keep secret the family's true background. Alexandra only gradually comes to realize the truth, and she finds that some friends see her differently when they learn that she is Jewish. "Young readers will have an easy time of imagining themselves in Alex's position and will become engrossed in her struggle to recover her identity," wrote Pam Klassen-Dueck in the *Canadian Review of Materials.* Paula J. LaRue, reviewing the novel for *School Library Journal,* called *No One Must Know* a "gentle and moving introduction to the enduring legacy of the Holocaust."

Wiseman's novel *Kanada* concerns Jutka Weltner, a fourteen year old living in Hungary who dreams of what life might be like in the far-off country of Canada. She has been sent a picture book depicting Canadian sights by a relative living there, and she hopes that someday she can move to that nation. World War II intervenes, however, and Jutka is sent to Auschwitz and put to work in the warehouses, which are, ironically, called Kanada. "The setting of the last third of *Kanada* are displaced persons camps, and this distinguishes the book from other Holocaust books written for young people," Wiseman noted on her home page. "Very few Holocaust books written for young people show what happened to the survivors after liberation." Victoria Pennell, writing in *Resource Links,* praised Wiseman's "captivating" prose and called *Kanada* "an excellent

read." Reviewing the work in *Booklist,* Heather Booth called Jutka "a resilient, realistically drawn heroine," and Klassen-Dueck deemed Wiseman's novel "a notable contribution to the genre of Holocaust literature for teens because of its interesting perspective of a Jewish-Hungarian teenager longing for Canada, despite the country's disinterest in her."

Wiseman's novel *Puppet* is based on the court proceedings of a trial set in nineteenth-century Hungary. When Julie's friend Esther goes missing, the townspeople behave hysterically, claiming that the local Jewish community is responsible. Julie's rational thinking on what might have happened to her friend is sidelined as a scapegoat is put on trial after being forced to testify. Reviewing *Puppet* in *Booklist,* Hazel Rochman called the story's denouement "electrifying with its public drama on the witness stand" and recommended Wiseman's novel for readers of all ages. *Puppet* provides "a valuable look at an historical phenomenon that contemporary readers would find difficult to comprehend," observed a *Publishers Weekly* contributor, and Rita Soltan remarked in *School Library Journal* that Wiseman's story "is a plausible retelling of a little-known episode in the long history of anti-Semitism."

Biographical and Critical Sources

PERIODICALS

Booklist, January 1, 2002, Jean Franklin, review of *My Canary Yellow Star,* p. 845; January 1, 2005, Kay Weisman, review of *No One Must Know,* p. 864; February 15, 2007, Heather Booth, review of *Kanada,* p. 90; February 15, 2009, Hazel Rochman, review of *Puppet,* p. 81.

Canadian Review of Materials, October 4, 1996, Helen Norrie, review of *A Place Not Home;* November 12, 2004, Pam Klassen-Dueck, review of *No One Must Know;* December 22, 2006, Pam Klassen-Dueck, review of *Kanada.*

Kliatt, March, 2002, Rebecca Rabinowitz, review of *My Canary Yellow Star,* p. 19; July, 2004, Maureen Griffin, review of *A Place Not Home,* p. 25.

Publishers Weekly, December 22, 2008, review of *Puppet,* p. 52.

Quill & Quire, May, 1996, Bridget Donald, review of *A Place Not Home;* January, 2002, Barbara Greenwood, review of *My Canary Yellow Star;* April, 2009, James Grainger, review of *Puppet.*

Resource Links, April, 1997, review of *A Place Not Home,* p. 176; February, 2002, Jill McClay, review of *My Canary Yellow Star,* p. 37; February, 2005, Teresa Hughes, review of *No One Must Know,* p. 42; February, 2007, Victoria Pennell, review of *Kanada,* p. 45.

School Library Journal, June, 2002, Martha Link, review of *My Canary Yellow Star,* p. 149; June, 2005, Paula J. LaRue, review of *No One Must Know,* p. 172; March 1, 2009, Rita Soltan, review of *Puppet,* p. 159.

Cover of Eva Wiseman's novel Puppet, *which focuses on a young woman dealing with anti-Semitism in nineteenth-century Hungary.* (Tundra Books, Inc. 2009. Copyright © 2009 by Eva Wiseman. Reproduced by permission.)

ONLINE

Canadian Broadcasting Corporation Web site, http://www.cbc.ca/ (October 16, 2007), "CanLit Heavyweights among Governor General Finalists."

Canadian Society of Children's Authors, Illustrators, and Performers Web site, http://www.canscaip.org/ (April 29, 2008) "Eva Wiseman."

Open Book Toronto, http://www.openbooktoronto.com/ (March 4, 2009), interview with Wiseman.

Tundra Books Web site, http://www.tundrabooks.com/ (April 29, 2008), "Eva Wiseman."*

* * *

WONG, Janet S. 1962-

Personal

Born September 30, 1962, in Los Angeles, CA; daughter of Roger and Joyce Wong; married Glenn Schroeder (an attorney); children: Andrew. *Education:* University of California—Los Angeles, B.A. (summa cum laude), 1983; Yale University, J.D., 1987; attended Université de Bordeaux.

Addresses

Home—Princeton, NJ. *E-mail*—janet@janetwong.com.

Career

Poet and children's book author. Attorney for GTE and Universal Studios Hollywood, Los Angeles, CA, 1987-91; writer, 1991—, public speaker and performer, 1994—. Writer-in-residence, University of Southern California Writing Project, 1995; visiting author, Singapore Society for Reading and Literacy, 1997. Founder of Immigrant Children's Art Project, University of California—Los Angeles; arbitrator/mediator for Arts Arbitration and Mediation Services, 1989-95.

Member

Society of Children's Book Writers and Illustrators, National Council of Teachers of English (member of commission on literature).

Awards, Honors

Books for the Teen Age citation, New York Public Library, and Notable Children's Trade Book in the Field of Social Studies citation, National Council for the Social Studies/Children's Book Council, 1996, and Stone Center Recognition of Merit, Claremont Graduate School, 1999, all for *A Suitcase of Seaweed and Other Poems;* Lee Bennett Hopkins Poetry Award Honor, for *The Rainbow Hand;* Oppenheim Toy Portfolio Gold Award, for *This Next New Year;* Asian Pacific American Award for Literature, for *The Trip Back Home;* International Reading Association Celebrate Literacy Award,

Janet S. Wong (Photograph by Anne Lindsay. Reproduced by permission.)

Foothill Reading Council, 1998; Stone Center Recognition of Merit, Claremont Graduate School, 1999, for *Good Luck Gold and Other Poems;* Charlotte Zolotow Award Highly Commended Book, 2002, for *Grump,* and 2003, for *Apple Pie Fourth of July.*

Writings

Good Luck Gold and Other Poems, Margaret K. McElderry Books (New York, NY), 1994.

(And illustrator) *A Suitcase of Seaweed and Other Poems,* Margaret K. McElderry Books (New York, NY), 1996.

The Rainbow Hand: Poems about Mothers and Children, illustrated by Jennifer Hewitson, Margaret K. McElderry Books (New York, NY), 1999.

Behind the Wheel: Poems about Driving, Margaret K. McElderry Books (New York, NY), 1999.

Night Garden: Poems from the World of Dreams, illustrated by Julie Paschkis, Margaret K. McElderry Books (New York, NY), 2000.

Buzz, illustrated by Margaret Chodos-Irvine, Harcourt Brace (Orlando, FL), 2000.

The Trip Back Home, illustrated by Bo Jia, Harcourt Brace (Orlando, FL), 2000.

This Next New Year, illustrated by Yangsook Choi, Farrar, Straus & Giroux (New York, NY), 2000.

Grump, illustrated by John Wallace, Margaret K. McElderry Books (New York, NY), 2001.

Apple Pie Fourth of July, illustrated by Margaret Chodos-Irvine, Harcourt Brace (Orlando, FL), 2002.

You Have to Write, illustrated by Teresa Flavin, Margaret K. McElderry Books (New York, NY), 2002.

Minn and Jake, illustrated by Geneviève Côté, Farrar, Straus & Giroux (New York, NY), 2003.

Knock on Wood: Poems about Superstitions, illustrated by Julie Paschkis, Margaret K. McElderry Books (New York, NY), 2003.

Alex and the Wednesday Chess Club, illustrated by Stacey Schuett, Simon & Schuster (New York, NY), 2004.

Hide and Seek, illustrated by Margaret Chodos-Irvine, Harcourt (Orlando, FL), 2005.

Before It Wriggles Away, photographs by Anne Lindsay, Richard C. Owen Publishers (Katonah, NY), 2006.

The Dumpster Diver, illustrated by David Roberts, Candlewick Press (Cambridge, MA), 2007.

Twist: Yoga Poems, illustrated by Julie Paschkis, Margaret K. McElderry Books (New York, NY), 2007.

Minn and Jake's Almost Terrible Summer (sequel to *Minn and Jake*), illustrated by Geneviève Côté, Farrar, Straus & Giroux (New York, NY), 2008.

Homegrown House, illustrated by E.B. Lewis, Margaret K. Elderberry Books (New York, NY), 2009.

Contributor to anthologies, including *Marvelous Math: A Book of Poems,* selected by Lee Bennett Hopkins, Simon & Schuster (New York, NY), 1997, and *I Am Writing a Poem About,* edited by Myra Cohn Livingston, Margaret K. McElderry Books (New York, NY), 1997. Contributor to periodicals, including *Instructor, Horn Book,* and *California English.*

Sidelights

Janet S. Wong is an Asian-American poet whose works employ a variety of voices and styles to explore her own heritage. Born in the United States, Wong is the daughter of a Korean-born mother and a Chinese-born father, and all three cultures have found a place in her books. In a review of her debut title, *Good Luck Gold and Other Poems, Voice of Youth Advocates* critic Anthony Manna stated that Wong has "distinctive gifts as a consciously cultural poet." Wong has also published a number of well-received picture books for children, including *Alex and the Wednesday Chess Club* and *The Dumpster Diver.*

A native of California, Wong spent several years working as a corporate attorney before she began writing. "There are many lawyers who are doing good work," she stated on the Scholastic Web site, "but I felt I was becoming a mean person. I didn't enjoy my work, and I wanted to do something more important with my life. I couldn't think of anything more important than working with kids." After deciding against a teaching career, Wong began writing for children, taking courses at the University of California—Los Angeles. With the help of Myra Cohn Livingston, a distinguished children's poet, she published *Good Luck Gold and Other Poems* in 1994.

Good Luck Gold and Other Poems is a collection of forty-two poems told from the point of view of Asian-American children, offering insight into their lives. Writ-

ten in rhyme, free verse, haiku, and other styles, the pieces explore everyday subjects such as food and shopping, as well as deeper topics, including racism, illness, and divorce. Several reviewers expressed the overall impression that *Good Luck Gold and Other Poems* is a powerful, positive contribution to Asian-American poetry for young people. Manna commented that the best pieces in this work are "characterized by technical competence and genuine emotional force." Writing in *Bulletin of the Center for Children's Books,* Deborah Stevenson noted that the book will be enjoyable to children from a variety of ethnic backgrounds.

Wong continues to explore her own mixed ethnic background in *A Suitcase of Seaweed and Other Poems,* published in 1996. The book is divided into three sections of poems—Korean, Chinese, and American—representing the poet's patchwork identity. As *Horn Book* contributor Nancy Vasilakis wrote, "the quiet, lyric poems acknowledge proudly, subtly, and with occasional touches of irony and humor the distinct strands within

Wong's middle-grade novel Minn and Jake *features animated pen-and-ink art by Geneviéve Côté.* (Illustration copyright © 2003 by Geneviéve Côté. Reprinted by permission of Farrar, Straus & Giroux, LLC.)

the weave of cultures of which she is a part." Each section is introduced with a short personal memoir, and Hazel Rochman commented in *Booklist* that these are "as interesting as the poems." As in *Good Luck Gold and Other Poems,* the pieces are often written from a child's point of view and explore topics such as family relations—particularly those between parent and child—and the poet's deeper Asian roots. Reviewers commented that many of Wong's subjects are universal and will be appreciated by children from all backgrounds.

Wong followed her early works with several volumes of poetry that explore specific themes, including *The Rainbow Hand: Poems about Mothers and Children, Behind the Wheel: Poems about Driving,* and *Night Garden: Poems from the World of Dreams.* Motherhood and the relationships between mothers and their children is the focus of *The Rainbow Hand.* There are eighteen poems in the collection, and "all of them hold a kernel of truth that readers of all ages will recognize," as GraceAnne A. DeCandido wrote in *Booklist. Behind the Wheel* examines issues of self and family through the lens of cars and driving. The poems deal with a range of driving-related issues, from learning to drive to car crashes to hitchhikers. Roger Sutton, writing in *Horn Book,* observed that "the timeworn idea that 'driving is like life' is simply a given here, and Wong relies on telling particulars rather than heavy universals." Although the book is aimed primarily toward young adults, in *Booklist* Gillian Engberg concluded that "readers of all ages will be moved by the intersection of poignancy and humor" in *Behind the Wheel.* In *Night Garden,* Wong explores different types of dreams, both good and bad, and the feelings that they evoke. A reviewer for *Publishers Weekly* wrote that "Wong's quiet yet haunting words skillfully simulate the reveries they recount," and Barbara Chatton predicted in *School Library Journal* that these poems will inspire children to "enjoy capturing their own dreams and giving them shape and meaning."

In *Knock on Wood: Poems about Superstitions* Wong examines the lore surrounding four-leaf clovers, black cats, and the number thirteen, among other rituals and beliefs. Engberg called the topic "compelling" and noted that "many of the poems have a sly humor and haunting, lyrical imagery." Other critics praised the combination of Wong's verse and Julie Paschkis's illustrations. "There is much to ponder in both words and pictures," remarked *School Library Journal* contributor Margaret Bush, who added that "the mixed poetic/visual brew is sophisticated." According to Susan Dove Lempke, writing in *Horn Book,* the duo "show[s] how a poet and painter in harmony can each enhance the other's work in this engaging and visually striking book." *Twist: Yoga Poems* contains sixteen original works that describe a variety of yoga poses, including the "lion," "mountain," and "warrior." "Wong's verses effectively evoke their subjects in different ways," observed *Horn Book* reviewer Bridget T. McCaffrey, and Susan Oliver similarly noted in *School Library Journal* that the po-

Wong tells the story of an enterprising and imaginative young man in **The Dumpster Diver,** *a picture book featuring art by David Roberts.* (Illustration copyright © 2007 by David Roberts. Reproduced by permission of Candlewick Press, Inc., Somerville, MA.)

ems "read almost like haiku, using imagery to get to the essence of the positions, rather than teaching how to perform them."

Picture books for young readers have proved to be another natural outlet for Wong's poetry. Two of these, *Buzz* and *Grump,* focus on babies and their reactions to the world around them. In *Buzz* a young child listens to the busy morning of the household around him. Everything, including a bumblebee outside, Daddy's electric razor, Mommy's hair dryer, and the coffee grinder, seems to coalesce in one great big buzz. Writing for *Booklist,* Kathy Broderick called *Buzz* "a great sensory experience for very young children." A tired, grumpy new mother in desperate need of a nap is the subject of *Grump.* While Mommy is at the end of her rope, Baby is wide awake and not quite ready for nap-time. A *Publishers Weekly* review noted that young children might not understand the ironic theme of the book, but that it "should strike a chord with frazzled mothers of toddlers." In a review for *School Library Journal,* Joy Fleishhacker praised the "poetic yet accessible text" in *Grump* and called Wong's language "inviting and fun to read aloud."

Three of Wong's picture books involve children exploring and reacting to their families' ethnic backgrounds. *The Trip Back Home,* inspired by Wong's own childhood experiences visiting family in Korea, tells of a young American girl who is taken to visit her grandparents and aunt in a rural Korean village. The girl joins into the family's daily routine, and her sensory experiences in this new place are described. *School Library Journal* critic Wendy Lukehart called it "a gentle celebration of family bonds," and praised the interplay between Wong's text and Bo Jia's watercolor illustrations. In *This Next New Year,* a Chinese-Korean boy tells how he and his friends from various backgrounds celebrate the lunar New Year. Engberg, writing in *Booklist,* found "optimistic activity and . . . yearning in the accessible, rhythmic text." Patriotism and what it means to be an American are the subjects of *Apple Pie Fourth of July.* A Chinese-American girl helps her parents prepare and sell Chinese food at their store on the Fourth of July, all the while warning the adults that no one will purchase Asian food on such an American holiday. The girl feels resentful of her separation from the community around her, but by evening she is surprised and proud to discover people lining up to eat Chinese food. The Fourth of July ends with the family eating apple pie with neighbors while watching fireworks. In *Booklist,* Engberg called *Apple Pie Fourth of July* "an appealing story with believable characters and emotions" that explore issues of identity and belonging.

A youngster rediscovers his love for the game he once abandoned in *Alex and the Wednesday Chess Club,* a chapter book. A talented chess player by the age of four, Alex decides to pursue other hobbies after losing an important match to a much older opponent. Years later, however, he cannot resist the lure of his school's chess team. "Wong's rhythmic, colloquial free verse combines the thrill of finding a talent with a child's anxieties," Engberg stated. In the counting book *Hide and Seek,* a father finds time to play with his son while they bake cookies. "Youngsters will love seeing how the hero's deductive reasoning garners him both a cool hiding place and a tasty reward," a *Publishers Weekly* contributor remarked. A free-spirited electrician enlists the help of his three young neighbors to locate discarded treasures in *The Dumpster Diver.* When Steve is injured during his collection efforts, the children band together to construct a wheelchair from found objects. *Horn Book* reviewer Barbara Bader complimented Wong's "deft, economical script," and Gloria Koster, writing in *School Library Journal,* reported that "this urban trash-to-treasure tale will resonate with city dwellers and send suburbanites and kids in rural areas searching for similar adventures."

In *Minn and Jake* ten-year-old Jake moves from Los Angeles to a new town and school and finds a new friend in Minn. The ten-year-old friends return in *Minn and Jake's Almost Terrible Summer* and this time they must spend the summer apart. Although Jake is visiting his old neighborhood, he soon misses Minn but is overjoyed when Minn and her family make a surprise visit to Los Angeles. A trip to Disneyland results in an argument between the friends, but ultimately the friendship survives. In reviewing *Minn and Jake's Almost Terrible*

Summer, Booklist reviewer Thom Barthelmes commented on the black-and-white illustrations by Geneviève Côté, and described the story as valuable for helping readers "learn about one another and discover ourselves in the process." Bethany A. Lafferty, writing in *School Library Journal,* also commented that Côté's ink sketches effectively bring to life Wong's "smart, endearing characters and humorous antics."

Wong once commented: "Since the time I was supposed to have learned all about fractions and decimals, I have known I would not be a mathematician. I knew, too, I never would be a neurosurgeon, which my father once wanted me to be. But I never thought I would be a poet, either. As far as I can remember—and at least since fourth grade—I remember hating poetry. I can't say, honestly, that I read much of it, but I did not like what I read—especially when I had to read it aloud! So why do I write poetry now?

"One Saturday in September 1991 I attended a workshop on writing for children. Myra Cohn Livingston, one of the speakers . . . recited the title poem from her book *There Was a Place and Other Poems.* . . . The next thing I knew, I was blinking back tears. What a powerful piece of writing!

"I like poems that are not afraid to talk about painful things. I like poems that make you laugh, or cry; poems that grab you and make you read them again; poems that make you think.

"Poetry is, in a way, like shouting. Since you can't yell at the top of your lungs for a very long time, you have to decide what you really need to say, and say it quickly. In a way, too, I suppose, poetry is like math. An idea for a poem is a problem that needs to be solved—and for me, the fun is in finding an answer."

Biographical and Critical Sources

PERIODICALS

Book, July-August, 2003, Kathleen Odean, "Unanimous Verdict: For These Lawyers, the Decision's In: Kids Are a More Rewarding Audience than Jurors," p. 31.
Booklist, November 15, 1994, review of *Good Luck Gold and Other Poems,* p. 600; April 1, 1996, Hazel Rochman, review of *A Suitcase of Seaweed and Other Poems,* p. 1362; April 1, 1999, GraceAnne A. DeCandido, review of *The Rainbow Hand: Poems about Mothers and Children,* p. 1412; January 1, 2000, Gillian Engberg, review of *Behind the Wheel: Poems about Driving,* p. 913; July, 2000, Kathy Broderick, review of *Buzz,* p. 2044; September 15, 2000, Gillian Engberg, review of *This Next New Year,* p. 251; July, 2002, Julie Cummins, review of *You Have to Write,* p. 1841; August, 2002, Gillian Engberg, review of *Apple*

Pie Fourth of July, p. 1963; November 15, 2003, Gillian Engberg, review of *Knock on Wood: Poems about Superstitions,* p. 596; October 1, 2004, Gillian Engberg, review of *Alex and the Wednesday Chess Club,* p. 339; May 1, 2005, Gillian Engberg, review of *Hide and Seek,* p. 1594; January 1, 2007, Gillian Engberg, review of *Twist: Yoga Poems,* p. 96; February 15, 2007, Jennifer Mattson, review of *The Dumpster Diver,* p. 76; June 1, 2007, Hazel Rochman, review of *Before It Wriggles Away,* p. 92; November 15, 2008, Thom Barthelmes, review of *Minn and Jake's Almost Terrible Summer,* p. 40.

Bulletin of the Center for Children's Books, January, 1995, Deborah Stevenson, review of *Good Luck Gold and Other Poems,* p. 181; April, 1996, review of *A Suitcase of Seaweed and Other Poems,* p. 282.

Horn Book, July-August, 1996, Nancy Vasilakis, review of *A Suitcase of Seaweed and Other Poems,* p. 475; November, 1999, Roger Sutton, review of *Behind the Wheel,* p. 755; September-October, 2003, Susan Dove Lempke, review of *Knock on Wood,* p. 624; May-June, 2005, Jennifer M. Brabander, review of *Hide and Seek,* p. 318; March-April, 2007, Bridget T. McCaffrey, review of *Twist,* p. 210; May-June, 2007, Barbara Bader, review of *The Dumpster Diver,* p. 276.

Kirkus Reviews, June 1, 2002, review of *You Have to Write,* p. 813; July 15, 2003, review of *Minn and Jake,* p. 969; August 1, 2004, review of *Alex and the Wednesday Chess Club,* p. 751; April 1, 2005, review of *Hide and Seek,* p. 429; January 15, 2007, review of *The Dumpster Diver,* p. 83, and *Twist,* p. 83; July 1, 2008, review of *Minn and Jake's Almost Terrible Summer.*

New York Times Book Review, November 19, 2000, Rebecca Pepper Sinkler, "Wild Pig-Rats and Carrot-Headed Dogs," review of *Night Garden: Poems from the World of Dreams,* p. 46; June 16, 2002, review of *Apple Pie Fourth of July,* p. 20.

Publishers Weekly, March 13, 2000, review of *Night Garden,* p. 84; January 1, 2001, review of *Grump,* p. 91; March 28, 2005, review of *Hide and Seek,* p. 78.

School Library Journal, January, 1995, Barbara Chatton, review of *Good Luck Gold and Other Poems,* p. 133; March, 2000, Barbara Chatton, review of *Night Garden,* p. 232; December, 2000, Wendy Lukehart, review of *The Trip Back Home,* p. 128; March, 2001, Joy Fleishhacker, review of *Grump,* p. 224; December, 2003, Margaret Bush, review of *Knock on Wood,* p. 140; July, 2002, Adele Greenlee, review of *You Have to Write,* p. 112; October, 2004, Linda L. Walkins, review of *Alex and the Wednesday Chess Club,* p. 136; April, 2005, Angela J. Reynolds, review of *Hide and Seek,* p. 116; February, 2007, Susan Oliver, review of *Twist,* p. 114; March, 2007, Gloria Koster, review of *The Dumpster Diver,* p. 191; August, 2008, Bethany A. Lafferty, review of *Minn and Jake's Almost Terrible Summer,* p. 106.

Voice of Youth Advocates, October, 1995, Anthony Manna, "Should We Read (More) Poetry (More Often)?," pp. 201-203; October, 1996, Anthony Manna, review of *A Suitcase of Seaweed and Other Poems,* pp. 241-242.

ONLINE

Blue Rose Girls Web site, http://bluerosegirls.blogspot.com/ (March 2, 2007), Elaine Magliaro, interview with Wong and Julie Paschkis.

Cynsations, http://cynthialeitichsmith.blogspot.com/ (March 12, 2007), Cynthia Leitich Smith, interview with Wong.

Harcourt Books Web site, http://www.harcourtbooks.com/ (January 10, 2010), interview with Wong.

Janet S. Wong Home Page, http://www.janetwong.com (January 10, 2010).

Scholastic Web site, http://www.scholastic.com/kids/ (May 27, 2009), "Janet S. Wong."*

* * *

WYNNE, Patricia J.

Personal

Female. *Education:* Illinois Wesleyan University, B.F.A., 1967; University of Iowa, M.A., 2003; postgraduate study at Wayne State University, 1970-73, and Columbia University, 1979-82, 2001-03.

Addresses

Home—New York, NY. *E-mail*—wynneart@aol.com; wynne@amnh.org.

Career

Illustrator. Macomb County Community College, Warren, MI, instructor in art history and design, 1970-71; Wayne State University, Detroit, MI, instructor in drawing, 1971-72; University of Windsor, Windsor, Ontario, Canada, instructor in prints and drawings, 1971-73; University of Michigan, Ann Arbor, senior scientific illustrator, 1973-74; American Museum of Natural History, New York, NY, contract artist, 1975—*New York Times,* New York, NY, illustrator, 1990-2000. *Exhibitions:* Paintings have been exhibited in collections at Chicago Art Institute, Carnegie-Mellon Institute, Field Museum of Natural History, American Museum of Natural History, St. Louis Botanical Garden, National Zoo, University of Wisconsin, Columbia University, Bronx Zoo, Detroit Zoo, and New York Aquarium, among others.

Writings

(Self-illustrated) *The Animal ABC,* Random House (New York, NY), 1977.

ILLUSTRATOR

The Wookiee Storybook, Random House (New York, NY), 1979.

The Empire Strikes Back, Random House (New York, NY), 1980.

Rith Dowling Bruun and Bertel Bruun, *The Human Body,* Random House (New York, NY), 1982.

George S. Fichter, *Rocks & Minerals,* Random House (New York, NY), 1982.

Donald M. Silver, *Life on Earth: Biology Today,* Random House (New York, NY), 1983.

Joanna Cole, *Hungry, Hungry Sharks,* Random House (New York, NY), 1986.

Donald M. Silver, *The Animal World,* Random House (New York, NY), 1987.

Donald M. Silver, *Indians,* Checkerboard Press (New York, NY), 1989.

Donald M. Silver, *Earth: The Ever-Changing Planet,* Random House (New York, NY), 1989.

Donald M. Silver and David Silver, *Sharks,* Checkerboard Press (New York, NY), 1989.

Donald M. Silver, *Dinosaurs,* Checkerboard Press (New York, NY), 1989.

Donald M. Silver, *The Checkerboard Press Nature Encyclopedia,* Checkerboard Press (New York, NY), 1990.

Andrew Chaikin, *When Dinosaurs Walked,* World Book (Chicago, IL), 1992.

An unusual animal family is the star of Patricia J. Wynne's art for Darrin Lunde's story in **Meet the Meerkat.** (Charlesbridge, 2007. Text copyright © 2007 by Darrin Lunde. Illustrations copyright © Patricia J. Wynne. Used with permission by Charlesbridge Publishing, Inc. All rights reserved.)

Phyllis Shalant, *Look What We've Brought You from Mexico: Crafts, Games, Recipes, Stories, and Other Cultural Activities from Mexican Americans,* Julian Messner (New York, NY), 1992.

Donald M. Silver, *Cave,* Scientific American Books for Young Readers (New York, NY), 1993.

Donald M. Silver, *Backyard,* Scientific American Books for Young Readers (New York, NY), 1993.

Donald M. Silver, *Seashore,* Scientific American Books for Young Readers (New York, NY), 1993.

Donald M. Silver, *Why Save the Rain Forest?,* Julian Messner (New York, NY), 1993.

Donald M. Silver, *Nighttime in My Backyard: A Pop-up Book,* W.H. Freeman (New York, NY), 1994.

Donald M. Silver, *Life on a Limb: A Pop-up Book,* W.H. Freeman (New York, NY), 1994.

Donald M. Silver, *Arctic Tundra,* W.H. Freeman (New York, NY), 1994.

Donald M. Silver, *African Savanna,* W.H. Freeman (New York, NY), 1994.

Donald M. Silver, *Take a Giant Step: A Pop-up Book,* Scientific American Books for Young Readers (New York, NY), 1994.

Donald M. Silver, *Prairie Dog Town: A Pop-up Book,* W.H. Freeman (New York, NY), 1994.

Donald M. Silver, *Pond,* Scientific American Books for Young Readers (New York, NY), 1994.

Donald M. Silver, *Busy Beaver Pond: A Pop-up Book,* Scientific American Books for Young Readers (New York, NY), 1995.

Donald M. Silver, *Cactus Desert,* Scientific American Books for Young Readers (New York, NY), 1995.

Donald M. Silver, *Extinction Is Forever,* Julian Messner (New York, NY), 1995.

Donald M. Silver, *Lion Cubs at Home: A Pop-up Book,* W.H. Freeman (New York, NY), 1995.

Donald M. Silver, *Woods,* Scientific American Books for Young Readers (New York, NY), 1997.

Donald M. Silver, *Swamp,* Learning Triangle Press (New York, NY), 1997.

Donald M. Silver, *Coral Reef,* Learning Triangle Press (New York, NY), 1998.

J. Willis Hurst and Stuart D. Hurst, *The Heart: The Kids' Question and Answer Book,* McGraw-Hill (New York, NY), 1999.

Sharon Katz, *In Search of Gorillas: Adventure in the Rain Forest,* Wildlife Conservation Society (New York, NY), 1999.

Donald M. Silver, *Colonial America,* Scholastic (New York, NY), 2002.

Caroline Arnold, *Birds: Nature's Magnificent Flying Machines,* Charlesbridge (Watertown, MA), 2003.

April Pulley Sayre, *The Bumblebee Queen,* Charlesbridge (Watertown, MA), 2005.

Darrin Lunde, *Hello, Bumblebee Bat,* Charlesbridge (Watertown, MA), 2007.

Ian Tattersall and Rob DeSalle, *Bones, Brains, and DNA: The Human Genome and Human Evolution,* Bunker Hill (Piermont, NH), 2007.

Darrin Lunde, *Meet the Meerkat,* Charlesbridge (Watertown, MA), 2007.

Caroline Arnold, *Super Swimmers: Whales, Dolphins, and Other Mammals of the Sea,* Charlesbridge (Watertown, MA), 2007.

Sidelights

Patricia J. Wynne is a scientific illustrator whose paintings are included in museum and university collections throughout the United States. She also has illustrated dozens of picture books for young readers, many concerning animals, birds, insects, and fish. In Donald M. Silver's *Woods* the reader is encouraged to examine a section of woods over the course of an entire year so as to learn the plants, animals, and insects that live there. Frances B. Spuler, writing in *Science Activities,* praised Wynne's artwork, stating that "the masterfully drawn illustrations include cross-sections, directions for activities, magnifications, life cycle charts, diagrams, and full-color drawings of all sorts of animals and plants attractively arranged on the pages."

In a review of *Birds: Nature's Magnificent Flying Machines* by Caroline Arnold, a *Kirkus Reviews* critic remarked that Wynne's "detailed, vibrant illustrations" for the book "enhance and enliven the text," and Sally Bates Goodroe wrote in *School Library Journal* that the book's "colorful artwork consistently clarifies the concepts being discussed." Reviewing Arnold's book *Super Swimmers: Whales, Dolphins, and Other Mammals of the Sea* for *School Library Journal,* Patricia Manning praised Wynne's "handsome, realistic watercolors," and *Booklist* critic Carolyn Phelan noted that the illustrator's "clearly delineated ink drawings, washed with delicate colors," are "precise yet lively."

Biographical and Critical Sources

PERIODICALS

Booklist, August, 1994, Julie Corsaro, review of *Cave,* p. 2040; March 1, 1995, Carolyn Phelan, review of *Pond,* p. 1239; March 1, 2005, Carolyn Phelan, review of *The Bumblebee Queen,* p. 1202; February 1, 2007, Carolyn Phelan, review of *Super Swimmers: Whales, Dolphins, and Other Mammals of the Sea,* p. 48; June 1, 2007, Carolyn Phelan, review of *Hello, Bumblebee Bat,* p. 76.

Childhood Education, summer, 2007, Ursula Adams, review of *The Bumblebee Queen,* p. 242.

Children's Bookwatch, April, 2005, review of *The Bumblebee Queen.*

Daily News (Los Angeles, CA), February 9, 1996, Jane Kurtz, review of *Extinction Is Forever,* p. L47.

Horn Book, May-June, 2005, Danielle J. Ford, review of *The Bumblebee Queen,* p. 350.

Kirkus Reviews, June 15, 2003, review of *Birds: Nature's Magnificent Flying Machines,* p. 855; June 1, 2007, reviews of *Hello, Bumblebee Bat* and *Meet the Meerkat.*

Publishers Weekly, August 9, 1993, review of *Backyard,* p. 479.

School Library Journal, December, 2003, Sally Bates Goodroe, review of *Birds,* p. 132; April, 2005, Patricia Manning, review of *The Bumblebee Queen,* p. 126; April, 2007, Patricia Manning, review of *Super Swimmers,* p. 154.

Science Activities, winter, 1997, Frances B. Spuler, review of *Woods,* p. 41.

Teacher Librarian, December, 2006, John Peters, review of *The Bumblebee Queen,* p. 15.

ONLINE

Charlesbridge Web site, http://www.charlesbridge.com/ (April 22, 2008), biography of Patricia J. Wynne.

Patricia Wynne Home Page, http://patriciawynne.com (April 22, 2008).*

DATE DUE

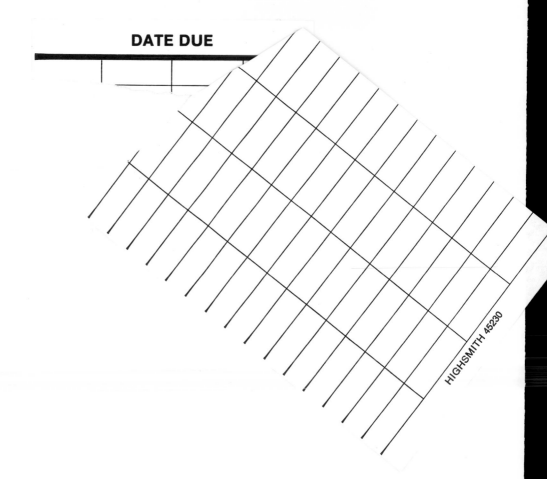